P9-DGH-059

D0014994

HANDBOOK
OF
PRACTICAL
PROGRAM
EVALUATION

Consulting Editor
Public Management and Administration
James L. Perry
Indiana University

HANDBOOK OF PRACTICAL PROGRAM EVALUATION

SECOND EDITION

JOSEPH S. WHOLEY
HARRY P. HATRY
KATHRYN E. NEWCOMER

EDITORS

JOSSEY-BASS
A Wiley Imprint
www.josseybass.com

Copyright © 2004 by John Wiley & Sons, Inc. All rights reserved.

Published by Jossey-Bass
A Wiley Imprint
989 Market Street, San Francisco, CA 94103-1741   www.josseybass.com

No part of this publication may be reproduced, stored in a retrieval system, or transmitted in any form or by any means, electronic, mechanical, photocopying, recording, scanning, or otherwise, except as permitted under Section 107 or 108 of the 1976 United States Copyright Act, without either the prior written permission of the Publisher, or authorization through payment of the appropriate per-copy fee to the Copyright Clearance Center, Inc., 222 Rosewood Drive, Danvers, MA 01923, (978) 750-8400, fax (978) 646-8700, or on the web at www.copyright.com. Requests to the Publisher for permission should be addressed to the Permissions Department, John Wiley & Sons, Inc., 111 River Street, Hoboken, NJ 07030, (201) 748-6011, fax (201) 748-6008, e-mail: permcoordinator@wiley.com.

Jossey-Bass books and products are available through most bookstores. To contact Jossey-Bass directly call our Customer Care Department within the U.S. at (800) 956-7739, outside the U.S. at (317) 572-3986 or fax (317) 572-4002.

Jossey-Bass also publishes its books in a variety of electronic formats. Some content that appears in print may not be available in electronic books.

Library of Congress Cataloging-in-Publication Data

Handbook of practical program evaluation/Joseph S. Wholey, Harry P. Hatry, Kathryn E. Newcomer, editors.—2nd ed.
    p. cm.
  Includes bibliographical references and index.
    ISBN 0-7879-6713-0 (alk. paper)
   1. Policy sciences. 2. Political planning—Evaluation. I. Wholey, Joseph S. II. Hatry, Harry P. III. Newcomer, Kathryn E., date.
    H97.H358 2004
    658.4—dc22
                                   2004001316

Printed in the United States of America
SECOND EDITION
HB Printing   10 9 8 7 6 5 4 3 2 1

Contents

Contents

Figures, Tables, and Exhibits

Chapter Four

Chapter Five

Chapter Seven

Chapter Eight

Chapter Nineteen

Chapter Twenty

Chapter Twenty-One

Chapter Twenty-Two

Chapter Twenty-Three

Preface

On the tenth anniversary of the publication of *Handbook of Practical Program Evaluation,* we are delighted to provide a new and improved edition. We address virtually all of the topics we originally identified as pertinent, and we cover additional issues and tools that we feel are critical for those working to improve public and nongovernmental organizations in the twenty-first century. We welcome a number of new chapter authors who offer fresh perspectives and approaches.

We remain enthusiastic advocates of efforts to assess systematically the performance, and particularly the outcomes and impacts, of public and nonprofit programs and policies. Given the heightened demand for documentation of program performance, together with ever present resource constraints, we believe there is even more need for practical evaluation advice than ever.

This handbook, as before, presents evaluation approaches that will enable policymakers and managers to obtain useful information more frequently, even under tight resource constraints. We asked the chapter authors to describe evaluation procedures that may not be ideal but nevertheless are likely to provide useful and reasonably reliable information at an affordable cost. At the same time, we gave them the latitude to suggest more sophisticated procedures to use when adequate resources are available to conduct more complex evaluations.

We hope that the variety of ideas presented in this book will encourage more use of systematic evaluation. We also hope that each reader will come away with at least one important new idea that he and she can put into practice to make program evaluation approaches more practical and more useful. Our philosophy in reissuing this new edition of the handbook continues to be, "It's better to be roughly right than to be precisely ignorant."

Acknowledgments

We thank the many good people who have assisted us in making this handbook a reality. We thank our chapter authors, who, with few complaints, produced draft after draft in response to our requests under tight time constraints. We thank the Jossey-Bass team, especially Allison Brunner and Johanna Vondeling, who produced this high-quality publication from our manuscript. Finally, we thank our cheerful, energetic, and capable support team, Michelle Amante, Cynthia Conner, Ben Licht, and Sarah Velasco of George Washington University (GWU), who have kept us on track throughout the entire process, and Mallory Barg, also of GWU, who provided essential analytical support. Our thanks to all who contributed to the success of this enterprise.

Washington, D.C.   Joseph S. Wholey
February 2004   Harry P. Hatry
                                                            Kathryn E. Newcomer

The Editors

JOSEPH S. WHOLEY is a professor in the University of Southern California's School of Policy, Planning, and Development. He received his B.A. in mathematics from Catholic University and his M.A. in mathematics and Ph.D. in philosophy from Harvard University. His work focuses on the use of strategic planning, performance monitoring, and program evaluation to improve the performance and accountability of public and nonprofit organizations. He is the author of many journal articles and is the author, coauthor, editor, or coeditor of seven books, including *Improving Government Performance* (1989, with K. E. Newcomer) and *Evaluation and Effective Public Management* (1983).

Wholey recently served as senior adviser for performance and accountability at the U.S. General Accounting Office and as senior adviser to the deputy director for management at the U.S. Office of Management and Budget. Before coming to the University of Southern California, he was deputy assistant secretary for planning and evaluation at the U.S. Department of Health and Human Services and director of program evaluation studies at the Urban Institute. He held elective office for eight years as a member of the County Board of Arlington, Virginia, serving as chairman for three years. He also chaired the Washington Metropolitan Area Transit Authority, the Virginia Board of Social Services, and the Arlington Partnership for Affordable Housing, and he was president of Hospice of Northern Virginia.

Wholey is a fellow of the National Academy of Public Administration. He received the 1983 Elmer B. Staats Award from the American Society for Public Administration, National Capital Area Chapter, and the Gunnar and Alva Myrdal Prize from the Evaluation Research Society. In 1999, he was recipient of the Joseph Wholey Distinguished Scholarship Award from the American Society for Public Administration.

HARRY P. HATRY is a principal research associate and director of the Public Management Program at the Urban Institute in Washington, D.C. He received his B.S. in engineering from Yale University and an M.S. from Columbia University's Graduate School of Business. He is a principal author of *Practical Program Evaluation for State and Local Government Officials* (second edition, 1981), *How Effective Are Your Community Services? Procedures for Measuring Their Quality* (second edition, 1992), and *Performance Measurement: Getting Results* (1999).

He has been a national leader in developing performance measurement and evaluation procedures for public agencies since 1970. He has led a number of efforts by public agencies to develop outcome measurement procedures for a number of public services.

Hatry is a fellow of the National Academy of Public Administration. He was a member of the U.S. Department of Education's Evaluation Review Panel and a member of the U.S. Office of Management and Budget's Performance Measurement Advisory Council (2002–2003). He received the 1985 Elmer B. Staats Award for Excellence in Program Evaluation and the 1984 American Society for Public Administration Award naming him Outstanding Contributor to the Literature of Management Science and Policy Science. In 1993, he received a National Public Service Award from the American Society for Public Administration and National Academy of Public Administration. In 1996, he received the Evaluator of the Year award from the Washington Evaluators Association. In 1999, the Center for Accountability and Performance of the American Society of Public Administration presented him with a lifetime achievement award for his work in performance measurement and established the Harry Hatry Award for Distinguished Practice in Performance Measurement. In 2000, he received a Fiftieth Anniversary Einhorn-Gary award from the Association of Government Accountants for "sustained commitment to advancing government accountability."

KATHRYN E. NEWCOMER is director of the School of Public Policy and Public Administration of Public Administration at the George Washington University, where she teaches public and nonprofit program evaluation, research design, and applied statistics. She conducts research and training for federal and local government agencies on performance measurement and program evaluation and has consulted for the governments of the United Kingdom, Ukraine, and Brazil on performance auditing. She has also conducted evaluations for many public agencies, including the U.S. Departments of Health and Human Services and Transportation.

Newcomer has published four books: *Improving Government Performance* (1989), *Handbook of Practical Program Evaluation* (1994, 2004), *Using Performance Measurement to Improve Public and Nonprofit Programs* (1997), and *Meet-*

ing the Challenge of Performance Oriented-Government (2002). She is as well the author of numerous articles in journals, including the *Public Administration Review.* She is a fellow of the National Academy of Public Administration.

Newcomer has won two awards for her teaching. In 1996, she was awarded the Peter Vail Excellence in Education Award, and in May 2000 she received the George Washington Award. She has received Fulbright awards in 1993 (Taiwan) and in 2002–2004 (Egypt).

Newcomer earned a B.S. in education and an M.A. in political science from the University of Kansas and the Ph.D. in political science from the University of Iowa.

The Contributors

HARVEY A. AVERCH is professor of public administration at Florida International University. He is an economist, policy analyst, expert on science and technology policy, and authority on heterodox methods of program evaluation. He has served as an economist at the RAND Corporation and has held posts at the National Science Foundation in Washington, D.C. At Florida International University, his research concerns science and technology policy, advice giving, and social and technological program evaluation. He received the B.A. in economics from the University of Colorado and the Ph.D. in economics from the University of North Carolina at Chapel Hill.

JAMES B. BELL is the president of James Bell Associates, a firm he founded in 1979 that specializes in health and human services program evaluation. From 1974 to 1979, Bell worked with Joseph Wholey and other members of the Urban Institute's Program Evaluation Studies Group to develop evaluability assessment and other approaches to planning useful evaluations of federal programs. He received the B.A. in political science from the University of California, Los Angeles, and M.A. in political science from California State University at Northridge.

DALE E. BERGER is professor of psychology at Claremont Graduate University, recently returning to full-time teaching after over twelve years of service as chair of the Psychology Department and dean of the School of Behavioral and Organizational Sciences. His research interests include research methodology, educational technology, and social and legal control of alcohol-impaired driving. A project using Internet technology in support of statistics teaching can be visited at http://wise.cgu.edu. Berger was president of the Western Psychological Association in 2002–2003 and recipient of its Outstanding Teaching Award in 1997. He earned the B.S. in mathematics from the University of Minnesota and M.A. and Ph.D. in psychology from the University of California, Los Angeles.

ROBERT F. BORUCH is University Trustee Chair Professor in the Graduate School of Education, the Statistics Department of the Wharton School, and the Fels Center for Government, all at the University of Pennsylvania. He is a recipient of the American Evaluation Association's Myrdal Award and the Policy Studies Organization's D. T. Campbell Award. He is a fellow of the American Statistical Association and the American Academy of Arts and Sciences and has been a fellow at the Center for Advanced Study in the Behavioral Sciences and the Rockefeller Foundation's Bellagio Center. His most recent books are *Randomized Experiments for Planning and Evaluation,* and with coeditor Frederick Mosteller, *Evidence Matters: Randomized Trials in Education Research.* He is a member of the boards of directors of the W. T. Grant Foundation and the American Institutes for Research, cochairs the Campbell Collaboration Steering Group, and serves as principal investigator for the U.S. Department of Education/Institute for Education Sciences' What Works Clearinghouse.

SHARON L. CAUDLE is a senior analyst with the U.S. General Accounting Office's Homeland Security and Justice Team and serves as adjunct faculty for the Office of Personnel Management's Management Development Centers and the George Washington University. She is a fellow of the American Society for Public Administration's Center for Accountability and Performance. Caudle specializes in homeland security management and national preparedness, organizational performance management and accountability, and intergovernmental relationships. She earned the M.P.A. and Ph.D. in public management from the George Washington University.

ROBERT GOLDENKOFF is an assistant director at the U.S. General Accounting Office, where he leads studies aimed at improving the accountability and performance of federal agencies and programs. His specific areas of responsibility have included oversight of the decennial census and right-sizing the federal workforce. He is the coauthor of *Federal Jobs: The Ultimate Guide,* and his articles on management, science policy, and other subjects have been published in *Technology Review, Government Executive, Policy Studies Journal,* and *Public Administration Review.* As a longstanding member of the American Society for Public Administration, he has held a variety of national and local positions. He received the B.A. (political science) and M.P.A. from the George Washington University and was a presidential management intern.

WILLIAM T. GORMLEY JR. is University Professor and professor of government and public policy at Georgetown University. He is the author or coauthor of many books and articles, including *Organizational Report Cards* (1999) with David Weimer, and *Bureaucracy and Democracy: Accountability and Performance* (2003) with Steven Balla. He is a fellow of the National Academy of Public Administration and a member of the executive council of the Association for Public Policy and Management. He is also a past president of the Public Policy Section of the American Political Science Association. He received the B.S. from the University of Pittsburgh and Ph.D. in political science from the University of North Carolina at Chapel Hill.

JOHN M. GREINER is a senior management and budget specialist with the Office of Management and Budget in Montgomery County, Maryland, where he coordinates the county's extensive performance measurement effort. He has also worked as a budget analyst in the budget offices of the Washington Suburban Sanitary Commission and Prince George's County (Maryland), as a private consultant, and for twelve years as a research associate at the Urban Institute. He has directed and participated in numerous projects on the development, testing, and evaluation of state and local government performance measures, productivity innovations and incentives, and responses to fiscal stress. His publications include two coauthored books, *Productivity and Motivation* (1981) and *How Effective Are Your Community Services?* (second edition, 1992), as well as "Positioning Performance Measurement for the Twenty-First Century," a chapter in *Organizational Performance and Measurement in the Public Sector* (1996). Greiner holds B.A. and M.S. degrees from Yale University and an M.S. in operations research from the University of Pennsylvania.

GEORGE F. GROB is deputy inspector general for management and policy at the U.S. Department of Health and Human Services. After being introduced to operations research analysis at the Department of Defense, he moved to the Department of Health, Education, and Welfare in 1973. He is still there, having filled the intervening thirty years both producing and consuming program evaluations. His work has centered on management and policy development. He received the B.A. in philosophy at Kilroe Seminary of the Sacred Heart in Honesdale, Pennsylvania, and M.A. in mathematics at Georgetown University.

GRETCHEN B. JORDAN is a principal member of technical staff with Sandia National Laboratories. She works with the U.S. Department of Energy (DOE) Energy Efficiency and Renewable Energy Office on evaluation and performance measurement and the DOE Office of Science and Sandia Labs on innovative methods of assessing the effectiveness of basic research organizations. She has edited two special issues and published articles and book chapters on assessing R&D performance and the research environment. She has consulted with Japan's Ministry of Economy, Trade and Industry on logic models and presented numerous workshops on logic modeling for energy program evaluators. She coauthored an article with John A. McLaughlin in *Evaluation and Program Planning* (1999) that trainers have translated into Russian and French. She has a Ph.D. in economics.

JAMES EDWIN KEE is a professor of public policy and public administration in the School of Public Policy and Public Administration at the George Washington University. He holds M.P.A. and J.D. degrees from New York University and the B.A. from the University of Notre Dame. Kee joined George Washington in 1985 after seventeen years in policy and management positions in government, including counsel to the New York State Assembly and budget director and executive director of finance and administration for the State of Utah. His research and teaching areas include public finance, intergovernmental relations, public management, privatization, and leadership. He has published in *Public Administration Review,* the *Harvard Law Review,* and *Public Budgeting and Finance.* He is the author of *Out of Balance* with former Utah governor Scott M. Matheson. His consulting has included work with the Chinese Ministry of Finance, the U.S. Department of Energy, the National Governors Association, the World Bank, and the Inter-American Development Bank. He also conducts training sessions on cost-benefit analysis and leadership.

MARY E. KOPCZYNSKI is a research associate with the Metropolitan Housing and Communities Center at the Urban Institute in Washington, D.C. Since joining the institute in 1995, her research has focused on strategic planning and assistance in the development of performance management systems for government agencies and nonprofit organizations. Her current interests include the design, implementation, and evaluation of strategies for increasing citizen involvement in their communities and government accountability. She received the B.A. from Bryn Mawr College and M.P.A. degree from American University.

ARNOLD LOVE is an internationally recognized program evaluation consultant based in Toronto, Canada. He has a special interest in evaluating the implementation of programs in the public and nonprofit sectors, building the capacity of organizations and communities to evaluate their own programs, and fostering the growth of the evaluation profession worldwide. He is a past president of the Canadian Evaluation Society (CES) and in 1996 received the CES Award for Distinguished Contribution to Evaluation in Canada. In 1998, he was honored by the American Evaluation Association for his contributions toward building a global evaluation community. More recently, his volunteer work has focused on facilitating the development of the International Organization for Cooperation in Evaluation, which brings together diverse regional and national evaluation associations and networks from around the world. In addition to consulting, he teaches program evaluation to leaders of public and nonprofit programs at York University and at institutions of higher learning overseas. He earned his interdisciplinary Ph.D. degree from the University of Waterloo.

MELVIN M. MARK is professor of psychology at Penn State. He is currently editor of the *American Journal of Evaluation*. His interests include the theory, methodology, practice, and profession of program and policy evaluation. His writings have addressed such issues such as the role of stakeholders in evaluation, systematic values inquiry, mixed methods, quasi-experimental design, and evaluation influence and use. He has been involved in evaluations in a number of areas, including prevention programs for at-risk youth, federal personnel policies, technology assistance programs for small manufacturers, and higher education. His most recent book (with Gary Henry and George Julnes) is *Evaluation: An Integrated Framework for Understanding, Guiding, and Improving Policies and Programs* (2000), and he is coeditor of the forthcoming *Handbook of Evaluation* with Ian Shaw and Jennifer Greene.

JOHN A. MCLAUGHLIN is an independent consultant in strategic planning, performance measurement, and program evaluation. He has assisted in the design, delivery, and evaluation of programs at federal, state, and local government levels and since the early 1990s has designed and implemented training and technical assistance for federal, state, and local managers as they moved their organizations to becoming performance based. Some of his clients in performance management have been Departments of Energy, Agriculture, Health and Human Services, and the Environmental Protection Agency; Centers for Disease Control and Prevention; National Institutes for Health; United Way of America; and Virginia Department of Education, Virginia Department of Environmental Quality, City of Williamsburg, Virginia, and James City County, Virginia. He has coauthored several books, including *Research Methods in Special Education* with Donna Mertens (1995), and a number of book chapters and journal articles. He has received more than thirty-five funded grants and contracts for research and training. He has been an active member of the American Evaluation Association, serving as annual conference chair from 1991 to 1997.

DEMETRA SMITH NIGHTINGALE is principal research scientist at the Johns Hopkins University's Institute for Policy Studies. Her research has concentrated on evaluating and analyzing social policies, particularly employment and training and welfare programs. She has developed and refined conceptual and theoretical models of implementation analysis and designed and directed numerous evaluations using multiple data collection and analytical methods. She publishes extensively and serves on many advisory groups and task forces. Among her books is *The Government We Deserve: Responsive Democracy and Changing Expectations,* coauthored with Eugene Steuerle, Edward Gramlich, and Hugh Heclo (1998). Before joining Johns Hopkins, she was principal research associate at the Urban Institute. She received a B.A. in political science and Ph.D. in public policy from the George Washington University.

ANTHONY PETROSINO is a research consultant specializing in studies relevant to criminology and justice, based in Amherst, New Hampshire. He serves as coordinator for the Campbell Collaboration Crime and Justice Group and as a researcher for the Study on Decisions in Education at Harvard University. After working as a researcher for several years in state justice agencies in New Jersey and Massachusetts, he completed his Ph.D. in criminal justice at Rutgers University and accepted a postdoctoral fellowship in evaluation at the Harvard Children's Initiative. He also was research fellow at the Center for Evaluation, American Academy of Arts and Sciences (1999–2002). Topics of recent articles include Megan's Law (*Crime and Delinquency,* 1999), causal model evaluation (*Canadian Journal of Program Evaluation,* 2000), community policing (*Police Quarterly,* 2001), Scared Straight and other juvenile awareness programs (*Cochrane Library,* 2002), school-based drug prevention (*Annals of the American Academy of Political and Social Science,* 2003), and convenience store robbery (*Crime Prevention Studies,* forthcoming).

THEODORE H. POISTER is a professor of public administration in the Andrew Young School of Policy Studies at Georgia State University, where he specializes in public management systems and applied research methods. He has published widely on the use of strategic planning, performance management, and quality improvement processes in governmental agencies, and his book *Measuring Performance in Public and Nonprofit Organizations* was published in 2003. In addition to working with numerous public agencies in the areas of program evaluation and performance measurement, he regularly teaches courses in applied statistics and performance measurement for the Evaluators' Institute. Previously he has taught at Southern University and Penn State University and served as a visiting faculty member at George

Washington University. Poister earned the M.P.A. and Ph.D. in social science from the Maxwell School at Syracuse University.

KATHLEEN PRITCHARD is director of Community Impact Product Development for the United Way of America. Previously she served as director of Community Impact for the United Way of Greater Milwaukee, where she designed and implemented the Outcomes Project and was responsible for planning, allocations, and evaluation for eighty-five local agencies. She served on the national Task Force on Impact for United Way of America and as a policy and research analyst, consultant, and trainer for state and local government. She has served as adjunct faculty at the University of Wisconsin-Milwaukee, Marquette University, and the National Academy of Voluntarism. She is president of the Village of Whitefish Bay, a trustee of the Public Policy Forum, and a member of the Executive Committee of Partnerships for Healthy Milwaukee. Pritchard holds the M.P.A. from the University of Wisconsin and Ph.D. in political science from the University of Wisconsin-Milwaukee.

CHARLES S. REICHARDT is professor of psychology at the University of Denver. His work focuses on research methodology and statistics in general and on the logic and practice of causal inference in particular. He is the coeditor of *Qualitative and Quantitative Methods in Evaluation Research* (with Tom Cook), *Evaluation Studies Review Annual* (with Will Shadish), and *The Qualitative-Quantitative Debate: New Perspectives* (with Sharon Rallis). He has worked with Arapahoe House in Thornton, Colorado, on federally funded projects to evaluate programs for substance abuse treatment, including an ongoing study involving women with co-occurring disorders and violence. He received the B.A., M.A., and Ph.D. degrees in psychology from Northwestern University.

SHELLI BALTER ROSSMAN is a senior research associate in the Justice Policy Center of the Urban Institute. She has more than twenty years of experience in program evaluation, policy analysis, and performance measurement. Her work has spanned criminal justice, public health and safety, and educational and environmental issues. She recently contributed to *How Federal Programs Use Outcome Information: Opportunities for Federal Managers* (with H. Hatry, E. Morley, and J. Wholey). She is also the coauthor of *Helping At-Risk Youth: Lessons From Community-Based Initiatives* (1997) and served as coeditor *for Safe Schools: Policies and Practices* (vol. 28 of *Education and Urban Society*, 1996). She received the B.A. in sociology from the University of Pittsburgh and M.A. in sociology from Temple University and has pursued other graduate studies in sociology at Temple University.

ROBERT G. ST. PIERRE is a vice president and principal associate in the Education and Family Support Area of Abt Associates. Since 1975, he has been principal investigator for educational research, evaluation, and policy analysis projects, conducting randomized experimental studies in such diverse areas as family literacy, case management, compensatory education, curricular interventions, school health education, and child nutrition. He currently directs research designed to improve the Even Start Family Literacy Program and has published on the effectiveness of popular social interventions in journals such as the *Early Childhood Research Quarterly,* the *American Journal of Evaluation,* the *Future of Children,* and the SRCD Social Policy Monograph series. St. Pierre received the B.A. in mathematics from Northeastern University and Ph.D. in educational research, measurement, and evaluation from Boston College.

TIMOTHY TRIPLETT is a survey associate at the Urban Institute and the survey manager for the Institute's National Survey of America's Families (NSAF). His work includes evaluating and monitoring sampling procedures and survey data collection for the NSAF and other projects and developing and improving NSAF public use files and internal survey data files. He conducts methodological research addressing such issues as estimating the nonresponse bias, weighting strategies, and imputation procedures. Prior to joining the Urban Institute, he was sampling and computer resources manager and senior project manager at Survey Research Center, University of Maryland, College Park. He has survey research experience, including responsibility for national, statewide, and regional projects; sample design; developing questionnaires; and managing statistical and computer programming. He has written and presented over twenty survey methodology papers and served as the program chair for the 1998 International Field Directors and Technology Conference. He received the B.A. and M.A. in economics and the M.P.P. from the College of Public Affairs, all at the University of Maryland.

MARGERY AUSTIN TURNER directs the Urban Institute's Metropolitan Housing and Communities policy center. A nationally recognized expert on urban policy and neighborhood issues, Turner served as deputy assistant secretary for research at the Department of Housing and Urban Development from 1993 through 1996, focusing the department's research agenda on the problems of racial discrimination, concentrated poverty, and economic opportunity in America's metropolitan areas. She has coauthored two national housing discrimination studies, which use paired testing to determine the incidence of discrimination against minority home seekers. She has also extended the paired testing methodology to measure discrimination in employment and in mortgage lending. Turner received the B.A. in government from Cornell University and M.A. in urban and regional planning from George Washington University.

PHILIP W. WIRTZ is professor of management science and psychology at the George Washington University. He has taught graduate-level research methods and statistics for over twenty years, is coauthor of the Adolescent Drinking Inventory instrument for identifying adolescents at long-term risk for alcohol problems, and is the author of numerous articles on substance abuse detection and prevention. He served as a methodological expert on a number of governmental review boards and recently served as a statistical consultant on the ten-year Project MATCH study for the National Institute on Alcohol Abuse and Alcoholism. He holds a Ph.D. in social psychology from the George Washington University, M.A. in computer science from Purdue University, and B.A. in psychology from the George Washington University.

WENDY ZIMMERMANN is a senior research associate at the Urban Institute. Since joining the institute in 1989, she has focused her research on immigration and immigrant policy and on testing for discrimination in the areas of employment and housing. Much of her recent work has examined the impacts of welfare reform on immigrants and their families. Her recent publications include *Immigrants and TANF: A Look at Immigrant Welfare Recipients in Three Cities* and *Patchwork Policies: State Assistance for Immigrants under Welfare Reform* (both with Karen Tumlin). Zimmermann received the B.A. in political science and French from Duke University and M.A. in Latin American studies from Stanford University.

In memoriam:
Kate Wholey

Meeting the Need for Practical Evaluation Approaches: An Introduction

Kathryn E. Newcomer, Harry P. Hatry, Joseph S. Wholey

The demand for systematic data on the performance of public and nonprofit programs continues to rise across the world. The supply of such data rarely matches the level of demand of the parties. Diversity in the types of providers of pertinent data also continues to rise.

Elected officials, foundations and other nonprofit funders, oversight agencies, and citizens want to know what value is provided to the public by the programs they fund. Program staff also want to know how their programs are performing so that they can improve them and learn from the information they gather. Increasingly, officials want to lead learning organizations, where staff systematically collect and learn from data about what works and does not work in their programs to improve their organizational capacity and services provided. And leaders and managers want to make evidence-based policy decisions, informed by data evaluating past programmatic performance.

The field of practice of program evaluation provides processes and tools that agencies of all kinds can apply to obtain valid, reliable, and credible data to address a variety of questions about the performance of public and nonprofit programs. Program evaluation is the systematic assessment of program results and, to the extent feasible, systematic assessment of the extent to which the program caused those results. Evaluation includes ongoing monitoring of programs, as well as one-shot studies of program processes or program impact. The approaches used are based on social science research methodologies and professional standards.

As we use the term in this handbook, a *program* is a set of resources and activities directed toward one or more common goals, typically under the direction of a single manager or management team. A program may consist of a very limited set of activities in one agency or a complex set of activities implemented at many sites by two or more levels of government and by a set of public, nonprofit, and even private providers.

Evaluation is accepted here as a valuable learning strategy to enhance knowledge about the logic of the underlying programs, as well as the practical results of programs. We use the term *practical program evaluation* because most of the procedures presented here are intended for application at reasonable cost and without extensive involvement of outside experts. We believe that resource constraints should not rule out evaluation. Ingenuity and leveraging of expertise can and should be used to produce useful, but not overly expensive, evaluation information. Knowledge of how trade-offs in methodological choices affect what we learn is critical.

A major theme throughout this handbook is that evaluation, to be useful and worth its cost, should not only assess program results but also identify ways to improve the program evaluated. While accountability, or demonstration of the value provided by programs, continues to be an important use of program evaluation, the major goal should be to improve program performance, thereby giving the public and funders better value for money. When program evaluation is used only for external accountability purposes and does not help managers improve their programs, the results are often not worth the cost of the evaluation.

Meeting the increasing demand for evaluation information to improve programs in a feasible and efficient manner is the objective of this handbook. This Introduction identifies the intended audience for the guidance offered here, outlines the scope of the subject matter covered, discusses the need for the content of the handbook, and describes the contents and organization of the material provided.

Intended Audience

The intended audience for this handbook includes (1) managers, management analysts, policy analysts, and evaluators in federal agencies, state and local governments, and school districts; (2) managers and analysts in nonprofit organizations; (3) independent auditors and management consultants; and (4) faculty members and students in professional schools, such as schools of public affairs and administration, business administration, education, public health, and social work.

The information presented here is intended to help those involved in program evaluation, those who fund programs, those who operate programs, staff members in the legislative and executive branches of government, those in universities, and those in the consulting world—both people new to evaluation and experienced evaluators who may find some new ideas to add to their current tool kit.

Scope

Considerable diversity exists in the training and skills possessed by both those charged with evaluating public and nonprofit programs and program managers seeking to collect useful data on their programs. In the box, we provide brief, practical definitions of terms used frequently in discussions about evaluation of public and nonprofit programs.

A Practical Program Evaluation Glossary

Case study: A description and analysis of a program in its context.

Comparison group design: Compares outcomes for program participants with outcomes for those in a comparison group.

Cost-benefit study: Compares the dollar value of program costs with the dollar value of program impacts.

Evaluation design: Specifies (1) a set of evaluation questions, (2) the data that will be collected and analyses undertaken to answer the evaluation questions, (3) the estimated costs and time schedule for the evaluation study, and (4) how the evaluation information will be used.

Experimental design: An experiment tests the existence of causal relationships by comparing outcomes for those randomly assigned to program services with outcomes for those randomly assigned to alternative services or no services.

Interrupted time-series design: Compares trends in outcomes before and after the program.

Logic model (or *program logic model*): A flowchart that summarizes key elements of a program: resources and other program inputs, program activities, and the intermediate outcomes and end outcomes (short-term and longer-term results) that the program hopes to achieve. Some logic models also identify program outputs (products and services to be delivered) and key external factors that are likely to affect program outcomes. In addition, a logic model shows assumed cause-and-effect linkages among elements in the model, showing which activities are expected to lead to which outcomes, and it may also show assumed cause-and-effect linkages between external factors and program outcomes.

Outcomes: Changes in clients or communities resulting from program activities and outputs.

Outputs: Products and services delivered to a program's clients.

Pre-post design: Compares outcomes before and after the program.

Process evaluation: Compares actual with intended inputs, activities, and outputs.

Program: Comprises resources and other inputs, program activities, outputs (products and services delivered), and outcomes (results).

Program logic model: See *logic model.*

Quasi-experimental design: Used to test the existence of a causal relationship where random assignment is not possible. Typical quasi-experimental designs include pre-post designs, comparison group designs, and interrupted time-series designs.

Stakeholder: An individual or group interested in or affected by the program.

Evaluators and program managers may have a variety of evaluation objectives in mind. They may have specific questions, or they may be unsure of how to frame useful questions about their programs.

Careful analysis of programs and the context in which they operate is a significant precursor to planning any sort of evaluation endeavor. Identification of the theory underlying programs and the sociopolitical contextual actors that affect the level and character of operations and success of programs is critical.

This handbook covers a variety of approaches to analyzing the operations and results of programs. Guidance for designing ongoing program performance monitoring systems is provided, along with advice on implementing one-shot studies of program processes and program outcomes.

Deductive, rigorous designs for measuring program impact are discussed, as well as more inductive, qualitative approaches to assess program quality. A variety of useful evaluation approaches are discussed, drawing on statistical and economic theory, as well as psychological measurement and group theory.

The handbook covers ongoing monitoring of program performance and ad hoc studies of past and existing programs. Except when evaluators develop recommendations for program improvement, our use of the term *program evaluation* excludes attempts to judge the worth of future programs.

The program evaluation approaches and tools covered here may provide feedback on program expenditures, program operations, or program results. They can be useful in developing new legislative proposals and in reauthorizing existing programs; in developing, debating, and deciding among budget alternatives; in implementing, operating, and improving public programs and programs operated by private or nonprofit organizations; and in managing, auditing, and reporting on the uses of public funds.

Need for Program Evaluation

The demand for program evaluation information is growing. The U.S. Congress, state legislatures, local legislative bodies, foundations, and other funding agencies are increasingly demanding information on how program funds were used and what those programs produced. Both program advocates and fiscal conservatives need information on program results. Performance management (or managing for results) initiatives are involving increasing numbers of program managers and staff in specifying performance measures and reporting data on program performance to inform decision making.

The U.S. Office of Management and Budget is requiring program performance monitoring and evaluation of program results through application of its Program Assessment Rating Tool. The Chief Financial Officers Act of 1990 requires federal agencies to provide "systematic measurement of performance" and information on the "results of operations" in audited financial statements (U.S. Office of Management and Budget, 1993). The Government Performance and Results Act of 1993 requires federal agencies to establish annual quantitative performance targets and report annually on actual results. The contributing public is also becoming more demanding about how its donated dollars are used in the nonprofit sector.

The environment in which evaluators work has become more challenging as taxpayers, legislators, the media, and the general public have increased requests for data on economy, efficiency, and return on investment. External entities are increasingly assessing the results of public programs. Auditing has evolved from concentration on financial issues toward performance auditing, a close relative of program evaluation. More and more audit organizations of government are being asked to undertake performance audits that explore both efficiency and effectiveness. National audit organizations in the United States, Australia, Canada, France, the Scandinavian countries, and the United Kingdom have developed experience with, and expertise in, program evaluation, or what they call performance audits or value-for-money audits.

At the federal level in the United States, a variety of staff offices provide oversight for service delivery and results. These bodies include the Congressional Budget Office, the Congressional Research Service, and the General Accounting Office, all of which report to the Congress; the Office of Management and Budget, which reports to the president; offices of the inspector general, reporting to Congress as well as to their agency heads; and planning and evaluation offices at agency and bureau levels. Congress has increasingly mandated program evaluation in authorizing legislation.

Paralleling oversight at the federal level, a growing number of state and local audit offices are being required by legislatures, boards of supervisors, and city councils to undertake performance audits of program results. The Governmental Accounting Standards Board, the Association of Government Accountants, and the National Association of Local Government Auditors have all made significant efforts to encourage a focus on performance results. Interest in program performance has generated interest in evaluation among state and local officials. A large number of state governments, including Oregon, Texas, Minnesota, North Carolina, Florida, and Virginia, are tracking the results of their programs. Requests for evaluative information from those outside government have grown, in part as a response to the antigovernment sentiment and taxpayer revolts.

Accountability issues have been the major motivating factor in the pressures. Other less dramatic movements also are increasing the demand for evaluation information. Heightened recognition of competition among service providers, especially in health care, has spurred on public assessments of service quality and customer satisfaction, and performance report cards and ratings have become commonplace.

Various governments have initiated attempts to link rewards or sanctions to results. Sometimes the rewards or sanctions apply to organizations and sometimes to individual employees. Under the banner of education reform, for example, some local school boards and state boards of education have reduced process requirements in return for improved school performance, with school performance defined in terms of agreed-on goals and performance indicators developed with the participation of school board members, principals, teachers, and parents. A growing number of federal laws specify that funds and grants will be awarded to "high performers." All of these trends increase the demand for useful and usable evaluation information.

Meeting the Need for Evaluation

Selection among evaluation options is a challenge to program personnel and evaluators interested in allocating resources efficiently and effectively. The value of program evaluation endeavors is likely to be enhanced when clients for the information know what they are looking for. Clients, program managers, and evaluators all face many choices.

Resources for evaluation and monitoring are typically constrained; prioritization among programs should therefore reflect the most urgent information needs of decision makers. Because there may be many demands for information on program performance, not all of which can be met at reasonable cost, what criteria can guide choices?

Three basic questions should be asked about any program being considered for evaluation or monitoring:

- Can the results of the evaluation influence decisions about the program?
- Can the evaluation be done in time to be useful?
- Is the program significant enough to merit evaluation?

More specific criteria for setting an evaluation agenda are presented in the box (see Hatry, Winnie, and Fisk, 1981).

Criteria for Setting an Evaluation Agenda

1. Can the results of the evaluation influence decisions about the program?
   Are decisions pending about continuation, modification, or termination?
   Is there considerable support for the program by influential interest groups that would make termination highly unlikely?
2. Can the evaluation be done in time to be useful?
   Are the data available now?
   How long will it take to collect the data needed to answer key evaluation questions?
3. Is the program significant enough to merit evaluation?
   Does the program consume a large amount of resources?
   Is program performance marginal?
   Are there problems with program delivery?
   Is program delivery highly inefficient?
   Is this a pilot program with presumed potential for expansion?

The watchword of the evaluation profession has been *utilization-focused evaluation* (see Patton, 2001). *Utilization-focused* means that an evaluation is designed to answer specific questions raised by those in charge of a program so that the information provided can affect decisions about the program's future. This test is the first criterion for an evaluation. Programs for which decisions must be made about continuation, modification, or termination are good candidates for evaluation, at least in terms of this first criterion. But programs for which there is considerable support, such as the Head Start program, are less likely candidates under this criterion.

Timing is important in evaluation. If an evaluation cannot be completed in time to affect decisions to be made about the program, the second criterion, evaluation will not be useful. Some questions about a program may be unanswerable because the data are not currently available and cannot be collected in a reasonable time period.

The last criterion deals with significance, which can be defined in many ways. Programs that consume a large amount of resources or are perceived to be marginal in performance are likely candidates for evaluation using this third test, assuming that evaluation results can be useful and evaluation can be done in a reasonable amount of time. New programs, and in particular pilot programs for which costs and benefits are unknown, are also good candidates.

Even with the explosion of quantitative and qualitative evaluation methodologies since the 1970s, evaluation remains more an art than a science. The planning of each evaluation effort requires difficult trade-off decisions as the evaluator attempts to balance the feasibility and cost of alternative evaluation designs against the likely benefits of the resulting evaluation work in improving program performance or communicating the value of program activities.

Wherever possible, evaluation planning should begin before the program does. The most desirable window of opportunity for evaluation planning opens when new programs are being designed. Desired data can be more readily obtained if provision is made for data collection from the start of the program, particularly for such information as clients' pre-program attitudes. These sorts of data would be very difficult, if not impossible, to obtain later.

Planning an evaluation project requires selecting a design, methods of data collection, and data analysis that will best meet information needs. Evaluators must be able to anticipate how the evaluation results might be used and how decision making might be shaped by the availability of the performance data collected.

Selecting an Evaluation Design

Identification of the key evaluation questions is the first, and frequently quite challenging, task faced during the design phase. Anticipating what clients need to know is essential to effective evaluation planning. For example, the U.S. General Accounting Office (GAO) conducts many program evaluations in response to legislative requests. These requests, however, are frequently fairly broad in their identification of the issues to be addressed. The first task of GAO evaluators is to identify what the committees or members of Congress want to know, and then to explore what information the legislative requesters really need to answer the questions they have defined.

Matching evaluation questions to a client's information needs can be a tricky task. When there is more than one client, as is frequently the case, there may be multiple information needs, and one evaluation project may not be able to answer all the questions raised. This is frequently a problem for nonprofit service providers who may need to address evaluation questions for multiple funders.

Identifying clear, useful, and answerable evaluation questions is probably the most difficult conceptual task in all evaluation work. Setting goals for information gathering can be like aiming at a moving target, for information needs change as programs and environmental conditions change. Negotiating researchable questions with clients can be fraught with difficulties for evaluators as well as for managers who may be affected by the findings.

A great deal of evaluation work performed for public and nonprofit programs is contracted out, and given current pressures toward outsourcing along with internal evaluation resource constraints, this trend is likely to continue. Contracting out evaluation places even more importance on the need to identify sufficiently targeted evaluation questions. Statements of work are typically prepared by internal program staff working with contract professionals, and these documents set in stone the questions the contractors will address, along with data collection and analysis specifications. Unfortunately the contract process may not leave evaluators (or program staff) much leeway in reframing the questions to adjust when the project gets underway and confronts new issues or when political priorities shift.

Balancing clients' information needs with resources affects selection of an evaluation design as well as specific strategies for data collection and analysis. Selecting a design requires the evaluator to anticipate the amount of rigor that will be required to produce convincing answers to the client's questions. Evaluators must specify the comparisons that will be needed to demonstrate whether a program has had the intended effects and other comparisons needed to clarify differential effects on different groups.

Resource issues will almost always constrain design choices; staff costs, travel costs, data collection burdens on program staffs, and political and bureaucratic expenses may limit design options. Evaluation design decisions, in turn, affect where and how data will be collected. To help evaluators and program personnel make the best design decisions, a pilot test of proposed data collection procedures should be considered. Pilot tests may be valuable in refining evaluation designs; they can clarify the feasibility and costs of data collection as well as the likely utility of different data analysis strategies.

Data Collection

Data collection choices may be politically as well as bureaucratically tricky. Exploring the use of existing data involves identifying potential political barriers as well as more mundane constraints, such as incompatibility of computer systems. Planning for data collection in the field should be quite extensive to help evaluators obtain the most relevant data in the most efficient manner.

Data Analysis

Deciding how the data will be analyzed affects data collection, for it forces evaluators to clarify how each data element will be used. Collecting too many data is an error that evaluators frequently commit. Developing a detailed analysis plan as part of the evaluation design can help evaluators decide which data elements are necessary and sufficient, thus avoiding the expense of gathering unneeded information.

An analysis plan helps evaluators structure the layout of a report, for it identifies the graphic presentations and tables through which the findings will be presented. Anticipating how the findings might be used forces evaluators to think carefully about presentations that will address the original evaluation questions in a clear and logical.

Getting Evaluation Results Used

Identifying relevant questions and answering them with data that have been analyzed and presented in a user-oriented format should help ensure that evaluation results will be used. However, communicating evaluation results entails more than simply drafting attractive reports. If the findings are indeed used to improve program performance, the evaluators must understand the bureaucratic and political context of the program and craft their findings and recommendations in such a way as to highlight their usefulness.

Program improvement is the ultimate goal for most evaluators. Consequently, they should use their skills to produce useful, convincing evidence to support their recommendations for program change.

The most effective evaluators are those who plan, design, and implement evaluations that are sufficiently relevant and credible to stimulate program improvement. In evaluation, effectiveness may be enhanced by efficiency, and use of practical, low-cost evaluation approaches will generally encourage the evaluation clients (the management and staff of the program) to accept the findings and use them to improve their services.

Handbook Organization

This handbook is divided into four parts: evaluation design, data collection, data analysis, and guidance on evaluation planning, management, and utilization issues. In Part One, the chapter authors explore different approaches to designing performance monitoring systems and evaluation studies. Evaluation design should ensure that the benefits of the evaluation strategy outweigh its costs. These chapters cover nonexperimental and quasi-experimental evaluation designs, including evaluability assessment, process evaluation, and performance monitoring. Then designs are presented that provide increasingly stronger evidence of the extent to which program activities caused program results. Each of the authors offers advice on the design of useful evaluations. They discuss the purpose of each of the evaluation designs examined, the types of questions that can be answered with these designs, and requirements that must be met to use them properly. They illustrate the use of alternative designs in evaluating public programs and programs operated by nonprofit agencies.

In Part Two, the chapter authors describe practical data collection procedures: methods for collecting data on program performance within tight time and resource constraints. They describe both well-established and newer procedures for collecting information on program performance, including ratings by trained observers, surveys, use of expert judgment, role playing, use of focus groups, fieldwork based on semistructured interviews, and use of agency records. They identify the uses of those data collection procedures in program evaluation and indicate the types of quality control needed to ensure that the resulting data are valid.

Because evaluation designs and data collection methods often include procedures for data analysis, some of the authors in Parts One and Two also discuss ways to analyze evaluation data. In Part Three, the chapter authors provide further advice on important methods for analysis: use of appropriate statistics and statistical tests, regression models, and cost-effectiveness and cost-benefit analysis. They also discuss requirements that must be met to use these data analysis techniques and present examples illustrating their application to the analysis of evaluation data.

In Part Four, the chapter authors describe methods for planning and managing evaluation projects, as well as procedures for getting the results used. They offer advice on how evaluators can manage evaluations effectively, develop effective recommendations, report their results persuasively with acknowledgment of limitations, craft compelling reports, and get evaluation used in small nonprofit agencies. An assessment of current use of organizational performance report cards is also provided.

The final chapter examines several additional evaluation topics, including the selection and training of evaluators, quality control of the evaluation enterprise, standards and ethics in evaluation work, and the creation of incentives for undertaking program evaluation and using its findings. The chapter and the handbook close with the editors' discussion of current and future trends in program evaluation.

References

Hatry, H. P., Winnie, R. E., and Fisk, D. M. *Practical Program Evaluation for State and Local Governments*. Washington, D.C.: Urban Institute Press, 1981.

Patton, M. Q. *Utilization-Focused Evaluation*. Thousand Oaks, Calif.: Sage, 2001.

U.S. Office of Management and Budget. *Budget Baselines, Historical Data, and Alternatives for the Future*. Washington, D.C.: Executive Office of the President, Jan. 1993.

HANDBOOK
OF
PRACTICAL
PROGRAM
EVALUATION

Part One

Designing Performance Monitoring Systems and Evaluation Studies

The chapters in Part One discuss a variety of techniques and strategies. The authors provide guidance relevant to designing ongoing evaluation (or monitoring) systems as well as one-shot studies. They offer designs for documenting program performance and designs to evaluate program impact. The chapters cover the following topics:

- Logic modeling.
- Evaluability assessment.
- Implementation evaluation.
- Ongoing performance monitoring.
- Quasi-experimental designs: before-after, interrupted time series, non-equivalent group, and regression-discontinuity designs, which provide evidence on the impact of program activities, that is, the difference between program outcomes and the outcomes that would have occurred without the program. Quasi-experimental designs may also involve explanation of how and why program activities have or fail to have the intended results.
- Randomized experiments, which provide the strongest evidence of program impact.
- Meta-analyses, systematic reviews, and research syntheses, which estimate program impacts using as data the results of past evaluations.

Evaluation design involves balancing the probable costs of answering evaluation questions with the likely credibility and usefulness of the evalua-

1

tion results. In general, the higher the level of precision, reliability, and generalizability, the higher the costs are in terms of time, staff, and other required resources. Evaluation costs are not limited to the evaluators' time and resources; they include as well the time of policymakers, program managers, program staff, clients, and others affected by the evaluation process; political and bureaucratic costs, including perceived disruptions and increased workload that may occur as a result of the evaluation process as well as possible loss of goodwill among those who are affected by data gathering; and the financial costs of data collection and analysis. The value of an evaluation is measured in the strength of the evidence produced; the credibility of the evaluation to policymakers, managers, and other intended users of the results; and the use of evaluation information in influencing public policies, program activities, or program results.

Evaluation designs that measure program outcomes and impact require more time and resources, but may yield stronger and more credible evidence for policymakers. Availability of in-house evaluation expertise and access to evaluation capacity will constrain design choices and limit the evaluation questions that can be answered. Matching design decisions to time and resources is an art, supported by the social sciences.

The design of an evaluation effort is the initial phase of conceptualizing how questions can be framed and strategies devised to address the questions within time and resource constraints. Whether the evaluation questions lead the evaluators to an ongoing performance monitoring system or a one-shot evaluation study, similar analytical activities are required. An evaluation design identifies the questions that will be answered by the evaluation, what will be measured, and what sets of analyses will be applied to the measures to answer the questions. Evaluation may entail description of program resources, activities, processes, or outcomes or estimation of the extent to which program activities cause program outcomes.

Each design illuminates an important aspect of program reality. Logic modeling is a useful strategy for identifying program components and outcomes, as well as critical contextual factors affecting program operations; it is useful to evaluators and program managers designing an evaluability assessment, implementation evaluation, performance monitoring system, or impact evaluation study. Evaluability assessment explores the information needs of policymakers and managers, the feasibility and cost of answering alternative evaluative questions, and the likely use of subsequent findings—for example, use of the evaluation information to improve program performance or communicate the value of program activities to higher levels. Implementation evaluation and performance monitoring systems are typically used to answer questions that ask for description: "What's happening?" Quasi-experiments, randomized experiments, and meta-analyses provide increasingly stronger evidence to answer questions that ask for explanation: "What difference does the program make?" Many evaluations use a combination of these approaches to answer questions about program performance.

John A. McLaughlin and Gretchen B. Jordan introduce logic models in Chapter One. They discuss the utility of these models and provide guidance on logic modeling. The chapter offers examples of logic models and practical tips on how to communicate effectively with program stakeholders to construct useful program logic models and how to avoid typical modeling pitfalls. The logic model has been used frequently during the past two decades to design performance monitoring systems for domestic programs, as well as for international assistance programs. Focusing on the theory underlying programs through developing logic models is a useful step in virtually any evaluation endeavor.

Joseph S. Wholey, in Chapter Two, discusses evaluability assessment, a process developed to help plan evaluations that are used to improve the performance of the programs being evaluated. Evaluability assessment can be used to evaluate program designs, explore program reality, and help ensure that programs and program evaluations meet three criteria: (1) program goals, objectives, important side effects, and priority information uses are well defined, (2) program goals and objectives are plausible, and (3) evaluators and clients agree on intended uses of evaluation information. The chapter describes the evaluability assessment process and illustrates how the process helps in planning useful program evaluation efforts in complex political and bureaucratic environments. The chapter also examines problems that arise in evaluability assessment and outlines workable solutions.

Arnold Love, in Chapter Three, describes and illustrates a number of practical methods to use in evaluating program implementation, especially when resources are limited. The role of systematic evaluation of implementation in performance management and building a performance-oriented organizational culture is noted. The chapter describes tools to use during the program life cycle: assessing the need for and feasibility of the program, planning and designing the program, program implementation, and program improvement. The tools are described for each stage, along with their potential benefits and challenges, and illustrative uses are showcased. For use in needs assessments, implementation research reviews and key information interviews are discussed. Program logic models, program templates, and outcome hierarchies are the tools discussed for use in program design. Tools to use in evaluating program delivery are coverage analysis, component analysis, program records reviews, and case studies. And service delivery pathways and client feedback analysis are tools discussed for use for improving programs. Actually, any of the tools highlighted can be used throughout the program life cycle to evaluate program reality.

Theodore H. Poister, in Chapter Four, describes the scope and purpose of performance monitoring, the types of measures typically incorporated in monitoring systems, and the ways in which performance monitoring can support program evaluation and performance management. He also describes the aspects of program performance that should be measured, ways to identify appropriate data sources and operational indicators, means for evaluating the quality of the measures, and ways to interpret performance data. The chapter offers examples of the performance comparisons provided by performance monitoring systems in a number of service areas. In addition, it pinpoints typical problems that arise in the design and use of performance monitoring systems.

Charles S. Reichardt and Melvin M. Mark, in Chapter Five, describe designs that can be used to estimate the net impact of a program when experimental design is not an option. These quasi-experimental designs provide means for comparing what happened after a treatment was implemented with an estimate of what would have happened had no treatment (or an alternative treatment) been implemented. The chapter describes and illustrates four prototypical quasi-experimental designs: before-after, interrupted time series, nonequivalent groups, and regression-discontinuity. Additional design features that can be used with any of the four basic designs are also described: treatment interventions, comparison groups, measurement occasions, and outcome variables. The chapter illustrates the designs with two treatment conditions. The limitations on drawing a causal link between the treatment and the measured program effect (that is, threats to internal validity) most likely to accompany use of each design are also elucidated.

Robert G. St. Pierre, in Chapter Six, discusses the use of experiments to evaluate program impact. The chapter provides guidelines for deciding when to use a randomized experiment, designing experimental evaluations, and working with program staff to put experiments in place and maintain them so that unbiased estimates of program effectiveness can be obtained. The chapter provides illustrations of the use of randomized experiments to assess the effects of a number of federal education and early childhood programs, and refers readers to centers that are currently aggregating findings from experimental evaluation, such as the Coalition for Evidence-Based Policy. Practical tips for evaluators to preserve randomization, estimate potential bias due to sample attrition, and work collaboratively with programs are also provided.

In Chapter Seven, the final one in this part addressing evaluation design issues, Robert Boruch and Anthony Petrosino offer guidance on conducting meta-analyses and systematic reviews that summarize studies of the effects of interventions, that is, impact evaluations. The chapter provides practical advice to evaluators and program staff who may be consumers of or contributors to meta-analyses of previous studies. Technical and training resources available to assist those interested in such systematic reviews, such as the Cochrane and Campbell Collaborations, are also cited.

All of the authors discuss the challenges and data demands of the evaluation designs they describe. They offer practical advice on implementing evaluation designs and illustrate how to use the designs in a variety of service delivery arenas. They often highlight data collection tools that are especially useful for specific evaluation designs, since design decision making encompasses data collection and analysis issues, topics addressed more thoroughly later in this handbook.

1

Using Logic Models

John A. McLaughlin, Gretchen B. Jordan

Those who are responsible for designing, conducting, reporting, and using program evaluations are the primary audience for this chapter. We believe that program managers and staff will also find the logic model tool useful for conceptualizing, planning, and communicating with others about their program. The logic model serves as a useful advance organizer for designing evaluation and performance measurement, focusing on the important elements of the program and identifying what evaluation questions should be asked and why and what measures of performance are key. The logic model also helps evaluators frame the evaluation reports so that findings from the evaluation and measurement can tell a performance "story," and results can be attributed to the program. Evaluators can use this tool when asked to evaluate a program during the design phase of a program, after it has ended, or at any point in a program life cycle. Managers may use this tool in planning and program design and to communicate the place of the program in a larger organization or context. The process of developing a logic model helps build shared understanding and expectations within program staff and others who participate.

We use the term *program* loosely throughout this chapter. We have used logic models to describe internal management functions, Web sites, and the performance-based management process itself. A program may be described as intentional transformation of specific resources (inputs) into certain activities (processes) to produce desired outcomes (results) within a specific context. We present a tool that evaluators and program managers can use to describe the unique program elements and show how they go together for the purposes of communicating and testing the assumptions that program staff made about the program theory.

A program can be thought of as a hypothesis: *if* a program is implemented, *then* the expected results will follow. Logic modeling is a tool that can be used to unpack this hypothesis in order to understand the underlying assumptions and create strategies to test the hypothesis.

The material in this chapter supports the chapters that follow in several ways. One of the assumptions that evaluators make is that a useful evaluation approach is based on an understanding of the objectives of the program and how it intends to achieve these. Conducting an evaluation of a program without this information can be both costly and potentially harmful. Logic models can be a useful tool for performing an evaluability assessment. The logic model can serve as an advance organizer for designing and conducting an implementation evaluation. The model presents a description of how the program staff members believe the program works. If the evaluation finds the program is successful in achieving its aims but works differently in practice, the logic model may be revised. If the evaluation determines that the program is not successful, it is possible for the evaluator to recommend that the staff exert more pressure on the actual delivery of the program to bring it in line with their logic. Collecting and interpreting evaluation information also is aided by the logic model, as it establishes a framework for understanding the elements of the program, assumed causal relationships, and the potential role of context. Finally, using the logic model in preparing and presenting the evaluation findings and recommendations can increase the probability that the evaluation results will be used.

What Is a Logic Model?

A logic model is a plausible and sensible model of how the program will work under certain environmental conditions to solve identified problems (Bickman, 1987). It can be the basis for a convincing story of the program's expected performance, telling stakeholders and others the problem the program focuses on and how it is uniquely qualified to address it. The elements of the logic model are resources, activities, outputs, short-, and intermediate- and longer-term outcomes (Wholey, 1983, 1987). Some have added the customers reached, as well as the relevant external contextual (antecedent and mediating) influences (McLaughlin and Jordan, 1991).

A basic logic model is shown in Figure 1.1, although logic models may take many different forms, including narrative and table form. Evaluators can prepare logic models at any time in the life cycle of the program, and they often revise them as more program information is collected.

Figure 1.1. Basic Logic Model

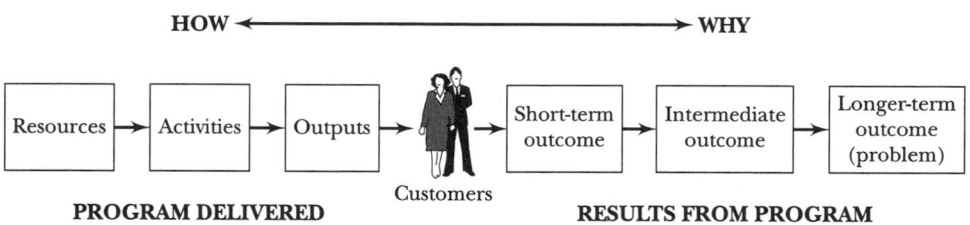

The model has the following basic features:

• *Resources*—human and financial resources as well as other inputs required to support the program such as partnerships. Information on customer needs is an essential resource to the program.

• *Activities*—all of the action steps necessary to produce program outputs.

• *Outputs*—the products, goods, and services provided to the program's direct customers or program participants. For example, the reports generated for other researchers and technology developers as a result of the activity of conducting research could be thought of as outputs of the activity.

• *Customers*—this feature had been dealt with implicitly in logic models until Montague added the concept of *Reach* to the performance framework. He speaks of the 3Rs of performance: resources, people reached, and results (Montague 1994, 1997). The relationship between resources and results cannot happen without people—the customers served and the partners who work with the program to enable actions that will lead to results. Placing customers, the users or receivers of a product or service, explicitly in the middle of the chain of logic helps program staff and stakeholders better think through and explain what leads to what and what population groups the program intends to serve.

• *Outcomes*—changes or benefits resulting from activities and outputs. Programs typically have multiple, sequential outcomes, sometimes called the program's outcome structure. First, there are *short-term outcomes,* the changes or benefits that are most closely associated with, or "caused" by, the program's outputs. Second are *intermediate outcomes,* which result from the short-term outcomes. *Longer-term outcomes* or program impacts follow from the benefits accrued though the intermediate outcomes. For example, an outcome structure for a teacher training program might be as follows. As a result of participating in training, teachers learn new skills and knowledge about classroom management techniques (the short-term outcome). Then they appropriately apply these new skills in their classrooms (the intermediate outcome), which leads to enhanced educational opportunities for the students, resulting in improved learning (the long-term impact the teacher training program was designed to achieve).

Key contextual factors external to the program and not under its control could influence its success either positively or negatively and are critical features of the logic model. Two types of contextual factors could influence the design and delivery of the program: antecedent and mediating (Harrell and others, 1996). *Antecedent variables* are those the program starts out with, such as client characteristics, geographical variables, and economic factors. *Mediating factors* are the influences that emerge as the program unfolds, such as changes in staff, new policies, a downturn (or uptick) in the economy, and new competing programs.

The Utility of Logic Models

The utility of logic models has increased as managers are being challenged by oversight agencies at all levels of government and in the nonprofit sector. At the federal level, Congress and the President's Office of Management and Budget are asking managers to tell their program's story in a way that both communicates the program's outcome goals and shows that these outcomes have been achieved. For many public programs, there is also an implicit question: "Are the results proposed by the program the correct ones?" That is, do the results address problems that are appropriate for the program and that stakeholders deem to be important to the organizational mission and national needs?

The emphasis on accountability and managing for results, which is found in state and local governments, as well as in nonprofit organizations such as the United Way of America and the American Red Cross, represents a change in the way managers have to describe their programs and document program successes. In the past, program managers were not as familiar with describing and measuring outcomes as they were with documenting inputs and processes. Program theory, the relationship between program actions and results, has not been made explicit. The problem is that program managers and evaluators have not used clear, logically consistent methods to make explicit their understandings about programs and how they work.

There is an increasing interest among program managers in continuous improvement and managing for quality. Choosing what to measure and then collecting and analyzing the data necessary for improvement is new to many managers. While tools such as flowcharts, risk analysis, and systems analysis are used to plan and describe programs, logic models more comprehensively address the increasing requirements for both outcomes measurement and measurement of how the program is being implemented to allow for improvement.

One of the uses of the logic model that should not be overlooked is communication. The process of developing a logic model brings people together to build a shared understanding of the program and program performance. The model also helps to communicate the program to those outside the program in a concise and compelling way and helps program staff to gain a common understanding of how the program works and their responsibilities to make it work.

Benefits of Using the Logic Model Tool

- Points to evaluation issues and a balanced set of key performance measurement points, thus improving data collection and usefulness and helping to meet performance reporting requirements
- Helps with program design or improvement by identifying projects that are critical to goal attainment, are redundant, or have inconsistent or implausible linkages to program goals
- Communicates the place of a program in the organization or problem hierarchy, particularly if there are shared logic charts at various management levels
- Builds a common understanding of the program and expectations for resources, customers reached, and results, and thus is good for sharing ideas, identifying assumptions, team building, and communication

Theory-Driven Evaluation

Assumptions about resources and activities and how these lead to realizing intended outcomes are often referred to as *program theory*. A logic model is a useful tool for describing program theory. The hypothesis, often implicit, is that if the right resources are transformed into the right activities for the right people, then these will lead to the results the program was designed to achieve. Some evaluators believe that making explicit the underlying assumptions about how a program is supposed to work increases the potential for evaluation utility (Rogers, Petroscino, Huebner, and Hacsi, 2000). While developing the program theory prior to the evaluation is considered most beneficial for *predicting* relationships, developing program theory at the end of the evaluation helps explain *observed* causal relationships.

Leeuw (2003) provides an excellent review of three approaches to restructuring program theories after the program has been implemented:

- The policy-scientific approach, which is more empirical and consists of generating a series of propositions or assumptions that have been made about how the program is supposed to work. The evaluator then tests these propositions through a review of relevant scientific research, interviews with key staff, and document reviews.
- The strategic assessment approach, which is driven through conversations or dialogues with program staff and participants. The focus is to draw out the underlying assumptions about how the program works and then subject these to open debate among stakeholders and staff.
- The elicitation method, which aims at recovering the mental models or cognitive maps that program staff hold about their program. The various maps are then compared and contrasted and assessed for their validity through open dialogue and reviews of existing related research.

The central theme in all three approaches is discovering the underlying assumptions held about how the program is believed to be working to achieve its outcomes and then testing these assumptions once they have been made public. All three approaches make the program transparent, allowing the evaluator and others to see how it is thought to be working from multiple perspectives. Logic modeling is a tool that can effectively be used to display the assumption pathways.

Chen and Rossi (1983) were among the first to recommend the program-theory-driven approach to evaluation, and they suggested tying it to social science theory. According to Chen (1990), program theory can be descriptive and prescriptive. That is, working with program staff, the evaluator might both describe the elements of the program and prescribe the logic of how the program should work—the underlying assumptions of the program staff and why the elements go together to cause the intended outcomes. Patton (1997) refers to a program description as an "espoused theory of action," that is, stakeholder perceptions of how the program will work to achieve its outcomes. Rogers, Petroscino, Huebner, and Hacsi (2000) and Birkmayer and Weiss (2000) present examples of theory-driven evaluations, but report that although theory-driven evaluation is conceptually sound, it is rare to find good examples of it in practice.

History of the Logic Model

Before the terms *logic model* or *program theory* became popular, there were models of evaluation that described programs similarly. Cooksy, Gill, and Kelly's brief history (2001) recalls that "Stake (1967) presented a model that calls for describing the intended antecedents (whatever needs to be in place before a program is operational), transactions, and outcomes of a program.

Stufflebeam's (1971) context-inputs-processes-products (CIPP) model is similar to Stake's in content and was designed to encourage a systems approach to evaluation and to interpret and understand outcomes. Weiss (1972) recommended using path diagrams to model the sequence of steps between a program's intervention and the desired outcomes."

Perhaps the first logic models were found in the discrepancy evaluation model, which was employed as a means to plan and evaluate educational programs for improvement and assessment (Provus, 1971). The model provided a tool for the evaluator to work collaboratively with the project staff to identify program inputs, processes, and outcomes. The emerging model served as the standard by which the program was evaluated. The purpose of the evaluation was to identify the degree to which program performance matched the standard. If there was a discrepancy, staff could revise the standard or put more pressure on implementation fidelity.

Rush and Ogborne (1991) describe the evolution of logic modeling during the 1970s and 1980s and point out that Suchman (1967) suggested the construction of a hierarchy of objectives when evaluators were presented with many short-term and longer-term goals and to help program managers make explicit their assumptions about cause and effect. Wholey's early use of the logic model (1983, 1987) emphasized the theories that program managers had about their programs for use in evaluability assessments during initial planning of an evaluation. Bennett developed a "chain of events" model in 1979 that appears in Patton's discussion of the logic model (1997). Mayeske (1999) suggests that an early version of the logic model was the "log frame," which the U.S. Agency for International Development (U.S. AID) used for years and that this developed somewhat separately but did influence Wholey and his associates at the Urban Institute in the late 1970s. den Heyer (2002) recounts how the logical framework analysis was invented by a team of consultants led by Rosenberg; it has become standard procedure for project and program management and evaluation at international development agencies in Canada, Denmark, Germany, Sweden, and Britain, in addition to the U.S. AID.

More recent work shows an expansion in the uses of the logic model and attempts to add features or depth. The program logic and linkages (ProLL) model of Rasappan (1995a) and Winston is a logic model that includes policy and objectives achievement in addition to the more traditional elements related to a program. Bennett's TOP model shows how the planning process is a mirror of the logic developed for evaluation design. Montague (1997) added the important concept of "reach" explicitly to the logic model, placing "who" as an element between the "how" and the "why." He and others often refer to logic models as "logical frameworks" or "performance frameworks." McLaughlin and Jordan (1991) were among the first to include the external context and notion of shared responsibility for outcomes into the model. Owen and Rogers (1999) describe its use in clarificative evaluation used during design of a program. Funnell's logic model (2000) helps managers deal with program delivery questions by asking that risk be defined at various steps so programs are aware of factors within and outside the program's control. Parsons (1999) is working with logic models that show systems and systemic change and is one of those modifying logic models for cultural differences. Fraser (2002) and others are developing logic models that show temporal dimensions more explicitly.

There are a variety ways of presenting logic models and differences in scope and uses. Some differences may be just in the translation, as is the case with "chains of reasoning" (Torvatn, 1999), or one of emphasis, as with theory of action (Patton, 1997) and "performance framework" (Montague, 1997; McDonald and Teather, 1997). But there are differences in the scope of the logic model and the process used to develop and use the model. Logic models are increasingly used for program design and management rather than for the evaluation of completed projects. Their growing use for planning and management usually requires increasing explanatory power, description of a theory of change, and more resources and time to complete and update the logic model. The more traditional linear, cause-and-effect logic models emphasize activities or sequence of outcomes and are often used for evaluability assessment, evaluation planning, or outcomes assessment. Logic models such as Funnell's are more dynamic, and they include behavior change, risk, context, and mediating variables. These take more time to develop, but have added utility as integrating frameworks for evaluation and performance measurement. The use of logic models for program and performance planning requires yet more time, more frequent updating, and models that are systemic and recursive and include organizational dynamics at more than one level. This emerging form of logic model is evident in conference presentations and discussions on evaluation listservs, but there is little written on the approach.

Building the Logic Model

The logic model is constructed in five stages:

   Stage 1—collecting the relevant information

   Stage 2—describing the problem the program will solve and its context

   Stage 3—defining the elements of the model in a table

   Stage 4—drawing the logic model

   Stage 5—verifying the model

> ### Tips to Consider Before Starting
>
> - Think of developing a logic model as a process. In general, it is important that program managers and staff be very involved in developing their logic model. The program should "do it themselves" after having had training in the logic modeling technique.
> - Do not try to do the job alone. It is important to involve in a work group a full range of stakeholders who are associated in some way with the implementation of the model and its results.
> - Be careful with jargon. Since logic modeling is often a new way of thinking about the program, using familiar language helps others understand it. The format and terminology used in creating the logic model should be adapted to the program.
> - View logic modeling as part of long-term cultural change. Do not shortcut the process. Make the model an iterative process, updating it as program and program context change.

Stage 1: Collecting the Relevant Information

Building the logic model for a program should be a team effort in most cases. If the evaluation function is external to the program, the evaluator, in collaboration with program managers and staff, should carry out the process of creating the model. If the program manager does the work alone, there is a great risk that others may leave out or incorrectly represent essential parts. In the following steps to building the logic model, we refer to the manager as the key player. However, we recommend that persons knowledgeable of the program's planned performance, including partners and customers, be involved in a work group to develop the model. As the building process begins, it will become evident that there are multiple realities or views of program performance. Developing a shared vision of how the program is supposed to work will be a product of persistent discovery and negotiation between and among stakeholders.

When a program is complex or poorly defined or communication and consensus are lacking, we recommend that a small subgroup or perhaps an independent facilitator perform the initial analysis and synthesis through document reviews and individual and focus group interviews. The product of this effort can then be presented to a larger work group as a catalyst for the logic model process.

Whether designing a new program or describing an existing program, it is essential that the evaluator or work group collect information relevant to the program from multiple sources. The information will come in the form of program documentation, as well as interviews with key stakeholders internal and external to the program. While strategic plans, annual performance plans, previous program evaluations, pertinent legislation and regulations, and the results of targeted interviews should be available to the manager before the logic model is constructed, this will be an iterative process requiring the ongoing collection of information. Conducting a literature review to gain insights on what others have done to solve similar problems, and on key contextual factors to consider in designing and implementing the program, can present powerful evidence that the program approach selected is correct.

Tips on Collecting the Relevant Information to Build the Logic Model

- Interview people associated with the program, starting with those closely associated with the design and implementation of the program and then moving to others either affected by the program or who have a stake in its results.
- Analyze documents with a small group, perhaps assisted by an independent facilitator, especially for complex, poorly defined programs or where communication and consensus is lacking.

Stage 2: Clearly Defining the Problem and Its Context

Clearly defining the need for the program is the basis for all that follows in the development of the logic model. The program should be grounded in an understanding of the problem that drives the need for the program. This understanding includes understanding the problems, who is involved, and what factors "cause" the problems. These are the factors that the program will address to achieve the longer-term goal of solving the problem.

For example, there are economic and environmental challenges related to the production, distribution, and end use of energy. U.S. taxpayers face problems such as dependence on foreign oil, air pollution, and the threat of global warming from burning of fossil fuels. The factors that might be addressed to increase the efficiency of the end use of energy include limited knowledge, risk aversion, consumers' budget constraints, lack of competitively priced clean and efficient energy technologies, externalities associated with public goods, and restructuring of U.S. electricity markets. To solve the problem of economic and environmental challenges related to the use of energy, the program chooses to focus on factors related to developing clean and efficient energy technologies and changing customer values and knowledge. As knowledge and values change, customer behavior changes lead to the use of technologies that will result in decreased use of energy, particularly of fossil fuels.

One of the greatest challenges that work groups developing logic models face is describing where their program ends and others start. For the process of building a specific program's logic model, the program's performance ends with the problem it is designed to solve with the resources it has acquired, with recognition of the external forces that could influence its success in solving that problem. Generally the manager's concern is determining the reasonable point of accountability for the program. At the point where the actions of customers, partners, or other programs are as influential on the outcomes as actions of the program, there is a shared responsibility for the outcomes and the program's accountability for the outcomes should be reduced. For example, the adoption of energy-efficient technologies is also influenced by financiers and manufacturers of those technologies.

Tips on Defining the Problem Addressed by the Program

- Look for what drives the need for the program. Some put client and customer needs as the first point in the model.
- Define all the major factors that "cause" the problem.
- Define which factors the program addresses and where it fits in the hierarchy of other programs addressing the problem.
- Seek agreement on a single problem statement, or assign priorities to competing goals or objectives.
- Clarify legislative language, perhaps by adding an additional layer of outcomes.

When defining the problem, it is important to examine the external conditions under which a program is implemented and how those conditions affect outcomes. Such explanation helps clarify the program niche and the assumptions on which performance expectations are set. Understanding program context provides an important contribution to program improvement (Weiss, 1997). Explaining the relationship of the problem addressed through the program, the factors that cause the problem, and external factors enables the manager to argue that the program is addressing an important problem in a sensible way.

It is important to recognize contextual factors before the program starts because the program may be able to do something about them. For example, we once were asked to participate in the evaluation of a preservice teacher training program before it started. When we met with staff, we began the logic modeling process to get a grasp on how they thought the program might work. When we finished the first draft, one outcome was that student teachers would practice technology integration in their practicum sites. We asked if there were any factors that could influence reaching this outcome. Staff said that participating classroom teachers would have to be skillful in the use of technology. As a result of this interchange, staff decided to amend their initial logic to include training for classroom teachers who would be working with the preservice teachers.

Many of the problems that programs address are highly complex, resulting from a number of causal factors. Most programs are uniquely qualified to address a few of these factors, but if the problem is to be solved, then many of these factors must be addressed. We recommend that the program staff identify all the factors that need to be addressed and then develop performance partnerships with other programs whose mission is to solve the same problem. Until the performance partnerships are established, all factors that are not under the control of the program fall into the context and may have a negative impact on the program's long-term success. For example, many federal programs depend on state and local programs to carry out policies established at the federal level. One of the performance goals of the U.S. Environmental Protection Agency is to ensure the availability of clean and safe water. This will not happen if localities do not develop and enforce guidelines for protecting waters.

Stage 3: Defining the Elements of the Logic Model

Building a logic model usually begins with categorizing the information collected into "bins," or columns in a table. The manager goes through the information and tags each as a resource, activity, output, short-term outcome, intermediate outcome, long-term outcome, or external factor. Since we are building a model of how the program works, not every program detail has to be identified and catalogued, just those that are key to enhancing program staff and stakeholder understanding of how the program works.

As the elements of the logic model are being gathered, the manager, evaluator, and work group should continually check the accuracy and completeness of the information contained in the table. The checking process is best done by involving representatives of key stakeholder groups to determine if they can understand the logical flow of the program from resources to solving the longer-term problem. Thus, the checking process goes beyond

Tips for Defining Contextual Factors Associated with Program Implementation

- Identify contextual factors that might influence the performance of the program: special features of the environment such as transportation restrictions, economic pressures, or clients' socioeconomic status, for example.
- Try to ascertain if there are changes in the context that could influence performance, such as staff turnover, new policies, or changes in the economy.
- Determine if the program can be modified to address or take advantage of the contextual factors identified.
- Identify possible performance partnerships with other programs whose results affect those of the program.
- Recognize that any factors not accounted for could influence the results, and remember to assess their influence in the evaluation.

determining if all the key elements have been identified to confirming that reading from left to right (or top to bottom), there is an obvious sequence or bridge from one column to the next.

One way to conduct the check is to ask "how" and "why" questions. Start with an entry in any column in the table, and ask, "How did we get here?" For example, "If we select a particular short-term outcome, is there an output statement that leads to this outcome?" Or for the same outcome, we could ask, "Why are we aiming for that outcome?" The answer lies in a subsequent outcome statement in the intermediate- or long-term outcome columns. Begin to organize the elements in the table into chains of activities, outputs, and a sequence of outcomes. If the work group cannot answer either the "how" or "why" question, then an element needs to be added or clarified by adding more detail to the elements in question. It is also helpful to inquire whom the action is for and who does the action, and further to ask "what else?" to account for any other programs that could be either a barrier or a boost to program activities. Ask these questions at any point in the logic modeling process, from inputs or resources to outcomes or results. The process of asking "how" and "why" questions is sometimes called *forward* and *backward mapping*.

Stage 4: Drawing the Logic Model

The logic model captures the logical flow and linkages that exist in any performance story. Using the program elements in the table, the logic model organizes the information, enabling the audience to understand and evaluate the hypothesized linkages. Where the resources, activities, and outcomes are listed within their respective columns in the story, they are specifically linked in the model, so that the audience can see exactly which activities lead to what intermediate outcomes and which intermediate outcomes lead to what longer-term outcomes or impacts.

Tips on Defining the Elements of the Logic Model

- Categorize the information into columns of the logic table. Later, organize rows to show logical links.
- Define the target audiences and expected effects of the program for each.
- Put the outcomes into a sequence.
- Map both forward and backward to develop and check logic and assumptions. Ask, "How do [did] we make this happen?" "Why do [did] we do this?" "If this, then that." "If that, then what?"
- Check up, down, and across for associations with other programs and partners.
- Combine and summarize program elements or activities, limiting the number of activity groups to no more than five to seven. These are the program strategies that lead to expected results.

Although there are several ways to present the logic model, usually the model is set forth as a diagram with columns and rows of boxes, with abbreviated text put in a box and causal linkages shown with connecting one-way arrows. (There are a number of tools that evaluators can use to construct the logic model including Inspiration, Microsoft PowerPoint, and Microsoft Visio.) We place inputs or resources to the program in the first column at the left of the model and the longer-term outcomes and problem to be solved on the far right column. In the second column, the major program activities are boxed. In the columns following activities, the intended outputs and outcomes from each activity are shown, listing the intended customer for each output or outcome. Another common format is showing the logic top to bottom rather than left to right, usually with resources and activities at the top and the goals at the bottom of the page.

An example of a logic model for an energy efficiency technology development program is depicted in Figure 1.2. This model shows the relationship of multiple program elements in a "Z" pattern, where one set of activities and outcomes leads to another. The rows are created according to activities or activity groupings. If there is a rough sequential order to the activities, as there often is, the rows will reflect that order reading from top to bottom of the diagram. This is the case if the accomplishments of the program come in stages, as demonstrated in our example of the if-then statements. When the outcomes from one activity serve as a resource for another activity chain, an arrow is drawn from that outcome to the next activity chain. The arrows represent the association between the program elements—the if-then relationship. The last in the sequence of activity chains could describe the efforts of external partners, as in the example in Figure 1.2.

Rather than a sequence, there could be a multifaceted approach with several concurrent strategies that tackle a problem. The arrangement of the boxes in the model would reflect that. For example, a program might do research in some areas and technology development and deployment in others, all working toward one goal such as reducing energy use and emissions. The reader is referred to Figure 2.1, Tennessee's prenatal program, for another example of a more complex logic model in which there are a number of activity groups: a central office, contract agency, local health department, regional office, and hospitals that contain activities that lead to the intended program outcomes.

Although the example in Figure 1.2 shows one-to-one relationships among program elements, this is not always the case. It may be that one program element leads to more than one outcome, all of which are of interest to stakeholders and are part of describing the value of the program. For example, the United Way might have identified infant mortality as a critical problem that needs to be addressed. One of its partners, the school division, discovers that several teenagers in the school are pregnant, and an after-school program is designed to address the needs of these students. The outcomes of the program are increasing the participants' knowledge and skills related to prenatal health *and* caring for newborns. The impact of the program is a reduction in infant mortality in the community.

Activities can be described at many levels of detail. Since models are simplifications, activities that lead to the same outcome may be grouped to capture the level of detail necessary for a particular audience. A rule of thumb is that a logic model should have no more than five to seven activity groupings. Most programs are complex enough that logic models at more than one level of detail are helpful. A logic model more elaborate than the simple one shown in Figure 1.1 can be used to portray more detail for all or any one of its elements. For example, research activities may include literature reviews, conducting experiments, collecting information from multiple sources, analyzing data, and writing reports. These can be grouped and labeled as research. However, it may be necessary to formulate a more detailed and elaborate description of research subactivities for those staff responsible and if this area is of

Figure 1.2. A "Z" Logic Model for a Research and Technology Development Organization

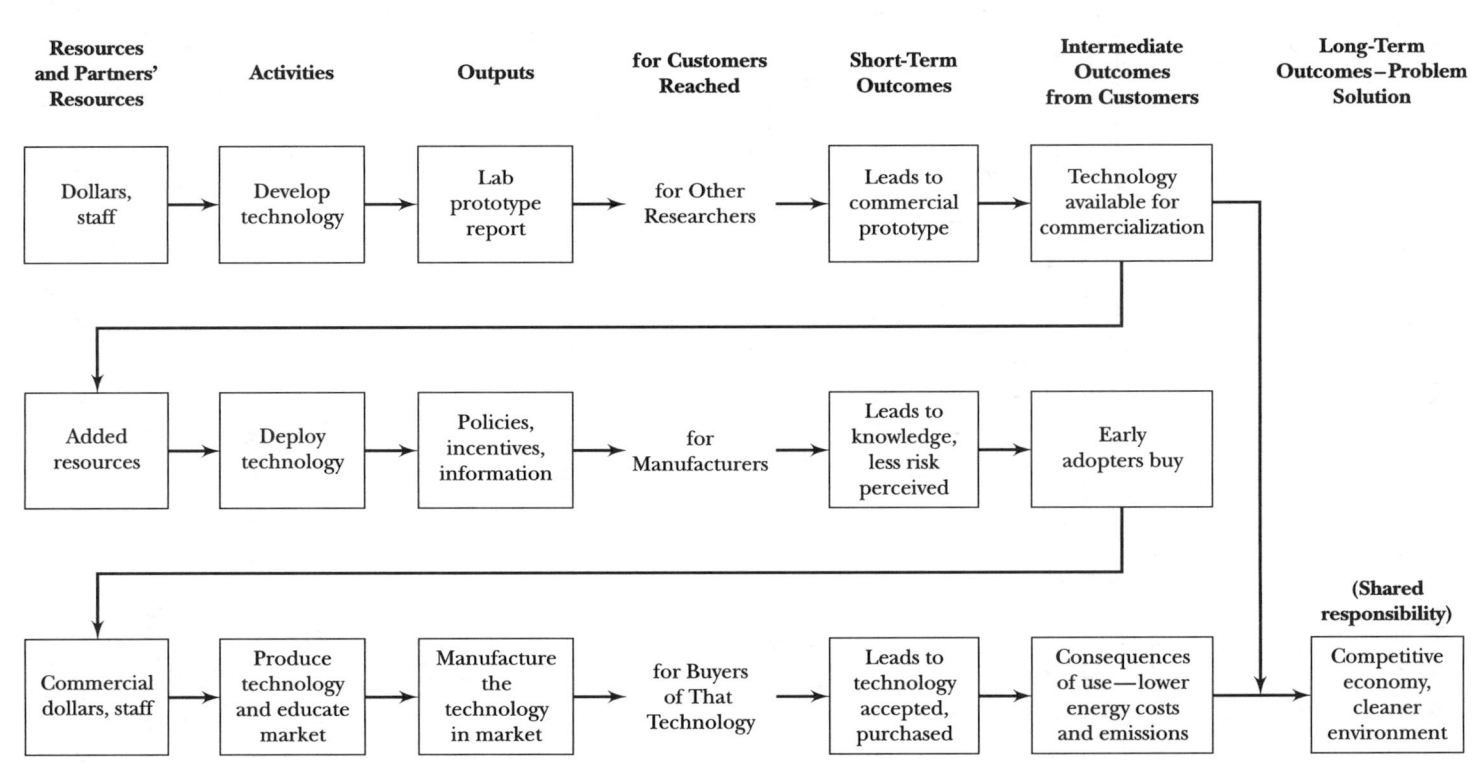

Resources and Partners' Resources | **Activities** | **Outputs** | **for Customers Reached** | **Short-Term Outcomes** | **Intermediate Outcomes from Customers** | **Long-Term Outcomes—Problem Solution**

Dollars, staff → Develop technology → Lab prototype report → for Other Researchers → Leads to commercial prototype → Technology available for commercialization

Added resources → Deploy technology → Policies, incentives, information → for Manufacturers → Leads to knowledge, less risk perceived → Early adopters buy

(Shared responsibility)

Commercial dollars, staff → Produce technology and educate market → Manufacture the technology in market → for Buyers of That Technology → Leads to technology accepted, purchased → Consequences of use—lower energy costs and emissions → Competitive economy, cleaner environment

External Influences: Price of oil and electricity, economic growth in industry and in general, perception of risk of global climate change and need for national energy security, market assumptions, technology assumptions

specific interest to a stakeholder group. For example, funding agencies might want to understand the particular approach to research that will be employed to answer key research questions.

The final product may be viewed as a network displaying the interconnections between the major elements of the program's expected performance, from resources to solving an important problem. External factors that influence the success of the program may be entered into the model at the bottom unless the program has sufficient information to predict the point at which they might occur. The external factors shown with the logic model serve to record the assumptions that went into the development of the model. They are helpful for people not familiar with the program and for evaluators and staff when using or revising the model.

Tips on Developing the Logic Model

- Start with simple forms of the diagram and then move to more complex diagrams.
- Be patient. Completed logic models are deceptively simple. In reality, it takes many drafts to describe the essence of a program.
- Consider having more than one model with different levels of detail, different groups of activities, different levels at which performance is measured, different stakeholder views, and different theories.
- Limit the words in the diagram. Provide more detail in separate charts or a written narrative.
- Limit the number of arrows. Show only the most critical relationships and feedback loops.
- Include outputs to external customers only, collapsing internal outputs such as management plans to one activity group or a separate document.
- Leave organizational charts separate, but use same activity descriptions in both.

Stage 5: Verifying the Logic Model with Stakeholders

As the logic model process unfolds, the work group responsible for producing the model should continuously evaluate it with respect to its goal of representing the program logic—how the program works under what conditions to achieve its short-, intermediate-, and long-term aims. The verification process should engage appropriate stakeholders in the review process. The work group will use the logic model diagram and the supporting table and text. During this time, the work group also can address the critical information they need about performance, setting the stage for evaluation and measurement plans.

A good way to check the logic model is to describe the program logic as hypotheses—a series of if-then statements (United Way of America, 1996): given observations of key contextual factors, *if* resources, *then* program activities; *if* program activities, *then* outputs for targeted customer groups. If outputs change behavior, first short- and then intermediate-term outcomes occur. If intermediate outcomes, then longer-term outcomes that lead to the problem being solved.

Given the problem of limited energy resources, the hypothesis might go something like this:

> Under the conditions that the price of oil and electricity increase as expected
>
> *If* the program performs applied research, *then* it will produce ideas for technology change.
>
> *If* industry researchers take this information and apply it to energy technologies, *then* the potential for technology changes will be tested and identified.
>
> *If* this promising new knowledge is used by technology developers, *then* prototypes of energy-efficient technologies will be developed.
>
> *If* manufacturers use the prototypes and perceive value and low risk, *then* commercially available energy-saving technologies will result.
>
> *If* there is sufficient market education and incentives and if the price is right, *then* consumers will purchase the new technologies.
>
> *If* the targeted consumers use the newly purchased technologies, *then* there should be a net reduction in the energy use, energy costs, and emissions, thus making the economy more competitive and the environment cleaner.

In addition to why, how, and if-then questions, we recommend four evaluation design questions be addressed in the final verification process:

- Is the level of detail sufficient to create understandings of the elements and their interrelationships?
- Is the program logic complete? That is, are all the key elements accounted for?

- Is the program logic theoretically sound? Do all the elements fit together logically? Are there other plausible pathways to achieving the program outcomes?
- Have all the relevant external contextual factors been identified and their potential influences described?

Pitfalls and Ways to Work Around Them

There are three primary areas of criticism of logic models. The first is that it can take so much time and so many resources that not enough energy and resources are left to complete whatever task the logic model was to facilitate. Some of the ways to ensure this does not happen are listed in Exhibit 1.1. Two of the four solutions are to use a broader definition of benefits when

Exhibit 1.1. Logic Modeling Pitfalls and How to Avoid Them

Pitfall	Work-Around
Time and resource sink	Avoid trying for perfection. Leave some elements unknown.
	Plan cost and schedule to include downstream activities such as choosing performance measures or planning next steps.
	Include all benefits in cost-benefit analysis of logic modeling, including team building and benefits to stakeholders as well as evaluator.
	Actual total costs might be lower if use of the logic model avoids costly premature impact evaluation or costly program design or implementation flaw.
Too linear	Recognize that the linear view can often be a helpful simplification.
	Use the Z form in Figure 1.2 to show concurrent or sequential logics with shared responsibility for impact.
	Indicate length of time for components of the logic model.
	Color-code to show aspects such as timing.
	Use a tree-type diagram with roots, trunk, branches, leaves, and fruit.
	Use spirals or three-dimensional drawings
Rigid use, not responsive to new information	Develop with program staff and stakeholders.
	Use and revisit the logic model regularly and recheck assumptions, since program operations often shift as staff measure and respond to performance.
	Keep an eye on developments in the program context that influence performance.

doing the cost-benefit analysis of developing the logic model. Consider the team-building and communication benefits, for example.

A second criticism is that logic models are too linear, but little in today's world is linear, and people tend to assume a temporal sequence that may not be the case. While linear models are often helpful and appropriate, some logic model developers look for alternative ways to describe program logic. Fraser (2002) proposes two new graphic conventions for logic models: a sequence map and a logic map. The sequence map illustrates when things can be expected to occur over a program's life cycle and beyond, using position and length of the box somewhat as a Gantt chart does. The logic map maps logic on a two-dimensional continuum. The "Z" model in Figure 1.2 is another workaround for this problem.

A third area of criticism is that the uses of the models are rigid rather than dynamic and thus do not capture the change inherent in the program and its circumstances. This criticism can be countered by changes in the way logic models are developed and the way they are used. Logic models should be updated regularly as new information is acquired and circumstances change. There is no need for them to be rigid. Linking logic models to organizational units can increase the likelihood that they are used and improvements and changes noticed.

The general view is that in spite of problems, the logic model is better than alternatives such as path diagrams, program templates, concept maps, and narrative.

Use of Logic Modeling in Measurement and Evaluation

Having a logic model in place at the beginning of the evaluation is important because it serves as an advance organizer or focusing mechanism for the evaluation and the measurement of key variables or performance indicators. Once the evaluator and staff agree on the logic, the evaluation questions and data collection strategies may be developed. We caution, though, that the logic model is a draft document that captures the program staff's concept of how the program works. Indeed, it may not work that way at all. Thus, the evaluator needs to test the logic model through an implementation assessment (see Chapter Three) to develop what Patton (1997) has called the theory in practice. If discrepancies are found, the evaluator and program staff should discuss the ramifications of the discrepancies and either redesign the program or increase implementation fidelity to enhance the chance for success.

Stufflebeam (2001) cautions that for many programs, it will be very difficult to establish a defensible theory of change either because previous social science research has not produced sufficient evidence to support theory development or there is insufficient time to develop the theory. He argues, as we do, that logic modeling is appropriate as long as too much time is not taken and that the evaluator understands that the model is a draft that needs to be assessed in reality.

Yin (1989) discusses the importance of pattern matching as a tool to study the delivery and impact of a program. The use of the logic model process results in a pattern that can be used in this way. It thus becomes a tool to assess program implementation and program impacts. An iterative procedure may be applied that first determines the theory in use, followed by either revisions in the espoused theory or tightening of the implementation of the espoused theory. Next, the resulting tested pattern can be used to address program impacts.

In addition to testing theory and logic, evaluation and measurement also serve the purpose of measuring the degree to which the program achieves specified performance objectives. Evaluation is the systematic investigation of the merit or worth of an object for the purpose of reducing uncertainty in decision making about that object. Evaluators often use the terms *merit* and *worth* synonymously. However, it is useful to contrast the two to focus the intent of evaluation more broadly. *Merit* focuses more on the effectiveness of the program to achieve its aims, while *worth* focuses on the broader impact of the program. Does achieving its aims add value to the community? The logic model helps the evaluator and project staff members focus the evaluation on questions of both merit and worth. Worth might be assessed from the standpoint of the degree to which the long-term impacts on which the program focuses have been achieved, while merit is addressed on the basis of the degree to which short-term and intermediate-term outcomes have been achieved. The program sphere of influence usually stops at the intermediate-term outcomes. Longer-term outcomes typically require the formation of performance partnerships because so many intervening variables cause variation in these strategic indicators of success.

Evaluation should examine or test the underlying assumptions about how the program works to achieve these outcomes. Weiss (1997), citing her earlier work, noted the importance of not only capturing the program process but also collecting information on the hypothesized linkages. According to Weiss, the measurement should "track the steps of the program" (p. x). In the logic model, the boxes are the steps that can often be simply counted or monitored, and the lines connecting the boxes are the hypothesized linkages or causal relationships that require in-depth study to determine and explain what happened. It is the testing of the linkages, the arrows in the logic chart, that allows the evaluator to determine if the program is working. Monitoring the degree to which elements are in place, even the intended and unintended outcomes, will not explain the measurement or tell the evaluator if the program is working. What is essential is the testing of the program hypotheses impact evaluation (see Chapters Five and Six). Even if the evaluator observes that intended outcomes were achieved, the following question must be asked: "What features, if any, of the program contributed to the achievement of intended and unintended outcomes?"

We should note that the verification and checking activities described with respect to steps 4 and 5 actually represent the first stages of performance measurement. That is, this process ensures that the program design is logically constructed, that it is complete, and that it captures what program staff and stakeholders believe is an accurate picture of the program.

The Community Anti-Drug Coalitions of America (2000) has developed a simple yet effective way of displaying the program logic, evaluation questions, and data sources. The model is set forth in Table 1.1. The model contains the problem on which the program focuses (column F) and the aspect of the problem that the program is uniquely qualified to address (column A). Next, it presents what is done by whom (column B) and to whom (column C) and the short-term outcomes that can be expected (column E). In the middle of the diagram (column D), the model presents the underlying assumptions of the program. Then, for each element of the logic, evaluation or monitoring questions are identified with probable sources of information. Thus, in a simple one-page framework, the model becomes an advance organizer for evaluation planning and a way to explain why results occurred (or did not occur).

Conclusion

Program managers across the public and nonprofit sectors are being asked to describe and evaluate their programs in new ways. People want managers to present a logical argument for how and why the program is addressing a specific customer need and how measurement and evaluation will assess and improve program effectiveness. Managers do not have clear and logically consistent methods to help them with this task, but evaluators do, and they can bring this tool to managers and help them meet the new challenges.

This chapter describes the logic model process in enough detail that evaluators as well as program managers and staff can use it to develop and tell the performance story for their program. The logic model describes the logical linkages among program resources, activities, outputs, customers reached, and short-, intermediate-, and longer-term outcomes. Once this model of expected performance is produced, critical monitoring and evaluation areas can be identified. Because the logic model and the measurement plan have been developed with the program stakeholders, the story these tell should be a shared vision with clear and shared expectation of success.

Table 1.1. Sample Program Logic for Community Drug Program

			Program Logic		
A *Goals*	*B* *Strategies*	*C* *Target Group*	*D* *If-Then Statements*	*E* *Short-Term Outcomes*	*F* *Long-Term Impacts*
Reduce academic failure through enhanced reading instruction for children in grades 1–3	Reading tutoring: three hours per week for one school year, fifty students by trained reading instructors	Children in grades 1–3 at the local elementary school who are struggling academically as identified by their teachers	If reading tutoring is offered to students having academic problems, then students will have the opportunity to improve their academic skills through enhanced reading skills. If students take the opportunity, they improve their academic skills. If they improve their academic skills, they will not fail in school. If they do not fail in school, they are less likely to abuse alcohol, tobacco, and other drugs.	Participants' grades improve; participants move to next grade level on time	Participants do not begin using alcohol, tobacco, and other drugs within three years after participating in the program
Measurement Was academic failure reduced in target population?	Did fifty students participate in tutoring program using trained tutors for three hours per week for one school year?	Were participants children from grades 1–3 who were struggling academically?	Did students who were selected for the program participate? Did students' reading skills improve? Did their grades improve? Were they advanced to the next grade on time?	Did participants' grades improve? Did participants move to next grade on time?	Did participants begin using alcohol, tobacco, and other drugs within three years after participating in the program?
Data Sources See column E for source	Program records from coordinator	Program records from coordinator	Program records from coordinator	Existing school records	Participant surveys conducted annually

Source: Community Anti-Drug Coalitions of America (2000), [http://www.cadca.org].

References

Bickman, L. "The Functions of Program Theory." In L. Bickman (ed.), *Using Program Theory in Evaluation*. New Directions for Program Evaluation, no. 33. San Francisco: Jossey-Bass, 1987.

Birkmayer, J. D., and Weiss, C. H. "Theory-Based Evaluation in Practice: What Do We Learn?" *Evaluation Review*, 2000, *4*(4), 407–431.

Chen, H. T. *Theory-Driven Evaluations*. Thousand Oaks, Calif.: Sage, 1990.

Chen, H. T., and Rossi, P. W. "Evaluating with Sense: The Theory-Driven Approach." *Evaluation Review*, 1983, *7*, 283–302.

Community Anti-Drug Coalitions of America. *Coalition Building 103: Strategic Planning*. Alexandria, Va.: Community Anti-Drug Coalitions of America, 2000.

Cooksy, L. J., Gill, O., and Kelly, P. A. "The Program Logic Model as an Integrative Framework for a Multimethod Evaluation." *Evaluation and Program Planning*, 2001, *24*, 119–128.

Corbeil, R. "Logic on Logic Models." *Evaluation Newsletter*, Sept. 1986.

Den Heyer, M. "The Temporal Logic Model Concept." *Canadian Journal of Program Evaluation*, 2002, *17*(2), 27–47.

Funnell, S. "Program Logic: An Adaptable Tool for Designing and Evaluating Programs." *Evaluation News and Comment*, 1997, *6*(1), 5–17.

Funnell, S. "Developing and Using a Program Theory Matrix for Program Evaluation and Performance Monitoring." In P. Rogers, New Directions for Evaluation, no. 87. San Francisco: Jossey-Bass, Fall 2000.

Harrell, A., and others. *Evaluation Strategies for Human Services Programs: A Guide for Policymakers and Providers*. Washington, D.C.: Urban Institute, 1996.

Jordan, G. B., and Mortensen, J. "Measuring the Performance of Research and Technology Programs: A Balanced Scorecard Approach." *Journal of Technology Transfer*, 1997, *22*(2).

Jordan, G. B., Reed, J. H., and Mortensen, J. C. "Measuring and Managing the Performance of Energy Programs: An In-Depth Case Study." Paper presented at Eighth Annual National Energy Services Conference, Washington, D.C., June 1997.

Jullian, J. A., Jones, A., and Dey, D. "Evaluation and the Logic Model: Program Planning and Evaluation Tools." *Evaluation and Program Planning*, 1995, *18*(4), 333–341.

W. K. Kellogg Foundation. *Logic Model Development Guide*. [http://www.wkkf.org/Pubs/Tools/Evaluation/Pub3669.pdf]. 2001.

Leeuw, F. L. "Restructuring Program Theories: Methods Available and Problems to Be Solved." *American Journal of Evaluation*, 2003, *24*(1), 5–20.

Management Systems International. "The Logical Framework." Unpublished paper, Washington, D.C., 1995.

Mayeske, G. W. *Life Cycle Program Management and Evaluation: An Organic and Heuristic Approach.* Washington, D.C. U.S. Department of Agriculture, 1999.

Mayeske, G., and Lambur, M. *How to Design Better Programs: A Staff Centered Stakeholder Approach to Program Logic Modeling.* Crofton, Md.: Program Design Institute, 2001.

McDonald, R., and Teather, G. "Science and Technology Policy Evaluation Practices in the Government of Canada." In *Policy Evaluation in Innovation and Technology: Towards Best Practices: Proceedings of the Organization for Economic Co-operation and Development.* 1997.

McLaughlin, J. A., and Jordan, G. B. "Logic Models: A Tool for Telling Your Performance Story." *Evaluation and Program Planning,* 1991, *22*(1), 65–72.

Millar, A., Simeone, R. S., and Carnevale, J. T. "Logic Models: A Systems Tool for Performance Management." *Evaluation and Program Planning,* 2001, *24,* 73–81.

Montague, S. "The Three R's of Performance-Based Management." *Focus,* Dec.–Jan. 1994.

Montague, S. *The Three R's of Performance.* Ottawa, Canada: Performance Management Network, Sept. 1997.

Owen, J. M., and Rogers, P. J. *Program Evaluation: Forms and Approaches.* Thousand Oaks, Calif.: Sage, 1999.

Parsons, B., "Making Logic Models More Systemic: An Activity." AEA Session, Boulder, Colo.: InSites, 1999.

Patton, M. Q. *Utilization-Focused Evaluation: The New Century Text.* Thousand Oaks, Calif.: Sage, 1997.

Perrin, B. "Performance Measurement: Does the Reality Match the Rhetoric? A Rejoinder to Bernstein and Winston." *American Journal of Evaluation,* 1999, *20*(1), 101–111.

Provus, M. *Discrepancy Evaluation for Educational Program Improvement and Assessment.* Berkeley, Calif.: McCutchan Publishing, 1971.

Rasappan. "How to Budget for Results." *Khidmat,* Sept. 1995a, pp. 18–20.

Rasappan. "Success Formula for Matchmaking." *Khidmat,* Dec. 1995b, pp. 13–16.

Rogers, P. J., Petroscino, A., Huebner, T. A., and Hacsi, T. A. "Program Theory Evaluation: Practice, and Problems." *New Directions for Evaluation,* no. 87. San Francisco: Jossey-Bass, 2000.

Rush, B., and Ogborne, A. "Program Logic Models: Expanding Their Role and Structure for Program Planning and Evaluation." *Canadian Journal of Program Evaluation,* 1991, *6*(2).

Rutman, L. *Planning Useful Evaluations.* Thousand Oaks, Calif.: Sage, 1980.

Scheirer, M. A. "Designing and Using Process Evaluation." In J. S. Wholey, H. P. Hatry, and K. E. Newcomer (eds.), *Handbook of Practical Program Evaluation.* San Francisco: Jossey-Bass, 1994.

Scheirer, M. A. "Getting More 'Bang' for Your Performance Measures 'Buck.'" Paper presented at the American Evaluation Association, November and later published in the American Journal of Evaluation, 1999.

Smith, M. F. *Evaluability Assessment: A Practical Approach.* Norwell, Mass.: Kluwer, 1989.

Suchman, E. *Evaluative Research: Principles and Practices in Public Service & Social Action Programs.* New York: Russell Sage Foundation, 1967.

Teather, G., and Montague, S. "Performance Measurement, Management and Reporting for S&T Organizations—An Overview." *Journal of Technology Transfer,* 1997, *22*(2).

Torvatn, H. "Using Program Theory Models in Evaluation of Industrial Modernization Programs: Three Case Studies." *Evaluation and Program Planning,* 1999, *22*(1).

United Way of America. "*Measuring Program Outcomes: A Practical Approach.*" Arlington, Va.: United Way of America, 1996.

University of Wisconsin Cooperative Extension. Evaluation Logic Model Bibliography, Program Development and Evaluation web site, Retrieved from [http://www.uwex.edu/ces/pdande/evaluation/evallogicbiblio.html], 2003.

Unrau, Y. "A Program Logic Model Approach to Conceptualizing Social Service Programs." *Canadian Journal of Program Evaluation,* 1993, *8*(1), 117–134.

U.S. Agency for International Development. "Results Framework: Introduction/Context for Planning System." [http://www.info.usaid.gov/pubs/sourcebook/usgov/mfr.html] Material developed by MSI, http://www.info.usaid.gov/pubs/r4workshop/STRATEG6/]. 1999.

Weiss, C. "Theory-Based Evaluation: Past, Present, and Future." In D. Rog and D. Founier (eds.), *Progress and Future Directions in Evaluation: Perspectives on Theory, Practice, and Methods.* New Directions for Program Evaluation, no. 76. San Francisco: Jossey-Bass, 1997.

Weiss, C. "Which Links in Which Theories Shall We Evaluate?" In Rogers, et. al. (eds.) New Directions for Evaluation, no. 87. San Francisco: Jossey-Bass, 2000.

Wholey, J. S. *Evaluation and Effective Public Management.* New York: Little, Brown, 1983.

Wholey, J. S. "Evaluability Assessment: Developing Program Theory." In L. Bickman (ed.), *Using Program Theory in Evaluation.* New Directions for Program Evaluation, no. 33. San Francisco: Jossey-Bass, 1987.

Yin, R. K. *Case Study Research: Design and Methods.* Thousand Oaks, Calif.: Sage, 1989.

2

Evaluability Assessment

Joseph S. Wholey

The planning and design of evaluations requires difficult decisions as evaluators identify the questions to answer, the evaluation criteria to use, the data to collect, and the analyses to undertake. Evaluators must balance the feasibility and cost of possible evaluations against the likely benefits of those evaluations. This chapter discusses evaluability assessment: a process that helps evaluators to identify evaluations that might be useful, explore what evaluations would be feasible, and design useful evaluations.

Evaluability assessment can be thought of as a form of market research that assesses the demand for information that might come from various possible evaluations, assesses the feasibility of various evaluations, and helps match evaluation supply with demand by helping select designs for evaluations that are feasible, relevant, and useful. Although many of the steps in evaluability assessment are present in many evaluation design efforts, only rarely do evaluators perform all of these steps. At a minimum, evaluators should be familiar with this process and know why evaluations might miss the mark if some of the steps are omitted.

In planning evaluations, evaluators begin by identifying program goals, performance indicators, and data sources. Evaluation is unlikely to lead to improved program performance in the following circumstances:

- The evaluators and intended users fail to agree on the goals and performance criteria to be used in evaluating the program.

- The program goals are unrealistic given the program design, the resources committed to the program, and the program activities currently under way.
- Relevant performance information cannot be obtained at reasonable cost.
- Policymakers and managers are unable or unwilling to change the program on the basis of evaluation information.

Unless these problems can be overcome, evaluation is unlikely to contribute to improved performance.

If evaluators and intended users fail to agree on program goals, information priorities, and intended uses of program performance information, those who are designing the evaluations may focus on answering questions that are not relevant to policy and management decisions. If program goals are unrealistic because insufficient resources have been applied to critical program activities, the program has been poorly implemented, or managers lack knowledge of how to achieve program goals, the more fruitful course may be for policymakers and managers to change program activities or goals before undertaking further evaluation efforts. If relevant data cannot be obtained at reasonable cost, subsequent evaluation work is likely to be inconclusive. If policymakers and managers are unable or unwilling to use evaluation information to change the program, even the most conclusive evaluations are likely to produce "information in search of a user." Unless these problems can be overcome, evaluation will probably not contribute to improved program performance.

An exploratory evaluation process, evaluability assessment, has been developed to detect and help correct these four problems before further evaluation work is undertaken. We call a program *evaluable* to the extent that the following four propositions are true:

- *Program goals and priority information needs are well defined.* There is a reasonable level of agreement on program goals and performance criteria. If important side effects have been identified, they have been incorporated into the goal framework (for example, as goals for minimizing or controlling those side effects).
- *Program goals are plausible.* There is some likelihood that the goals will be achieved.
- *Relevant performance data can be obtained at reasonable cost.* There are feasible measures of key program inputs, program activities, program outputs (products and services delivered), and program outcomes (results).
- *Intended users of the evaluation results have agreed on how they will use the information,* for example, to improve program performance or communicate the value of program activities to higher policy levels.

Evaluability assessment is a process for clarifying program designs, exploring program reality, and, if necessary, helping to redesign programs to ensure that they meet these four criteria. Evaluability assessment not only shows whether a program can be meaningfully evaluated (any program can be evaluated) but also whether evaluation is likely to contribute to improved program performance. The original purposes of evaluability assessment were to determine whether formative evaluation was likely to help policymakers and managers to improve the performance of their programs and to get management agreement on specific evaluations to be undertaken and specific uses that would be made of the resulting information. As in the two examples presented in this chapter, evaluability assessment can also be used in designing summative evaluations to meet policymakers' needs for information about the impacts of programs.

Evaluability assessment is appropriate if there is policy- or management-level interest in improving program performance and a willingness to invest in evaluation, but managers have not yet defined program performance in terms of realistic, measurable goals or decided on intended uses of specific evaluation information. Evaluability assessment is most useful in large, decentralized programs in which policymaking and management responsibilities are dispersed, evaluation criteria are unclear, and program results are not readily apparent. Evaluability assessment may be a separate process or an initial step in a larger evaluation effort. When a reasonable set of evaluation criteria has been specified or the purpose of evaluation is accountability rather than program improvement, evaluability assessment may not be appropriate.

Rather than having the evaluator construct an evaluation design that may prove to be irrelevant, infeasible, inconclusive, untimely, or otherwise useless to those who wish to improve program performance, evaluability assessment begins the evaluation planning process by carrying out a preliminary evaluation of the program design. Evaluability assessment:

- Compares and contrasts the expectations and assumptions of those who have the most important influence over the program
- Compares those expectations with the reality of program activities underway and program outcomes that are occurring or are likely to occur
- Determines whether relevant program performance information is likely to be obtainable at reasonable cost
- Explores which of the evaluations that could be conducted would be most useful

The commitment that may be required to plan relevant, feasible evaluation work is likely to pay for itself by averting the greater costs of irrelevant, inconclusive evaluations that contribute little to improved program performance. The most time-consuming step that may occur in evaluability assessment, helping managers and policymakers to redesign their program prior to further evaluation work, is likely to be appropriate only when evaluability assessment reveals that specific program goals are unrealistic given the resources that have been allocated and the program activities that are underway and intended evaluation users believe that the program should be redesigned before further evaluation is done.

This chapter describes the evaluability assessment process, presents examples of evaluability assessment, and suggests solutions to problems that arise in the evaluability assessment process. The chapter draws on and reflects developments in evaluability assessment over the past thirty years (Horst, Nay, Scanlon, and Wholey, 1974; Schmidt and Waller, 1976; Nay, Scanlon, Graham, and Waller, 1977; Schmidt, 1977; Wholey, Bell, Scanlon, and Waller, 1977; Schmidt, Scanlon, and Bell, 1979; Rutman, 1980; Nay and Kay, 1982; Smith, 1989; Strosberg and Wholey, 1983; Wholey, 1983, 1987, 1994, 2002).

Key Steps in Evaluability Assessment

Although each step in evaluability assessment is important, it is essential not to get bogged down in any one of them. Evaluability assessment can take days, weeks, or months depending on the time available and the magnitude of the likely evaluation efforts. To keep the project moving, the key steps should be touched but not lingered on.

Evaluability Assessment: Key Steps

1. Involve intended users of evaluation information.
2. Clarify the intended program from the perspectives of policymakers, managers, those involved in service delivery, and other stakeholders.
3. Explore program reality, including the plausibility and measurability of program goals.
4. Reach agreement on any needed changes in program activities or goals.
5. Explore alternative evaluation designs.
6. Agree on evaluation priorities and intended uses of information on program performance.

Step 1: Involve Intended Users

Evaluators often operate in isolation from policymakers, managers, and program staff. Evaluability assessment, on the contrary, encourages interactions with key policymakers, managers, and staff. These interactions help to ensure that to the extent possible, program designs as seen by evaluators conform to both the expectations of key stakeholders and the reality of program operations. Evaluability assessment also helps shape stakeholders' expectations by informing key policymakers and managers of the expectations and priorities of others, by confronting them with the reality of the program as it is currently operating, and in some cases by helping them to explore the implications of possible changes in program activities or goals.

Evaluability assessments may use policy groups and work groups to facilitate policymaker, manager, and staff participation in evaluation. Work groups generally involve managers, program staff, and evaluators (Rog, 1985). Policy groups tend to involve higher-level managers and policymakers, who are briefed periodically on findings and options as the assessment and subsequent work proceed (Wholey, 1983).

Step 2: Clarify Program Intent

For many programs, the program design is vague or implausible. This vagueness may have been a deliberate strategy of the initial planners; perhaps too much precision about intended program activities or goals might have inhibited the political compromises needed to initiate the program and gain the resources needed for its maintenance and expansion. Thus, an important early task in evaluability assessment is to clarify the assumed relationships among program inputs, program activities, and intended program outcomes from the perspectives of key policymakers, managers and staff, and interest groups.

Here the evaluator documents program goals, expectations, causal assumptions, and the information needs and priorities of key stakeholders, clarifying the performance indicators, or types of evidence, in terms of which the program could be evaluated. The evaluators use two sources of information on program intent. The first is program documentation, including the program's authorizing legislation, if it is in the public sector, and the grant or contract document if it is private; they also examine, where appropriate, legislative history, regulations, guidelines, budget justifications, grant applications, monitoring and audit reports, research and evaluation studies, and other reports of program accomplishments. The second information source is interviews with policymakers, managers, and other stakeholders. The interviews focus on program priorities, expected program accomplishments, problems facing the program, and information needs. The questions that evaluators should explore in their review of relevant program documentation and in interviews and meetings with key stakeholders are listed in the box.

Guide for Review of Documentation and Interviews with Key Policymakers, Managers, and Interest Group Representatives

- From your perspective, what is the program trying to accomplish, and what resources does it have?
- What results have been produced to date?
- What accomplishments are likely in the next year or two?
- Why would the program produce those results?
- What are the program's main problems?
- How long will it take to solve those problems?
- What kinds of information do you get on the program's performance and results? What kinds of information do you need?
- How do you (how would you) use this information?
- What kinds of program performance information are requested by key stakeholders?

On the basis of information from these sources, the evaluators should now develop two sets of products that promote fruitful dialogue between evaluators and intended users of evaluation information: logic models (see Chapter One, this volume, and Figures 2.1 and 2.2) and lists of currently agreed-on program performance indicators. These products document the extent of agreement on program goals among policymakers, managers, and interest groups and the types of information that could be developed in terms of agreed-on performance indicators.

Logic models are flowcharts that identify program activities, intended program outcomes, and assumed causal linkages between activities and outcomes, as seen by policymakers, managers, those involved in service delivery, and other stakeholders. Some logic models also identify program inputs (human, capital, information, and other resources allocated to the program); program outputs (products and services delivered by the program); customers or participants served by the program; and relevant external contextual factors (Chapter One, this volume). Some also identify performance monitoring and evaluation activities included in the program. An important part of developing logic models is identifying the intermediate outcome goals that connect program activities to end outcomes. Logic models focus the attention of policymakers, managers, and evaluators on the kinds of evaluation that might be useful: occurrence of intended program results can be tracked in performance monitoring systems or management information systems (Chapter Four, this volume), and assumed causal connections can be tested through the use of one of the impact evaluation designs discussed below (Chapters Five and Six, this volume).

In evaluability assessment, evaluators do not hypothesize the program design. Instead, they extract the program design—in particular, the outputs and intermediate outcomes expected to connect program activities to end outcomes—from relevant documentation and from key actors in and around the program. The evaluators ensure that the program design is acceptable to the primary intended users of evaluation information before undertaking a full-scale evaluation. The intended users' program design, which may evolve during the course of an evaluability assessment, is the framework for decisions on the collection and analysis of program performance data.

In many programs, policymakers and managers agree on the intended program in all important respects. In other instances, however, there will be conflict among policymakers and managers over program goals or the relative importance of different goals. As long as some of the key stakeholders are interested in a particular goal, it will often be included in management's program design as a guide to possible monitoring and evaluation efforts.

In meetings with program managers and policymakers, evaluators should use models of program inputs, activities, intended outcomes, and assumed causal linkages to highlight differences in expectations and to facilitate agreement on the intended program between themselves and the primary intended users of evaluation information. Those meetings should also review possible measures of program performance to ensure a common understanding of the goals and performance indicators to be used in subsequent evaluation activities.

Step 3: Explore Program Reality

The second focus of evaluability assessment is on program reality. The evaluator documents the feasibility of measuring program performance and estimates the likelihood that program goals will be achieved. Believing that evaluators too often attempt measurements and comparisons that later prove to be unrealistic or too costly, Nay and his colleagues recommended that those planning and designing evaluations spend some time documenting program reality (Nay, Scanlon, Graham, and Waller, 1977; Nay and Kay, 1982). A preliminary examination of program operations and results may reveal that program reality is far from the program design envisioned by those at higher management and policy levels.

Using existing documentation (program data systems, monitoring reports, reports of project accomplishments, research and evaluation studies, and audit reports), site visits to a small number of projects, and information obtained from knowledgeable observers of the program, the evaluators should compare the intended program with actual program inputs, activities, and outcomes; identify problems inhibiting effective program performance; and identify feasible measures of program performance. Issues that evaluators should explore through review of relevant documents and discussions with those involved in service delivery and other knowledgeable observers are presented in the box.

Guide for Review of Documents and Interviews with Operating-Level Managers and Staff

- What are your goals for the project or program?
- What are the major project activities?
- Why will those activities achieve those goals?
- What resources are available to the project? Number of staff? Total budget? Sources of funds?
- What evidence is necessary to determine whether goals are met?
- What happens if goals are met or not met?
- How is the project related to local priorities?
- What data or records are maintained? Costs? Services delivered? Service quality? Outcomes? Something else?
- How often are these data collected?
- How is this information used? Does anything change based on these data or records?
- What major problems are you experiencing?
- What results have been produced to date?
- What accomplishments are likely in the next two to three years?

Step 4: Reach Agreement on Any Needed Changes in the Program Design

Evaluability assessment, in addition to its role in evaluation planning, is itself a qualitative process that is closely related to implementation evaluation (Chapters Three and Thirteen, this volume). Evaluability assessment goes beyond implementation evaluation by using site visits, agency and program data systems, prior audits and evaluations, and interviews with knowledgeable observers to produce preliminary estimates of the program's likely success in producing intended outcomes. As such, evaluability assessment may lead to changes in program design or improvements in program implementation before further evaluation efforts occur.

Using the information gathered and analyzed in the first three evaluability assessment steps, the evaluators now work with management to examine the implications of what has been learned and, if necessary, to explore options for program change and program improvement. Comparing the intended program with program reality may indicate that changes should be made in the program prior to further investments in evaluation. In some cases, the evaluability assessment reveals that some program goals are implausible given the manner in which the program is being operated. Insufficient resources may have been allocated for effective program performance, the intended program may have been poorly implemented in the field, or available technology may be insufficient to achieve program goals. In other cases, higher-level managers and policymakers may find that the program's actual accomplishments suggest the desirability of adding program goals that capture some of those accomplishments. At this point, the evaluator may suggest changes in the program design that appear likely to improve program performance. Such changes might include either changes in program activities or deletion of rhetorical program goals that seem unattainable at current or probable resource levels.

Step 5: Explore Alternative Evaluation Designs

Although reality is complex, the portion of reality that can usefully be evaluated is relatively simple, especially when time and other resources are limited. The next five chapters describe specific evaluation design options; succeeding chapters discuss data collection procedures, data analysis techniques, and ways to ensure that evaluation efforts are useful. The decision to proceed with an evaluation usually focuses on specific portions of the intended program: measuring specific variables or testing specific causal assumptions to provide information that policymakers or managers intend to use in specific ways. At this point, the evaluator should identify a set of evaluation design options that outline the following factors:

- Data that could be collected
- Analyses that could be undertaken
- The likely costs of such data collection and analysis (dollar costs and costs in terms of the time of evaluation staff, program managers and staff, and clients)
- Calendar time
- Political and bureaucratic costs
- The uses that would be made of the resulting information

Step 6: Agree on Evaluation Priorities and
Intended Uses of Evaluation Information

When policymakers or managers select an evaluation design of the form just suggested, they will at least tentatively be agreeing on how the resulting evaluation information will be used. By explaining the implications of the status quo option (no further evaluation) and the costs and potential uses of other specific evaluation options, the evaluator encourages policymakers and managers to commit themselves to using evaluation information at the time that they decide on the collection and analysis of specific data on program performance.

Tennessee's Prenatal Program

Evaluability assessment of the Toward Improving the Outcome of Pregnancy (TIOP) project and related prenatal programs provides an early example of how a useful evaluation can be designed. In July 1981, the Tennessee Department of Public Health began the last year of TIOP, a five-year, federally funded, $400,000-per-year project. The TIOP grant and other federal, state, local, and foundation resources provided funds for prenatal and infant care for low-income patients in nineteen counties in rural Tennessee. Pilot projects in local health departments provided community outreach, screening and diagnostic services, treatment, education, and referral and follow-up of women with high-risk pregnancies and high-risk infants. The Department of Public Health faced the end of the TIOP project grant and likely constraints on state funding for prenatal care. An evaluation of the project was required under the terms of the federal grant. Evaluability assessment was used to clarify the design of the department's prenatal care program in the nineteen rural counties and determine the evaluation activities that would be most useful as the TIOP grant funding came to an end (Wholey and Wholey, 1981a, 1981b, 1982; Smith, 1986; Wholey, 1987).

In forty-eight staff days of effort over a five-week period, two evaluation consultants worked with Department of Public Health staff to plan an evaluation of the prenatal program and establish a decision process that would use the evaluation findings. During this time, the evaluators held a series of working meetings with managers and staff, reviewed documents describing the TIOP project and related prenatal services, and visited one of the six regional projects that then made up the program. (Originally there had been seven regional projects but one had closed, reducing the number of counties served from nineteen to eighteen.) These activities helped the evaluators to (1) identify likely users of the planned evaluation; (2) clarify the program design; (3) compare the intended prenatal program with actual program inputs, activities, and outcomes; (4) determine the likely availability of relevant data; and (5) determine which of the feasible evaluation options would be most relevant and useful.

Involving Intended Users

To facilitate evaluation and the use of evaluation findings, the department established a work group and a policy group that would provide ongoing input to the evaluation. The work group members were key central office maternal and child health staff, staff from three of the regional prenatal TIOP projects, and the evaluation consultants. The policy group members were executive and management staff from region, section, and bureau levels; the deputy commissioner of health; and key budget staff from the Department of Public Health and the Department of Finance and Administration.

Documenting the Intended Program

The evaluators identified prenatal program inputs, activities, intended outcomes, and assumed causal linkages by analyzing program documentation and holding interviews and working meetings with managers and staff. From the perspective of policymakers and managers in the Department of Public Health, TIOP and related prenatal care program activities were intended to achieve the process, output, and outcome goals displayed in boxes 2, 3, 4, 6, 8, 9, 10, and 11 in Figure 2.1, the logic model presented to the department.

Through implementation of model projects in selected high-risk areas across the state, Tennessee's prenatal program sought to bring together state, regional, and local agencies and private providers to develop comprehensive systems for the delivery of prenatal care to low-income patients. Central office staff were expected to provide planning, guidelines and standards, training, monitoring and evaluation, and technical assistance. Regional office staff were expected to assist in project development, hiring and training of staff, and coordination with local health departments and private providers. Local health departments were expected to provide community outreach, screening and diagnostic services, comprehensive prenatal services, and referral and follow-up of women with high-risk pregnancies and high-risk infants. Private providers were asked to provide cooperation and support, including consultation and backup, staffing of clinics, management of high-risk cases, and delivery (with or without partial payment from project budgets). The program was expected to achieve the following goals:

- Increase the number of low-income women entering prenatal care in their first trimester of pregnancy.

**Figure 2.1. Tennessee's Prenatal Program:
Resources, Activities, and Intended Outcomes**

Resources Allocated and Expended	**Central Office**	**Contract Agency**	**Local Health Department**

1.1: $400,000 TIOP
1.2: $300,000 ICHP
1.3: $400,000 MCH
1.4: $X   RO
1.5: $Y   Local Health
1.6: $Z   RWJ
	2.1: Establish priorities
	2.2: Identify needs
	2.3: Allocate resources to regions
	2.4: Assist regions in selecting counties
	2.5: Motivate local health departments
	2.6: Prepare guidelines and standards
	2.7: Train staff
	2.8: Monitor
	2.9: Evaluate
	2.10: Provide technical assistance
		3.1: Fiscal management
		3.2: Employ staff
		
		Regional Office
		4.1: Develop project
		4.2: Expand project to counties in greatest need
		4.3: Hire staff
		4.4: Train staff
		4.5: Coordinate with local health departments
		4.6: Coordinate with providers
			6.1: Recognize need
			6.2: Community outreach, education, use of mass media
			6.3: Medical/socioeconomic screening
			6.4: Liaison with physicians and hospitals
			6.5: Provide comprehensive prenatal and postpartum services
			  a. to teenagers
			  b. to nonwhites
			  c. to high-risk women
			  d. to all women
			6.6: Diagnostic/preventive services
			6.7: Referral and follow up of high-risk pregnancies and high-risk infants

Physician/Hospital

7.1: Cooperation and support
7.2: Consultation/backup
7.3: Staffing of clinics
7.4: High-risk OB management
7.5: Delivery (free/paid)

Local Support

5.1: Local support

Key:

☐ Activity/expected outcome ("Event")

→ Assumed causal connection

Source: Wholey, J. S., and Wholey, M. S. *Evaluation of TIOP and Related Prenatal Care Programs: Proposed Approach to Parts A, B, and C of the Evaluation.* Arlington, Va.: Wholey Associates, 1981, pp. 111-3a– 111-3b.

**Figure 2.1. Tennessee's Prenatal Program:
Resources, Activities, and Intended Outcomes,** *continued*

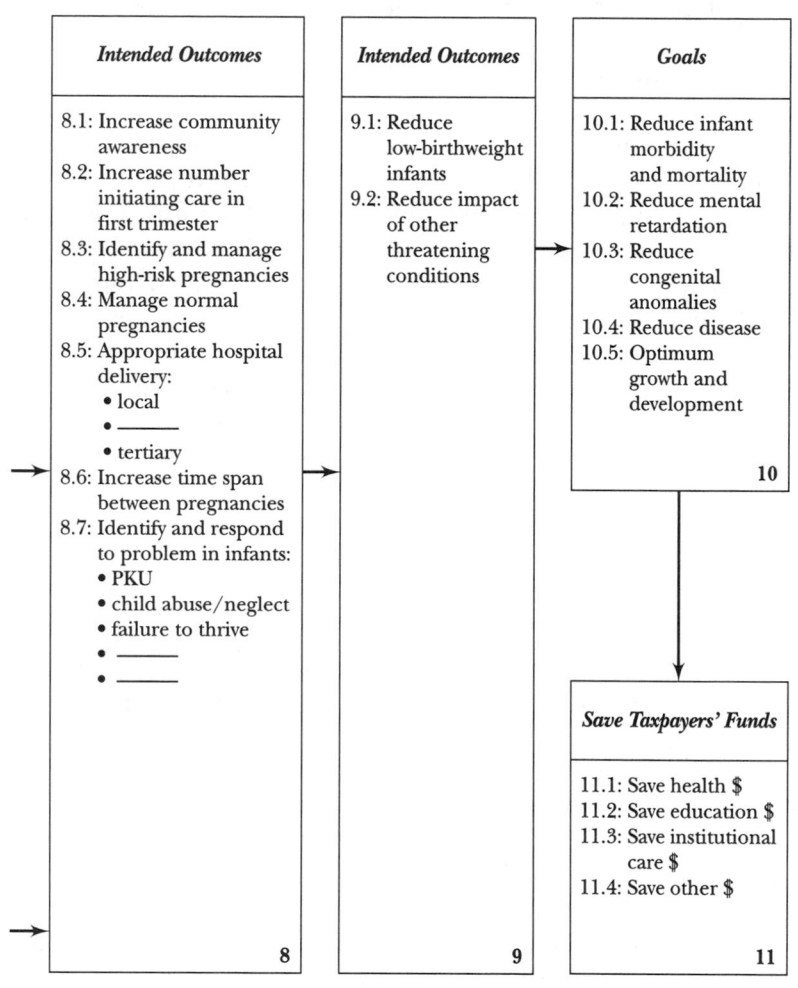

Intended Outcomes	*Intended Outcomes*	*Goals*
8.1: Increase community awareness 8.2: Increase number initiating care in first trimester 8.3: Identify and manage high-risk pregnancies 8.4: Manage normal pregnancies 8.5: Appropriate hospital delivery: • local • _____ • tertiary 8.6: Increase time span between pregnancies 8.7: Identify and respond to problem in infants: • PKU • child abuse/neglect • failure to thrive • _____ • _____	9.1: Reduce low-birthweight infants 9.2: Reduce impact of other threatening conditions	10.1: Reduce infant morbidity and mortality 10.2: Reduce mental retardation 10.3: Reduce congenital anomalies 10.4: Reduce disease 10.5: Optimum growth and development 10

Save Taxpayers' Funds

11.1: Save health $
11.2: Save education $
11.3: Save institutional care $
11.4: Save other $

8   9   11

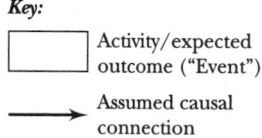

Key:

☐ Activity/expected outcome ("Event")

⟶ Assumed causal connection

- Reduce the number of low-birthweight infants (infants weighing less than 5.5 pounds at birth).
- Reduce infant morbidity, infant mortality, and mental retardation.

Through review of Department of Public Health documents and interaction with staff in central, regional, and local health department offices, the evaluation team found broad agreement on the types of evidence that could be used to assess the performance of TIOP and related prenatal care activities. The team identified approximately sixty possible indicators of program performance (inputs, activities, and outcomes). Quantitative performance measures were available for most of the events in the department's intended program (Figure 2.1), such as trimester of pregnancy in which prenatal care was initiated and infant birthweight. Qualitative performance information could be obtained for other important events, such as descriptions of the support provided by the local medical community. Agreed-on performance indicators were lacking, however, for some of the project goals, such as provision of prenatal services to high-risk patients.

Exploring Program Reality

The evaluators interviewed Department of Public Health staff and reviewed annual reports from regional health offices and prenatal projects, project budgets and expenditure reports data from the prenatal program's quarterly reporting system, and annual monitoring reports by central office staff; they also made a site visit to one of the regional projects. Using these data, the evaluators made preliminary assessments of fiscal flows, services being delivered, outcomes of services, and flows of information on the prenatal program. They concluded that Tennessee's actual prenatal program closely resembled the intended program but had a number of problems that might have threatened effective performance. Based on the information available, none of the program goals appeared to be unrealistic. No changes in program activities or goals were suggested at that time.

Development of Evaluation Options

The evaluation team next developed a set of evaluation options for the work group and the policy group to consider. The group members were asked to review a list of sixty possible indicators of program performance and to select the specific types of quantitative and qualitative data that would be of greatest use to policymakers and managers. Using these indicators, the evaluation team outlined several sets of comparisons that could be made:

- TIOP success in meeting statewide standards
- Intraprogram comparisons among TIOP projects or counties
- Before-and-after comparisons and interrupted time-series analyses using data on all births in the counties served by TIOP
- Before-and-after and interrupted time-series comparisons using data on all births in counties served by TIOP and data on all births in other counties in the same region not served by TIOP
- Before-and-after and interrupted time-series comparisons among TIOP projects offering different services at different costs

If the evaluation team were to identify especially effective projects or types of projects, the evaluation options provided for the evaluators to make site visits to document project resources, services, and service outcomes. To the extent that time and funds permitted, the evaluation team was also to examine the existing service delivery system and make recommendations on maintenance and expansion of prenatal services after federal TIOP funding was to end in fiscal year 1982.

Decisions on Evaluation Priorities

In early July 1981, the work group and the policy group met separately to react to the evaluability assessment. Prebriefings and individual meetings were held with key members of both groups. The evaluability assessment resulted in agreement among evaluators and key policymakers, managers, and staff on the design of Tennessee's prenatal care program (intended program inputs, activities, and outcomes, and assumed causal linkages among these) and on the goals and performance indicators that would be the major focus of the evaluation. The evaluation would focus particular attention on whether the prenatal care program was effective in achieving an intermediate outcome goal: reducing the number of low-birthweight infants. Low birthweight was known to be closely associated with infant morbidity and mortality and with mental retardation; reducing the incidence of low birthweight was an outcome goal that program managers considered realistic and one for which they believed they could fairly be held accountable. Although they did not believe that they could demonstrate significant impact on infant mortality rates, they retained reduction of infant mortality as a focus of the evaluation because the deputy commissioner of health believed that questions would be asked on that subject.

After reviewing the information on the intended program and program reality, the department agreed to focus the evaluation on a subset of the intended program that included resources expended, numbers of patients served, types of services delivered, trimester in which prenatal care was initiated, incidence of low birthweight, and infant mortality rates (see Figure 2.1). It was agreed that the evaluation would be used in making budget decisions for fiscal year 1983, planning for the prenatal care to be provided in fiscal year 1983 and beyond, developing formulas for allocating funds to maintain or expand prenatal services, reexamining the guidelines and standards for prenatal care, and making regional and local decisions on the types of prenatal care to be provided.

The evaluation contract had included a planned evaluation of the prenatal program in terms of the input and process goals stated in the original TIOP grant application. The decision was made, however, not to focus on the project's input and process goals because the annual project reports to the federal government had monitored progress in terms of those goals; moreover, interviews with Department of Public Health managers and staff had revealed relatively little demand for additional information on progress toward those goals.

Results

The evaluability assessment resulted in the decision to add to the evaluation an interim report that would be available for use in the state's budget process for fiscal year 1983. The interim evaluation (Wholey and Wholey, 1981b) showed that the prenatal program had reduced the incidence of low birthweight. Information compiled by the evaluators from project reports and other available data indicated that the incidence of low birthweight among infants born to prenatal program patients was well below the rate in appropriate comparison groups.

Exhibit 2.1. Tennessee's Prenatal Program: Key Performance Indicators

Event	Performance Indicator	Data Source
1. Patients served	1. Number of new admissions	1. Quarterly reports admissions
2. Costs	2a. Staff time	2a. Project records
	2b. Funds expended	2b. Annual reports
	2c. Cost per patient	
3. Physician support	3. Staffing of clinics	3. Survey of project staff
4. Early initiation of care	4. Trimester in which care was initiated	4. Quarterly reports
5. Morbidity	5. Birthweight	5. Quarterly reports
6. Infant mortality	6a. Neonatal mortality	6a.[a]
	6b. Postneonatal mortality	6b.[a]

[a]Data source not identified in the evaluability assessment.

Smith (1986) notes that the interim evaluation was used in preparing the department's plan to extend prenatal care throughout Tennessee and also in budget deliberations over the proposed statewide program. In addition, the interim evaluation was used in establishing realistic goals for improved prenatal care throughout Tennessee:

- Securing the cooperation of private physicians
- Maximizing Medicaid reimbursement to local health departments for prenatal care
- Ensuring early initiation of prenatal care
- Reducing the incidence of low birthweight, neonatal mortality, and infant mortality

Although the politically powerful Governor's Task Force on Mental Retardation had earlier called for improvements in prenatal care and the Department of Public Health and the Department of Finance and Administration had reached agreement that the governor would request a $500,000 appropriation to continue the pilot projects, it appears that the interim evaluation was a factor in the executive branch decision to propose $2 million in state appropriations for initiation of a statewide prenatal program. The positive evaluation findings were used in successful advocacy within the executive branch for inclusion of the $2 million request in the governor's fiscal year 1983 budget at what otherwise was a time of budget retrenchment in Tennessee.

Family Preservation Programs

Evaluability assessment does not depend on production of logic models. The key is to involve intended users in clarifying and, if necessary, refining the program design, defining the criteria to be used in evaluating the program, and specifying evaluation work that is likely to be useful to managers and policymakers. In 1992, in the context of rising foster care caseloads and increasing federal and state foster care costs, both the states and the federal government were interested in time-limited, very intensive home-based services to families in crisis. The aims were to improve family functioning when children were at imminent risk of placement in foster care and to prevent this placement. Given the likelihood of major federal investments in such "family preservation" programs and the lack of prior authoritative research, a definitive impact evaluation was needed. In response to a request for proposals from the U.S. Department of Health and Human Services, evaluators used evaluability assessment to develop a design for evaluating family preservation programs (James Bell Associates, 1992; Kaye and Bell, 1993).

The evaluators formed an intergovernmental work group and a technical advisory panel to provide input into the evaluability assessment. (The two groups were later merged into a single technical advisory committee that consisted of twenty-five policymakers, managers, and evaluators.) The evaluators held discussions with federal agency staff and national private sector organizations to learn the views of national policymakers on the definition of family preservation programs, services provided, target populations, and expected program outcomes (James Bell Associates, 1992). The evaluators reviewed thirty-one documents—literature on family preservation programs and earlier evaluations—to identify variations in family preservation efforts, the findings of past evaluations, and the methodologies used. They talked by telephone with state and local representatives of family preservation programs (in ten states, five counties, and five cities) to get descriptions of their programs and identify relevant unpublished research and evaluation studies. The evaluators made site visits to four family preservation programs to develop models of program operations, obtain information from state and local policymakers on expected program outcomes, and explore the feasibility of implementing alternative evaluative designs. They held meetings with members of the technical advisory committee to discuss key issues, implications for evaluation design, and evaluation design alternatives (Kaye and Bell, 1993).

The evaluability assessment compared and contrasted the views of policymakers (federal agency staff, congressional staff, and state legislative staff), program managers, and operating-level staff (child protective services and foster care workers, family preservation program staff, and other child welfare services personnel) on four key dimensions:

- The goals of family preservation programs and related outcome measures
- Aspects of child welfare systems that affect family preservation programs
- The target population for family preservation programs ("imminent risk" criteria)
- The characteristics that distinguish family preservation programs from other home-based services

The evaluability assessment concluded that current family preservation programs were not consistently targeted at families with children who were at imminent risk of foster care placement and that as a result, the primary goal of policymakers could not be achieved as these programs were currently operated (Kaye and Bell, 1993).

The evaluability assessment then explored three other issues that affected the feasibility of impact evaluation:

- Whether existing program operations could be modified to achieve the consistency needed for a useful impact evaluation
- Whether program sites would be willing to employ a design that called for random assignment of families to treatment and control groups
- Whether the data needed to describe the services, costs, and outcomes associated with family preservation programs and other parts of the child welfare system were available and accessible

To measure the impact of family preservation programs on foster care placements and related costs, the evaluators recommended a design based on random assignment of cases in which children were at risk of imminent placement as determined by a judge, a child welfare agency attorney, or senior program managers. The recommended evaluation design would "establish . . . a set of procedures for determining that cases referred for family preservation are those that would otherwise be placed in foster care. . . . Cases in which there was a determination that it was unsafe or not feasible to avoid placement would be excluded from the evaluation and presumably placed in foster care" (Kaye and Bell, 1993, pp. 30–31).

Issues, Problems, and Solutions

This section examines issues and problems that arise in performing evaluability assessments and suggests solutions based on past experience. The box summarizes the suggestions presented in this and the other sections.

Gaining and Holding the Support of Managers

Evaluators often take a long time to complete their work, while the time frame of their intended audiences tends to be highly compressed. Moreover, it takes time to gain managers' confidence and produce program change. Evaluators need mechanisms that will convince managers that it is worth their while to become and stay engaged in the evaluation process.

Getting off to a good start can be a problem. At a minimum, evaluators should begin an evaluability assessment by clarifying the types of products and results expected from evaluability assessment and from subsequent evaluation work.

By quickly providing objective, credible information relevant to problems that managers face, the evaluability assessment process tends to overcome managers' skepticism. The steps in an evaluability assessment facilitate the briefings and discussions needed to keep evaluators' work relevant to management needs. Each briefing can be used to present a preliminary evaluability assessment product (for example, information on the expectations of policymakers, managers, those involved in service delivery, and other key stakeholders; findings from site visits; options for changes in program activities; or options for collection, analysis, and use of information on program performance) and to get the feedback needed to reach agreement on a revised product or identify the need for collecting and analyzing additional data. These meetings allow the evaluator to determine which policymakers and managers want evaluation information and what information evaluation they need.

Practical Suggestions for the Evaluability Assessment Process

Gaining and Holding the Support of Managers

- Form a policy group and a work group to involve policymakers, managers, and key staff in evaluation.
- Clarify the types of products and results expected.
- Use briefings to present the perspectives of policymakers, managers, those involved in service delivery, and other stakeholders; the reality of program operations; and options for changes in program activities or collection, analysis, and use of information on program performance.

Clarifying Program Intent

- Develop logic models documenting program inputs, program activities, intended program outcomes, and assumed causal linkages from the perspectives of policymakers, managers, those involved in service delivery, and other stakeholders.
- Develop logic models at varying levels of detail.
- Use more detailed logic models to ensure that evaluators and intended users of evaluation information have a common understanding of the intended program, including any important negative side effects to be minimized.
- Use less detailed logic models to focus briefings and discussions on key issues.
- Develop lists of currently agreed-on performance indicators and possible new performance indicators to ensure a common understanding of the goals and performance indicators to be used in subsequent evaluation work.

Exploring Program Reality

- Focus on descriptions of actual program activities and outcomes, reviews of performance monitoring systems currently in use, and descriptions of especially strong project performance and problems inhibiting effective program performance.

- Use site visits, prior reports, and information from knowledgeable observers to make preliminary estimates of the likelihood that program goals will be achieved.
- Identify feasible measures of program performance.

Reaching Agreement on Any Needed Changes in Program Design

- If appropriate, suggest changes in program design that appear likely to improve program performance.
- Proceed by successive iterations, spelling out the likely costs and likely consequences of the program change options of greatest interest to program managers.

Exploring Alternative Evaluation Designs

- Spell out the costs and intended uses of evaluation options: measurements of specific variables or tests of specific causal assumptions.
- Present examples of the types of information that would be produced.
- Interact with the intended users of evaluation information at frequent intervals.
- Hold managers' interest by providing early evaluability assessment products.
- Brief key managers and policymakers on evaluability assessment findings and evaluation options.
- Explain the implications of the status quo option (no further evaluation) and the costs and potential uses of various other evaluation options.
- Ensure that a mechanism is available for speedy initiation of follow-on evaluation efforts.

Documenting Policy and Management Decisions

- Conclude each phase of an evaluability assessment with a brief memorandum documenting significant decisions made in meetings with managers and policymakers.

Proceeding by Successive Iterations

- Do the entire evaluability assessment once early in the assessment; obtain tentative management decisions on program goals, important side effects, evaluation criteria, and intended uses of evaluation information; and redo portions of the evaluability assessment as often as necessary to obtain informed management decisions.

Reducing Evaluability Assessment Costs

- Minimize the number of intermediate written products.
- Use briefings that present the information required for management decisions.

Clarifying Program Intent

Logic models can be developed at varying levels of detail. These models help build a common understanding between evaluators and intended users of evaluation information on program inputs, program activities, intended program outcomes, and assumed causal linkages. Such agreement is a prerequisite for evaluation work that is likely to be useful to management. The logic models display, in shorthand form, the relevant evaluations that could be conducted, since they display the key events (inputs, activities, outcomes) that could be monitored and the assumed causal linkages that could be tested through impact evaluations.

The question here is one of the appropriate level of detail in the logic model. More detailed logic models, like that shown in Figure 2.1, are useful in ensuring that the evaluator has a clear understanding of the program and that evaluators and managers have a common understanding of the way the program is intended to achieve its results. These models are best communicated in papers that managers and staff can study before meeting with the evaluator.

For briefings and discussions with higher management and policy levels, evaluators should use less detailed logic models (see, for example, Figure 2.2). Simpler logic models allow the evaluator to focus briefings and discussions on key issues. They also facilitate clear distinctions between those program goals for which management will take responsibility and those for which managers believe that they cannot fairly be held accountable.

Exploring Program Reality

The second phase of the evaluability assessment is carried out to document program reality. In some evaluability assessments, however, efforts to document the actual program have resulted only in additional, more detailed models of intended program activities and outcomes; in other cases, site visit reports have required a long preparation time but have yielded little useful information. In this phase, the evaluators' activities should focus on descriptions of program activities that are actually occurring and program outcomes that are actually being achieved; reviews of program and project monitoring systems currently in use; descriptions of especially strong project performance and of problems inhibiting effective program performance; and collection of project estimates of likely accomplishments over the new few years.

A key evaluability assessment product is the evaluator's preliminary evaluation of the likelihood that program goals will be achieved. Such a preliminary evaluation may be based on firsthand contact with program reality through relatively small numbers of site visits or on second-hand contact with

Figure 2.2. Tennessee's Prenatal Program: Resources, Activities, and Important Outcomes

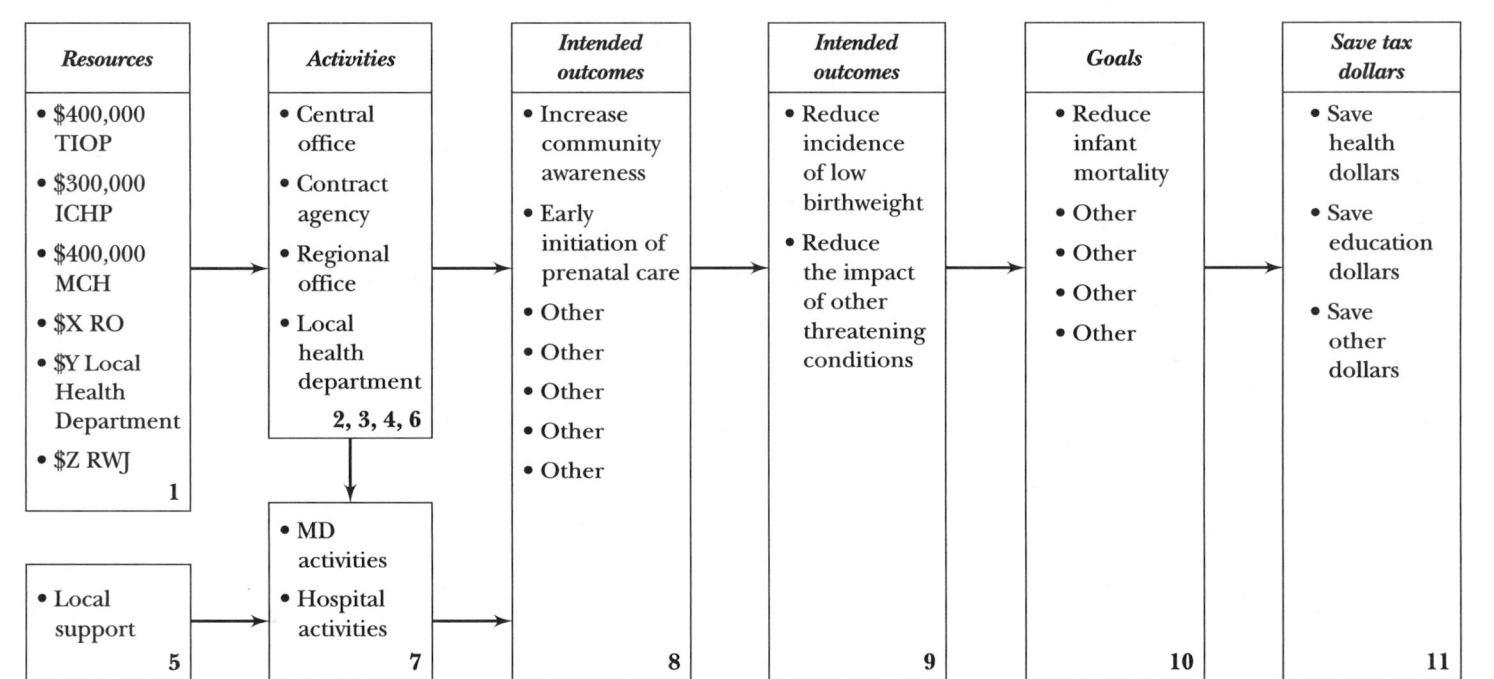

the program through analyses of program expenditures, project reports, monitoring reports, audits, research reports, and evaluation studies, and through collection of information from knowledgeable observers of the program.

Reviews of successful and unsuccessful evaluability assessments strongly suggest that a small number of site visits are helpful early in the assessment. Guided by a preliminary version of the program design model, the evaluators can gather information about actual levels of resources being used, program activities actually under way, program outcomes actually occurring, and trouble spots that seem to be emerging. The evaluators can then make preliminary judgments as to the likelihood that program goals will be achieved. Presentation of new information from the field helps give the evaluators credibility. The early warning nature of this plausibility analysis allows the evaluators to identify problems in the program design or in program reality while there is still time for policymakers and managers to act.

Reaching Agreement on Any Needed Changes in Program Design

Reviews of successful and unsuccessful evaluability assessments suggest the advisability of successive iterations in getting management and policy-level agreement on any needed changes in the program design. After identifying problems inhibiting effective performance, the evaluators should get preliminary management reactions as to any program changes that appear to be worth pursuing. The evaluators can then spell out the preferred options in more detail to allow more informed management commitment to specific changes in the program and effective implementation of any program change options that are selected. An important part of the job of spelling out options for changes in the program design is that of clarifying the likely costs of such changes in terms of dollars, staff time, management time, calendar time, and other resources.

In a number of the more successful evaluability assessment efforts, continual interaction between evaluators and managers led to agreement on implementation activities needed to improve program performance. As a result, assistance in some of the needed implementation activities was either incorporated into the evaluability assessment or commissioned as specific follow-on work for the evaluation team.

Exploring Alternative Evaluation Designs

Exploration of evaluation design options should include estimates of the costs of the various options. These include the expense of collecting, analyzing, and using specific types of program performance data. Also included should be hypothetical or real examples of the types of data that would be produced and specific indications of how that information would be used.

Agreeing on Evaluation Priorities and Intended Uses of Evaluation Information

The most important step in evaluability assessment is getting decisions from intended evaluation users on the program goals and performance indicators that will be used to evaluate the program and how the resulting information will be used. There appear to be four keys to securing the necessary decisions:

- Holding the interest of those in charge of the program through provision of early evaluability assessment products
- Continuing interaction with intended evaluation users
- Briefing key managers and policymakers on evaluability assessment findings and options to clarify the findings and get their positions on the options
- Providing the additional information needed to clarify the findings and prepare for implementation of the highest-priority options

When the evaluability assessment is the initial phase of a larger evaluation effort or another mechanism is available for speedy initiation of follow-on evaluation work, implementation of useful evaluation work is more likely.

Documenting Policy and Management Decisions

Some evaluability assessments have failed to document policy and management decisions on the goals and performance indicators in terms of which the program is to be evaluated, an omission that can lead to later misunderstanding. Evaluators should conclude each phase of an evaluability assessment with a brief memorandum documenting significant decisions made in meetings with managers and policymakers.

Proceeding by Successive Iterations

Evaluators have sometimes exhausted the resources available for evaluability assessment without achieving management decisions on the goals on which the program is to be held accountable, the types of information to be used to assess progress toward those goals, or the intended uses of program performance information.

Evaluability assessment is often more successful when it proceeds by successive iterations. With this strategy, the evaluators perform all the steps of the evaluability assessment once early in the process; they obtain tentative management decisions on program goals, evaluation criteria, and intended uses of evaluation information; then they redo portions of the evaluability assessment as often as necessary to achieve informed management decisions and, if necessary, a better-designed program. Each iteration of the evaluability assessment allows the evaluator to provide new information and get a better sense of management's positions on which options appear most useful.

Reducing Evaluability Assessment Costs

Some evaluability assessments have been heavily procedural, requiring many intermediate written products. In more effective evaluability assessment efforts, evaluators have emphasized the spirit of evaluability assessment, communicating the information required for decision making through briefings rather than written reports. Focusing on the essentials makes the evaluability assessment process more efficient and thus reduces its costs.

Conclusion

A program may be any policy, program, project, function, agency, or activity that has an identifiable purpose or set of goals (U.S. General Accounting Office, 1998). It may be a set of activities in one organization or a set of activities in a number of organizations. Scheirer (1994) distinguishes *aggregate programs* from *targeted programs:* in the former, the specific activities undertaken locally may be quite diverse at different sites; in the latter, the program design specifies local activities in some detail.

Program evaluation remains more an art than a science. It may be accomplished through regular monitoring of program performance or through evaluation studies that examine a broader range of information on program performance and program context (U.S. General Accounting Office, 1998, 2000). It is especially challenging in decentralized programs and in cross-cutting programs and partnership efforts that represent the contributions of a number of agencies to common goals.

Useful program evaluation is inhibited by four problems:

- Lack of agreement on the goals and performance criteria to be used in evaluating the program
- Program goals that are unrealistic given the program design, the resources that have been committed to the program, and the program activities that are under way
- Inability to obtain relevant performance information at reasonable cost
- Inability or unwillingness of policymakers or managers to act on the basis of evaluation information

When evaluation has been requested in terms of appropriate, clearly specified evaluation criteria or the purpose of evaluation is not performance improvement, evaluability assessment may not be needed. When appropriate evaluation criteria have not been identified or the intended uses of evaluation are unclear, evaluability assessment can be very useful.

Much of the early evaluability assessment work focused on exploration of the goals and expectations of policymakers and managers, to clarify the extent to which those in charge had agreed on program goals and the extent to which they had the ability and willingness to act on the basis of program performance information (Horst, Nay, Scanlon, and Wholey, 1974; Schmidt, 1977). Nay and others added an emphasis on the need to examine program operations in order to clarify the functions actually being performed and the feasibility of measuring actual program inputs, activities, and results (Nay, Scanlon, Graham, and Waller, 1977; Nay and Kay, 1982). Schmidt, Nay, Scanlon, Waller, and others emphasized the identification of options under which management would be able to set realistic goals, monitor and evaluate performance, and demonstrate effective program performance (Schmidt and Waller, 1976; Nay, Scanlon, Graham, and Waller, 1977; U.S. Comptroller General, 1977; Wholey, Bell, Scanlon, and Waller, 1977).

In evaluation planning efforts that use the evaluability assessment approach, evaluators do not select the evaluation criteria by relying only on their own knowledge and expertise. Instead, as in the prenatal program and family preservation program examples, they involve policymakers, managers, those involved in service delivery, and other stakeholders in activities that clarify program intent and identify criteria that could be used in evaluating the program. In such evaluation planning efforts, the evaluators collect data on the expectations of key actors and the reality of program operations. When a program has been designed on a sound theoretical base, evaluability assessment makes the program design explicit before choices are made concerning evaluation measures, sample sizes, and tests of specific causal assumptions. When a program lacks a sound theoretical base, evaluability assessment can make policymakers and managers aware of this lack and suggest options for program redesign.

Evaluability assessment helps evaluators and program managers to understand, and in some cases modify, the expectations of those who have the most important influence over the program. It clarifies similarities and differences among the assumptions and expectations of policymakers, managers, those involved in service delivery, and other stakeholders, and it documents differences between intended and actual program inputs, activities, and outcomes.

Evaluability assessment can be a useful tool in strategic planning efforts, especially when programs are decentralized, effective program performance requires the efforts of a number of agencies, the program is a performance-oriented partnership among agencies, or the program is an entire agency or bureau.

Evaluability assessment helps policymakers, managers, and evaluators to explore the feasibility, costs, and likely usefulness of alternative evaluation designs and plan data collection and analysis that will produce useful information on program performance. It can help policymakers and managers to reach a reasonable level of agreement on the program activities and outcomes that will be monitored, the types of process and outcome data that will be collected, and the causal assumptions that will be tested in subsequent program evaluation work. Evaluability assessment tends to focus evaluation resources on intermediate outcomes that are subject to the influence, but not under the control, of program managers.

Finally, evaluability assessment encourages policymakers and managers to act on the basis of evaluation results. Evaluability assessment can be useful in planning evaluations that will be used to help improve program performance. On occasion, evaluability assessment can also be useful in planning evaluations that executives and managers will be able to use to build support for the program.

References

Horst, P., Nay, J. N., Scanlon, J. W., and Wholey, J. S. "Program Management and the Federal Evaluator." *Public Administration Review,* 1974, *34*(4), 300–308.

James Bell Associates. *Evaluation Design: Evaluability Assessment of Family Preservation Programs.* Arlington, Va.: James Bell Associates, 1992.

Kaye, E., and Bell, J. *Final Report: Evaluability Assessment of Family Preservation Programs.* Arlington, Va.: James Bell Associates, 1993.

Nay, J., and Kay, P. *Government Oversight and Evaluability Assessment.* San Francisco: New Lexington Press, 1982.

Nay, J. N., Scanlon, J. W., Graham, L., and Waller, J. D. *The National Institute's Information Machine: A Case Study of the National Evaluation Program.* Washington, D.C.: Urban Institute, 1977.

Rog, D. J. "A Methodological Analysis of Evaluability Assessment." Unpublished doctoral dissertation, Vanderbilt University, 1985.

Rutman, L. *Planning Useful Evaluations: Evaluability Assessment.* Thousand Oaks, Calif.: Sage, 1980.

Scheirer, M. A. "Designing and Using Process Evaluation." In J. S. Wholey, H. P. Hatry, and K. E. Newcomer (eds.), *Handbook of Practical Program Evaluation.* San Francisco: Jossey-Bass, 1994.

Schmidt, R. E. *Serving the Federal Evaluation Market.* Washington, D.C.: Urban Institute, 1977.

Schmidt, R. E., Scanlon, J. W., and Bell, J. B. *Evaluability Assessment: Making Public Programs Work Better.* Rockville, Md.: U.S. Department of Health and Human Services, Project Share, 1979.

Schmidt, R. E., and Waller, J. D. *Appalachian Regional Commission Health and Child Development Program: Final Evaluation System Design.* Washington D.C.: The Urban Institute, 1976.

Smith, J. D. "Communicating the Value of Tennessee's Prenatal Program." In J. S. Wholey, M. A. Abramson, and C. Bellavita (eds.), *Performance and Credibility: Developing Excellence in Public and Nonprofit Organizations.* San Francisco: New Lexington Press, 1986.

Smith, M. F. *Evaluability Assessment: A Practical Approach.* Boston: Kluwer-Nijhoff, 1989.

Strosberg, M. A., and Wholey, J. S. "Evaluability Assessment: From Theory to Practice in the Department of Health and Human Services." *Public Administration Review,* 1983, *43*(1), 66–71.

U.S. Comptroller General. *Finding Out How Programs Are Working: Some Suggestions for Congressional Oversight.* Washington, D.C.: U.S. General Accounting Office, 1977.

U.S. General Accounting Office. *Performance Measurement and Evaluation: Definitions and Relationships.* Washington, D.C.: U.S. General Accounting Office, 1998.

U.S. General Accounting Office. *Program Evaluation: Studies Helped Agencies Measure or Explain Performance.* Washington, D.C.: U.S. General Accounting Office, 2000.

Wholey, J. S. *Evaluation and Effective Public Management.* New York: Little, Brown, 1983.

Wholey, J. S. "Evaluability Assessment: Developing Program Theory." In L. Bickman (ed.), *Using Program Theory in Evaluation.* New Directions for Program Evaluation, no. 33. San Francisco: Jossey-Bass, 1987.

Wholey, J. S. "Assessing the Feasibility and Likely Usefulness of Evaluation." In J. S. Wholey, H. P. Hatry, and K. E. Newcomer (eds.), *Handbook of Practical Program Evaluation.* San Francisco: Jossey-Bass, 1994.

Wholey, J. S. "Evaluability and Evaluability Assessment." Unpublished paper, World Bank, 2002.

Wholey, J. S., Bell, J. B., Scanlon, J. W., and Waller, J. D. *Evaluability Assessment for the Bureau of Health Planning and Resources Development.* Washington, D.C.: Urban Institute, Report 1977.

Wholey, J. S., and Wholey, M. S. *Evaluation of TIOP and Related Prenatal Care Programs: Proposed Approach to Parts A, B, and C of the Evaluation.* Arlington, Va.: Wholey Associates, 1981a.

Wholey, J. S., and Wholey, M. S. *Evaluation of TIOP and Related Prenatal Care Programs: Interim Report.* Arlington, Va.: Wholey Associates, 1981b.

Wholey, J. S., and Wholey, M. S. *Toward Improving the Outcome of Pregnancy: Implications for the Statewide Program.* Arlington, Va.: Wholey Associates, 1982.

3

Implementation Evaluation

Arnold Love

Program evaluations routinely show that many programs are not producing the positive outcomes that their sponsors and other stakeholders anticipated. Likewise, on a daily basis, a steady stream of news about troubled programs that have failed to meet expectations fills the media. Some programs are based on apparently sound ideas but fail in practical application. Others are failures because they are not used in the way they were intended or not used at all. Why this is the case can often be traced to the way the program was implemented.

The tragic loss of the space shuttle *Columbia* in 2003 is a very public example of this failure. Framed by the headline, "Same Problems Haunt NASA 17 Years After Challenger Loss," an angry editorial in *USA Today* pointed to the recurrence of problems first identified and supposedly solved following the *Challenger* disaster. The editorial emphasized the failure of NASA to learn from past errors and implement safety reforms that could lessen the chances of another deadly accident. The editorial continued relentlessly with the rebuke of retired admiral Herald Gehman, who heads the *Columbia* probe, that the NASA safety office created in response to the *Challenger* explosion was a facade "with no people, money, engineering expertise, analysis." Without proper implementation, how could anyone expect the safety program to be effective?

Implementation is an integral part of the program cycle, popularized by the management mantra: plan, implement, evaluate, improve. *Implementation* refers to all of the activities focused on the actual operation of a program once it moves from the drawing board and into action. In their seminal book *Implementation: How Great Expectations in Washington Are Dashed in Oakland,* Pressman and Wildavsky portrayed the intimate connection between implementation and evaluation (1984): "Implementation and evaluation are the opposite sides of the same coin, implementation providing the experience that evaluation interrogates and evaluation providing the intelligence to make sense out of what is happening" (p. xv).

The evaluation of implementation has become particularly important during the past decade. Spurred by major management reforms and demand by the public, organizations in all sectors (private, public, and nonprofit) have given greater attention to achieving measurable results and to the active management of program operations needed to attain those results. These reforms include giving primacy to identifying and meeting the needs of the customer or citizen, delivering high-quality programs, continuously improving business and service delivery processes, applying evidence-based practices, demonstrating accountability for achieving outcomes, and using performance measures to bridge the gap between strategic planning and program implementation. These new management approaches are highly data driven. Program evaluators have much to contribute by assisting managers and staff in strengthening program implementation, achieving results, and building a performance-oriented organizational culture. In this context, implementation evaluations are used for a wide variety of purposes—for example:

- Actively aiding in the design of programs (both theoretical and operational)
- Achieving "ordinary excellence" by validating program models and their results
- Generating ongoing information that ensures program implementation is successful
- Continuously improving program operations
- Supplying rapid feedback about operations and outcomes that guides program evolution in an increasingly dynamic and turbulent environment
- Demonstrating the value of implemented programs to funders, donors, and the public

This chapter introduces the concept of implementation evaluation and highlights practical strategies and tools for evaluating implementation in organizations with limited resources. The tools and techniques range from ways of providing insight into potential implementation problems during the planning phases, to systematic descriptive information about program operations, to methods for strengthening outcomes evaluation. Because implementation evaluation data are often used to manage change and drive organizational improvements, this chapter also explores the use of implementation evaluation as part of a process to foster organizational development and organizational learning.

Beyond the "Black Box": Adopting an Expanded Paradigm of Evaluation

The complementary role of implementation evaluation for examining the dynamic interplay of theory, practice, and outcome was recognized more than twenty years ago: "Indeed, by expanding evaluation beyond the mere measure of outcomes to cover the causes of the consequences observed, we can use such knowledge to alter programs or their mode of implementation. Whether evaluation is used to check progress or to change direction, it involves the analysis of implementation" (Browne and Wildavsky, 1983, p. 101). In practical terms, implementation evaluation enables evaluators to be clearer about what worked and what did not to produce the intended program outcomes (Bickman and Heflinger, 1995).

In the "black box" paradigm of classical experimental evaluation, evaluators assume that the program "technology" (that is, theory as applied in program activities) is controlled by the program staff and observed outcomes are caused by the program. To evaluate program results, the evaluators assess program participants before they begin the program and at one or more points after completing it. A major criticism of black box evaluations is that they reveal little about the process of program delivery or how to improve programs. They do not adequately describe the relationship of program activities, program context, and outcomes. Instead, attention to treatment often is limited to a description of client characteristics and service "dosage," usually measured by number of contacts or the participant's length of participation in program activities.

In contrast to the black box paradigm, the dynamic and interactive nature of modern programs has led many evaluators to adopt an expanded, or "transparent box," paradigm of program evaluation. The transparent box paradigm adopts an ecological systems perspective that nests the program technology within the context of the organization and embeds both the program and the organization within the broader environment.

The simplified diagram of the transparent box paradigm that appears in Figure 3.1 shows two very important features. First, it encourages the careful study of program delivery, including an assessment of how well programs are implemented and the relationship among theory, program activities, and program outputs and outcomes. Second, it explicitly considers organizational and environmental factors outside the program itself and how they influence

Figure 3.1. The Transparent Box Paradigm

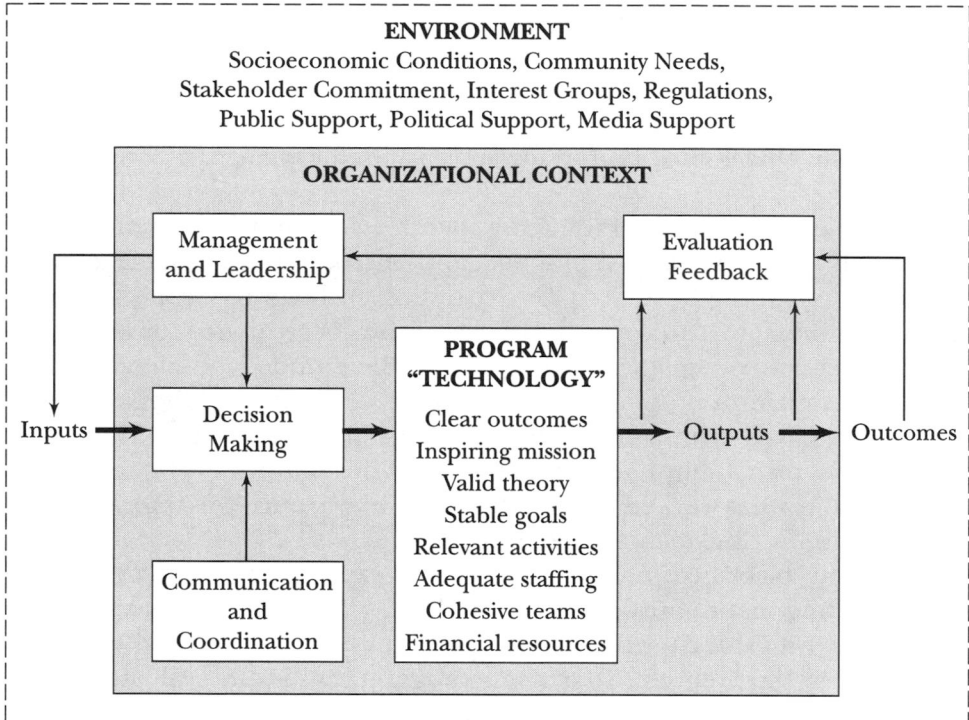

intake into the program, the acceptance and value of program activities, and the achievement of program outcomes. The transparent box paradigm highlights the complexity of the program delivery process and places programs in context as just one among many sets of factors that influence outcomes. It thus provides a model of the program that avoids the explanatory gaps inherent in the black box and enhances the ability to tell a "performance story" that illuminates the logic and rationale of how various aspects of the program interact with each other to produce results.

Program evaluations based on the expanded transparent box paradigm can produce valuable insights into the relationship between the characteristics of the participants within their life context, the contribution of program "technology" within the service delivery context, the direct outcomes of a program, and the contributions to the outcomes by organizational and environmental factors. Implementation evaluations that employ the expanded transparent box paradigm can provide a more realistic appraisal of factors that produce program outcomes and thereby assist program managers and staff to strengthen programs and modify factors outside the program to the advantage of the participants.

Practical Methods for Evaluating Program Implementation

During the past twenty years, evaluators have devised a wide array of approaches and techniques for evaluating program implementation and an equally diverse set of names to label them. Among the methods of evaluating implementation are formative evaluation, process evaluation, descriptive evaluation, performance monitoring, and implementation analysis, to mention only some of the most common. Because of potential confusion, let us look at these terms a moment to distinguish their similarities and differences:

- Formative evaluation refers to the use of evaluation to improve a program during the development phase. It is contrasted with summative evaluation after completion of the program.
- Process evaluation traditionally examines how well the services delivered match those that were planned.
- Descriptive evaluation provides extensive details about programs so their implementation can be compared across sites or replicated elsewhere. Although it is similar to process evaluation, the usual distinction is that descriptive evaluation provides rich description and process evaluation draws evaluative conclusions about the match between the actual and planned program.
- Performance monitoring connotes an ongoing system of measurement and feedback of program operations and results, usually through the use of administrative information systems and performance indicators.
- Implementation analysis ordinarily examines what happened to a policy after it had been formulated and during its implementation in real-world settings.

More information about these terms may be found in Scriven (1991), Owen and Rogers (1999), and Rossi, Freeman, and Lipsey (1998).

In fact, a wide variety of program evaluation methods may be used to evaluate at least some aspect of program evaluation. A two-step approach was used to filter this overwhelming range of potential methods into a small number of practical methods. The first step was to apply the chronological mode of program development (Berk and Rossi, 1999) to implementation evaluation. The chronological model is a widely used way of describing the program life cycle and then matching appropriate evaluation methods to each stage. This process identified four stages that are especially relevant for implementation evaluation:

Stage 1: Assess need and feasibility.

Stage 2: Plan and design the program.

Stage 3: Deliver the program.

Stage 4: Improve the program.

A core set of implementation evaluation questions matched to each stage appears in the box. These questions can provide a useful start for developing an implementation evaluation plan.

Key Implementation Evaluation Questions

Stage 1. Assess Need and Feasibility

- What are the needs of the target group?
- What attempts have been made to implement programs to meet these needs?
- What were the major implementation obstacles faced by existing programs?
- What do implemented programs tell us about the best practices in this area?
- What resources are needed to implement an effective program?
- Among program alternatives, what are the best choices to make in the light of the implementation issues and implementation constraints?

Stage 2. Plan and Design the Program

- How is the theory of the program designed to achieve the intended outcomes?
- What program operations are needed to make the theory effective?
- Does the implementation setting of the program support or impede the program design? How?
- What aspects of this program design need to be modified to achieve the intended outcomes in this implementation setting?
- How will we monitor the implementation of this program and make any necessary changes?

Stage 3. Deliver the Program

- Is the program serving the right target groups?
- Are potential clients rejecting the program or dropping out? Why?
- Is the program design being implemented according to plan?

- Is the program producing the expected outputs (such as services or products) that were planned?
- Is the program meeting its standards of quality?
- Is the program producing its intended short-term outcomes for clients?
- What implementation obstacles are being encountered?
- What differences are there between sites?

Stage 4. Improve the Program

- Is the program meeting its implementation goals and targets?
- Are the clients receiving the outcomes they expected?
- Is the program producing any unintended positive or negative results?
- Are significant internal or external events affecting the program, its staff, or its clients?
- What are the program's strengths and weaknesses?
- What are the differences in strengths and weaknesses between sites? Why?
- What are the areas of requiring improvement?
- Are the efforts to improve the program working?

The next step was to select a core set of practical methods for implementation evaluation that were matched to each stage. The working definition of "practical" was that the methods could be applied in a broad variety of program settings and used by organizations that had limited time and resources. The overall advantage of this strategy is that most programs go through developmental stages or a life cycle, and it provides a simplified framework to select useful implementation evaluation methods. A disadvantage is that a program may not systematically progress from one developmental stage to another but rather jump from one stage to another, depending on program or external pressures. On balance, however, the chronological model has proven itself as a useful strategy for selecting appropriate evaluation methods and it is a offered here as a point of departure.

The following sections describe each of the selected methods for implementation evaluation organized according to the four stages. They represent a small but highly practical subset of available implementation evaluation methods. Although these methods may be used for other evaluation purposes, each section outlines the application of the method as it is used for implementation evaluation, provides tips and suggestions, and includes a brief example to make the application clear.

Selected Implementation Evaluation Methods

Stage 1: Assess Need and Feasibility of Program

- Implementation research review
- Key informant interviews about implementation factors

Stage 2: Plan and Design the Program

- Program logic models
- Program templates
- Outcomes hierarchies

Stage 3: Deliver the Program

- Coverage analysis
- Component analysis
- Program records
- Case studies

Stage 4: Improve the Program

- Service delivery pathways
- Client feedback

Stage 1: Assessing the Needs and Feasibility of the Program

Over the past twenty years, one of the major changes in the evaluation field has been the realization that programs do not produce tangible outcomes simply on the basis of clearly formulated program goals and program plans. Implementation is not automatic. The achievement of program outcomes is now recognized as a complex interplay of program technology, organizational context, and broader environmental forces (see Figure 3.1).

These changes have been accompanied by a greater awareness that potential implementation issues must be identified and assessed before a program is designed. By using implementation research reviews and key informant interviews, evaluators can draw on over a quarter-century of evaluation findings and the practice experience of experts to assess which program models are more likely to meet the needs of the target groups and identify the specific implementation factors that must be considered in an analysis of implementation feasibility. These tools can help answer the fundamental question, "Is the proposed program capable of being implemented and producing the intended outcomes for the target group given the organizational and environmental contexts?" Answering this question at the start can improve the selection of program models that will produce the desired outcomes and reduce the risk of program failure during implementation.

Implementation Research Review

The implementation research review synthesizes the research relevant to a specific program area. The purpose of the review is to identify the implementation variables associated with program success or failure. (For more information about systematic research reviews and evaluation synthesis, see Chapter Seven, this volume.) It has these benefits and challenges:

> Benefits: It counterbalances the tendency to reinvent the wheel and identifies important implementation factors that affect program performance.

> Challenges: Interpreting research that involves different methods and settings can be difficult.

Synopsis of Method

1. Assemble a small team of managers and front-line staff knowledgeable about the program area.
2. Identify keywords related to the program client group, program purpose, and program model.
3. Conduct a literature review using computerized library searches, complemented by Internet searches.
4. Document the review and obtain source articles.
5. Examine source articles to identify implementation factors that are related to program performance.
6. Identify leading evaluators, researchers, and program managers from the literature review.
7. Contact these key informants and request further information or an opportunity for a telephone interview regarding implementation issues, problems, and suggestions based on their experience.
8. Describe key implementation factors in the research that are linked to program success and failure.
9. Integrate this information into the program plan.

   Example. To achieve greater protection of children at risk of abuse and neglect, a government department wished to introduce a standardized approach to assessing eligibility for services, risk assessment, and risk management in child protection services. The project evaluator conducted a literature review to assemble the research evidence about the design parameters and the psychometric properties of the major instruments currently in use by child protection agencies. The evaluator also used the literature review to identify the strengths and weaknesses of each instrument, including its cultural sensitivity, and to describe critical factors that were essential for implementation.

Key Informant Interviews About Implementation Factors

Key informant interviews collect informed opinions, perceptions, and facts from people with special knowledge and expertise about the implementation of the type of program being considered. Usually key informant interviews take place by telephone, but they may be face-to-face in certain situations (with homeless people or special needs populations, for example). They have the following benefits and challenges:

> Benefits: This rapid method takes advantage of informants' expert knowledge to identify important implementation issues and help assess the feasibility of implementing various program options.

> Challenges: It requires an experienced interviewer to ask relevant questions within a short period of time and to establish the rapport needed to encourage honest answers. It is also subject to expert bias and shared perceptions of those selected through the sampling process.

Synopsis of Method

1. Assemble a committee to investigate the need and feasibility of a program and to suggest several "experts" who have special knowledge of the target group and operate programs that respond to the target group's needs.
2. Contact the initial group key informants, describe the purpose of the interview, and ask the initial group to suggest other key informants to interview.
3. Add the names of key informants identified in the review of the research to the list.
4. Continue developing this "snowball sample" until the informants do not suggest any new names. Typically fifteen to twenty key informants are identified.
5. Send the interview questions in advance to the key informants and arrange a time for the interview.
6. Develop an interview script and use it to guide the interview process. When used for implementation evaluation, interview questions ask key informants to identify obstacles, problems, issues, and hidden costs regarding the implementation of various program options that are under

consideration. Typically key informants also are asked to assess the feasibility of the different options given additional information about program parameters that are supplied by the program evaluator. All key informants who participate in the interviews usually receive a copy of the findings.

7. Supply a synopsis of the findings to all key informants who participate in the interviews.

Example. To provide detailed information about the critical factors necessary for implementing each major standardized instrument for assessing the risk of child abuse and neglect, the evaluation consultant supplemented the literature review with key informant telephone interviews with a sample of child protection professionals who had experience using the instruments, government staff who were responsible for child protection risk assessment, and the developers of the major assessment instruments. Implementation questions included the ease of use in terms of training time, time to complete, case recording, and computer use and the consistency of implementation within individual agencies and across the jurisdiction. The evaluator also asked the key informants to identify the major barriers to implementing a standardized risk assessment instrument and suggestions for ensuring successful implementation. For example, the key informants identified the need for training both supervisors and front-line workers in the use of the instrument, ongoing support, an adequate implementation time line, and placing assessment for risk of abuse and neglect as part of ongoing case assessment and case planning.

Stage 2: Program Planning and Design

In times of limited resources, governments and other funders are under enormous pressure to implement effective and efficient programs. The public demands evidence that their taxes and donations are well spent. This requires carefully designed programs and effective implementation. Evaluation has a complementary role in program planning and design by ensuring that program plans are responsive to the needs of the target groups, giving attention to implementation issues, and verifying that program plans are translated into effective interventions that produce the intended outcomes.

The transparent paradigm of implementation (see Figure 3.1) includes the design of the program, the internal structure and organizational factors (communication, coordination, resources) that shape service delivery, and the external factors that facilitate or constrain program delivery and the achievement of program outcomes. Taken together, these sets of factors affect both program planning and implementation and the relationship between the program and its context.

At this stage, there are three practical tools to build the bridge between planning and implementation and to illuminate the relationship between program technology and program context: program logic models, program templates, and outcomes hierarchies. The program logic model is an essential tool because it clarifies the intended outcomes of the program and requires reflection by program planners about the specific activities needed to achieve those outcomes, together with a consideration of the deployment of program resources.

Program templates incorporate the program logic model, and then go beyond by developing a brief but clear picture of the program in its context, including its rationale, mission and major goals, organizational structure, and program implementation plan. By completing the program template, program managers and staff are walked through a planning process that includes implementation issues. In the space of a few pages, they have a complete view of their program that may be shared with board and senior managers, funders, and service delivery partners. It is also a dynamic tool that is designed to be easily updated once the program is implemented. In that way there is a "diary of development" and a mechanism for implementation evaluation findings to shape program design.

The outcomes hierarchy provides another view of the program. It links together program outcomes and program theory, but places both within the context of a sequence of program operations needed to achieve the outcomes. It also clearly identifies the specific measures needed to monitor program progress and to identify early warning signs of problems in program design or implementation during the program delivery stage.

Program Logic Models

Program logic models are brief diagrams that give a picture of how the program theoretically works to achieve benefits for participants. They are typically diagrammed on a flowchart representing program components, activities, goals, outputs, and outcomes. They clarify the cause-and-effect relationship among program resources, activities, and outcomes from key stakeholder perspectives (McLaughlin and Jordan, 1999). Logic models are typically diagrammed on a flowchart representing program components, activities, goals, outputs, and outcomes. (For additional information about logic model development, see Chapter One, this volume.) They have the following benefits and challenges:

> Benefits: Logic models can help identify problems in the design of programs. The most common problem regarding poor performance of a program is faulty program design. Logic models provide a useful framework for examining the relationship between program components

and outcomes. They can help determine whether a proposed program has the capacity to achieve program outcomes or results. Logic models can help identify the key indicators that need to be tracked to assess program implementation and outcomes.

Challenges: Developing logic models requires expertise or instruction in model building and in specifying performance outcomes and indicators. Programs may have little documentation about their activities and unrealistic notions about the relationship of program theory, program activities, and outcomes.

Synopsis of Method

1. Form a work group that includes key program stakeholders.
2. Clarify the overall program purpose or overall program outcomes.
3. Specify the long-term outcomes, that is, the changes or improvements expected for the client some time after the program has been completed.
4. Specify the short-term outcomes, that is, the changes or improvements expected for the client close to the time of participating in the program that lead to long-term outcomes
5. Identify each program activity that leads to the short-term outcomes
6. Identify service delivery objectives (outputs) that state what each program activity will produce (for example, kinds of services, intensity, or units of service).
7. Link long-term and short-term outcomes in the diagram.
8. Link program activities with their service delivery objectives (outputs).
9. Link short-term outcomes with service delivery objectives.
10. Identify duplicate and missing components.

Example. Disabled persons with chronic disabilities in a midsized city have experienced limited access to employment services, resources, training opportunities, and employers. They need career planning and supports to ensure that they are aware of their rights and receive the services they need for sustainable employment. For their part, employers need skilled and dependable workers. The employment services staff formed a small work group with experienced managers, staff, several disabled workers, and several representatives from the local chamber of commerce.

The group decided to develop a logic model that clearly identified the desired outcomes for the disabled workers, the resources and program activities needed to achieve those outcomes, and the indicators of performance so that implementation and outcomes could be tracked and progress measured. The long-term outcomes were to retain employment eighteen months or more, improve client access to mainstream and specialized employment opportunities, and improve employer acceptance of qualified workers who may have chronic disabilities. The work group then identified the shorter-term outcomes, such as improving job skills and obtaining a job placement, that would eventually lead to the longer-term outcome of obtaining and retaining employment. In turn, the work group outlined the activities, such as career counseling and employer incentives, that would produce the shorter-term outcomes. Finally, the work group set the expectations for service levels by defining the outputs, such as "50 percent increase in job placements," that would be necessary to achieve the intended outcomes.

Program Templates

A program template is a summary of the key aspects of a program in a format that is clear to managers, staff, and program evaluators. Program templates may be updated at regular intervals to provide an ongoing "diary of program development." They have the following benefits and challenges:

> Benefits: Program templates systematically describe the contents inside the "black box." Templates help assess the extent and process of program implementation by providing a checklist of what program components should be delivered and what is actually delivered at a program site. Templates can help determine if a program includes all components recommended for best practice for this type of program.

> Challenges: Because program templates provide a comprehensive view of the program implementation, they require assembling data from different sources and then editing the information into a coherent document. Usually the program evaluator coordinates the team effort and edits the template.

Synopsis of the Method

1. Conduct a formal and informal review of the literature based on the program type, giving careful attention to the findings of the research and practice experience about the components necessary for programs to be effective (Loucks-Horsley, 1996).
2. Assemble a writing team comprising program managers, program staff, and the person facilitating the program evaluation. When used to improve program implementation, template data are usually collected by program managers and others close to the program.
3. Identify the key components of the program being evaluated. Table 3.1 provides a list of the common program components and a brief description of each.

Table 3.1. Description of Program Template Categories

Program Template Category	Description of Contents
1. Need or problem addressed by the program	Describe the major needs or difficulties addressed by the program
2. Program target group	Define the target group(s) clearly
3. Rationale for the program	Explain how the program responds to the needs of the target group(s)
4. Origin and history of the program	Trace how the program started and any major changes since start-up
5. Program mission and major program goals	State the mission and major goals in a few paragraphs
6. Shorter and longer term outcomes	Start with the longer term outcomes the program intends to achieve, then the shorter term outcomes that will contribute to attaining the long-term outcomes
7. Major service activities and program components	Briefly describe the program's theory of program delivery, the activities used to deliver the program, and how they are organized (for example, intake, assessment, home visits, follow-up)
8. Program flow-chart	Draw a flow-chart of client flow through the program, including major decision points
9. Program logic model	Develop a program logic model and append it here
10. Program organizational structure	Describe briefly (or diagram) how the program is structured, including major accountability and reporting relationships
11. Program leadership and staffing	Explain the human resources devoted to the program
12. Program financial resources	Describe the financial resources available to the program and major breakdown of the program budget
13. Program linkages	Note program's referral sources, service delivery partners, participation in major collaborative provider networks
14. Program implementation plan	Define the implementation objectives, amount and intensity of services to be delivered, and intended outputs and outcomes
15. Program evaluation plan	Describe the major evaluation questions being addressed, how the program is monitoring and evaluating its service delivery and outcomes, and the reporting process

4. Pilot-test the draft program template on one or two program locations if possible.
5. Identify the persons (managers, staff, evaluators) who will complete each of the program template categories.
6. Assemble the descriptions for each category, and then edit for content and consistency.
7. Distribute the completed program templates to all program managers and staff.
8. Use the template to compare actual versus intended program, assess the presence of best practices, and track organizational development (Scheirer, 1996).
9. At designated intervals, usually every six months, revise the template to reflect current practice.

Example. Program managers and staff developed a program template to describe the implementation of an innovative program that combined specialized mental health services with a wraparound service delivery approach. The program evaluator worked with the program team to explain the concept of the program template, define and explain each template category, distribute writing tasks, and then edit the final template. Because there were no published evaluations or program descriptions to guide program development, the first program template documented the program as it was initially implemented, and this information was used to give rapid feedback to program managers, staff, government funders, and a community steering committee. Government policymakers also made use of the program template description during their deliberations about the transferability of the model to other locations.

After considering the findings of the interim evaluation, the managers and staff decided to modify the program model. These changes were captured in an updated program template. The second phase of the study included an implementation evaluation of the revised program model, an evaluation of the shorter-term outcomes for clients, and an assessment of the strengths, weaknesses, benefits, and costs of the revised model in comparison with alternative services.

Outcomes Hierarchies

An outcomes hierarchy identifies the key program outcomes and places them in a sequence (hierarchy) from shorter- to longer-term outcomes, according to their order of implementation. The outcomes hierarchy is a simple tool for avoiding the three main causes of program failure: faulty program theory, an inability to translate theory into programs, and inadequate program implementation. It does this by clearly defining the implementation sequence of program outcomes and then relating them specifically to the program theory that stands behind each step, called the "linking validity assumptions." It has the following benefits and challenges:

> Benefits: An outcomes hierarchy provides a clear description of a program's change strategy. It sharpens the definition of the scope of the problem or opportunity the program addresses, the program theory and rationale, and the factors that may affect the ability of the program to attain the intended outcomes. In this way, an outcomes hierarchy helps to identify areas of possible implementation failure, explain results, and recognize areas for possible improvement.
>
> Challenges: The concept of outcomes hierarchies is not widely promoted, so explanation of the concept and its applications may be needed. Program managers and staff often are not experienced in linking program theory closely to program outcomes and operations; learning to use outcomes hierarchies may take formal instruction and coaching.

Synopsis of Method

1. Form a work group comprising program managers, staff, evaluation facilitator, and key stakeholders.
2. Define the major problem the program is attempting to solve or the issues the program intends to address—the ultimate, or long-term, outcomes of the program.
3. List the context and environmental factors that might influence the ability of the program to achieve outcomes for participants (for example, risk or protective factors or the economic environment).
4. List successful implementation strategies or best practices that literature reviews and practice experience show have helped achieve desired outcomes in similar programs.
5. Roughly sketch out the overall program theory (or strategic initiatives) to employ to achieve the long-term goal.
6. Start building the hierarchy by identifying the first short-term outcome needed to begin the program response.
7. In the second column of the hierarchy, state assumptions about why the first outcome is needed to implement the program. That is, relate the outcome to the program theory.
8. Continue building the outcomes hierarchy by writing the second outcome in the cause-and-effect chain.
9. State the assumptions about why the second outcome is needed to implement the program.

10. Continue this process until you reach the ultimate, or long-term, outcome of the program. The outcomes hierarchy is now complete.

Example. To develop consensus around program theory, program activities, and realistic program outcomes, the staff of a mentoring program developed an outcomes hierarchy (see Table 3.2). The core strategy for this program was to change the behavior of youth who were in danger of expulsion from school by matching them with a mentor. The mentor would form a strong bond with the youth, serve as a positive role model and guide, and apply a cognitive-behavioral program to help the youth develop positive behaviors. Because youth experiencing behavior problems in school often have poor peer role models, another aspect of the program was to encourage them to develop a positive peer group by participating in after-school programs. Table 3.2 provides an example of an outcomes hierarchy for a mentoring program.

The program staff began the outcome hierarchy by specifying the long-term outcomes in terms of intended benefit for the youth. The ultimate outcome was graduation from school rather than dropping out or expulsion. To achieve this, longer-term outcomes, such as the ability to show self-control under stress and demonstrating positive behaviors in school, were necessary.

The program staff began with the first logical short-term outcome needed to begin the process toward achievement of the ultimate outcome. Strictly speaking, some of the shorter-term and intermediate outcomes are program objectives rather than outcomes for the youth themselves. The first shorter-term outcome was the recruitment of mentors. In the second column, this is linked with the validity assumption that the program will not achieve its longer-term outcomes and performance targets (number of students who graduate) unless there are enough mentors.

The program staff then repeated this process by carefully considering the next outcome needed to move toward the longer-term outcomes and the rationale for that outcome. Table 3.2 shows how the staff related the outcomes to program theory (validity assumptions), such as the need for mentor and youth to sign a contract, the importance of frequent meetings, and the necessity for the youth to take responsibility by selecting an activity and calling the mentor.

Stage 3: Program Delivery Stage

The heart of implementation evaluation is the evaluation of program delivery. This has two major sets of issues: program coverage and the service delivery process. Coverage measures the actual participation by the intended

Table 3.2. Example of an Outcomes Hierarchy for a Mentoring Program

Hierarchy of Outcomes	*Linking Validity Assumptions*
I. Shorter-term	
1. Recruit mentors	Adequate number of mentors needed to achieve long-term outcomes and performance targets
2. Determine eligibility of mentors	Services must be delivered by mentors who are qualified
3. Accept qualified mentors who are low risk	Qualified mentors must pass risk assessment screening
II. Intermediate	
4. Youth accepts "match" with mentor	Mentoring has greatest impact when youth meets mentor first and then accepts the match
5. Youth and mentor sign contract	Mentoring causes changes when expectations for youth and mentor are stated clearly and accepted by both in writing
6. Youth and mentor meet weekly for one year	Mentoring causes changes only when contact is frequent and sustained over time
7. Youth is responsible for selecting one activity and initiating one call with the mentor a month	Youth will experience change only if actively involved in mentoring relationship
8. Youth participates in one agency group activity per month	To sustain change, youth must become part of a new peer group that has positive values, attitudes, and behaviors
III. Longer-term	
9. Youth accepts limits set by mentor on weekly outings	Long-term change depends on youth accepting authority of adults and complying with limits
10. Youth demonstrates self-control in a difficult situation with mentor, parent, teacher, or other adults once a month	Through the application of cognitive-behavioral strategies learned and practiced in the mentoring relationship, youth acquires self-control in difficult situations
11. Youth demonstrates positive behaviors in school (for example, cooperates with others, accepts class rules, no suspensions, no expulsions)	Increased self-control results in positive behaviors and reduced problem behaviors that had been serious obstacles to school success
12. Youth graduates from school	School graduation fulfills intended outcomes of youth, mentor, agency, and funding body

target groups. Coverage analysis is a tool used to shed light on the key coverage concerns, especially the extent of participation by the target group, possible bias in selecting program participants, and participation by the wrong persons.

Component analysis is a tool that carefully describes the program operations at each phase (component) of service delivery, such as intake, assessment, treatment, and follow-up. The initial description is based on the components needed to execute the program theory. The initial description is then compared with evaluation data about the program as implemented. Component analysis can identify potential problems in service delivery that might jeopardize the ability to deliver its intended outcomes.

Virtually all programs keep records, and these are a common source of information about service delivery. Program records, whether on paper or computerized, provide a ready source of data about client characteristics, participation in program activities, type and intensity of services, and achievement of short-term outcomes. When combined in an implementation evaluation, these data can demonstrate whether the program delivery was faithful to the program plan, differences in implementation by program site or client characteristics, and the relationship between implementation and outcomes.

Case studies are frequently used for implementation analysis, primarily to compare the fidelity of the implemented program to the program plans. With the growing awareness that programs delivered in real-world settings must adapt to the organizational context and local conditions, case studies often are the method of choice to examine variations in program implementation and outcomes across sites. The strength of case studies is their flexibility and ability to assemble a comprehensive array of quantitative and qualitative data to provide in-depth analysis and valuable insight.

Coverage Analysis

Coverage analysis provides information about the acceptance of the program by the target group and the extent of participation by the target group in the program. It is one of the fundamental measures of program implementation, and it helps ensure accountability that the target population is reached by the program (Rossi, Freeman, and Lipsey, 1998). It has the following benefits and challenges:

> Benefits: The analysis provides feedback about participation in the program and can detect implementation bias by examining differences in participation by subgroups of the target population (such as voluntary self-selection, intentional "creaming" of easier-to-serve clients by staff,

and location of program). It also helps identify bias in comparison and control groups when an experimental evaluation design is employed.

Challenges: It requires clear definition of the target group during program planning and accurate monitoring of key target group characteristics during program implementation.

Synopsis of Method

1. During program planning phase, develop a clear definition of the target population.
2. Identify key characteristics of the target population for monitoring. These will vary according to program but typically include age, gender, ethnicity, socioeconomic status, geographic location, and place of residence.
3. Identify any specific characteristics that may affect ability to participate in the program (examples are transportation, child care, distance from program site, and hours of operation).
4. Collect data on the identified characteristics for the target population. Check for data accuracy.
5. Analyze the data about characteristics for the target population to determine if the persons served are the ones specified in the program plan. This provides a measure of program coverage. Responsible use of program resources requires minimizing the number of persons who are not in need of the program.
6. Analyze the data to determine if the persons served by the program meet the program eligibility criteria. These data help identify bias.
7. Using the identified characteristics for the target population, determine which subgroups are underrepresented or overrepresented among program participants. This analysis detects program bias.
8. Analyze the characteristics of program dropouts from program records. These data examine bias and provide insight into possible program changes that are needed to attract and engage more of the target population.

Example. A project for immigrant women addressed problems of isolation, health, parental concerns, and lack of information about community services and schools. The project provided a weekly support group for immigrant women and a project for their preschool children. The target population was recent immigrant women with preschool children at home who were socially isolated. From the sponsor's perspective, the main implementation question was whether the project was able to reach isolated immigrant women and engage them in the project.

To analyze coverage, the evaluator used several data sources. The first was a client information system with specific questions regarding length of time in the country and a number of indicators of isolation, such as language spoken on arrival, the presence of close relatives, and participation in community activities. An activities tracking system was used to monitor participation by the immigrant women and their children in the project. Individual and group interviews were conducted with women, staff, and collateral professionals, such as settlement workers and staff of ethnic-cultural organizations.

The coverage analysis showed that the project provided tangible benefits for women of diverse cultures and their children, but it was not able to attract the target population. For example, the majority of women spoke English, were not isolated, worked outside the home, and were active in a variety of community activities. There were high levels of satisfaction with the project, and an implementation analysis of each session showed that the actual project closely matched its intended design. Although the original sponsor ended project funding, a few months later, on the strength of the evaluation, a new sponsor reinstated the project as a program for the cultural integration and mutual support of new immigrants and their families.

Component Analysis

A component analysis maps the relationship between program operations and outcomes for each major component of a program (Bickman and Heflinger, 1995; Bickman, 1985). For example, the major components of a treatment program may be outreach, intake, assessment, treatment, and follow-up. The component analysis is usually conducted at the program planning stage, during program implementation to provide feedback, and after program implementation for comparison with the planned program. It has the following benefits and challenges:

> Benefits: It helps to detect problems with program theory and program implementation, helps ensure that the right clients receive appropriate services, and can improve the coordination between program activities. It also strengthens the ability of field experimental designs and quasi-experimental designs to interpret outcome data.

> Challenges: Component analysis requires a good understanding of the underlying program theory. Logic model or outcomes hierarchy (or both) may be necessary before undertaking a component analysis.

Synopsis of Method

1. Form a component review team of program managers, staff, program evaluation facilitator, and key stakeholders.
2. Describe the program theory, including the assumptions underlying the program intervention and the cause-and-effect links.

3. Draw a logic model or outcomes hierarchy for the program that reflects the program theory accurately.
4. Identify each major component of the program based on the program theory. A component is the largest homogeneous unit or building block of a service.
5. Define the program operations that are necessary for achieving the short-term outcomes and the intermediate outcomes for each program component.
6. Draw a flowchart or complete a table that illustrates clearly (1) the relationship between program operations and the short-term and intermediate outcomes for each program component and (2) the longer-term outcomes for the overall program.
7. Identify any contextual, structural, or broader environmental (social, political, economic) factors that may influence program implementation.
8. Use data from multiple sources during the process of program implementation and after the program is implemented to provide accurate information about the structure, operations, and short-term and intermediate outcomes needed to validate and revise the component model. Data sources typically include documents (policies and procedures, minutes, program descriptions), key informant interviews with stakeholders, administrative and program monitoring data about client and program characteristics, and client-staff feedback surveys or interviews.

Example. Bickman and Heflinger (1995) offer a good example of a component analysis used in the evaluation of the Fort Bragg Child and Adolescent Mental Health Demonstration Project. To provide a fair test of the program theory, the evaluators first conducted a component analysis to verify that the key program components had been properly implemented. As part of the component analysis, they developed a descriptive graph of the program that linked program operations to theory for each of three major components of the program: intake, assessment, and treatment. For example, during the intake component, the clinic was required to engage in a public information and marketing campaign that was hypothesized to lead to the short-term outcome of better awareness (see Figure 3.2). When coupled with better access through a single point of entry, no copayments and no deductibles, and prompt intake, the intake operations were hypothesized to lead to the intermediate outcomes of increasing the number of clients served, treating milder and more severe cases, and increasing client satisfaction about the intake process when compared to traditional services. The analysis of the components required to operationalize the theory showed that they had been properly implemented.

**Figure 3.2. Component Analysis of the Intake Process
for the Fort Bragg Child and Adolescent Demonstration Project**

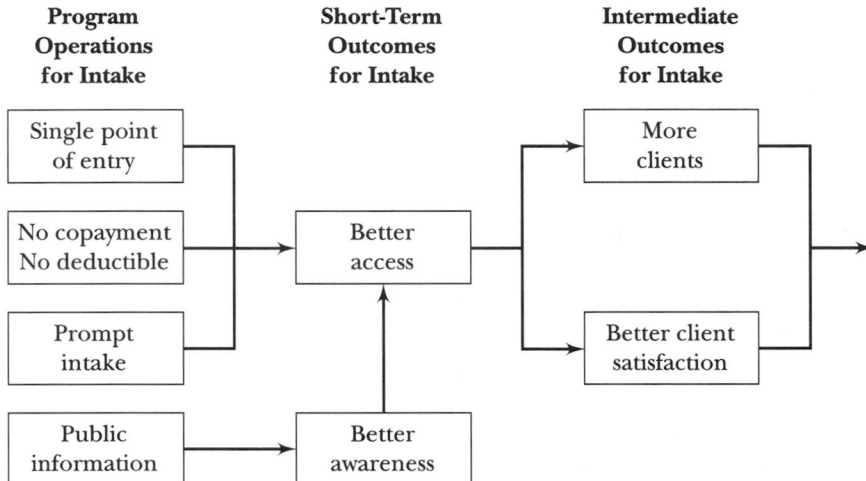

Source: Bickman, L., and Heflinger, C. A. "Seeking Success by Reducing Implementation and Evaluation Failures." In L. Bickman and D. J. Rog (eds.), *Children's Mental Health Services: Research, Policy, and Evaluation.* Thousand Oaks, Calif.: Sage, 1995, p. 180. Copyright ©1995 by Sage Publications. Reprinted by permission of Sage Publications, Inc.

Program Records

Program records may be paper or computerized. They include client files and administrative data that, when combined, provide a continuous source of data about client needs and characteristics, program resources and delivery, program outputs, and indicators of short-term outcomes, all very useful for monitoring service delivery. They have the following benefits and challenges:

> Benefits: Program records are a source of rapid feedback information needed to change a faulty program design, manage a program well, and document delivery of the program over time that permits ongoing monitoring of program changes and improvements. They also help ensure that all target subgroups receive equitable services.

> Challenges: Good mastery of target group needs, program theory, and program operations is needed to define data elements clearly. Computer software and hardware must be affordable, user friendly, capable of providing the required analyses and reports, and easily maintained and updated. Unfortunately, this is the exception rather than the common situation. Data collection and entry can take time from service

delivery. Data quality may be poor or deteriorate over time unless staff are trained and data quality is audited regularly.

Synopsis of Method

1. Bring together a team of program managers, staff, evaluation facilitator, and key stakeholders.
2. Specify evaluation questions that address program delivery issues—for example: Is the program serving the right persons? Are program activities being implemented according to plan? Is the program producing the expected outputs (number of clients served, number of units of service)? Is the program meeting its standards of quality? What program areas need improvement or fine tuning?
3. Identify the sources of data needed to answer each question.
4. Study the data sources to determine which questions may be answered by data from program records. Program records typically include the following materials:

> Client intake and referral forms
>
> Assessments
>
> Service activity forms (type, duration, intensity, units of service)
>
> Case notes
>
> Records of goal attainment and client progress
>
> Financial records
>
> Service statistics reports
>
> Quality reports
>
> Weekly and monthly variance reports
>
> Quarterly and annual reports

5. Examine existing program records to assess the adequacy of current data (it is much less expensive and time-consuming to use or modify existing data).
6. Identify data that must be collected from new types of program records.
7. If feasible, design and pilot-test new data collection forms.
8. Develop a data collection plan that includes sources of data, who will collect data, and strategies for ensuring data quality (training, auditing).
9. Develop an analysis plan for presenting the data from program records (tables, graphs, or figures, for example).

10. Develop a reporting plan that reduces redundancies and workload on data entry and analysis staff while providing timely reporting.

Example. Multiple sources of data were used in the evaluation of the implementation of a multisite prevention and early intervention program designed to reduce the incidence of premature and low birthweight babies, reduce the risk factor associated with abuse and neglect, and promote positive child development in high-risk families. A number of types of program records were used in the evaluation:

- Service request and general intake forms
- Individual client questionnaires that collected demographic information, pregnancy history, utilization of services, lifestyle and risk behaviors, and pregnancy and breastfeeding outcomes
- Weekly debriefing forms completed by staff after every session that recorded attendance, issues discussed, follow-up, or action needed
- Final review and wrap-up notes completed by staff after every program
- A follow-up questionnaire that measured parent and child involvement in the community before and after the program, as well as implementation feedback, such as accessibility of the program

In addition to the program records, several standardized evaluation tools were used to measure program outcomes. The implementation analysis based on the program records showed that the programs were successful in targeting the most disadvantaged families and that they had reached a substantial proportion of the neediest families, that the participation rate was fairly high, and that the programs were able to reach and engage families that were disadvantaged socioeconomically. The prenatal follow-up questionnaire identified areas of concern that needed to be better addressed by the parenting courses (such as how to know whether the baby was receiving enough milk). The weekly debriefing forms provided a way to check the intended plans for program sessions against the actual topics discussed.

Case Studies

The case study is the most frequently used method for implementation evaluation. Case studies integrate quantitative and qualitative information from a variety of sources to give an in-depth picture of the implemented program, its organizational context, and the broader environment. Depending on the evaluation questions, case studies may include single or multiple locations and involve a wide variety of data-gathering strategies. More details may be found in Yin (2002). They have the following benefits and challenges:

Benefits: Case studies are a flexible way of providing a detailed picture of program operations, often at different sites. The inclusion of qualitative information allows for deeper understanding of how and why program operations relate to outcomes, especially if there are implementation problems. Case studies are especially useful for understanding the implementation of innovative programs or demonstration projects.

Challenges: Because of the multiple sources of data and depth of analysis, case studies can be time-consuming and costly. Several cases usually are needed to portray a range of issues or program responses. Often it is difficult to generalize the findings to other program settings.

Synopsis of Method

1. Assemble a team of program managers, staff, evaluation facilitator, and key stakeholders.
2. Specify the evaluation questions that the implementation case study will address. Usually these are descriptive questions that describe the program implementation or normative questions that ask how well the program complies with legislation, regulations, or demands for corrective action.
3. Select the program locations that will be included in the case study. Usually the sample of program locations will select sites with average or representative programs or those that bracket the best and worst scenarios.
4. Select evaluators. The quality of case studies depends largely on the expertise and experience of the program evaluators.
5. Plan the evaluation to allow enough time on each site to collect data from multiple sources and confirm the validity of the data gathered.
6. Collect data from multiple sources, including program documentation (policies and procedures, minutes, reports), direct observation of program operations, and individual or group interviews.
7. Analyze the quantitative and qualitative data. In analyzing implementation case studies, take special care to avoid bias, consider different views about program operations and results, check the quality of data, and validate the findings.

Example. In the evaluation of the Fort Bragg Demonstration Project, Bickman and Heflinger (1995) used a case study approach to describe the structure and processes of the demonstration. The approach used multiple methods, including program documentation (correspondence, program descriptions, administrative reports), semistructured interviews with key stakeholders, utilization and outcome data describing participants at the demonstration and comparison sites, and a series of interviews with service providers and service agency representatives about the mental health of children and their families at the demonstration and comparison sites. These data were used to compare the program as implemented with the program as planned. The case study approach provided a comprehensive description of how the demonstration was implemented and also showed that the demonstration was implemented faithfully enough to plan to provide an excellent test of the program theory.

Stage 4: Program Improvement Stage

During the past decade, there has been growing recognition that programs are continuously changing and that program evaluation is important for managing the change process. This has sparked a proactive approach to program management that ensures positive outcomes, high-quality programs, and responsiveness to changing needs. As part of the transparent paradigm of program evaluation (see Figure 3.1), there also has been increasing awareness of contributions of evaluation as an essential part of organizational development and learning, as well as a necessary adjunct to achieving community outcomes.

In keeping with these changes, evaluation has moved from a one-time report card model to a continuous and interactive process for program improvement. At the program improvement stage, implementation evaluation is used to improve program design, modify program plans, strengthen service delivery, and give program staff greater understanding about the relationship of program operations and outcomes.

Service delivery pathways are a useful tool for program improvement. At first glance, they appear similar to client flow diagrams. A key difference with this tool is the need for program and evaluation staff to work closely together to understand the milestones or operational benchmarks to be expected and achieved at each step of service delivery implementation. This knowledge is crucial in situations where programs are paid for results. For example, an employment program might need to enroll five hundred clients initially if it expects to have two hundred graduates who have full-time jobs. Through previous implementation evaluations, the program knows that if five hundred are not enrolled, two hundred will not graduate. Monitoring this milestone provides early warning of service delivery problems and a measure for assessing program improvements, for example, in the referral and outreach processes.

Client feedback is another essential tool for improving program implementation. Although monitoring quantitative data through information systems is helpful for identifying problem areas, there is no substitute for direct client feedback. Given its relatively low cost and flexible administration, the questionnaire survey tends to be the practical method of choice for obtaining reliable feedback.

Service Delivery Pathways

Service delivery pathways are flow diagrams that map the key program activities needed to achieve positive outcomes. They have the following benefits and challenges:

> Benefits: Service delivery pathways identify the program milestones (outputs) that need to be achieved to reach outcome targets. When used for program monitoring, they can spot implementation problems early so that they can be corrected before they damage outcomes. Service delivery pathways can help ensure the achievement of intended outcomes, service targets, and quality of services. They are an essential tool for programs that receive payment based on program outcomes.

> Challenges: Creating service delivery pathways requires a good understanding of program theory and the links between program operations and outcomes. In practice, an outcomes hierarchy or logic model would be developed before formulating the pathway. Maximum benefit is obtained when monitoring or trend data are available to calibrate the targets of program operations.

Synopsis of Method

1. Appoint a project team.
2. Develop a logic model and outcomes hierarchy.
3. Study current operations.
4. Conduct a literature review and key informant interviews of similar programs.
5. Agree on output and outcome measures and procedures.
6. Develop the service delivery pathway.
7. Pilot-test the service delivery pathway.
8. Revise the service delivery pathway based on the pilot test.
9. Implement the service delivery pathway.
10. Collect output and outcome data.
11. Review the service pathway on a regular basis looking for differences between intended and actual outputs and outcomes.
12. Treat these differences as possible early warning signs, and make changes to program operations if necessary.

Example. A service delivery pathway was used to document the implementation of an innovative gang prevention and school retention program. Figure 3.3 traces the service delivery pathway for the program. The wraparound process required a two-stage assessment process. Referrals usually came from the school, child protection agencies, or juvenile justice authorities. There also was the opportunity for self-referrals or referrals from participants, parents, and friends. A key aspect of the service delivery pathway is the inclusion of implementation milestones. These milestones are based on program experience, and they represent targets (for example, "recruit sixty youth") that must be achieved if the program is expected to attain the milestones. For example, experience with service delivery implementation has shown that the program must recruit sixty youth in order to have fifty youth attend the information session, forty youth to return signed consent forms, and thirty youth to complete six program sessions. If these milestones are not met, they provide early warning that the targets of having eighteen youth participate in at least one social and recreational activity and twelve youth to reduce their disruptive school behavior will not be attained.

The service delivery pathway was drawn and revised several times during the course of the implementation evaluation. It not only traced client progress through the system, but it caused program staff and sponsors to examine the theoretical and service delivery model very carefully and document needed changes to reach milestones or remediate problems. In many respects, the pathway served as a simulation of the program delivery and the relationships with youth, schools, service delivery partners, and the broader community. Revisions to the pathway often led to revisions in the guiding principles for the program, the implementation of the program model in the specific service setting, and new relationships with partners and sponsors. It also helped to document program changes that were useful for policy analysis.

Client Feedback

Client feedback measures how well program services meet participants' expectations about service delivery and the achievement of short-term outcomes. It has the following benefits and challenges:

> Benefits: Meeting client expectations is important to organizations in all sectors, and it usually is directly linked to an organization's funding success or profit levels. Client feedback helps to ensure accountability for meeting client outcomes, maintain the quality of service delivery, and fix implementation problems.

Figure 3.3. Service Delivery Pathway with Program Implementation Milestones

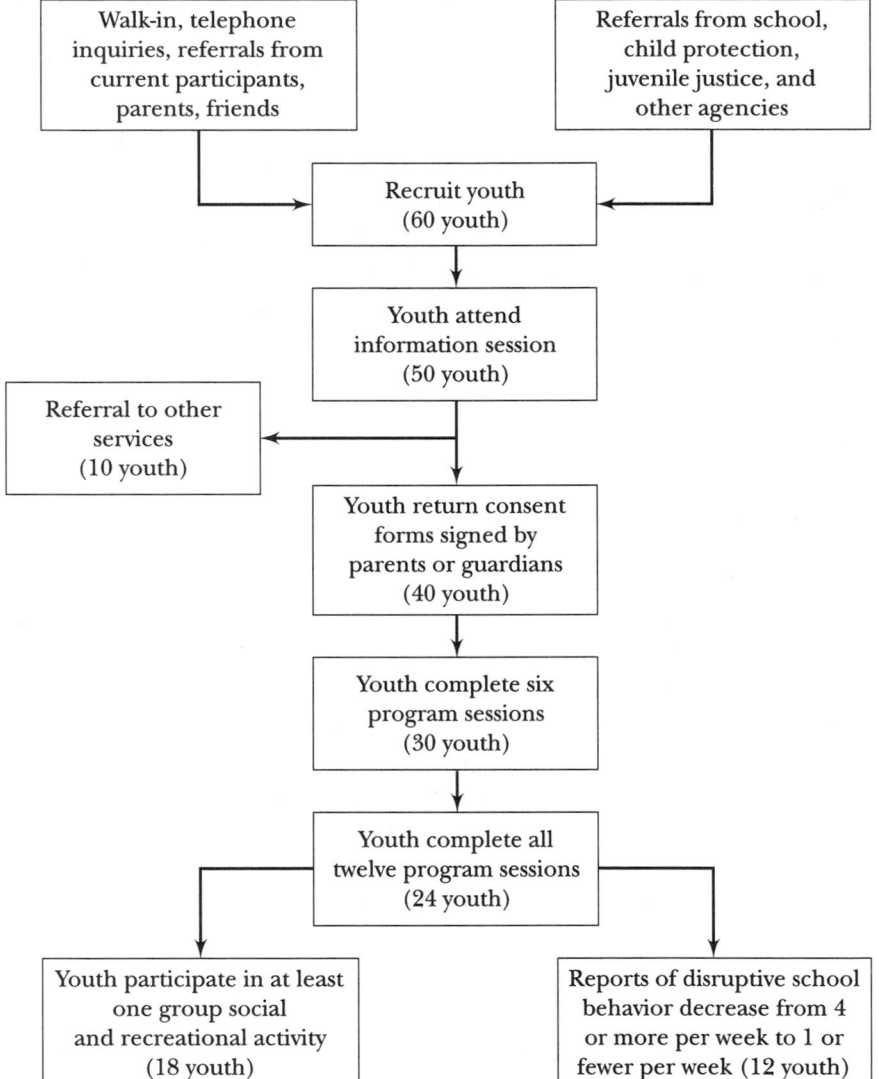

Challenges: Care must be taken to compensate for the known positive bias in client feedback surveys; that is, participants who are not satisfied with the program are less likely to return feedback questionnaires and those who do return them are more likely to have higher-than-average levels of satisfaction. Often it is difficult to obtain representative samples or adequate rates of return.

Synopsis of Method

1. Define the relevant clients (customers) for the specific program being evaluated.
2. Invite several groups of clients to participate in a group interview or individual interviews.
3. During the group interview, ask the clients to identify the performance attributes or factors that capture their expectations about your program. The performance attributes must be important to the clients, although a similar process may be repeated with staff and managers to identify differences in perception. Some "universal" performance attributes related to services include location, hours of operation, courtesy of staff, competence of staff, receiving services as promised, quality of services received, complaint handling, and resolution of problems.
4. For implementation evaluation, pay special attention to performance attributes related to service delivery and short-term outcomes
5. To reduce bias, follow the general formatting and key evaluation questions found in standardized client feedback measures used for program evaluation, such as the Larsen Scale (Larsen, Attkisson, Hargreaves, and Nguyen, 1979).
6. For programs with small numbers of clients (fewer than one hundred), distribute the client feedback questionnaire to all participants.
7. For larger numbers of clients, obtain professional consultation regarding the method of sample selection and sample size. In general, it is important to remember the rule that the larger the sample, the more precise the generalization to the overall population. See Henry (1990) for more information about sampling.
8. Use professional methods for ensuring higher return rates for mail surveys (cover letters, clear questions, clean layout, follow-up, incentives). (See Goldenkoff, Chapter Twelve, this volume for more suggestions about mail and telephone surveys.)

Example. Client and client representative participation and support is a crucial element of the Individual Program Planning (IPP) process for developmentally disabled persons. An implementation evaluation of the process in a large agency sought information directly from the developmentally disabled clients and client representatives concerning their satisfaction with the IPP conference process and the quality of the IPP plans.

Together with the IPP Implementation Committee, the evaluators developed and tested a questionnaire that met the standards for the design of client feedback instruments with developmentally disabled persons. The client questionnaire used a pictorial representations, and clients were asked to choose between pairs of cartoon drawings that pictured positive or negative IPP process outcomes, for example, "I felt I was part of the conference" or "I felt left out of the conference." A more traditional client feedback questionnaire was developed for interviews with parents and other client representatives.

Building Implementation Evaluation into the Organizational Culture

Implementation evaluation is one part of a performance-based management process (Scheirer and Newcomer, 2001; Wholey, 1999). As a result, it is important to involve managers and staff closely in the implementation evaluation process. Not only does participation help ensure buy-in and utilization of evaluation findings, it also helps to ensure the quality of evaluation data. Resistance by managers and staff can sabotage an implementation evaluation and impair the use of evaluation results. Resistance to evaluation is a normal response to the perceived threat that the evaluation will be used in a pass-fail manner to cut or continue the program and to judge individual performance. Furthermore, when managers and staff must supply data, a normal response to the evaluation paradox is that "those who provide the data may be hurt by it." Experienced evaluators reduce resistance and improve use by adopting a participatory approach and involving program personnel as partners in the evaluation process. A partnership is essential since the evaluators must rely on program staff to collect accurate data and supply crucial information, such as program descriptions. In organizations with their own internal evaluators, a partnership also may be forged between external evaluators, who bring their special expertise and objectivity, and the internal evaluators, who contribute their knowledge of the organizational context and its programs.

Experienced evaluators also know that adopting a participatory approach requires an investment in evaluation process and interaction with program personnel (Preskill and Torres, 1999). Rather than devoting the lion's share of evaluation resources to data collection and analysis, useful implementation evaluations place greater emphasis on front end analysis, frequent feedback of results, and follow-through activities. At the front end, this may include highly structured methods, such as evaluability assessments, that help program personnel describe their activities and understand their programs better (see Chapter Two, this volume). During the evaluation, it may mean regular feedback meetings to provide timely information about program strengths and weaknesses. Toward the end, it may include involving staff in briefings and presentations tailored to various stakeholders and working with them to monitor action plans and program performance indicators. This strategy permits higher participation by managers and staff in the evaluation process and contributes to the acceptance and utilization of evaluation findings.

Implementation evaluations must examine the organizational context of programs closely. This includes program structure, policies, management, methods, resources, and the outside environment. Often the best people for this aspect of the implementation evaluation are not evaluators but managers and senior staff persons, who are knowledgeable about program operations. They may become part of the evaluation study team. Clients also provide a valuable perspective about the organizational context, and their perceptions may be obtained by brief interviews or surveys.

The final decisions about how to modify the process of program delivery are usually left to program managers. Evaluators should not be surprised that feedback from implementation evaluations will be only part of the information that managers use to modify the program. Managers rarely make decisions based on research without significant staff input. They also need to consider their budgets, staff skills and staff availability, space requirements, past experiences with similar programs, and the advice of people they respect. The process of implementation evaluation, however, shows managers and staff where attention should be focused, and it facilitates staff training and supervision.

It is hard to imagine an evaluation study today that should not include some aspect of implementation evaluation. Implementation evaluation serves many useful purposes. It enhances program accountability by documenting program activities and efforts, provides objective evidence that a program is being delivered as planned, and helps senior managers and policy analysts make informed decisions about program design and policy direction.

References

Berk, R. A., and Rossi, P. H. *Thinking About Program Evaluation.* (2nd ed.) Thousand Oaks, Calif.: Sage, 1999.

Bickman, L. "Improving Established Statewide Programs: A Component Theory of Evaluation." *Evaluation Review,* 1985, *9,* 189–208.

Bickman, L., and Heflinger, C. A. "Seeking Success by Reducing Implementation and Evaluation Failures." In L. Bickman and D. J. Rog (eds.), *Children's Mental Health Services: Research, Policy, and Evaluation.* Thousand Oaks, Calif.: Sage, 1995.

Browne, A., and Wildavsky, A. "Should Evaluation Become Implementation?" In A. J. Love (ed.), *Developing Effective Internal Evaluation.* New Directions for Program Evaluation, no. 20. San Francisco: Jossey-Bass, 1983.

Henry, G. T. *Practical Sampling.* Thousand Oaks, Calif.: Sage, 1990.

Larsen, D., Attkisson, C., Hargreaves, W., and Nguyen, T. "Assessment of Client/Patient Satisfaction: Development of a General Scale." *Evaluation and Program Planning,* 1979, *2,* 197–207.

Loucks-Horsley, S. "The Design of Templates as Tools for Formative Evaluation." In M. A. Scheirer (ed.), *A User's Guide to Program Templates: A New Tool for Evaluating Program Content.* New Directions for Evaluation, no. 72. San Francisco: Jossey-Bass, 1996.

McLaughlin, J. A., and Jordan, G. B. "Logic Models: A Tool for Telling your Program's Performance Story." *Evaluation and Program Planning,* 1999, *22,* 65–72.

Owen, J., and Rogers, P. *Program Evaluation: Forms and Approaches.* Thousand Oaks, Calif.: Sage, 1999.

Preskill, H. S., and Torres, R. T. *Evaluative Inquiry for Learning in Organizations.* Thousand Oaks, Calif.: Sage, 1999.

Pressman, J. L., and Wildavsky, A. *Implementation: How Great Expectations in Washington Are Dashed in Oakland: or, Why It's Amazing That Federal Programs Work at All, This Being a Saga of the Economic Development Administration as Told by Two Sympathetic Observers Who Seek to Build Morals on a Foundation of Ruined Hopes.* (3rd ed.) Berkeley, Calif.: University of California Press, 1984.

Rossi, P. H., Freeman, H. E., and Lipsey, M. W. *Evaluation: A Systematic Approach.* (6th ed.) Thousand Oaks, Calif.: Sage, 1998.

"Same Problems Haunt NASA 17 Years After Challenger Loss." *USA Today,* May 16, 2003, p. 14A.

Scheirer, M. A. "A Template for Assessing the Organizational Base for Program Implementation." In M. A. Scheirer (ed.), *A User's Guide to Program Templates: A New Tool for Evaluating Program Content.* New Directions for Evaluation, no. 72. San Francisco: Jossey-Bass, 1996.

Scheirer, M. A., and Newcomer, K. "Opportunities for Program Evaluators to Facilitate Performance-Based Management." *Evaluation and Program Planning,* 2001, *24,* 63–71.

Scriven, M. *Evaluation Thesaurus.* (4th ed.) Thousand Oaks, Calif.: Sage, 1991.

Wholey, J. S. "Performance-Based Measurement: Responding to the Challenges." *Public Productivity and Management Review,* 1999, *2*(3), 288-307.

Yin, R. K. *Case Study Research.* (3rd ed.) Thousand Oaks, Calif.: Sage, 2002.

4

Performance Monitoring

Theodore H. Poister

The question of how to measure agency and program performance effectively is one of the big issues in public and nonprofit management (Behn, 1995; Young, 1997; Plantz, Greenway, and Hendricks, 1997; Wholey, 1999). Performance measurement systems are descriptive evaluation tools that complement, inform, and support more methodologically rigorous evaluation studies. Although they are obviously more superficial than intensive evaluation studies, they can often provide a timely and comprehensive view of program or agency performance on an ongoing basis. Thus, government and nonprofit organizations that are interested in managing for results and improving their performance are increasingly using performance measurement systems or performance monitoring systems (Aristiqueta, 1999; Poister and Streib, 1999; Berman and Wang, 2000; Julnes and Holzer, 2001; United Way of America, 1998; Hendricks, 2002).

Scope and Purpose

Performance measures are quantitative indicators of various aspects of the performance of public or nonprofit programs, agencies, or other entities that can be observed on a regular basis. Most often they focus on programs or service delivery, in which case they tend to relate most closely with evaluation. However, they are also used to track the performance of agencies or organizations themselves, perhaps focusing on a number of programs as well as other aspects of organizational performance, such as employee development and control over administrative overhead.

Sometimes performance measures pertain to an entire governmental jurisdiction, as in the case of a city government's measurement system that tracks performance over a large number of departments, programs, and services. Finally, performance measures may focus on a larger system, such as a state's transportation system or a health care system such as the sexually transmitted diseases prevention system, which may encompass multiple levels of government as well as nonprofit agencies, private corporations, and community organizations.

Performance monitoring systems are designed to track selected measures of program, agency, or system performance at regular time intervals and report them to managers and other specified audiences on an ongoing basis. Their purpose is to provide objective information to managers and policymakers in an effort to improve decision making and thereby strengthen performance, as well as to provide accountability to a range of stakeholders, such as higher-level management, central executive agencies, governing bodies, funding agencies, accrediting organizations, clients and customers, advocacy groups, and the public at large (Epstein, 1984; Wholey and Hatry, 1992; Broom, Caudle, Jennings, and Newcomer, 2002; Hendricks, 2002). Thus, performance monitoring systems are critical elements in a variety of approaches to results-oriented management.

Types of Performance Measures

A number of useful sources are available to program evaluators who are interested in learning about methodological approaches to developing performance monitoring systems (Ammons, 1995, 2001; Hatry, Van Houten, Plantz, and Greenway, 1996; Broom, Harris, Jackson, and Marshall, 1998; Hatry, 1999; Poister, 2003). One of the initial issues concerns the types of measures to emphasize in any particular performance measurement system.

Resources. The various types of resources going into a program (for example, the number of teachers, school buildings, classrooms, textbooks, or computer work stations in a local school system) can be measured in their own natural measurement units, or they can be measured and aggregated in their common measurement unit, dollar cost. Although resources are often not considered to represent true performance measures in their own right, when managerial objectives focus on controlling costs or improving the mix and quality of resources, such as maintaining a full complement of teachers or increasing the percentage of teachers who have master's degrees in their primary fields of instruction, it will be appropriate to track resources measures as indicators of performance.

Outputs. Output measures are critical because they represent the immediate products or services produced by public and nonprofit organizations.

They typically measure the amount of work performed or units of service produced, such as the number of seminars presented by an AIDS prevention program, the number of detoxification procedures completed by a crisis stabilization unit, the hours of routine patrol logged in by two-officer teams in a local police department, or the miles of guardrail replaced by highway maintenance crews. Sometimes output measures focus on the number of cases dealt with, such as the number of crimes investigated by the police or the number of clients served, such as the number of individuals who have received counseling in a drug abuse prevention program.

Productivity. Productivity indicators measure the rate of output production per unit of some specific resource over some particular unit of time. Usually these measures focus on labor productivity, such as the number of flight segments handled per air traffic controller per hour, the miles of highway resurfaced per maintenance crew per day, the number of clients counseled per vocational rehabilitation counselor per month, or the number of claims processed per disability adjudicator per week.

Efficiency. Like productivity indicators, measures of operating efficiency relate outputs to the resources used in producing them, but efficiency measures focus on the ratio of outputs to the dollar cost of the collective resources consumed in producing them. Thus, the cost per crime investigated, the cost per AIDS seminar conducted, the cost per ton of residential refuse collected, and the cost per client completing a job training program are all standard efficiency measures. Although the most useful efficiency measures focus on the cost of producing specific outputs, such as the cost per psychiatric assessment completed or the cost per group therapy session conducted in a crisis stabilization unit, performance monitoring systems sometimes incorporate efficiency measures relating cost to more general outputs, such as the cost per highway lane mile maintained or the cost per client per day in group homes for mentally disabled persons.

Service Quality. The most common dimensions of the quality of public and nonprofit services are timeliness, turnaround time, accuracy, thoroughness, accessibility, convenience, courtesy, and safety. Thus, the percentage of customers who wait in line more than fifteen minutes before being able to renew their driver's license, the number of calls to a local child support enforcement office that are returned within twenty-four hours, the percentage of claims for disability benefits that are not adjudicated within seventy working days, and the number of air traffic controller errors per 1 million flight segments handled are typical quality indicators. Quality indicators are often process indicators measuring compliance with established standards, such as the percentage of highway maintenance jobs that are performed according to prescribed operating procedures; others focus on the quality of the outputs themselves and the need for rework, such as the number of completed highway crack sealing projects that have to be repeated within a year.

Outcomes. Measures of outcomes tend to be strongly emphasized in the kinds of monitoring systems developed today because they represent the extent to which a program is effective in producing its intended outcomes and achieving desired results. Thus, the outcomes of a state's highway traffic safety program would be measured by the numbers of accidents, injuries, and fatalities occurring each year, and the overall effectiveness of the sexually transmitted diseases prevention system would be monitored by examining trends in incidence and prevalence rates of syphilis, gonorrhea, chlamydia, and AIDs.

Outcome measures can be challenging and costly to operationalize because they often require follow-up with clients after they have completed programs, as is the case with respect to the percentage of crisis stabilization unit consumers who are readmitted within thirty days of discharge, the percentage of youths discharged from juvenile detention centers who are attending school or engaged in gainful employment one year later, or the percentage of job training program participants who have been placed in jobs, and perhaps the wages they are earning, six months after completing the program.

To convey a comprehensive view of program effectiveness, monitoring systems often include measures of immediate outcomes, intermediate outcomes, and longer-term outcomes. The immediate outcomes of a teen mother parenting education program might well concern pregnant teens' knowledge of prenatal nutrition and health guidelines and their behavior in actually following these guidelines in practice. The intermediate outcomes might focus on pregnant teens' delivering healthy babies, and the longer-term outcomes would include babies achieving appropriate twelve-month developmental milestones.

Cost-Effectiveness. Whereas indicators of operating efficiency represent the unit costs of producing outputs, cost-effectiveness measures relate costs to outcome measures. Thus, for a crisis stabilization unit, cost-effectiveness would be measured as the cost per successfully discharged consumer. For a vocational rehabilitation program, the most relevant indicators of cost-effectiveness would be the cost per client placed in suitable employment and the cost per client successfully employed for six months or more; the cost-effectiveness of a local police department's criminal investigation activity would be measured as the cost per crime solved.

Customer Satisfaction. Measures of customer satisfaction are often closely related to service quality and program effectiveness, but it may be more helpful to consider them as constituting a separate category of performance measures. For example, measures of customer satisfaction with a vocational rehabilitation program might be based on data from client evaluation forms asking how satisfied they were with various aspects of the training, counseling, and placement assistance they received. They might also incorporate survey-based measures of former clients' satisfaction with their jobs after they have been employed for six months, relating more to outcomes. Such customer satisfaction ratings may or may not square with more tangible measures of service quality and program effectiveness, but they do provide a complementary perspective.

Range of Applications

Performance monitoring systems are evaluation tools that track a variety of measures of program or agency performance over time on a systematic basis. The data they generate are basically descriptive, and these systems by themselves do not provide a rigorous methodology for isolating cause-and-effect relationships and attributing observed results as the impact of a particular program. While monitoring systems track what is in fact occurring with respect to program outputs and outcomes, on their own they cannot "address the how and why questions" (Newcomer, 1997, p. 10). Nevertheless, monitoring outputs is often very important to program and agency managers, and when they are confident about the underlying program logic connecting outputs to outcomes, they can track the outcomes generated by monitoring systems and interpret them as real results of their programs. In addition, performance monitoring systems build up databases that often lend themselves to more rigorous program evaluations, especially those employing time-series designs (Harkreader and Henry, 2000).

Performance monitoring systems are also tied to a variety of other management processes in public and nonprofit organizations. In addition to stand-alone reporting systems and measurement systems designed to enhance program management and evaluation, they are also used for other specific purposes, such as strategic planning and management (Vinzant and Vinzant, 1996; Poister and Van Slyke, 2002), budgeting and financial management (Melkers and Willoughby, 1998; Joyce and Tompkins, 2002), performance management (Swiss, 1991; Poister and Streib, 1995), productivity and quality improvement (Rosen, 1993; Milakovitch, 1995; Berman, 1998), contract management (Baker, 1992; Behn and Kant, 1999), and external benchmarking (Keehley, Medlin, MacBride, and Longmire, 1997; Ammons, Coe, and Lombardo, 2001; Morley, Bryant, and Hatry, 2001). Performance monitoring systems designed for these applications need to be tailored to serve their intended purpose in terms of the kinds of measures tracked, reporting frequencies, audiences to whom the data are distributed, the level of aggregation of the data, and the kinds of comparisons to be emphasized.

Focusing on Results

Among the systematic approaches to identifying the kinds of results to be tracked by a performance monitoring system are (1) formal goals, objectives, standards, and targets, (2) program logic models, and (3) the balanced score-card. Hierarchies of goals and objectives often signal the kinds of outcomes that should be monitored, and increasingly public and nonprofit agencies are identifying indicators to track success in accomplishing them and setting target levels on these measures to be achieved within specified time frames.

For example, in support of its goal to reduce the major threats to the health and productivity of all Americans, the U.S. Department of Health and Human Services (DHHS) has established an objective of reducing tobacco abuse, especially among youth. One of four effectiveness measures linked to this objective is the proportion of adolescents age twelve to seventeen years who have used cigarettes in the past month, monitored through the national household survey on drug abuse. The proportion using cigarettes, estimated at 35 percent in 1999, is targeted to be reduced to 16 percent by the year 2010 (DHHS, Healthy People 2010). Similarly, the United Way of Metropolitan Atlanta identified a number of key results areas, such as nurturing children and youth and strengthening families, and then it established targets on one or more performance indicators for each result, as illustrated in Exhibit 4.1.

Program Logic Models

Program logic models, discussed in depth in Chapter Two of this book, can be extremely helpful in identifying the kinds of results to be monitored by performance measurement systems. Although logic models often do not elaborate the process side of program performance pertaining to how a program operates, they are often useful in clarifying the logic of how program outputs are supposed to be linked with immediate, intermediate, and longer-term outcomes. Figure 4.1 illustrates a logic model of the national sexually transmitted disease prevention effort spearheaded by the U.S. Centers for Disease Control (CDC). Interestingly, although the conventional wisdom holds that it is usually more difficult to measure performance as the logic moves from the process side to the outcome side of the model, because outcomes tend to be more diffuse and often require going out into the field to observe, this is not always true. In the CDC case, for instance, the longer-term effectiveness measures regarding the incidence and prevalence of these diseases have been monitored for some time, whereas defining and tracking many of the outputs and earlier-stage outcomes represent a new and more challenging effort.

Exhibit 4.1. United Way of Metropolitan Atlanta Results and Targets

Results	Targets for 2003
Nurturing Children and Youth Outcomes	
1. Affordable, quality preschool and child care	(A) Approximately 20,000 new licensed or registered child care spaces for 0–4-year-olds in working-parent households by 2005
	(B) 300 new accredited child care centers by 2005
	(C) 250 accredited family child care providers by 2005
2. Safe, productive, structured group activities outside of school hours	(1) Number of safe, structured and productive out-of-school slots and activities
3. Parents involved in their children's education	(A) Move from 33.1 to 28 percent of middle school students missing 10 or more days
	(B) Move from 39.6 to 32 percent of high school students missing 10 or more days
4. Positive aspirations for the future and a belief they can attain them	(A) Percentage of youth who remain stable one year after transitioning out of foster care (twice baseline but not less than 50 percent
	(B) Move from 5.5 to 4.5 percent of students dropping out in grades 9–12
Strengthening Families Outcomes	
5. Parenting skills and knowledge	(A) 3,000 parents will increase their parenting knowledge and/or skills through United Way facilitated partnerships and initiatives by 2003
	(B) Move from 4,659 to 4,300 the number of substantiated child abuse cases
6. Problem resolution and coping skills	(A) Reduction in the number of inpatient days spent for mental health reasons
	(B) Reduction in the number of emergency room visits due to mental health reasons

Note: (A), (B), and (C) identify separate targets for a given desired result.
Source: United Way of Metropolitan Atlanta (2001). Used by permission of United Way of Metropolitan Atlanta.

The Balanced Scorecard

Over the past several years, many public agencies have used the balanced scorecard as a framework for developing performance measures. Originally developed for private sector applications, the balanced scorecard prompts managers to develop goals and associated performance measures in each of four perspectives focusing on financial performance, customers, internal business processes, and innovation and learning (Kaplan and Norton, 1992). This model has become popular in the public sector as well because it

Figure 4.1. The STD Prevention System

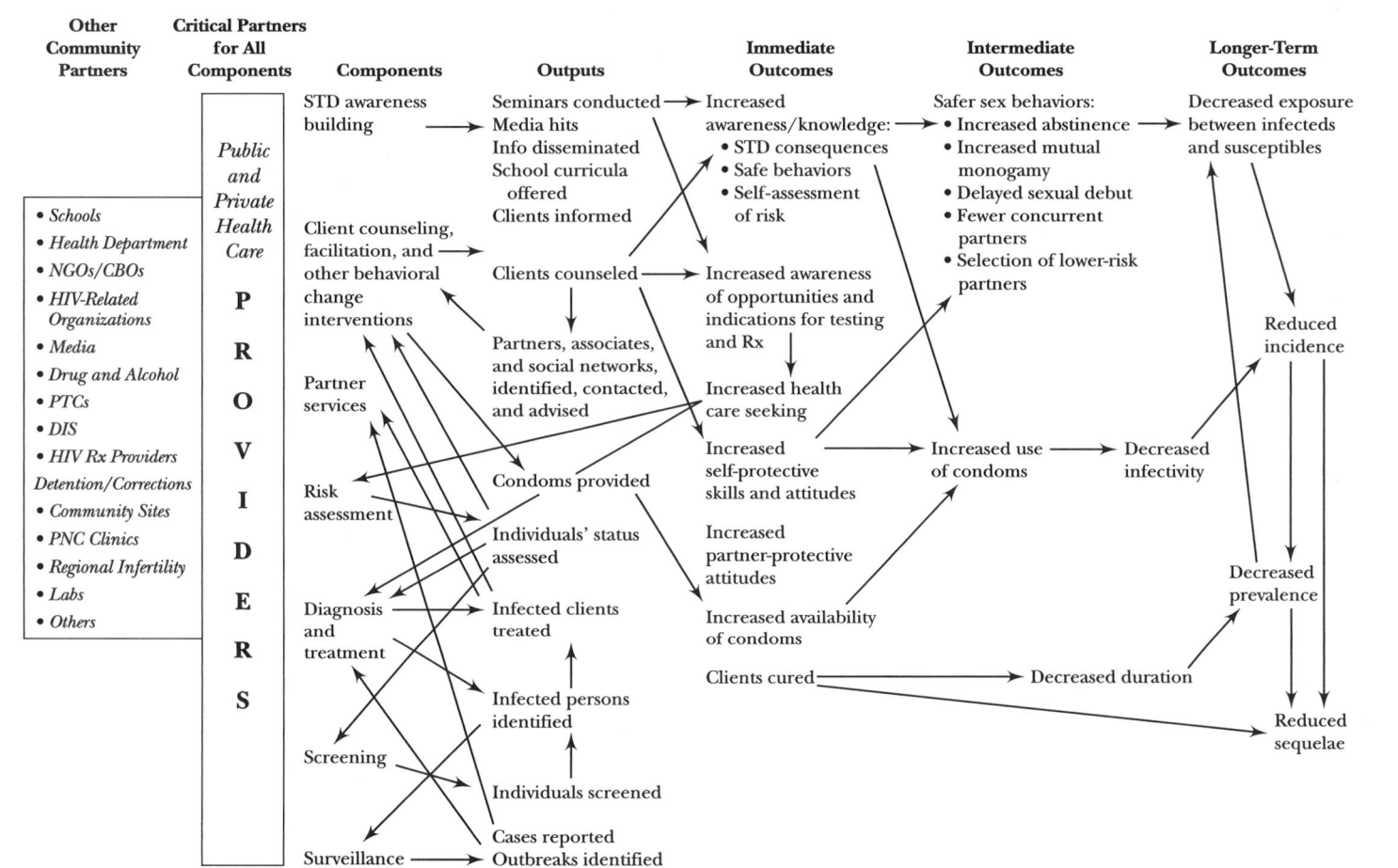

encourages managers to take a holistic view of performance, ties performance measures to goals, and imposes discipline on work planning and decision making by emphasizing the alignment of goals and measures at lower levels in the organization with those at the executive level. Some governmental agencies have modified the model to fit public sector applications better. For example, as shown in Figure 4.2, the Texas Department of Transportation focuses on customer satisfaction, outreach to partners, internal process efficiency, and employee actualization in its performance measurement process (Doyle, 1998).

One of the early pioneers in implementing the balanced scorecard in the public sector was the City of Charlotte, North Carolina. At the suggestion of the city manager, the city council developed a "corporate-level" scorecard consisting of goals, but not measures, beginning with substantive policy goals from the customer perspective and fleshing out supporting priorities from the financial, internal process, and learning perspectives. The council then asked the city's department of transportation to pilot the effort at the department level, with more specific supporting goals, objectives, and associated lead and lag performance measures, as shown in Exhibit 4.2. The transportation department uses the scorecard (currently being updated) to manage work programs and ongoing activities, monitoring the performance measures annually or more frequently.

Program evaluators should understand that program logic models and the balanced scorecard framework are complementary approaches to identifying performance measures. Whereas logic models focus directly on the performance of specific public or nonprofit programs, the balanced scorecard focuses on overall organizational performance, which might incorporate multiple programs as well as other dimensions of performance.

Data and Measures

Given agreement on the dimensions of performance that need to be captured in a monitoring system, the challenge for program evaluators and other system designers is to identify appropriate data sources, operationalize measures, and develop data processing support and quality assurance procedures.

Data Sources

As is the case with program evaluations, performance monitoring systems use data from a wide variety of sources. A lot of measures, particularly those regarding internal processes, service delivery, and outputs, are based on transactional data that agencies maintain on an ongoing basis regarding requests

Figure 4.2. The Balanced Scorecard for the Texas Department of Transportation

External

Outreach Effectiveness	Customer Satisfaction
How well do we involve partners? How easy are we to work with?	Are we meeting our customers' expectations?
Goals Measures	Goals Measures

Process ————————————————————————————— Results

Internal Process Efficiency	Employee Actualization
How do we do work faster, better, cheaper, and right the first time?	Do employees have the support, motivation, tools and skills to "be all they can be"?
Goals Measures	Goals Measures

Internal

Source: Doyle (1998).

for service, clients admitted and discharged, production records, inventories, permits issued or revoked, activity logs, incident reports, claims processed, treatments administered, follow-up visits made, and complaints from clients or others. Such data are usually maintained in management information systems and therefore often are readily available.

Performance measures, particularly outcomes, however, often require additional sources and data collection procedures developed specifically to measure performance. These include direct observation, such as trained observer surveys of street cleanliness or mechanized counts of traffic volumes, as well as medical or psychiatric examinations of clients, and tests typically used in measuring the effectiveness of education and training programs. Outcomes measures are often operationalized most directly through follow-up contacts or interviews with clients at specified lengths of time after they have completed programs. Finally, surveys of clients, employees, or other stakeholders administered on a regular basis are often important sources of data used in performance monitoring systems, as are customer response cards. Monitoring performance through trained observer surveys, clinical examinations, special testing procedures, follow-up contacts, and surveys entails significantly greater effort and cost than relying on existing agency records. Nevertheless, these tools are often the only means of obtaining suitable measures of performance, particularly in terms of effectiveness and client satisfaction.

Exhibit 4.2. Scorecard for Charlotte Department of Transportation

Objective	Lead Measures	Lag Measures
C-1 Maintain the transportation	C-1 Repair Response: repair response action	
	C-1 Travel Speed: average travel speed by facility and selected location	C-1 High Quality Streets: condition of lane miles ≥ 90 rating
C-2 Operate the transportation system	C-2 Commute Time: average commute time on selected roads	C-2 Safety: citywide accident rate; number of high accident locations
	C-2 On-Time Buses: public transit on time	
C-3 Develop the transportation system	C-3 Programs Introduced: newly introduced programs, pilots, or program specifications	C-3 Basic Mobility: availability of public transit
C-4 Determine the optimal system design	C-4 Plan Progress: percent complete on 2015 Transportation Plan	
C-5 Improve service quality	C-5 Responsiveness: percent of citizen complaints and requests resolved at the CDOT level	
F-1 Expand non-city funding	F-1 Funding Leverage: dollar value from non-city sources	
	F-1 New Funding Sources: dollar value from sources not previously available	
F-2 Maximize benefit per cost	F-2 Costs: costs compared to other municipalities and private sector competition	

I-1 Gain infrastructure capacity	I-1 Capital Investment: dollars allocated to capital projects in targeted areas	I-1 Capacity Ratios: incremental capacity built versus required by 2015 Plan
I-2 Secure funding and service partners	I-2 Leverage Funding and Service Partners: new funding and resource partners identified	I-2 Number of Partners: number of partners
I-3 Improve productivity	I-3 Cost Per Unit: cost per unit	I-3 Street Maintenance Cost: cost per passenger
	I-3 Competitive Sourcing: percent of budget bid	
	I-3 Problem Identification: source and action	
I-4 Increase positive contacts with community	I-4 Customer Communications: number, type, frequency	I-4 Customer Surveys: survey results concerning service quality
L-1 Enhance automated information systems	L-1 IT Infrastructure: complete relational database across CDOT	L-1 Information Access: strategic information available versus user requirements
L-2 Enhance "field" technology	L-2 Information Tools: strategic tools available versus user requirements	
L-3 Close the skills gap	L-3 Skills Identified: key skills identified in strategic functions	L-3 Skills Transfer: skill evidence in task or job performance
L-4 Empower employees	L-4 Employee Climate Survey: results of employee survey	L-4 Employee Goal Alignment: training and career development aligned with mission

Source: Charlotte Department of Transportation. Used by permission.

Quality of Measures

From a methodological perspective, the hallmark of good measurement is a high degree of validity and reliability. Thus, in developing measurement systems, program evaluators must try to anticipate and guard against such problems as observer bias or subject bias, systematic overreporting or underreporting, poor instrument design, tenuously connected proximate measures of outcomes, and nonresponse biases due to missing cases. The last can be particularly problematic when performance measures are operationalized by follow-up contacts with clients initiated after they have completed a program or left an agency, when the intended results might be expected to materialize.

Since performance monitoring systems are designed to track the same set of performance measures at regular intervals over time, the problem of instrument decay is of particular concern. Thus, it is important to maintain consistency in data collection procedures in order to generate valid trend data over time. In addition, data input in many monitoring systems is decentralized, with data fed in by numerous local offices around a state, for instance. In such cases, the need to guard against sloppy reporting in the field and to ensure comparable measurement and data collection procedures among reporting units is of paramount importance.

Performance monitoring systems are evaluation tools that are often tied directly to other ongoing management processes. Thus, monitoring systems are less "researchy" but often more immediately linked to decision-making processes than are more rigorous discrete program evaluations. Beyond validity and reliability, then, system designers need to be concerned with a number of other criteria of good measures as well.

Meaningful and Understandable Measures. Performance data measures must be meaningful to decision makers; they should focus on the goals and objectives, priorities, and dimensions of performance that are important to them. In addition, the measures should be readily understandable by their intended audiences. Thus, the measures should have an obvious face validity to the users and be clear in terms of where they come from and what they mean. More complicated or less obvious indicators should be accompanied by clear definitions of what they represent.

Balanced and Comprehensive Measures. Collectively, the set of measures tracked by a monitoring system should provide a balanced and comprehensive picture of the performance of the program or agency in question, in terms of both the components covered and the classes of measures employed. Using program logic models or a framework such as the balanced scorecard can be immensely helpful in this regard.

Timely and Actionable Measures. Performance monitoring systems sometimes fail to provide results to decision makers on a timely basis. When the data are no longer fresh or are not provided to decision makers when they need the information, monitoring systems are not particularly useful. In addition, performance measures are useful to decision makers only if they are actionable, focus on results over which decision makers can exert some leverage, and are dimensions that can be affected by program elements or organizational strategies. Otherwise, the performance data may be interesting but will not serve to improve decisions and strengthen performance.

Goal Displacement. Performance measurement systems are intended to stimulate improved performance. In addition to providing information to higher-level decision makers, the very fact of measuring performance on a regular, ongoing basis provides a powerful incentive for managers and employees to perform well on the measures being tracked. However, with inappropriate or unbalanced measures, this can lead to goal displacement in which people will perform toward the measures but sacrifice the real programmatic or organizational goals in the process. Thus, in designing monitoring systems, it is critical to ensure that indicators are directly aligned with goals and objectives, anticipate problems such as the selective treatment of cases, or "creaming," that can result from overly simplified measures, avoid focusing on some parts of program logic or goal structures to the exclusion of others, focus directly on real outcomes as well as outputs wherever possible, and incorporate balanced performance criteria, such as quality and customer satisfaction measures, along with efficiency and effectiveness indicators.

Practical Considerations and Cost. Countervailing the desire to incorporate well-balanced and meaningful sets of measures that are highly reliable and resistant to goal displacement is a set of more practical considerations and the need for monitoring systems to be cost-effective. Although for some measures, the data will be readily available, others will require the development of new instruments or data collection procedures. Some measures may be too difficult or time-consuming to collect in the field in a systematic and consistent manner, and others might impose undue burdens on employees at the operating level who would have to keep track of different things and be responsible for reporting the data. In comparing different candidate measures, system designers must often weigh trade-offs between the usefulness of the measures and the quality of the data against issues of feasibility, time, effort, and costs. Ultimately, such decisions should be made on the basis of ensuring accurate and reliable data whose usefulness exceeds the cost of maintaining the system.

Data Processing

Performance monitoring systems require data processing support to input and extract data from existing record-keeping systems into organized files, convert raw data into performance measures, often at different levels of aggregation, and produce reports, sometimes for a variety of audiences, on an ongoing basis. There are a number of commercially available performance measurement applications, such as FlexMeasures, Comshares, and dbProbe, that might be used to support an agency's measurement system. For very complicated measurement systems, it might be preferable to contract with information technology or computer design specialists to develop custom-made software applications. For relatively simple systems at the other end of the spectrum, program or agency staff might develop an in-house system using a generic spreadsheet program, such as Microsoft Excel, perhaps in combination with database management software and a graphics program.

Quality Assurance

Because the quality of the data are crucial for maintaining the credibility and usefulness of a performance monitoring system, it is important to have procedures in place for ensuring data integrity. Thus, procedures for collecting and processing the data should provide clear data trails for tracking the data back to records of initial transactions or observations in order to reproduce the results. Although it is usually not necessary to check all the data along these lines, conducting selective data audits on a small random sample basis can go a long way toward ensuring high-quality data. Such an audit process provides an overall reading on the accuracy of reported data, identifies problems in data collection that can then be resolved, and serves as an incentive for people to guard against sloppy reporting. Moreover, conducting data audits, even on a small sample basis, provides a safeguard against deliberate false reporting or other manipulation of the system, particularly if appropriate sanctions or penalties against such forms of cheating are in place.

Examining Performance Data

Although selecting appropriate measures and maintaining the integrity of the data are of critical importance, performance monitoring systems can be effective only if they provide information that is useful for management and decision making. Thus, the performance data need to be examined in some kind of comparative framework: comparisons over time, actual performance against targets, comparisons among operating units, other kinds of breakouts, or comparisons against external benchmarks.

Trends over Time

Because monitoring systems make repeated observations of a set of indicators at regular time intervals, they automatically accumulate time-series databases that facilitate tracking trends over time. For example, one of the strategic priorities emphasized by the Pennsylvania Department of Transportation (Penn-DOT) over the past several years has been to improve the ride quality on its highway system, focusing on interstate highways and other higher-level roads in particular because they have been notably worse than in many other states (Pennsylvania Department of Transportation, 2000). PennDOT uses the international roughness index (IRI) as the principal measure of ride quality. It "runs" these roads with special vehicles and equipment to measure IRI every fall at the conclusion of the highway maintenance season to determine whether ride quality has improved, remained the same, or regressed over the past year. Higher IRI values represent rougher roads and inferior ride quality, whereas lower IRI values indicate smoother roads and better ride quality. As shown in Figure 4.3, the median average ride quality on Pennsylvania interstate highways has improved substantially over the past decade to a level that is comparable with national averages.

Actual Performance Versus Targets

In the context of results-oriented approaches to managing public and non-profit organizations, monitoring systems often track actual performance against previously determined goals, objectives, standards, or targets. For example, Table 4.1 shows some of the data reported by the Connecticut Works initiative, a collaboration of state, regional, and local organizations addressing the state's workforce development needs. Interestingly, this quarterly report focuses first on outcome measures and then on process measures and compares the current data against the same measures for the four preceding

Figure 4.3. Ride Quality of Pennsylvania Highways Compared with National Averages

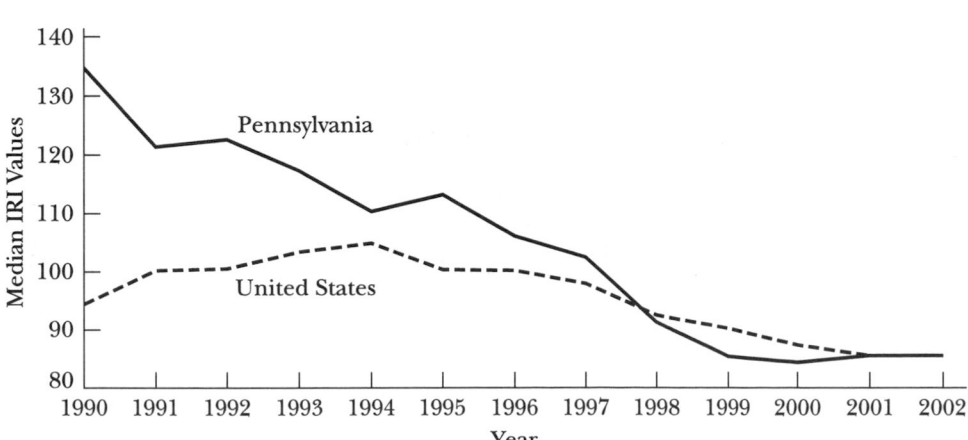

Table 4.1. Job Center Performance Overview, Connecticut Works Initiative, Period Ending March 31, 1999

		Outcome Measures						
		Statewide Quarter Ending					Best Practice [a] (Connecticut)	Goal
Activity Area	Indicator	Mar. 1999	Dec. 1998	Sept. 1998	June 1998	Mar. 1998		
Entered employment	O-1. Percentage of applicants who entered	5.7	6.9%	5.7	7.6	6.3	12.7%	17
	O-2. Percentage of applicants receiving services who entered employment	11.2	13.5	11.0	15.1	12.4	23.4	
Job Bank	O-3. Percentage of purged job orders with at least one placement	10.6	12.3	10.8	10.3	10.6	22.7	38
	O-4. Percentage of applicants with wages in five quarters	56.5	64.3				71.9	
	O-5. Median percentage wage gain	28.1	25.5				39.3	

		Process Measures						
		Statewide Quarter Ending					Best Practice [a] (Connecticut)	Goal
Activity Area	Indicator	Mar. 1999	Dec. 1998	Sept. 1998	June 1998	Mar. 1998		
Applicant/ claimant satisfaction	P-1. Index of overall applicant/claimant satisfaction	83.1			90.2		90.5	100

Wait Time	P-2. Percentage of applicants/claimants who waited too long	14.7			8.4		0.0.	
	P-3. Average number of minutes claimants who waited too long	15.7			10.3		4.3	
UI	P-4. Percentage of nonmonetary decisions made on time	84.0	87.9	85.3	85.9	82.3	93.6	85.0
	P-5. Percentage of first payments made within 21 days	95.5	96.1	95.5	95.5	95.4	97.4	93
Employability services	P-6. Percentage of applicants receiving employability or other services	50.5	51.4	51.9	49.9	50.9	64.7	66
	P-7. Percentage of newly registered applicants assessed	60.8	60.7	58.4	63.8	64.6	99	100
	P-8. Percentage of applicants receiving a service within 30 days of assessment	22.1	23.5	22.9	22.6	20.7	43.8	45
Career Resource Center	P-9. Percentage of individuals receiving services who used the Career Resource Center	17.9					76.7	

[a]The highest four-quarter office average for outcome measures and process measures.
Source: Connecticut Works. Available at www.ctdol.state.ct.us/ctworks/ctworks.htm

quarters in order to track performance over time, as well as gauge any patterns of seasonal variation. However, goals or target levels have been established for many of these measures, and the results for spring 1999 show that while actual performance came fairly close to the goals for some of the process measures, it fell dramatically short of the targets on the two outcomes measures for which goals had been established.

Comparisons Among Units

While governing bodies, funding organizations, and chief executive officers tend to be interested principally in tracking performance data for a program or agency as a whole, senior and middle managers often find it useful to compare these measures across operating units or project sites. For example, PennDOT breaks the annual IRI data shown in Figure 4.3 down to its eleven engineering districts and further down to the sixty-seven highway maintenance units that make up the districts in order to monitor regional and local variation in ride quality and to examine where it has been improving and where it has not. In addition, targets are set for individual districts and county maintenance units regarding ride quality, and their actual performance is assessed each year against these targets. Similarly, the Connecticut Works collaboration tracks the performance measures shown in Table 4.1 for each of its eighteen local offices and uses the data to compare performance on these outcome and process measures around the state. Indeed, the data in the "Best Practice" column show the performance of the local office that scored the highest on each particular measure for the current quarter.

Other Breakouts

Performance data are often much more meaningful when they are broken out by different types of cases. For example, in support of an effort to improve safety at its nine city parks and recreation areas, a medium-size suburban municipality might track the number of reported personal injuries at these facilities on a monthly basis. While reducing the total number of injuries is officials' principal concern here, breaking these incidents down by type of venue will help pinpoint where the problem areas are. Thus, the monitoring system may display the number of reported injuries occurring on sports fields, tennis courts, jogging trails, swimming pools, picnic areas, parking lots, and other venues on a monthly basis.

Often the most relevant breakouts of performance data focus on different groups of agency clients or program participants. For example, the federal No Child Left Behind Act of 2001 requires all states to maintain accountability systems, including annual standardized testing of all students in grades 3 through 8 and other measures of academic achievement and safety in all public schools. Schools that fail to meet adequate yearly progress toward statewide proficiency goals on a consistent basis are identified as needing improvement and subject to corrective and restructuring measures aimed at getting them back on track to meet the standards. In addition to tracking the proportion of all students who are reading, writing, and doing math at grade level, these annual performance data are tracked separately for white, black, Latino, and Asian students and for low-income students, disabled students, special education students, and non-English-speaking students for purposes of evaluating each school's performance.

External Benchmarking

Increasingly, public and nonprofit agencies are experimenting with external benchmarking, comparing their own performance data against the same measures for other similar agencies or programs (Bruder and Gray, 1994; Morley, Bryant, and Hatry, 2001). Such a comparative framework can help an agency assess its own performance and perhaps set future target levels within the context of its larger public service industry. For example, Figure 4.4 shows a variety of performance data for a public hospital in Georgia based on an intensive survey of patients who were discharged during a particular three-month period. The survey is conducted for the hospital by an independent firm that conducts the same survey for twenty such hospitals on a quarterly basis. The data reported to each individual hospital show not only its own scores on a number of indicators but some comparisons against the other hospitals being surveyed. The hospital's overall performance is benchmarked against the system of twenty hospitals and is further compared against a leading institution that represents the hospital's aspirations on indicators of several specific dimensions of performance.

External benchmarking is often facilitated when funding organizations impose uniform reporting requirements on all their grantees. Thus, a local job training and placement program funded by the federal work investment program, for instance, must report prescribed performance measures to the U.S. Department of Labor on a regular basis, but it can also access the national database in order to gauge its performance against that of other similar programs. Similarly, the Pennsylvania Department of Transportation requires annual reports from local transit agencies on a variety of measures regarding service levels, operating efficiency, service quality, and ridership, and it also requires these agencies to conduct on-board passenger surveys every three years that contain a minimum of six uniform questions. Thus,

Figure 4.4. Hospital Patient Survey for a Georgia Hospital

Summary of Outcomes

400 completed interviews

	Benchmark	Hospital
Quality of Care Score	91.1	87.7
Overall Nursing	95.1	91.8
Overall Physician	95.9	95.9
Willingness to Return	96.9	93.5
Willingness to Recommend	96.7	93.2
Helpfulness of Visit	95.7	94.8

Overall Assessment

The overall quality of care score for the hospital is

87.7

This puts the hospital *8th* among 20 hospitals measured.

The aggregate score (computed by taking the average score for all attributes and functional area items) is

92.0

Inpatient Survey Results

THIRD QUARTER

From patients discharged August 21 through September 30

Quality of Care Score

Benchmark
Hospital System Mean
Low Score

How would you rate the overall quality of care?

Reasons for Visits

Reason	Hospital	System
Physician	31.9%	48.5%
Convenient	15.8%	33.0%
Friend recommend	17.4%	14.8%
Care better	39.4%	29.4%
Insurance	15.8%	12.3%
Cost lower	1.3%	0.5%
Only hospital in area	5.5%	5.4%

Percent of Respondents

Source: Satisquest^SM. Reprinted with permission.

the local agencies have ready access to statewide performance data for benchmarking their own performance against other systems in terms of customer satisfaction as well as service quality, efficiency, and effectiveness.

In other instances, governmental units or nonprofit agencies can agree to enter into comparative performance measurement arrangements on a voluntary basis, for example, when the transportation departments in two or more neighboring states share selected performance data on a regular basis in order to identify superior performance and best practices in one department that the others might adopt. At the local level, a number of U.S. cities (Kopczynski and Lombardo, 1999), in one instance, and a number of local jurisdictions within North Carolina (Coe, 1999), in another instance, have established consortia for the purpose of identifying common indicators to measure performance in selected service areas and then share the data on these measures annually as an aid to helping them assess and improve their performance in these areas. Although issues concerning the availability, reliability, and comparability of data, as well as differences in operating conditions, create challenges for defining measures, collecting the data, and interpreting the results, participants tend to report that such efforts are worthwhile (Ammons, Coe, and Lombardo, 2001).

Design and Implementation

The process of designing and implementing performance measurement systems is described elsewhere in detail (Ammons, 1995; Hatry, 1999; Poister, 2003). Briefly, the following steps are essential for building a workable monitoring system:

1. Secure management commitment.
2. Clarify the purpose, intended audiences, and system parameters.
3. Identify the relevant outcomes and other performance criteria to be covered.
4. Define, evaluate, and select appropriate indicators.
5. Develop data collection procedures and a process for quality assurance.
6. Specify reporting frequencies and develop reporting formats.
7. Develop software applications.
8. Assign responsibilities for data input and system maintenance.
9. Provide training as necessary to staff, intended users, and other stakeholders.
10. Conduct a pilot test, and revise measures and system design if necessary (optional).
11. Implement the full-scale system, and use, evaluate, and modify it as appropriate.

The design process may be relatively simple and straightforward in some cases, or it may be much more complicated depending on the size and complexity of the organization or program and the scope of the system envisioned at the outset. Program evaluators should recognize, however, that organizational and process issues are likely to arise that will be just as challenging, or more challenging, to deal with than the strictly methodological issues they will face. Thus, careful structuring of a systematic design and implementation process and thoughtful consideration regarding stakeholder involvement in that process are critical for success.

Common Problems with Monitoring Systems

Measurement systems are not panaceas for improving the performance of public programs and managing them effectively. Sometimes the data are not good enough to have any reasonable credibility. Noncomparability of data from different sources can create serious reliability problems, especially, but not only, with respect to benchmarking efforts. Even with a high degree of validity and reliability, the data generated by performance monitoring systems are basically descriptive and limited in terms of evaluating cause-and-effect relationships regarding program effectiveness. Sometimes real outcomes are too elusive to measure (an example is the impacts of a federal agency's research program) and do not lend themselves to regular, systematic, quantitative measurement on a real-time basis.

Interpreting performance data out of context can be misleading and produce erroneous impressions regarding performance. The data can also be overinterpreted in terms of cause-and-effect relationships and lead to unwarranted conclusions that a program is in fact producing desired outcomes. Worse, perhaps, the data generated by measurement systems can be misused or abused in ways that are unfair to managers and employees and counterproductive in terms of program or agency performance. Measurement systems can also set up unbalanced or suboptimal incentive structures that result in goal displacement and "gaming" the system at the expensive of overall effectiveness.

Another common problem concerns unrealistic expectations regarding the costs and benefits of performance measurement systems. Most monitoring systems of any substantial size and complexity require a significant investment of time, effort, and money, and if this is not clearly understood at the outset, enthusiasm for a system may wane as the costs mount up. In addition, there is often internal resistance to monitoring systems on the part of managers and staff who feel threatened by the measures or concerned that they might be face adverse system impacts. Finally, monitoring systems often fail to make a difference because they are not responsive to other stakeholder concerns or the decision makers do not deem them useful by decision makers.

Strategies for Developing Useful Performance Measurement Systems

Strategies are available for overcoming the problems noted here and developing effective performance monitoring systems (Kravchuk and Schack, 1996; Plantz, Greenway, and Hendricks, 1997; Hatry, 1999; Poister, 2003). First, with respect to building credibility for the system and increasing the likelihood that it will in fact be used, those who are developing monitoring systems should:

- Secure a commitment from the top to support and use the system.
- Communicate realistic expectations regarding the benefits of the system, as well as the time and effort required to develop and maintain it.
- Be candid about the limitations of the system with all concerned.
- Involve stakeholders in identifying criteria, measures, targets, and data.
- Tailor measures and design features to users' needs and preferences.
- Communicate how and why measures are being developed, and prompt management to demonstrate commitment to using the measures.
- Provide training to managers on using performance data to improve their programs.

At the core of the process, developing a measurement system is both an art and a science, and it often involves weighing trade-offs among competing criteria. Thus, program evaluators who are designing systems should:

- Tie measures directly to mission, goals, objectives, service standards, and targets.
- Use program logic models or other relevant frameworks to ensure a systematic and comprehensive approach.
- Be results driven rather than data driven in defining measures, but use available data when appropriate.
- Be pragmatic in evaluating measures in order to build a workable system that produces worthwhile information.
- Try to anticipate likely goal displacement or gaming strategies, and balance measures in order to avoid such reactions.
- Install procedures to ensure data integrity.

Finally, it is important to build features into a monitoring system that will help generate acceptance and encourage its use. Thus, system designers should:

- Keep measures and presentations simple and straightforward and not employ more measures than are necessary.
- Emphasize useful comparisons in reporting systems, and break out data by key clientele groups and other important characteristics.
- Provide adequate explanatory information along with the performance data, and provide fields in reporting formats for explanatory comments.
- Give program managers and others a chance to see the performance data first and make corrections and comments before reports go to higher-level management.
- Avoid overinterpreting the data and drawing unwarranted conclusions regarding cause and effect relationships between programs and outcomes.

Every instance of performance measurement will be unique in terms of program, setting, and purpose, and therefore the particular challenges that arise in designing and implementing a monitoring system will vary by application. Although effective performance measurement is not easy, it is not rocket science either (Hatry, 1999). Rather, it is a commonsense approach to results-oriented management that can be useful in providing descriptive information on program performance on an ongoing basis. Stability in measures and data collection procedures is therefore prized, but program evaluators should also understand that it is important to gauge the usefulness of monitoring systems themselves and to make adjustments as necessary to increase their worth to program managers and decision makers.

References

Ammons, D. N. *Accountability for Performance: Measurement and Monitoring in Local Government.* Washington, D.C.: International City/County Management Association, 1995.

Ammons, D. N. *Municipal Benchmarks: Assessing Local Performance and Establishing Community Standards.* Thousand Oaks, Calif.: Sage, 2001.

Ammons, D. N., Coe, C., and Lombardo, M. "Performance-Comparison Projects in Local Government: Participants' Perspectives." *Public Administration Review,* 2001, *61*(1), 100–111.

Aristiqueta. M. P. *Managing for Results in State Government.* Westport, Conn.: Quorum Books, 1999.

Baker, F. "Incentive Contracts and Performance Measurement." *Journal of Political Economy,* 1992, *100*(31), 598–614.

Behn, R. D. "The Big Questions of Public Management." *Public Administration Review,* 1995, *55*(4), 313–324.

Behn, R. D., and Kant, P. A. "Strategies for Avoiding the Pitfalls of Performance Contracting." *Public Productivity and Management Review,* 1999, *22*(4), 470–490.

Berman, E. M. *Productivity in Public and Nonprofit Organizations.* Thousand Oaks, Calif.: Sage, 1998.

Berman, E., and Wang, W. "Performance Measurement in U.S. Counties: Capacity for Reform." *Public Administration Review,* 2000, *60*(5), 409–420.

Broom, C., Caudle, S., Jennings, E. T., and Newcomer, K. "Meeting the Challenges of Performance-Oriented Government." In K. Newcomer, E. Jennings, C. Broom, and A. Lomax (eds.), *Meeting the Challenges of Performance-Oriented Government.* Washington, D.C.: American Society for Public Administration/Center for Accountability and Performance, 2002.

Broom, C., Harris, J., Jackson, M., and Marshall, M. *Performance Measurement Concepts and Techniques.* Washington, D.C.: American Society for Public Administration/Center for Accountability and Performance, 1998.

Bruder, K. A., Jr., and Gray, E. M. "Public Sector Benchmarking: A Practical Approach." *Public Management,* 1994, *76,* S9-S14.

Coe, C. "Local Government Benchmarking: Lessons from Two Major Multi-government Efforts." *Public Administration Review,* 1999, *59*(2), 110–123.

Department of Health and Human Services. *Healthy People 2010.* [http://www.healthy people.gov./Data/]. Jan. 8, 2002.

Doyle, D. "Performance Measurement Initiative at the Texas Department of Transportation." *Transportation Research Record,* 1998, *1649,* 124–128.

Epstein, P. D. *Using Performance Measurement in Local Government.* New York: Van Nostrand, 1984.

Harkreader, S. A., and Henry, G. T. "Using Performance Measurement Systems for Assessing the Merit and Worth of Reforms." *American Journal of Evaluation,* 2000, *21*(2) 151–170.

Hatry, H. P. *Performance Measurement: Getting Results.* Washington, D.C.: Urban Institute Press, 1999.

Hatry, H., Van Houten, T., Plantz, M. C., and Greenway, M. T. *Measuring Program Outcomes: A Practical Approach.* Alexandria, Va.: United Way of America, 1996.

Hendricks, M. "Outcome Measurement in the Nonprofit Sector: Recent Developments, Initiatives, and Challenges." In K. Newcomer, E. Jennings, C. Broom, and A. Lomax (eds.), *Meeting the Challenges of Performance-Oriented Government.* Washington, D.C.: American Society for Public Administration/Center for Accountability and Performance, 2002.

Joyce, P. G., and Tompkins. "Using Performance Information for Budgeting: Clarifying Terms and Investigating Recent State Experience," In K. Newcomer, E. Jennings, C. Broom, and A. Lomax (eds.), *Meeting the Challenges of Performance-Oriented Government.* Washington, D.C.: American Society for Public Administration/Center for Accountability and Performance, 2002.

Julnes, P. L., and Holzer, M. "Promoting the Utilization of Performance Measures in Public Organizations: An Empirical Study of Factors Affecting Adoption and Implementation." *Public Administration Review,* 2001, *61*(6), 693–708.

Kaplan, R. S., and Norton, D. P. "The Balanced Scorecard—Measures that Drive Performance." *Harvard Business Review,* Jan.-Feb. 1992, pp. 71–79.

Keehley, P., Medlin, S., MacBride, S., and Longmire, L. *Benchmarking for Best Practices in the Public Sector.* San Francisco: Jossey-Bass, 1997.

Kopczynski, M., and Lombardo, M. "Comparative Performance Measurement: Insights and Lessons Learned from a Consortium Effort." *Public Administration Review,* 1999, *59*(2), 124–134.

Kravchuk, R. S., and Schack, R. W. "Designing Effective Performance Measurement Systems Under the Government Performance and Results Act of 1993." *Public Administration Review,* 1996, *56*(4), 348–358.

Melkers, J. E., and Willoughby, K. G. "The State of the States: Performance-Based Budgeting Requirements in 47 out of 50." *Public Administration Review,* 1998, *58*(1), 66–73.

Milakovitch, M. E. *Improving Service Quality: Achieving High Performance in the Public and Private Sectors.* Boca Raton, Fla.: St. Lucie Press, 1995.

Morley, E., Bryant, S. P., and Hatry, H. P. *Comparative Performance Measurement.* Washington, D.C.: Urban Institute Press, 2001.

Newcomer, K. E. "Using Performance Measurement to Improve Public and Nonprofit Programs." In K. E. Newcomer (ed.), New Directions for Evaluation, no. 75. San Francisco: Jossey-Bass, 1997.

Pennsylvania Department of Transportation. *Moving Pennsylvania Forward: Journey to the Strategic Agenda.* Harrisburg, Pa.: Pennsylvania Department of Transportation, 2000.

Plantz, M. C., Greenway, M. T., and Hendricks, M. "Outcome Measurement: Showing Results in the Nonprofit Sector." New Directions for Evaluation, no. 75. San Francisco: Jossey-Bass, 1997.

Poister, T. H. *Measuring Performance in Public and Nonprofit Organizations.* San Francisco: Jossey-Bass, 2003.

Poister, T. H., and Streib, G. "MBO in Municipal Government: Variations on a Traditional Management Tool." *Public Administration Review,* 1995, *55*(1) 48–56.

Poister, T. H., and Streib, G. "Performance Measurement in Municipal Government: Assessing the State of the Practice." *Public Administration Review,* 1999, *59*(4), 325–335.

Poister, T. H., and Van Slyke, D. M. "Strategic Management Innovations in State Transportation Departments." *Public Performance and Management Review,* 2002, *26*(1), 58–74.

Rosen, E. D. *Improving Public Sector Productivity.* Thousand Oaks, Calif.: Sage, 1993.

Swiss, J. E. *Public Management Systems: Monitoring and Managing Government Performance.* Upper Saddle River, N.J.: Prentice Hall, 1991.

United Way of America. *Outcome Measurement Activities of National Health and Human Service Organizations.* Alexandria, Va.: United Way of America, 1998.

United Way of Metropolitan Atlanta. *Indicator and Targets Chart.* Atlanta: United Way of Metropolitan Atlanta, 2001.

Vinzant, D. H., and Vinzant, J. "Strategy and Organizational Capacity: Finding a Fit." *Public Productivity and Management Review,* 1996, *20*(2), 139–157.

Wholey, J. S. "Performance-Based Management: Responding to the Challenges." *Public Productivity and Management Review,* 1999, *2*(3), 288–307.

Wholey, J. S., and Hatry, H. P. "The Case for Performance Monitoring." *Public Administration Review,* 1992, *52*(6), 604–610.

Young, D. R. "The First Seven Years of NML: Central Issues in the Management of Nonprofit Organizations." *Nonprofit Management and Leadership,* 1997, *8*(2), 193–201.

5

Quasi–Experimentation

Charles S. Reichardt, Melvin M. Mark

Evaluations often involve estimating the effect of a program, policy, or other kind of treatment. In this chapter, we describe a set of designs that can be used to estimate the effect of a treatment. We do not deal here with the issue of how those involved in an evaluation decide that they are interested in assessing a treatment's effects, though that is an important consideration in the design of evaluations. We do note, however, that the question of a treatment's effect is often central to evaluation. What is the effect of welfare reform on welfare recipients, and especially on children? What is the effect of Head Start? What are the consequences of tort reform? These and many other causal questions often emerge as important for evaluation.

Estimating the effect of a treatment requires a comparison between what happens after a treatment is implemented and what happens or would happen after no treatment or an alternative treatment is implemented (Reichardt and Mark, 1998). In research-based evaluation, the comparison between a treatment and its alternative is made in one of two forms of research designs: randomized experiments or quasi-experiments. In randomized experiments (the subject of Chapter Six), study participants are assigned to treatment conditions at random. In quasi-experiments, which we focus on here, the treatment conditions are assigned nonrandomly.

In general, randomized experiments produce more credible estimates of treatment effects than quasi-experiments do, but they tend to be far more difficult to implement than quasi-experiments. To implement a randomized experiment, researchers must have considerable latitude to intervene in an established setting, such as an ongoing program, or be able to create their own settings in which to administer treatments. In the case of ongoing programs, the requirements of randomized experiments are often unpalatable to administrators, service providers, service recipients, and other stakeholders. In addition, some treatment effects are impossible to assess with randomized experiments for ethical or practical reasons (or both). For example, it would be unethical (and probably infeasible) to study the effects of smoking by randomly assigning individuals to smoking or nonsmoking treatment conditions. And it is physically impossible to study the effects of natural disasters by randomly assigning communities to receive earthquakes or hurricanes. In contrast, quasi-experiments can often be implemented with minimal, or even no, intervention in the ongoing delivery of treatment services, and they tend to be more agreeable to a wide variety of stakeholders. And in some cases, they are the only morally and practically feasible designs for assessing treatment effects. For these reasons, evaluators concerned with assessing program effects are well advised to be familiar with quasi-experimentation.

We look at four prototypical quasi-experimental designs: before-after, interrupted time-series, nonequivalent group, and regression-discontinuity designs. These four designs can be partitioned into two classes based on the nature of the comparison that is being drawn. The before-after and interrupted time-series designs estimate treatment effects by drawing comparisons over time. The nonequivalent group and regression-discontinuity designs estimate treatment effects by drawing comparisons across participants.

Each of the prototypical quasi-experiments can be embellished with a variety of design features to create more elaborate designs (Shadish and Cook, 1999): treatment interventions, comparison groups, measurement occasions, and outcome variables. We describe each of these design features. By combining the four prototypical quasi-experiments with the embellishing features, evaluators can select from a vast pool of designs to craft a study that fits the demands and opportunities of the specific research setting and provides the most trustworthy estimates of treatment effects.

For simplicity, we will assume that only two treatment conditions are being compared (for example, an innovative program versus a standard treatment), but the designs and design features we discuss easily can be applied to comparisons of more than two treatment conditions.

Before-After Comparisons

In a before-after comparison, a participant is measured both before and after a treatment is introduced. The participant can be an individual or a group of individuals such as a classroom, business, or community. In before-after designs, the difference between the before measurement, commonly known as the pretest, and the after measurement, called the posttest, is used as the estimate of the effect of the treatment.

Using the notation of Campbell and Stanley (1966), the before-after design is represented schematically as

O X O

where the Os represent observations (that is, measurements) and X represents the implementation of a treatment. Time flows from left to right, so the O to the left is the before measurement, or pretest, and the O to the right is the after measurement, or posttest. The difference between the mean of the pretest observations and the mean of the posttest observations is the estimate of the effect of the treatment (as compared to no treatment or whatever treatment was in effect before the intervention).

Before-after comparisons are widely used because they are easy to implement and the results as reported, for example, in the mass media, often appear credible to lay audiences. Nevertheless, most before-after comparisons are susceptible to a number of plausible and potentially severe biases. In the nomenclature of Campbell and Stanley (1966) and their successors (Cook and Campbell, 1979; Shadish, Cook, and Campbell, 2002), sources of potential bias are called *threats to internal validity*. These threats are alternative explanations for an effect that a researcher would like to attribute to the treatment intervention. Seven threats to internal validity are plausible most often in before-after comparisons. We describe these threats using an example: a before-after design to assess the effects of a program for improving middle school students' self-esteem. In our hypothetical example, the self-esteem-enhancing program is implemented at the start of a school year and continues until the traditional holiday break in December, and self-esteem is assessed using a self-report measure:

- History. History is a threat to internal validity that arises when an event, besides the treatment, takes place between the pretest and the posttest, and that event either lowers or elevates the posttest scores compared to the pretest scores. To the extent such a historical event is present, a bias is introduced into the estimate of the treatment effect. For example, the students in the self-esteem program might have been members of a sports team that was particularly successful, and therefore self-esteem enhancing, during the fall.
- Maturation. Maturation is a threat to internal validity that arises because study participants grow steadily older, wiser, more tired, hungrier, and the like. In the assessment of our hypothetical self-esteem program, the study participants might have shown an improvement in self-esteem between the pretest and posttest due to trends in emotional change that would have

occurred even in the absence of an intervention. For example, perhaps the middle school years are characterized generally with a rise in self-esteem as students move past the initial self-doubts and uncertainty caused by adolescence and the transition to middle school. If this is the case, students would exhibit an increase in self-esteem between the pretest and posttest even if the program made no difference.

- Seasonality. Perhaps self-esteem among middle schoolers varies naturally with the seasons, tending to be lower at the end of summer than at the start of winter. This could be a recurring cycle due to anxieties at the beginning of each school year that subsides as the year goes on. If so, the change in seasons that occurred during the implementation of the self-esteem program could have produced a change in self-esteem even in the absence of the program. The resulting bias in the estimate of the treatment effect is said to be due to the threat to internal validity of seasonality.

- Testing. The threat to internal validity of testing arises when the pretest itself causes a change in the outcome variable. For example, reporting their level of self-esteem might cause the students in the self-esteem program to recognize their deficits for the first time, and thereby to confront them in ways that lead to improvement. Such an improvement could arise due to the effects of the pretest measurement, even if the content of the program were ineffective.

- Instrumentation. Another threat to internal validity, instrumentation, occurs when the measurement instrument changes between pretest and posttest measurements. A bias due to instrumentation could arise if the students in the self-esteem program changed the way in which they judged their level of self-esteem from the time of the pretest to the time of the posttest.

- Attrition. Some of the students enrolled in the self-esteem-enhancing program might have dropped out before the program was completed. Students might tend to drop out because their self-esteem was so low they were embarrassed to continue in the program. In this case, the mean level of self-esteem would increase from before to after the program because the lowest scores were included in the before measurement but excluded from the after measurement. Or those who dropped out might tend to be those with the highest levels of self-esteem, and so they found the program unnecessary. In this case, the mean level of self-esteem would decrease from before to after the program because the highest scores would have been included on the before measurement but excluded on the after measurements. Biases like these are said to be due to the threat to internal validity of attrition.

- Statistical regression. A threat of statistical regression would arise if students chose to attend or were assigned to the program because their level of self-esteem was atypically low at the time the program began. When levels of a variable are unusually high or unusually low, they will often become more normal over time without any intervention. Thus, if the students entering the program have an unusually low level of self-esteem at the start of the program, their self-esteem is likely to return (that is, regress) to a more usual level at the end of the program, even if the program were ineffective. As a result, the program would look more effective than it is.

Research settings may sometimes arise where none of the preceding threats to internal validity is plausible. For example, some instructional programs are focused on such narrow and unique areas of knowledge (such as idiosyncratic procedures on an assembly line) and assessed using objective measures closely tailored to that content that performance could improve only because of the program (Eckert, 2000). Or the effect of a treatment might be so large that it dwarfs any possible biases due to threats to internal validity. Under such circumstances, the before-after design can be a credible method for estimating treatment effects. But such circumstances are rare. In most instances, one or more threats to internal validity will plausibly introduce biases of such severity that a before-after design can be more misleading than informative.

In general, we recommend one of the alternative designs described next. Many of these designs are elaborations of the before-after comparison, intended to take account of the threats to internal validity described.

Interrupted Time-Series Designs

The interrupted time-series design extends the before-after comparison by adding further measurements over time. In the elementary interrupted time-series (ITS) design, an outcome variable is measured at multiple time points before and after a treatment is introduced. In schematic form, the design is:

$$O \quad O \quad O \quad O \quad OXO \quad O \quad O \quad O \quad O$$

where the different Os represent measurements at repeated times. In essence, the effect of the treatment is estimated in the following way:

1. The researcher models the trend in the pretreatment observations over time and, based on that model, projects that pretreatment trend forward in time. The projected trend provides an estimate of what the trend in the posttreatment observations would have been in the absence of the treatment.
2. The projected trend is compared to the actual trend in the posttreatment observations, and differences between the two trends are attributed to the effect of the treatment.

A treatment that had an immediate and abrupt effect would produce a discontinuity, or interruption, between the projected and actual posttreatment trends (hence the name *interrupted time-series design*).

The data in Figure 5.1 were used to assess the effectiveness of a protest to a planned increase in a bank's mortgage rates (Steiner and Mark, 1985; Mark and Reichardt, 2004). The protest, organized by a community action group, called for a mass withdrawal of savings from the bank. Figure 5.1 plots the bank's savings balances over time. The protest began at month 35 on the horizontal axis, which is marked by the vertical line in the figure. The overall trend in savings balances before the protest is upward, as revealed by the regression line drawn through the pretreatment observations. An abrupt shift in savings balances occurs at month 35, and the subsequent trend in savings balances is relatively flat, as revealed by the regression line drawn through the posttreatment observations. Projecting the pretreatment trend forward in time and comparing to the posttreatment trend suggests that the protest produced an immediate drop in savings balances and slowed the rate of growth in savings balances.

The elementary ITS design rules out some of the threats to internal validity that can arise in the before-after design. In particular, the effect of maturation is taken into account when the trend in the pretreatment observations is modeled and that model is used to project the pretreatment trend forward in time. In general, a researcher can have more confidence that the effects of maturation have been modeled and removed when the treatment effect is abrupt and immediate rather than gradual and delayed. Similarly, the effects of seasonality can also be modeled based on the pretreatment observations and removed, assuming that the time series includes several cycles of observations so that the seasonal pattern can be assessed.

An examination of the trend in the pretreatment observations can also rule out statistical regression as a threat to validity. If statistical regression is operating, the observations shortly before the treatment implementation will be unusually high or low, which can be detected from a plot of the data. Finally, having multiple pretreatment observations over time reduces the plausibility that substantial testing effects are confounded with the implementation of the treatment, because the effects of testing would typically die out during the earliest, repeated pretest measurements, and therefore would not be operating by the time the treatment is introduced.

Nonetheless, the threats to validity of history, instrumentation, and attrition remain as potential alternative explanations for the results of an elementary ITS design. The plausibility of these threats can be assessed by embellishing the elementary design with additional design features, which we describe next.

**Figure 5.1. Data from an Interrupted Time-Series Design Used
to Assess the Effects of a Community Action Campaign**

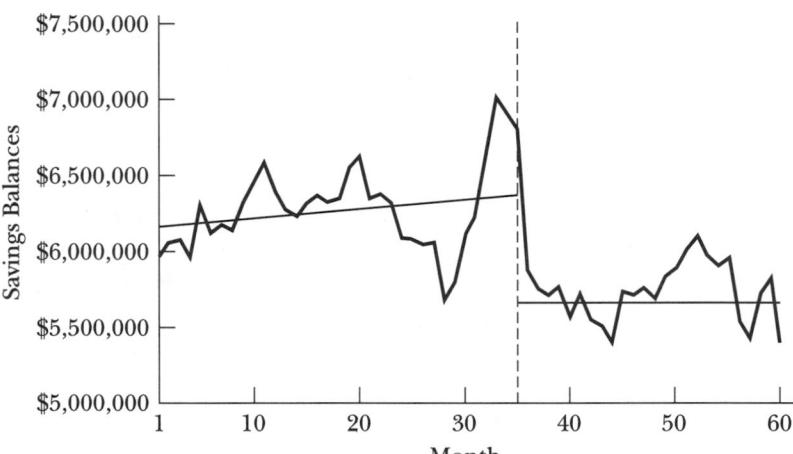

Source: Mark, M. M., and Reichardt, C. S. "Quasi-Experimental and Correlational Designs." In C. Sansone, C. C. Morf, and A. T. Pauter (eds.). *Handbook of Methods in Social Psychology.* Thousand Oaks, Calif.: Sage, 2004. Copyright © 2004 by Sage Publications. Reprinted by permission of Sage Publications, Inc.

Treatment Interventions

The elementary ITS design contains a single intervention. It can be elaborated by incorporating additional interventions. In the simplest case, an intervention is added that consists of removing or reversing the treatment that was introduced earlier. This design is schematically represented as:

O   O   O   O   O X O   O   O   O   O–X O   O   O   O   O

where X and –X denote the treatment that was originally introduced and the removal or reversal of that treatment, respectively. For example, the design was used to assess the effects of a federal law requiring that motorcycle riders wear helmets (General Accounting Office, 1991). The rate of fatalities from motorcycle accidents was reduced following the enactment of the law in 1965 and then rose again after 1975 when the law was repealed.

    In a more complex variation, called the ITS design with multiple replications, the treatment is repeatedly implemented and removed. The design is diagrammed as:

O   O   O X O   O   O–X O   O   O X O   O   O–X O   O   O

    For example, Schnelle and others (1978) estimated the effect on home burglaries of using a police helicopter for surveillance in a high-crime area.

Over several months, helicopter surveillance was implemented, withdrawn, implemented, and once again withdrawn. The number of home burglaries per day was recorded. Each time that helicopter surveillance was implemented, the number of burglaries decreased. Each time that helicopter surveillance was removed, the number of burglaries increased.

The relatively complex pattern of results produced in ITS designs with multiple treatment implementations reduces the plausibility of the threat to validity due to history. That is, to explain the pattern of results in a multiple intervention ITS design, history effects would have to occur multiple times, in opposite directions, and in synchrony with the implementation and removal of the treatments. It is generally far less plausible that such a complex pattern of history effects would occur than it is that the treatment interventions produced the changes. Following the same logic, the plausibility of threats to validity due to instrumentation and attrition is also diminished in ITS designs with multiple treatment implementations as compared to elementary ITS designs.

Comparison Groups

An alternative embellishment to the elementary ITS is the addition of one or more comparison groups. An ITS design with an experimental and a comparison group is diagrammed as:

$$
\begin{array}{cccccccccc}
O & O & O & O & OXO & O & O & O & O \\
\hline
O & O & O & O & O & O & O & O & O
\end{array}
$$

The top row of time-series observations is obtained from a group of participants who receive the treatment (the experimental group). The bottom row is obtained from a group of participants who do not receive the treatment (the comparison group). The dashed line between the two rows indicates that the two groups of participants are not formed at random but are nonequivalent. For example, Guerin and MacKinnon (1985) assessed the effects of a California law requiring passenger restraints in automobiles for children from birth to three years old. A time series of observations of the number of automobile fatalities of children in this age group was compared to the number of fatalities for children four to seven years old, who were not required to wear passenger restraints.

Adding comparison groups is another way to reduce the plausibility of threats to internal validity. For example, if you add a comparison group that receives no treatment but shares the same history effects as the experimental group, the threat of history is ruled out to the extent that there is an interruption in the experimental series but not in the comparison group. We will use Guerin and MacKinnon's evaluation (1985) of the effect of the law requiring passenger restraints for young children again. The fatality rates for the comparison time series of the older children should share with the experimental series, the younger children, the same history effects due to weather conditions or advances in automobile safety or other such factors. But only the number of injuries for the younger group declined after the law was enacted, a pattern of results more plausibly explained as the effect of the treatment than as the effects of history.

Outcome Variables

Instead of adding a comparison time series derived from study participants who do not receive the treatment, a comparison time series could be added that is derived from an alternative measure. Such a design is diagrammed as:

$$O_A \quad O_A \quad O_A \quad O_A \quad O_A X O_A \quad O_A \quad O_A \quad O_A \quad O_A$$
$$\cdots\cdots\cdots\cdots\cdots\cdots\cdots\cdots\cdots\cdots\cdots\cdots\cdots\cdots\cdots\cdots\cdots\cdots\cdots$$
$$O_B \quad O_B \quad O_B \quad O_B \quad O_B \quad O_B \quad O_B \quad O_B \quad O_B \quad O_B$$

where O_A and O_B represent separate measures collected on the same participants. The dotted line indicates that the A and B observations are collected on nonequivalent measures (rather than nonequivalent groups, which we represent with a dashed line). For example, to assess the effects of the British Breathalyzer crackdown, made famous by Campbell and Ross (1968), Anderson (1989) compared a time series of the number of fatalities to a time series of the number of drivers' licenses. That the number of fatalities declined while the number of licenses increased following the intervention reduces the likelihood that the decline in fatalities was due to the threat to validity of attrition that would have arisen, for example, if there had been fewer drivers on the road. The outcome measure, which provides the comparison time series of observations, is often called a *nonequivalent dependent variable* (Shadish, Cook, and Campbell, 2002).

Combinations of Design Features

More than one embellishment can be added to a design. For example, an interrupted time-series design with switching replications combines a comparison group and repeated treatment interventions. The design is diagrammed in the following way:

$$O \quad O \quad O \quad O \quad OXO \quad O \quad O \quad O \quad O \quad O \quad O \quad O \quad O \quad O$$
$$- -$$
$$O \quad O \quad O \quad O \quad O \quad O \quad O \quad O \quad O \quad O \quad OXO \quad O \quad O \quad O \quad O$$

The first row of Os represents observations on participants who receive the treatment the first time (but not the second time) it is implemented. The second row of Os represents observations on participants who receive the treatment the second time (but not the first time) it is implemented. When the treatment is introduced, the second time series serves as a control comparison for the first time series. When the treatment is introduced the second time, the first time series serves as a control comparison for the second time series. When the treatment is introduced the first time, there should be an interruption in the first time series but not the second time series, and vice versa when the treatment is introduced the second time. The advantage of such complex patterns of results is that they are relatively unlikely to arise through threats to internal validity. The ITS design with switching replications is particularly useful when an organization can offer services to only a limited number of participants at any one time but can offer treatment to batches of participants at later times.

Strengths and Weaknesses of Interrupted Time-Series Designs

Because they can rule out more threats to internal validity, ITS designs tend to be inferentially stronger than before-after designs. For the same reason, ITS designs with added treatment interventions, comparison groups, and outcome variables tend to be inferentially stronger than elementary ITS designs. Another advantage of ITS designs is that the multiple posttreatment observations enable the researcher to assess whether the effects of a treatment increase or decline over time, as well as whether increases or decreases in effects over time are linear or nonlinear. Another advantage is that an ITS design can be implemented without a comparison group, which means the treatment need not be withheld from any potential service clients. It is also possible to implement an ITS design with a very small group of participants or even a single participant, as is often done in the field of applied behavioral analysis.

An obvious disadvantage of ITS designs is that they require multiple observations over time, which often is beyond the resources of an evaluation. The burden of multiple observations can sometimes be reduced by using archival records or logs, including time series of observations collected in the ordinary operations of a service organization, business, or community.

In addition, ITS designs often require sophisticated statistical procedures. Observations in a time series are likely to be correlated, with adjacent observations more similar to each other than to distant observations. Correlations among observations in a time series are called *autocorrelations*. Classic statistical procedures such as multiple regression assume that observations are uncorrelated. Autocorrelation does not bias estimates of the treatment effects but does bias (usually attenuating) estimates of their standard errors. As a result, both tests of statistical significance and confidence intervals are biased (usually producing p-values that are too small and confidence intervals that are too narrow). The biasing effects of autocorrelation can be taken into account by using sophisticated statistical procedures such as autoregressive integrated moving average (ARIMA) models. In addition, multivariate statistical procedures are required for what are called cross-sectional ITS designs, where the experimental and comparison groups contain multiple participants, each of whom contributes separate time series of observations, but such designs and analyses are beyond the scope of our presentation here (see Mark, Reichardt, and Sanna, 2000).

Nonequivalent Group Designs

In these designs, comparisons are drawn between participants who receive different treatments and have been assigned to the treatments nonrandomly. Nonrandom assignment arises, for example, when participants select the treatment conditions they are to receive based on personal preferences. Or treatment conditions could be assigned by others, such as administrators, based on convenience or some other nonrandom criteria. Alternatively, treatment conditions could be assigned to preexisting groups (such as schools, communities, or businesses) that were created nonrandomly.

The most elementary nonequivalent group design compares two groups, where one receives the treatment and the other does not, and both groups are assessed on an outcome measure. Such a design is called a posttest-only nonequivalent group design and is schematically depicted as:

$$\begin{array}{c} \text{X O} \\ \hline \text{O} \end{array}$$

where the two rows represent the two nonequivalent groups. The first row represents the group that receives the treatment (X), and the second row represents the group that receives no treatment. In this design, the treatment effect is estimated as the mean difference between the groups on the posttest outcome measure.

The primary threat to internal validity in nonequivalent group designs is due to selection differences, which are differences between the treatment groups in the composition of the participants. For example, if only the most motivated individuals receive the treatment and only the least motivated individuals are included in the comparison group, selection differences include the difference between the groups in level of motivation. If the outcome measure is influenced by motivation, a mean difference between the groups on the outcome measure would arise even if the treatment were ineffective. In other words, the effects of selection differences can create the appearance of a treatment effect when none actually exists or can mask a treatment effect that does exist.

Because of the effects of selection differences, the posttest-only nonequivalent group design produces credible results only to the extent a researcher can be confident that the participants in one group are similar to the participants in the other. Using cohorts is one way to create similar groups. For example, the groups could be composed of different waves (cohorts) of first-year students at a university where the first-year class from one year would not receive the treatment and be compared to the first-year class from the year after, which does receive the treatment. Such a comparison would be diagrammed as:

$$O_{\text{year K}}$$
$$\sim \sim \sim \sim \sim \sim \sim \sim \sim \sim \sim \sim \sim \sim$$
$$X \qquad O_{\text{year K+1}}$$

where the first row of data is collected at the end of year K from first-year students who entered the university in year K and did not receive the treatment. The second row of data is collected at the end of year $K + 1$ from first-year students who entered the university in year $K + 1$ and received the treatment during that year. The underlying assumption is that the characteristics of first-year students are sufficiently constant from year to year that the different classes would perform the same on the outcome measure, in the absence of a treatment effect. (The wavy line used to separate the two groups denotes that the groups, while still nonequivalent, are also cohorts.) But such an assumption can be difficult to test. With or without cohorts, the posttest-only nonequivalent group design provides no way by itself to assess the similarity of the treatment groups, and therefore little reassurance that groups are sufficiently similar to justify credible inferences about treatment effects.

Measurement Occasions

Adding a pretest measure to the posttest-only nonequivalent group design produces the pretest-posttest nonequivalent group design, which is diagrammed as:

$$\begin{array}{ccc} O & X & O \\ \hline O & & O \end{array}$$

The difference between the groups on the pretest measure is used to try to take account of the effects of selection differences. In general, the kind of pretest that will best take account of selection differences is one that is operationally identical to the posttest, that is, when the pretest and posttest are collected in the same way using the same instruments or rating scales. But pretest measures could also be collected on background characteristics and any other constructs on which the treatment groups are thought to differ and to be related to the outcome.

A wide variety of statistical procedures have been developed for taking account of the effects of selection differences using pretest measures (Reichardt, 1979; Winship and Morgan, 1999). These procedures include change score analysis, standardized change score analysis, analysis of covariance, analysis of covariance with corrections for measurement error in the pretest, selection modeling, and matching on propensity scores. Fundamental differences among the analyses are the following. In change score analysis, the outcome variable is the difference between the pretest and posttest scores. The other analysis strategies use the posttest as the outcome variable, but differ in the types of covariates that are included in the statistical model. In the analysis of covariance, the pretest with or without a correction for unreliability is used as the covariate. In selection modeling and matching on propensity scores, the covariate is a derived estimate of the likelihood that an individual is in the different treatment conditions. Selection modeling adjusts for the estimated likelihood mathematically, while matching controls with physical equating.

Each statistical procedure imposes different assumptions about the nature of selection differences. Unfortunately, there is no guarantee that any of the sets of assumptions are correct and therefore no guarantee that any procedure will properly take account of the selection differences so as to produce unbiased estimates of the treatment effect. We recommend using a range of statistical procedures where some impose assumptions that will likely produce underestimates of the treatment effect, while others impose assumptions that will likely produce overestimates. In this way, the researcher attempts to bracket the size of the treatment effect within a likely range of estimates rather than to try (inappropriately) to estimate the treatment effect precisely.

Even more pretests can be added over time to produce designs such as:

$$
\begin{array}{cccc}
O & O & X & O \\
\hline
O & O & & O
\end{array}
$$

Taken together, the two pretests provide additional information about the nature of selection differences. For example, when there is only one pretest, groups that appear similar on the pretest may nonetheless be maturing at different rates, so that differences on the posttest would arise even in the absence of a treatment effect (this is called a *selection by maturation* interaction). By comparing scores on an earlier pretest to the scores on a later second pretest (as obtained from a design as diagrammed above), the researcher can diagnose and thereby remove the effects of differential trends in maturation (for an example, see Wortman, Reichardt, and St. Pierre, 1978). Another approach is to use the double pretests as a dry run for assessing the effectiveness of different statistical analyses (Boruch, 1997). That is, the researcher conducts an analysis that treats the second pretest as though it were a posttest. Such an analysis should find no treatment effect because no treatment has yet been administered. Nonetheless, selection differences are present. As a result, analysis strategies that properly remove the effects of selection differences should estimate the (nonexistence) treatment effect to be zero. A nonzero estimate (again, using only the two pretests) indicates that selection differences are not being properly removed by the analysis.

Comparison Groups

To assess the effectiveness of the Salk polio vaccine, rates of polio infection for second graders who were given the vaccine were compared to rates of infection for two comparison groups, consisting of first and third graders who were not inoculated (Meier, 1972). The resulting design is diagrammed as:

$$
\begin{array}{cc}
 & O_{\text{grade 1}} \\
\hline
X & O_{\text{grade 2}} \\
\hline
 & O_{\text{grade 3}}
\end{array}
$$

where each row represents the nonequivalent groups distinguished by grade level. The results revealed that the rates of polio infection for the second graders were lower than the rates for first or third graders. If only one comparison group had been used, maturation might plausibly account for the findings. The design that was used is inferentially strong because, in general, selection differences would be expected to affect the three groups in the order of their grade level. Adding the comparison group in this case greatly enhanced the credibility of the otherwise inferentially weak posttest-only nonequivalent group design.

Treatment Interventions

In dose response studies, different groups of participants receive different levels of treatment. For example, to assess the effects of supervision on factory output, supervision could be implemented at three levels: the current amount of supervision (X), an increased amount of supervision (X+), and a reduced amount of supervision (X–). Such a design would be diagrammed as:

```
        O  X+  O
        ---------
        O  X   O
        ---------
        O  X−  O
```

The expected pattern of results would be for the X+ group to exhibit more pretest-posttest change than the X group, which in turn would exhibit more change than the X− group. Under many conditions, such a pattern of results would be difficult to explain as an effect of selection differences, especially if the three groups started at similar levels on the pretest.

Outcome Variables

Braucht and others (1995) compared those who received a substantial amount of alcohol abuse services to those who received relatively little on two outcome variables: alcohol use and quality of family relationships. The design is diagrammed as:

$$O_A \; X+ \; O_A$$
$$\cdots\cdots\cdots\cdots$$
$$O_B \; X+ \; O_B$$
$$-----$$
$$O_A \; X- \; O_A$$
$$\cdots\cdots\cdots\cdots$$
$$O_B \; X- \; O_B$$

where the dashed line demarcates the two groups, with X+ denoting the group that received the greater amount of services and X− indicating the group that received the lesser amount of services. As before, the dotted line indicates alternative measures, and the O_A and O_B denote, respectively, the measures of alcohol use and quality of family relationships, which were collected on each of the two groups of participants. Two comparisons were drawn across the two nonequivalent groups: one using the O_A (alcohol use) outcome measure and one using the O_B (quality of family relationships) outcome measure.

The comparison involving alcohol use exhibited a cross-over interaction. That is, the X+ group had greater alcohol abuse than the X− group before treatment but less after treatment. Typically, cross-over interactions cannot be plausibly explained by selection differences. But in the design, a cross-over interaction could have occurred because individuals self-selected the amount of treatment services they received, and those who were the heaviest users of alcohol at the start might have been the most motivated to change. As a result, the most motivated might have reduced their drinking more than those who were less motivated, even in the absence of the differential amounts of treatment.

Braucht and others (1995) examined the second outcome measure, the quality of family relationships, to assess the plausibility of this alternative explanation. The quality of family relationships showed no differential change between the treatment groups. This pattern would not be predicted by differences in motivation because those most motivated to reduce their alcohol use would also likely be those most motivated to improve the quality of their lives in other ways as well, such as with regard to their family relationships. In contrast, the alcohol abuse services should produce little, if any, effect on the quality of family relationships because the treatment was directed only toward alcohol use and not to interpersonal or family relationships. Thus, the observed pattern of results suggests a treatment effect, and this conclusion was strengthened by the inclusion of the nonequivalent dependent variable.

Combinations of Design Features

If services are limited and cannot be given to all eligible individuals at the same time, different groups of individuals could be given services at different times. Adding measurements before and after different groups receive services at different times could result in a design such as:

$$
\begin{array}{cccc}
O & X & O & O \\
\hline
O & & O \; X & O
\end{array}
$$

where the first row represents a group receiving services first and the second row represents a group receiving services later (sometimes called a wait-list comparison group). This design is the nonequivalent-group version of the switching-replication ITS design. Compared to the elementary pretest-posttest nonequivalent group design, the switching-replication nonequivalent group design adds both a measurement occasion and a treatment implementation. To the extent the treatment is effective, the first group would show greater change from the first measurement to the second as compared to the second group, while the second group would show greater change from the second measurement to the third. In most instances, such a complicated pattern of outcomes is not plausibly produced by selection differences.

Strengths and Weaknesses of Nonequivalent Group Designs

Nonequivalent group designs can be easy to implement. Data must be collected from two groups, but this often can be done with little, if any, disruption in ongoing services delivery, and measurements need to be collected at only a few occasions. But although easy to implement, nonequivalent group designs are susceptible to threats to internal validity due to selection differences, whose effects can be severe and difficult to assess and remove.

The credibility of the results from nonequivalent group designs is enhanced by using groups that are as similar as possible and by diligently assessing the degree of similarity. For example, Langer and Rodin (1976) used a pretest-posttest nonequivalent group design to assess the effects on nursing home residents of increased opportunities for decision making. The different treatments were given to the residents of different floors of a nursing home. Incoming residents were not assigned to floors randomly, but were nonetheless assigned without any obvious tendency to send one type of resident to one floor rather than another. In addition, pretests, institutional records, and reports of the staff suggested no obvious initial selection differences. In such situations, where the nonequivalent groups are initially similar on the available pretreatment measures, statistical procedures will produce similar estimates of treatment effects. As a result, researchers can have greater confidence that the range of estimates brackets the size of the treatment effect. As we have shown, credibility can also be enhanced by adding design elaborations, such as additional comparison groups, treatment interventions, measurement occasions, and outcome variables, to create complex patterns of outcomes that are predicted by the treatment effect but not by threats to internal validity.

Regression-Discontinuity Designs

In a regression-discontinuity design, participants are ordered on a quantitative assignment variable (QAV) and allotted to treatment conditions based on a cutoff score on that variable. Participants with scores above the cutoff point are assigned to one treatment condition, and those with scores below the cutoff point are assigned to the other condition. The most common QAVs are measures of need or merit. An ameliorative program would be assigned to those with high need. A program designed to reward meritorious performance (such as high grade point average or distinguished sales volume) would be assigned to those with the highest scores on merit. But any quantitative variable can be used as the QAV. For example, participants could be assigned to a desirable treatment based on the time at which they apply for the services, using the first-come, first-served principle. If everything else is the same, the best QAV is one that is highly correlated with the outcome measure.

The effect of the treatment in a regression-discontinuity design is estimated by regressing the outcome scores onto the QAV separately in each treatment group. The treatment has no effect if the two regression lines have the same intercept and slope. In contrast, the presence of a treatment effect is evidenced by a difference between the two regression lines in height, slope, or both height and slope.

Figures 5.2 and 5.3 are plots of data from two hypothetical regression-discontinuity designs. In both plots, scores on the QAV vary along the horizontal axis, and scores on the outcome variable vary along the vertical axis. The vertical line in the middle of each plot denotes the cut-off score on the QAV that is used to assign the participants to the different treatments. In both plots, the cut-off point is at a score of 55 on the QAV. The scatter of data to the left of the cut-off score comes from the treatment group. The data points on this side of the cut-off score are represented by squares. The scatter of data to the right of the cut-off score comes from the comparison group. The data points on this side of the cut-off score are represented by circles. The slanted lines drawn through the scatter of data in each treatment condition are the regression lines.

The data in the plot in Figure 5.2 show no treatment effect. The scatters of data flow smoothly from one side of the cut-off score to the other. As a result, the regression lines in the two treatment groups have the same intercepts and slopes. In contrast, a treatment effect is present in the data in the plot in Figure 5.3 because the two regression lines do not coincide; one regression line is higher than the other, and there is an abrupt discontinuity in the regression lines at the cutoff score (hence the name *regression-discontinuity*). That the regression line for the treatment group is higher than for the comparison

Figure 5.2. Hypothetical Data from a Regression-Discontinuity Design with No Treatment Effect

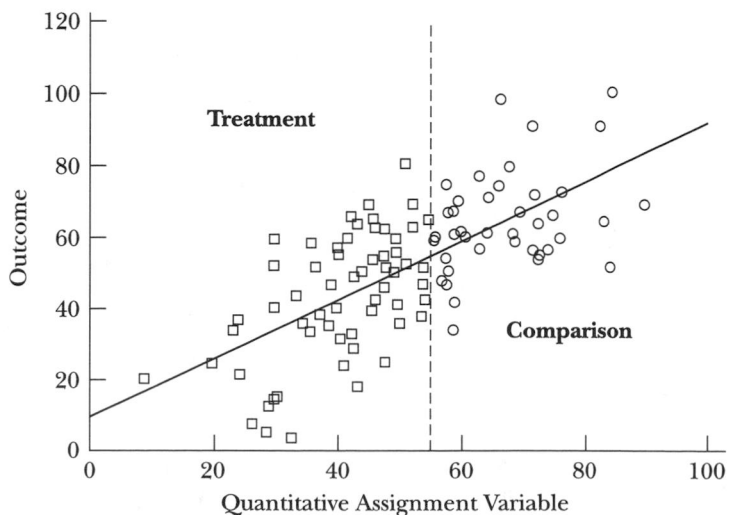

Figure 5.3. Hypothetical Data from a Regression-Discontinuity Design with a Positive Treatment Effect

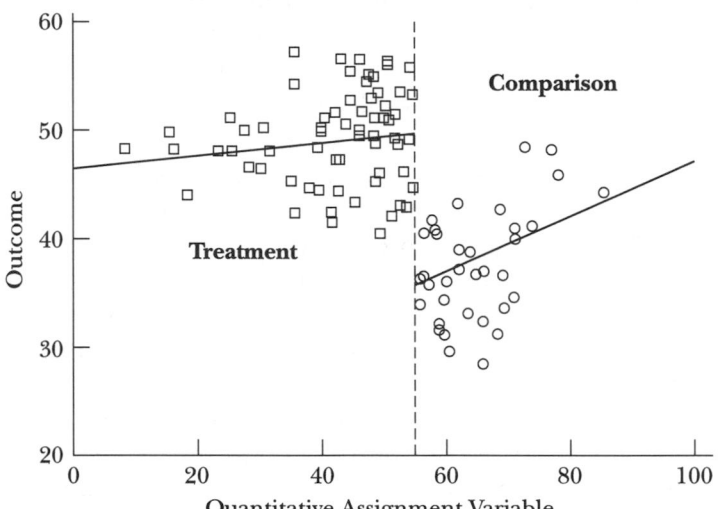

group indicates that the treatment raises scores on the outcome measures. That the regression line in the treatment group is flatter than in the comparison group means that the treatment has a larger effect for participants who have lower scores on the QAV than for those who have higher scores.

Analyzing the data from a regression-discontinuity design requires statistically modeling the shape of the regression surface between the scores on the outcome variable and the QAV. The most common statistical models assume the shape of the regression surface is a straight line (as in Figures 5.2 and 5.3). However, fitting a straight line leads to biased estimates of treatment effects if the true regression surface is curvilinear. Consider Figure 5.4. The scatter in the data has been removed so that the underlying, curvilinear relationship between the QAV and outcome can be clearly seen. (Such a curvilinear relationship might arise, for example, because of a ceiling effect.) There is no treatment effect because there would be no discontinuity at the cut-off score (which is equal to 70) if a correctly fitted, curvilinear line were plotted. However, the straight lines that are fit to the data in the figure do not meet at the cut-off score. Fitting straight, rather than curvilinear, lines therefore makes the treatment appear to have an effect, even though it does not.

Curvilinearity can be modeled by adding polynomial terms to a regression equation because polynomial terms allow for curved fits. Curvilinearity can often be diagnosed by examining the raw data, plots of the residuals from both straight line and curvilinear regression analyses, and parameter estimates

Figure 5.4. Regression-Discontinuity Design Demonstrating a Bias Resulting from Fitting Straight Lines to a Curvilinear Regression Surface

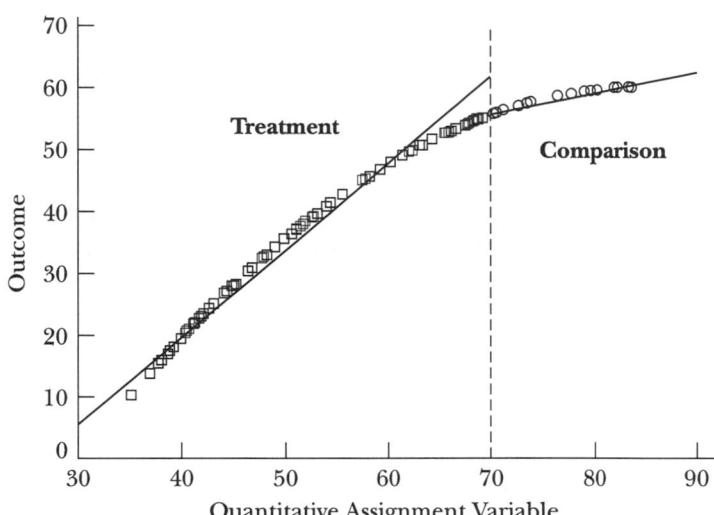

from models with polynomial terms. When curvilinearity is present, treatments that dramatically raise or lower the level of the regression line at the cut-off score (as in the plot in Figure 5.3) can be estimated with the greatest degree of confidence. Curvilinearity is most problematic when the effect of the treatment alters the slope, but not the level, of the regression line at the cut-off score. (For more detail on the analysis of the regression-discontinuity design, see Trochim, 1984, and Reichardt, Trochim, and Cappelleri, 1995.)

Additional Design Features

Like the other quasi-experimental designs, the regression-discontinuity design can be embellished with additional design features. Because the same four types of design features can be added to the regression-discontinuity design as to the ITS and nonequivalent group designs, we will consider only two types of additional design features here.

First, treatment implementations can be added. By incorporating a second cut-off score, three treatment conditions can be compared instead of only two. For example, Lipsey, Cordray, and Berger (1981) used a regression-discontinuity design to compare three treatments for reducing recidivism among arrested juveniles: counsel-and-release, diversion from the juvenile justice system, and probation. The QAV was a quantification of the decision rules that were already being used in the disposition of an arrested juvenile.

Juveniles below the first cut-off score were assigned to the counsel-and-release program, those between the two cut-off scores were placed in the diversion program, and those above the second cut-off score were assigned to probation. Recidivism increased with the QAV, but this trend was interrupted for those in the diversion program. Across all three groups, the regression surface looked roughly like the letter M, which effectively ruled out the threat to validity of curvilinearity because curvilinearity could not plausibly have such a shape in the absence of a treatment effect.

Second, additional measurement occasions can be added. For example, a regression-discontinuity design was used to assess the effects of Medicaid, which, starting in 1965, provided funds for medical care to families with yearly incomes below $3,000 (Marcantonio and Cook, 1994). One way Medicaid was intended to improve physical health was by increasing the number of visits to physicians. Based on data from *Current Population Reports,* the number of physician visits in 1967 decreased as income decreased up to an income of $3,000, whereupon physician visits dramatically increased, producing an obvious discontinuity in the regression surface. An alternative explanation other than that Medicaid caused the discontinuity is that low incomes produce proportionately more physician visits even without Medicaid, perhaps because particularly poor health causes incomes to drop to poverty levels. To evaluate the plausibility of this alternative explanation, the number of physician visits was plotted for incomes in 1964, the year before Medicaid was introduced. If the discontinuity in the 1967 data was due solely to Medicaid, a discontinuity should not appear in the 1964 data. In contrast, the alternative explanation predicts discontinuities in the data from both the years. There was no discontinuity in the data from 1964, ruling out the alternative explanation and strengthening the case for the effectiveness of Medicaid.

Strengths and Weaknesses of Regression-Discontinuity Designs

A regression-discontinuity design often produces more credible results than an elementary nonequivalent group design. The difference in credibility arises because the effects of selection differences are typically difficult to remove in nonequivalent group designs. However, adding design embellishments to the nonequivalent group design can increase the credibility of its results to more nearly rival the credibility of the results from a regression-discontinuity design. In addition, because it requires strict adherence to a quantitative rule for assigning participants to treatment conditions, a regression-discontinuity design is harder to implement in most settings than is a standard nonequivalent group design.

Although the regression-discontinuity design is a relatively strong quasi-experimental design, in general a randomized experiment is preferable for two reasons. First, a randomized experiment imposes fewer assumptions, such as those concerning the proper way to fit the regression surface between outcome scores and QAV (for example, linear versus nonlinear). Second, even ignoring differences in assumptions, the randomized experiment is more powerful than a regression-discontinuity design. Even under ideal conditions, a regression-discontinuity design requires approximately 2.7 times as many participants to have the same power as a randomized experiment. In addition, when researchers have enough control in a research setting to implement a regression-discontinuity design, they often have sufficient control to implement a randomized experiment. Nonetheless, a regression-discontinuity design is an attractive option when neither elementary nor elaborate nonequivalent group designs can well rule out threats to validity due to selection differences and when randomized experiments cannot be implemented. Sometimes the regression-discontinuity design will satisfy the ethical or practical requirement that the treatment be given to those most in need or, alternatively, to those most meritorious. In such a case, if a QAV can be devised and used in assigning participants to conditions, the regression-discontinuity design may be acceptable in settings where random assignment is not.

Conclusions

Estimating the effect of a program or policy requires a comparison between what happened when the program or policy was implemented and what would have happened if the program had not been implemented. Such a comparison can be drawn across different times or different participants. The before-after design and the interrupted time-series design are the two prototypical quasi-experiments that draw comparisons across different times. The nonequivalent group design and the regression-discontinuity design are the two prototypical quasi-experiments that draw comparisons across different participants. Neither class of comparison is inherently superior to the other. Which is to be preferred depends on the research circumstances, the plausibility of various threats to internal validity, and the types of design features that can be added to the prototypical designs.

The design features that can be added to a prototypical quasi-experiment are treatment interventions, comparison groups, measurement occasions, and outcome variables. Adding design features tends to blur the distinction between over-time and across-participant comparisons. For example, adding comparison groups to a comparison over time gives the design attributes of an across-participant comparison. Conversely, adding measurement occasions to an across-participant comparison gives the design attributes of over-time comparisons. The more important point, however, is that design embellishments can greatly strengthen the credibility of the results that are produced by quasi-experiments. With careful forethought, design features can be added so as to create elaborate patterns of results that make alternative explanations implausible.

The four prototypical types of quasi-experimental designs, combined with any number of the four types of additional design features, provide a vast array of design possibilities. Alone, each design and each design feature is susceptible to different patterns of threats to internal validity. In more complex combinations, the plausibility of validity threats will generally be reduced.

References

Anderson, A.J.B. *Interpreting Data: A First Course in Statistics*. London: Chapman and Hall, 1989.

Boruch, R. F. *Randomized Experiments for Planning and Evaluation: A Practical Guide*. Thousand Oaks, Calif.: Sage, 1997.

Braucht, G. N., and others. "Effective Services for Homeless Substance Abusers." *Journal of Addictive Diseases*, 1995, *14*, 87–109.

Campbell, D. T., and Ross, H. L. "The Connecticut Crackdown on Speeding: Time-Series Data in Quasi-Experimental Analysis." *Law and Society Review*, 1968, *3*, 33–53.

Campbell, D. T., and Stanley, J. C. *Experimental and Quasi-Experimental Designs for Research*. Skokie, Ill.: Rand McNally, 1966.

Cook, T. D., and Campbell, D. T. *Quasi-Experimentation: Design and Analysis Issues for Field Settings*. Skokie, Ill.: Rand McNally, 1979.

Eckert, W. A. "Situational Enhancement of Design Validity: The Case of Training Evaluation at the World Bank Institute." *American Journal of Evaluation*, 2000, *21*, 185–193.

Guerin, D., and MacKinnon, D. P. "An Assessment of the Impact of the California Child Seat Restraint Requirement." *American Journal of Public Health*, 1985, *75*, 142–144.

Langer, E. J., and Rodin, J. "The Effects of Choice and Enhanced Personal Responsibility for the Aged: A Field Experiment in an Institutional Setting." *Journal of Personality and Social Psychology*, 1976, *34*, 191–198.

Lipsey, M. W., Cordray, D. S., and Berger, D. E. "Evaluation of a Juvenile Diversion Program: Using Multiple Lines of Evidence." *Evaluation Review*, 1981, *5*, 283–306.

Marcantonio, R. J., and Cook, T. D. "Convincing Quasi-Experiments: The Interrupted Time Series and Regression-Discontinuity Designs." In J. S. Wholey, H. P. Hatry, and K. E. Newcomer (eds.), *Handbook of Practical Program Evaluation*. San Francisco: Jossey-Bass, 1994.

Mark, M. M., and Reichardt, C. S. "Quasi-Experimental and Correlational

Designs." In C. Sansone, C. C. Morf, and A. T. Panter (eds.), *Handbook of Methods in Social Psychology.* Thousand Oaks, Calif.: Sage, 2004.

Mark, M. M., Reichardt, C. S., and Sanna, L. J. "Time Series Designs and Analyses." In H.E.A. Tinsley and S. R. Brown (eds.), *Handbook of Applied Multivariate Statistics and Mathematical Modeling.* Orlando, Fla.: Academic Press, 2000.

Meier, P. "The Biggest Public Health Experiment Ever: The 1954 Field Trial of the Salk Poliomyelitis Vaccine." In J. M. Tanur and others. (eds.), *Statistics: A Guide to the Unknown.* San Francisco: Holden-Day, 1972.

Reichardt, C. S. "The Statistical Analysis of Data from Nonequivalent Group Designs." In T. D. Cook and D. T. Campbell (eds.), *Quasi-Experimentation: Design and Analysis Issues for Field Settings.* Skokie, Ill.: Rand McNally, 1979.

Reichardt, C. S., and Mark, M. M. "Quasi-Experimentation." In L. Bickman and D. Rog (eds.), *Handbook of Applied Social Research.* Thousand Oaks, Calif.: Sage, 1998.

Reichardt, C. S., Trochim, W.M.K., and Cappelleri, J. C. "Reports of the Death of Regression-Discontinuity Analysis Are Greatly Exaggerated." *Evaluation Review,* 1995, *19,* 39–63.

Schnelle, J. F., and others. "Police Evaluation Research: An Experimental and Cost-Benefit Analysis of a Helicopter Patrol in a High-Crime Area." *Journal of Applied Behavior Analysis,* 1978, *11,* 11–21.

Shadish, W. R., and Cook, T. D. "Comment-Design Rules: More Steps Toward a Complete Theory of Quasi-Experimentation." *Statistical Science,* 1999, *14,* 294–300.

Shadish, W. R., Cook, T. D., and Campbell, D. T. *Experimental and Quasi-Experimental Designs for Generalized Causal Inference.* Boston: Houghton Mifflin, 2002.

Steiner, D., and Mark, M. M. "The Impact of a Community Action Group: An Illustration of the Potential of Time Series Analysis for the Study of Community Groups." *American Journal of Community Psychology,* 1985, *13,* 13–30.

Trochim, W.M.K. *Research Design for Program Evaluation: The Regression-Discontinuity Approach.* Thousand Oaks, Calif.: Sage, 1984.

U.S. General Accounting Office. *Motorcycle Helmet Laws Save Lives and Reduce Costs to Society.* Washington, D.C.: U.S. General Accounting Office, 1991.

Winship, C., and Morgan, S. L. "The Estimation of Causal Effects from Observational Data." *Annual Review of Sociology,* 1999, *25,* 659–707.

Wortman, P. M., Reichardt, C. S., and St. Pierre, R. G. "The First Year of the Educational Voucher Demonstration: A Secondary Analysis of Student Achievement Test Scores." *Evaluation Quarterly,* 1978, *2,* 193–214.

6

Using Randomized Experiments

Robert G. St. Pierre

The United States seeks to ameliorate the social ills that low-income populations face by developing, implementing, and evaluating a wide range of social programs. (In this chapter, *program, intervention,* and *treatment* are used as interchangeable terms, referring to any educational or social program.) As examples, in fiscal year 2002, the United States spent $6.5 billion on Head Start to help preschool-age children from low-income homes enter school on a par with their more advantaged age-mates, $10.7 billion on child nutrition programs such as the National School Lunch Program and the School Breakfast Program so that children from low-income families are ensured of adequate nutrition while they attend school, and $12.3 billion on education for disadvantaged children including Title I programs so that elementary school children who attend schools in high-poverty neighborhoods can get extra help in reading and math.

These are substantial investments of taxpayer dollars, and we have a national interest in making the best possible use of these funds. We regularly have national debates about the effectiveness of these investments—about the payoffs for the costs incurred. These national forums draw on ideological stances, personal testimony, and an array of surveys, research studies, evaluations, and policy analyses that provide information about federal expenditures and their effectiveness. The same kinds of debates take place in state legislatures and local governments. To the extent that these discussions call for assessments of the effectiveness of investments in social programs, we want to be able to answer questions such as: Does Head Start work? Does Title I really help children read better, and if so, how much better? Are children who participate in the National School Lunch Program better off than they would have been if they did not participate?

How do we best answer these questions about the impacts and effectiveness of social programs? There has been a growing call for evidence obtained from evaluations that are based on randomized experiments. This chapter provides guidelines for deciding when to use a randomized experiment, designing such studies, and working with program staff to put experiments in place and maintain them so that unbiased estimates of the effectiveness of educational and social programs can be obtained.

Why Rely on Experimental Studies?

The value of randomized experimental studies is apparent when we want to draw causal inferences about the effectiveness of interventions (Shadish, Cook and Campbell, 2002; Mosteller and Boruch, 2002). In short, random assignment of people or institutions to intervention or control groups is the best way to determine the effectiveness of an intervention because that procedure allows the strongest possible causal connection between provision of the treatment and observed outcomes. No other research designs offer the benefits of a randomized experiment, although some quasi-experimental designs allow much stronger causal inferences than others (Cook and Campbell, 1979), and many alternative evaluation approaches are appropriate for addressing noncausal questions.

Although experimental research has been the method of choice in medical effectiveness studies for many decades (Meinert, 1986), the social sciences have been slower to recognize the benefits of randomized experiments that, when well done, produce irrefutable evidence about a social program's effects. Because they were relatively rare events in the 1960s and 1970s, and to encourage their wider application, Boruch and his colleagues started documenting the use of randomized experiments (Boruch, 1974; Boruch and Wothke, 1985). By the late 1990s, randomized experiments had become widely used for determining the effectiveness of social science interventions, and Greenberg and Schroder (1997) compiled a lengthy book chronicling recent experiments in the social sciences. (The box sets out some important studies.)

Assessments of the effectiveness of federal education and early childhood programs provide examples of the recent application of randomized experiments. For example, Head Start has a history of experimental examinations of demonstration programs. In the 1990s, Head Start demonstration and evaluation activities included randomized experimental studies of the Comprehensive Child Development Program (Goodson and others, 2000), the Head

Selected Resources for Practical Experiments

Digest of Social Experiments (Greenberg and Shroder, 1997). A lengthy compendium of brief summaries on 143 social experiments.

Evidence Matters (Mosteller and Boruch, 2002). An edited volume on randomized experiments in education that addresses politics of random assignment, the importance of randomized studies, how experiments have been neglected in education, and how to counter arguments against experiments.

Validity and Social Experimentation (Bickman, 2000). An edited volume in tribute to Donald Campbell, a leading contributor to social science methodology from the 1950s to the 1990s, that addresses issues of evaluation theory, research synthesis, statistical power and effect sizes, units of randomization, the experimenting society, and the politics of experimentation.

Toward Reform of Program Evaluation (Cronbach and others, 1980). Examines issues in planning, designing, and carrying out evaluations.

Experimental and Quasi-Experimental Designs for Generalized Causal Inference (Shadish, Cook, and Campbell, 2002). Covers experimental theory, quasi-experimental design, randomized experiments, and causal inference.

Start Family Service Centers (Swartz, Bernstein, and Levin, 1998), the Head Start Transition Study (Ramey and others, 2000), and the Head Start Family Child Care Demonstration (Faddis and Ahrens-Gray, 2000). In the late 1990s and early 2000s, Head Start continued to study the effectiveness of demonstration programs by funding a random assignment evaluation of the Early Head Start program (Love and others, 2002). Most recently, and at the insistence of the General Accounting Office and the Congress, the Department of Health and Human Services funded a random assignment evaluation of the Head Start program itself (Bell and Puma, 2002).

In recent years, the U.S. Department of Education has sponsored only a few experimental evaluations, including studies of the Even Start Family Literacy program (St. Pierre and others, 1995, 2003), the 21st Century Community Learning Centers program (Dynarski and others, 2003), dropout prevention programs (Dynarski, Gleason, Rangarajan, and Wood, 1998), and Upward Bound (Myers and Schirm, 1997). However, the U.S. Department of Education has begun to embrace research studies based on randomized designs for the purpose of assessing program effectiveness. After years of rejecting randomized studies, the education community is succumbing to pressures brought by researchers and policymakers who are convinced of the importance of obtaining evidence of effectiveness from randomized experiments—for example:

- The National Institute of Child Health and Human Development has published findings based on more than thirty years of experimental research on how to strengthen the reading achievement of children with learning disabilities (Lyon, 1999). This research led to the development of the term *scientifically based reading research,* and the No Child Left Behind legislation (2002) uses this terminology in reference to many different federal programs for children, including Title I, Even Start, Head Start, Reading First, and Early Reading First.
- The National Academy of Sciences sponsored a series of reports summarizing research on reading, preschool education, and early childhood development (National Research Council, 1998, 2000, 2001). In drawing conclusions, these reports give greater weight to experimental research.
- Based on President George Bush's belief that "government should be results-oriented—guided not by process but guided by performance," the Office of Management and Budget is systematizing its program reviews through the development of program assessment rating tools. Reviews and ratings of programs, and subsequent recommendations for funding in the president's budget, rely heavily on the results from experimental evaluations when such evaluations are available.
- The Coalition for Evidence-Based Policy, sponsored by the Council for Excellence in Government, was formed with the mission to promote government policymaking based on rigorous evidence of program effectiveness. A report from the coalition in 2002 recommended to the U.S. Department of Education that knowledge in education be built on the basis of interventions proven effective through randomized controlled trials.
- Individual researchers have called for the reform of federal efforts to synthesize existing research and have advised the Department of Education to fund experiments when trying to assess the effectiveness of educational interventions (for example, Cook and Payne, 2002; Mosteller and Boruch, 2002; Vinovskis, 2002; Carnine, 1997).
- A group of evaluation methodologists formed the international Campbell Collaboration to prepare, maintain, and make accessible systematic reviews of studies of the effectiveness of programs in crime and justice, education, social work and social welfare, and other social and behavioral areas. The Department of Education has funded the Campbell Collaboration to operate the What Works Clearinghouse, an effort designed in part to collect

and report experimental evidence about the effectiveness of educational interventions.

In 2002, congressional legislation reorganized the Department of Education's program evaluation functions and assigned specific responsibility for assessing the effectiveness of educational interventions to the National Center for Educational Evaluation within the newly created Institute of Education Sciences (formerly the Office of Educational Research and Improvement). This reorganization brought with it a new emphasis on high-quality research. Experiments are being designed and implemented to assess the relative impacts of various preschool curricula, and randomized designs are being developed to assess the impacts of the Reading First and Early Reading First programs, comprehensive school reform programs, promising family literacy interventions, Title I preschool, charter schools, educational technology, after-school programs, various approaches to English literacy for non-English-proficient students, promising models of adult education, and different models of teacher preparation, among other programmatic activities. All of this activity is being undertaken with the hope that higher-quality research based on experimental studies will result in better information about the impacts of educational and social programs and an eventual improvement in the effectiveness of those interventions.

When Is an Experiment Warranted?

An experiment should be included as part of a program evaluation when there is an interest in assessing the impact of the program. Otherwise, there is no reason to consider an experiment. For example, when a new social program is funded, policymakers typically want to know how many families are being served, the kinds of services being delivered, how long families participate, and so on. Surveys of program participants and program providers are appropriate to deal with these issues. Questions about program impacts are premature for new programs, and hence experiments are not warranted. However, when policymakers want to understand the impacts of a program, experimental research is called for. Examples of questions that call for experimental evidence are, "Does Head Start work?" "Are children better off if they participate in Title I?" "What are the benefits of the National School Lunch Program?"

Given a desire to obtain evidence about an intervention's impacts, the next issue to be addressed is whether time, financial resources, and political will exist to support an experiment. A randomized experiment is complicated and expensive, and its design and implementation require time, research expertise, and adequate resources, so it ought not to be undertaken lightly. Certainly, a

The Comprehensive Child Development Program

The evaluation of this program involved random assignment of 4,410 families in twenty-one programs to participate in the program or to be in a control group (Goodson and others, 2000). Randomization was done in each of the twenty-one projects, and families assigned to the program were enrolled for an average of 3.3 years. During this time, they were provided with intensive case management and home visiting, with the intent of increasing participation in a range of social and educational services. Families in the control group participated in a normal mix of social and educational services. Child, parent, and family outcomes were measured annually for five years. The researchers found that the program had no effect on child outcomes (cognitive and socioemotional development, and health) or parent outcomes (parenting, family economic self-sufficiency, or maternal life course) and concluded that the combination of case management and parenting education, delivered primarily through home visits, is not an effective means of improving developmental outcomes for low-income children.

randomized experiment is expensive and time-consuming when compared with the alternative of doing no research at all. But any quasi-experimental study in which data are collected from a treatment group and a nonequivalent comparison group is just as expensive and takes just as long as a randomized experiment. Some alternative research designs are quick and inexpensive, for example, relying on data collected for other purposes. However, even if alternatives to random assignment are less expensive, require less time, and are easier to implement, they rarely are worth the time and money spent on them because the results are not helpful for their intended purpose: understanding program impacts. Hence, the expense and difficulty of randomized studies ought not to be used as an argument in favor of alternative designs that may be easier to implement—not if the purpose is to assess program impacts.

Finally, evaluators must determine whether there is a research platform for the experiment, such as a set of projects, schools, or sites in which the study can reasonably be conducted. For example, a question about the impacts of Head Start could be answered by an experiment in which Head Start projects with waiting lists are recruited to participate. Eligible children on each project's waiting list would be randomly assigned to participate in Head Start or to be in a control group (not allowed to be in Head Start). Thus, in the case of an existing service program such as Head Start, local projects generally serve as the research platform. But what about studying the effectiveness of a comprehensive school reform program such as Success for All that has been developed for use in almost any school system (Slavin and Madden, 2001)? There is no built-in research platform for Success for All as there is for Head Start, and so it would be necessary to negotiate with potential research sponsors. One possible research platform would be provided by a public school system or a group of school systems that are struggling to strengthen students' academic skills. If approached and offered reasonable incentives, these schools might be willing to take part in an experiment in which schools are randomly assigned to intervention (Success for All) or control group (continued normal operations) status. A similar approach would have to be taken to evaluate the impacts of almost any curricular intervention.

How Do We Implement an Experimental Evaluation?

Given the desire to design and implement an experimental evaluation, researchers have to consider a myriad of design issues, such as defining the desired experimental contrasts, specifying an appropriate unit of random assignment, setting a desired level of statistical power, dealing with nonparticipation, crossovers and attrition, and designing methods to preserve randomization.

Defining the Experimental Contrasts

Questions such as, "Does Head Start work?" or "Are children better off if they participate in Title I?" seem simple enough. But the simplicity masks the implicit comparison that is required. "Does Head Start work?" might be restated in several different ways:

> "Do children in Head Start do better than children who get no preschool education at all?"

> "Do children in Head Start do better than they would have had they not been in the program?"

> "Do children in Head Start do better than children in state-funded preschool programs?"

> "Do children in Head Start do better than children in family day care programs?"

Each of these (and other) questions specifies a comparison and hence defines an experimental contrast. The first question calls for a comparison between children in Head Start and children who are not enrolled in any formal preschool education. The second calls for a comparison between children in Head Start and children who are not in Head Start and hence who participate in the mix of preschool services that is available in their communities. The third and fourth questions are more specific about the desired comparison, calling for studies of the relative effectiveness of Head Start, state-funded preschool programs, and family day care programs.

Early Head Start

Seventeen Early Head Start programs participated in an evaluation in which 3,001 families that wanted to participate in Early Head Start were randomly assigned to Early Head Start or a control group within each project (Love and others, 2002). Families in Early Head Start participated for an average of twenty-one months and were provided with a range of educational and social services. Families in the control group availed themselves of the normal set of educational and social services to which they were entitled. Data were collected annually over a three-year period, from the time a child was born to age three. Several modest impacts were detected (effect sizes of 10 to 20 percent) in areas such as child cognitive development and language development, as well as social-emotional development. Early Head Start parents were found to have improved parenting skills and to have fewer subsequent births. Impacts were found only for African American families.

Hence, an evaluator needs to discuss the desired contrast with policymakers to be certain that the evaluation is answering the most important question. In many cases, policymakers want a study of the effectiveness of a program compared with no services. But in education and the social sciences, this is rarely possible, and individuals in a control group often receive services similar to those offered to the intervention group. For example, low-income families typically have multiple options when searching for early childhood services. Head Start, Early Head Start, Title I preschool, Early Reading First, Even Start, state-funded preschools, family day care, and other similar services often are available in the same communities. Furthermore, mothers who seek to enroll their children in, say, Head Start, almost always are looking for either full-day or part-day care for their child. The implication for experimental studies of such programs is that mothers of children assigned to a control group (instead of Head Start) are likely to enroll their children in another program that provides similar services, such as Even Start or Title I preschool. The resulting impact estimates will be attenuated since the experimental contrast is not between Head Start and no preschool but between Head Start and an unspecified mix of preschool services.

Similar issues are faced when trying to evaluate school reform models. It would be difficult to find any school in the nation that is not currently engaged in some sort of school reform effort: school improvement teams, creating small schools within schools, coordinating support services for students, involving parents more fully, and so on. So what is the appropriate control condition for formal school reform models such as Success for All and the Comer School Development Program?

One solution to this problem is to avoid a no-treatment control condition and instead to specify all of the experimental conditions by conducting planned variation experiments to formally test the relative effectiveness of various approaches to solving a given problem. For example, after two impact evaluations found that the Even Start family literacy program had no measurable positive effects on the literacy levels of participating children and their parents (St. Pierre and others, 1995, 2003), the Department of Education is designing a study in which the effectiveness of a small number of specified family literacy approaches will be tested. Even Start projects that volunteer to participate in the study will be randomly assigned to implement one of the new family literacy models or to continue with their current family literacy operations. Thus, the regular Even Start program forms the control group against which the new family literacy models will be tested.

Specifying the Unit of Random Assignment

When designing an experiment, researchers often have a choice of several different units of random assignment, for example, children, families, classrooms and teachers, schools, or school districts. Designs in which individual children or families are randomly assigned to interventions are the most efficient, because a given level of statistical power can be obtained with the smallest sample of individuals. This type of random assignment works best with interventions that are delivered at the child, student, or family level. Examples include pull-out programs in which children are taken out of their regular classes to receive special services, after-school programs for which children volunteer, or family literacy programs where families select from a menu of available services.

Designs that assign individuals to educational interventions have disadvantages despite their benefits in terms of statistical power. Parents and school-level personnel are understandably resistant to the random assignment of individual students because it interferes with normal school operations and with teacher and classroom assignments. In addition, it may be seen as unethical to randomly assign some students to participate in a particular

> ### Even Start
>
> Eighteen Even Start projects in two cohorts participated in an evaluation in which 463 families were randomly assigned to participate in Even Start or to a control group within each project (St. Pierre and others, 2003). Pretest and posttest data were collected in the 1999–2000 and 2000–2001 school years; follow-up data were collected a year later. Control group families were guaranteed participation in Even Start during the follow-up year. Families participated in Even Start for an average of ten months and were offered four instructional services: early childhood education, adult education, parenting education, and parent-child literacy activities. Families assigned to the control group participated in a mix of educational services that they found on their own. Even Start had no impact on any of a variety of outcomes including child reading and math literacy, adult reading literacy, child behaviors in school, and parent education, employment, and income. The researchers concluded that families participate in only a small amount of instruction relative to their needs, that the early childhood classrooms did not place sufficient emphasis on language acquisition and reasoning, and that high-quality family literacy curricula need to be developed.

intervention that confers a perceived benefit while denying other students that same service. A researcher who wants to evaluate the relative effectiveness of a new one-semester health education curriculum would be more likely to find school personnel willing to cooperate if, instead of randomly assigning students, the evaluation randomly assigned classrooms or even entire schools either to implement the new health education curriculum or to continue to implement the health education curriculum that already existed in the school.

Random assignment within a particular school or school district carries with it the risk of diffusion of the intervention to other students or classrooms within that school or district. Consider the situation where all kindergarten classrooms in a school district are randomly assigned to implement a new literacy-based curriculum or to continue with the existing curriculum. Teachers of kindergarten classrooms that are assigned to implement the new curriculum will receive training and new curriculum materials, whereas the other teachers in the district do not. To the extent that kindergarten teachers in the district spend considerable time together, it is reasonable to expect that they will share information about what they are doing in their classrooms, so there may be diffusion or spillover of the new curriculum to the control classrooms. Assuming that the degree of implementation of the new curriculum is being assessed as part of the evaluation, then the same measurements can be made in control classrooms in an attempt to assess the extent of such spillover effects.

Setting a Desired Level of Statistical Power

The power of an evaluation design is the probability that it will yield statistically significant results when, in fact, there is a true difference between the intervention and control groups. Evaluators need to understand that many of their design decisions have a direct effect on power. In particular, the power of an evaluation design depends on many factors, such as the size of the treatment and control difference that the evaluators wish to be able to detect, the significance level of the statistical tests to be used, the number of interventions being tested and consequently the number of comparisons being made among the various treatments, the number of units randomly assigned, and the number of smaller-level units (say, students) within the units (a classroom) that are randomly assigned (Cohen, 1977).

Perhaps most important for setting a desired level of statistical power is for the evaluator to have a reasonable understanding of the size of the treatment and control difference that is expected. Some of the largest effects in education (greater than 1.0 standard deviation units difference in cognitive development between intervention and control children) have been pro-

Nutrition Education and Training

An evaluation of a one-semester Nutrition Education and Training (NET) program was conducted in twenty volunteer elementary schools (St. Pierre, Cook, and Straw, 1981). Thirteen schools serving 1,651 children in grades 1 through 6 were randomly assigned to the treatment group, and seven schools serving 700 children were assigned to a control group. Schools in the control group were guaranteed participation in NET the following year. The evaluation included pretest and posttest data collection during the spring 1980 school semester and follow-up data collection a year later. The evaluation found that teachers implemented an average of 80 percent of the planned NET activities. Strong positive effects were found in all grades on several measures of nutrition knowledge, positive effects on reported food preference, and willingness to select new foods. No consistent effects were found on food attitudes, reported food habits, or plate waste. The researchers concluded that it was possible to change nutrition-related knowledge and food preferences, but that behaviors were more difficult to change.

duced by high-quality model early childhood education programs such as the Abecedarian program (Ramey and Campbell, 1988), Project CARE (Wasik, Ramey, Bryant, and Sparling, 1990), and the Infant Health and Development Program (Infant Health and Development Program, 1990). A broad review of the effectiveness of preschool education by Barnett (1995) documented average effects of about 0.5 standard deviation in cognitive development after a year of preschool intervention. And a review of the effectiveness of large-scale service or demonstration programs by St. Pierre and Layzer (1998), as well as individual studies of Early Head Start (Love and others, 2002), Even Start (St. Pierre and others, 2003), the Comprehensive Child Development Program (Goodson and others, 2000), and the New Chance program (Quint, Bos, and Polit, 1997), have shown either no effects or very small effects, on the order of 0.1 standard deviation. Thus, small-scale, well-controlled model early childhood programs produce the largest effects on children's cognitive development, and large-scale preschool programs with great site-to-site variation in activities produce small effects at best. Such an understanding of the effect sizes documented in previous related research will help evaluators determine what size effect a given evaluation ought to be designed to detect. An alternative approach is to set an absolute standard for success wherein evaluators, policymakers, and program staff all agree ahead of time that a particular intervention needs to produce an effect of a given size in order to be considered cost-effective.

Sample size may be the most obvious contributor to statistical power, and although studies based on large samples have greater statistical power than studies based on small samples, large samples are expensive. When it is not feasible, financially or otherwise, to increase the number of units participating in an evaluation, it may be possible to increase the precision of impact estimates in other ways, for example, by controlling for differences in the baseline characteristics of sample members that are related to outcomes. Using baseline data in the analysis allows higher levels of statistical power by reducing variance in the outcome measure by a factor of $(1 - R^2)$, where R^2 represents the proportion of variation in the outcome explained by the baseline characteristics. This has the same effect on statistical power as multiplying the sample size by a factor of $1/(1 - R^2)$. For example, baseline characteristics that explain 50 percent of the variance in the outcome measure have the same analytic effect as would be obtained by doubling the sample size.

Finally, it is important to decide on the level of statistical power needed for subgroup analyses. For example, an evaluation of the overall effectiveness of Head Start might be designed to detect subgroup effects on boys and girls, or on children in different regions of the country. Evaluation designers need to determine ahead of time whether there are enough subgroup members in the study to obtain accurate estimates of the impact of an intervention on a

The Abecedarian Study

This experiment tested the impacts of a very intensive (all-day, year-round), long-lasting (five years) early childhood program (Campbell and others, 2001). One hundred eleven children from volunteer low-income families participated in the evaluation: 57 were randomly assigned to the treatment group and 54 to the control group. Assessments of children were done at three, four, five, six, eight, twelve, and fifteen years of age. At age twenty-one, 104 of the 111 originally assigned children participated in the data collection. The evaluation found large effects on cognitive development (1.75 standard deviations on IQ) at age three, effects that persisted even at age twenty-one (0.87 standard deviations on reading and math achievement). The researchers concluded that intensive early childhood education can have lasting effects on the cognitive and academic development of children from economically disadvantaged families and that programs that work directly with children produce larger effects than programs that hope to help children by working with their parents.

particular subgroup. If it is important for policy purposes to obtain separate estimates for a small subgroup, it may be possible to oversample that group.

The power of a design also is affected by the number of interventions being tested and hence the number of analytical comparisons being made. We may be satisfied with the power of a design that includes two hundred children randomly assigned to participate in a new preschool intervention or a control group (one hundred children in each group). Now suppose that there is an interest in testing the relative effectiveness of four different preschool curricula against each other and against a control group. On the face of it, we might want to include five hundred children (one hundred in each group) to achieve the same statistical power as the earlier design. But with five treatment groups, we may well want to make all ten possible treatment versus treatment comparisons as opposed to the single comparison being made in the two-group example. This means that the sample size in each group must be even larger in order to avoid declaring an effect statistically significant when, in fact, it could have occurred by chance alone.

Dealing with Nonparticipation, Crossovers, and Attrition

While randomized experiments produce efficient and unbiased estimates of program impacts, bias or statistical inefficiencies can be introduced during the implementation of randomized designs. One problem occurs when individuals assigned to an intervention do not take full advantage of it. Suppose that students are randomly assigned to participate in an after-school tutoring program but not all of those students attend the program. Or suppose that a family is randomly assigned to a family literacy program offering multiyear services but participates for only a week or a month. In such cases, the outcomes of intervention and control group members can still be compared and will still provide unbiased estimates of the effect of making the intervention available to eligible students or families. But, in addition, policymakers are generally interested in estimating the impact of an intervention on students and families that actually participated. Such an estimate can be obtained by dividing the impact estimate for all students or families assigned to receive the intervention by the proportion of the intervention group that actually participated (Bloom, 1984). Although this operation may change the size of the effect estimate, it does not change the statistical significance of the estimate.

Just as some members of an intervention group may not participate fully in the treatment, some control members may receive a form of the intervention. For example, if students were randomly assigned to classrooms implementing different math curricula, midyear transfers from a control class to a treatment class would create crossovers. To the extent that the intervention affects the outcomes of the crossover students, treatment control outcome differences will be reduced, and the estimated impact of the intervention will be biased downward.

Randomized designs can also suffer from sample attrition. Students drop out of school, families move away, and subjects refuse to participate in data collection activities. Sample attrition is less problematic if the attrition occurs randomly in both the intervention and control groups, even if the rate of attrition is not equal in both groups. Nonrandom attrition, however, can bias impact estimates. For example, if low-achieving students are more likely than the control group to drop out of the intervention group, impact estimates may be biased upward.

One way to estimate the potential bias due to sample attrition is to use administrative records that are available on the entire sample. For example, in an evaluation of the Moving to Opportunity program (Goering, Feins, and Richardson, 2002), both administrative data (through employment records) and survey data (through in-person surveys) were collected from study participants. Subsequent to random assignment, some participants were lost or refused to cooperate with the study. Although it was not possible to collect survey data from respondents who left the study, administrative data continues to be available for the full sample and can be used to compare the employment characteristics of the full sample to the reduced sample. This information provides an estimate of the bias that is introduced into the survey data through attrition, and impact estimates can be adjusted accordingly. If the employment characteristics of the full sample and the reduced sample are similar, then it is unlikely that differential attrition has occurred, and hence there should be no bias in the survey data. But if there are important differences between the employment characteristics of the two groups, then the survey data may be similarly biased. (Other methods for determining whether attrition is related to the treatment and ways of dealing with this problem are discussed by Cook and Campbell, 1979.)

21st Century Community Learning Centers

An evaluation of the 21st Century program was conducted in seven elementary schools where there were more applicants than could be accepted for after-school programs (Dynarski and others, 2003). The study involved random assignment of one thousand children to treatment and control groups. Children in the treatment group were eligible to participate in school-based academic and recreational activities when school was not in regular session (after school, on weekends and holidays, and during the summer) and did so for an average of fifty-eight days. Children in the control group did not participate in after-school activities. Baseline and follow-up data were collected at the start and end of the 2000–2001 school year. Although the programs increased the amount of time students spent at school, they had no effects on reading or math grades or reading test scores. Nor did the programs appear to improve students' effort in school. The researchers concluded that too few children received sustained, substantive academic support and that both participation rates and the academic content of the program need attention.

In some cases it is possible to ameliorate the effects of attrition by using matched pairs in the random assignment process. For example, families with similar background characteristics could be paired, and then one member of each pair would be randomly assigned to the intervention or control group. If either the intervention or the control family drops out of the study, then both members of the pair would be dropped, ensuring that the remaining sample would still be unbiased. The drawback of this approach is that it may reduce the sample size and hence the statistical power of the study.

Preserving Randomization

Implementing random assignment is so difficult that, once it is achieved, we want to do all we can to help preserve it throughout the life of an evaluation. One consideration, requiring that we make trade-offs between generalizability and internal validity, has to do with when randomization takes place. For example, families interested in participating in the Even Start family literacy program could be randomized as soon as they are recruited for the program or after they have had the evaluation explained to them and have indicated their willingness to accept any of the intervention alternatives, or after they have completed a one-month tryout period during which they can try Even Start to see whether they truly are interested in the program. Early randomization draws on the largest possible pool of families (increased generalizability) but risks losing many families (decreased internal validity) who find out that they are not assigned to the desired group or leave the program after a tryout period. Late randomization winnows the pool of families (decreased generalizability) to those who are most likely to participate in the program (increased internal validity). Gueron and Pauly (1991) and Riecken and others (1974) give additional examples.

There are several ways to reduce the likelihood that subjects will refuse to go along with the randomization or refuse to participate in the study:

- Plan the study so that subjects who agree to participate in the randomization have a better chance of getting the desired intervention than they would have if the study had not existed. This works best when there is a waiting list and the intervention has a large number of openings relative to the number of subjects needed for the study.
- Offer a competing intervention to members of the control group, for example, a financial or in-kind incentive for participating in the study or a reduced or modified version of the treatment being studied.
- Offer control group subjects the opportunity to enroll in the desired intervention at a later time.

How Do Researchers Best Work with Program Staff?

The most difficult part of experimental research in the social sciences is implementing the planned experiment. This calls for:

- Explaining the purposes, advantages, and disadvantages of experiments to the staff who are implementing the program being studied and dealing with and countering objections to randomization
- Searching for situations in which randomization can be most easily implemented and providing incentives for program staff to go along with the experimental research
- Preparing and entering into a written evaluation agreement
- Ensuring the integrity of the randomization process
- Assessing the fidelity of the intervention being tested

Explaining Experiments and Dealing with
Common Objections to Random Assignment

Randomized experiments are tricky for evaluators to design and devilishly difficult for program staff to go along with. To be respectful of the requirements that we are asking program staff to accept and endure, research staff must appear in person to explain a planned random assignment study to program staff. When researchers explain the strengths and weaknesses of random assignment studies, program staff are better able to understand the rationale underlying random assignment and sometimes can be convinced to participate in random assignment designs on the basis of a clear and honest explanation of the reasons for and benefits of the experiment. Monetary or in-kind incentives can be helpful, and projects often are offered a financial honorarium, a computer, assistance with recruiting, or something else. Project staff can be offered the opportunity to meet on an ongoing basis with staff from other projects participating in the study, as well as the chance to get free publicity, for example, through published case studies. Researchers who are working with schools, classrooms, and community-based organizations can provide data about the students and families participating in an intervention, and school or classroom profiles can be prepared to help principals and teachers understand how their students are performing. Researchers can support participating schools by making presentations before local school boards or other agencies, pointing out the importance of the evaluation and ways in which the school system could benefit.

Most of the common objections that program staff make to random assignment in studies of program effectiveness do not dispute its utility as a

Greater Avenues for Independence

The Greater Avenues for Independence (GAIN) evaluation assessed the impacts of a mandatory welfare-to-work program (Riccio, Friedlander, and Freedman, 1994). More than thirty-two thousand recipients of Aid to Families with Dependent Children (AFDC) were randomly assigned to the treatment (twenty-four thousand) or to a control group (eight thousand). Adults assigned to the treatment group were provided with basic education, job search, and skills training. Adults in the control group were precluded from receiving these services, but they could seek other services on their own. Data were collected over four and a half years. Findings were that GAIN significantly increased earnings and reduced AFDC benefit payments for single parents. Impacts were statistically significant, but smaller, for two-parent families.

tool for understanding causal connections. Instead, objections take other forms—for example, that random assignment is unethical or means denying services to some individuals. These statements are generally made in an attempt to retain control over which subjects are to be served by a given social program. When there is excess demand for a social intervention, program operators are in the position of denying services to eligible families every day as they make decisions about which families are the neediest or the most deserving. As long as a randomized experimental study of such an in-demand program does not reduce the total number of subjects served, then there is no denial of services: the same aggregate number of children and families are served with or without an experiment. What an experiment does change is the mechanism for selecting which families receive the services; random assignment is used to decide who participates in the program instead of the judgment of program staff. Thus, when program operators say that random assignment is unethical or involves denying services, they usually are saying that they do not want to give up the power to determine which families are served.

An underlying, and typically unvoiced, objection to random assignment is that program staff or funders often would rather assume that social programs are effective instead of worrying about whether scarce resources are being spent in the most appropriate manner. This is understandable, since scientific skepticism seems to counteract the ability of program operators to do their best work. This issue needs to be discussed openly and honestly with program staff. While the idea of subjecting what appears to some to be an obviously successful social program or a new intervention to a rigorous test of effectiveness is likely foreign to them, an acknowledgment of the need for such testing is the key justification for most social science experiments.

Another objection to random assignment is that assignment of any children to a control group feels wrong to program staff and the families they serve. The argument that randomization is like a lottery and hence is a fair way of determining which families get an intervention that is in short supply does not work in many social program settings because a lottery usually has only one winner, and the losers can take solace in the fact that they are in the great majority. But those assigned to the control group in a randomized study of a social program do not view their assignment the same way they view a lottery loss, since the odds of winning the lottery are minuscule, whereas the odds of being randomly assigned to the desired social program are usually fifty-fifty.

Situations Conducive to Randomized Experiments

There are circumstances that reduce the difficulty of implementing random assignment studies. Suppose an intervention program is in short supply and there is a list of subjects waiting to participate. This can happen with Head

Start projects in large metropolitan areas. If being placed on a waiting list means that a family is likely to miss a substantial portion of the Head Start year, then being part of a study in which children are randomly assigned from the waiting list to be in Head Start or in a control group might well be preferable to being on the waiting list with certainty. The absence of a waiting list does not mean that subjects are uninterested in a program. It often means that program staff members do not want to spend time and energy on recruiting until they have openings. Thus, it sometimes is possible for researchers to work with program staff, help to recruit subjects, and inform them about the planned study, and in this way generate a waiting list.

Another fortuitous situation occurs when a treatment can be delayed with no ill effect on the participants. This is likely the situation in a school that wishes to test the short-term effectiveness of a one-semester school health curriculum. In this case, it would be possible to randomly assign students to take the school health course in the fall semester or the spring semester. Parents, students, and school administrators rarely object to this kind of a design.

It sometimes is possible to conduct a large-scale experiment while minimizing the unpleasant effects of random assignment for a project. Suppose that a social program has many local projects, for example, the Head Start program has about sixteen hundred local projects, and the Even Start program has about a thousand projects. An experimental evaluation of these programs could be done be selecting a relatively large number of projects and randomly assigning only a few subjects within each project. Random assignment of only a half-dozen or so children might make participation in an experiment more palatable to program staff.

Modifying the design in response to the concerns of project or school staff helps to encourage cooperation with an experiment. Such willingness on the part of evaluators to make design concessions demonstrates sensitivity to local concerns and allows local staff to deal with cases where random assignment creates the greatest difficulty. For example, a small number of students and families perceived by program staff to be most in need of intervention services could be identified, set aside from the pool of families to be included in the evaluation, and provided with the intervention. Such modifications entail an analytic cost—in this case, the evaluation would not be able to estimate the impact of the intervention on the neediest students and families. However, if the number of exemptions from random assignment is small enough, it will have little effect on the evaluation.

Assigning higher-level units is another way to enhance the acceptability of random assignment. For example, a federal agency could hold a grant competition to test three different approaches to early education. School districts interested in improving their early education programming would be encouraged to apply, with the understanding that they could receive a grant

Nurse Home Visiting

This study tested the effects of nurse home visits on pregnant women and their children (Olds and others, 1999). Four hundred families were randomly assigned to four treatment groups: (1) developmental screening, (2) treatment 1 plus free transportation for prenatal and well-child care, (3) treatment 2 plus bimonthly home visits by nurses during pregnancy, and (4) treatment 3 plus nurse home visits through age two. Data were collected from birth to age four. Evaluation findings were that the program benefits the neediest families (low-income unmarried women) but provides little benefit for the broader population. Among low-income unmarried women, the program helps reduce rates of childhood injuries and ingestions that may be associated with child abuse and neglect, and helps mothers defer subsequent pregnancies and move into the workforce. Children also benefited from the program: by the time they were age fifteen, they had fewer arrests and convictions, smoked and drank less, and had fewer sexual partners. Researchers concluded that the use of nurses as home visitors is key and that services should be targeted to the neediest populations.

only if they were willing to implement any of the three approaches. School districts that received grants would then be randomly assigned to implement one of the three approaches. This strategy allows an experiment to be implemented in a setting where all participating schools receive a presumably beneficial intervention.

Finally, experimental evaluations are more likely to be accepted by program staff when such studies have political backing and monetary implications. For example, the ongoing experimental evaluation of the Head Start program is characterized by a high degree of cooperation on the part of local Head Start staff. In large part, this cooperation was the result of strong statements from the Department of Health and Human Services that informed Head Start grantees that cooperation with the study was a condition for the continued receipt of funding.

Preparing a Written Evaluation Agreement

Once evaluation staff and program staff have met, discussed the evaluation, agreed on a design and on incentives, reviewed the measured to be used, and so on, each of these aspects of the evaluation ought to be formalized in a written evaluation agreement so that there is a clear and complete understanding of the intervention and the evaluation. The agreement should:

- Spell out the roles and responsibilities of each actor in the evaluation: evaluation staff, program staff, funding agency, and study participants.
- Describe the intervention being assessed, the roles of each group in implementing the intervention, and the expected duration of the intervention.
- Specify the evaluation design, the measures to be made, and the frequency of measurement.
- Document agreements about incentives, honoraria, publicity, confidentiality, and data to be shared with program developers.
- Describe the processes agreed on for recruiting families, children, students, teachers, schools, projects, or communities to participate in the study and for randomly assigning participants to intervention and control conditions.

Ensuring the Integrity of the Random Assignment Process

Random assignment is more likely to be successfully implemented if it is done by researchers and research organizations with prior experience in conducting experimental studies. Certain research organizations have built the capacity to and reputation for conducting random assignment studies, and Greenberg, Shroder, and Onstott (1999) reported that almost half of the social experiments started in the United States since 1983 have been done by three large research organizations. This does not mean that only these groups are qualified to conduct experimental evaluations, but it does mean that experience is important. Randomized experimental research in the social sciences is one of those areas where textbook learning is helpful, but there is no substitute for real-world experience.

Another condition that strengthens the likelihood of a successful randomized experiment is when randomization is under the control of researchers rather than program implementers (Conner, 1977). Implementers are likely to make exceptions or may misunderstand random assignment rules, even if researchers carefully prepare those rules. The research team does not have to be physically present in order to control the random assignment. Program staff can be responsible for recruiting subjects, explaining the experimental alternatives, and transmitting lists of study subjects to the research team by fax, e-mail, or other means. The research team then does the random assignment and sends back listings of research subjects, sorted into treatment and control groups. A related approach is for the research team to prepare a random assignment computer program for use by program staff who recruit subjects and enter basic data on a microcomputer that does the random assignment on the spot.

The way in which random assignment is implemented depends on the method used to recruit applicants for an intervention. Sometimes a large pool of applicants is recruited. In these cases, information on the entire pool can be sent to the research team at the same time, simplifying the random assignment. The process is more complicated when applicants are recruited to enter a program on a rolling basis. In these cases, a random assignment algorithm has to be developed so that applicants are told their treatment or control status soon after they apply. However, simple assignment rules, such as assigning the first applicant to the treatment, the second to control, and the third to treatment, are easily manipulated by program staff who have control over the flow of applicants. More complex assignment systems are less subject to local control. For example, random assignment of families to an intervention could be done in blocks of four, where the order of treatment and control assignment is random within each block.

Ensuring That the Intervention Is Implemented Properly

Interventions in education and other social sciences generally involve complex processes designed to change human behaviors or improve learning or development. Furthermore, teachers or other social service professionals or paraprofessionals implement these interventions, each with unique skills, experience, and training. Therefore, it is hardly surprising that the implementation of social science interventions can exhibit a great deal of variability across sites. Acknowledging the existence of this variability, our ability to draw correct causal inferences from a randomized evaluation still depends on

---

Parents as Teachers

Two evaluations assessed the impacts of Parents as Teachers (PAT), a home visiting parent education program that offers monthly home visits from birth through a child's third birthday (Wagner and Clayton, 1999). One evaluation randomly assigned 497 families to PAT (298) and control (199) groups. Home visits covered lessons from the national PAT curriculum, and program participants received an average of twenty visits over three years. Control group families did not participate in the home visits. A second evaluation randomly assigned 704 families to PAT (177), case management (174), PAT plus case management (175), or a control group (178). Program participants received an average of ten visits over two years. The evaluations revealed small and inconsistent positive effects on parent knowledge, attitudes, and behavior and no gains in child development or health. Some subgroups (children in Spanish-speaking Latino families) benefited more than others.

proper implementation of the intervention being evaluated. Hence, in multisite randomized studies, evaluators have to be concerned with the amount of cross-site variation that occurs in the implementation of an intervention.

The degree to which a particular intervention has specific and consistent programmatic features that can easily be replicated has a significant impact on the fidelity of its implementation in multiple sites. Some interventions have clearly defined components, complete with curricular materials, lesson plans, and training manuals, whereas others have general guidelines, organizational features, and recommended instructional approaches but not a specified curriculum. The more specific a program is, the easier it is to measure its implementation.

In a randomized evaluation, quantifiable information on the extent to which the intervention is implemented should be collected and used analytically to explain outcome differences across sites. Depending on the nature of the intervention, implementation data can be collected through surveys of teachers and students, interviews with school administrators, logs of time spent on various activities, attendance logs, and so on.

The Worth of Randomized Experiments

Randomized experiments are the most practical kind of studies for assessing the effectiveness of a social intervention. They require mutual respect, teamwork, coordination, understanding, and sympathy on the part of both evaluators and program staff. They are not easy to design, they are not easy to implement, they are not easy to maintain, and they are not inexpensive. Nevertheless, they produce information that can be believed, information that provides unbiased estimates of the effectiveness of a program, and information that is convincing to policymakers.

References

Barnett, W. S. "Long-Term Effects of Early Childhood Programs on Cognitive and School Outcomes." *The Future of Children: Long-Term Outcomes of Early Childhood Programs,* 1995, *5*(3), 25–50.

Bell, S., and Puma, M. *Building Futures: The Head Start Impact Study. Analysis Plan: Discussion Draft.* Washington, D.C.: Urban Institute, Feb. 2002.

Bickman, L. (ed.). *Validity and Social Experimentation: Donald Campbell's Legacy.* Thousand Oaks, Calif.: Sage, 2000.

Bloom, H. "Accounting for No-Shows in Experimental Evaluation Designs." *Evaluation Review,* 1984, *8*(2), 225–246.

Boruch, R. F. "Bibliography: Illustrative Randomized Field Experiments for Program Planning and Evaluation." *Evaluation,* 1974, *2*, 83–87.

Boruch, R. F., and Wothke, W. "Randomization and Field Experimentation." *New Directions for Program Evaluation,* 1985, *28.*

Campbell, F. A., and others. "The Development of Cognitive and Academic Abilities: Growth Curves from an Early Childhood Educational Experiment." *Developmental Psychology,* 2001, *37*(2), 231–242.

Carnine, D. "Bridging the Research-to-Practice Gap." *Exceptional Children,* 1997, *63*(4), 513–521.

Coalition for Evidence-Based Policy. *Bringing Evidence-Driven Progress to Education: A Recommended Strategy for the U.S. Department of Education.* Washington, D.C.: Coalition for Evidence-Based Policy, Nov. 2002.

Cohen, J. *Statistical Power Analysis for the Behavioral Sciences.* Orlando, Fla.: Academic Press, 1977.

Conner, R. F. "Selecting a Control Group: An Analysis of the Randomization Process in Twelve Social Reform Programs." *Evaluation Quarterly,* 1977, *1,* 195–244.

Cook, T. D., and Campbell, D. T. *Quasi-Experimentation: Design and Analysis Issues for Field Settings.* Boston: Houghton Mifflin, 1979.

Cook, T. D., and Payne, M. R. "Objecting to the Objections to Using Random Assignment in Educational Research." In F. Mosteller and R. F. Boruch (eds.), *Evidence Matters: Randomized Trials in Education Research.* Washington, D.C.: Brookings Institution Press, 2002.

Cronbach, L. J., and others. *Toward Reform of Program Evaluation.* San Francisco: Jossey-Bass, 1980.

Dynarski, M., Gleason, P., Rangarajan, A., and Wood, R. *Impacts of Dropout Prevention Programs: Final Report.* Princeton, N.J.: Mathematica Policy Research, 1998.

Dynarski, M., and others. *When Schools Stay Open Late: The National Evaluation of the 21st-Century Community Learning Centers Program: First Year Findings.* Princeton, N.J.: Mathematica Policy Research and Decision Information Resources, 2003.

Faddis, B. J., and Ahrens-Gray, P. *Evaluation of Head Start Family Child Care Demonstration: Final Report.* Portland, Ore.: RMC Research Corporation, Feb. 2000.

Goering, J., Feins, J., and Richardson, T. "Across-Site Analysis of Initial Moving to Opportunity Demonstration Results." *Journal of Housing Research,* 2002, *13*(1), 1–30.

Goodson, B. D., and others. "Effectiveness of a Comprehensive Five-Year Family Support Program on Low-Income Children and Their Families: Findings from the Comprehensive Child Development Program." *Early Childhood Research Quarterly,* 2000, *15*(1), 5–39.

Greenberg, D., and Shroder, M. *The Digest of Social Experiments.* (2nd ed.) Washington, D.C.: Urban Institute Press, 1997.

Greenberg, D., Shroder, M., and Onstott, M. "The Social Experiment Market." *Journal of Economic Perspectives,* 1999, *13*(3), 157–172.

Gueron, J. M. "The Politics of Random Assignment: Implementing Studies and Affecting Policy." In F. Mosteller and R. F. Boruch (eds.), *Evidence Matters: Randomized Trials in Education Research.* Washington, D.C.: Brookings Institution Press, 2002.

Gueron, J. M., and Pauly, E. *From Welfare to Work.* New York: Russell Sage Foundation, 1991.

Infant Health and Development Program. "Enhancing the Outcomes of Low-Birth-Weight, Premature Infants." *Journal of the American Medical Association,* 1990, *263*(22), 3035–3042.

Love, J. M., and others. *Making a Difference in the Lives of Infants and Toddlers and Their Families: The Impacts of Early Head Start: Executive Summary.* Washington, D.C.: Mathematica Policy Research, June 2002.

Lyon, R. "Overview of Reading and Literacy Initiatives." In Consortium of Reading Excellence, *Reading Research Anthology: The Why? of Reading Instruction.* Emeryville, Calif.: Arena Press, 1999.

Meinert, C. L. *Clinical Trials: Design, Conduct, and Analysis.* New York: Oxford University Press, 1986.

Mosteller, F., and Boruch, R. F. (eds.). *Evidence Matters: Randomized Trials in Education Research.* Washington, D.C.: Brookings Institution Press, 2002.

Myers, D., and Schirm, A. *The Short-Term Impacts of Upward Bound: An Interim Report.* Princeton, N.J.: Mathematica Policy Research, 1997.

National Research Council. *Preventing Reading Difficulties in Young Children.* Washington, D.C.: National Academy Press, 1998.

National Research Council. *From Neurons to Neighborhoods: The Science of Early Childhood Development.* Washington, D.C.: National Academy Press, 2000.

National Research Council. *Eager to Learn: Educating Our Preschoolers.* Washington, D.C.: National Academy Press, 2001.

Olds, D. L., and others. "Prenatal and Infancy Home Visitation by Nurses: Recent Findings." *The Future of Children: Home Visiting: Recent Program Evaluations,* 1999, *9*(1), 44–65.

Quint, J. C., Bos, J. M., and Polit, D. *New Chance: Final Report on a Comprehensive Program for Disadvantaged Young Mothers and Their Children.* New York: Manpower Demonstration Research Corporation, July 1997.

Ramey, C. T., and Campbell, F. A. "Preventive Education for High-Risk Children: Cognitive Consequences of the Carolina Abecedarian Project." *American Journal of Mental Deficiency,* 1988, *88*(5), 515–523.

Ramey, S., and others. *Head Start Children's Entry into Public School: A Report on the National Head Start/Public Early Childhood Transition Study.* Birmingham, Ala.: Civitan International Research Center, Nov. 2000.

Riccio, J., Friedlander, D., and Freedman, S. *GAIN: Benefits, Costs and Three*

Year Impacts of a Welfare to Work Program. New York: Manpower Demonstration Research Corporation, 1994.

Riecken, H. W., and others. *Social Experimentation: A Method for Planning and Evaluating Social Innovations.* Orlando, Fla.: Academic Press, 1974.

Shadish, W. R., Cook, T. D., and Campbell, D. T. *Experimental and Quasi-Experimental Designs for Generalized Causal Inference.* Boston: Houghton Mifflin, 2002.

Slavin, R. E., and Madden, N. A. (eds.). *One Million Children: Success for All.* Thousand Oaks, Calif.: Corwin, 2001.

St. Pierre, R. G., Cook, T. D., and Straw, R. B. "An Evaluation of the Nutrition Education and Training Program." *Evaluation and Program Planning,* 1981, *4,* 335–344.

St. Pierre, R. G., and Layzer, J. I. "Improving the Life Chances of Children in Poverty: Assumptions and What We Have Learned." *Social Policy Report: Society for Research on Child Development,* 1998, *12*(4), 1–25.

St. Pierre, R. G., and others. *National Evaluation of the Even Start Family Literacy Program: Final Report.* Cambridge, Mass.: Abt Associates, 1995.

St. Pierre, R. G., and others. *Third National Even Start Evaluation: Program Impacts and Implications for Improvement.* Cambridge, Mass.: Abt Associates, 2003.

Swartz, J. P., Bernstein, L., and Levin, M. *Evaluation of the Head Start Family Service Center Demonstration projects. Volume 1: Final Report from the National Evaluation.* Cambridge, Mass.: Abt Associates, 1998.

Vinovskis, M. A. "Missing in Practice: Development and Evaluation at the U.S. Department of Education." In F. Mosteller and R. F. Boruch, (eds.), *Evidence Matters: Randomized Trials in Education Research.* Washington, D.C.: Brookings Institution Press, 2002.

Wagner, M. M., and Clayton, S. L. "The Parents as Teachers Program: Results from Two Demonstrations." *The Future of Children: Home Visiting: Recent Program Evaluations,* 1999, *9*(1), 91–115.

Wasik, B. H., Ramey, C. T., Bryant, C. M., and Sparling, J. J. "A Longitudinal Study of Two Early Intervention Strategies: Project CARE." *Child Development,* 1990, *61,* 201–217.

7

Meta–Analysis, Systematic Reviews, and Research Syntheses

Robert F. Boruch, Anthony Petrosino

A variety of phrases have been used to describe reviews that are scientifically disciplined, transparent, and uniform in regard to searching literatures, assembling studies for review, coding and combining studies, and interpreting and reporting the results. Here, we adopt the definitions given in the *Dictionary of Epidemiology* and quoted in Chalmers, Hedges, and Cooper (2002):

> *Systematic review:* The application of strategies that limit bias in the assembly, critical appraisal, and synthesis of all relevant studies on a specific topic. Meta-analysis may be, but is not necessarily, used as part of this process.

> *Meta-analysis:* The statistical synthesis of the data from separate but similar (that is, comparable studies), leading to a quantitative summary of the pooled results.

The definition of a systematic review is pertinent to a meta-analysis in that good meta-analysis usually depends on a good systematic review. The definition of *research synthesis* here capitalizes on Cooper and Hedge's characterization:

Work reported in this chapter has been funded partly by the Institute for Education Sciences (U.S. Education Department), the Rockefeller Foundation, Knight Foundation, and Smith-Richardson, among others. The views expressed here do not necessarily reflect the views of these organizations.

> *Research synthesis:* An attempt to "integrate empirical research for the purpose of creating generalizations . . . [in a way that] is initially non-judgmental vis a vis the outcomes of the synthesis and intends to be exhaustive in the coverage of the research base" (1994, p. 5).

Implicit in this complicated definition is the idea that generalization is based on and informs one or more theories, and vice versa.

The word *bias* in the basic definition of *systematic review,* and implied in the other definitions, has several distinct and important meanings that are made plain in the best of the guidelines on how to do reviews. Identifying and depending on only reports that suit the reviewer's ideological or theoretical preference is an obvious source of bias, for example. That tactic has been exploited shamelessly, of course, in political, professional, and even ostensibly dispassionate arenas such as the university. Paying attention only to reports that are published in refereed academic journals also implies a biased sample (or census) of pertinent reports; those not published in journals are ignored or not identified.

Bias also refers to the design of each study in an assembly of studies considered in a review and the statistical estimates of an intervention's effect that is produced by each. Randomized trials, for instance, produce statistically unbiased estimates of the relative effect of an intervention when they are carried out well. The statistical bias in estimates of effect that are produced by alternative approaches, such as a before-after evaluation, cannot always be identified, much less estimated.

Simple definitions are necessary. They are not sufficient to carry out systematic reviews, meta-analysis, and research syntheses. As Light and Pillemer (1984) suggest, there is science of reviewing research, including evaluations. The rationales, the principles, and the procedures that are used, the steps taken from start to finish, and the scientific standards of evidence have to be made clear.

Why Bother to be Conscientious in Reviewing? What Is the Value Added?

The rationales for conscientiousness hinge on the fact that examining an assembly of related, well-conducted studies is more productive than relying on a single study—that is, examining the assembly permits us to map the evidential terrain. Being conscientious in exploiting the state of the art in meta-analysis and systematic reviews and syntheses also reduces mistakes. Each value added is considered in what follows.

Multiple Evaluations versus a Single Evaluation

Other things being equal, examining multiple, independent, and high-quality evaluations of an intervention or a class of interventions is a better way to understand an intervention's effects than examining just one high-quality evaluation of it. Findings from a single study done in one place, by one team, with one actualization of the intervention, usually cannot be generalized to other settings, other teams, or other actualizations. Replication or near replication is important to science if the aim is to make careful statements about how often, to what degree, and in what circumstances the intervention works. Meta-analysis, disciplined systematic reviews, and research syntheses try to get beyond the single study.

A massive randomized trial on a conditional income transfer program to help children stay out of the agricultural fields and in school may work in Mexico, for example. But without similar trials in Honduras, say, we will not have a basis for generalization on empirical grounds as opposed to theoretical ones (Rawlings, forthcoming). Mandatory arrest of an offender for domestic violence may work in Minneapolis, based on a trial there. But it may not, and did not, work to reduce violence to judge from subsequent trials in five other cities (Sherman, Schmidt, and Rogan, 1992).

Dry Land, Deep Water, and the Swamps

Part of the value of high-end systematic reviews, meta-analyses, and research syntheses lies in determining where good evidence has been produced on the effects of interventions, where good evidence is absent, and where the evidence is ambiguous—respectively, the dry land, deep water, and swamp.

Petrosino, Turpin-Petrosino, and Buehler (2002), for instance, examined hundreds of abstracts of studies of Scared Straight programs for their Cochrane/Campbell review. Both the Cochrane Collaboration in health care and the Campbell Collaboration in the social sector stress inclusiveness in searches of the literature so as to ensure that all relevant reports on studies are identified. Most of these studies were not designed well, and most concluded that the program worked to reduce delinquent behavior.

The authors discovered some dry land by focusing on randomized trials in this assemblage of studies. They found clear evidence that such programs have no discernible positive effect and in some cases even increase the likelihood that youth will commit crime. That is, the programs effects are negative despite claims, based on untrustworthy evaluations, to the contrary.

The value of some systematic reviews lies in establishing that no high-quality evaluations have been carried out on a particular topic. Claims that the water is deep is one thing. Producing evidence that the water is indeed deep, based on transparent standards and procedures, is another. So, for example, hundreds of articles and reports have been written about teacher development programs and their purported effects. Credibly maintaining that none of these were based on relatively unequivocal evidence requires deep searches of published and unpublished reports, surveys and personal networks, and other resources. Nonetheless, a thorough search is essential in justifying a country's ministry or a department of education's investments in such programs.

Comprehensive school reform in the United States had been a topic of serious interest since 1994 when the U.S. Congress passed a law that would support this initiative. Thousands of schools engaged in reform efforts, and many based their efforts on "studies." Until the 1999 review by Herman and others, none of the studies had been subject to a serious review. The review's authors began the effort to find the dry spots in the swamps, with financial support from the American Federation of Teachers, American Association of School Administrators, and other groups that were willing to fund an independent review of evidence. Only one of twenty-four comprehensive school reform efforts appears to have been based on randomized trials, to judge from the report by Herman and others (1999). New trials were carried out after this report so as to understand that one intervention, the School Development Program, worked when implemented well and did not work when implemented poorly (Cook, Murphy, and Hunt, 2000).

Flaws in Conventional Literature Reviews

Few of us are without sin, of commission or omission, in reviewing a body of literature. We fail at times by relying on searches based on the World Wide Web, when it is known that hand searches are superior. People and organizations often rely only on published literature when we understand that unpublished reports are potentially important. We often fail to understand systematic review or meta-analysis in basic scientific terms: framing a question properly, identifying a target population of studies, and sampling the studies well. And people who do literature reviews often fail to make standards of evidence and procedures explicit, much less transparent. The modern approaches assist us in being virtuous, or at least understanding what virtue is.

Farrington and Petrosino (2000) put the imperfections of "common reviews of the literature" in contrast to what is produced by the international Cochrane Collaboration in health care. Both the Cochrane Collaboration in health and its younger sibling, the Campbell Collaboration in the social, behavioral, and education sectors, have developed operating principles that contrast, sometimes sharply, with the practices associated with conventional literature review. Farrington and Petrosino point out that common reviews are usually "one-off" exercises that fail to be updated or to exploit new technologies of searching, reviewing, and summarizing studies. Cochrane and Campbell, in contrast, try to capitalize on contemporary technical methods and attempt to update reviews. The authors remind us that conventional reviews are usually based on one country's research and on English-language publications. The Cochrane Collaboration and the Campbell Collaboration are intensely international in their intent and operations and in products, partly because studies of the effects of interventions and reviews of them transcend geopolitical boundaries.

Finally, Farrington and Petrosino point out that conventional reviews are published in a variety of outlets that each have their own jargon and standards of evidence. This presents substantial difficulties for policy people, practitioners, and researchers who work across disciplines. Cochrane uses uniform procedures and ways to present the information so as to make it easy for readers.

When Light and Pillemer (1984) wrote *Summing Up,* they announced that reviews were subjective because independent reviewers might not have common standards of evidence and might not have an opportunity to make the standards plain, much less to agree or disagree on the standards. They showed that reviews were often statistically unsound because they ignored basic rules of statistical evidence. And they maintained that the traditional review was not an efficient way to extract evidence. Things have improved since 1984.

How Are the Best Approaches Employed at Their Best?

As a practical matter, one can learn about systematic reviews, syntheses, and meta-analyses in several ways. Reading is good. Listening is good. Actually becoming engaged, at the margins or centrally, is very good. Most of the readers of this chapter recognize the options. Taking advantage of the options given here is no mean task, however.

Read or Take a Course

Evaluators and other applied researchers who know nothing about a systematic review but want to learn should read a conscientious systematic review. Since 1993, the best and most uniform of the genre on health care are given in Web-accessible form at http://cochrane.org. In the social, behavioral, and education sectors, cross-nationally, the Campbell Collaboration has tried to develop protocols (plans) for systematic reviews that are also uniform and transparent, and aspire to high standards of evidence.

A younger effort, but one with some money and lots of moxie, is at the Institute for Education Sciences' What Works Clearinghouse (WWC). The publications on these sites are peer reviewed. Variations on the products of each are also published in peer-reviewed journals.

The contents of these reviews will improve as the state of the art improves. For instance, the Quality of Reporting on Meta-Analysis (QUOROM) Group has developed guidelines to advance agreement on exactly what a meta-analysis should contain (Moher and others, 1999). We capitalize on this guidance here. Related efforts include the development of uniform guidelines for evidence reports produced by the WWC, which are likely to be adopted or tailored to special applications by others (http://w-w-c.org.).

People who are serious in their interest read a book. Perish this thought for those who look only at a Web site. The books referenced in this chapter, and the books referenced by their authors, belong on one's five-foot shelf on this topic.

Short courses on systematic reviews, meta-analysis, and the activities they require, such as hand searches of journals and adherence to explicit standards, are valuable. The Cochrane Collaboration in health care offers short courses at annual meetings and at other times (http://cochrane.org). The Campbell Collaboration's effort to foster systematic reviews has been supported by short courses and presessions at each annual meeting since 2000. (See also the Campbell Methods Group Web site at http://www.missouri.edu/percent7EC2Method/ and the Proposal on Training by Becker and Pigott, 2002.) The WWC is developing training courses for reviewing education evaluations in its purview. At least one professional organization, the Society for Prevention Research, initiated presessions led by Betsy Becker at Michigan State University on the topic at its Eleventh Annual Meeting in 2003 (http://www.preventionscience.org/meeting.php#ProgramHighlights).

Contribute to a Meta-Analysis, Systematic Review, or Research Synthesis

Contributing to a meta-analysis, systematic review, or research synthesis that is governed by high standards can be demanding. The opportunities for both voluntary and paid contributions are ample. The Cochrane Collaboration and Campbell Collaboration have depended on both kinds of contributions.

Some government initiatives invite contributions. In the United States, for example, the WWC has invested in developing procedures and articulating high standards of evidence for reviews. Interested people can contribute through a WWC Network and in other ways because all relevant information is public. In the Nordic countries, Copenhagen's Nordic Campbell Center (http://nc2.org) seeks talented people who want to contribute to systematic reviews that are far better than the reviews of literature that are common.

Contributing can be done at a variety of stages in a review.

Produce a Meta-Analysis, Systematic Review, or Research Synthesis

The major steps in a systematic review, meta-analysis, or research synthesis are easy to lay out but not easy to take. Analogous steps are not easy to take in field evaluations and other applied research. The following material is based on Sutton and others (2002) in the health sector and Lipsey and Wilson (2001) in the social sector, who themselves depend on others referenced in their books and in this chapter. We also capitalize on the Quality of Reporting of the Meta-Analysis Group's guidelines for reporting on a meta-analysis (Moher and others, 1999).

Specify the Topic Area. In the WWC, for instance, specifying the topic means identifying:

- A rationale for addressing the problem
- The specific questions that will be addressed
- The relevant outcome variables
- The relevant target populations and subpopulations of interest
- The relevant interventions or a class of interventions that address the problem

In justifying a systematic review of peer-assisted learning, for example, evidence on teachers' frequent use of the approach was reported in protocols developed by Ginsberg-Block and Rohrbeck (2003). The protocol then had to pose specific questions about the effects of the approach, relative to controls or alternative conditions, outcomes such as mathematics and reading achievement, and target populations or subpopulations such as elementary school children at risk of academic failure including low-income families and children whose first language is not English.

Specify the Search Strategy. Specifying what literatures that will be searched, how, and with what resources is crucial. One may focus on only reports published in peer-reviewed social science journals, or on reports issued by organizations with high-quality editorial screening, or on both. Doing both is better, at least in the United States, where some evaluation organizations have peer review systems with standards that go beyond the standards of some science journals. The people who do Cochrane or Campbell systematic reviews strive to include other studies that are unpublished and found only in researchers' file drawers if resources permit.

One may undertake hand searches of peer-reviewed journals, knowing that the hand search yields a far more reliable complete assembly of relevant studies than a machine-based search. The best systematic reviews under Campbell and Cochrane guidelines make plain what literatures are covered in a search.

Beyond identifying the target for the literature search, the way the search is conducted has to be specified. What key words, constructed how, and why will be used with what electronic search engine and with what electronic databases? Randomized trials are especially hard to locate given that relevant key words in a social science journal often do not appear in an article's abstract, key word lists, or title. Consequently, trying out different words in each database may be warranted. In searching for trials in the crime and justice arena, Petrosino's search (1995) suggested that the following key words had a high yield: *random, experiment, controlled, evaluation, impact, effect,* and *outcome.* Depending on the vernacular in the discipline, databases, search engines, and so on, the list could be appreciably different from this. (See, for instance, Petrosino, Turpin-Petrosino, and Buehler, 2002, based on a joint Cochrane-Campbell Collaboration review.)

Will organizations that produce relevant evaluations also be surveyed to learn about them? Many organizations, for-profit and otherwise, do not publish reports widely and do not submit manuscripts for publication in peer-reviewed journals. School district offices of research and vendors of education software are among these. Similarly, many local health care providers may be well positioned to do a randomized trial and contribute to a systematic review, but they do not issue a report that is readily accessible. Police jurisdictions that cooperate in evaluations of crime prevention interventions are also vulnerable in this respect. Nonetheless, conscientious reviewers must learn about these efforts. The systematic review team has to decide whether to survey these resources and how to do so.

In their systematic review of evidence on discrete education software, for example, Murphy and others (2002) list the vendors whose Web sites were surveyed or whose staff were otherwise contacted for reports that were not accessible through journals, conference proceedings, and the like. The WWC posts the topical protocol for each review that is planned on its public Web site. It tells the formal WWC Network about each, so as to invite people to submit studies that seem pertinent for inclusion in a review.

Develop Inclusion and Exclusion Criteria for Studies in the Review. This step focuses on what studies will be regarded as potentially legitimate ingredients for a systematic review. Efforts to make standards more uniform and explicit, and clearly scientific in orientation, have been made by the international Cochrane Collaboration and the Campbell Collaboration, and the What Works Clearinghouse, among others.

The WWC approach is reflected partly in the Design and Implementation Assessment Device (DIAD). This tool requires that each study in a review be included or excluded on the basis of four global standards, which are themselves informed by a series of detailed questions whose answers depend on the contents of each study's report.

The WWC standards have the following implication. A study that (1) fails to report on construct validity that ties interventions and outcomes, (2) fails to employ an evaluation design that permits statistically unbiased and unequivocal estimates of effects, (3) does not test the intervention on appropriate target populations, and (4) fails to report information sufficient to estimate effect sizes is ruled out of a review. Studies that do report information on all these are tentatively included in the review.

Once a study is included, more detailed questions on implementation fidelity, attrition rates, quality of measurement, and so on are posed. Answers are coded so as to permit further determinations about how much one can depend on the study at hand (Valentine and Cooper, 2002). For instance, a randomized trial or quasi-experiment with a 50 percent difference in the attrition rates among groups that are being compared would be ruled out as a dependable resource by reviewers who understand how vulnerable this makes the study results—unless evidence can be produced to argue that plausible biases are indeed negligible.

As the definitions given here suggest, inclusion criteria in high-end systematic reviews focus on bias in estimates of the effects of interventions. Generalizability of the results is important in many studies, notably probability sample surveys. But it is secondary in systematic reviews of the effects of interventions because the value of an estimate that is biased but based on a large sample is still biased, and consequently misleading.

The WWC standards of evidence for including studies in a review are public. These standards are being considered for adoption by the Campbell Collaboration. The Cochrane Collaboration's handbook contains similar ingredients, put into the vernacular of health research (Clarke and Oxman, 2003), that have guided Cochrane reviews and were used in early reviews in the Campbell Collaboration such as Petrosino, Turpin-Petrosino, and Finckenauer (2000).

Compute Effect Size Estimates, Code Them, and Estimate Their Variances. An effect size in any science is estimated relative to some basis for comparison, reference, or benchmark. In a two-arm randomized trial in the social sector, for instance, the common estimate of effect size involves computing the difference between mean outcomes for the two interventions that are compared, and then dividing this difference by the square root of a pooled estimate of variance within groups. In the health care sector, odds ratios are more common. (See Lipsey and Wilson, 2001, for more detail on good professional practice.)

Neither of these statistical indicators (and many others) is easily understandable to many people. Graphical indicators are better. Some of them embody good statistical standards. (Figure 7.1, discussed later in this chapter, is a good example.)

Impact evaluation reports do not always contain sufficient information for the reviewer to estimate effect size. For example, over 40 percent of the evaluations of discrete educational software packages that Murphy and others (2002) reviewed were discarded. This was because they had neither comparison groups nor sufficient information to permit estimating effect size. When an evaluation report's contents are insufficient, the people who are doing the systematic review must address direct questions to the report's authors. Efforts to ensure that journals routinely require their authors to provide sufficient information are underway (Mosteller, Miech, and Nave, forthcoming).

Develop a Scheme for Coding Studies and Their Properties, and Then Screen. Research syntheses, systematic reviews, and meta-analyses direct attention to an assembly of studies. The assembly is often a mob. So-called evaluations of Scared Straight, for instance, included polemical essays, before-after studies, testimonials, randomized trials, and quasi-experimental studies. The Scared Straight program targets might include children from elementary school or high school. They might include programs that differ in frequency, intensity, or character of service, despite the common "Scared Straight" label.

The implication is that evaluations of the effects of interventions, when included in a disciplined review, need to be categorized in a variety of ways. As a practical matter, this means that the reviewer must code each evaluation in a way that is uniform and transparent.

In best practice, coding and abstracting each study considered for a systematic review typically involves development of coding schema, training of coders, and the use of at least two independent coders (double coding) so as to provide reliability checks. Cochrane Collaboration reviews do this. The codes include details of the health intervention, characteristics of the samples used in the study, and definitions of specific outcomes such as perinatal mortality and dose levels.

Consider an example. Wilson, Lipsey, and Soydan's award-winning review (2003) of the effect of mainstream delinquency programs on minorities, rather than majorities, is based on double coding about 150 features of each study in the review. The early detail in coding studies permitted the authors to focus on subsamples of minority youth in evaluations that included small to moderately sized samples of subpopulations. Coding categories in this review are similar to those used in Cochrane, at least with respect to the evaluation's design; for example, randomized trials are opposed to nonrandomized trials. They include detailed features of the interventions, such as the kinds of personnel delivering the treatment, format (group versus individual), site, and so on. Some of the coding is reflected in statistical description of the studies given in tables that Wilson, Lipsey, and Soydan provide.

For transparency, coding categories that are used in a systematic review and the way each study is coded for each category ought to be public. For the science of reviews, the categories ought to be uniform. The standards for coding studies that are embodied in the WWC are public, for example.

Expect to work hard at screening after this coding. The review by the U.S. General Accounting Office (GAO) of sixty-one Women, Infants, and Children (WIC) studies depended heavily on only thirty-seven, which were declared "relatively credible" (Hunt, 1997, p. 41). GAO's review of studies of the effect on accidents of age-related drinking laws in the states involved four hundred documents, "only 14 of which met all its criteria for inclusion. . ." in the review (Hunt, 1997, p. 148).

Lipsey's review depended initially on his "amassing more than eight thousand citations" and after screening depended on 443 that met their standard for good design and execution (Hunt, 1997, p. 129). Smith and Glass "amassed a thousand titles" and screened them on the basis of their standards of evidence at the time down to 375 (Hunt, 1997, p. 28). In a review of effects of a marital and family therapy, a year and a half of such efforts "netted Shadish a mighty haul of roughly two thousand references" (Hunt, 1997, p. 45). About 160 met reasonable and explicit standards of evidence and were included in the review.

Develop a Management Strategy and Procedures. Managing a single systematic review, meta-analysis, or research synthesis requires a strategy that does not differ in principle from the management requirements of a field study. The tasks include identifying who will do what tasks in the long task list, when, with what resources, and under what ground rules.

Information about the management of producing a single systematic review and in conducting high-end evaluations, including randomized trials, is not often published. After all, knowing how to do these things can be construed as intellectual and financial capital. Sharing this knowledge permits others to do equally good work. In a competitive environment, sharing such information could lead to financial bankruptcy. In a scientific environment, it is a fine intellectual virtue.

The best of systematic reviews based in universities have resources and schedules that depend on talented faculty, graduate students, academic schedules, and university business offices. The best of systematic reviews based in a research organization have resources and schedules that depend on talented people and staff, contract schedules, and the organization's business offices. The best of systematic reviews generated with support of federal government organizations depend on talented people, schedules for testimony for the Congress or legislatures, and the particular government's business office.

We have no practical advice on this except this: organizations vary in their capacities, just as individuals do. Learn what you and your organization can do to produce excellent systematic reviews, meta-analyses, and research syntheses. This is trite but important.

Develop an Analysis Strategy. The purpose of a systematic review, meta-analysis, and research synthesis is to reach conclusions that are based on a summary of results from an assembly of studies.

First, arrange one's thinking about the data at hand, studies of interventions, in terms of the target population of studies, the sample observed and the sample of the population that was not observed, and the effect sizes that the studies produce. Ensure that these effect sizes are constructed so as to make their interpretation plain. And ensure that outliers and artifacts of particular studies are identified and taken into account.

Second, focus attention on the distributions of the effect sizes. For instance, any given randomized trial on X produces an effect size. A confidence interval can be constructed for this effect size. The next five studies also produce effect sizes, each associated with a confidence interval. All this can plotted out in a chart of the distribution of effect sizes. Systematic reviews under the definition given earlier involve statistical description of the distribution of effect sizes. A meta-analysis involves combination of effect sizes and (often) the analysis of effect sizes as a function of the coded characteristics of the studies that are included in the review.

Describing the effect sizes and their distribution for an assembly of interventions in a class is essential for the Cochrane and Campbell Collaboration. Petrosino, Turpin-Petrosino, and Finckenauer (2000) did so in their review of Scared Straight (Figure 7.1). This satisfies the interest of some readers who want to know about when an intervention resulted in doing some good, relative to high standards of evidence, and when it did no good, relative to the same standards.

This description satisfies some appetites for evidence. Schools and social organizations that handle potential delinquents, for instance, would be interested to know that Scared Straight has no positive effects if they are seriously interested in evidence on the matter.

Beyond this, sophisticated statistical machinery and substantive understanding might be brought to bear on the question: What seems to "explain" the variation in effect size among studies that were reviewed? For instance, one may examine effect size for each study as a linear statistical function of characteristics of the study's design, such as whether the design is a randomized trial or not and sample size. One may examine effect size as a function of coded characteristics of the intervention.

Lösel and Beelman (2003), for instance, undertook a meta-analysis of eighty-four reports on randomized trials that were designed to estimate the effect of child skills training on antisocial behavior. They depended on different kinds of statistical models to understand the relationship between effect sizes (the dependent variable in their study) and characteristics of each study, the interventions, and the children in each study sample. They found

Figure 7.1. Effects of Scared Straight and Other Juvenile Awareness Programs on Juvenile Delinquency: Random Effects Models, "First Effect" Reported in the Study

Study	Treatment n/N	Control n/N	OR (95% CI Random)	Weight %	OR (95% CI Random)
Finckenauer 1982	19/46	4/35		9.8	5.45 (1.65, 18.02)
GERP & DC 1979	16/94	8/67		14.7	1.51 (0.61, 3.77)
Lewis 1983	43/53	37/55		15.3	2.09 (0.86, 5.09)
Michigan D.O.C 1967	12/28	5/30		9.5	3.75 (1.11, 12.67)
Orchowsky and Taylor 1981	16/39	16/41		15.2	1.09 (0.44, 2.66)
Vreeland 1981	14/39	11/40		13.9	1.48 (0.57, 3.83)
Yarborough 1979	27/137	17/90		21.6	1.05 (0.54, 2.07)
Total (95% CI)	147/436	98/358		100.0	1.72 (1.13, 2.62)

Test for heterogeneity chi-square = 8.50   df = 6   p = 0.2

Test for overall effect z = 2.55   p = 0.01

0.1   0.2   1   5   10

Favors Treatment   Favors Control

Note: n = number of failures; N = number of participants; CI = confidence intervals; Random = random effects model assumed.

Source: Petrosino, Turpin-Petrosino, and Finckenauer (2000).

that studies with smaller samples tended to be associated with larger effect sizes, for instance, and that dosage appeared not to be related to effect size. Interventions administered by study authors or research staff or supervised students were associated with larger effect sizes. No remarkable difference in associations appeared for the different kinds of interventions included: behavioral, cognitive, cognitive behavioral, and counseling.

As Lipsey (2003) and others point out, statistical modeling in this context has the same merits and shortcomings of modeling data that are based on passive observation in other contexts. That is, the studies under review are the units of observation, observed passively by the reviewer. The conventional regression analyses of effect size then can help to illustrate relationships. But misspecification of the model, unobserved variables that are related to variables in the model, and relations among the independent variables do not permit unequivocal statements about what causes the effect size to vary.

Interpret and Report the Results. In the best systematic reviews, reports of at least two kinds are produced. The first is exquisitely detailed and contains all information that would be sufficient for another reviewer to conduct an identical review. That is, the systematic review permits others to replicate it. As a practical matter, such detailed reviews are published in electronic libraries that, unlike hard copy reports and research journals, have no page limitations. In the best, the topical coverage is uniform and standards uniformly transparent, to make it easy for readers to move from one systematic review to the next. The Cochrane Collaboration has this character. The Campbell Collaboration aims to do so. The WWC has a similar aim.

A second kind of report, a summary in hard copy or electronic form (or both), is crucial to users of research who are not themselves researchers. Users require a summary that is uniform from one review to another and in language that is as plain as possible. The Cochrane Collaboration's reviews in recent years have included such summaries. The WWC plans to produce these in education. The Campbell Collaboration aspires to do so.

Reporting in the most sophisticated production of systematic reviews includes an entire system. That is, networks of users who were a party to choosing a topic for review and contributing to the review's design are part of a larger reporting system. Networks of users who were a party to a review's production, networks of potential users who might repackage and distribute the results, information brokers, and so on are part of "reporting" writ large. The hard problem is developing networks of users and information brokers.

The Institute of Education Sciences has invested resources in developing a network to ensure that products of the WWC are understood and influenced by a network of potential users. The Campbell Collaboration, which supports the WWC but is independent of it, has also initiated efforts through an Internationalization and Communications Group.

The practical advice on this is from the WWC: engage potential users at the front end.

Readers need no reminder that pictures are important. Figure 7.1, for example, makes it plain that most effect sizes and lower bounds on confidence intervals fall above the zero point, implying trustworthy evidence that the interventions had negative effects. An error bar chart lays out each study that is used in a systematic review along the vertical axis. The horizontal axis is numerical and standardized at zero to indicate no discernable difference between interventions that are being compared. The indicators to the left of zero reflect findings that are positive, that is, the intervention is better than the comparison or control group. The indicators to the right of zero reflect findings, that is, effect sizes, that the particular intervention under examination works worse than the comparison. The estimated effect size for each study is bounded by a confidence interval.

What Resources Can Be Employed to Do the Job Well?

Here we look at a variety of resources on which one might depend.

International Resources

Until the 1990s, no organization had taken a leadership role in routinely producing systematic reviews, meta-analyses, or research syntheses that meet standards that are uniform, transparent, and high in the sense of focusing on the least equivocal evidence. This changed in 1993 with the creation of the Cochrane Collaboration in the health care sector and in 2000 with the Campbell Collaboration in the social, criminological, and education sectors. It also changed in the sense that governments took an interest in high-end systematic reviews. This interest is related to, but different from, government interests in identifying model programs.

The international Cochrane Collaboration was formed in 1993 to prepare, maintain, and make accessible systematic reviews of evaluations of the effects of health-related interventions. As of 2003, it had produced over fifteen hundred systematic reviews based on explicit and uniform operating principles and transparent standards of evidence. One of the Cochrane Collaboration's electronic accessible libraries is unique in the world in covering randomized trials in health care. It contains over a quarter of a million entries. Its methods groups provide training at annual meetings and at other times. Cochrane people also do studies that advance the state of the art in a systematic review and their ingredients.

The international Campbell Collaboration is the Cochrane Collaboration's young sibling. Created in 2000, its aims are identical to Cochrane's: to prepare, maintain, and make accessible systematic reviews of studies of the effects of interventions. This is to inform people in their decisions about what works in arenas of crime and justice, education, and social welfare. Campbell people also do studies that help advance the state of the art in doing reviews, and they design the studies that are ingredients for reviews. See the Glazerman, Myers, and Levy (2002) protocol on comparing estimates of effect based on randomized trials against estimates of effect from parallel nonrandomized studies.

Several dozen reviews were put into the Campbell Collaboration's pipeline from 2002 to 2004. Procedures were developed to vet protocols for these reviews. Annual meetings in Philadelphia in 2000 and 2001 and Stockholm in 2002 included training sessions and workshops. An electronic archive on randomized and possibly randomized trials, C2-SPECTR, which includes about twelve thousand entries, has been created and made accessible to the public.

The Methods Groups of both the Campbell Collaboration and the Cochrane Collaboration learn from one another. Both are a resource for those who are interested in serious systematic reviews, meta-analyses, and research syntheses. For instance, methodological study of how estimates of an intervention's effect differ depending on whether the studies under review are randomized trials, or quasi-experiments, or econometric models based on surveys, are especially important. (See the Glazerman, Myers, and Levy (2002) protocol at the Campbell site. Also see issues of the Cochrane Collaboration's Methods Group newsletter at the Cochrane Web sites.)

Government Organizations and Government-Sponsored Entities

In the United States, a variety of government organizations have undertaken systematic reviews of the applied research and evaluation literature or have provided funds to others to do so. Some of these have helped to advance the state of the art. The GAO's cross-design synthesis of trials of interventions for breast cancer is a case in point (U.S. General Accounting Office, 1992; Droitcour, Silberman, and Chelimsky, 1993). Others have helped to develop a public appetite to better and more trustworthy summaries of evidence, such as GAO's work on WIC.

In 2002, the Institute of Education Sciences at the U.S. Education Department launched the WWC to provide a "central, independent, and trusted source of information" on effects of education interventions. The effort led to technical resources, such as uniform standards and procedures, for determining whether each evaluation study in an assembly of studies can be used as a basis for a causal inference about an intervention's effect. See http://w-w-c.org on the Design and Implementation Assessment Device and on procedures and organization.

Technical Resources

Technical resources include the contents of monographs, such as Lipsey and Wilson's *Practical Meta-Analysis* (2001). The book's appendixes contain a listing of databases that can be searched electronically for studies and the contents of manuals for coding the studies' characteristics, including study design, outcome variables, and effect sizes. The appendixes give detailed formulas on computing effect sizes and the code for an EXCEL program. A macro SPSS program is given in another appendix to support meta-analysis.

Sophisticated software developed partly for the health research sector, and applicable to the social sector, is available. Comprehensive Meta-Analysis (Biostat), for instance, helps to automate a review in entering a reference to a study and the study's relevant properties, importing abstracts from electronic databases, and identifying and coding study characteristics that will be used in the review. The graphical displays are automated and capitalize on the state of the art.

Many of the technical resources produced by individuals or small organizations are used by government agencies that commission or produce systematic reviews, advance the resources, and make them accessible to others. A case in point is the WWC, whose DIAD (Valentine and Cooper, 2002), for instance, frames four basic questions:

- Was the intervention or approach, and outcome, properly described?
- Was the intervention or approach the cause of the change in the outcome?
- Was the intervention or approach tested on relevant participants and in relevant environments?
- Could accurate effect sizes be derived from the study report?

It then drives deeper to pose more technical questions that help to ensure we understand each study in an assembly of studies used in a systematic review. The system for addressing these questions is automated.

Technological Resources Now and the Near Future

Web-oriented databases and search engines that furnish the ingredients for an research synthesis are low cost in that access to them is easy. PsychInfo and ERIC, for instance, are databases that are accessible in many universities and research and evaluation organizations. Each is accessed by different vendors' search engines. The costs and benefits of these may differ appreciably.

These electronic resources are less helpful than one might expect. Web-based search engines, for example, typically rely on the reviewers' specifying certain key words and on matching these to the same or similar words in the information on each study in a database. In particular, the machine attempts to match the reviewers' key words with those appearing in the title, abstract, or key word listing for a report on evaluation.

The machine typically does not search the full text of the evaluation report for the key words. As a consequence, studies are missed. For instance, a PsychInfo search of the *Journal of Educational Psychology* (1997–2000) for randomized trials yielded about thirty reports on trials. A search of the full text of the journal's contents for the same years yields one hundred trials (Turner and others, 2003). Electronic searches by C. Leow and R. Boruch of *American Education Research Journal* (1963–2000) yielded less than a third of the randomized trials in math and science education that were actually reported in the journal.

To complicate matters, abstracts of refereed journals in evaluation and applied research are not uniform. As a consequence, Web-based search engines that depend on key words and phrases in an abstract cannot be exploited well until certain information appears routinely in the abstract. Mosteller, Miech, and Nave (forthcoming) have proposed uniform structured abstracts for education journals, building on the experience of the *Lancet,* the *British Medical Journal,* and others. The Campbell Collaboration has begun to develop uniform synopses of evaluations to include C2-SPECTR (Turner and others, 2003).

One technological advance that constitutes a major resource in systematic reviews and meta-analyses is that peer-reviewed scientific journals can publish full texts of journal articles and books. This greatly facilitates full text searches, including immediate demarcation and reproduction of pertinent reports or portions of them. A hand search of the American Psychological Association's *Journal of Educational Psychology,* for instance, was relatively easy in locating randomized trials because the full text is on-line. The abstracts are insufficient for identifying trials, but the full text (the methods and procedures section) is sufficient for identifying trials. The same is true for recent issues of Sage Publications' *Evaluation Review.* Publication of the full text of books is not common. But organizations such as the National Academy of Sciences are leading the way in making these readily accessible on the Web.

Resources and Issues for the Future: Scenarios

Organizations, technical methods, and technologies will advance, of course, and eager readers will have to learn how to anticipate advances. Consider some plausible scenarios.

The first scenario lies in the fact that most systematic reviews, meta-analyses, and research syntheses of the disciplined sort that are considered have relied mainly on reports of studies. Most reviewers do not reanalyze microrecords from each study in the assembly of studies that they review. Relying on published reports is necessary. In any case, the published reports may be the only material at hand.

Part of the future lies in the reviewer's access to microrecords from each study that is used in a review. During the 1970s, for instance, evaluation studies of programs began to yield microrecord data that were made available at times for the secondary analysis of the data. Microrecords from original evaluations on the effects of capital punishment on crime in the United States, of randomized trials on the effects of cultural enrichment programs on children in Colombian barrios, of randomized trials on graduated taxation plans, and others were made accessible. The data were reanalyzed to confirm earlier analyses, test new hypotheses, and for other reasons (Boruch, Wortman, and Cordray, 1981).

During the 1980s, the National Academy of Sciences Committee on National Statistics (Fienberg, Martin, and Straf, 1985) reinforced the idea of open scientific inquiry partly by encouraging access to microrecords. More recently, Mosteller (1995) and Krueger (1999) reanalyzed microrecords from the Tennessee Class Size randomized trial to verify an earlier analysis by Finn and Achilles (1990), which found that reducing class size led to substantial effects on children's achievement. After 2000, the life sciences made a commitment to share data. (See Marshall, 2003, on the Universal Principle of Sharing Integral Data Expeditiously in the genome research arena and others.)

As a practical matter, the Web makes access to machine-readable microrecords on impact evaluations far more feasible. This means that people who undertake systematic reviews, meta-analyses, and research syntheses will be able to undertake deeper reviews that capitalize on microrecords rather than only on evaluation reports.

The research literature on systematic reviews, meta-analysis, and research synthesis cited here is disconnected from the research literature on data sharing and secondary analysis. Sieber (1991), for instance, covered data sharing that is, microrecord access, in anthropology, psychology, sociology, criminology, and education, and some of the normative and government standards that affected data sharing in the 1990s. None of the texts at hand on systematic reviews cites the Sieber collection. None of the authors in the Sieber volume cited the people who have advanced the state of the art in systematic reviews. The two crowds ought to talk to one another. Eventually they will.

To What End? Value Added and Usefulness

The indicators of a review's usefulness include learning unexpected lessons, the increasing frequency in the production of reviews, and their production in different academic disciplines.

Surprises

What can we learn from a disciplined meta-analysis or systematic review? Surprises are important.

The Cochrane Collaboration and Campbell Collaboration systematic review of Scared Straight (Petrosino, Turpin-Petrosino, and Finckenauer, 2000) focused on randomized trials. We learn that Scared Straight had negative effects: delinquency increased for youth exposed to the program. This is in sharp contrast to news coverage and reports by police and school people. These anecdotes and the nonrandomized trials suggested positive effects and extolled the program's virtues. The results of the randomized trials are more credible, of course, for the same reasons they are credible in the medical sector.

Roberts and Kwan (2002) reviewed randomized trials on driver education programs to understand whether they worked. Given substantial investments in such programs in the United Kingdom, the United States, and elsewhere, the public would expect that the programs are effective. Using Cochrane Collaboration standards and procedures, Roberts and Kwan found that the programs did not lead to lower accident rates among graduates. Because students got licenses earlier as a consequence of graduating from the programs, their exposure risk was higher, leading to more accidents. Achara and others (2002) suggest that the review has been greeted with sturdy indifference by the relevant government agencies that support driver education in England.

Shadish and his colleagues (1993) produced an award-winning systematic review showing that marital and family therapy, on average, placed about 70 percent of participants above the mean of control group members (50 percent base). The work took a decade, involving reviews of over two thousand references that were winnowed down to fewer than two hundred trustworthy ones (Hunt, 1997). The review's origins lay in serious doubts about the effectiveness of such therapy, including criticism of it by therapists whose work focused on individuals rather than couples or families. The doubts were put to rest for a while, at least on scientific grounds.

Cooper (2001) examined a topic that brings anxiety, if not fear and loathing, to many parents, not to speak of children or teachers: homework. His systematic review of studies of the effect of homework in elementary, middle, and high school led to recommendations that in elementary school, one ought not expect the homework assignments to yield better test scores. Rather, one should expect better study habits. This study led to recommendations, based on reliable studies, that assignments ought to be short for elementary school students and engage materials found at home and lead to successful experiences (Hunt, 1997). The academic functions of homework kicked in at middle school and could be regarded as an extension of classroom and curriculum in high school. Cooper's reviews and the recommendations based on it have been featured in the *Wall Street Journal* and *New York Times,* on TV shows (Oprah and Larry King's shows), and in forums at the local school and national levels.

In the medical sector, Chalmers and others recognized that over a twenty-year period, over fifteen different approaches to handling acute myocardial infarction had been tested in randomized trials. Results varied. Hunt (1997) gives the storyline with ample footnotes. The message, roughly speaking, is this: meta-analyses of diverse evaluative studies showed that anticlotting drugs "almost certainly" reduced the risk of dying by 10 to 20 percent. Further, streptokinase is among these drugs, tested in over thirty trials. Over reported trials, cumulative odds ratios favor this (Hunt, 1997). Part of the surprise in all this is that many physicians paid no attention to the early evidence (Hunt, 1997).

Contemporary History and Academic Disciplines

An indirect indicator of how systematic reviews add value is the number of published products of these efforts. Between 1974 and 1989 the number of "integrative reviews" and "meta-analyses" grew from roughly zero to about three hundred articles per year in refereed academic journals. This is a lower-bound estimate because only three engines (PsychInfo, ERIC, and SocScience) and associated databases and two search terms were used in a restricted time frame (White, 1994). This indicator reflects the increasing important of reviews in some arenas. It says nothing about the quality of the reviews or how they are used, of course, and in this sense the indicator is only indirectly related to the value of reviews.

Books

The books that are cited in this chapter are excellent and contain practical advice. The production of books on this topic is an indirect indicator of the topic's importance.

Academic Disciplines

An indirect indicator of value added is that meta-analyses and systematic reviews are undertaken in many disciplines (see Chalmers, Hedges, and Cooper, 2002, for specific references in each area):

- Agricultural sciences (for example, on fertilizers)
- Physiological experiments

- Psychology (for example, on expectations of children and behavior)
- Education (for example, on, class size, homework, summer school)
- Health research (for example, on, aspirin, myocardial infarction, cardio-vascular disease)
- Physical sciences (for example, on estimating physical constants)

One practical implication is that the rules of evidence that are used to reach conclusions in systematic reviews in each of these areas are similar. A second is that procedures used to screen evidence can usually be applied to other areas.

Valuable By-Products

Some by-products of organized efforts to produce systematic reviews are also essential to review production. This includes uniform transparent guidelines on classifying evaluations on the basis of their design and execution. This sets an explicit standard for judging the extent to which a particular evaluation can sustain a causal inference about an intervention's effect. Higher-order guidelines make explicit the standards used in deciding whether an assembly of evaluations justifies a systematic review or meta-analysis.

To take a simple example, the Campbell Collaboration and the Cochrane Collaboration require that each review make the standards explicit and, moreover, abide by collaboration guidelines in doing so. Randomized trials (experiments) are put high in the priority of designs that justify a causal inference. Simple before-after studies are low in priority unless some remarkable evidence or theory can be invoked to justify causal claims based on the results. The WWC has developed the DIAD, among other instruments, to guide and better articulate the process (Valentine and Cooper, 2002).

To the extent that reviews and organizational efforts make standards of evidence explicit, we expect that the number of new studies that can sustain causal inferences will increase. For instance, we would expect randomized trials to increase as a consequence of identifying such trials as high in priority. The annual meetings of the Campbell Collaboration and the questions put to the WWC suggest that this is a potential and important by-produced disciplined efforts to generate systematic reviews on effects of interventions.

Another by-product is the development of better databases that serve as the reservoir from which studies are drawn for review. For instance, Medline searches often failed to identify "randomized trial" in its database until the 1990s. The Cochrane Collaboration's hand searches of journals revealed that these searches had a far higher yield of trials than Medline-based searches. Medline changed its database policy to ensure that trials are more easily detectable to anyone, including Cochrane people who do reviews, trialists who are designing a study, and so on (see Turner and others, 2003, for references).

In the Campbell Collaboration's ambit, ERIC, PsychInfo, and other databases are pertinent. We expect that the Campbell Collaboration's experience in trying to identify reports on trials and to place them into C2-SPECTR, C2-PROT, and other registers will lead to recommendations for improving these databases. See Turner and others (2003) for C2's planning.

A third by-product of organized efforts to generate systematic reviews, supported by individual efforts, is an international network of people who have an interest in the ideas. The Cochrane Collaboration has developed a network of over ten thousand people involved in health-related reviews in nearly thirty countries, for instance. Cochrane's sibling, the Campbell Collaboration, has involved people from eight to fifteen countries in annual meetings since 1999. The people in these networks include evaluators and other applied researchers and policymakers and practitioners of other kinds. The WWC is taking a far more structured approach.

Model Programs, Exemplary Programs, and Systematic Reviews, Meta-Analyses, and Syntheses

The relationship among efforts to identify exemplary or model interventions and systematic reviews begs to be clarified. Contemporary efforts to identify models typically focus on one particular package and then examine the study or studies on the package's effect. If the studies are deemed trustworthy, and results suggest the intervention's effect is positive, then the intervention is declared a "model" or "exemplary." Examples of systems of this type include the National Register of Exemplary Programs in the drug abuse arena and blueprints in delinquency prevention (Petrosino, 2003). The system of the Food and Drug Administration (FDA) for permitting drugs to be marketed is based on a similar idea.

The FDA requires that two studies be completed before the approval process can begin, and legal sanctions can be applied against companies that withhold evidence or fabricate it. Efforts such as blueprints require at least one replication of an initial study.

The studies may be poorly designed, or there may be no discernible positive effect of the package. In either case, the package presumably is not declared a model. Furthermore, in many such systems, the packages that fail to become models are not identified.

In contrast, systematic reviews typically focus on an assembly of studies—more than two. In the Cochrane Collaboration, for instance, the typical number of studies is 6, but the range is large: 0 to 136. The Petrosino, Turpin-Petrosino, and Finckenauer (2000) Scared Straight review depended on seven randomized trials, for example. Meta-analysis often usually deals with more studies, a large enough number to permit complex statistical modeling of effect size. Lösel and Beelman's meta-analysis (2003) of child skills training depended on 84 reports on randomized trials. Shadish's award-winning meta-analyses of family therapy studies depended on 160 of them.

Unlike systems for finding model programs, systematic reviews and meta-analyses typically describe the distribution of effect sizes for the interventions reviewed, including sizes that are zero and negative rather than only the positive ones. They also try to identify all the studies in a review, not just those that yielded a positive finding.

A further difference between "model"-oriented systems and review-oriented systems meta-analyses is that the latter often get beyond the description of effect sizes to estimate the relationships' associations between effect size and characteristics of the studies and interventions that are the targets for study. Model-based systems and systematic reviews with small numbers of studies typically cannot be used in statistical analysis of this kind.

Of course, it will not always be possible to capitalize on systematic reviews of assemblies of studies. The supply of studies of interventions may be very small for a specialized outcome and target populations, for example, eleven-year-old Polish boys who attempt to derail locomotives, as in Jerzy Kosinski's *The Painted Bird*. And so we need something like model systems for these cases, and we expect the supply to be very small until research policy does more to make the portfolio of studies more coherent.

Of course, nothing prevents using a systematic review or meta-analysis to inform the search for "exemplary" interventions. That is, the standards of evidence in either case have some things in common, such as unbiased estimates of relative effect.

There are potential advantages to this strategy. First, model program systems generally do not engage in deep searches of published and unpublished literature of the sort that the best systematic reviews engage. Consequently, model program systems have no protection against sandbagging. That is, model advocates provide only the studies that show positive results to the system; less complementary studies are not brought forward. If all pertinent studies are located, one has more confidence in judgments about whether the model really is a model.

Second, the systematic review results provide statistical context. Knowing that four interventions have similar and notable effect sizes is better than knowing that one intervention has a notable effect size. This provides users with a choice among four goods rather than a choice of yes or no on the one.

This suggests that the model systems can then inform systematic reviews. In particular, as models and related studies accumulate, these become part of the ingredients for systematic reviews. No formal mechanism exists at yet for doing this.

Conclusion

The title of this chapter could easily have been, "Try all things and hold fast to that which is good," which exploits one of St. Paul's letters to the Thessalonians. We can find the same idea in medieval Arabic literature, notably Ibn Khaldun, Florence Nightingale's writings, and elsewhere.

People who do high-end systematic reviews stand on the shoulders of these people in at least two respects. They try to understand what is good. That is, what evidence justifies the claim that the intervention, program, or policy worked better than a specified alternative and works better relative to a fair comparison. Contemporary systematic reviewers also try to bring order out of the assembly of experience, studies. They do so in ways that make the processes and standards plain. Iba Khaldun would have admired. Ditto for Florence. Maybe even Paul.

References

Achara, S. et al. "Evidence Based Road Safety: The Driving Standards Agency's Schools Programme." *Lancet,* 2002, *358,* 230–232.

Becker, B., and Pigott, T. "Proposal for a Campbell Collaboration Training Group Within the Campbell Methods Group." East Lansing: Michigan State University and Chicago: Loyola University, 2002. [http://www.missouri. edu/ percent&7EC2 method/TrainingGroup.htm].

Boruch, R. F., Wortman, P. M., and Cordray, D. S. (eds.). *Reanalyzing Program Evaluations: Policies and Practices for Secondary Analysis of Social and Educational Programs.* San Francisco: Jossey-Bass, 1981.

Chalmers, I. "Trying to Do More Good Than Harm in Policy and Practice: The Role of Rigorous, Transparent, and Up-to-Date Replicable Evaluations." *Annals of Political and Social Science,* forthcoming.

Chalmers, I., Hedges, L. V., and Cooper, H. "A Brief History of Research Synthesis." *Education and the Health Professions,* 2002, *25,* 12–37.

Clarke, M., and Oxman, A. D. (eds.). *Cochrane Reviewers Handbook 4.2.0.* 2003. [http://cochrane.dk/cochrane/handbook/handbook.htm].

Cochrane Collaboration. *Cochrane Collaboration Methods Group Newsletter,* 2003, *1,* 1–44.

Cook, T. D., Murphy, R. F., and Hunt, H. D. "Comer's School Development Program." *American Educational Research Journal,* 2000, *37,* 535–597.

Cooper, H., *The Battle over Homework: Common Ground for Administrators, Teachers, and Parents.* Thousand Oaks, Calif.: Corwin Press, 2001.

Cooper, H., and Hedges, L. V. (eds.). *The Handbook of Research Synthesis.* New York: Russell Sage Foundation, 1994.

Droitcour, J., Silberman, G., and Chelimsky, E. "Cross-Design Synthesis: A New Form of Meta-Analysis for Combining the Results from Randomized Clinical Trials and Medical-Practice Databases." *International Journal of Technology Assessment in Health Care,* 1993, *9,* 440–449.

Editorial. *Journal of Educational Sociology,* 1933, *7*(4), 267–272.

Farrington, D. P., and Petrosino, A. "Systematic Reviews of Criminological Interventions: The Campbell Collaboration and Crime and Justice Groups." *International Annals of Criminology,* 2000, *38*(5), 49–66.

Fienberg, S. E., Martin, M. E., and Straf, M. L. (eds.). *Sharing Research Data.* Washington, D.C.: National Academy Press, 1985.

Finn, J. D., and Achilles, C. M. "Answers and Questions About Class Size: A Statewide Experiment." *American Educational Research Journal,* 1990, *27,* 557–577.

Ginsburg-Block, M., and Rohrbeck, C. "Peer-Assisted Learning in Elementary Schools." Paper presented at the Third Annual Campbell Collaboration Colloquium, Stockholm, Sweden, 2003.

Glazerman, S., Myers, D., and Levy, D. "Nonexperimental Replications of Social Experiments in Education, Training, and Employment Sciences (Revised Protocol)." 2002. [http://Campbellcollaboration.org/doc-pdf/ged.prot.pdf].

Herman, R., and others. *An Educator's Guide to Schoolwide Reform.* Washington, D.C.: American Institutes for Research, 1999.

Hunt, M. *How Science Takes Stock: The Story of Meta Analysis.* New York: Russell Sage Foundation, 1997.

Krueger, A. B. "Experimental Estimate of Education Production Functions." *Quarterly Journal of Economics,* May 1999, pp. 497–532.

Light, R. J., and Pillemer, D. B. *Summing Up: The Science of Reviewing Research.* Cambridge, Mass.: Harvard University Press, 1984.

Lipsey, M. W. "Those Confounded Moderators in Meta-Analysis: Good, Bad, and the Ugly." *Annals of the American Academy of Political and Social Science,* 2003, *587,* 69–83.

Lipsey, M. W., and Wilson, D. B. *Practical Meta-Analysis.* Thousand Oaks, Calif.: Sage, 2001.

Lösel, F., and Beelman, A. "Effects of Child Skills Training in Presenting Antisocial Behavior: A Systematic Review of Randomized Evaluations." *Annals of the American Academy of Arts and Science,* 2003, *587,* 84–109.

Marshall, E. "The UPSIDE of Good Behavior: Make Your Data Freely Available." *Science,* 2003, *299,* 990.

Moher, D., and others. "Improving the Quality of Reports of Meta-Analyses of Randomized Controlled Trials: The QUOROM Statement." *Lancet,* 1999, *354,* 1896–1900.

Mosteller, F. M. "The Tennessee Study of Class Size in the Early School Grades." *Future of Children: Critical Issues for Children and Youth,* 1995, *5,* 113–127.

Mosteller, F., Miech, E., and Nave, W. "Structured Abstracts." *Educational Researcher,* forthcoming.

Murphy, R. F., and others. *E-DESK: A Review of Evidence on the Effectiveness of Discrete Educational Software.* Palo Alto, Calif.: SRI International, 2002.

Petrosino, A. J. "The Hunt for Randomized Experimental Reports: Document Search Efforts for a 'What Works' Meta-Analysis." *Journal of Crime and Justice,* 1995, *18*(2), 63–80.

Petrosino, A. "Standards of Evidence and Evidence for Standards: The Case of School Based Drug Prevention." *Annals of the American Academy of Political and Social Science,* 2003, *587,* 180–207.

Petrosino, A., Turpin-Petrosino, C., and Buehler, J. *Scared Straight and Other Juvenile Awareness Programs for Preventing Juvenile Delinquency (Cochrane Review).* Cochrane Library, no. 1. 2002.

Petrosino, A., Turpin-Petrosino, C., and Finckenauer, J. "Well Meaning Can Have Harmful Effects: Lessons from Experiments on Scared Straight and Like Programs." *Crime and Delinquency,* 2000, *42*(3), 354–379.

Rawlings, L. "Operational Reflections on Evaluating Development Programs." In *Proceedings of the Operations Evaluation Department, World Bank Conference on Evaluation.* Washington, D.C.: World Bank, forthcoming.

Roberts, I., and Kwan, I. "School Based Driver Education for the Prevention of Traffic Crashes." *Cochrane Database of Systematic Reviews,* 2002, *4.*

Shadish, W. R., and others. "Effects of Family and Marital Psychotherapies: A Meta-Analysis." *Journal of Consulting and Clinical Psychology,* 1993, *6,* 992–1002.

Sherman, L. W., Schmidt, J. D., and Rogan, D. P. *Policing Domestic Violence: Experiments and Dilemmas.* New York: Free Press, 1992.

Sieber, J. E. (ed.). *Sharing Social Science Data.* Thousand Oaks, Calif.: Sage, 1991.

Sutton, A. J., and others. *Methods for Meta-Analysis in Medical Research.* New York: Wiley, 2000.

Turner, H., and others. "Populating International Register of Randomized Trials: C2-SPECTR." *Annals of the American Academy of Political and Social Science,* 2003, *589,* 203–223.

U.S. General Accounting Office. *Cross-Design Synthesis: A New Strategy for Medical Effectiveness Research.* Washington, D.C.: U.S. General Accounting Office, 1992.

Valentine, J., and Cooper, H. *Design and Implementation Assessment Device.* Washington, D.C.: U.S. Department of Education, 2002.

White, H. D. "Scientific Communication and Literature Review." In H. Cooper and L. V. Hedges (eds.), *The Handbook of Research Synthesis.* New York: Russell Sage Foundation, 1994.

Wilson, S. J., Lipsey, M. W., and Soydan, H. "Are Mainstream Programs for Juvenile Delinquency Less Effective with Minority Youth Than Majority Youth? A Meta-Analysis of Outcomes Research." *Research on Social Work Practice,* 2003, *13*(1), 3–26.

Part Two

Practical Data Collection Procedures

Evaluation design is usually considered the glamorous part of program evaluation. Evaluators love to discuss and debate ways to link program activities to outcomes. Equally important, however, is collecting the data once the evaluation design has been selected. Even the best evaluation designs come to naught if accurate data cannot be obtained or data are not collected in a reasonably reliable and valid way.

The seven chapters in Part Two discuss approaches to data collection: trained observer approaches, systematic surveys, the systematic use of expert judgment, use of role playing, focus groups, field interviewing, and use of agency record data. Some of these approaches are well known, such as use of agency record data and surveys. Others are not as common, such as using trained observer ratings and role playing. Most evaluations will need to use more than one, and possibly several, of these approaches.

John Greiner, in Chapter Eight, provides detailed procedures for undertaking trained observer ratings. Such ratings can provide data on a variety of physical conditions. These procedures can be used to evaluate changes in street cleanliness, street "ride-ability," park and playground maintenance, housing conditions, the condition of schools and other buildings, and the maintenance quality of child care and institutional facilities, among other uses. Ratings before and after specific program actions can be taken to help determine the effectiveness of those actions. Less widely used in program evaluations have been trained observer ratings of client functioning, such as in assessing the rehabilitation of persons with physical and mental disabilities.

The chapter describes systematic procedures that can be used to achieve reasonable inter-rater and across-time reliability for use in program evaluations. Because many public agencies have staff members who already undertake some form of inspection, they may find these procedures particularly feasible. As Greiner describes, the increasing availability of low-cost hand-held computers has given considerable impetus to the use of trained observer ratings, greatly facilitating data entry and the preparation of quick turnaround rating reports.

Kathryn Newcomer and Timothy Triplett, in Chapter Nine, discuss a better-known procedure, undertaking systematic surveys, whether surveys of a whole population or surveys of the clients of particularly programs. No book on data collection for program evaluation would be complete without examining survey procedures. The chapter discusses many of the key elements needed for quality surveys. Sample surveys have been used by agencies to track such conditions as employment, housing, and health conditions. Surveys have been used by evaluators for decades. Often they are the key data collection procedure used to evaluate human services programs. Surveys are the only way to obtain statistically reliable data from respondents on ratings of services they have received. They can be a major way to obtain factual information on changes in the behavior and status of respondents, especially after customers have completed the service. Surveys can also provide demographic information on customers and their perceptions of what needs to be improved in the service and how much the service contributed to any improvements they identified. The targets of surveys might be clients of particular services, households, businesses, or other agencies or levels of government that are customers of a service.

Most of the procedures described in Chapter Nine can be applied whether a sample of a population or the full population is surveyed. Surveys of a program's customers will be particularly feasible if the program keeps records of clients' names, addresses, and telephone numbers. Surveys are especially attractive when costs can be kept relatively low, such as when mail administration is feasible. As Newcomer and Triplett indicate, mail surveys are becoming more attractive and more competitive with telephone procedures because of growing problems in achieving high telephone response rates and the introduction of better mail survey procedures. Mail surveys can often provide sufficiently accurate information if multiple mailings and telephone reminders or interviews are used to achieve reasonable response rates. Telephone surveys are practical when relatively small samples can be used to obtain the needed information. The authors also note the growing potential for and attractiveness of electronic surveys, at least for situations where the respondents can be expected to have ready access to computers.

Harvey Averch, in Chapter Ten, discusses the systematic use of expert judgment, a technique rarely thought of as a way to collect data for program evaluations. Usually expert judgment procedures, such as Delphi, are used to provide estimates about the future. However, in some types of programs, such as research and planning, evaluators may need to fall back on the judgments of knowledgeable persons. Such procedures also can be applied to programs for which hard data cannot be obtained for certain outcomes. Some evaluators may scoff at the systematic use of expert judgment, but it may be the only way to get reasonable information on some aspects of service quality.

Although individual experts can have all sorts of biases, the collective use of experts in a systematic way can sometimes be helpful for an evaluation, probably in more situations than evaluators currently recognize. This chapter addresses many of the issues that arise, including selection of the experts and how to collect and combine their ratings.

Margery Austin Turner and Wendy Zimmermann, in Chapter Eleven, describe a procedure that has been gaining attention: role playing. This technique has been applied particularly to assess discrimination in housing and employment. In these cases, paired role players, two or more individuals with different racial and ethnic or gender characteristics but who are otherwise similar, apply for housing or jobs. The differences in the treatment each member of these pairs receives can provide powerful evidence of how well equal opportunity programs have—or have not—achieved fairness in consideration of applications.

Turner and Zimmermann also point out the many applications of the procedure where paired role playing is not needed. One role player can call or visit facilities sponsored by a public agency to test the quality of the information or service the role player requests. This is a technique the Internal Revenue Service has used to evaluate the quality of its agents who provide tax information to the public. Single role players can be used, for example, to assess the quality of responses to requests for information from government tourist offices, public assistance offices, or almost any other office that directly serves customers. While such strategies can be, and have been, used to bring discrimination cases against individual firms, that is not the function here. Rather, we are concerned with the procedure's use to provide aggregate data on many cases to help evaluate the quality and success of public programs.

To provide reliable statistical data, the key concern is to use systematic, reliable procedures on enough cases or situations to be reasonably representative of the population of interest. Evaluators may not always have sufficient resources to obtain statistically representative information; however, in such cases, the evaluators can use role playing at the beginning of evaluations to identify issues that the evaluation should cover.

Robert Goldenkoff, in Chapter Twelve, describes the use of focus groups, a popular information-gathering procedure. This approach is not normally intended to collect actual evaluation statistics since the number of persons involved in the groups is intentionally kept quite small. Focus group information is not intended to be statistically representative of the full population. These groups are frequently used in case study and other fieldwork evaluations to provide clues to how well a program is working. Respondents in such instances are often program personnel as well as clients.

Focus groups can be important to program evaluators at the front end of their evaluations to help identify customer concerns that should be included in the evaluation design—both outcome and process characteristics.

In addition, the groups can assist evaluators after data are collected to help them interpret the data. This is done by asking focus group members to identify reasons that the particular findings occurred.

Focus groups usually represent a very low-cost procedure, thus adding to their attractiveness to evaluators. They also offer a way that sponsors of the evaluation, and subsequently the users of the evaluation report, can gain assurance that the evaluation has considered the interests of the program's customers.

Demetra Nightingale and Shelli Rossman, in Chapter Thirteen, describe field data collection issues and procedures, particularly those involving interviews with persons knowledgeable about program implementation, quality, or outcomes. Evaluators use such fieldwork to obtain qualitative and quantitative information on how programs are working. They often seek information on both successes and problems in implementing programs in order to provide feedback to agencies for improving their programs.

A major problem for evaluators is deciding what procedures they should use to make the information more systematic and therefore more valid and credible. The authors provide numerous suggestions for accomplishing this. Many large-scale, federally sponsored evaluations in recent years have involved such examinations. Other chapters in this book have discussed qualitative, implementation, and case study type evaluations. The fieldwork that Nightingale and Rossman discuss is particularly applicable to these types of evaluations.

Harry Hatry, in Chapter Fourteen, discusses the collection of data from agency, archival, and administrative records—probably the most common source of information for an evaluation. Most, and possibly all, public program evaluations require data from agency records, if only to obtain counts of the number of customers or cases the program has served. Agency records can pose a considerable challenge to evaluators, however. The field of evaluation is littered with examples of missing and incomplete records, differences in definitions and in data collection procedures for desired data elements, difficulties in gaining access to records, and other problems. The author identifies and discusses such problems and provides a number of suggestions for alleviating them.

Agency records are the source on which public agencies sponsoring evaluations will most likely depend initially. Information from records is, in general, the cheapest, most readily available source of data. Unfortunately, existing agency records seldom provide adequate information on the outcomes of program activities, and one or more of the procedures described in Chapters Eight through Fourteen will also be needed.

The chapters in Part Two do not cover all the data collection procedures that evaluators might use. For some public programs, mechanical or electronic recording devices are increasingly used to track program outcomes. Examples are the use of various instruments to assess air and water quality and noise levels. "Ride meters" are used by some transportation agencies to measure the bumpiness of roads. If the readings from such equipment can be correlated with more end-oriented outcomes, they can be even more effective.

For example, in some instances, ride meters have been correlated with driving comfort and potential car damage, and air and water pollution levels have been correlated with levels of health hazards. Some of the measuring devices can be quite expensive, such as those that test water for toxic pollutants and condition of fish tissue. In such instances, the evaluators may need to use smaller samples and test less frequently.

Cost is an important consideration in all data collection procedures. Some of these chapters attempt to identify some of the less costly ways to acquire information. A common cost-reduction scheme in surveys, trained observer, and role-playing procedures is to use sampling with smaller samples and reduced precision levels. Evaluators in all cases should review their precision needs. Calling for more precision than necessary will add to the cost of the evaluation. For example, 95 percent confidence levels might be more than is needed for many evaluation applications. How often do decision makers, those using evaluation findings, have such certainty in their decisions? Why not 90 percent, or even lower levels?

Another key issue for data collection is quality control. This element should be given explicit attention when data collection is planned. Quality control should be built into the data collection process. This means such steps as:

- Training all data collection personnel thoroughly
- Checking the definitions and data obtained from other sources thoroughly
- Attempting to triangulate field findings with confirmatory responses from more than one respondent and from multiple sources

- Pretesting data collection procedures before full use
- Checking questionnaire wording for ambiguity and biases

One special way to ensure better data quality is for all members of the evaluation team to visit the program, at least one of its sites, possibly as part of a pretest. This on-site experience can give the evaluators a reality check and enable them to do a better job of planning data collection.

Finally, evaluators will need to make important decisions about the amount of data to be collected. They may be tempted to seek large amounts of information about a wide range of program and service quality characteristics. At some point, overcollecting will overload the collection resources and cause significant difficulties in data analysis. In their initial planning, the evaluators should make sure that each data element they include has a specific purpose and is likely to provide useful evaluative information. Advocates for particular data elements should be required to justify each element's inclusion. Otherwise, the evaluation may dissipate the data collection efforts and produce more quantity than quality.

8

Trained Observer Ratings

John M. Greiner

Evaluators often encounter situations in which the outcomes of interest involve qualitative phenomena, conditions, or behaviors that can be classified, counted, or rated on an ordinal scale (for instance, dirtier, bumpier, less responsive). In such circumstances, an accurate, systematic technique for directly assessing these conditions using one's eyes, ears, and other senses can serve as an important evaluative tool. Indeed, as Yogi Berra succinctly put it, "You can observe a lot just by watching" (Peter, 1977, p. 295).

Consider, for instance, the following potential program evaluation tasks:

- Compare the effectiveness of private contractors versus municipal forces in providing park maintenance services.
- Evaluate the relative effectiveness of alternate street cleaning programs and identify factors that influence the results.
- Evaluate the impact of a tax limitation initiative (such as Massachusetts's Proposition 2½) on the quality and equity of street maintenance services.

This chapter draws heavily from discussions of trained observer techniques in two International City/County Management Association/Urban Institute publications: Hatry, Greiner, and Swanson (1987) and Hatry and others (1992). The discussion of technological innovations has benefited from extensive discussions with Barbara Cohn of the Fund for the City of New York, Michael Meotti and Michelle Doucette Cunningham of the Connecticut Policy and Economic Council, and Roberta Schaefer and Richard Beaman of the Worcester Regional Research Bureau.

- Evaluate the effectiveness of efforts to encourage businesses, government agencies, and private property owners to maintain and improve the streetscape in commercial areas.
- Assess the accessibility, courtesy, and responsiveness of public agencies to routine in-person and telephone requests for service.
- Assess the physical condition of a city's housing stock or public facilities (for example, classrooms), and subsequently evaluate the effectiveness of policies and programs undertaken to address the needs identified.
- Evaluate the responsiveness of city agencies in addressing street-level problems identified by neighborhood residents.
- Evaluate the relative effectiveness of alternate mental health programs based on changes in observed client behavior.
- Assess the quality of the care provided by nursing homes.

In these and many other situations, a systematic technique for assigning accurate, reliable grades based on direct visual observations can be—and has been—employed to support program evaluation efforts. This technique involves the use of trained observers.

The Nature and Application of Trained Observer Ratings

Trained observers make ratings of conditions or events by comparing their perception of the condition to a prespecified rating scale. Most trained observer ratings have been based on visual perceptions of conditions, but any of the senses can be used: touch, smell, hearing, and even taste. The rating scales should incorporate detailed written definitions or photographic benchmarks, or both, that enable the observers to assign precise grades to the conditions they see. The technique should include systematic procedures to ensure the accuracy and consistency of the ratings between raters and over time. When properly used, trained observers can provide accurate, reliable, quantitative measures of program outcomes for use in program evaluation.

Most applications of trained observers have focused on assessing facility maintenance, such as the care and appearance of public parks and beaches; the condition of recreation centers, schools, dwellings, and other public and private facilities; the bumpiness and safety of streets and sidewalks; the visibility of street signs and pavement markings; street cleanliness and other aspects of neighborhood appearance; the condition of the streetscape in commercial districts; and the condition of public transportation facilities. Trained observers have also been used to evaluate the impacts of mental health programs on client behavior (here, the observers are usually trained clinicians), the responsiveness of employees to citizen requests, and the quality of the care provided by nursing homes (see the box).

The Use of Trained Observers to Help Evaluate the Quality of Care in Nursing Homes

Federal law requires that all nursing homes be inspected annually in order to be certified to receive Medicare and Medicaid payments. Since 1990, these inspections have emphasized outcomes: quality of care, patient quality of life, protection of patient rights, and the quality of dietary, nursing, pharmacy, and other support services. The inspections have drawn on a variety of data collection techniques: trained observer ratings of physical facilities, group activities, and a sample of residents (and their rooms); interviews of residents and staff; physical measurements; reviews of records; and various specialized procedures (such as checking the accuracy of a sample of medications as they are distributed and quizzing randomly selected staff concerning proper emergency procedures). These techniques have been used to obtain information on a lengthy list of items that jointly characterize various aspects of the quality of nursing home services: quality of life, quality of care, and so forth.

Among the many trained observer ratings used to help assess quality of life have been ratings of accommodation to resident needs, resident clothing and grooming, the cleanliness and orderliness of resident rooms, the comfortableness of sound and temperature levels in resident rooms, and the degree to which the resident's room provides a homelike environment. The evaluation of quality of care has included trained observer ratings of the amount eaten by residents, the degree to which the dining environment enhances resident independence and well-being, and potential safety hazards. Trained observers have rated dietary services in terms of the timeliness, appearance, flavor, temperature, and nutritional balance of the meals served. And the physical environment has been evaluated with the help of trained observer ratings of the degree of visual privacy, lighting, ventilation (including the presence of odors), and numerous other characteristics. Both two-level (yes-no) and three-level (A-B-C) rating scales have been employed. Definitions have been provided in a comprehensive manual prepared by the federal Health Care Financing Administration (HCFA), now called the Centers for Medicare and Medicaid Services, which has also supplied detailed rating forms used by all inspectors.

HCFA has contracted for the inspections with state health departments. The fieldwork has been undertaken by full-time, multidisciplinary teams of four to seven professionals—nurses, dietitians, social workers, pharmacists, sanitarians, and so forth. A typical certification inspection has required three to four days and can result in a list of citations for the major problems identified. These can have serious consequences for the nursing home, including decertification.

Nursing home inspectors have received extensive training using materials prepared by HCFA (see, for example, Health Care Financing Administration, 1992). For instance, in Michigan new inspectors have undergone four weeks of full-time training, followed by on-the-job training with a survey team under the guidance of a trainer (who was not a regular member of the team). It has taken six months for an inspector to be fully qualified. HCFA has also required that all nursing home inspectors complete a one-week training course at HCFA's Baltimore headquarters during their first year on the job.

Quality control for these inspections has been exercised by HCFA and the state health departments. For instance, in Michigan, the quality of nursing home inspections has been controlled through monthly in-service training of all staff, analysis of complaints, and observation of survey teams by trainers working with new inspectors. In addition, HCFA personnel have completely resurveyed a 5 percent random sample of inspected nursing homes in each state. These reinspections occurred within two months of the state inspection. HCFA has also implemented joint nursing home inspections (independent, parallel surveys with both state and federal inspection teams on site at the same time) and required that all surveyors pass a standard test designed by HCFA.

Trained observer procedures can also provide a practical, systematic approach for tallying specific items or conditions associated with the impacts of a program. Examples include the number of safety hazards in parks or playgrounds, "abandoned" vehicles left on private property, and evidence of criminal activity such as drug paraphernalia and broken car windows (for the use of trained observers to track petty street crimes in New York City's Times Square area, see Fund for the City of New York, n.d.).

Among many other potential applications, trained observers can be used to rate buses, subways, parks, and libraries in terms of how crowded they are. Observers can evaluate the effectiveness of noise ordinances; the walkability of neighborhood streets; the courtesy, professionalism, and respect shown to citizens by police (City of New York, 2003); the ease of filing complaints at city hall; and the presence of hazards, odors, and vermin at a landfill. Trained observers can also be used to count and characterize homeless persons and to determine the incidence of potholes, stray animals, malfunctioning traffic signals, abandoned buildings, or diseased shade trees. And such observers can be used to evaluate a neighborhood's social environment, including the people on the street and their activities (children playing, teenagers loitering or fighting, homeless persons, drug sales), the police presence, and the types of businesses and institutions in the neighborhood (bars, strip clubs, pawnshops, churches, schools, police and fire stations, and so forth).

Table 8.1 lists several of the characteristics that have been rated with the help of trained observers as well as some of the places where the technique has been employed. It also provides selected references to more detailed information on the scales and procedures that have been used in connection with trained observer ratings of specific types of conditions. (For descriptions of program evaluations involving trained observer ratings, see "Before and After," 1985; Fund for the City of New York, 1983; Greiner, 1984; Greiner and Peterson, 1986; Riccio, Miller, and Litke, 1986; Thomas, 1980; and "A Ticket to Clean Streets," 1982.)

The information produced by trained observer ratings can be used in connection with most of the evaluation designs discussed in this handbook. The ratings can serve as outcome measures (the dependent variables) for before-after assessments, controlled experiments, or quasi-experiments involving comparison groups or interrupted time series. By providing a systematic inventory of potential service needs (for example, the condition of the housing stock, the number of poorly maintained classrooms), trained observer ratings can serve as the basis for assessing the percentage of unmet need—a key indicator of effectiveness for many programs. The ratings can also be used to measure certain independent or explanatory variables—for instance, to initially classify clients of mental health programs by problem severity for evaluating the effectiveness of alternate service delivery options.

Potential Advantages, Disadvantages, and Limitations

Trained observer ratings offer a number of potential advantages in connection with program evaluation:

- They provide a relatively easy and often inexpensive way to quantify conditions—and program outcomes—that would otherwise be quite difficult to measure.
- Despite their inherent subjectivity, trained observer ratings, when done properly, can achieve considerable objectivity and reliability. Under such circumstances, they have been accorded a high degree of validity and credibility by researchers and decision makers.
- Public administrators (and the public) can readily understand trained observer results, especially when photographic rating scales are used or when the findings are accompanied by pictures of the conditions encountered. Hence, trained observer ratings can serve as an excellent communications tool and can contribute to the acceptance and use of the evaluation results.

Table 8.1. Some Applications of Trained Observer Ratings

Characteristic Rated	Jurisdiction(s) Rated	Rating Scales and Procedures[a]
Park maintenance	Alexandria, Va.[b] Arlington County, Va.[b] Boston, Mass.[b] Charlotte, N.C. Charlottesville, Va.[b] Greenville, S.C. Hartford, Conn. Honolulu, Hawaii Kansas City, Mo. King County, Wash. New York City San Diego (city), Calif. San Francisco, Calif. Savannah, Ga. Sunnyvale, Calif. Six jurisdictions in the State of Florida[b] Seventeen jurisdictions in the State of Massachusetts[b]	Hatry and others, 1992 City of Greenville, 1990 Wilson, 1989 TriData Corporation, 1986 Fund for the City of New York, 1978 Ammons, 2001 City of Kansas City, n.d.
Beach maintenance	West Haven, Conn. Five jurisdictions in Volusia County, Florida[b]	Urban Institute, 1983
Building maintenance (public buildings)	Alexandria, Va.[b] Charlottesville, Va.[b] Dayton, Ohio New York City (schools) Sunnyvale, Calif.	Moore, 1988 TriData Corporation, 1986
Housing stock/ public housing	Albany, N.Y. Charlotte, N.C. Charlottesville, Va. Dallas, Texas Kansas City, Mo. York, Pa. State of Texas	Hatry, Morley, Barbour, and Pajunen, 1991 City of Kansas City, 1989
Street cleanliness[c]	Alexandria, Va.[b] Boston, Mass.[b] Charlotte, N.C. Charlottesville, Va.[b] Nashville, Tenn.[b] New York City St. Petersburg, Fla.[b] Savannah, Ga. Sunnyvale, Calif. Washington, D.C.	Hatry and others, 1992 Thomas, 1980 Blair and Schwartz, 1972

Table 8.1. Some Applications of Trained Observer Ratings, *continued*

Characteristic Rated	Jurisdiction(s) Rated	Rating Scales and Procedures[a]
	Eight jurisdictions in Volusia County, Florida[b] Seventeen jurisdictions in the State of Massachusetts[b]	
Abandoned vehicles	Charlotte, N.C.[b] Nashville, Tenn.[b] Prince George's County, Md. St. Petersburg, Fla.[b] Washington, D.C.	Hatry and others, 1992
Street rideability, bumpiness[c]	Alexandria, Va.[b] Boston, Mass.[b] Charlottesville, Va.[b] Nashville, Tenn.[b] New York City St. Petersburg, Fla.[b] Eight jurisdictions in Volusia County, Florida[b] Seventeen jurisdictions in the State of Massachusetts[b]	Hatry and others, 1992 TriData Corporation, 1986
Street maintenance	Kansas City, Mo.	City of Kansas City, 2000
Sidewalk walkability[c]	Alexandria, Va.[b] Charlottesville, Va.[b] Nashville, Tenn.[b] St. Petersburg, Fla.[b]	Hatry and others, 1992 TriData Corporation, 1986 "Walkable America Checklist," 1999
Streetscape conditions[d]	Des Moines, Iowa Montgomery County, Md. New York City Worcester, Mass. Seven jurisdictions in the State of Connecticut	"Neighborhood Data: ComNET," n.d.
Responsiveness to citizen requests	Kansas City, Mo. Montgomery County, Md. Saratoga, Calif. Washington, D.C.	Center for Excellence in Local Government, 1988 Herman and Peroff, 1981 "Telephone Tester Program," n.d. Milford, Dougherty, and Bradbury, 2000
Functioning of social service and mental health clients	Denver, Colo. Jefferson County, Colo. State of Michigan State of Oklahoma State of West Virginia	Millar and Millar, 1981

Table 8.1. Some Applications of Trained Observer Ratings, *continued*

Characteristic Rated	Jurisdiction(s) Rated	Rating Scales and Procedures[a]
Quality of nursing home care	Nationwide (all nursing homes receiving Medicare or Medicaid payments)	Health Care Financing Administration, 1992
Subway conditions	New York City	Institute for Public Transportation, 1980
Petty street crime	New York City	Fund for the City of New York, n.d.
Solid waste disposal	Nashville, Tenn. St. Petersburg, Fla.	Hatry and others, 1992

[a]These references provide detailed information on some of the scales and procedures that have been used to rate the given characteristic.

[b]This condition was rated as part of a multiservice trained observer assessment covering a variety of services and characteristics: street cleanliness; bumpiness of streets and sidewalks; condition of signs, stoplights, and pavement markings; park maintenance; and/or the condition of public buildings.

[c]Ratings of street cleanliness, street rideability, and/or sidewalk walkability have frequently been coupled with ratings of curb and gutter conditions, street and traffic sign visibility and condition, traffic light operability, shade tree condition, abandoned vehicles, and similar conditions that can be observed along a street.

[d]Streetscape ratings usually focus on many of the maintenance characteristics listed above, as well as items such as vacant buildings, vacant lots, bus shelters, public telephones, police and fire call boxes, fire hydrants, parking meters, street lights, street furniture (benches, bike racks, bollards, planters, trash receptacles), curbs and handicapped cuts, catch basins, illegal posters and handbills, graffiti, odors, encroaching vegetation, animals running loose, parking violations, and evidence of criminal activity.

- Trained observer ratings tend to focus on conditions as experienced by a typical citizen or other user of a service or facility. Thus, they can complement technical assessments of program outcomes by professionals.
- In most cases, trained observer ratings can be made by ordinary citizens without the need for expensive experts. For many applications, existing government staff, students, or citizen volunteers can be trained to be competent raters.
- The results can be readily applied by management, especially when physical conditions are assessed. Because precise information is usually available on the location of problem conditions, the data can be grouped and sequenced to ensure efficient prioritization and routing of remediation efforts, while facilitating follow-up and verification of those efforts.

Despite these advantages, trained observer ratings must be used with caution. A number of potential disadvantages and practical limitations need to be kept in mind when deciding whether—and how—to employ trained observers:

- Trained observer ratings are designed for assessing characteristics that can be readily and directly sensed or experienced by the rater—observed, felt, heard, smelled, or tasted. They are not suited for determining the less obvious underlying factors and technical details associated with a condition.
- Because they often depend on visual observations of conditions or behavior, trained observer ratings can be hampered—and in some cases precluded—by uncontrollable situations that limit observability: crowds, parked cars, snow, privacy requirements, and so forth. To avoid such problems, the observations might have to be scheduled at times that may be inconvenient from the rater's standpoint (for instance, on evenings, weekends, or holidays).
- Because the raters must observe conditions firsthand, some applications of trained observers can pose potential physical dangers. For instance, ratings of dangerous neighborhoods or isolated parks, or "windshield" ratings made while driving slowly on congested or high-speed roads can be hazardous to the observer.
- Many trained observer ratings involve nominal or ordinal scales that cannot be interpreted in the usual absolute quantitative sense. Numbers are often used to distinguish between the various conditions that make up a nominal scale, despite the fact that there is no consistent, quantitative relationship between the conditions (for instance, 1 = "safe," 2 = "hazardous," and 3 = "safety unknown"). Ordinal rating scales can involve the assignment of numbers to conditions that exhibit a qualitative ordering (for instance, cleanliness ratings of 1, 2, and 3, where 1 is "cleaner than" 2 and 2 is "cleaner than" 3). For many such scales, the numbers merely serve as labels and can be replaced by letters or other symbols with no loss of information. (For instance, the above cleanliness rating levels could be designated A, B, and C.) In these situations, the nominal or ordinal scale can limit the applicability of certain familiar and convenient statistical measures and techniques (averages, standard deviations, regression analyses, and so forth), which are valid only when the "distance" between adjacent rating levels is a constant.
- Trained observer ratings are not usually suitable for assessing subtle changes or especially complex conditions. The primary "instruments" used in making trained observer measurements are the human senses, and the ratings are strongly constrained by the physiological limitations of human perceptions and mental processes. For instance, trained observer scales usually involve relatively few distinct gradations (typically two to five grades). The number of different levels that can be used depends on the observer's ability to perceive differences in the characteristics being rated and to accurately remember and apply the detailed definitions associated with all the levels.

• Without considerable care in their design and implementation, trained observer ratings can easily become subject to the problems that potentially threaten any inherently subjective assessment process: imprecision, poor repeatability, and lack of inter-rater comparability. An evaluator choosing to use trained observers must put the necessary effort into systematic design of the rating scales, careful validation, adequate training, and extensive quality control. One must avoid the temptation to use trained observers as a "quick and dirty" way to quantify outcomes and identify problems, especially if the ratings are to be used for systematic program evaluations. Rigorous program evaluation requires rigorous statistical design and quality control of the trained observer procedure.

• The credibility of the trained observer results may be suspect if the observer is also involved in providing the service being rated. This sets up a potential conflict of interest that can compromise the rater's objectivity. Even if the rater remains unbiased, the external credibility of the evaluation may be damaged in such a situation. Such considerations can limit the applicability of trained observer ratings in cases where program staff must be used as the raters (because of access or confidentiality restrictions, for example, or the need for special expertise).

• There is a danger (present in any evaluation effort) that trained observer ratings will become intrusive—that the observations will alter the conditions or outcomes being measured and hence affect the evaluation results. For instance, the presence of the raters may focus the attention of service delivery personnel on addressing the specific items or conditions being measured.

Most of these concerns can be addressed through proper design and sensitive implementation of the rating procedures: carefully selecting the characteristics to be graded, developing adequate rating scales, properly choosing and training the raters, providing adequate quality control, and properly analyzing the results.

Selecting the Characteristics to Be Rated

The first step in implementing trained observer ratings is to identify the specific features and conditions that will be rated. In some cases, the appropriate characteristics will be obvious from the program being evaluated. For instance, if the outcome of interest is the number of abandoned vehicles, the cleanliness of a park, the bumpiness of a road, or the odor of a landfill, the evaluator can develop straightforward trained observer ratings focusing on a single attribute.

In other cases, the evaluator will have to analyze the various program objectives, breaking the relevant constructs into elements (and results) that can be more readily observed and rated. For example, if the objective is to evaluate the effectiveness of a building maintenance program, the concept of "building maintenance" might first be broken down into distinct maintenance concerns: maintenance of rooms, restrooms, halls and corridors, staircases, elevators, building exterior, and building grounds. Each of these elements can then be subdivided into more narrowly defined maintenance issues and responsibilities. Thus, "room maintenance" involves the condition of the ceiling, walls, windows, doors, floors, lighting and other electrical fixtures, other utilities (heat, ventilation), and any special equipment or conditions. For each of these items, one can either define an overall maintenance rating based on an assessment of the feature as a whole (for instance, an overall ceiling maintenance rating of 1, 2, 3, or 4 based on various combinations of observable conditions), or further disaggregate the item into a set of potential problems whose individual ratings will jointly provide an assessment of the maintenance of the feature. (For ceilings, potential problems might include cracks or bulges, missing or damaged tiles, stains or other painting needs, and dirt or dust.) In general, the trade-off is between having a few complex rating scales versus many relatively simple ratings.

Greenville, South Carolina, has broken park maintenance into ten maintenance elements: paths, walks, and parking areas; benches and picnic tables; shelters, restrooms, and water fountains; play areas; ball fields; basketball courts; tennis courts; grass and lawns; shrubs, trees, and plantings; and litter (Wilson, 1989). Each of these elements is further subdivided into specific observable maintenance problems, such as the existence of weeds, broken glass, and overturned or damaged benches. The trained observer ratings then focus on assessing the presence and extent of each potential problem. Charlottesville, Virginia, has used a similar approach (see Exhibit 8.5 later in this chapter).

New York City's Department of Parks and Recreation has focused its park maintenance ratings directly on the overall condition of key aspects of its park facilities: benches, comfort stations, fences, playground equipment, ball fields, shrubs, and so forth. There has been no effort to assess the presence of specific types of problems.

A number of sources can be helpful in identifying the most relevant attributes, conditions, and potential problems to look for. The evaluator should consult program and service delivery staff, top-level management, members of relevant advisory and advocacy groups, and users of the service in question concerning the results they expect and the potential problems of greatest importance to them in connection with the service or program. Field observations of a range of situations and facilities can be especially helpful. Maintenance checklists, inspection forms, standard operating procedures, published standards, and trained observer procedures used by other jurisdictions and organizations can also suggest key factors and conditions to monitor (see, for instance, Ammons, 2001).

The Fund for the City of New York and the Connecticut Policy and Economic Council in Hartford have emphasized the importance of letting neighborhood residents and community organizations identify what conditions are important to rate. In effect, the definition of effective government services is that of the residents. Focus groups, meetings with neighborhood organizations, and citizen surveys have been used to identify the conditions and problems that the community wants to be assessed.

Evaluators should exercise care in choosing the final list of features and problems to be rated. The characteristics selected should be readily observed or sensed by a rater. Check also for completeness (do they address all key aspects of the construct or outcome in question?), the absence of overlaps or redundancy, and the clarity and directness of the presumed association between the characteristic to be observed and the construct of interest.

Another important issue is the degree of disaggregation—how far to go in breaking a complex concept into discrete components. The list of items to be rated should be limited because a lengthy list will dilute the impact of the results for any one item while increasing the stress on the rater, the potential for error, and the time and cost associated with completing the assessment. (Nevertheless, a more detailed listing is likely to be especially helpful for operating personnel in identifying where problems exist and what needs to be done to remedy them.)

Trained observers in Worcester, Massachusetts, assess up to one hundred streetscape characteristics, and raters in Montgomery County, Maryland, evaluate fifty-seven conditions. Trained observers assessing street maintenance in Kansas City, Missouri, focus on thirty-seven different conditions with very precise (and distinct) scales and criteria for each (City of Kansas City, 2000). Greenville's park rating procedure has explicitly addressed forty-two different types of maintenance problems; New York City's has focused on seventeen general features but with more complex rating scales. The ComNET trained observer procedure developed by the Fund for the City of New York (Cohn, 1999; "Computerized Neighborhood Environment Tracking: ComNET," 2002) begins with thirty-eight core streetscape conditions, which are selectively supplemented or deleted by neighborhood groups from the area being rated. The City Scan trained observer procedure developed by the Connecticut Policy and Economic Council ("City Scan: People, Technology, Results," n.d.; "City Scan Project: Contract for Results," n.d.; "City Scan: Current Measurable Conditions," n.d.) allows its raters to focus on no more than eight conditions at a time. (The use of more than eight has led to consistency problems between rating teams and information overload for the neighborhood groups that use the results.) Note that if the ratings focus on the presence of specific problems, an open-ended "other" category can always be included to catch any problems or concerns not explicitly listed.

Developing the Rating Scales and Forms

The next step is to specify the rating scales and the associated forms. Before developing a new rating scale, explore the feasibility of using existing, pretested scales such as those cited in Table 8.1. In addition to the cost saving, the use of existing scales has the advantage of drawing on tested, validated ratings, many of them complete with photographic standards. Literature from the fields of survey research, observational methods, and psychometrics can also be helpful (see, for instance, Miller, 1983, Cronbach, 1960, and Edwards, 1957).

General Guidelines for Developing the Rating Scales

Several guidelines should be followed when developing a new rating scale for trained observers. If possible, the evaluator should first observe numerous examples of the phenomenon of interest to record, and perhaps photograph, the full range of potential conditions. (A digital camera can greatly facilitate the latter effort.) Special situations and potentially difficult distinctions should be noted so that procedures or conventions can be developed to deal with them clearly and consistently.

No more than four or five major rating levels should be established, although midpoint ratings (2.5, 3.5) are usually allowed for conditions that fall between the major rating levels. It is essential that the conditions constituting each major level be defined with sufficient clarity and detail that a trained observer using the definitions can make accurate ratings with a minimum of guesswork and a high degree of consistency. The definitions should cover the entire range of conditions likely to be encountered, and each level of the scale should correspond to a meaningful perceived distinction. It is often conceptually useful to initially anchor the ratings by characterizing each grade in general terms, such as "very clean," "moderately clean," "dirty," and "very dirty." When a scale has more than three major rating levels, it is especially important to supplement the verbal descriptions with reference photographs that clearly depict the conditions and distinctions associated with each level.

The form of the rating scale will depend in part on the level of disaggregation used. At one extreme (no disaggregation), the evaluator could employ a single, composite multiattribute scale that simultaneously addresses all relevant aspects (and distinctions) regarding the given condition. At the other extreme (extensive disaggregation), the evaluator can use many simple, independent, single-attribute rating scales that jointly capture the important aspects of the condition—in effect, an elaborate checklist of key features, each addressing a distinct aspect of the condition or concept of interest (and each rated separately).

Simple (Single-Attribute) versus Complex (Multiattribute) Scales

The simpler conditions—involving single problems or attributes—can usually be adequately characterized using two- or three-level scales (present/not present, or present/partly present/not present). More complex, multiattribute constructs usually require the development of more elaborate scales containing four or more grades, each anchored by extensive definitions and reference photographs. The added complexity is needed to capture in a few grades the many important combinations, distinctions, and interactions among the characteristics that jointly define the overall condition or quality being assessed.

To illustrate these options, consider some simple two- and three-level scales that have been widely used in rating park and building maintenance. For each of several specific types of potential maintenance problems listed on the rating form (for ceilings, these might include cracks or bulges, missing or damaged tiles, and the need for repainting), the trained observer assesses the presence and extent of the problem using a scale such as the following:

NP = No problems

LIM = Limited problems

WID = Widespread problems

A problem is limited if it involves one-third or less of the feature rated. A problem is defined as widespread if it is extensive in scope or frequency—that is, if it involves over one-third of a given feature or facility. Detailed written definitions are provided to allow the raters to identify each type of potential maintenance problem. For instance, the need for repainting a ceiling can be defined as the presence of chipped or peeling paint, the existence of stains or graffiti, or the presence of bare, untreated surfaces.

The evaluator may wish to add a separate assessment to determine whether each of the problems identified constitutes a hazard, perhaps using a two-level scale (present or not present). Hazards can be defined as problems that are potentially dangerous to health or safety, regardless of their extent.

The four-level rating scale used in connection with the City Scan trained observer technique to assess streetscape and other conditions in Connecticut cities represents a combination of the two foregoing scales, with "hazardous" added as a fourth level. The general model for a City Scan scale is: no problem; minor problem/ugly; major problem; safety hazard/needs immediate attention. The nomenclature for each of the rating levels is adapted to the conditions being rated. For instance, vacant property and abandoned buildings are rated as: secure, clean; secure, eyesore; unsecured, eyesore; or unsecured, hazardous. Abandoned vehicles are rated as: removed; no apparent danger; eyesore but no apparent danger; or safety hazard. And catch basins are rated as: clean; minor nuisance; major nuisance; or safety hazard.

"Street cleanliness" illustrates a construct whose complex and potentially subtle distinctions justify a four-level scale with extensive written and photographic definitions for each grade. Exhibit 8.1 provides an example of a street cleanliness scale that has been used by several governments. Note that the written criteria specify the distinctions between the severity of combinations of conditions (scattered trash versus piles of trash) that help to jointly define and distinguish the various levels of cleanliness. Photographic standards illustrating the distinctions between each of the four major grades have been developed to assist with the ratings (see Exhibit 8.2).

Exhibit 8.1. Example of a Multiattribute Scale for Rating Street Cleanliness

Rating	Description
1	Street completely clean or almost completely clean; up to two pieces of litter are permitted.
2	Street largely clean; a few pieces of litter observable, but only in the form of a few isolated discarded items. On a generally clean blockface that otherwise merits a rating of 1, a single accumulation of uncontained trash (not set out for collection) with a volume less than or equal to the volume of a grocery bag should be rated 2.
3	Lightly scattered litter along all or most of the street or one heavy pile of litter, but no accumulations of litter large enough to indicate dumping. On a generally clean blockface otherwise meriting a rating of 1, a single accumulation of litter with a volume larger than that of a grocery bag but smaller than a standard 30 gallon garbage can (and not set out for collection) should be rated 3.
4	Heavily littered street; litter accumulation in piles or heavy litter distributed down all or nearly all of the blockface. On a generally clean blockface that would otherwise be rated 1 or 2, a single accumulation of litter with a volume greater than that of a standard 30 gallon garbage can (and not set out for collection) should be rated 4.

Intermediate ratings of 1.5, 2.5, and 3.5 can also be used when appropriate.

Source: Hatry, H. P., and others. *How Effective Are Your Community Services? Procedures for Measuring Their Quality.* (2nd ed.) Washington, D.C.: Urban Institute and the International City/County Management Association, 1992, p. 266. Used by permission.

Exhibit 8.2. Examples of Photographic Standards for Rating Street Cleanliness

Rating 1: Clean

Rating 2: Moderately clean

Source: Hatry, H. P., and others. *How Effective Are Your Community Services? Procedures for Measuring Their Quality.* (2nd ed.) Washington, D.C.: Urban Institute and the International City/County Management Association, 1992, p. 10. Used by permission.

Rating 3: Moderately littered

Rating 4: Heavily littered

New York City's Department of Parks and Recreation has used several multiattribute, multilevel rating scales for assessing park and recreation facilities. The four-level scale shown in Exhibit 8.3 has been used by the department to rate restrooms.

New York's Board of Education has used a combination of simple (two-level) scales and more complex multilevel scales for rating the condition of schools and playgrounds (Moore, 1988). Seven-level scales were used to rate the material integrity, surface quality, and cleanliness of classroom ceilings and walls. Two-level (yes-no) scales were used to assess certain specific types of problems (door appearance, door operation, damaged or inoperable lights, and the like). Individual pieces of playground equipment were graded using a four-level scale (severe, moderate, minor, no problems), with a separate assessment of hazards.

Advantages and Disadvantages of Single-Attribute and Multiattribute Scales

An increasing number of trained observer procedures are forgoing multi-level scales in favor of simple two-level rating scales. The ComNET technique pioneered by the Fund for the City of New York (see "Computerized Neighborhood Environment Tracking: ComNET," 2002) uses a checklist approach that is, in effect, a two-level scale: a problem condition is either present or not present. For example, trained observers using the ComNET technique in Worcester, Massachusetts, record utility covers that are missing, not level with the sidewalk, not level with the street, or unstable; they note streetlights with a missing or open baseplate, posted bills, exposed wires, broken glass, or graffiti ("Neighborhood Data: ComNET," n.d.). A specific address is entered for each problem noted. Kansas City's Department of Public Works uses trained observers to rate a variety of street maintenance features and conditions using a two-level pass-fail scale with distinct, precisely defined criteria for each item (City of Kansas City, 2000). Scales such as these simplify the rating process by focusing the ratings on the underlying reason for conducting the observations: the action or decision that depends on the rating produced. By ignoring rating distinctions and levels that are irrelevant to the action or decision of interest, the trained observer's workload is eased and the ratings focus on the problem at hand.

Indeed, even when a multilevel rating scale is adopted, the ratings frequently have to be translated into the equivalent of a two-level scale for the results to be used. For instance, although the cleanliness ratings shown in Exhibit 8.1 can range from 1 to 4, in practice ratings of 2.5 or higher are often considered unsatisfactory—a dirty street. If the primary reason for conducting the cleanliness rating is to identify dirty streets or the percentage of

Exhibit 8.3. Example of a Multiattribute Scale for Rating Restrooms

Rating	Description
1	All fixtures (sinks, bowls, and urinals) are intact and operating. Floors, walls, and ceilings are free from cracks and holes.
2	Some fixtures may be slightly damaged (for instance, chipped sinks or bowls, and/or leaky faucets). Walls, floors, and ceilings may be slightly cracked but are essentially intact.
3	Interior deterioration is evident. One or two fixtures may be inoperable; lighting fixtures, mirrors, and/or partitions may be broken or missing. Significant number of cracks exist in floors, walls, and/or ceilings.
4	Interior deterioration is widespread. Three or more fixtures may be inoperable; lighting fixtures, mirrors, and/or partitions are broken or missing. Extensive cracks and/or holes are present in floors, walls, and/or ceilings.

Source: City of New York (n.d.).

streets with unsatisfactory cleanliness ratings, the observer could use a two-level scale (clean-dirty) from the beginning, with "clean" corresponding to ratings of 1 to 2 on the four-level scale and "dirty" to ratings of 2.5 or higher. Of course, it then becomes essential to focus the definitions and the training (supplemented by appropriate photographs) on distinguishing between what would have merited a rating of 2 (on the four-level scale) and what would have corresponded to a rating of 2.5. There is no longer any need to consider the distinctions between ratings of 1 and 2 or between 3 and 4. But a two-level scale will tend to mask more subtle improvements or degradations in cleanliness that would be captured by a four-level scale.

Each type of scale has other advantages and disadvantages. The more elaborate multilevel, multiattribute scales can allow an observer to assess a given outcome relatively quickly (with only a single rating), while providing the additional precision possible by having several intermediate grades. The results are likely to be easier to understand since they compress numerous conditions and contingencies into a single rating. The frequent use of photographic standards in connection with such scales also enhances the reliability of the ratings.

However, such scales can also be difficult (and costly) to develop and validate. Unlike simple problem-oriented scales with only two or three rating levels, the attributes, distinctions, and definitions that form the basis for multilevel scales tend to differ considerably from feature to feature. A completely new scale must be developed, tested, *and remembered* by the person making the ratings for each feature or condition rated (although the use of hand-held computers, described later, can reduce the memory burden). Furthermore, because the ratings produced in connection with these scales are highly aggregated, the individual magnitudes and effects of the various underlying attributes are not available for further analysis.

In contrast, two- and three-level single-attribute (problem-oriented) scales are fairly similar from one type of problem to another, requiring simpler judgments and fewer subtle distinctions. It is also usually easier to check on the accuracy and validity of the trained observer ratings when fewer distinctions are required and the ratings focus on a single problem at a specific address. This greatly simplifies training and quality control and makes it easier to assess a large number of diverse items, including unexpected problems. (The list of potential problems can be readily modified to reflect new issues or concerns.)

However, some precision is sacrificed in relying on only two or three rating levels: subtle changes in individual conditions or problems may go undetected. (Nonetheless, the increased difficulty of applying multilevel scales accurately and consistently may dilute the benefits of the added precision afforded by the extra rating levels.) Moreover, it is likely to take longer to assess a given overall outcome (for instance, the quality of the housing stock) if it is decomposed into ratings of numerous individual problems than if a few less disaggregated, overall rating scales are used.

Clearly, selection of the appropriate rating scale depends on a variety of sometimes conflicting considerations: the use to be made of the results, the users of the results and their ability to understand the information produced, and the cost (and difficulty) of developing, conducting, and validating the ratings. The more different observers involved in the process, the more important it is for the rating scales to be clearly defined and simple to apply.

Anchoring the Scales

Regardless of the number of rating levels used, one should consider anchoring the definition of one or two levels to conditions that trigger special actions by program staff. For instance, in Dallas, where trained observer procedures have been used to assess the condition of the housing stock in certain neighborhoods, the rating levels were defined so that a grade of 3 was just sufficient to require action by a city building inspector. Toronto has used a ten-part street condition rating scale in which the lowest grades require no repair work, the highest rating requires complete reconstruction of the road, and the remaining grades correspond to various less extensive repairs. Two-level scales such as those used by ComNET and Kansas City's Department of Public Works are designed to focus directly on the conditions or situations that are severe enough to trigger the decision or action of interest.

Using Photographic Benchmarks

The accuracy and consistency of trained observer ratings can often be improved by providing the observers with photographs illustrating the distinctions between rating levels. In some cases, existing reference photographs, such as those in Exhibit 8.2 and in several of the references at the end of this chapter, can be used. When a new set of reference photographs has to be developed, the following procedure can be employed. It is based on Thurstone's "method of equal-appearing intervals," a general approach for developing an equal interval scale often called the "Q sort" technique (see Thurstone and Chave, 1929; Edwards, 1957; Cronbach, 1960):

1. Take a large number of pictures (fifty to one hundred) of each facility or condition of interest (for instance, litter or cracks in walls). A digital camera can be very helpful here. The photographs should include examples of the entire spectrum of conditions that can be encountered. Close-ups should be used to provide detail on small features.
2. The photographs for a given condition should be numbered and given to five to ten "judges" for review. Each judge is asked to sort the photographs for the condition independently, placing them in separate piles representing significantly different gradations in the condition. Each pile should correspond to a distinct rating on the desired scale and should be characterized in a word or two (for instance, very clean, moderately clean, moderately littered, very littered).
3. Analyze the results to determine how frequently each photograph was assigned to each category by each judge. Determine the photographs for which there is the most agreement between the judges concerning the rating category to which they belong. These should serve as the benchmarks for the corresponding rating level. One can also use the sophisticated yet simple statistical techniques associated with the Q-sort method to assign each photograph to a rating category and assess its value as a standard (see, for instance, Edwards, 1957).

If, in the opinion of the evaluator, the final set of photographs does not adequately cover—or distinguish between—the full range of conditions expected, additional photographs should be taken, and the process should be repeated.

Photographs are especially helpful in connection with scales that involve four or more levels or complex, multiattribute definitions of the ratings. In such cases, the distinctions between rating levels may be rather subtle (especially for ratings toward the middle of the scale), and rating accuracy and consistency can often be improved by providing the trained observers with reference photographs illustrating those distinctions. The need for photographic anchors tends to be less critical in connection with two- or three-level scales focusing on individual problems since the distinctions tend to be clearer. However, the same potential ambiguity will characterize observed conditions that are visually "close" to the threshold that separates adjacent ratings, whether part of a two-level or a five-level scale. Reference photographs for such borderline conditions can be very helpful, especially for training.

Aggregating Ratings into an Overall Assessment

A final issue in developing trained observer scales is how to aggregate individual ratings of several items into an overall assessment of a given feature or construct. One approach is to develop a combined distribution (or score) for the ratings of all relevant items. (Of course, this is practical only if the rating scales for the various items all have the same number of levels.) For the two- and three-level park maintenance scales discussed previously, this approach corresponds to determining the total number and percentage of "limited," "widespread," "no problem," and "hazard" ratings for all the potential problems examined in connection with a given feature or facility (see Exhibit 8.5 later in this chapter). Such an analysis is also possible if "no problem" ratings are ignored, as in the ComNET trained observer technique; however, the interpretation of the aggregate percentages will be different.

The procedure just described assumes that each rating has the same importance in determining the overall score. However, it may be appropriate to weight the various items differently when preparing the overall assessment. For instance, in developing a combined assessment of overall housing conditions, the City Development Department of Kansas City, Missouri, has multiplied each of eight ratings (for roofs, exterior wall surfaces, windows, and so forth) by prescribed weights before computing the overall score. The weights were developed from prior studies designed to determine the relative importance of each housing characteristic to overall conditions (Hatry, Morley, Barbour, and Pajunen, 1991).

Alternatively, a set of rules can be developed to create an overall rating from a set of individual ratings. Exhibit 8.4 illustrates a procedure that has been used by Alexandria, Virginia, and other jurisdictions to combine the ratings of park or building problems for a given feature or facility into a single overall rating. Kansas City's Department of Parks and Recreation has established precise rules for determining whether a park is considered acceptable or unacceptable, based on ratings of numerous distinct park maintenance conditions. For instance, a park is unacceptable if it receives any unacceptable cleanliness

**Exhibit 8.4. A Procedure for Deriving an Overall
Facility Rating from Ratings of Individual Problems**

Overall Rating	Ratings of Individual Problems
1	No problems
2	A few "limited" problems
3	Many "limited" problems or one "widespread" problem
4	More than one "widespread" problem

Note: Half-point ratings (1.5, 2.5, 3.5) can be used to indicate conditions that fall between the defined points.

ratings, if there are any hazards requiring immediate attention, or if three or more other features are rated unacceptable (City of Kansas City, n.d.).

Note that many jurisdictions prepare aggregate overall assessments by averaging the relevant (numerical) ratings. Although this is convenient, the validity of such averages may be compromised by the nominal or ordinal nature of the relevant rating scales.

Forms for Recording the Results

To facilitate the trained observer process (and subsequent aggregation of the ratings), a convenient form should be designed for recording the results. This form should indicate the date, time, and location of the ratings, the names of the raters, and perhaps the weather (since weather conditions may affect the observations). Space should be provided on the form for the rater to record any other characteristics and potential explanatory factors that could be helpful in analyzing the data. (Connecticut's City Scan makes a point of asking responders—city agencies, private property owners, and so forth—at the outset what information they will need to make an effective response to the problems identified; raters are required to provide such information in connection with the ratings.)

If the rating process is based on identifying and rating specific problems, the most common types of anticipated problems (as well as those whose importance merits a special search effort) should be listed explicitly on the rating form. The form should also provide places for the rater to record and assess any other problems encountered.

Exhibit 8.5 is an example of a paper form for recording and aggregating problem-based trained observer ratings of park maintenance conditions. It is designed to lead the rater through each step of the rating process,

Exhibit 8.5. Form for Recording Trained Observer Ratings of Parks and Recreation Facilities

Name of Park/Facility: _____

Location (Streets): _____ Neighborhood Area: _____

Type of Park: _____

Date: _____ Weather: _____ Name: _____ Time of Day: _____

Key:
"–" – No such facility/not applicable
NP – No Problem
Lim. – Limited
Wide. – Widespread
Haz. – Hazard

Aspect	Element	STEP 1: Identification of Problem		STEP 2: Rating of Each Problem	STEP 3: Element Totals	STEP 4: Aspect Totals
		Potential Problem	Notes and Comments on Problems Found			
Landscaping	Grass and lawns	Grass unmowed, unkempt			NP ___ Lim. ___ Wide. ___ Haz. ___	NP ___ Lim. ___ Wide. ___ Haz. ___
		Weeds present in grass, fences				
		Grass not trimmed				
		Grass not properly edged				
		Grass brown, unhealthy, worn				
		Broken glass hazard				
		Other				
	Shrubs, trees, plantings	Require trimming			NP ___ Lim. ___ Wide. ___ Haz. ___	
		Weeds present in planted areas				
		Dead shrubs, trees, foliage				
		Broken glass hazard				
		Other				
Cleanliness	Litter	Litter rating of 2.5 or worse	Overall litter rating: ____			
Playgrounds and playing fields	Play areas	Equipment broken, cracked, or loose			NP ___ Lim. ___ Wide. ___ Haz. ___	
		Equipment defaced				
		Equipment needs repainting or refinishing				

		Area infested with weeds			NP ___
		Broken glass hazard			Lim. ___
		Other			Wide. ___
	Playing fields and courts	Basketball/tennis court lines or surface in poor condition			Haz. ___
		Equipment broken or damaged		NP ___	
		Base paths rutted, muddy		Lim. ___	
		Base paths, skinned areas poorly defined		Wide. ___ Haz. ___	
		Playing fields infested with weeds			
		Broken glass hazard			
		Other			
Restrooms	Odors and cleanliness	Objectionable odors			
		Toilets, basins, mirrors, etc.		NP ___	
		Walls dirty or stained		Lim. ___	
		Floors dirty, stained, littered, or wet		Wide. ___ Haz. ___	
		Broken glass hazard			NP ___
		Other			Lim. ___
	Maintenance	Lack of toilet paper, towels, etc.			Wide. ___
		Broken/leaking/inoperable fixtures		NP ___ Lim. ___	Haz. ___
		Need for repainting (due to graffiti, etc.)		Wide. ___ Haz. ___	
		Other			
Other facilities	Paths, walks, parking areas	Dirt/gravel paths rutted, overgrown, muddy, blocked, etc.		NP ___	
		Paved walks have holes, ruts, water, defects, etc.		Lim. ___ Wide. ___	
		Parking area pavement rated 2.5 or worse	Overall pavement rating: _____	Haz. ___	
		Broken glass hazard			
		Other			

Exhibit 8.5. Form for Recording Trained Observer Ratings of Parks and Recreation Facilities, *continued*

Aspect	Element	STEP 1: Identification of Problem		STEP 2: Rating of Each Problem	STEP 3: Element Totals	STEP 4: Aspect Totals
		Potential Problem	*Notes and Comments on Problems Found*			
	Park benches and picnic tables	Tables broken, overturned, or damaged			NP ___ Lim. ___ Wide. ___ Haz. ___	NP ___ Lim. ___ Wide. ___ Haz. ___
		Table surfaces dirty, littered, greasy, etc.				
		Benches broken, overturned, or damaged				
		Benches need painting or refinishing				
		Broken glass hazard				
		Other				
	Structures and other facilities	Structures dirty or stained			NP ___ Lim. ___ Wide. ___ Haz. ___	
		Structures damaged or broken, parts missing				
		Need for repainting (due to graffiti, etc.)				
		Lights/electric services broken or hazardous				
		Broken glass hazard				
		Other				

Source: City of Charlottesville, Virginia, and TriData Corporation, Arlington, Virginia. Used by permission.

from problem identification to the preparation of overall summary ratings for each aspect of park maintenance examined. The basic definitions of the rating levels are repeated on the form as a convenience to the rater.

Although paper forms are easy and inexpensive to prepare, they can be cumbersome to use, and the need to hand-tally the ratings on such forms or to transfer the information to a computer database can be daunting. Such difficulties have reportedly sometimes been a factor in discouraging or limiting the use of trained observer ratings, especially when volunteers must conduct the coding and analysis. Working with paper forms can also introduce additional errors, for instance, in tallying the ratings and in deciphering the rater's handwriting. The use of hand-held computers, which provide electronic rating forms, can avoid these problems. Nevertheless, some jurisdictions have found that retirees and other older observers prefer paper rating forms.

Testing the Rating Procedures

Regardless of the technology used, it is essential that all rating scales, forms, and data collection techniques be carefully pretested by several persons before proceeding with the ratings to ensure that the procedures produce consistent results. Special attention should be given to the middle rating categories, which are usually the most difficult to distinguish.

Hand-Held Computers and Other Technology

In recent years, trained observers have benefited from an infusion of technology. The introduction of hand-held computers, digital cameras, camcorders, and other technologies has had a profound effect on the rating procedures and the analysis and presentation of the results.

Hand-Held Computers

The use of hand-held computers in connection with trained observer ratings is growing in popularity. One of the first such efforts was the School Scorecard program operated by New York City's Board of Education, which used hand-held computers to record ratings of playgrounds and school buildings. The computers weighed four and a half pounds and were about the size of a legal pad in 1992, although they have become considerably smaller since then. Using a stylus wired to the unit, the rater "wrote" the necessary information—for example, the playground name, the number and type of equipment—on a form displayed on the screen. The computer then displayed the appropriate rating forms, one after the other, for each maintenance element or piece of equipment associated with the given playground. Each form included a list of potential problems and ratings tailored to the item. The rater assessed each feature or potential problem using the appropriate scale (which was provided by the computer) and noted whether it represented a hazard. The computer prompted the rater to provide all the necessary information, checked the rater's entries for completeness and logical consistency, and tallied the results as appropriate. At the end of the day, each rater's entries were uploaded to School Scorecard's main computer system, where all the trained observer results were checked and compiled.

The Fund for the City of New York has pioneered in using hand-held computers to facilitate trained observer ratings. The ComNET (for Computerized Neighborhood Environment Tracking) technique developed by the fund employs palm-sized computers with attached digital cameras to help in rating and recording a wide variety of street-level conditions (see Cohn, 1999; "Computerized Neighborhood Environment Tracking: ComNET," n.d.). This approach is being used in connection with trained observer ratings in Worcester, Massachusetts (Worcester Regional Research Bureau, n.d.) and by eighteen neighborhood organizations in New York City, including a number of the city's Business Improvement Districts. Drawing on the ComNET concept, the Connecticut Economic and Policy Council has developed a trained observer approach it calls City Scan that makes extensive use of hand-held computers and other technologies ("What Is City Scan?" n.d.; "City Scan Project: Contract for Results," n.d.). City Scan has been used to undertake trained observer ratings in a number of Connecticut cities, including Hartford, Norwalk, Stamford, Bridgeport, and Danbury. Both ComNET and City Scan rely heavily on neighborhood residents and community groups to identify the conditions to be rated and to provide the raters. Des Moines, Iowa; San Francisco, California; and Montgomery County, Maryland are also using hand-held computers in connection with trained observer ratings (see, for instance, "ParkScan Home," n.d.).

In each of these examples, the ratings are recorded using specially designed software running on the hand-helds. When a feature or condition is selected by the rater, the computer brings up the appropriate rating form, including the scale to be used and (in some cases) suggested problems that the rater should look for in assessing the condition. There are usually provisions for entering (sometimes automatically) other important descriptive and identifying information. In some instances, the route to be traversed by the raters is preprogrammed, block by block, on the hand-held. Detailed maps and aerial photographs of the neighborhood, downloaded from a Geographic Information System (GIS), can also be included to help the raters. At the end of the day, the teams' ratings are uploaded back at the office into a central database that compiles and organizes the information, linking it as necessary to photographs, maps, and other pertinent files.

Benefits of Hand-Held Computers

Although they may increase the cost of conducting trained observer ratings, hand-held computers can provide some significant benefits. They can enhance the completeness and consistency of the ratings through their ability to show in detail the specific scale used to rate a given condition (including the relevant definitions, and prompts concerning the types of problems to look for) and by encouraging (or requiring) the rater to provide other key information needed to characterize or remediate the given problem. Hand-held computers can improve the accuracy of the ratings by facilitating the inclusion of detailed information on problem location, in some cases linked electronically to digital maps and photographs (this helps in verifying and validating the ratings); by making reference photographs for any scale readily available to the rater in the field; by reducing the need for raters to recall the many scales, problems, and features of interest; and by avoiding the introduction of errors associated with the need for manually tallying the ratings and for deciphering the raters' handwriting. In some cases, users of paper rating forms have reported that the tedious work of tallying and transcribing the forms has made it difficult to recruit and retain volunteers. On the contrary, the opportunity to use hand-held computers and other high-tech equipment has often served to attract volunteers (although some jurisdictions have found that older raters, while needed for their knowledge of the conditions of interest, are sometimes reluctant to use the hand-helds).

The hand-held computers have proven to be easy to operate ("as easy as an ATM," in the words of one observer) while sturdy enough to absorb rough treatment. In contrast to paper rating forms, the software running on a hand-held can be quickly and easily revised to reflect new or modified conditions or to focus on specific items of interest for a particular neighborhood or evaluation problem. The fact that the output provided by hand-held computers is already organized as a digital database has additional advantages. Foremost among these, in the view of many users, is the rapid turnaround of the results: tallies can be produced almost as soon as the data are uploaded from the hand-held to the central database. The output can be presented as familiar, easy-to-manipulate spreadsheets, can be transmitted over the Web to take advantage of remote database and data analysis resources, and can in principle be directly linked to the municipal systems that record and track complaints and that write work orders to ensure that problems are addressed on a timely basis. The digital output facilitates, and perhaps encourages, extensive analysis of the data and provides great flexibility for displaying the results and linking them to maps, photographs, and other types of information.

Digital Cameras

Digital cameras have been closely associated with the use of hand-held computers for trained observer ratings. The ComNET process usually uses a digital camera that is attached to the hand-held computer: the resulting photographs are automatically linked within the database to the appropriate trained observer ratings. ComNET's policy has been to use the digital camera as an optional supplement to the ratings: observers can take a picture whenever they feel it is necessary or helpful, for example, to document a safety hazard, a new condition, or a particularly egregious situation. Under City Scan's procedures, a digital photograph is taken for every condition rated as a problem. Since this policy requires a large amount of memory, City Scan uses a separate digital camera containing a removable floppy disc for storage. Special software links the digital photographs to the rating database.

     The availability of a digital camera can have many advantages for trained observer ratings. Digital photographs provide an inexpensive way to document, verify, and track the conditions found. This can be very helpful for following up on the findings and their remediation (for example, using before and after photos), publicizing the results, protecting against possible challenges to the ratings, or justifying potentially controversial follow-up actions (for instance, when evaluating the performance of contractors). Digital cameras can also be helpful in defining the rating scales and training the observers. This technology makes it possible for staff to record key conditions quickly and inexpensively, even before the rating scales are completely specified. This capability could be helpful when the evaluation gets off to a late start, the conditions of interest are changing rapidly, or one cannot be sure at the outset that a formal evaluation is going to be necessary.

Camcorders

Camcorders can be used for many of the applications noted in connection with digital cameras: developing rating scales, documenting ratings, and assisting with training. Videotapes can be especially useful for documenting extended conditions and for demonstrating (for training purposes) specific behaviors to be rated in connection with human services clients. Indeed, camcorders capable of recording sound can assist in documenting and validating trained observer assessments of such clients (any such recordings generally require the permission of the client).

     One potential disadvantage of camcorders is the difficulty associated with accessing videotaped results. Videotaped information can be difficult to incorporate into the written reports that often are preferred by local governments and neighborhood organizations for transmitting trained observer results. But videotaped results can be very effective when displayed on a Web site or included in formal presentations to city and community organizations.

The availability of camcorders or digital cameras can also reduce the number of trained observers needed and the time necessary to complete the ratings. Conditions at widely separated locations can be photographed or videotaped simultaneously by relatively untrained staff and subsequently rated by a single trained observer. Videotaped or digitally photographed conditions recorded by the trained observer can also be used by the rating supervisor for quality control. In some cases, an evaluator might be able to take advantage of existing videotape records. For instance, many state highway departments periodically videotape every mile of state-maintained highway, a process known as "photologging."

Other Technologies

A variety of other technologies have been used to facilitate and enhance trained observer ratings. Custom-designed software has been developed for organizing and analyzing the data collected, preparing reports, and linking the rating results with maps, photographs, and other information to provide what is, in effect, a visual database of the trained observer results. GIS software has been used to provide up-to-date maps for the raters (in some cases, displayed on their hand-held computer), plot the location of the problems or conditions identified, and overlay aerial photographs of the neighborhood or of the route taken by the trained observers to enhance the presentation of results (or to help orient the raters). Kansas City's Department of Public Works uses its GIS database to prepare a stratified random sample of eighteen hundred street segments to be rated by trained observers (a new sample is drawn each year). In Hartford, Connecticut, Global Positioning Satellite (GPS) receivers have been used by City Scan teams to determine the precise location of problem conditions found in parks, where no address is available. The GPS coordinates have been electronically linked to the relevant maps and ratings to provide a graphical display of the park conditions identified (see the City Scan Web site, www.city-scan.com). City Scan staff have also experimented with the use of wireless modems to transmit field ratings to the base office, avoiding the need for the trained observer teams to return to the office at the end of the day. Bandwidth problems have limited the usefulness of this technology so far. However, if those limitations can be overcome in the future, this technology may make it possible to transmit "before" photographs of a specific location to the raters in the field for direct comparison with current conditions.

Trained observers have also taken advantage of the Internet. In addition to being an excellent medium for presenting and publicizing the rating results (including maps, photographs, and videotapes of the findings), the Internet can provide a convenient tool for storing and using the rating results. For example, the Fund for the City of New York has developed and hosts a Web-based database that ComNET users in remote locations can access for compiling their ratings, analyzing the results, and preparing reports. (Users are assigned their own section of this database; they do not have access to the results of other teams that use the database.)

Selecting and Training the Raters and Conducting the Ratings

The accuracy and usefulness of trained observer ratings also depend on how the ratings are implemented: the raters used, the training they are given, and the observational protocols they follow.

Selecting the Raters

Although nearly anyone can be a trained observer, the best raters will have good eyesight and concentration, will be observant and conscientious about detail, and will be skilled at reading maps. Since the ratings can be tedious, the observers should be able to sustain their motivation and concentration for long periods. (The opportunity to use high-tech equipment such as hand-held computers and GPS receivers can help maintain rater interest.)

Persons of many backgrounds and ages have successfully served as trained observers, from high school students to senior citizens. (The use of high school students as observers can impose additional burdens such as obtaining parental consent, unique supervision requirements, and the need to provide transportation and exclude dangerous locations.) To avoid the possibility or appearance of bias, at least one member of each trained observer team (and preferably all members) should be neutral—that is, not involved in the program being assessed.

Trained observer ratings can (and sometimes must) be conducted by individuals, but the use of teams is preferable. Two pairs of eyes to identify problems and two opinions on ambiguous rating decisions are better than one. Team members can share the workload, each rating different conditions or handling different functions. (City Scan teams in Connecticut consist of a spotter who identifies problem conditions, a recorder who enters the rating in a hand-held computer, and a photographer who documents each problem identified.) Teaming can also contribute to the safety of the raters if that is of concern (for instance, if the observations are made from motor vehicles or in isolated areas). However, the use of teams may also increase the total cost of the ratings. A balance must be struck between ensuring the quality of the ratings and limiting their cost.

If the number of ratings needed is small (or there is plenty of time), all ratings should probably be conducted by a single trained observer or team of observers to minimize inter-rater consistency problems. For faster ratings or for assessing a large number of facilities or events, several different raters or rating teams can be used. To economize on the number of trained observers needed, consider having relatively untrained personnel make photographs or videotapes of the conditions of interest; these can be brought to a single observer or team to be rated.

Training the Raters

The provision of adequate training is critical to the reliability and ultimately the credibility of the trained observer procedure since the quality of the training will determine rater accuracy and inter-rater consistency to a great extent. This is especially important when the procedure is used for program evaluation, as opposed to merely identifying, assessing, and following up on problems. Although the actual time needed to train the raters will depend on the number and complexity of the characteristics rated (and the scales used), no more than two or three days of training will usually be necessary. When the observations focus on only one or two simple characteristics, training can often be completed in one to two hours.

Each rater or rating team should receive copies of the written definitions for each scale, any photographic standards, a training manual, and related equipment, such as rulers or a hand-held computer. After a general introduction and classroom discussion of photographs, slides, or videotapes of the conditions of interest, the trainees should accompany the trainer to several preselected sites. The trainer should demonstrate how various conditions or events are rated and recorded and discuss the considerations that come into play in each case. The trainees should be shown examples of the full spectrum of possible ratings—the very bad as well as the very good—to help ensure that they do not rate moderate conditions too severely.

Two tests should be administered. The first is a practice test: all trained observer teams should independently rate a preselected site or event just as if they were making an actual rating in the field. Any difficulties with the procedures or inter-rater differences in the ratings should be discussed, with additional field training provided as needed.

The raters should then be given a realistic qualifying test involving several preselected sites or conditions. The team pairings for this test should be those that will subsequently be used for the actual ratings. The teams should summarize their results at the end of the field test, using the appropriate forms and procedures. The trainer should check the rating forms, computer dumps, and summaries prepared by each team to identify any errors (or bad habits). The ratings should then be compared rater by rater (or team by team) with those of the trainer or judge. Individual biases or errors should be identified and corrected, with supplemental instruction and fieldwork provided as necessary. The training should continue until the rater and the trainer are in exact agreement for at least 70 percent of the ratings and agree within half a rating level for 90 percent of the ratings.

Conducting the Ratings

If there are numerous facilities or events to be rated, the evaluator may need to specify a sample (or sampling rules) before proceeding with the ratings. Standard sampling techniques can be used. For each grouping of interest (for instance, units participating in the program being evaluated, units not participating in the program), a sample of perhaps one hundred units should be selected.

Ratings of street or housing conditions can be made from a sample of blockfaces or road segments. The individual blocks or road segments can be chosen randomly, or one can lay out a random route of 100 to 150 blocks through each neighborhood of interest. A sample of rooms for assessing conditions in buildings can be obtained by establishing a simple sampling rule (for instance, walk along every corridor and rate every third room or enclosed area).

To rate a park, the trained observer team should begin by systematically walking around the facility, taking extensive notes on any problems encountered. After covering the entire facility, the team should complete the rating form, referring to the notes they made and reobserving items where there is a disagreement. (If a hand-held computer is being used and the focus is on individual problems, each problem should be assessed and entered into the computer, along with its location, as it is encountered.) For assessing linearly distributed features such as street cleanliness or housing conditions, "windshield" ratings from a moving vehicle can be used. The rating team drives slowly along the street in question, recording the ratings on the appropriate forms, on a hand-held computer, or into a tape recorder.

Regardless of the procedure employed, the raters should refer frequently to the photographs and written definitions of the various scales. (Periodically reviewing reference photographs of the worst conditions can help raters in relatively "good" areas avoid the tendency to overreact to a few moderate problems by assigning overly severe ratings.) The raters should be provided with good maps or floor plans for the features of interest. Although it can sometimes be efficient to have the raters assess several kinds of facilities or conditions at one time, the observers should not be overloaded with too many simultaneous ratings or accuracy and consistency will suffer.

Quality Control Procedures

Because of the inherently subjective nature of trained observer ratings, adequate quality control is critical to ensuring the validity and credibility of the results. This is especially important when the technique is used for program evaluation. Key features to monitor (and control) include inter-rater reliability, repeatability, and accuracy with respect to the written and visual (photographic) rating standards.

The accuracy and validity of the trained observer results can be greatly affected by the design of the rating procedure. A number of considerations can affect the quality of the results:

- The number of teams used (fewer teams mean fewer potential consistency problems)
- The source and qualifications of the raters (they should have no vested interest in the results)
- The number of persons on a rating team (and thus the need for a broad consensus on the ratings)
- The number of specific conditions to be rated
- The variety and complexity of the rating scales used
- The focus and effectiveness of the training provided

Providing for or requiring photographs of the problems identified and precise information on the location of those problems can facilitate subsequent review and validation of the ratings. To provide oversight and ensure the consistency of the assessments made by its raters (who are usually drawn from the neighborhood being rated), the Worcester Regional Research Bureau in Worcester, Massachusetts, requires that a specially trained staff member accompany each of its trained observer teams.

There are also a number of procedures that can be undertaken to monitor and control the quality of the trained observer ratings. In addition to the quality control checks built into the initial training, the following procedures should be used:

- The supervisor of the trained observer effort should periodically rerate 5 to 10 percent of the facilities or events assessed by each individual or team. The percentage of agreement between each rater and the supervisor should be computed and any discrepancies discussed. (The observers should be informed that a sample of their ratings will be checked.)

Special emphasis should be given to rechecking those items that received the "worst" assessments since these determine many of the key effectiveness measures. Verification of several of the worst ratings will also indicate whether the observers are rating some problems too harshly. (There is often a tendency to become too severe in rating moderate problems, especially when most facilities are in good condition.) Some ratings toward the middle of the scale should also be checked since these tend to be the hardest for the raters to distinguish accurately.

• The ratings should be turned in as they are completed and reviewed by the judge or rating supervisor for errors, omissions, and logical consistency. If the ratings are entered directly into a hand-held computer, the computer can perform logical checks as the ratings are recorded and can require that any errors or omissions be corrected before the ratings proceed.

• If the ratings are conducted over several months or years, the trained observers should be periodically retested by the judge or rating supervisor. This can be done by having the observers rate photographs, slides, or videotapes of specific conditions or events or by having them all rate the same sites. The retest results should be compared with those of the judge and, where appropriate, analyzed for inter-rater reliability.

• When extensive trained observer ratings are to be conducted on a continuing basis, it can be helpful to create special computer programs for analyzing the ratings and identifying potential discrepancies. New York City developed a number of programs for analyzing the weekly and monthly ratings prepared in connection with Project Scorecard (street cleanliness) and School Scorecard (condition of schools and playgrounds) (see Fund for the City of New York, 1983; Moore, 1988). The software estimated the reliability of individual raters and of the rating process as a whole from a statistical analysis of periodic rater cross-checks (in which all trained observers rated the same series of slides, buildings, or blockfaces). The cross-check data were also used to analyze differences between raters and to determine whether there was sufficient inter-rater consistency. In addition, each rater's latest ratings were checked against his or her past assessments of the same block or facility to identify unexplainable trends that might suggest that the rater was drifting from the prescribed rating standards.

If any of the quality control procedures indicate errors, discrepancies, or inter-rater reliability levels that exceed the established tolerances, the relevant problems should immediately be discussed with the observers in question, with remedial training provided as necessary.

Analyzing and Presenting the Results

A wide variety of performance indicators can be prepared from the information collected by trained observers. For instance, such indicators can address the overall characteristics of facilities and events (an example would be the average number of maintenance problems found in a given type of building). It is also possible to prepare performance indicators that focus on the effectiveness of specific activities or the incidence of specific types of problems.

The problem-based park maintenance ratings described previously illustrate the range of indicator options available. These results can usually be expressed in several alternate forms:

- As an "average" rating (average park cleanliness)
- As a percentage of the facilities rated (the percentage of ball fields with widespread maintenance problems)
- As a percentage of all the individual observations made (the percentage of all maintenance ratings that were "unsatisfactory")
- As an extreme (the number or percentage of park ratings that exceeded a certain critical level, the "worst" parks, the most common problems)

For some indicators, the trained observer results for specific items or features will first have to be classified as "satisfactory" or "unsatisfactory." For instance, a number of governments have determined that, for their purposes, a cleanliness rating of 2.5 or more on the four-point scale described in Exhibits 8.1 and 8.2 should be considered "unsatisfactory." Similarly, using the problem-oriented park rating scale described above (and illustrated in Exhibit 8.5), one could define a park or playground as being in "unsatisfactory" condition if it contains, say, one or more "widespread" maintenance problems, or—alternatively—if more than one-third of all the major park maintenance elements examined (ball fields, play areas, grass and lawns, and so forth) exhibit at least some problems. Dallas designed its housing condition scale so that a rating of 3 or more corresponded to an unsatisfactory situation (that is, one potentially in violation of city housing codes).

Unless the intervals between the points of the rating scale are equal in some absolute sense, the use of average ratings is not strictly correct and can distort the results. Although averages constitute a popular way to summarize numerical trained observer ratings, it is safer methodologically to use percentages (for instance, the percentage of ratings that exceed a given level). Percentages also have the advantage of being able to highlight the presence of serious problems, results that might be lost in an average rating.

The ratings can often be usefully disaggregated on the basis of geographical, demographic, and operational factors. For instance, park maintenance ratings can be broken down using the following categories:

- Type of facility (mini-park, neighborhood park, recreation center)
- Neighborhood area, ward, or councilmanic district
- Maintenance district or service area

- Demographic characteristics of the neighborhood or clientele served (for example, income, racial mix, education)

Such breakouts can also be used to assess the equity with which services are being provided, that is, to identify differences in service outcomes between various neighborhoods and socioeconomic groups. In addition, the data can be grouped to examine the effects of potential confounding factors—weather, the timing of the observations, seasonality, traffic levels, or specific raters.

One of the advantages of trained observer ratings is that the results can be easily understood by the average citizen. Appropriate displays of the data can further enhance the accessibility and utility of the information. Figure 8.1 illustrates one such display, using classroom maintenance ratings from New York's School Scorecard project. See also the Worcester Regional Research Bureau (2001 and 2002) for examples of reports summarizing trained observer results. These reports can be downloaded from the Web.

Because the geographical location of each trained observer rating is precisely known, the results can often be usefully mapped and displayed using a GIS. Figure 8.2 illustrates such a display. The availability of digital photographs and digital maps linked to the trained observer results offers many opportunities for creatively displaying the findings in reports and on Web sites. For example, to obtain additional information on the park rating results shown on the maps of Hartford's parks appearing on the City Scan Web site (www.city-scan.com), one can click on the icons that denote the locations of observed problems. This will bring up information on the nature of the problem found, its precise location, the date of the observation, and a picture of the relevant condition.

Time, Cost, and Staffing Requirements

The cost of a trained observer effort is usually relatively modest, especially if existing personnel or citizen volunteers are available to conduct the ratings. Total expenditures will depend on the number and type of facilities or events rated, whether the evaluator develops new rating scales or adapts materials from others, the type of scales employed (multilevel, multiattribute scales with photographic anchors versus single-problem "checklist" scales), and the frequency with which the ratings are repeated. Preparation of new, photographically anchored multiattribute rating scales can require four weeks or more, whereas a set of single-attribute, problem-oriented rating scales can usually be developed in one to two weeks. Training typically requires no more than two to three days.

Some relatively small out-of-pocket expenses are likely to be necessary. These include printing and reproducing the reference photographs (which

Figure 8.1. Presenting Trained Observer Results: An Example

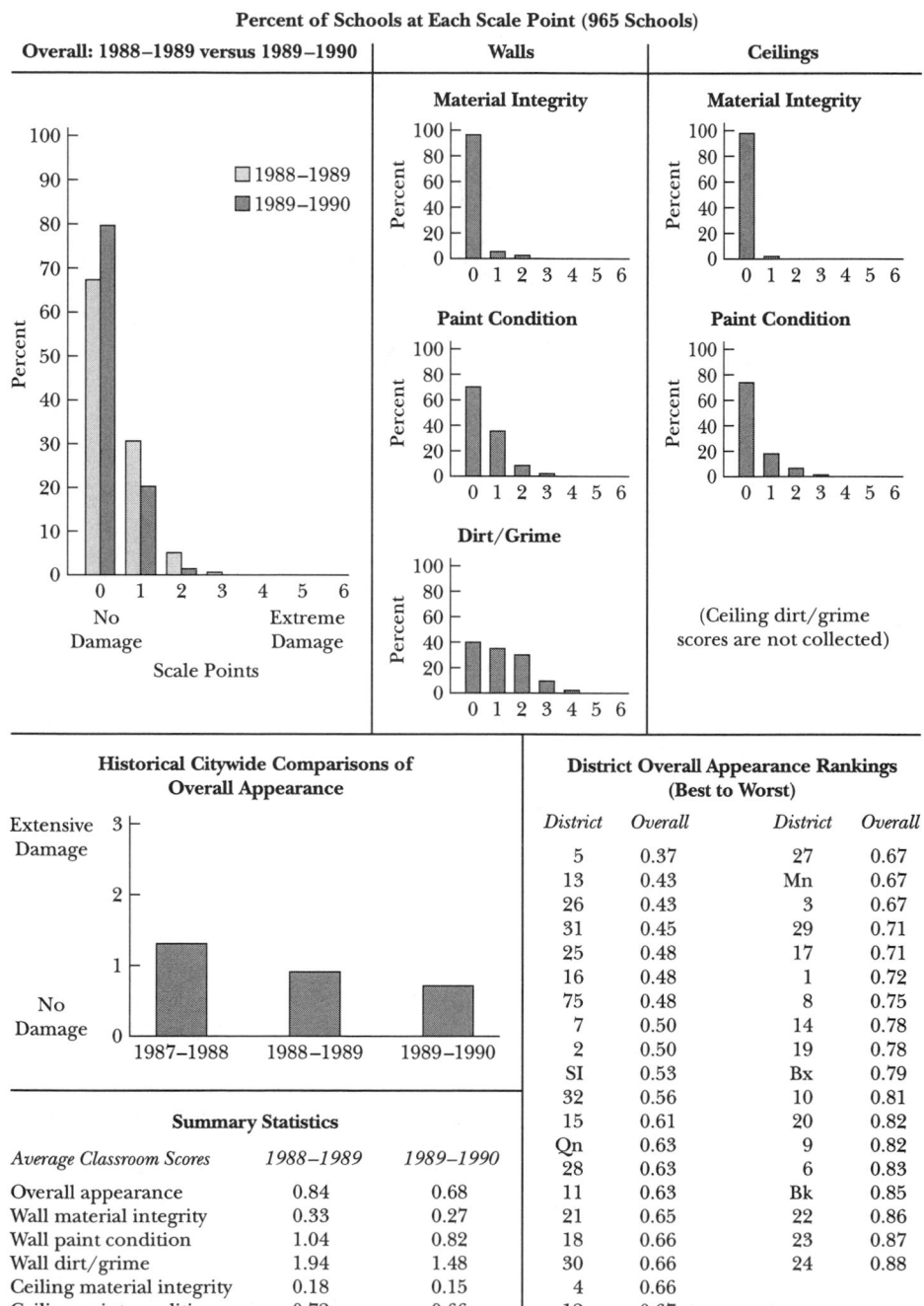

Percent of Schools at Each Scale Point (965 Schools)

Source: Liebmann (1990, p. 7).

Figure 8.2. Using Maps to Present Before and After Trained Observer Results

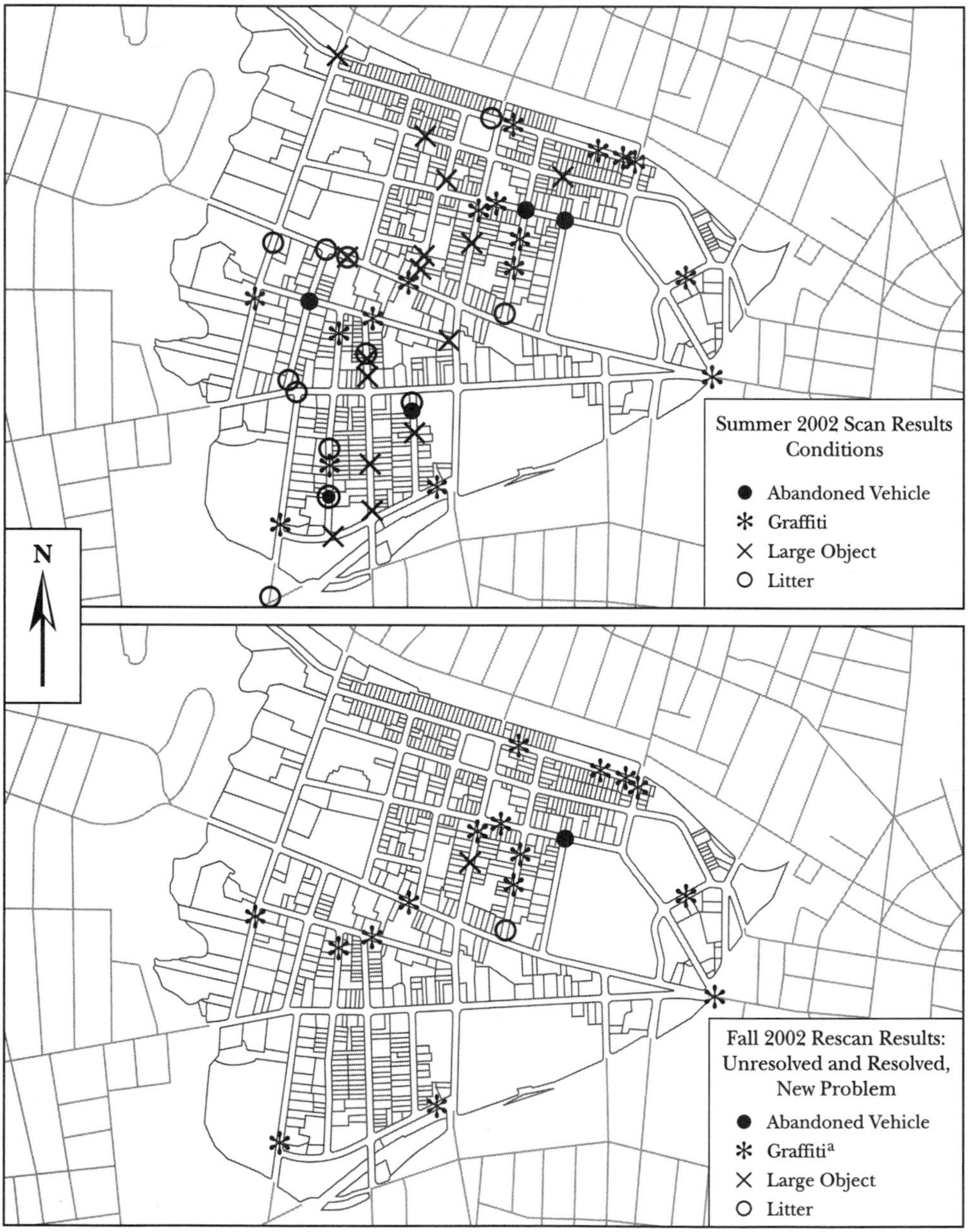

Summer 2002 Scan Results
Conditions

● Abandoned Vehicle
✳ Graffiti
✕ Large Object
○ Litter

N

Fall 2002 Rescan Results:
Unresolved and Resolved,
New Problem

● Abandoned Vehicle
✳ Graffiti[a]
✕ Large Object
○ Litter

[a]Due to an early snowfall, the fall graffiti clean-up was postponed.

Source: "City Scan Results, Asylum Hill Neighborhood: Summer 2002 Scan and Fall 2002 Rescan" (n.d.).
Used by permission of Connecticut Policy and Economic Council.

can be minimized by the use of digital cameras), copying the forms and training manuals, underwriting vehicle expenses, and—in some cases—providing box lunches for volunteer raters during training. While the trained observers have often been volunteers, a number of organizations have paid their raters up to ten dollars an hour.

The use of technology in conjunction with the trained observer ratings can add to these costs, although the benefits can be substantial. Acceptable hand-held computers can be purchased for $200 to $250, and appropriate digital cameras start at $100 each. A desktop computer is needed to upload the data from the hand-helds. One-time software costs usually come to about $400, although development of more specialized software can be quite expensive, depending on the capabilities required. Enhancements such as GPS receivers, wireless modems, and GIS software can add considerably to the cost but are optional.

In some cases, groups undertaking trained observer ratings have been able to use hardware and software owned by other organizations. For instance, the Fund for the City of New York and the Connecticut Policy and Economic Council have made hand-held computers, digital cameras, appropriate software, and (in the case of the Fund for the City of New York) a specially designed Web site available free of charge to groups using the ComNET and City Scan trained observer procedures developed by those two organizations. The use of loaned equipment and software can be especially economical when the ratings are conducted only a few times a year. A number of groups began by using borrowed hardware and software and subsequently purchased their own equipment, while licensing the software from the organization that developed it.

The actual observations usually proceed rather quickly. On the average, an experienced trained observer team can rate a park in about thirty minutes. Trained observer assessments of classrooms, offices, public housing units, and similar facilities usually require twenty to thirty minutes per room. Skilled teams simultaneously rating several types of street conditions (rideability, cleanliness, traffic signs and signals) have been able to grade as many as five hundred blocks a day traversing continuous, prespecified routes.

Adequate time, staff, and resources must also be devoted to quality control. As emphasized above, 5 to 10 percent of the results should be rerated by a "judge" or supervisor. A day or two should also be set aside for analyzing the follow-up results and for any retraining needed. The development of computer software for statistical analyses of rater and inter-rater reliability is potentially expensive and time-consuming unless one can adapt packages already used by other organizations. Such software is likely to be justified only in connection with extensive, multiperiod trained observer efforts.

Conclusions

Trained observer ratings can serve as an important program evaluation tool for assessing differences in key service quality conditions over time or in response to alternate programs. While not yet widespread, the technique can play a major role in program monitoring and in-depth program evaluation. Indeed, trained observer ratings are merely a systematic version of the kinds of inspections already used in connection with many government services. While most applications of trained observers up to now have focused on streetscape conditions and facility maintenance, the technique can be applied to a wide variety of conditions and outcomes—from assessing how crowded a bus is or how many petty street crimes occur to observing the posttreatment behavior of mental health patients and the quality of the care provided by nursing homes.

With proper training and supervision, trained observer ratings exhibit a high degree of consistency between raters and over time. The resulting information can serve as the basis for accurate, reliable assessments of program outcomes and other key program characteristics. The technique offers a number of potential advantages. For instance, trained observer ratings tend to focus on conditions as experienced by citizens—the users of a program or facility. Such ratings can serve as a relatively inexpensive way to quantify conditions that would otherwise be difficult to measure. The ratings can usually be conducted by ordinary citizens, without the need for expensive "experts," and can serve as a means for getting citizens interested and involved in improving their neighborhood services. And the approach can be readily understood by the public and by public administrators, which can help ensure the acceptance and utilization of the results.

These advantages must be balanced against a number of potential disadvantages. For instance, trained observer ratings are usually practical only for assessing characteristics that can be readily and directly sensed or experienced by the rater. They are not usually suitable for rating complex or subtle conditions. The nominal or ordinal nature of many trained observer rating scales may preclude the use of averages and other familiar statistical measures and techniques. And considerable care must be exercised to ensure that the inherent subjectivity of the rating process does not impair the precision, repeatability, and inter-rater comparability of the results.

Most of these concerns can be addressed through careful design and implementation of the rating procedures—by appropriately selecting the characteristics to be graded, systematically developing the rating scales, maximizing the use of available technology such as hand-held computers and digital cameras, carefully choosing and training the raters, ensuring adequate quality control, and properly analyzing the results. The importance of investing adequate time and resources on quality control cannot be overemphasized. The attention given to quality control, plus the care taken in developing and clearly documenting the various scales and procedures, elevates trained observer ratings from the status of "just watching" to a valid, systematic measurement technique capable of providing useful evaluative information for program managers, elected officials, and the general public.

References

Ammons, D. N. *Municipal Benchmarks.* (2nd ed.) Thousand Oaks, Calif.: Sage, 2001.

"Before and After: Streets and Parks and the Returnable Container Law." *Public Papers of the Fund for the City of New York,* 1985, *4* (entire issue 3).

Blair, L. H., and Schwartz, A. I. *How Clean Is Our City?* Washington, D.C.: Urban Institute, 1972.

Center for Excellence in Local Government. "Achieving Excellence in Customer Service." Palo Alto, Calif.: Center for Excellence in Local Government, 1988.

City of Greenville. "City of Greenville Photographic Guide for the Evaluation of Park Maintenance." Greenville, S.C.: Office of Management and Budget, 1990.

City of Kansas City. "Housing Conditions: Survey Results." Kansas City, Mo.: City Development Department, May 1989.

City of Kansas City. "S.H.A.P.E. Program." Kansas City, Mo.: Department of Parks and Recreation, n.d.

City of Kansas City. "SMCAP Data Collection Training Course: Instructor's Guide." Kansas City, Mo.: Department of Public Works, June 2000.

City of New York. "Detailed Condition Assessment." New York: Department of Parks and Recreation, n.d.

City of New York. *The Mayor's Management Report: Preliminary Fiscal 2003.* New York: Office of Operations, Feb. 2003. [http://nyc.gov/html/ops/pdf/2003_mmr/0203_mmr.pdf].

"City Scan: Current Measurable Conditions." Hartford, Conn.: Connecticut Policy and Economic Council, n.d.

"City Scan: People, Technology, Results." Hartford, Conn.: Connecticut Policy and Economic Council, n.d.

"City Scan Project: Contract for Results." Hartford, Conn.: Connecticut Policy and Economic Council, n.d. [http://www.city-scan.com/homepage.htm].

"City Scan Results, Asylum Hill Neighborhood: Summer 2002 Scan and Fall 2002 Rescan." Hartford, Conn.: Connecticut Policy and Economic Council, n.d.

Cohn, B. J. "Public-Minded Measurement." *New Public Innovator,* Spring–Summer 1999, pp. 18–20.

"Computerized Neighborhood Environment Tracking: ComNET." New York: Fund for the City of New York, Center on Municipal Government Performance, 2002. [http//www.FCNY.ORG/cmgp/comnet.htm].

Cronbach, L. J. *Essentials of Psychological Testing.* (2nd ed.) New York: Harper-Collins, 1960.

Edwards, A. L. *Techniques of Attitude Scale Construction.* New York: Appleton-Century-Crofts, 1957.

Fund for the City of New York. "Development of Scorecard Monitoring System for the Department of Parks and Recreation." New York: Fund for the City of New York, Feb. 1978.

Fund for the City of New York. "Litter Survey Project." New York: Fund for the City of New York, August 1983.

Fund for the City of New York. *Police Patrol and Street Conditions.* New York: Fund for the City of New York, n.d.

Greiner, J. M. "The Impacts of Massachusetts' Proposition 2½ on the Delivery and Quality of Municipal Services." Washington, D.C.: Urban Institute, Sept. 1984.

Greiner, J. M., and Peterson, G. E. "Do Budget Reductions Stimulate Public Sector Productivity? Evidence from Proposition 2½ in Massachusetts." In G. E. Peterson and C. W. Lewis (eds.), *Reagan and the Cities.* Washington, D.C.: Urban Institute, 1986.

Hatry, H. P., Greiner, J. M., and Swanson, M. *Monitoring the Quality of Local Government Services.* Washington, D.C.: International City Management Association, Feb. 1987.

Hatry, H. P., Morley, E., Barbour, G. P. Jr., and Pajunen, S. M. *Excellence in Managing: Practical Experiences from Community Development Agencies.* Washington, D.C.: Urban Institute, 1991.

Hatry, H. P., and others. *How Effective Are Your Community Services? Procedures for Measuring Their Quality.* (2nd ed.) Washington, D.C.: Urban Institute and the International City/County Management Association, 1992.

Health Care Financing Administration. *State Operations Manual: Provider Certification.* Baltimore, Md.: Health Care Financing Administration, Apr. 1992.

Herman, R. D., and Peroff, N. C. *Measuring City Agency Responsiveness: The Citizen-Surrogate Method.* Washington, D.C.: International City Management Association, May 1981.

Institute for Public Transportation and the New York Public Interest Research Group. *Off the Track: Subway Service Derailed.* New York: Institute for Public Transportation and the New York Public Interest Research Group, 1980.

Liebmann, T. "School Scorecard Report (Academic Year 1989–90)." New York: New York School Scorecard Unit, New York City Board of Education, Oct. 1990.

Milford, R. L., Dougherty, G. W., and Bradbury, M. D. "Improving Customer Services." Paper presented at the University of Georgia Institute of Government and the Georgia City/County Management Association, ICMA Best Practices 2000, Savannah/Chatham County, Ga., Mar. 30–Apr. 1, 2000.

Millar, R., and Millar, A. (eds.). *Developing Client Outcome Monitoring Systems: A Guide for State and Local Social Service Agencies.* Washington, D.C.: Urban Institute, 1981.

Miller, D. *Handbook of Research Design and Social Measurement.* (4th ed.) New York: Longman, 1983.

Moore, J. "School Scorecard Report (October, 1987—January, 1988)." New York: School Scorecard Unit, New York City Board of Education, Mar. 1988.

"Neighborhood Data: ComNET." Worcester, Mass.: Worcester Regional Research Bureau, n.d. [http://www.wrrb.org/Neighborhood/conditions.html].

"ParkScan Home." San Francisco: Neighborhood Parks Council, n.d. [http://www.parkscansf.org].

Peter, L. J. *Peter's Quotations: Ideas for Our Time.* New York: Bantam Books, 1977.

Riccio, L. J., Miller, J., and Litke, A. "Polishing the Big Apple: How Management Science Has Helped Make New York Streets Cleaner." *Interfaces,* 1986, *16*(1), 83–88.

"Telephone Tester Program." Washington, D.C.: Office of the Mayor, n.d. [http://www.washingtondc.gov/mayor/telephone_tester/call_agency.html].

Thomas, J. S. "Scorecard: Measuring Street Cleanliness." In F. O'R. Hayes and others, *Helping City Government Improve Productivity: An Evaluation of the Productivity Projects of the Fund for the City of New York.* New York: Fund for the City of New York, May 1980.

Thurstone, L. L., and Chave, E. J. *The Measurement of Attitude.* Chicago: University of Chicago Press, 1929.

"A Ticket to Clean Streets: Enforcing the Health and Administrative Code." *Public Papers of the Fund for the City of New York,* May 1982, *1* (entire issue 2).

TriData Corporation. "Rater's Manual for Capital Plant Assessment." (2nd ed.) Arlington, Va.: TriData Corporation, 1986.

United Way of America. *Measuring Program Outcomes: A Practical Approach.* Alexandria, Va.: United Way of America, 1996.

Urban Institute. "Guidelines for Trained Observer Ratings of Parks and Beaches." Washington, D.C.: Urban Institute, October 1983.

"Walkable America Checklist." Itasca, Ill.: National Safety Council, June 1999. [www.nsc.org/walk/wkchecklist.htm].

"What Is City Scan?" Hartford, Conn.: Connecticut Policy and Economic Council, n.d. [http://www.city-scan.com/overview.htm].

Wilson, D. "The Use of Trained Observers to Evaluate Park Maintenance." Greenville, S.C.: Office of Management and Budget, City of Greenville, Oct. 1989.

Worcester Regional Research Bureau. "Center for Community Performance Measurement." Worcester, Mass.: Worcester Regional Research Bureau, n.d. [http://www.wrrb.org/CCPM/what.html].

Worcester Regional Research Bureau. "Results, ComNET Project: Bell Hill." Worcester, Mass.: Worcester Regional Research Bureau, July 26, 2001. [http://www.wrrb.org/Neighborhood/BellHillResults.pdf].

Worcester Regional Research Bureau. "ComNET Project Resurvey Report: Bell Hill Neighborhood." Worcester, Mass.: Worcester Regional Research Bureau, June 17, 2002. [http://www.wrrb.org/Neighborhood/BellHill2002.pdf].

9

Using Surveys

Kathryn E. Newcomer, Timothy Triplett

Listening to citizens, program beneficiaries, public and nonprofit program managers and employees, elected and appointed officials, relevant substantive experts, and other stakeholders is frequently necessary to evaluate program delivery and results, whether for ad hoc evaluations or for ongoing monitoring of service. Reaching the appropriate respondents to learn about their experiences and measure their attitudes and opinions can be challenging. Capturing information reliably and efficiently through surveying is rewarding.

Surveying a representative and sufficiently large number of target respondents has been affected both positively and negatively by recent advances in technology and survey research methods. Advances in telecommunications technology have changed telephone use patterns in ways that directly affect surveying. Answering machines and caller ID are ubiquitous in homes and in offices and present a new hurdle for telephone surveying. And the increased use of cell phones, with a related decline in the importance of residential phones, presents another potential obstacle to reaching respondents. This has contributed in many instances to more reliance on mailed questionnaires, perhaps in combination with other modes of administration.

The availability of the Internet has provided new means of reaching respondents. Surveys increasingly are being administered by e-mail. With rising Net literacy rates, respondents can also be asked to traverse the Internet to Web sites that present surveys in graphically attractive and enticing formats.

Advances in computer technology also have provided streamlined and cost-efficient means for inputting data collected from respondents in person or by telephone, e-mail, and Web directly into computers to facilitate analysis. Hand-held computers and computer-assisted telephone surveying methodologies have reduced survey costs while adding greater flexibility in designing survey instruments.

Commercial use of surveying the public has increased as the technological advances have reduced costs. The result is a much more skeptical public that is reluctant to answer questions by any survey mode. Americans have tired of marketers' interrupting their leisure time, and they share concerns about the invasion of their privacy. The technological advances that have made it faster and cheaper to obtain data from the public have raised levels of cynicism among the public about surveying. Concern with response rates, or the proportion of those surveyed who responded, plagues evaluators. Creativity in boosting response rates and in examining limitations introduced by rates lower than desired is more essential than ever before.

Survey research methodologies have improved over the past two decades, bolstered by both technological advances and learning through expanded experience. The number of survey research firms has increased dramatically to meet increased demands from both private and public sector clients. Levi Jeans, General Motors and Victoria's Secret rely on survey data, as do the U.S. Census, Internal Revenue Service, and the United Way. Surveying has become a growth industry. There are now many options for surveying support available to private, public, and nonprofit organizations.

In addition, survey researchers have become more skilled in their craft. Survey research has become a discipline whose practitioners are more knowledgeable and skilled in statistical and technological methods than ever before. Options for survey mode and sampling strategies have increased along with choices for analysis and reporting.

This chapter clarifies the options available and provides practical guidance for program managers and evaluators who choose to survey relevant target populations to help them learn about their programs.

Planning the Survey

Before you can begin designing survey instruments, develop sampling plans, and decide on data collection strategies, you need to establish evaluation questions.

Evaluation Questions

Use of a design matrix arrays the design choices, such as data collection mode, sampling, and questions, that are made to address your survey objectives is especially useful. Table 9.1 provides an example of the types of categories of

Table 9.1. Survey Design Matrix

Evaluation Questions	Information Source	Sampling	Data Collection	Survey Questions	Pretesting	Data Quality Assurance	Presentation Format
Identify the questions to be addressed by the data collection methods that are: • Specific in terms of concepts, time frame, and unit of analysis • Clear and understandable by both involved stakeholders and "cold readers" • Objective and neutrally stated • Appropriately framed in terms of scope and time frame • Likely to produce information of interest and usefulness to the audience (client)	Specify target respondents who: • Possess relevant knowledge or perceptions relevant to addressing the research questions • Are accessible • Are representative of the population to which generalization is desired • Provide multiple and complementary perspectives to answer questions	Design a means of selecting respondents from the targeted respondents that: • Allow generalization to the desired population • Allow an appropriate amount of subgroup analysis • Does not have too large a sampling error	Select modes of data collection that will: • Ensure that data collected directly and adequately address the evaluation questions • Are reliably implemented • Permit sufficient ability to probe accuracy of responses • Achieve sufficient response rates • Will provide findings within the time available • Are within budget	Craft questions to be used in survey mode that: • Address one or more of the evaluation questions • Are clear, understandable, and easy for respondents to answer • Permit adequate generalizability of findings • Permit adequate opportunity for desired quantitative analysis • Are appropriate for your mode of data collection	Design a means of pretesting all survey questions that will: • Provide feedback to clarify all wording in questions • Identify any unanswerable questions • Reveal any assumptions made about respondents' willingness or ability to answer questions that are not supported	Devise procedures to continually obtain feedback on data collection processes and wording of survey questions that: • Provide feedback to clarify wording in questions • Reveal inconsistencies in data collection procedures or coding • Improve interviewers' skills	Plan for analysis of the data obtained through the surveying that: • Clearly displays the data that address the evaluation questions • Permits a sufficient level of disaggregation to be useful for the audiences (clients)

design choices that are made. The design matrix summarizes virtually all of the design decisions in a succinct format that facilitates communication among and between program staff and evaluators. In order to design a survey, define the evaluation questions in terms of your specific information needs or issues to be addressed. Table 9.2 provides a sample design matrix to illustrate how it may be used. Formulating specific evaluation questions will help you determine who you need to interview, help you write good survey questions, and provide a solid foundation for presenting the results. The evaluation questions should be clear and understandable and produce useful information. In addition, the questions should be objective, neutrally stated, and specific in terms of time frame and unit of analysis (for example, persons, classrooms, or larger entities).

Determining If a Survey Is Necessary and Feasible

Once you have established evaluation questions you should decide, first, if a survey is necessary, and second, if surveys are within your time and budget constraints and will address your evaluation objectives. A survey may not be necessary if the answers to your evaluation questions can be obtained from information that has already been collected. For example, college students often complain about being asked to complete a survey that consists of questions that they already had to answer when they registered for classes. An important part of the planning stage is searching for and reviewing surveys that address issues related to your objectives. You probably will not find the information you need to answer your evaluation questions, but finding similar surveys will be extremely helpful in designing your own survey. The second reason for not conducting a survey is that obtaining the information you need would take too long or cost too much. Suppose you want to find out if the number of homeless shelters are adequate and located in appropriate areas. Given the difficulty of reaching and communicating with homeless people, a survey to collect this information would certainly be expensive and take a long time, and even with enough time and resources, this information still may not be attainable.

Determining the Population of Interest

As you establish your evaluation questions, you are also deciding on your population of interest: individuals or an organization or group (for example, school superintendents, principals, or state school officials). If the population of interest is an organization or group, you also need to think about who within this group would be the most knowledgeable person in providing information for the group (for example, school superintendents, principals, or state social service officials). In some situations, surveys of several different groups of respondents may be necessary to address the evaluation questions. Besides identifying the population of interest, you also need to consider whether there any groups or individuals within this population to exclude because of a lack of pertinent experience. For instance, you might exclude part-time workers from an employee survey, businesses with fewer than five employees from a business study, or graduating seniors for a survey about future student housing needs. Usually you exclude groups or individuals whom you believe would not contribute useful information, but you also should consider limiting your population to save time and money. Limiting the population geographically is often done to save money. For instance, to save money, Alaska and Hawaii are often excluded in nationwide surveys. (Such exclusions should be made clear when reporting the findings.)

After defining the population of interest, consider whether there is anyone else to obtain information from. For instance, had we limited the population of interest to individuals who had been represented by legal aid attorneys in the sample survey design matrix in Table 9.2, we would not have fully answered our evaluation question. To fully understand how effective legal aid services are in meeting the needs of the community, we need to expand the population of interest to include individuals who potentially could have used legal aid services as well as those who were denied services.

Analysis Plan

Think about the analysis plan. How likely are you to analyze any subgroups within your population? If you plan on analyzing a group that constitutes a very small portion of your population of interest, the survey design will probably include oversampling this group. Careful consideration of the sorts of disaggregation that may be desirable for data analysis is needed from the start, for by the time report preparation begins, it is probably too late to boost subgroup sample sizes.

A Plan for Collecting the Data

The next important decision will be deciding how to collect the data. Table 9.3 lists the advantages and disadvantages of the most common modes of data collection. Much of the work involved in preparing the survey instrument depends on the mode of data collection. Therefore, a decision on which data collection mode to use should be made early on, so that there is enough time left in the schedule for preparing the survey instrument.

Mail Surveys. Even with the increasing number of e-mail and Web surveys, traditional mail surveys are still a popular form of data collection. The

Table 9.2. Example of a Survey Design Matrix

Evaluation Questions	Information Source	Sampling	Data Collection Mode
Over the past 12 months, how well is Legal Aid Services meeting the needs of those eligible for services in the community	• Beneficiaries who have been represented by the Legal Aid attorneys	• A systematic random sample of names taken off agency records with potential stratification by gender, race, and crime	• Mail survey with monetary incentives
	• Applicants for services who were denied		• Analysis of archival records indicating reasons for denial[a]
	• Potential beneficiaries who did not apply for Legal Aid Services but would have been eligible	• A systematic random sample of those who represented themselves in court taken from court records	• Mode will depend on availability of contact information

[a]A more expensive analysis would entail following up with court records to track the experience of applicants who were denied and locate them for subsequent contact.

Table 9.2. Example of a Survey Design Matrix, *continued*

Survey Questions	Pretesting	Data Quality Assurance	Presentation Format
How satisfied were you with: Not satisfied / Extremely satisfied a. Responsiveness of your attorney to your questions 1 2 3 b. Effectiveness of the representation afforded you by your attorney 1 2 3 c. Amount of time your attorney devoted to your case 1 2 3 d. Ease of obtaining legal representation 1 2 3 e. Courteousness of the Legal Services Staff 1 2 3 f. Timeliness of the response of the Legal Services staff to your request for assistance 1 2 3	• Mail survey of a small systematic sample	• Write clear introduction that assures respondents of of the anonymity of their responses • Send a pilot survey to reveal any problems before • Train coders before they access records	• A table that arrays percentage frequencies for respondents broken out by key demographic characteristics N.A.
N.A.	N.A.	N.A.	N.A.
How important was each of the following reasons that you did not seek assistance from Legal Aid Services? Not a Factor / An Important Factor / Not Applicable a. Did not think I would qualify 1 2 3 9 b. Did not think I I had enough time 1 2 3 9 c. Heard unfavorable reviews from friends or acquaintances 1 2 3 9 d. Never heard of this service 1 2 3 9	Same as above	Same as above	Same as above

Table 9.3. Comparison of Survey Modes

Criteria	Mail	Internet	Telephone	In Person[a]
Quality of data				
• Ability to locate respondent	High	**Low**[b]	Medium	High
• Ability to probe	Low	Low	Medium	**High**
• Response rates	Low-Medium	Low-Medium	Medium	**High**
• Protect respondent anonymity	High	Medium-High	Medium	Low
• Ability to ask sensitive topics	High	Medium-High	Medium	**Low**
• Ability to interview less educated	Low-Medium	Low	Medium-High	High
• Quality of recorded response	Low-Medium	Medium	High	High
• Question complexity	**Low**	Medium	Medium	**High**
Opportunities for analyses				
• Ability to use larger scales	High	High	Low	Medium
• How quickly you can post results	Low	**High**	Medium-High	Low
• Ability to collect anecdotes	Low	Low	Medium	**High**
• Number of questions asked	**Low**	Low-Medium	Medium	High
• Ability to adjust for nonresponse	Medium	**Low**	Medium	High
• Ability to add sample frame data	High	Low	Medium	High
Resources required				
• Time required for preparation	**Low**	Medium	High	High
• Time required for collection	High	**Low**	Medium	High
• Expertise required for design	Medium	**High**	Medium	Medium
• Survey research expertise	Medium	Medium	Medium-High	High
• Staffing requirements	Low	Low	High	High
• Equipment requirements	**Low**	Medium	Medium	Medium
• Travel requirements	Low	Low	Medium	**High**
• Costs per survey	Low	Low-Medium[c]	Medium-High	High

[a]If it is appropriate to ask clients to complete the survey at an agency's facility, the ratings will not be as low (or costs as high).

[b]Bold font indicates a particularly strong advantage or disadvantage.

[c]Costs for e-mail- and Web-based survey decrease as sample size increases.

three distinct advantages of mail surveys are that they are relatively inexpensive, a complete list of addresses is usually obtainable, and they yield less response bias when the questions are sensitive. Some disadvantages of mail surveys are lower response rates, response bias toward more educated respondents, higher nonresponse rates for individual questions, and the questionnaire needs to be short, with minimal or no skip patterns (that is, instructions that ask respondents to ignore certain questions).

Telephone Surveys. Telephone surveys have been very popular because they often yield high response rates and less item nonresponse, provide more control of the question ordering, allow you to use longer questions and skip patterns, and ask for respondents to recall information during the interview. Some disadvantages of telephone surveys are that they are relatively more expensive, it may be more time-consuming to write and test questions, and there is more bias when asking for sensitive or personal information. Higher cooperation rates and the ability to reach people by telephone have been two major advantages of telephone surveys, but these advantages are now on the decline. There are no longer big differences in terms of response rate between a properly administered household mail survey and a telephone survey. However, if the population being surveyed has a strong interest or feels some ethical obligation to respond when contacted personally, telephone surveys may still be a good choice. For instance, response rates among college students are often two to three times higher on telephone surveys versus mail surveys.

Face-to-Face Surveys. The oldest method, face-to-face surveys, still yields the highest response rates and is the best method for asking open-ended questions (questions that do not limit response to predefined response options) or questions requiring visual aids. However, these surveys are usually prohibitively expensive, require longer testing and data collection periods, and are inappropriate for surveys that include sensitive questions. In addition, sampling usually involves interviewers' conducting several interviews in a small geographical area, which can create a clustering effect that will decrease the precision of some of your estimates. These are appropriate for captive audiences, such as institutionalized clients.

E-Mail and Web Surveys. Until recently e-mail surveys were seen as a good alternative to mail surveys for conducting surveys with populations where you could obtain e-mail addresses. You can collect the data faster and potentially more efficiently through e-mail. However, confidentiality concerns about who has access to e-mail messages, filters and firewalls that prevent unsolicited e-mail, and increases in computer viruses sent by e-mail are all contributing to a declining interest in e-mail surveys.

Improvements in the development of Web surveys are perhaps the most important reason for the declining importance of e-mail surveys as a mode of data collection. Now that almost everyone with e-mail access has access to a Web browser, sending a short message about the survey with a link to the questionnaire has for the most part replaced e-mail as a mode of data collection. With e-mail surveys, the questionnaire has to be a simple text-based message, and short to accommodate the variety of systems people use to read e-mail. Web surveys can take advantage of the established html and Java script standards that make it possible for survey designers to create complex questionnaires that can handle skip patterns and recall information from earlier questions. In addition, Web surveys can provide enticing graphics or visual aids to help guide respondents. Although there is some concern with providing information over the Internet, the data are actually more secure than information provided by e-mail, and people are starting to understand this better, as evidenced by the increasing willingness of people to complete forms and make purchases on the Internet. Web surveys are currently limited to populations that use the Internet, but that population continues to grow and there are now organizations (such as Knowledge Networks and Harris Interactive) that are conducting national studies that are representative of the nation by providing free Web access to randomly selected respondents.

Other Methods. There are many other ways to conduct surveys. You may use pencil-and-paper questionnaires when you have a captive audience—for instance, asking people to complete a survey at the end of a meeting, surveying students in the classroom, or having clients complete a survey while they fill out required forms. It is often possible to bolster the response rate by taking advantage of a captive audience. Another important point is that if you plan to compare results with a previous survey, try to use the same mode of data collection; using a different mode of data collection could introduce some unintentional bias.

Finally, for some programs, you may consider a combination of data collection modes. For instance, when conducting a job satisfaction survey, you may be able to collect most responses using the Web, but for employees who do not use a computer, you may need to call them or provide them with a paper survey.

Identifying Who Will Conduct the Survey. While deliberating on the most desirable mode of data collection, you will also be considering whether to conduct the survey yourself or contract out. The "When Should You Contract Out?" box helps to identify factors to consider in making decisions about whether to conduct the survey in-house or contract out the work. The most common reason people choose to conduct their own survey is to save money. However, often when one factors in all the hours staff spend working on the project, you may be surprised how little you actually save by not contracting out. Much of this chapter is written assuming you plan to collect your own data, but the information in this chapter is almost equally important to those who select and work with contractors. If you are planning to contract out, the "Who Will Be the Right Consultant or Contractor for You?" box provides useful tips. In general, it is much easier to collect your data if you are choosing a self-administered mode of data collection, such as mail surveys, because interviewer-administered surveys have much higher start-up costs. For outcome monitoring purposes, it is typically the agency that regularly surveys clients to obtain useful feedback about program operations and to estimate program outcomes. Less costly and easier-to-administer surveys will be especially appropriate for these purposes.

When Should You Contract Out?

Do you have staff to perform all required work?

- Do staff have the needed expertise for survey design?
- Are staff skilled and available for interviewing?
- Do staff have the requisite expertise for analysis of the survey findings?
- Are staff available and skilled to write the report and prepare the graphics needed to support the findings in the report?
- Do the results benefit from being able to claim that the data were collected by an independent contractor?

Is there adequate technological support to support the survey?

- Do you have adequate hardware and software capabilities to collect data?
- Do you have the type of hardware and software needed to analyze the data?

Can staff complete the survey in time?

- How quickly do you need the data reported?

Timing of the Data Collection

You need to decide when would be a good time to collect your data. Think about collecting during a time when reaching your population is least difficult. Often you should avoid conducting surveys around the holidays or during the summer months when people may be on vacation. However, if your

Who Will Be the Right Consultant or Contractor for You?

Does the consultant have enough relevant experience?

- How much experience does the consultant have with the service delivery or policy being addressed in the survey?
- How much experience does the consultant have with the survey mode you think you want?

What about the quality of the consultant's communication skills?

- How compatible is the consultant's communications style with yours?
- How clearly does the consultant communicate orally and in writing?
- How responsive is the consultant in reacting to your requests and suggestions?
- How accessible is the consultant in communicating with all relevant stakeholders involved with the survey project?
- What do previous clients say about the consultant's communications skills in their recommendations?

What about the quality of the consultant's written reports?

- How clearly written are the consultant's previous reports?
- How effective are the presentations of graphics and analyses provided by the consultant in previous reports?

Is the consultant in your price range?

- How competitive is the cost estimate the consultant provides?
- How responsive is the consultant when asked to unbundle the tasks he or she will provide to reduce costs?
- Is the consultant willing to allow your staff to perform some tasks to reduce costs?

project involves recalling an event, the survey needs to occur shortly after the event. Although surveys are often scheduled to accommodate important meetings or presentations, the quality of the survey will benefit from placing a higher priority on accommodating the respondents. For many customer surveys, especially for outcome monitoring, it is often more useful to collect data continuously, say, at a fixed period of time after each client has completed services (such as three, six, nine, or twelve months after departure).

A continuous data collection process avoids seasonal or other fluctuations in satisfaction that often occur over time. If all clients are to be covered, it avoids worries about sampling, the subject of the next section.

Selecting the Sample

The first question should be: Do I need to try and interview everyone, or should I select a sample of the population to interview? If the population of interest is quite large, then you almost certainly need to select a sample. However, even if you think that you can survey all customers, selecting a relatively small number of respondents may provide reasonably precise estimates of the entire population at a much reduced cost. For routine outcome monitoring, many benefits accrue to covering all clients if the number is not too large. Many one-time studies end up spending too much money trying to interview everyone, when they may have been able to get better estimates by spending more resources on getting a high response rate from a sample of the population. In general, sample sizes of one thousand, five hundred, and even two hundred or fewer can provide sufficient precision as long as the sample has been selected at random from the overall population.

If you are planning to conduct separate analysis on a subgroup of the population, you may need to choose a larger overall random sample or select at random additional respondents who meet the definition of the subgroup you want to analyze. How many interviews you need to complete depends on a number of things (for example, types of analysis planned, variability of key variables, total population size), but most of it all it depends on how much precision is needed for the study. Although the goal should always be to achieve the highest-quality project possible, most surveys do not need the same level of precision. That is why many successful surveys have published results based on samples sizes of five hundred or fewer.

Table 9.4 provides an overview of the various sampling options to consider. The table includes what is usually described as a convenience sample, meaning that it relies on contacting population members who are easily located and willing to participate. Convenience samples are not recommended for evaluations that involve making an inference about the population as whole, but they can be justified when trying to interview hard-to-find populations or if the evaluation objective is not to produce estimates but rather to learn more about some of the key issues. As discussed in Chapter Seventeen in this book, statistically significant findings that are generalizable to whole client populations require probability samples, but some evaluation questions may not require this level of coverage. For example, investigations of specific problems with program implementation or service quality may only require targeted surveys.

Table 9.4. Sampling Options

	Description	*Types of Studies*	*Analysis Concerns*
Census	Interviewing the entire population	Small populations. E-mail and Web surveys where most of the costs are incurred in designing the survey.	Possibly need some nonresponse weights adjustment, but usually no weight is needed.
Simple random sample	Every person in the population has an equal chance of being chosen.	Studies where it is possible to obtain a list of all eligible and a census is too expensive or unnecessary.	Possibly need some nonresponse weights adjustment, but often a weighting adjustment is not needed.
Stratified random sample	Every person in the population has an equal chance of being chosen. Sample is sorted by key variables before the sample is selected. For example, if the list includes postal code and gender, you could stratify (sort) it first by postal code and then within postal code by gender.	Studies where it is possible to obtain a list and the list contains useful information about the respondent.	Possibly need some nonresponse weights adjustment or some adjustment due to having differential response rates in the different subgroups.
Stratified with unequal probability of selection	Every person in the population has a known probability of selection. However, certain groups of people have a greater or lesser chance of being sampled.	Studies where you want to make sure to collect enough interviews with specific groups within the population in order to perform separate analysis on those groups.	In order to look at the population as a whole, you will need to weight respondents by the inverse of their probability of selection. In addition, you may need to do two or more nonresponse adjustments: one for the overall sample and one for each of the groups specifically oversampled. The key here is to use a weight variable when analyzing the overall population, but no weight or only a nonresponse adjustment weight is needed for analyzing the groups you over sampled.

Table 9.4. Sampling Options, *continued*

	Description	Types of Studies	Analysis Concerns
Multistage sample designs	Multistage sample designs are usually very complex and require the assistance of a sampling statistician. For these studies, you would be advised to have the data collected by a survey shop.	These are usually large household surveys where it is often unknown who you want to speak with until after information about the household has been obtained.	Requires both sample design weights and poststratification weights. Also, estimates will be subject to design effects. To correctly estimate the variance of the measurements, you need to use special data techniques.
Convenience samples	Sampling populations at places where they can be easily reached—for example: homeless in homeless shelters, drug users at drug treatment clinics.	Hard-to-locate populations. Limited budget.	Should not generalize your results to the population as a whole.

Designing the Survey Instrument

We want both good, relevant answers to our questions and a high response rate. To accomplish these two important objectives requires:

- Designing the survey and formulating the questions with the target respondents in mind.
- Writing extremely compelling introductions to get our foot in the door.
- Wording questions that are easy to answer for the respondents and provide pertinent data for the intended users of the information.
- Pretesting and continually reassessing the usefulness of the instrument in obtaining accurate and useful data.

The Target Respondents

Before writing survey questions, think about the target respondents. Many characteristics of target respondents are especially pertinent to considerations about survey layout and questions. Think about how receptive the respondents will be to being surveyed, how much they know about the subject matter, and how sensitive they may feel about the questions asked.

The educational background of the target respondents is a key characteristic that will affect the sophistication of the terms to use in the survey.

Writing questions directed to scientists and engineers presents different challenges from writing questions to ask of recipients of food stamps. Other demographic characteristics of the target respondents are also pertinent, such as their age and primary language spoken.

The receptivity of the target respondents to answering questions about the issues may also reflect whether or not they have the desired information, how easy it is for them to get the information requested, and how willing they are to part with the information. We need to think through any assumptions we make about the knowledge or experience the target respondents have that is relevant to their ability to answer the questions. For example, we may assume that target respondents are more familiar with service delivery procedures or with the acronyms we use than they may actually be. Or we may be overly optimistic in assuming that respondents can provide reliable estimates about their experiences, such as reporting how many hours they watch television. Memories are fleeting, and respondents' abilities to recall experiences or impressions may not be sufficient to provide accurate data.

We need to anticipate how receptive target respondents will be to the questions asked of them. Ordering questions should reflect how respondents would perceive the intrusiveness or sensitivity of the questions. Typically, surveys start with straightforward, factual questions that are extremely easy to answer and inoffensive. The questions then move toward more sensitive areas, such as requesting respondents to evaluate services, and end with requests for demographic information that will help to disaggregate responses.

Getting a Foot in the Door

The introduction to a survey conducted by any mode is critical to boosting the likelihood that the respondents will participate. Introductions are more likely to be effective in convincing the respondent to answer questions if the following information is explained:

- The purpose of the survey
- Who will use the data they provide (such as by a city council to improve city services)
- Who is funding or sponsoring the survey
- What benefits the respondent will enjoy by participating in the survey

Providing incentives to participate, such as enclosing money in mail surveys or promising that money or in-kind awards will be sent to respondents will help convince respondents to participate as described in the box displaying "Tips on Incentives" (Singer, 2002).

Tips on Incentives

- Incentives improve response rates on all modes of data collection.
- Incentives are more effective on self-administered surveys.
- Prepaid incentives are more effective on mail surveys than are promised incentives.
- Response rate gains are the same when using prepaid or promised incentives in telephone or face-to-face surveys.
- Money is more effective than gifts (equal in value) for all modes of data collection.
- A positive linear relationship exists between money and response rate.
- On average, there is a one-third percentage point gain in response rate per dollar spent on incentives in telephone surveys.
- On mail surveys, incentives have been found to increase response rates as much as twenty percentage points.
- The more burdensome a survey is, the more effective are incentives.

Good Questions

Questions are only as good as they are clear and answerable for respondents. Crafting questions should be undertaken with the target respondents in mind. We need to anticipate target respondents' receptivity to different sorts of question formats and their willingness to volunteer responses to open-ended questions. Asking open-ended questions works best in face-to-face interviews. Most questions in all other surveys should provide easy-to-understand options for the respondent to select.

A first step in formulating questions should be to look for questions on the intended topic that have been used before—in a previous survey or in customer surveys in another governmental jurisdiction, for example. Of course, just because the questions have been used previously does not mean they are ideal, but they do present options to consider and perhaps pretest. For use in outcome monitoring, questions should be asked with the same wording from year to year.

A second step in question preparation is to estimate how many total questions can feasibly be asked and how many questions are needed to address all of the evaluation questions. Since asking too many questions will hurt the response rate, the need to ask more questions must be balanced against the negative impact a lengthier survey may have in discouraging respondents. For mail surveys, try to keep the number of questions limited, to require perhaps two to four pages.

When asking respondents to give their opinions or evaluations of services, scales are typically used. Using a numerical scale in which only the end points are defined, such as a 1 to 7 scale where 1 equals "not at all useful" and 7 equals "extremely useful," are preferable to using adjectives such as "poor," "fair," and "above average," because numbers are less fraught with connotations that vary across respondents. The box on "Wording Questions" contains tips for writing questions that will obtain reliable answers from respondents.

Wording Questions to Measure Attitudes and Perceptions Reliably

- Use scales with numbers, not fuzzy adjectives, for respondents to assess their attitude.

Example: On a scale from 1 to 7, where 1 = Not at All Clear, and 7 = Extremely Clear, how clear were the instructions in the manual?

          1   2   3   4   5   6   7   N.A.

- Ask respondents to rate each factor that you want to evaluate rather than asking them to rank a list of factors (from first to last).

Example: Please rate the usefulness of *each* of the following sources in helping you select a graduate program on a scale from 1 to 7 where 1 = Not Useful at All and 7 = Extremely Useful:

a. Web site	1	2	3	4	5	6	7	N.A.
b. Written brochure	1	2	3	4	5	6	7	N.A.
c. Campus visit	1	2	3	4	5	6	7	N.A.
d. Interview with faculty member	1	2	3	4	5	6	7	N.A.
e. Calls from current students	1	2	3	4	5	6	7	N.A.
f. Any other useful sources: Please specify _____	1	2	3	4	5	6	7	N.A.

- Keep the questions brief. Rather than confuse respondents with long statements, break up inquiries into clear components.

Example: On a scale from 1 to 3 where 1 = Not at All Satisfied and 3 = Extremely Satisfied, how satisfied were you with:

a. The clarity of the written training materials?	1	2	3	N.A.
b. The availability of the trainer for consultation outside class?	1	2	3	N.A.

c. The trainer's knowledge of the materials he
or she covered? 1 2 3 N.A.

- Provide definitions in the survey instrument for any terms or concepts you see that may be vague or not understood in the same manner by all respondents. For example, *team building* may mean different things to different respondents.
- Use easy-to-answer close-ended questions. Since respondents will not likely spend much time answering open-ended questions by mail, e-mail, or the Web, ask only a few open-ended questions that will provide especially helpful information.
- Select the length of the scales based on the respondents' ability to discriminate, and then use the same scale for all questions in the survey. For example, engineers should be comfortable with longer scales, like 1 to 7 or 1 to 10, but elderly recipients of Meals-on-Wheels might feel more comfortable answering 3-point scales.
- Ask an open-ended question at the end that requests respondents to identify an additional issue, factor, or quality (or whatever else is relevant) that was not addressed in the survey.

One question that typically arises about the use of scales to measure respondents' perceptions is whether to provide a middle value. In other words, some experts advocate forcing respondents to choose a positive or negative response rather than give them a midpoint (neutral) such as 3 on a 1 to 5 scale. The view against providing a middle value is based in large part on the fear that too many respondents will prefer to give the neutral (middle) response. Our own experience is that offering midpoints does not lead to an overreliance on that neutral response by respondents. In fact, we advocate the use of an odd-numbered scale such as 1 to 5 or 1 to 7. However, once you decide what scale to use, stick with it for the entire survey; changing scales will lead to reporting errors.

A good rule-of-thumb in formulating questions is to provide a thorough and mutually exclusive list of options for respondents to consider or rate rather than asking them to volunteer responses. For example, rather than using an open-ended question to ask respondents what they liked about a training course or an encounter with an emergency squad, it is preferable to provide a list of aspects that is developed and refined through pretesting, and ask them to evaluate each aspect on the list. Question sequencing is also important, and developing effective lead questions is critical. Tips on sequencing appear in the box on page 276.

Tips on Question Sequencing

- Ask more specific items first. As an example, consider rating community recycling services and garbage collection. People's rating of garbage collection is likely to be influenced by the recycling services provided. Asking first, "How would you rate recycling services in your community?" before asking, "How would you rate garbage collection in your community?" cues the respondents that you want them to consider garbage collection separate from the recycling services.
- Consider a lead-in statement for items in which there is likely to be an order effect in either direction. For example, let's say that a respondent is trying to evaluate how well the police, the courts, and local leaders have been doing in preventing crime in the community. No matter what order you choose, there is likely to be some order effect, so use a lead-in statement similar to the following: "Now, I'd like you to tell me how effective the police, the courts, and local leaders have been in preventing crime in your community. First, how about . . . "

Ease of answering from the respondents' point of view should be a driving principle, no matter what sort of question format is used. The box about "Common Mistakes" lists the most common mistakes people make in writing survey questions. Well-written questions do not break any of these rules.

Instructions should be given to respondents about how many responses to provide for each question and which option to select if they feel they cannot or should not answer a question due to lack of knowledge or experience. The box on "No Opinion" explains how to address the "no opinion" issue. (See also McClendon and Alwin, 1993, and Krosnick and others, 2002.)

Pretesting

Pretesting a survey instrument with a representative sample of the population of target respondents is essential. The questions, mode of administration, and procedures should be the same in the pretest as planned for the survey. Even if questions are borrowed from previous studies or other agencies or jurisdictions, the questions need to be asked of a set of the target respondents to ensure clarity and understandability. Often more than one pretest is necessary; in general, the final pretest should look as much like the actual survey as possible. A good size sample for a pretest is generally twenty to twenty-five completed interviews with more interviews needed with questionnaires that have lots of skip patterns. If the total population is very small,

> ## Common Mistakes in Writing Questions
>
> - The question asks about more than one thing.
> - Some of the terms used are not familiar to some respondents.
> - The response options are not exhaustive and mutually exclusive.
> - The scale questions do not have balanced alternatives.
> - The information is redundant since it can be obtained from another source.
> - Not all respondents will have the same interpretation of the question.
> - The time frame is not clearly stated and is not reasonable for recall questions.
> - There will not be variation in response because almost everyone will provide the same answer.
> - The question contains double negatives.
> - You are asking respondents to rank too many items or some other difficult task.
> - There is an unnecessary neutral, "don't know," or "no opinion" option.
> - The intervals for numeric response options are not reasonable.
> - The wording seems to advocate a particular answer (that is, it leads the respondents).

you will probably need to include the findings from the pretest interviews in the analysis, noting the changes that were made as a result of the pretest. However, if the overall population is large enough, we recommend not including pretest interviews in the analysis results.

Focus groups of target respondents are useful in identifying pertinent aspects of experiences or services that should be included in surveys. A group

> ## The "No Opinion" or "Don't Know" Option
>
> - Less educated respondents are more likely to choose this category.
> - Offering this option increases the likelihood of other item nonresponse.
> - Studies have shown that including these items does not improve the consistency of respondents' attitudes over time.
> - For questions that require some thought, these items discourage respondents from thinking about the issue.
> - Respondents who do not have clearly formulated opinions usually lean in one direction or the other.
> - Recent cognitive studies have shown that when encouraged, respondents who choose these options would have provided substantive answers.

of target respondents can help operationalize what "quality" means to them in a specific type of service or program, for example. (For more on focus groups, see Chapter Twelve.)

Collecting the Data from Respondents

Getting respondents to complete the survey is a vital part of the survey process. If you do not follow up all the planning and design with a good data collection effort, you will negate your preparation work. Nevertheless, designing a good and flexible data collection operation can overcome some preparation oversights.

Mail Surveys

For optimal response rates on mail surveys, the total design method (Dillman, 1978, 2000) remains the most popular mail survey procedure used. It calls for a series of steps to achieve a satisfactory response rate:

1. Include in the first mailing a questionnaire, a separate cover letter, and a postage-paid return envelope (a stamp appeals more to respondents than a business permit).
2. Approximately ten days later, send the entire sample a reminder postcard that emphasizes the importance of the study and thanking people who have already responded.
3. About two weeks later, mail all nonrespondents another questionnaire, but with a new shorter cover letter. If you have enough funds, you may increase your response rate by using monetary incentives, using express mail, or sending a postcard prior to the first mailing announcing the survey. If you can afford it, you should also consider calling the nonrespondents and asking them to return their questionnaire. For many agencies, such as health and human service agencies, staff should be asked to encourage clients to complete the questionnaire.

E-Mail Surveys

For optimal response rates on e-mail surveys, the methodology is similar: send the questionnaire with a cover letter, followed by a short e-mail reminder, followed by another questionnaire to nonrespondents. One major difference is the timing of mailings. With e-mail, most people who are going to respond will do so the same day they receive the e-mail. Hence, instead of waiting ten days to send a reminder, it is best to send the reminder just after you see a significant decline in return responses (usually three to four days). After the reminder is sent, there should be some increase in returns. Once these returns significantly decline, the second questionnaire to nonrespondents should be sent out. Another key aspect of e-mail surveys is that the questionnaire should be included in the message text and not as an attachment. With so many computer viruses and virus warnings, many potential respondents will not open the attachment. It is also important to restrict the length of the e-mail survey to no more than a few pages, because some e-mail systems automatically turn longer messages into attachments or the scrolling length of the message itself may reduce the respondent's willingness to participate. Also, try to send the e-mail at times when people are most likely to receive them; thus, avoid weekends. Resend nonrespondents an e-mail at different times and days of the week than in the initial mailing. Finally, it is very useful to get someone with name recognition to send out a global announcement just prior to the start of data collection, explaining the importance of the study.

Web Surveys

The number of Web surveys that are being designed and implemented is increasing at a fast pace. They are cheaper and give the designer more flexibility in designing the survey, since the computer can handle skip patterns and process information on the fly. Most Web surveys rely on an e-mail being sent that contains a description of the study and a Web link to a server on which the survey resides. Thus, you should use the same mailing procedures that you would use in conducting an e-mail survey. Keep the e-mail message short so that it is easy for the respondent to see the Web link, and it is preferable to have an embedded password in the link so that people can be connected to their own unique questionnaire without having to be given a password and log-in. Also, make sure the Web link fits on one line, or it becomes difficult for some respondents to click the link from within their Web browser.

Some early comparison studies of e-mail versus Web surveys indicated that respondents prefer completing Web surveys (Triplett, 2001). There is also some evidence that people are more willing to provide sensitive information on a Web survey than through e-mail, where often an employer is legally the owner of employees' e-mail messages. Web surveys offer a wide range of options for the survey designer; however, this increase also means a greater need to test and understand the effects of various visual designs. Currently, there is much exploratory research being conducted as to the best ways of designing Web surveys. Although you need access to a Web server and probably some technical support, there are now many software applications that make it easy for a novice to design a Web survey; among them are EZ-Survey, Perseus, Apian, SurveySaid, SumQuest, Remark Web Survey, Survey Monkey, and Snap Survey Software. However, before designing a Web survey, you should browse the Web to examine survey examples. In addition, read the current literature about Web design (Dillman, 2000; Couper, Traugott, and Lamias, 2001). One thing is certain: with e-mail penetration increasing, Web surveys are going to be an increasingly important mode of data collection.

In-Person Surveys

Face-to-face or in-person interviewing is the oldest form of data collection. Face-to-face interviewing also still provides the highest response rate. It works best for both open-ended questions and longer surveys. In addition, the sampling frame bias is usually lowest for face-to-face studies. Ease of administration is greatest if target respondents are together at a facility, such as a recreation center or hospital, and they can be interviewed or given pen-and-paper questionnaires to complete. Usually, though, interviewing in-person requires that interviewers travel to a place (usually a home or office) where the respondent can be interviewed. Thus, the cost of conducting face-to-face interviews makes this mode of data collection impractical for most survey studies. In addition to cost, two other disadvantages of face-to-face interviewing are that respondents do not usually report sensitive behavior in the presence of an interviewer, and it takes much longer to complete the survey study (Fowler, 1993). In addition, gaining access to respondents in their homes may be difficult due to fear of allowing a stranger into their home or danger to the interviewers. Although the use of hand-held computers using computer-assisted personal interviewing (CAPI) software has reduced the time it takes to retrieve information from the interviewers, the field periods for personal interviewing still remain longer than the other modes of data collection.

Telephone Surveys

Because of the cost of face-to-face interviewing and the difficulty in getting good response rates on mail surveys, telephone surveys have been very popular over the last twenty years. Although they are still a viable mode of collecting survey data, changing technology, such as answering machines, cell phones, and call screening, has made it more difficult to achieve high response rates on telephone surveys. Nevertheless, decent response rates can still be achieved using the telephone as the mode of data collection.

Now there is added importance in scheduling enough time to make multiple calls at varying times and days of the week. Most survey methodologists agree that for household surveys that rely on a random digit dial sample design, up to fifteen to twenty call attempts is an optimal level of effort. After that, response rate gains for additional calls are very small relative to the added costs. A major difference between conducting telephone (and face-to-face) surveys and self-administered surveys (mail, e-mail, and Web) is the need to recruit and train interviewers to ask the questions.

Training and Interviewing

Recruiting and training face-to-face and telephone interviewers are time-consuming and difficult. For most good survey shops, maintaining a core staff of good interviewers is a high priority. The fact that a survey shop already has an available group of interviewers is probably one of the most important considerations when deciding whether to contract out data collection (budget probably being the most important). What makes recruiting and training interviewers especially difficult is that there are lots of people who are just not good at it.

In general, it helps to have a more mature-sounding voice and be female; however, there have been many successful male and young interviewers. For many studies, you may need to choose interviewers who have characteristics similar to the respondents. For instance, it is not advisable to have men ask women questions about domestic violence programs, and when surveying in populations for whom English is not their first language, having interviewers with relevant language abilities may be necessary. Usually, people with high levels of enthusiasm tend to be more successful at getting others to respond to surveys, but their enthusiasm sometimes biases the actual interview, especially when they are asking sensitive questions. Screening potential interviewers on the phone to assess the clarity of their speech before deciding whether training them to be interviewers is worthwhile. Even with this prescreening, often as many as half the new interviewers who start out in training will not make it as useful interviewers.

Interviewer training should be broken into two separate sessions: general training, followed by a specific training session. The general training should cover the basics, such as reading verbatim, neutral probing, dealing with difficult respondents, and learning the computer-assisted telephone interviewing CATI/CAPI system if the interviewer will be using the computer. Although experienced interviewers may not need to attend this training, it is often a good refresher for them.

Specific training, which should occur after general training, primarily consists of taking the interviewers through the survey instrument question by question. It is also important during the specific training to provide interviewers with information about the purpose of the survey. There is a lot of information passed along to the interviewer during a good training session; therefore, interviewers should also be provided with a training manual that they can use as a reference. It is easy to locate good examples of interviewer training manuals by searching the Web with the key phrase "survey interviewer training manual."

After the training, most survey shops have new interviewers conduct live practice calls before conducting interviews with respondents who were selected to be included in the final sample. This procedure helps protect the quality of the study since you will be able to assess whether a new interviewer will be able to do the job before he or she begins calling actual respondents. In fact, it is very important to remove interviewers early on who are having problems. Some people do not make good interviewers, and it is better to catch the problem early rather than deal with a bigger problem later. Although retraining is an option, it is usually less effective than replacing an interviewer with a new person.

If you plan to try to recontact respondents who initially refuse, provide special refusal conversion training. This has been found to help interviewers who are asked to try and convert refusals. Emphasis on getting your foot in the door rather than conducting the interview is emphasized during the refusal conversion training.

Quality Control

Although no interviewer training is needed for mail, Web, and e-mail surveys, you will need to train someone to monitor, track, and institute quality control measures. For traditional mail surveys, the person should be detail oriented and carefully check a random sample of the mailing before sending it out. On days when mailings are being sent out, things are generally quite hectic; having a person in charge of quality control at this time will go a long way in avoiding embarrassing mistakes, such as enclosing cover letters that do not match the label or not stuffing the envelopes correctly.

For e-mail and mail surveys, it is important to find someone who is competent in using the e-mail system and also has experience using distribution lists. In addition, with Web and e-mail surveys, someone needs to be available for a few days after each mailing who can answer e-mail questions, check address problems, and track the number of completed interviews that have been submitted or returned. Unlike traditional mail studies, it has been found that a majority of people who participate do so shortly after receiving the e-mail survey or the e-mail that provides a link to the Web survey. Because of this quick response time, consider sending out the survey in batches by creating smaller distribution lists. For example, if you are conducting a job satisfaction survey, the employer may not appreciate having all employees completing a survey at the same time. It should be noted that with both mail or e-mail surveys, it is essential to track returned surveys if second or third mailings are used.

Monitoring telephone interviews is a standard quality control practice. Most survey shops aim to monitor 10 to 20 percent of all interviewers' work, with more frequent monitoring at the beginning of the project. The person responsible for monitoring should try to listen in on various parts of the survey, especially to hear how well the interviewer performs on the introduction. Monitoring telephone interviews requires a centralized phone facility with proper equipment. If you do not have proper monitoring equipment, consider using some call-back verification as a quality control alternative. Call-back verification involves having a supervisor contact a respondent who was recently interviewed to verify that the interview was completed and ask the respondent if he or she experienced any problems with the interviewer or the survey. Although we generally think of monitoring and call-back verification as tools to catch and solve data collection problems, it is equally as important to provide interviewers with immediate and positive feedback. For face-to-face interviewing, a combination of call-back verification and having someone observe the interview is the best strategy, since monitoring at random is operationally more difficult for in-person interviewing.

Good record keeping and tracking relevant information during data collection is an underappreciated but important part of the survey process. Proper tracking and recording procedures always yield higher response rates, in addition to demonstrating a high level of professionalism to both respondents and audience.

For all types of surveys, but especially telephone and face-to-face interviews, good record keeping is essential since a respondent is often unavailable to complete the interview during the first contact attempt. The timing of contact attempts is critical in completing telephone and face-to-face interviews. Most CATI and CAPI software includes features that keep track of previous call attempts and schedule future call attempts. If you are not using computer-assisted software, have interviewers fill out information about all contacts on a contact record sheet (see Exhibit 9.1). In addition, to maintaining information on the date, time, and result of each contact attempt, the interviewer should record his or her initials (or ID number), and provide comments that may be useful in future contact attempts.

For mail, Web, and e-mail surveys, keeping track of when all mail-outs (or e-mails) were sent, including postcard reminders, and when completed surveys were returned is an important part of the data collection process. This can be accomplished manually or, preferably, with standard spreadsheet or database software that allows you to manage and update mailing lists so that people who complete the survey can be excluded from follow-up mailings. For e-mail or Web surveys, it is important to have the program automatically send a thank-you reply acknowledging receipt of the survey. For traditional

Exhibit 9.1. Sample Telephone or In-Person Contact Record Sheet

Caseid: 10001	Phone Number:	(301) 555– 9999			
Interviewer ID:	**Interview Date**	**Interview Time Start**	**Interview Time End**	**Outcome Code**	**Comments**
414	Mon 03/13	7:30pm		callback	Will be home this weekend
523	Sat 03/18	5:05pm	5:23pm	complete	

mail surveys, a thank-you postcard is especially useful for populations you are likely to survey again. With Web, e-mail, and mail surveys, use tracking to determine when to send the next reminder. For nonrespondents, send reminder e-mails at a different time of day and on a different day of the week from the original mailings. Also, if most of the e-mail addresses in the sample are work addresses, do not send the e-mail out on Friday afternoon or on Saturday, Sunday, or Monday morning.

Since it is becoming increasingly difficult to reach respondents, many survey designs now use combinations of ways through which respondents can respond (telephone, mail, Web or e-mail). With mixed-mode data collection efforts, a record of both when and what method has already been offered must be carefully kept.

Response Rates

Getting people to respond to the survey is the main goal of the data collection process. If everyone you are trying to contact is eligible to complete the survey, the response rate is the total number of people interviewed divided by the total number of people you attempted to interview (anyone ineligible to complete the study should be removed from the denominator). The lower the response rate is, the more likely the study is vulnerable to nonresponse bias. Unlike sampling error, the effect that nonresponse error has on the quality of the survey is not easy to quantify because we do not know whether the nonrespondents differ from the respondents in terms of how they would have responded to the survey.

Although there is no such thing as an official acceptable response rate, response rates are the industry's standard for which people judge the quality of a survey. Surveys that achieve a response rate of 70 percent or higher are generally thought of as being high-quality surveys, and nonresponse is not usually a concern. Studies that have response rates between 50 and 70 percent can use some nonresponse weighting adjustment to reduce potential nonresponse bias. Nonresponse adjustments usually involve weighting the data set to increase the overall impact of the data that were collected from people who have characteristics similar to the nonrespondents. For example, if you are attempting to measure employee satisfaction, but while collecting your data you found that support staff were less likely to participate, you can reduce the potential nonresponse bias in the measurement by increasing the weighting factor for the support staff who did complete the survey. The adjustments apply to responses aggregated over different client groups and do not help in reducing errors due to nonresponses among individual client groups. Typically, adjustments are not made for small agency surveys, especially for local and nonprofit service providers.

If the budget is tight, try not to cut back on efforts to achieve a higher response rate. Reducing sample size or questionnaire length is usually a more appropriate way of trying to save money than reducing the level of contact effort during data collection. A low response rate often negates what may have been, on the whole, good survey design work.

The most important factor in getting good response rates is making additional contact attempts. Most telephone and in-person interviews are not completed on the first call attempt. With household telephone surveys that rely on calling randomly selected telephone numbers, the average number of call attempts needed to complete an interview has risen to over five. Telephone studies that make fewer than five call attempts are not likely to achieve a 50 percent response rate. For mail, e-mail, and Web surveys, a single mailing often yields a very low response rate. The standard is two or three mailings, with at least two mailings having a reminder postcard or e-mail messages sent a few days after the initial mailing reminding people to participate. Of course, the more professional the survey looks or sounds, the more likely it is that a respondent will decide to participate. A good introduction is particularly important for interviewer-administered surveys, and a strong cover letter and an attractive instrument design are key to gaining cooperation on self-administered surveys. For surveys by agencies of their own clients, if the agency has established a reasonable level of trust with clients, the key problem will be gaining contacts with clients, not client refusals to respond.

Besides the overall response rate, you should be concerned with item nonresponse. During data collection, it is very important (especially at the beginning) to check the quality of the respondents' answers. This usually is referred to as performing data checks. Data checks performed during data collection often uncover interviewer problems, procedural problems, or questionnaire problems. Although it may be too late to fix problems that are discovered during data collection, the damage can often be contained or minimized during data analysis.

Preparing Data for Analysis

Interview-administered and Web surveys that use CATI and CAPI have the distinct advantage of providing a useful data file immediately after the data have been collected. For mail and paper surveys, a coder must enter the data into a data file. To reduce entry errors, it is recommended that at least 5 percent of a coder's work be checked for accuracy. If you find lots of errors during the checking, you may need to retrain the coder or there may be something wrong with the coding procedures. If the project has enough funding, consider doing double entry and fixing all errors found between the two data files. Regardless of how data were entered, by a coder, respondent, or an interviewer, you usually find yourself needing to fix or change answer responses. *Never alter the original raw data file.* It is better to make all edits and corrections and fix input errors using the statistical software package you plan to use for the analysis, thus creating an edited version of the original data file, preserving original data file, and also being able to keep a record of all edits made.

Backcoding data is a special type of data editing that involves giving a coder some rules for interpreting a respondent's open-ended response to a question that included "other" as a response category. Sometimes when the respondent has a series of response options that includes an "anything else" or "other specify" option, the respondent chooses the "other response" category, but actually provides an answer that is equivalent to an existing response option. For instance, a respondent asked, "Do you consider yourself white, black, Asian, or some other race?" may record "African American" under "other." Backcoding procedures would most likely change the respondent's answer from "other" to "black."

To categorize responses to an open-ended question, break the task down into three distinct tasks: develop categories, code the responses, and do the data entry that includes an identification variable so the new variable can be merged on to the existing data set.

In some situations, you may want to weight the responses of subgroups of respondents. There are two main reasons to include a weight variable in the data file: the sample design was not a random sample or the selection was random but the final sample of respondents significantly differs on key characteristics from the overall population you are trying to generalize to. If you need to weight for both of these reason, create a weight that corrects for the sample design and then, using this weight, adjust the sample to match the key characteristics of the population. For example, consider a study of engineers where you purposely gave women twice the chance of selection to ensure that enough interviews would be completed with women. Comparing men and women would not require using a weight. However, to calculate the overall percentage of engineers giving a particular response, you would need to weight women's responses by one-half. Suppose that when you look at the weighted estimates, you realize that nuclear engineers were far less likely to complete the survey. If having too few nuclear engineers affects the result, adjust the weight (increasing the weight for nuclear engineers and reducing it for all other engineers) so that in the weighted estimates, the proportion of nuclear engineers in the sample is the same as the proportion of nuclear engineers in the overall population.

Presenting Survey Findings

The most important objective when reporting findings is to present the data in a format that is accessible and clear for the intended audience. Knowing the audience is key. You need to:

- Anticipate what the audience is most interested in seeing
- How much and what sort of disaggregation of responses the audience will want
- How sophisticated an analysis the audience expects and needs
- How long a report (or briefing) the audience will prefer

As you decide which data to report and how to report them, think about the audience's priorities and then remember that less is better and clarity is essential when planning a presentation. (See the box for tips on table preparation.)

The priorities of the audience should drive decisions on what to include and in what order findings should be presented. The first table should present demographic or relevant background on the respondents to the survey. A table titled something like "Profile of the Sample," which displays pertinent data about who (or which jurisdictions) responded to the survey, should be provided first. Comparable data on the population demographics should be arranged in this table as well (if they are available), so that the relative representativeness of the sample can be related to the audience. Decisions on what to include in the profile table should reflect the audience's interests. Sometimes, for example, the answer to a key question, such as whether a jurisdiction has adopted an innovative tax or regulation, might be included in the first table.

For tables, basic contingency tables that present percentages of units selecting each response for questions in the survey are the most user-friendly mode of presentation. (See Tables 9.5 and 9.6.) The percentages should be disaggregated according to background (or demographic) characteristics that are of interest to the audience. Factors that are used to disaggregate responses might be simply demographic differences, such as levels of education

Designing Effective Tables

Less is better:

- Consolidate by grouping related questions together to minimize the total number of tables.
- Reduce the number of entries in each table, for example, reporting only the percentage of yes (or no) responses, or reporting only the percentage of agree (or disagree) responses.
- When reporting on the statistical significance of the findings, report only whether the results were or were not statistically significant at the level selected rather than giving values for the statistical test.

Clarity is essential:

- Give each table a clear, descriptive title that identifies which variables are related in the table.
- Label each variable with sufficient detail for the audience.
- Provide the exact wording of a question in the first table in which the question appears.
- When collapsing a variable, clarify which values are in each group rather than just labeling values as "high" or "low."
- Provide the number responding to the particular items in each table, since the number may vary from table to table.
- Specify which units are in the denominator when reporting percentages such as "of those responding."
- If a measure of the strength of the relationship between a pair of variables is provided, briefly define it the first time it is provided in a footnote to the table.
- When providing data from another source to compare to your survey data, identify that source with sufficient documentation in the footnote to the table.

or geographical location, or behavioral factors, such as frequency of contacts with an office or with a specific service.

It is crucial to report response rates, and even the rates among subgroups, if relevant, no matter how you selected the sample. Sampling error is only one source of error, and not necessarily the major one; thus, analysis of the impact of nonrespondents is always required. When response rates are less than 70 percent, extra effort should be undertaken to ensure that there is no evidence of nonresponse bias. Only if assurances are sufficient to con-

Table 9.5. Contingency Table Presenting Survey Findings

Level of Satisfaction with Legal Aid Services by Type of Criminal Prosecution[a]

How satisfied were you with the responsiveness of your attorney to your questions?[b]	Drug Charges (N = 352)	Misdemeanor (N = 85)	Theft/Robbery (N = 122)
Not satisfied	5%	8%	10%
Somewhat satisfied	10	12	18
Extremely satisfied	85	80	72
	100%	100%	100%

[a]The differences found in satisfaction levels across the subgroups divided by type of crime are statistically significant at a 95 percent level of confidence. However, this does not preclude nonsampling errors. One source of nonsampling error is nonresponse bias. In this case, only 63 percent of the sample responded.

[b]Totals may not add up to 100 percent due to rounding in this and all subsequent tables.

vince the most critical audience that the sample is fairly representative of the target population should statistical significance tests be used. The most common test used in contingency tables is the chi-square test. It simply reports whether the differences between subgroups are statistically significant (and thus generalizable to the target population) given the decision rule used, such as a 95 or 99 percent confidence level, rather than reporting actual values of a statistic such as the chi square. (See Chapter Sixteen for more guidance on statistical analyses of survey data.)

Although the actual number of tables and analysis reported should be limited by the targeted length of a presentation, the data should be analyzed from many different angles. Thorough analysis of the data means that many more potential tables can be produced and reviewed than are reported. Simply searching for interesting relationships should not be frowned on. Sometimes the most interesting findings are not anticipated.

In addition to reporting the survey data in a user-friendly format, information on the methodology used to obtain the data is also extremely important. A "Scope and Methods" section should be included (possibly as an appendix) to describe the decisions you made and reasoning behind them regarding sampling, wording of questions, and other pertinent decisions that may affect interpretation. It is also important to be explicit about how response rates were computed. Sufficient detail on how many mailings were sent and other means that were used to test the generalizability of the results should be given. The key is to provide clear, understandable background information on the methodology without overwhelming and boring the audience.

Table 9.6. A Contingency Table That Consolidates Multiple Variables

Proportion of Respondents Who Are Satisfied
with Legal Aid Services by Type of Criminal Prosecution

Proportion of Respondents Reporting Extremely or Somewhat Satisfied (2 or 3 on a 1 to 3 scale) with:	Drug Charges (N = 352)	Misdemeanor (N = 85)	Theft/Robbery (N = 122)
Responsiveness of your attorney to your questions	95%	92%	90%
Effectiveness of the representation afforded you by your attorney	90	83	88
Amount of time your attorney devoted to your case	88	81	78
Ease of obtaining legal representation	85	84	86
Courteousness of the Legal Services staff	95	94	93
Timeliness of the response of the Legal Services staff to your request for assistance	84	80	72

Conclusion

There are many options for surveying stakeholders in public and nonprofit programs. Certain aspects of survey methodology have remained constant and are likely to remain so into the future, while others continue to change. Principles of survey design, protection of confidentiality, sampling protocols, data analytical approaches, and audience-oriented presentation skills are fairly impervious to change. Technological improvements in means for reaching and encouraging respondents, and capturing data continue to modify the ways in which we conduct surveys.

The keys to obtaining valid, useful data about programs are to rigorously plan and pretest the survey and the sampling strategy, and then meticulously oversee data collection and analytical processes. Many key decisions are made during the design phase that can make or break the entire endeavor. Careful consideration of the relative advantages and disadvantages of different survey modes, types of incentives, and types of questions to employ is essential. And then open discussion about the decisions made and the rationale underlying them is necessary for strengthening the legitimacy and credibility of the findings. As technological innovations open yet more choices, the key is to systematically weigh the options and choose wisely to provide the most valid and reliable information possible.

References

Couper, M. P., Traugott, M. W., and Lamias, M. J. "Web Survey Design and Administration." *Public Opinion Quarterly,* 2001, *65*(2), 230–253.

Dillman, D. *Mail and Telephone Surveys: The Total Design Method.* New York: Wiley, 1978.

Dillman, D. *Mail and Telephone Surveys: The Tailored Design Method.* New York: Wiley, 2000.

Fowler, F. J. *Survey Research Methods.* (2nd ed.) Thousand Oaks, Calif.: Sage, 1993.

Krosnick, J. A., and others. "The Impact of 'No Opinion' Response Options on Data Quality: Non-Attitude Reduction or an Invitation to Satisfice?" *Public Opinion Quarterly,* 2002, *66*(3), 371–403.

McClendon, M. J., and Alwin, D. F. "No Opinion Filters and Attitude Measurement Reliability." *Sociological Methods and Research,* 1993, *20,* 60–103.

Singer, E. "The Use of Incentives to Reduce Nonresponse in Household Surveys." In R. M. Groves, D. Dillman, J. L. Eltinge, and R.J.A. Little (eds.), *Survey Nonresponse.* New York: Wiley, 2002.

Triplett, T. "Comparing an E-Mail Survey with a Web Survey." Paper presented at the International Field Directors and Technology Conference, Montreal, Canada, May 2001.

10

Using Expert Judgment

Harvey A. Averch

Any public sector program may be evaluated by applying expert judgment. However, standard texts argue that such an approach must be scientifically inferior to randomized experiments—the "flagships of evaluation" (Rossi, Freeman, and Lipsey, 1999, p. 305). Compared to the massive literature on using experts in quantitative or qualitative forecasting or in estimating technological parameters, the reported cases on expert program evaluation are thin (Nevo, 1989; Geis, 1987; Weston, 1987). The evaluation profession has its methodological roots in traditional social science, where the use of experts is not common. Evaluators trained in the mainstream profession do not often work in agencies where expert judgment may be appropriate or the only alternative, for example, as it is in public or private research and development laboratories.

Yet evaluation by experts persists. For some types of programs and decisions, there may be no alternative way to evaluate. For some, there may be no more cost-effective way. If we believe that the information to be gained by evaluation should be proportional to decision makers' needs, time, budget, and attention, then conventional quantitative evaluations may be infeasible or inappropriate. If so, properly designed expert evaluations may be cost-effective alternatives. For example, expert evaluation is very common in evaluating the results of science and technology programs or higher education programs. Actually, it is the preferred method in these domains, although its validity and reliability remain relatively unresearched. Today, the federal Office of Management and Budget (OMB) asks agencies to do expert evaluations and uses them in judging whether programs are effective or not as inputs to budget decisions.

Deciding to Use Expert Evaluations

Decision makers and program evaluators should consider using expert evaluation when the effectiveness of programs is subject to high uncertainty. Program uncertainty can be defined and identified by the following situations and conditions:

- *A public agency has been operating a "program" for a number of years, and it cannot be certain about the effective quantity or quality of inputs it has bought during those years, and there is no easy way to measure these.* For example, research and development agencies frequently cannot specify the real quantity and quality of scientific labor and capital they invest in or the factor proportion— the number of senior researchers, assistants, and instruments that will lead to significant research output.
- *The expected "benefits" or "outcomes" of the program are highly uncertain in the present or must occur in the future.* Education is an example. Although some educational outcomes may be measured by standardized or criterion-referenced tests, the true educational program output is multidimensional. It can be known only in the very long run, and knowing it takes significant investment, as, for example, in tracking students over many years. Whether schools produce both skilled, flexible workers capable of operating a complex modern economy and good citizens capable of operating a competent democracy cannot be known in the short run. It is difficult to know in the long run. Indeed, such uncertainty is characteristic of any program that produces a multipurpose public good distributed over large numbers of consumers in different geographical areas.
- *The agency does not know with precision whether decision-relevant outcomes can be attributed to the inputs and the design of the program.* Contrary to what economists usually assume, suppose the relationship between inputs and outcomes (the production function) is not technologically determined, but instead twists and bends according to the mix of inputs purchased and the institutional arrangements in which they will be applied. In other words, the program design and the choice of inputs interact in unpredictable ways in producing final outcomes (Murnane and Nelson, 1984).

At time $t+1$, agency sponsors or managers need to make a decision about the program. They may want information to improve current performance (formative evaluation). They may want to learn whether the program is worth the amount that has been invested in it or achieved its intended purpose (summative evaluation). Up to time t, the program has been operating under input uncertainty, outcome uncertainty, and uncertainty about causal relationships; therefore, expert evaluation will be either the sole alternative or the most cost-effective alternative. Under such conditions, the job of the evaluator is to work collaboratively with decision makers or program operators to clarify uncertainties and make connections so as to improve internal management and ultimate outcomes. But working in this mode means that the evaluator has become an expert adviser to the program.

Translating Expert Judgment Techniques to the Evaluation Domain

Given a decision that expert evaluation is the preferred mode, significant choice remains over the particular procedures to be used. Procedures unique to evaluation purposes have not yet been developed. Rather, expert evaluation procedures must be carefully adapted from standard uses such as parameter estimation and forecasting.

For example, reliability in estimation or forecasting ordinarily means the certainty with which an expert judgment reflects the true parameter and is not a result of random error. Reliability is necessary for validity in estimating the distribution of a parameter but not sufficient. In an evaluation context, this means that other experts looking at the same information would come to approximately the same judgments. Some group judgment procedures, however, use initial nonreliability and conflict among experts to try to get valid and reliable estimates by mean of formal or informal interaction among the experts. Similarly, accuracy in estimation or forecasting is defined as the correspondence between an a priori expert judgment about a parameter and its real world value or between a forecast and its realization. Accuracy in a priori estimation corresponds to validity in ex post program evaluation. In conventional evaluations, validity is the correspondence between the actual program outcomes and the evaluation findings. However, expert evaluations are most appropriate when such a correspondence is difficult to establish. So the validity of expert judgment in program evaluation means that if a decision maker accepts some individual or collective expert judgment about a program and acts on its basis, social benefits are realized or costs avoided.

Evaluators looking to use expert judgment need to be sensitive to trade-offs in validity, reliability, time required, information and operating costs, and clarity to prospective users. No procedures so far devised clearly dominate. More elaborate procedures are not necessarily more reliable or valid than less elaborate ones. The procedures I analyze here are not exhaustive, only suggestive. Variants on each major procedure are easy to invent, depending on the particular trade-offs that evaluators and decision makers want to make. I have sorted the procedures according to whether the technical experts work inside or outside the evaluating organization, and if outside, according to their structure and modes of interaction.

Expert Evaluations from the Inside of Agencies

Inside government, the people who manage a program or support its budget are experts. They have access to the information a program creates and records in the standardized, routine reporting its parent agency requires. They also have immediate access to the views of working staff, constituents, and clients. If one wants to evaluate a public program subject to uncertainty, then a crude but rapid way to obtain performance information is to use the judgment of operating managers, higher-level administrators, and budgetary sponsors. Obtaining judgments from those closest to a program is the most common kind of evaluation. All budget offices and legislative committees carry out such evaluations. OMB requests federal agencies to provide cost and performance information in preparing the president's annual budget (Office of Management and Budget, 2003).

Operating managers tell budget or oversight agencies a "story" about their program's performance and cost over a budget or life cycle. The stories are, of course, highly stylized and inherently self-serving. However, budget and oversight agencies are rarely under illusions about administrators' incentives to find that the outcomes of the programs for which they are responsible are always both positive and intended. They know managers and administrators have incentives to blame reported problems on shortages of funds or personnel. They are well aware of the perceived and real costs to a program of reporting problems or failures. However, if evaluators of budget and oversight agencies can specify the ways in which administrators present information, they can control incentives to deceive to a considerable extent. And when they discover deception, they can impose penalties in budget or staff or remove decision making (Bendor, Taylor, and Van Gaalen, 1985). Thus, it is possible to judge whether a program's claims about its outcomes have warrants or justifications. Depending on the credibility of the claims, the people running a program receive rewards or punishments in the form of budget, staff, or other things of value.

Customarily, budgetary and oversight agencies check the stories programs tell by using analysis from government experts and consultants or by the testimony of interested witnesses. Evidence from clients and constituents is given heavy weight in budget and legislative agencies on both substantive and political grounds. The degree of credibility in administrators' stories can be checked by collating multiple, simultaneous accounts of program performance, Assigning the appropriate degree of credibility requires good contextual information on the relations among programs, clients, and constituents, but sophisticated sponsors will be sensitive to these.

Using Internal Program Evaluation Staff

Many agencies recognize a necessary, if limited, evaluation function and assign separate staff to carry it out, although the staff may not always be formally trained in standard evaluation techniques. Today, many federal and many state agencies contain evaluation offices designed to be semi-independent from programs and to have no immediate stake in program outcomes. Such offices track programs and evaluate them objectively, without the perspectives and biases of managers and operating staff. They carry out routine internal evaluations and display expertise on any performance questions that come up during ordinary bureaucratic transactions, including questions about short-run or long-run effectiveness raised by sponsors and constituents. When a rapid, low-cost expert evaluation is needed, the agencies evaluation staff can be asked to provide it.

Checks on validity and reliability may be horizontal: the evaluation staff may ask the program being evaluated for a reply to some draft evaluation, or it may ask other people in the agency with technical knowledge to review an evaluation. Alternatively, checks may be vertical: superiors at different levels in an evaluation office hierarchy may review a draft evaluation for technical merit, organizational feasibility, and political acceptability.

For a variety of technical and political reasons, an agency may prefer to use outside experts in universities or contract research organizations to obtain estimates of outcomes. Given such a preference, the agency supplies the experts with questions about a task, problem, or program; allows them to review available data; and then asks them to pool their knowledge and come to some collective judgment or recommendation. A single outside expert will not ordinarily be asked to make a formal systematic evaluation, since the research literature on making judgments suggests that collective ones are more accurate than individual ones (Woudenberg, 1991). In any case, politically astute agencies know that it is much more difficult to attack collective judgments than individual judgments. Evaluations by prestigious, credible outside experts may give parent or oversight agencies an upper hand in forcing acceptance of recommendations that are unpleasant to the program being evaluated.

Selection of outside experts can be accomplished in many ways. For example, to get technical experts, an agency may use its past grant or contract experience, publications or citations in the field of interest, or recommendations from the members of a relevant "invisible college," the set of peers recognized by all in a given discipline or substantive area. Technical experts may be mixed with political experts, or even program constituents and clients, to bring different perspectives to bear in the evaluation process.

The Government Performance and Review Act (GPRA) in 1993 mandated performance budgeting for the federal government. Performance budgets, in principal, relate agency strategic plans, programs, budget requests, interim indicators of performance, and, if at all possible, the marginal social impacts on an agency's clients or constituents. The OMB has a long history of trying to make budget formats reveal rational trade-offs among programs, and the passage of the GPRA gave impetus to this effort. Today, federal agency budgets are supposed to contain transparent connections between budgets and the proximate outcomes and social impacts achieved (Daniels, 2003).

The OMB has developed a set of thirty questions, the so-called Program Assessment Rating Tool (PART), organized in four sections: (1) program purpose and design, (2) strategic planning, (3) management, and (4) results. Depending on the fractions of satisfactory responses about its performance, programs receive a score of "effective," "moderately effective," "results not demonstrated," or "ineffective." Table 10.1 shows the PART evaluations of three programs in the Department of Justice using the evaluation categories.

About 20 percent of federal programs were evaluated using the PART in 2003. Budgetary rewards, in theory, come from having a high fraction of programs judged to be effective or from making good progress toward being effective. In years of budget constraint, "effective" programs are likely to be held level, while those judged "ineffective" are likely to be cut or even eliminated. In the fiscal year 2004 budget, OMB reports that all programs rated as effective received budget increases or were held level. For example, the Department of Commerce's Bureau of Economic Analysis (BEA) received a rating of effective and gained an increase. Department of Health and Human Services Health Centers received increases for the same reported reason. OMB does not report how its examiners mapped its individual indicators of effectiveness into its aggregated categories. How the responses from thirty or so dichotomous yes-no questions per program were mapped into the simpler aggregate ratings is not clear, and there are various alternatives for doing this job.

An Alternative Format for Information-Producing Agencies

Some agencies produce public goods for third parties to use. Their cost-effectiveness and outcomes do not lie within their own power to manage. For example, information-producing agencies such as the National Science Foundation (NSF) and the Office of Naval Research (ONR) produce information for social use by anyone who can appropriate the information and congeal it

Table 10.1. Sample Justice Department Evaluations

Program	Rating	Explanation	Recommendation
Bureau of Prisons (BOP)	Moderately effective	BOP was established seven decades ago and represents over 15 percent of the Department of Justice total budget authority. It has seen a dramatic increase in funding and inmate population over the past decade. While rated moderately effective, BOP lacks long-term, measurable goals with associated targets and time frames.	The budget requests the activation of newly constructed prison facilities and increased reliance on contract bed space for low, minimum, and special category inmates.
Drug courts	Results not demonstrated	The program has been instrumental to the creation of hundreds of drug courts throughout the country. Independent studies indicate these courts can provide an effective intervention to substance abusers who might not otherwise receive treatment and generally result in lower rearrest rates. There is room for improvement in clarifying this program's long-term scope and goals and in collecting grantee data	The budget proposes a $16 million increase, which will support the creation of additional courts, as well as initiatives to lower the program's dropout rate and improve long-term effectiveness.
Juvenile accountability block grants	Ineffective	The program lacks clear objectives, performance goals, or measurable results. Application criteria are minimal. Grants can be used for sixteen different activities and there is no consistent definition of accountability. As a result, it is not currently possible to link funding to performance.	The budget requests no funding for this program in 2004.

Source: Adapted from a table in http://www.whitehouse.gov/omb/budget/fy2004/justice.html.

into products and services. The evaluation categories used for service delivery agencies that nominally link strategies to service flows to outcomes cannot easily be employed for basic research programs. For example, NSF mapped its programs into "successful" and "minimally effective." How a program rated in the NSF was determined, as usual in this agency, by outside expert peer review. As could be predicted from an agency that relies on external peer review by experts to allocate funds at the microlevel, the NSF used its committees of visitors (COVs) to review entire programs.

The COVs consist of distinguished scientists asked to take a broad view of a discipline, a field, or a program. They ask a now-standardized set of questions about the substantive distribution of grants and the implied research trajectories of a field instead of evaluating the scientific merits of particular grants.

Eliciting Systematic Judgments

Once experts have been selected, many alternatives exist for eliciting judgments. Judgments can be individual but aggregated in some way, or they can be collective. Since ex post program evaluation is not a job for which expert judgment is commonly considered, the discussion here concentrates on options that have been used and documented, could plausibly be adapted to evaluation purposes, and been partially tested for validity and reliability.

Informed Dialogue: Unstructured, Direct Interaction

In an informed dialogue procedure, an agency brings a group of experts together for informed, face-to-face exchange of views. The agency's evaluation staff provides initial questions or terms of reference, collects pertinent information, and records the proceedings. The experts conduct face-to-face conversations resulting in agreements and disagreements. They may hold their conversations iteratively, in a series of meetings, in which they try to achieve an informal consensus. Reaching a consensus by formal voting and polls is rare because it might reveal and record conflict. The idea is for the experts to talk long enough and intensely enough so that everyone arrives roughly at the same view.

During their meetings, the experts may obtain information from the program being evaluated, constituents, possibly clients involved in the program, and even bureaucratic competitors of the program at hand. Side conversations and consultations outside formally scheduled meetings are generally permitted, since they are not controllable anyway and may help form the desired consensus.

Most evaluations of the information and education outcomes of science and technology programs follow this informed dialogue format. Strategic behavior by the experts in promoting their own views and achieving their own private agendas through biased or self-interested evaluation of the outcomes is, in principle, controlled by the norms of science and engineering practice—the so-called Mertonian norms of disinterestedness, organized skepticism, and willingness to share data and findings with the larger community working in the field (Merton, 1973). The Mertonian norms provide grounding for the conventional image of the way scientific research is done. They lead to "certifiable" knowledge in the conduct of research.

While highly common, the structured direct mode of expert judgment is one of the least formally researched. We do not really know whether the Mertonian norms prevail in expert scientific evaluations or what conditions guarantee that they will prevail. The reported, finished consensus findings or recommendations rarely document the evolution of the experts' dialogue or the measures evaluation staff may have had to take to keep the dialogue on track and moving. In most cases, therefore, additional layers of technical, bureaucratic, and political review will be applied to a draft consensus report to check both substance and style. Whether a consensus is valid and reliable is not well known. A good expert evaluation in science and technology fields is one that turns out to be useful to the sponsor. When scientific agencies like the National Science Foundation or the National Institutes of Health or advisory organizations like the National Academy of Science use expert advice in evaluating programs, they assert two things: (1) they have engaged the best experts and (2) standard scientific committee procedures are effective in assessing program performance. Consequently, (3) judgments offered should be accepted and acted on. But we do not know whether self-interest and the ordinary afflictions of committee procedures, such as logrolling or dominance by strong personalities, are overcome by adherence to the norms for scientific discourse. Indeed, fear that the norms could not apply to estimating and forecasting served as the impetus for inventing the structured, indirect forms of obtaining collective expert judgment. By controlling, channeling, and aggregating interactions, the inventors of the structured forms of expert dialogue hoped that bias and self-interest would be controlled.

Structured, Indirect Interactions

Structured, indirect procedures, that is, procedures that are not face-to-face, characteristically impose constraints on direct information flows and expert interchange to control common afflictions, for example, the pursuit of private agendas or the emergence of groupthink. An ideal format, if it could be designed and executed, would force rapid convergence to reliable and valid estimates, predictions, or problem solutions. However, no such ideal has yet emerged, although each procedure that has been tried has its own champions. As a limited sample of such procedures, in addition to the very well-known Delphi procedure, we might list QCF (quantitative controlled feedback; Press, Ali, and Chung-Fang, 1979), NGT (nominal group technique; Delbecq, van de Ven, and Gustafson, 1977), devil's advocate (DA), and dialectical inquiry (DI; Mason, 1969; Schwenk, 1990).

   Delphi. Delphi's essence is structured, indirect, iterative interaction among experts with centralized control, tabulation, and feedback of information and judgments. Delphi was invented in the 1960s to assist in addressing problems for which there could be little real-world operating experience (Dalkey and Helmer, 1963). Traditionally, decision makers used Delphi to elicit estimates of unknown parameters in new, complex technological systems or to make forecasts of the new policy environment emerging from unanticipated political or economic developments. It has been adapted to decision making and policymaking, and nothing in its design prevents its use in ex post program evaluation. In the evaluation case, the collective judgment to be made is the current or expected worth of a particular program or the comparative worth of alternative programs.

In Delphi, the experts do not have direct contact with each other. On successive iterations, every expert submits his or her responses to a central "control agent" by memo, mail, or electronic medium. The control agent aggregates the information and circulates the collective findings to the experts. The collective judgment on each round is presented statistically without any backup reasoning, although the experts may be asked to give the reasons for their judgment. Asking for reasons is more common in later iterations, especially if there is no convergence. No one knows who has contributed what judgment to the collective statistical judgment. After seeing summaries of the total response distributed by the control agent, the experts then adjust and revise their estimates.

By aggregating and filtering the individual estimates or forecasts centrally and feeding them back on successive rounds, Delphi's inventors hoped that the collective estimate would converge, and, ideally, converge to a valid estimate or forecast. By providing for controlled, structured dialogue and immediate feedback and interchange by participants, they hoped that biases would be reduced or eliminated. Of course, Delphi's inventors did not deal much with science advising or technological evaluations, where, it could be argued, the direct exchange of ideas is what is desired and the Mertonian norms work to control the biases.

In an evaluation context, the experts would be given a series of structured questions about a program or would be asked to make qualitative or quantitative estimates of performance. Then the standard procedures would be applied. The steps in using the Delphi procedure for program evaluation are in the box.

Woudenberg (1991) reviewed 102 published studies in which a Delphi technique was applied. Based on the weight of the reported evidence, he concluded it is no more accurate than other collective judgment procedures. Although Delphi does achieve consensus or convergence, Woudenberg determined that it is achieved by tacit group pressures to conform to the group estimate and not by coherent, individual reprocessing of the common, ordered information received on successive rounds of estimation. In comparing the Delphi technique with alternative expert procedures, Woudenberg

Delphi Procedure for Program Evaluation

1. Develop the evaluation issues and questions that the experts will address.
2. Obtain data that the decision maker wishes experts to examine, and arrange any interviews with program staff desired. (The data can be agency records as defined in Chapter Fourteen, this volume, including previous evaluations, or the data can be interviews with people who hold relevant information about the program. The latter could include focus groups as discussed in Chapter Twelve, this volume.)
3. Design the instrument for addressing the issues and questions (for example, qualitative assessments, questions with numerical scales).
4. Select and contact the experts.
5. Administer the instrument in round 1.
6. The control agent collates, aggregates, and sends the judgments from round 1 back to the experts. (In estimation and forecasting, quartile and median responses are traditionally presented. The same can be done with a series of closed evaluation questions.)
7. Administer the instrument, round 2.
8. Repeat step 6.
9. Administer the instrument, round 3.
10. Repeat step 6.
11. Prepare the final report on results. (Provide draft report to experts if appropriate.)

found that Delphi alternatives generally perform as well as Delphi and frequently are superior for the task selected.

Some Procedures with Built-In Conflict: Devil's Advocate and Dialectical Inquiry. In DA procedures, a recommended course of action or a plan is defined and presented by the experts to the control agent or the direct user, along with the assumptions and data that support it (Mason, 1969). Then an adversary is designated to carry out the most rigorous critique possible of the current plan or action on the table. The critique elicits the tacit assumptions in the recommendations or plans and forces the user to account for them in settling on particular actions or plans. However, the advocate will offer no counterrecommendation. In program evaluation using DA, a recommended position on the program would be offered by the experts along with supporting reasons and data, and the user or his agent would then critique it or hire someone to do it.

In DI procedures, a feasible, credible counterrecommendation is derived and presented along with its accompanying assumptions and data (Mason, 1969). The user then weighs the recommendation and the counterrecommendation side by side. One of the two recommendations may be accepted. Alternatively, out of dialectical inquiry, that is, systematic comparisons and contrasts, a third alternative may be generated with more strength and less weakness.

The box sets out the steps in the DI process as adapted to program evaluation.

The Dialectical Inquiry Process Adapted to Program Evaluation

1. Select and convene the experts along with the sponsor and users of the evaluation.
2. Designate a subset of experts to make an initial evaluation or assessment of the program. Suppose the initial evaluation is positive.
3. Designate another subset of experts to make the best case possible against the (positive) case made in step 2.
4. The users or their designees conduct a structured debate between the two subsets of experts.
5. The user selects the best-argued case as presented in steps 2 and 3 or creates a new synthesized evaluation. For example, in an educational program evaluation, the experts persuaded the user that results were positive on cognitive dimensions and negative on affective dimensions.

DA and DI procedures assume that open, direct conflict between experts will reveal tacitly held information and demonstrate clearly why experts disagree. Knowing the initial reasons for disagreement will, it is hoped, eventually lead to a reliable and valid consensus. Proponents of dialectical procedures argue that either one is superior to expert procedures without formal conflict, for example, Delphi. Standard Delphi results prevent the experts from articulating their assumptions and making them known to others. It follows that Delphi users may be unaware of perhaps critical assumptions (Mason, 1969).

Schwenk (1990) carried out a meta-analysis of the published empirical research on the validity and reliability of Delphi, DA, and DI. The meta-analysis is suggestive but not definitive for selecting among the procedures. Almost all of the reported tests on these procedures involve undergraduate college students, not public decision makers. Schwenk reports that DA procedures are superior to unstructured expert-based approaches in terms of predictive validity and quality of solutions with respect to the problems attacked. However, DI did not prove clearly superior to other structured approaches, at least when applied to ill-structured decision problems of the kind we would have in using DI as an evaluation procedure. Compared to each other, neither of the two conflict-based approaches was clearly superior.

Because I have defined programs with high uncertainty about inputs and outcomes as being appropriate for evaluation by experts, it follows that procedures that reveal assumptions will probably serve better than those that do not. However, no particular assumption-revealing procedure will dominate independent of the trade-offs mentioned before: validity, reliability, time required, information and operating costs, and clarity.

Characteristics of Experts

Traditionally, there are three traits and characteristics that we want participating experts to have: coherence, reliability, and resolution, that is, validity (Chan, 1982):

- Coherence. A coherent expert is one who obeys the standard dictates of logic and probability. For example, an expert does not assert that A and not-A exist simultaneously or that a conditional probability is higher than an unconditional one.
- Reliability. For making forecasts, a reliable expert is one whose prior probabilities of events conform well to actual probabilities when they become known. Weather forecasting provides the standard example. Thus, when a weather forecaster predicts a 60 percent chance of rain and it does in fact rain 60 percent of the time, we say we have a reliable expert (a well-calibrated expert, in forecasting parlance). In other words, the forecaster is consistent with observed real-world frequencies and so can be "trusted."

In program evaluation, reliability is defined by the expert's agreement with other experts. We want reliable, trustworthy experts because in many uncertain decision situations, say, judging the merit of a mental health program, there is no other way of checking for the absence of random error or the presence of bias than by comparing judgments across experts.

- Validity. Reliability is not sufficient to make a good forecaster. A forecaster who was only reliable could simply keep delivering a standard forecast of 60 percent rain all the time. When a forecaster is also able to specify with precision the actual probability of rain on any given day, then we say the forecaster makes valid forecasts (has a high degree of resolution). Since we will incur costs in acting or not acting on particular weather forecasts, we want forecasters who can make reliable and valid forecasts. Similarly, we incur costs in using or not using an expert evaluation. We want evaluators whom we know make reliable and valid judgments about program performance.

The very large literature on experts and on making judgments suggests that experts frequently do not possess all the properties we desire, especially in situations with high uncertainty. To the extent they do, they use certain strategies for enhancing their information and judgments, and these strategies suggest ways of formulating an appropriate evaluation process (Shanteau, 1988).

Experts for example, rely on others in making their estimates. They obtain feedback and opinion from other experts and use informal decision aids to avoid the biasing effects of heuristics. For example, they break problems into small pieces, examine the prior decisions of other experts, and learn from each other. Whatever procedure for expert program evaluation one chooses, its design should assist the experts in implementing their personal strategies.

Identifying Experts and Composing the Group

Experts may be identified in a number of alternative ways. Evaluation users generally find experts through direct or indirect reputational procedures. In the direct procedure, the user's staff identifies one or more experts by consulting with the program, clients, constituents, prominent academics, professional associations, or invisible colleges. Experts initially identified may then be consulted about additional experts, thus using a snowball selection process. In other words, the evaluator tries to assemble an unusually knowledgeable and respected cadre of experts, not a random sample of them. The danger of the standard snowball process is that one may reduce the breadth and variation required for a sound evaluation.

Using indirect procedures, one may find scientific and technical experts in a relatively objective way by counting their past publications and, more important, their citations. High publication and citation counts in peer-reviewed journals reflect the scientific utility that complementary and competing experts find in a person's work. Such counts can be a check on snowball procedures, since reputation, significant publications, and citations should all correlate. As computing costs continue to fall and the number of organized databases continues to rise, publications and citations can become a way of checking on the standard reputational procedures, at least for experts who publish in scientific or technical journals. There may be desired expert skills, of course, that leave no trace in any published record. For example, in evaluating a homelessness program, one might want a homeless person to be on an expert panel.

In the case of a formative evaluation, if the evaluator could track program events with the advice and estimates some experts gave at some prior time, then the evaluator might be able to estimate the actual quantity and quality of information received. However, ordinarily, a group of experts called together to do an evaluation will offer judgment only once. The group will not usually be brought together again for updated evaluation. (In evaluating small research projects, experts sometimes provide ex ante estimates of quality and then examine the actual output through site visits or publication review.)

A major and unavoidable difficulty with constructing a cadre of experts in the standard way is that the experts cannot have entirely independent perspectives and information. They will usually know each other directly or know of each other, their professional styles, and their substantive output. The information they have will be partially redundant, so the actual amount of useable information per dollar invested in the evaluation process will have definite limits.

It follows that to maximize the amount of information from an evaluation for fixed evaluation outlays, the expert cadre should include more than technical, substantive experts. In addition to substantive experts, the cadre might include general-purpose policy analysts, philosophers of evaluation, or stakeholders. This reduces the dependence among experts, widens the base of experience in the group, and allows important nontechnical questions to be raised. Furthermore, the diversity in perspectives may force clarity of argument and recommendations, although consensus may be more difficult to achieve. Such mixed groups of experts have been tried in evaluating energy and naval basic research with some success, as judged by sponsors and users (Kostoff, 1988). The box contains the procedure for an evaluation by the Office of Naval Research (ONR) using such mixed groups (Kostoff, 1988).

Procedure Using Mixed Groups for an Office of Naval Research Evaluation

1. Classify all accelerated research initiatives (ARIs) into common scientific fields. (ARIs are priority research areas designed to extend over five years.)
2. Convene mixed panels of detailed technical experts, experts with systems knowledge, and ARI users, naval officers, and civilians from the operating branches.
3. Panels meet for one day to hear verbal presentations by ARI program officers, give written evaluations, and score and rank individually.
4. Construct a consensus score on each evaluation issue (predefined by the ONR).
5. Conduct a panel discussion of individual rankings on each evaluation issue, and assign a consensus score on the issue.
6. Provide a panel view of the overall quality of the ARI.
7. Conduct a reliability check by ONR to see if consensus scores were related to the individual issues that had been predefined.

The costs of evaluating the output of the ARIs were substantial. Expert evaluation, by definition, is labor intensive. ONR's out-of-pocket costs for expert panels ranged between $5,000 and $20,000 for salaries or consulting fees, travel time, and document preparation (Kostoff, 1988). In this example, ONR did not have to pay all the costs of all those involved. If this had been required, given the large number of projects evaluated, the real costs would have been significantly greater. However, the costs of a scientific evaluation, for programs like those run by ONR, even if one could be defined and even if it were technically feasible, would also be very high. For example, a "traces" type of study might have been a feasible alternative here (Illinois Institute of Technology Research Institute, 1968). In such a study, investigators would sift the historical record, carry out interviews of researchers and users, and then estimate the critical economic outcomes attributable to research. For several hundred interconnected projects or programs, the costs would also be very high and the results certainly not as timely. Cost is itself a trade-off relative to the demands and requirements of end users.

The Prospects for Expert Program Evaluation

Using the tacit and explicit knowledge of experts to make evaluations is not considered best practice in the evaluation profession compared to random assignment experiments or ex post statistically controlled analysis of the relations between program inputs and outcomes. However, for some programs, the use of experts in some form is the only feasible way to conduct an evaluation. For others, it can be a timely, cost-effective way.

A large variety of procedures can be adapted for evaluation, but few have been. Although some comparisons of the performance of alternative procedures exist for parameter estimation and forecasting, we still do not have them for the evaluation task. From the perspective of cost-effective evaluation techniques, it would be nice to know how well an expert evaluation would correlate with one based on experimental or quasi-experimental methods. One could, in theory, compare evaluations of the same program using both methods and assess the trade-offs, including their relative decision utility.

Technical issues are unlikely to be decisive in program evaluations subject to uncertainty as in education, science, or health. Indeed, they are rarely decisive at all, since evaluations are part of a political and bureaucratic process. Programs with demonstrable valid, high-quality outcomes may not prosper, and, conversely, those with demonstrably valid, low-quality outcomes may well do so. Assuming that some decision maker is interested in, or impelled by, bureaucratic requirements into doing expert evaluation, then what form might be chosen? There are not many experts on expert evaluation or many experts who have participated in them.

In my own experience as an evaluator of science and technology programs and as a decision maker who has used expert evaluations, I have found that procedures that force a wide range of participants to provide their reasoning and assumptions about a program turn out to be superior for decision making compared to narrow, prespecified, tightly centrally controlled procedures like Delphi. Where uncertainties are high about inputs, outcomes, and their relations, all the experts need to be made aware of them in relatively graphic ways rather than have uncertainties filtered in some way. Direct exposure to the biases of evaluators is probably a better way to correct for them rather than by preventing exposure through central filtering and aggregation. In other words, the unstructured procedures carried out in science and technology program evaluation seem most appropriate.

Having good and defensible reasons in arguing outcomes, positive or negative, may be more important than the actual outcomes. For the kinds of programs discussed here, the actual outcomes may never be available or available only long after the decision required. Decisions on whether to continue, stop, or modify a program require defensible reasons, since it is these reasons that will be examined closely by program advocates and opponents. Expert procedures characterized by participants with different skills and perspectives and intense dialogue among them almost by their nature will produce a broader range of defensible reasons for decision making.

References

Bendor, J. S., Taylor, S. and Van Gaalen, R. "Bureaucratic Expertise versus Legislative Authority." *American Political Science Review,* 1985, *79,* 755–769.

Blair, A. R., Nachtman, R., Saaty, T. L., and Whitaker, R. "Forecasting the Resurgence of the U.S. Economy in 2001: An Expert Judgment Approach," *Socio-Economic Planning Sciences,* 2002, *36,* 77–91.

Chan, S. "Expert Judgments Made Under Uncertainty: Some Evidence." *Social Science Quarterly,* 1982, *63,* 428–444.

Chelimsky, E., and Shadish, W. R. (eds.). *Evaluation for the Twenty-First Century: A Handbook.* Thousand Oaks, Calif.: Sage, 1997.

Dalkey, N., and Helmer, O. "An Experimental Evaluation of the Delphi Method to the Use of Experts." *Management Science,* 1963, *9,* 458–467.

Daniels, M. Jr. "Program Assessment Rating Tool (PART) Present in Congressional Justifications." 2003. [www.whitehouse.gov/memoranda/m].

Delbecq, A. L., van de Ven, A. H., and Gustafson, D. H. *Group Techniques for Program Planning: A Guide to Nominal Group and Decision Processes.* Glenview, Ill.: Scott, Foresman,1977.

Geis, G. L. "Formative Evaluation: Developmental Testing and Expert Review." *Performance and Instruction,* 1987, *26,* 1–8.

Illinois Institute of Technology Research Institute. *Technology in Retrospect and Critical Events in Science.* Chicago: Illinois Institute of Technology Research Institute, 1968.

Kostoff, R. "Evaluation of Proposed and Existing Accelerated Research Programs by the Office of Naval Research." *IEEE Transactions in Engineering Management,* 1988, *35,* 271–279.

Mason, R. O. "A Dialectical Approach to Strategic Planning." *Management Science,* 1969, *15,* B403–414.

Merton, R. K. "The Normative Structure of Science." In R. K. Merton, *The Sociology of Science.* Chicago: University of Chicago, 1973. (Originally published 1942.)

Murnane, R. J., and Nelson, R. R. "Production and Innovation When Techniques Are Tacit." *Journal of Economic Behavior and Organization,* 1984, *5,* 353–373.

Nevo, D. "Expert Opinion in Program Evaluation." In R. F. Conner and M. Hendricks (eds.), *International Innovations in Evaluation Methodology.* San Francisco: Jossey-Bass, 1989.

Press, S. J., Ali, M. W., and Chung-Fang, E. Y. "An Empirical Study of a New Method for Forming Group Judgments: Qualitative Controlled Feedback." *Technological Forecasting and Social Change,* 1979, *15,* 171–189.

Rossi, P. H., Freeman, H. E., and Lipsey, M. W. *Evaluation: A Systematic Approach.* Thousand Oaks, Calif.: Sage, 1999.

Schwenk, C. R. "Effects of Devil's Advocacy and Dialectical Inquiry on Decision Making." *Organizational Behavior and Decision Processes,* 1990, *47,* 161–176.

Shanteau, J. "Psychological Characteristics and Strategies of Expert Decision Makers." *Acta Psychologica,* 1988, *68,* 203–215.

U.S. Office of Management and Budget. *Budget of the United States Government.* Washington, D.C.: U.S. Government Printing Office, 2003.

Weston, C. "The Importance of Involving Experts and Learners in Formative Evaluation." *Canadian Journal of Educational Communication,* 1987, *16,* 45–58.

Woudenberg, F. "An Evaluation of Delphi." *Technological Forecasting and Social Change,* 1991, *40,* 131–150.

11

Role Playing

Margery Austin Turner, Wendy Zimmermann

Every day government agencies interact with the public, providing information, processing applications, responding to complaints, and delivering services. How well are these interactions handled? Do people receive prompt responses from their government? Is the information provided to them accurate? Does everyone receive the benefits or services to which they are entitled? Are all individuals—men and women, minorities and whites, young and old, literate and illiterate, handicapped and able—treated fairly? One way to address these questions is through the use of role playing evaluation.

The complexity and cost of implementing role playing vary with the objectives and scope of analysis. In addition, role playing raises significant ethical and legal concerns that warrant serious consideration. These range from the legality of using government employees as role players to the ethical implications of deceiving service providers or businesses and making false requests or applications. Nevertheless, role playing offers distinct advantages that make it a unique and convincing method for documenting the character and quality of service provided by government agencies and for determining whether systematic differences in treatment may be undermining program equity and effectiveness.

What Is Role Playing?

Role playing offers a methodology for directly assessing the overall quality of services provided to or treatment received by the public. In such an evaluation, individuals pose as job seekers, home buyers, benefit applicants, information seekers, or any other type of customer or client in order to document service or treatment quality directly. Role playing can be performed by single individuals to assess an agency's responses to requests for information or to complaints. And it can be performed by matched pairs or teams of individuals to evaluate whether different groups of applicants receive equal treatment.

Unlike most other research tools, role playing allows evaluators to observe directly the treatment that people receive when they apply for services, ask for information, or complain about a problem. The methodology can be used to follow up on individual complaints of inadequate or inequitable service, monitor the quality and evenness of service, spot-check and provide feedback to service providers, or evaluate treatment quality and equity comprehensively.

The simplest applications of role playing use any number of individuals to spot-check consistency or assess the quality of information or services provided to the public. The application of this type of role playing, which has been used for over twenty years, has expanded greatly in recent years. The accuracy of information provided over the telephone by Internal Revenue Service (IRS) employees was evaluated by having individual role players call with carefully scripted questions (U.S. General Accounting Office, 1989, 1990). And the Texas Department of Human Services used limited-English-speaking role players to determine whether local welfare offices provided them with needed services (Business Resources, 2001). Large numbers of private businesses offer "mystery shopper" services, targeted at both the private and public sectors, offering to examine customer service quality for clients ranging from banks and restaurants to doctors' offices and public welfare agencies. In applications such as these, evaluators can observe directly how employees treat their clientele in known circumstances. Because many interactions between government workers and members of the public generally go unobserved, role playing may provide the only feasible methodology for objectively assessing public program performance.

A unique strength offered by paired role playing is in determining whether different groups of clients receive comparable treatment or services. In a paired role-playing evaluation, carefully matched teams are formed, with each team consisting of one member from each population group of interest—one man and one woman, for example, or one white person and one African American, or one able-bodied person and one person with a disability. Both teammates apply for the same service or benefit, presenting themselves as equally eligible and equally in need. Often, characteristics are assigned to teammates such that the disadvantaged group role player is slightly better qualified than the majority group role player. Because both teammates are eligible for the same service or benefit, systematic differences in treatment across a significant number of cases provide convincing evidence of discrimination on the basis of race, sex, disability, language, education, or any other attribute of concern to evaluators.

Paired role playing has been used since the 1970s by private and public fair housing organizations to test for discrimination against minority home seekers by real estate and rental agents. Teams of African Americans and whites (also Hispanics and non-Hispanic whites, as well as Asians and whites) pose as home seekers with comparable family characteristics, housing needs, and financial resources. Teammates visit real estate and rental agents to inquire about the availability of houses and apartments and about the terms and conditions of rent or sale. Agents who systematically treat comparable customers differently are, in effect, caught in the act of discriminating. Findings from such fair housing tests (also known as audits) have been admitted as evidence in state and federal courts and have been used by local governments in determining the severity of discrimination in their communities (Fix and Struyk, 1993; Boggs, Sellers, and Bendick, 1993). In addition, the U.S. Department of Housing and Urban Development has sponsored major role-playing studies to determine the incidence and severity of housing discrimination nationwide (Wienk and others, 1979; Turner, Struyk, and Yinger, 1991; Turner, Ross, Galster, and Yinger, 2002).

Building on the fair housing experience, the paired role-playing methodology has been extended to test for discrimination in many other kinds of transactions. For example, two exploratory studies—one focusing on the treatment of Hispanic men and the other on the treatment of African American men—have established the applicability of matched role playing beyond the housing context. In these studies, pairs of young men—African American or Hispanic and white—were matched on major characteristics relevant to the hiring decision; they then applied for entry-level positions advertised in the newspaper. Unfavorable treatment of African American and Hispanic applicants was recorded whenever they were unable to advance as far in the hiring process as their white counterparts (Cross, Kenney, Mell, and Zimmermann, 1990; Turner, Fix, and Struyk, 1991). The same basic methodology has also been used to determine whether car sales representatives consistently quote women and African Americans less attractive terms than they do males and whites, whether taxi drivers deny service to African Americans who are trying to hail cabs on the street, whether home insurance companies provide comparable price quotes for homes in white and African American neighborhoods, and whether minorities receive the same information as whites when they visit lending institutions to inquire about mortgage loans (Ayres, 1991, 2001; Ridley, Bayton, and Outtz, 1989; Wissoker, Zimmermann, and Galster, 1998; Turner and others, 2002). In almost any situation where one group of consumers may be treated less favorably than another, matched role playing can be used to obtain direct evidence of any differences in treatment that actually occur.

Sampling

The first set of issues to address in designing role playing for evaluation is sampling. No evaluation, however ambitious, can record information about every transaction of interest; evaluators must select a sample of transactions for which role playing will be conducted. The generalizability of evaluation results hinges on the representativeness of this sample. In this section, we discuss three critical sampling issues:

- What the universe of transactions is
- How big the sample needs to be
- How a sample should be selected from the universe of transactions

Regardless of the scope and objectives of an analysis, these three issues should be resolved before role playing begins.

Universe of Transactions

Every application of role playing should be explicit about the universe of transactions or encounters to which its results apply. For example, if applications for permits or employment openings are accepted at five locations around the city, analysts need to decide in advance whether the results of their evaluation should be used to evaluate the treatment members of the public receive at one office, or whether results should assess treatment received regardless of the office visited. Evaluators might choose to send individual role players to all five locations to assess differences among the offices or choose to target one office to analyze differences among staff members there.

When paired role playing was used to test for discrimination against African Americans and Hispanics in employment, analysts initially hoped to analyze all entry-level hiring. To do so, however, would have required a sample representative of all entry-level job openings: every opening would have to have had a measurable chance of being selected for inclusion. In a simple random sample such as this one, every case in the universe would need to be identified so that it has an equal chance of being selected (see Chapter Sixteen, this volume).

Many entry-level jobs are advertised in newspapers; others are advertised with "help wanted" signs in the window, through employment agencies, or simply by word of mouth. Analysts concluded that it would be extremely difficult to identify all jobs advertised by word of mouth or with "help wanted" signs (Cross, Kenney, Mell, and Zimmermann, 1990). Therefore, the universe for analysis in the initial hiring discrimination studies was narrowed to openings advertised in the newspaper. Consequently, results from these studies reflect the incidence of discrimination in entry-level jobs that are advertised in the newspaper, not the incidence of discrimination in all entry-level hiring.

An alternative strategy, used by a group of fair employment advocates, targeted employment agencies. Role players were sent to major employment agencies in a particular city, with repeat visits to agencies that showed evidence of possible discriminatory treatment. This sampling strategy did not yield definitive estimates of the incidence of discrimination in hiring, but it did yield convincing evidence of discrimination by individual employment agencies (Boggs, Sellers, and Bendick, 1993). Thus, the scope and objectives of a role-playing effort, as well as the characteristics of transactions under investigation, need to be considered in defining the universe of transactions from which to draw a sample.

Sample Size

There is no single, easy answer to questions about required sample sizes. The answer depends on the purpose of the analysis, the desired degree of precision, and the extent to which comparisons will be made for subgroups within the sample. Small sample sizes—as few as ten or fifteen tests (each inquiry that an individual or a matched team of role players makes is a test)—may be sufficient for complaint investigations or compliance monitoring, but may yield ambiguous results if differences in treatment turn out to be small. Much larger sample sizes—250 tests or more—are required to support definitive measures of the incidence of discrimination, or if analysts wish to explore outcomes for different subgroups within the total sample.

Many local fair housing groups use paired role playing to investigate complaints that real estate agents or landlords are discriminating against minorities, families with children, persons with disabilities, or other legally protected groups. The objective of these investigations is to determine whether there is support for a complaint or suspicion of discrimination and to assemble evidence that may be used in court. Experienced fair housing groups typically send up to five or six pairs of role players to a given agent or landlord. If several of these pairs experience differential treatment (or if differences in treatment are particularly flagrant for only one or two pairs), then there is good reason to pursue the matter legally, and the evidence from this small sample is likely to be very convincing in the courtroom (Boggs, Sellers, and Bendick, 1993).

When the objective of role playing is to yield definitive measures of the incidence of a particular problem, sample sizes must be substantially larger than five or six tests to provide statistically significant results. Most discussions of sampling error and statistical significant focus on the chance that what appears to be an important finding is in fact the result of random events or the chance that another sample from the same population would not support the same finding. This approach is sufficient for applications of role playing that do not compare the experiences of two or more matched teammates. For example, a role-playing study designed to determine whether a tourist information office or IRS help line is giving accurate information would need a sample large enough to minimize the chance of a false-positive result—of incorrectly concluding that the public is being misinformed (see Chapter Sixteen, this volume). However, in paired role playing, it is equally important to guard against the opposite kind of error: mistakenly concluding that there is no difference in treatment. In other words, the sample needs to be large enough to make it unlikely that evaluators observe a difference in treatment that does not really exist in the full population (a false-positive, or type I, error) *and* to protect them from concluding that there is no difference in treatment when in fact a small but meaningful difference exists in the full population (a false-negative, or type, II error).

To illustrate, in three studies of hiring discrimination, white applicants were favored over their African American teammates 12 to 33 percent of the time, as shown in Table 11.1 (Cross, Kenney, Mell, and Zimmermann, 1990; Turner, Fix, and Struyk, 1991; James and Del Castillo, 1992). The African American partner was less likely to be favored, but this result did occur between 7 and 26 percent of the time. The first two studies summarized in Table 11.1, which were conducted by the Urban Institute, found large and statistically significant differences between the percentage of times the majority was favored and the percentage of times the African American was favored. This result strongly suggests that majority job applicants were considerably more likely to be favored than African American applicants. However, in the third study, conducted by the University of Colorado at Denver, the differences were relatively small. Because of the small sample size in the Denver study, analysts concluded that outcomes favoring African American and majority job seekers essentially balanced each other out—that minorities were not subject to systematically unfavorable treatment. There is a risk in relying heavily on this result, however, because the small sample size leaves a high probability that the true differences in treatment may exist but go undetected.

In designing a full-scale evaluation in which statistically reliable results are an important objective, evaluators should obtain advice from a sampling expert. However, a rough rule of thumb is shown in Table 11.2, which provides estimates of the probability of detecting a difference in treatment of 5 to 20 percent, given sample sizes of 50 to 250. The table shows that if there

**Table 11.1. Selected Results from Hiring
Discrimination Studies Using Paired Role Players**

	Percentage of Times Majority Teammate Favored	Percentage of Times African American Teammate Favored	Net Difference	Sample Size (Numbers of Pairs)
Chicago: Hispanic-Anglo study	33	8	25[a]	169
San Diego: Hispanic-Anglo study	29	13	16[a]	191
Chicago: Black-white study	17	8	9	197
Washington, D.C.: Black-white study	23	7	16[a]	241
Denver: Hispanic-Anglo study	19	26	-7	140
Denver: Black-white study	12	10	2	145

Note: The Chicago and San Diego Hispanic-Anglo studies were conducted in summer 1989. The Chicago, Washington, D.C., and Denver black-white studies and the Denver Hispanic-Anglo studies were conducted in summer 1990, and they remain valid more than a decade later.

[a]Indicates that the difference between the percentage of times the majority was favored and the percentage of times the African American was favored is statistically significant at a 95 percent or higher confidence level.

Sources: Cross, Kenney, Mell, and Zimmermann (1990); Turner, Fix, and Struyk (1991); James and Del Castillo (1992).

is a true difference of 10 percentage points between preference for the majority and preference for the African American, the chance of discovering this difference is only 40 percent with a sample size of fifty, but it rises to 93 percent with a sample size of two hundred. In other words, if whites are 10 percent more likely to be treated favorably than African Americans, a sample size of fifty or one hundred would probably be too small to detect this difference with statistical certainty.

Selecting the Sample

Once the universe of transactions has been defined and a suitable sample size has been identified, a systematic procedure must be defined for selecting cases from the universe for inclusion in the sample. Sometimes the selection process will be straightforward, focusing on all transactions in a particular, narrowly defined category. If there have been complaints about a specific office or individual, for example, evaluators may decide to conduct several role-playing visits targeted at that office or individual. In most circumstances, however, there will be good reasons to draw a random sample of locations,

**Table 11.2. Probability of Discerning Differences
Between Pairs with Samples of Varying Size**

| Sample Size[a] | True Difference in Treatment Between Two Groups (Percentage Points) | | | |
	5	10	15	20
50	.171	.400	.671	.872
10	.256	.630	.907	.990
15	.333	.783	.977	.999
20	.404	.877	.995	1.00
25	.470	.932	.999	1.00

Note: This table sets the likelihood of a false positive at 5 percent, and estimates the likelihood of a false negative for different sample sizes and true differences. For these calculations, variance estimates are based on the Urban Institute's black-white employment discrimination study, conducted in Washington, D.C., and Chicago, Illinois.

The first column assumes that the true difference between outcomes for whites and African Americans is 5 percentage points. Entries in the column indicate the chance of discerning this difference, with statistical confidence of at least 95 percent, for various sample sizes.

[a]A sample size of fifty means that fifty paired tests would be conducted. In a paired housing study, for example, each sample test is a visit by two teammates to a real estate office.

individuals, days, or times of day at which role-playing encounters will be conducted. To ensure an unbiased, random sample, every case in the universe has to have a known probability of being selected for inclusion.

In the 1989 and 2002 national housing discrimination studies, random samples of advertisements for apartments and homes were selected from the classified sections of newspapers. A three-step procedure was used to select the sample ads:

1. All the advertisements that qualified for selection were numbered sequentially.
2. A computer program was used to generate enough random numbers to produce the required sample size (for example, if a sample of fifty ads was needed from a total of one thousand, the computer generated fifty random numbers between 1 and 1,000).
3. The ads whose numbers corresponded to the random numbers generated by the computer were selected for inclusion in the sample.

This procedure ensured that ads at the end of the classified section were just as likely to be selected as ads at the beginning and that there was no element of human choice in the decision to include or exclude an eligible advertisement from the sample.

Many other techniques can be designed to yield a reasonable probability sample. For example, evaluators could make an exhaustive list of all offices in which permit applications are accepted and select every third (or sixth, or tenth) office to produce the desired sample of offices to visit. Any systematic procedure that gives every case in the universe a measurable chance of inclusion should generate a defensible random sample, and such procedures should produce comparable results.

Selecting and Training Role Players

One of the keys to conducting role playing effectively lies in carefully selecting the role players and ensuring they have the relevant characteristics. The results of any role-playing application are based on the treatment or services received by individuals with known qualifications and characteristics. Therefore, evaluators will need to determine the major characteristics that are relevant to the study and decide which of those can be assigned (that is, fictitious) and which must be innate to the role players. They will also need to determine what qualities they want in the individual role players themselves to ensure that they do the job properly.

In evaluating whether two groups of individuals (African American and whites, or men and women, for example) are treated equally, evaluators will need to select pairs, or teams, of role players. These individuals need to be matched on all characteristics relevant to the evaluation except for the one under examination (such as race, gender, or age). For nonpaired role-playing evaluations, in which role players would individually assess, for example, the quality or consistency of services provided by a public agency, selection and training of role players is still important but is considerably more straightforward.

Determining Key Characteristics for Role Players

Role players should be selected based on all characteristics that are relevant to the treatment or service provision being evaluated. For some evaluations, this includes only objective characteristics, such as gender, age, or income, which are easily determined. However, it may also be necessary to select candidates according to intangible characteristics, such as personality and demeanor, which are more difficult to define and involve more subjectivity in the selection process.

Clearly, the purpose of the evaluation will determine the relevant characteristics. For example, a nonpaired evaluation of a program that provides services to the elderly may require the role players to be elderly. In paired role playing, matching the role players presents a greater challenge. In the studies of housing discrimination where pairs of role players appear to be equally qualified home buyers or renters, they were matched on age and gender and then assigned fictitious qualifications, including income, age, marital status, family size, occupation, assets and debts, and housing needs. For the employment discrimination studies, the role players were matched on age, education, work experience, skills, and physical build as well as on such intangible factors as articulateness, personality, and demeanor. Since employers may base their decisions on how friendly or outgoing a person is, the role players had to appear equally shy, gregarious, or aggressive.

Matching two individuals according to such characteristics as age, education, or physical build can be done in a straightforward and objective manner. However, in matching on such intangible traits as personality and articulateness, the process becomes much more subjective. For this reason, having more than one person interview the role players and agree on teams will help ensure well-matched pairs. Preferably, three or more should interview each candidate and participate in the matching decisions. In the Urban Institute employment studies, members of the research team who varied in age, gender, and race participated in the pairing decisions. This mix was to ensure agreement on the pairing among individuals with different perspectives. Evaluators may also want to consider using independent observers or program stakeholders to participate in the matching process.

Role players can assume many fictitious characteristics relevant to the evaluation, but other attributes, such as sex or skin color, cannot be assigned or changed. Some evaluations may require role players to have a certain physical appearance, level of articulateness, or unaccented speech, in which case role players with those actual attributes have to be recruited. It may be appropriate, however, to alter other characteristics, such as income, education, or home address. Which characteristics can be altered also depends on the nature of the study. If, for example, role players may be required to present documentation such as a driver's license or proof of income, the information that appears on that document cannot be altered. In evaluations using pairs of role players, certain characteristics might be altered for one of the role players in a pair while others could be altered for both.

Role players should also be selected on the basis of some criteria that are not directly relevant to the evaluation but may bear on outcomes. For example, if a government agency wants to evaluate whether women and men are treated differently when they request information, both teammates should appear as similar as possible in every respect except gender. Consequently, evaluators should control for such attributes as regional or foreign accents, extreme differences in height, and distinct differences in personality, such as aggressiveness or passiveness, even though these are not relevant to the subject of the evaluation. In this way, if the person providing the information happens to discriminate against southerners, or particularly assertive people, or people with visible tattoos, the results of the study will not reflect a separate type of differential treatment from the one being evaluated.

Varying the Qualifications of the Role Players

One common strategy for conducting paired role playing is to make the minority group role player slightly more qualified than the majority group role player with whom he or she is paired. The Fair Employment Council of Greater Washington conducted an employment discrimination study in which Latino job applicants were given better credentials than their Anglo counterparts. For example, Latinos could type sixty words per minute and Anglos only forty-five, or Latinos had managed a retail department while Anglos had worked as senior sales staff. In addition, when initial contact was by phone, Latinos always phoned first and Anglos second rather than alternating (Bendick, Jackson, Reinoso, and Hodges, 1992). Similarly, an exploratory study of discrimination by mortgage lending institutions assigned slightly higher income levels to minority applicants than to their white teammates (Turner and others, 2002). Varying the qualifications of role players in this way can provide even stronger evidence of differential or discriminatory treatment when the less-qualified role player is treated more favorably than the better-qualified role player. If a public agency wants to determine whether African American applicants for a job opening are treated the same as white applicants, evaluators might use an African American role player with slightly better qualifications (more experience or better grades, for example) in conducting the evaluation. This weighting reduces the possibility that the white role player could be chosen over the African American for legitimate or unobservable reasons and could strengthen the credibility of a finding of discrimination.

The disadvantage of making one partner slightly more qualified than the other is that if the differential treatment or discrimination is subtle, the evaluation may not reveal significant levels of difference. In other words, an employer might consistently prefer an equally qualified white applicant over an African American applicant but might be swayed to hire an African American who is clearly better qualified. Since differential treatment of this kind might be rarer, a larger sample size would probably be needed to discern smaller incidences of differential treatment.

Recruiting and Selecting Role Players

Recruiting individuals who will be dependable role players and are capable of role playing and recording treatment is central to conducting a good evaluation. Aside from the characteristics relevant to the role being played, a number of characteristics are also desirable for the role players themselves. Because the outcomes of an evaluation depend on what the role players observe and record, it is imperative that role players be reliable and honest and that they provide accurate information about their experiences. The role players should also be objective about the issue in question, particularly if the study is potentially controversial or political, such as testing for race-based discrimination.

Other factors important for those participating in any type of role playing are that they be organized, timely, detail oriented, reliable, and motivated. Role players should also be able to act, or portray someone different from themselves if the evaluation requires it, and to think on their feet, responding in an appropriate way to unanticipated questions or circumstances that may arise in the course of their inquiry.

Certain evaluations may have practical constraints. If the evaluation requires the role players to travel around a city, visiting various agencies, for example, then the evaluation may require that role players have cars and know the city or town well enough to be able to get around easily. If the role players will be involved in detailed or complicated interactions, such acquiring a business license, they may need to know a substantial amount about the issue in question. For certain issues, role players can be trained; for others, it may be necessary to hire individuals with substantive knowledge of the subject.

Some government agencies use their own employees as role players. The General Accounting Office has used the role-playing methodology to evaluate the IRS's responses to questions about tax returns. Subsequently, the IRS began evaluating its own services, using employees as role players (U.S. General Accounting Office, 1989, 1990). The Justice Department's Civil Rights Division operates a fair housing testing program in which government employees sometimes pose as home seekers. Role players who are government employees may have the advantage of being knowledgeable about the service delivered or program in question and about how the system works. However, since confidentiality is key to a successful study, it is important that the role players not be recognized by the persons with whom they are likely to interact. The legality and perceived acceptability of using government employees as role players may also vary by agency and by program. Analysts should therefore review the appropriateness of using employees for each evaluation.

In both of the Urban Institute employment discrimination studies, students from nearby universities were recruited to act as role players. These students provided the benefits of relatively inexpensive labor and a pool of individuals who were interested in social science research and able to work during the summer on a full-time but short-term basis. In Kansas City, Missouri, students were also used as participant observers, or role players. In this study, the students presented city agency employees with standardized questions and then recorded employees' responses (International City Management Association, 1981).

Conducting Role Playing for Evaluation

Regardless of the type of evaluation—testing for discrimination, evaluating the timeliness of a telephone response, or analyzing the quality of a complicated service delivery—certain implementation issues are always relevant. These issues include developing a comprehensive data collection instrument, training the individuals who will be role playing, managing the study, maintaining quality control, and keeping costs low.

Developing Data Collection Instruments

On completing a role-playing encounter (or one stage of a complex transaction), each role player records the treatment he or she received. Subsequently, the experiences and outcomes reported by all the role players can be objectively compared to assess treatment and determine whether systematic differences occurred. For paired role playing, data collection instruments should be completed independently by each member of a pair, not jointly by a team of role players. To ensure consistency and credibility, differences in treatment should not be assessed or reported by the role players. Instead, each individual reports on the treatment he or she received. Analysts then use these data to make comparisons between the experiences of two matched partners or among a group of role players in nonpaired role playing.

New technologies can make it easier for role players to record their experiences immediately. In the Urban Institute's most recent housing discrimination study, reporting forms are completed through a Web-based data entry system, similar to the forms we increasingly use for Internet purchases. Role players access a secure Web site using individual passwords, enter the unique identification number for the transaction they have just completed, and fill in the required information items. This system automatically checks for completeness and consistency of responses and immediately prompts the role player to make corrections or complete missing items. In addition, this approach eliminates the costs and errors involved in entering paper reports into an electronic database.

To capture all relevant information about the transaction under evaluation, the data collection instrument should, to the extent possible, be structured unambiguously, anticipate all possible outcomes (intermediate as well as final), and account for all important elements of treatment. In order to measure treatment or quality of service, as much information as possible should be quantifiable. Although it is always a good idea to allow role players to comment in narrative form, the amount of subjectivity and quality judgments that role players make should be minimized.

A key factor in determining an instrument's format and complexity is the number of stages in the transaction. Many transactions may have only one stage. For example, an evaluation of how a local tourist office delivers information would involve a single interaction: a phone call, a walk-in visit, or perhaps a written request for information. Data collection for this type of study would consist of reporting all relevant information related to this one encounter.

More complex transactions might have multiple stages, with numerous measures at each stage. The employment discrimination studies used a three-stage analysis: application, interview, and job offer. Role players reported whether they were able to complete and submit an application for the job advertised, whether they obtained an interview, and whether they received a job offer. In these studies, the data collection instruments also recorded the treatment a role player received at each stage, including such information as how long they had to wait, the questions they were asked, the number of follow-up phone calls they had to make, and the salary they were offered. If a study is evaluating the treatment that applicants for public benefits receive, the data collection instrument might capture not only whether a role player was found to be eligible for assistance but also whether the appropriate questions were asked during the interview and whether relevant documents were requested and reviewed.

Analysts may want to measure qualitative aspects of the treatment role players receive by asking them to record negative or positive remarks made to them about race, gender, or other attributes. These aspects of treatment are difficult to quantify and subject to the interpretation of the role players. Urging the role players to record comments of this type word for word is likely to increase accuracy. These comments are useful for adding texture and anecdotal detail to the more objective and quantitative results of the study. For example, in the recently completed pilot study of discrimination by mortgage lending institutions, quotations helped illustrate important differences in the willingness of loan officers to assist white and minority customers.

Training Role Players

Role players should always be systematically trained so that their behavior is consistent and the treatment they receive is recorded fully and objectively. Thus, training should include practice in playing the assigned role and in completing data collection instruments. When the paired team methodology is used, another integral part of the training is to familiarize role players with their shared characteristics. In the lending discrimination study, for example, role players had to be trained to remember all of their assigned characteristics, such as income, employment, and details of their financial situation. In addition, the pairs had to be trained to approach the agents in the same manner and express interest in the same kinds of mortgage products.

Training role players to act in a controlled manner—that is, following the script—is key for making later assessments of the treatment they received and for aggregating data. This uniformity is particularly important for paired role playing. For example, in the employment discrimination studies, it was assumed that employers may make hiring decisions based on the enthusiasm and personality of an applicant. Therefore, role players were trained to ask employers similar questions and to behave similarly in the interview. Practice interviews were conducted in which each member of the team watched the other so that he or she could imitate the teammate's responses and manner as well as practice those characteristics that had been assigned to both.

A more superficial but important element when role players appear in person (rather than calling on the telephone) is physical appearance (age, gender, and approximate build). For paired studies, role players should be matched according to physical appearance, and they should also dress similarly. In the car sales discrimination study, role players who were sent to buy cars needed to project the same image. A well-dressed role player might make a better and more serious impression on a car salesperson than one who is poorly dressed (Ayres, 1991). This rule also applies to the role players who participated in the housing and employment studies and is applicable to some extent to all evaluations in which the role players make personal contact with the person or office being evaluated.

Also important to the training of role players is coordination among role players and accurate and timely reporting of treatment. For paired evaluations, the order in which teammates visit or call should alternate (or vary randomly). For example, in both the employment and housing discrimination studies, half the time the African American testers called first; white testers called first the other half. If an evaluation requires role players to respond to an advertisement, for example, it is important that both members of a team respond at about the same time. In the employment discrimination studies, role players were required to phone an employer in response to an advertisement between ten and thirty minutes of one another. If the advertisement required going directly to the employer, they were required to visit between fifteen minutes and one hour of one another. Teammates also need to coordinate the number of phone calls made to ensure that both displayed the same amount of interest in obtaining the job, house, or service.

Evaluators should also train role players to record information accurately on the data collection instruments. This accuracy can be achieved by having them conduct practice tests and practice filling out the instruments. Practicing the actual steps that role players will have to take has proven invaluable in previous studies. In the employment discrimination studies, for example, the role players remarked that the practice tests were the most valuable part of the training to them. If the role players will be dealing with other types of forms, such as applications, they should practice filling out these forms. Such trial runs will also help them remember their assigned characteristics or biographies.

A key part of the training lies in emphasizing the confidential nature of the study as well as the importance of it. For any role playing to succeed, the nature and timing of the evaluation must remain secret. At the same time, role players should understand the purpose and seriousness of the evaluation, as well as the importance of their part in it.

Management and Quality Control

The importance of close supervision and careful management of role playing cannot be underestimated. The validity of an evaluation's data depends critically on the reliability of information recorded by the role players. Therefore, the methods used to ensure that role players are honest and accurate in their record keeping may come under close scrutiny. There should be sufficient oversight of the role players that a manager can follow the course of each individual interaction closely. The level of management needed depends on the number of sites, the number of role players, and the nature of the study. If the role playing is undertaken by telephone only, managers can simply listen to and observe the role players. This type of supervision is more straightforward than that required for in-person fieldwork. In the employment discrimination studies, for example, one manager in each site supervised four to five teams, or eight to ten individuals. This level of supervision ensured that the manager was able to keep close track of every step in the interactions. If there are more than two or three sites, an additional staff member may be needed to coordinate.

Another way to maintain close supervision is to meet with each of the role players daily or, if appropriate, require them to call the office daily. In the employment discrimination studies, where close supervision and coordination were essential, the role players were required to visit the office once a day and to call in at least twice a day. Managers should also review the data collection instruments as soon as they are completed to ensure that the role players are filling them out right after a transaction, when the information is fresh in their minds. Reviewing the instruments for completeness and accuracy also improves the quality of the data and makes it possible to correct or retrain role players who may be making mistakes. In the pilot study of discrimination by mortgage lending institutions, centralized management staff carefully reviewed completed test forms and tester narratives daily, identifying mistakes or ambiguities and contacting testers immediately to address them.

Throughout the history of role playing, observers have had concerns about quality control—more specifically, about the possibility of role players' recording false information. As in all other research that uses human subjects, this is a possibility. There are ways to minimize the likelihood of its occurrence. One way is for role players themselves to be audited. For instance, one of the phone numbers they are given to call could be a member of the evaluation team who would ensure that both members of the pair, or the nonpaired individuals, are completing the transaction completely and comparably. In addition, a number of the management techniques already noted serve to control the quality and validity of the data. Close supervision, checking the data collection instruments, and having the role players make phone calls from the evaluation office all help the manager maintain control over the quality of the data collection. Evaluators may also consider making teammates double-blind, where they do not know the outcomes of their partner's actions. The advantage of this approach is that the role players will not be influenced in any way by the knowledge of what has happened to their partner. The disadvantage is that coordination becomes more difficult and must be handled entirely by a supervisor.

Cost Considerations

A number of decisions made in designing a role playing application affect its cost. The type of interaction being simulated obviously has an impact on how much it will cost. An evaluation that can be conducted entirely by mail or telephone clearly requires less labor and costs less than one in which role players must travel around a city visiting numerous sites. Because simpler types of evaluations require less time and labor per transaction and can probably be done from a single location, the costs would be considerably lower than the costs of a more complex evaluation. The employment discrimination studies, for example, involved more than one round of contact through telephone calls and in-person visits. The complexity of the study required one week of training, which also increased costs. Tests of discrimination against home buyers typically use two visits: one to gather general information about available homes and the second to drive around and inspect one or more of these homes. Less complex evaluations, such as one that assesses the quality and accuracy of telephone requests for information from an agency, probably could be conducted with fewer role players and less training.

Certain costs, however, are constant across most evaluations: role players' salaries (some studies have used unpaid volunteers), managers' salaries, office space, production of training materials and collection instruments, and the costs of data analysis. Other possible expenses are telephone lines, postage, and travel expenses. Using government employees as role players, if they do not use overtime, helps reduce costs for public agencies.

Another important issue in determining cost is sample size and personnel time needed to conduct the evaluation. In the Hispanic-Anglo employment discrimination study, for example, eight pairs of role players worked full time for five weeks (plus one week of paid training), conducting 360 tests. In the black-white study, ten pairs worked full time for six weeks, finishing 476 tests. Each pair of role players completed an average of 10 tests per week, not including the last week of the study, which was used to complete tests started in the previous weeks. In both studies, role players were paid a fixed amount for the weeks worked so that there was no financial incentive to fabricate data. Evaluators should also take into account the time it may take to initiate tests that ultimately cannot be included in the sample. The employment studies required initiating many more tests (50 to 100 percent more) than were ultimately included in order to achieve the desired sample size because role players called and visited employers who had already filled the jobs or the role players were unable to reach an employer to submit an application.

In a less labor-intensive and less complex evaluation, however, role players working full time may be able to complete many more than ten tests per week and, consequently, work for a shorter period of time. In addition, if the goals of the evaluation are to obtain a general assessment of how a program or office is operating or to evaluate complaints received about a program activity, a large and statistically valid sample might not be needed and the purposes of the study could be achieved in a short time, with only a few tests, and at low cost. Thus, the cost of a study can vary widely depending on its goals, its complexity, the sample size, and how long it takes to conduct the evaluation.

Statistical Analysis

Role playing is an extremely powerful methodology because its results are intuitively clear and compelling to nontechnical audiences. The public can clearly understand findings that minors attempting to buy cigarettes were successful in three of every five establishments they visited, or that information provided by a tourist bureau was accurate 85 percent of the time. Paired role playing is particularly effective because its results directly document unfair differences in treatment. In the study of hiring discrimination against African Americans, 20 percent of the time that young African American men applied for entry-level jobs, they were unable to advance as far in the hiring process as equally qualified white applicants. This kind of result and the individual case examples that can accompany it are clear and convincing to policymakers and to the general public.

Analysis of outcomes using simple role playing in an evaluation of program performance does not present any special statistical challenges. However, analyzing data from paired role playing requires considerable caution. This section focuses on three key issues to address at the data analysis stage for paired role playing: basic measures of differential treatment, procedures for testing the statistical significance of these measures, and the issue of random and systematic factors that contribute to the differences in treatment observed in paired role playing. All three of these issues apply specifically to analysis of paired outcomes. Analysis of results from nonpaired role playing is much more straightforward and can be accomplished with more conventional measures and statistical tests.

Measuring Differences in Treatment

The key building block for analysis of data from paired role playing is a case-by-case determination of whether the two members of each team were treated the same or differently, and if there was a difference, which teammate was favored. In this analysis, the unit of observation is the team, and variables are constructed from the experience of the two teammates to measure relative outcomes.

To illustrate, in the studies of employment discrimination, analysts determined how far in the hiring process each applicant was able to progress. Specifically, was he able to submit an application (stage 1)? Was he granted a formal interview (stage 2)? And did he receive a job offer (stage 3)? Then outcomes for the two members of each team were brought together to determine whether one partner advanced further than the other. A test was classified as white favored (if the white partner advanced to a higher stage than the African American partner), African American favored (if the African American partner advanced farther), or no difference (if they both reached the same stage). Finally, results were tabulated across tests to report the share of cases in which the white advanced further than an equally qualified African American and the share in which the African American advanced further. Analysis can also be conducted using the individual teammates' experience as the unit of observation and comparing the overall outcomes for teammates of one type to the overall outcomes for teammates of the other type. For example, in the Hispanic-Anglo hiring discrimination study, analysts found that the Hispanic applicants received formal interviews 48 percent of the time they applied for entry-level jobs compared to 64 percent for the white applicants.

Sometimes it is difficult to decide whether the two members of a team have actually been treated differently or whether the differences are so negligible that they should be ignored. To illustrate, the housing discrimination study focused on the racial and ethnic composition of neighborhoods where African American and white teammates were shown houses in order to determine whether African American home seekers were being steered away from predominantly white neighborhoods (or vice versa). For each teammate, analysts calculated the average percentage African American for neighborhoods where houses were shown. In other words, if a person was shown three houses—one in a neighborhood that was 10 percent African American, one in a neighborhood that was 13 percent African American, and one in a neighborhood that was 5 percent African American—the average racial composition for houses shown to this partner was 9.3 percent African American. Next, average neighborhood characteristics were compared for the two members of each team to determine whether the African American partner was shown houses in more predominantly African American neighborhoods than the white partner.

At this stage, a threshold was established to define a nonnegligible difference in neighborhood composition. Analysts decided that small differences in average racial composition were not meaningful from a policy perspective and should not be counted as steering. If an African American was shown houses in neighborhoods averaging 3 percent African American while his white partner was shown houses in neighborhoods averaging 2.5 percent African American, it would be imprudent to classify this difference as a case of racial steering. In the housing discrimination study, analysts classified a team's experience as steering only if the difference in neighborhood racial composition exceeded a threshold of 5 percentage points. Thresholds were also defined for differences in average per capita income and differences in average house values.

Results like those outlined above represent the share of cases in which two comparable teammates received different treatment. In other words, they reflect the incidence of differential—or unequal—treatment. For many forms of treatment, this is the most logical measure. If the treatment of concern is categorical, then teammates are either treated the same or one of them is favored over the other, with no degrees of difference. Examples of such categorical outcomes include the following:

- Did an applicant receive a job offer?
- Did a loan office provide information about mortgage products?
- Was an advertised apartment available for rent?
- Did a taxi driver stop to pick up the passenger?

Other outcomes, however, may vary in terms of degree:

• What hourly wage was the applicant offered?
• What loan amount was the home buyer quoted?
• How many apartments were made available for consideration?
• How long did the passenger have to wait for a taxi?

The incidence of differential treatment can certainly be calculated for these continuous outcome measures, possibly using thresholds like those discussed in the racial steering example. In addition, analysts can compute the severity of differential treatment for continuous outcome variables.

Severity measures reflect the magnitude of differences in outcomes between teammates. They are constructed by (1) calculating the average value of a given treatment measure across all teammates of each type and (2) comparing the averages for the two types of teammates. To illustrate, Table 11.3 presents several measures of the severity of discrimination in housing. On average, white home buyers were told about 2.3 possible houses per visit to a real estate agent, compared to an average of 1.8 possible houses shown or recommended to their African American counterparts. Thus, the severity of discrimination can be expressed as 0.5 houses on average per visit—or as 21 percent fewer houses for African American home buyers than for comparable whites.

In presenting measures of the differential outcomes, it is important to recognize that the average outcome measures incorporate cases in which (1) no differences in treatment occurred, (2) one type of partner was favored, and (3) the other type of partner was favored. Thus, this type of severity measure reflects the average difference in treatment across all cases, including those in which no difference was recorded. This measure indicates how big an impact differential treatment has on overall outcomes, not how severe the differences are when they do occur. Alternatively, severity measures can be constructed for the subset of cases in which one teammate was favored over the other to reflect how severe differential treatment is when it does occur (Yinger, 1993).

Tests of Statistical Significance

In studies that are based on a probability sample of encounters and whose goal is to describe the total universe of such encounters, the next important analysis step is to test the statistical significance of incidence and severity measures. Suppose that in a sample of one hundred cases, members of group A received more favorable treatment than their group B partners fifteen times, members of group B received more favorable treatment than their

**Table 11.3. Measures of the Severity of Discrimination in Housing
from a Study Using Paired Role Players**

	Difference[a]	Percentage Difference[b]
African American and white home buyers	0.476	20.8
Hispanic and Anglo home buyers	0.522	22.1
African American and White renters	0.404	24.5
Hispanic and Anglo renters	0.176	10.9

[a]Average number of houses shown or recommended to the majority auditor minus the average number shown or recommended to the African American.

[b]Difference in houses shown or recommended as a percentage of the number shown or recommended to the majority auditor.

Source: Turner, Struyk, and Yinger (1991).

group A partners five times, and partners (A and B) were treated equally eighty times. Can the analyst reasonably conclude that group A is consistently favored over group B in the universe of all such transactions, or is there a real chance that this result is idiosyncratic—that another sample would have shown no such difference in treatment?

In more formal terms, one must test the null hypothesis that the incidence of preferential treatment for Group A (I_a – 15 percent in the example above) is actually zero. This hypothesis can be tested with a standard t statistic, which is calculated by dividing the incidence of preferential treatment by its standard error and determining from a table of t statistics how likely it is that the resulting ratio could occur by chance. Analysts typically reject the null hypothesis if there is a 5 percent chance or less that the observed results could occur when there is no real difference for the population as a whole. Sometimes a more rigorous statistical standard is applied, requiring a 1 percent chance or less. In paired role-playing studies, there are three possible outcomes for any test. Specifically, the analyst actually needs to test (1) the hypothesis that the incidence of group A being favored (I_a) is zero, (2) the hypothesis that the incidence of group B being favored (I_b) is zero, and (3) the hypothesis that both are treated equally. Some researchers might also test that the difference between I_a and I_b is zero. In the example, these would mean testing the hypothesis that 15 percent A favored is significantly different from 5 percent B favored.

Similar tests of statistical significance need to be conducted for measures of the severity of differential treatment. In this case, the appropriate measure is a difference-of-means test, which also produces a standard t statistic. Again, the observed difference in outcomes (D) is divided by its standard error, and a table of t statistics is used to determine whether the resulting ratio could reasonably have occurred by chance. If not, the analyst can reject the null hypothesis that D is actually equal to zero in the population as a whole.

Systematic versus Random Differences in Treatment

In addition to statistical significance tests, an analyst using the paired role-playing methodology must be aware of the distinction between systematic and random differences in treatment. Differential treatment of teammates can occur for both systematic and random reasons. To illustrate, suppose a landlord showed one apartment to a white home buyer but no apartments to the African American partner, so that the case was classified as white favored for the outcome measure. This unfavorable treatment of the African American teammate might have occurred for systematic reasons: perhaps the landlord wants to keep African Americans out of his building because he considers them poor tenants or because he fears that he will lose white tenants if there are African Americans in the building. But the same unfavorable treatment may also have resulted from random factors. Perhaps the landlord received a call between the visits from the two teammates indicating that a tenant had been found for the apartment. Or perhaps the agent felt tired or ill at the time of the African American partner's visit. Any number of random events might result in differential treatment of two customers—differential treatment unrelated to race.

Simple measures of the incidence of differential treatment inevitably include some cases in which the majority role player was favored because of systematic discrimination and some in which he was favored for random reasons. In fact, the share of cases with white-favored outcomes may either over- or understate the true incidence of systematically unfavorable treatment of African Americans, and there is no foolproof mathematical or statistical procedure for disentangling the random and systematic components of these measures.

One strategy for estimating systematic discrimination, that is, to remove the cases where nondiscriminatory random events are responsible for differences in treatment, is to subtract the incidence of African American–favored treatment from the incidence of white-favored treatment to produce a net measure. This approach essentially assumes that all cases of African American–favored treatment are attributable to random factors—that systematic discrimination never favors African Americans—and that random white-favored treatment occurs just as frequently as random African American–favored treatment. If these assumptions hold, the net measure subtracts differences due to random factors from the total incidence of white-favored treatment.

However, it seems unlikely that all African American–favored treatment is the result of random factors; sometimes African Americans may be systematically favored on the basis of their race or ethnicity. For example, an African American landlord might prefer to rent to families of his or her own race or a real estate agent might think that African American customers need extra assistance. Other instances of African American–favored treatment might reflect a form of race-based steering in which white customers are discouraged from considering units in African American neighborhoods or developments. Therefore, the net measure subtracts not only random differences but some systematic differences, and therefore it probably understates the frequency of systematic discrimination. Thus, net measures provide lower-bound estimates of systematic discrimination and reflect the extent to which the differential treatment that occurs (some systematically and some randomly) is more likely to favor whites than African Americans.

Advanced statistical procedures can offer some insights into the relative importance of random and systematic differences in treatment in a paired role-playing evaluation. For example, multivariate regression or logistical analysis can be used to quantify the independent impacts of various observed factors on treatment outcomes and to estimate the residual role of random factors (Yinger, 1991). However, these procedures are technically complex and must be tailored to the circumstances of a particular data set.

It may also be possible to empirically observe differences in treatment between paired testers of the same race. If same-race testers are carefully matched and follow the protocols of a conventional paired test, any differences in treatment that are observed between them must reflect random factors (both observable and unobservable). The most recent national study using role playing to measure racial and ethnic discrimination in housing experimented with three-part tests, including tests involving visits by two whites and an African American as well as tests involving two African Americans and a white. Analysis of these "triad" tests suggests that the incidence of same-race differences in treatment is generally not significantly different from the incidence of African American–favored treatment. In other words, African American–favored treatment may be a reasonable proxy for random differences in treatment, and the net measure may provide a good estimate of systematic discrimination. However, because sample sizes are small, these preliminary results should be interpreted cautiously (Turner and Ross, 2003).

Researchers continue to explore the issue of random and systematic contributions to observed differences in treatment and to refine statistical and other procedures for disentangling the effects of random factors. In the meantime, however, simple measures of the incidence of differential treatment are straightforward and informative. It is reasonable to report that, for example, African American job applicants receive less favorable treatment than comparable whites 20 percent of the time. Although not all of these cases of unfavorable treatment necessarily reflect systematic discrimination, they do reflect the incidence of unequal treatment. At the same time, it would make sense to report the incidence of white-favored outcomes. If the limitations of these simple measures are understood and the potential role of random factors is acknowledged, then complex statistical adjustments are not necessary.

Expanding Applications of Role Playing

In recent years, the use of the role-playing technique has greatly expanded. Although the major studies using role playing have tested principally for racial and ethnic discrimination in housing and employment, increasing numbers of researchers and evaluators have conducted smaller studies using the technique in new and innovative ways. Role players have been used to assess doctors' interpersonal skills, to examine whether airport screeners effectively detect weapons after 9/11, and to determine whether employers discriminate against applicants based on their criminal history.

In addition to rapid expansion in the use of role players by private businesses to measure customer satisfaction, role playing has increasingly been used by government agencies to examine the quality and equity of services provided by public programs. Federal and state governments have used role playing to help enforce their own regulations. While role playing is an effective tool for many types of evaluations, it does have limitations that should be considered. These range from the legality of using government employees to the ethical implications of making false requests or applications (Fix and Struyk, 1993). However, role playing has distinct advantages that make it a unique and convincing method for evaluating programs and for measuring discrimination.

Innovative Applications for Role Playing

Researchers have used the role-playing methodology to test for racial and ethnic discrimination in entry-level employment, housing rentals and purchases, car sales, and taxi service. The methodology has also been modified for application to mortgage financing (Turner and others, 2002) and home insurance (Galster, 1993). The use of role playing in employment has especially grown, with evaluators, including some outside the United States, conducting studies of discrimination based on a person's age, weight, sexual orientation, and criminal history (Bendick, Jackson, and Romero, 1996; Puhl and Brownell, 2001; Weichselbaumer, 2001; Pager, 2002).

The simplest applications of role playing are for evaluations that do not use pairs or teams at all. Many of these types of evaluations have also been conducted. Health researchers in Minnesota and Massachusetts have used teenagers posing as cigarette purchasers to determine whether restaurants, bars, stores, and hotels are locking vending machines and limiting sales to minors as required by law ("Smoking and Teens . . .," 1992). Similarly, evaluators can analyze the quality of information given to the public on request generally (as opposed to whether two groups received different quality information) using the simple role-playing methodology, as was done in an assessment of city employees' responses to requests for services and information conducted in Saratoga, California (Center for Excellence in Local Government, 1988).

Nonpaired testing can also be used to detect discrimination. The Texas Department of Human Services used limited-English-speaking role players to examine whether local welfare offices were providing required information and services. The evaluation examined overall results for the two groups rather than results for matched pairs (Business Resources, 2001). The Department of Health and Human Services' Office of Civil Rights used limited-English-speaking role players to determine if state and local welfare offices were violating Title VI by not providing interpreters to persons with limited English proficiency (see www.hhs.gov/ocr/selectacts/lep.html, March 2002).

For these types of applications, role players can be trained in a group instead of in pairs so that all testers have the same relevant traits and knowledge but sufficient differences to appear believable as ordinary citizens. Data collection and analysis can be based not on the differences within pairs but across the group of testers.

To test for differences among more than two categories of clients, teams of three, or possibly more, could be arranged. A team could have one white, one African American, and one Hispanic role player. This arrangement provides information on discrimination against members of two minority groups at once, as well as the relative extent of discrimination against each group. This technique would provide a direct comparison of the levels of discrimination against, for example, African Americans and Hispanics. However, using teams of three or more would add certain complications. Recruiting and forming these teams would take more time and effort than would forming pairs. Management and coordination would also be more complex, and a slightly larger sample size might be needed for analysis purposes. In some circumstances, three-way tests might seriously increase the risks of disclosure, endangering the validity of the study as a whole. For example, three-way tests were considered in the most recent national study of housing discrimination, but there was great concern that agents in white neighborhoods would be tipped off by visits from both African Americans and Hispanics in quick succession.

Potential Problems and Limitations

Despite the significant growth in the uses of role playing, the methodology has significant limitations and poses some potential problems. Probably the major constraint on the use of this methodology is its cost. Because role playing is labor intensive, cost considerations may severely limit sample sizes and the extent to which results can be generalized. In addition, there are some areas to which the methodology cannot be applied for practical reasons. To evaluate discrimination in hiring for jobs beyond entry-level openings would be extremely difficult because the qualifications of applicants are greater and matching pairs of role players becomes more complicated as the relevant criteria expand. Personal references take on more importance at higher skill levels, and verifying references and previous employment therefore poses a serious problem. Another difficulty within the area of employment is evaluating promotions, where role players could not be used at all. Placing role players in jobs and ensuring that they conduct equivalent quality work over an extended period of time would be impractical and would raise ethical issues.

Particularly complex transactions, such as evaluating the driver's license application process where official documentation is required and tests must be taken, are more complicated to evaluate using the role-playing methodology. Similarly, an evaluation that would require role players to have very specific traits or knowledge, such as obtaining a liquor license for a restaurant, would also be problematic to implement on a large scale. In order for the role players to have the necessary traits, such as proof of restaurant ownership, the pool of potential role players becomes very small and recruitment becomes more difficult. In addition, to obtain statistically significant results, sample size and cost issues make the use of role playing in these types of evaluations impractical to do on a large scale.

Ethical and Legal Issues

A number of ethical and legal issues have been raised by the paired role-playing studies that should be considered in future evaluations. Some observers have criticized the methodology for deceiving or entrapping subjects of an evaluation. Alan Greenspan, chairman of the board of governors of the Federal Reserve, has objected to the use of testing because it involves deception (see Edley, 1993). These observers are concerned about the implications of deceiving for purposes of research and about the privacy rights of the person or office being evaluated. Is it right to intrude on someone's business without that person's knowledge? Is that intrusion harmful because of the cost of interacting with role players—even if the cost is only lost time? These are valid concerns.

Nevertheless, a convincing argument can be made that the benefits of role playing far outweigh the drawbacks. Also, role playing can be designed to pose as limited an intrusion as possible, taking up the minimum amount of time necessary. In terms of privacy, most of the studies discussed here involve responding to offers (for homes, apartments, jobs, and services) that were publicly advertised and are subject to laws or regulations barring discrimination. As for such studies' constituting entrapment, there is no lure or incentive for people to act any differently from the way they would otherwise (Fix and Struyk, 1993).

Another issue is whether a government agency can use its own employees as role players for an evaluation. Although many of the studies cited in this chapter were conducted by public agencies, only one used its own employees as role players. To avoid any possible conflict of interest, a public agency might choose to contract with an independent outside entity that would conduct the evaluation. Government audit agencies, however, have unique roles and therefore may not face the same problems as other public agencies. Because the legal issues vary according to the evaluation being conducted, each agency should independently examine the legality of conducting role playing, as well as the legality of using its own employees as role players.

Conclusion

Role playing is a unique and innovative evaluation tool used in a wide range of settings. Individuals can act as role players in order to evaluate the quality of services or information provided by public agencies, giving evaluators direct observations on which to base their assessments. Similarly, the paired role-playing methodology allows analysts to directly observe differences in treatment between population groups. Other variations on the methodology are also possible, including using teams of three or more role players. Because role playing involves direct human observation, the results produced are particularly powerful. They also provide the power of narrative: role players can give anecdotal evidence of their own experiences. For these reasons, this approach to information-gathering produces results in a form that is clear and convincing to the public and to policymakers and, at the same time, is useful to program evaluators.

References

Ayres, I. "Fair Driving: Gender and Race Discrimination in Retail Car Negotiations." *Harvard Law Review,* 1991, *104*(4), 817–872.

Ayres, I. *Pervasive Prejudice? Unconventional Evidence of Race and Gender Discrimination.* Chicago: University of Chicago Press, 2001.

Bendick, M., Jr., Jackson, C., Reinoso, V. A., and Hodges, L. E. *Discrimination Against Latino Job Applicants: A Controlled Experiment.* Washington, D.C.: Fair Employment Council of Greater Washington, 1992.

Bendick, M., Jackson, C., and Romero, J. H. "Employment Discrimination Against Older Workers: An Experimental Study of Hiring Practices." *Journal of Aging and Social Policy,* 1996, *8*(1), 25–46.

Boggs, R.V.O., Sellers, J., and Bendick, M. "The Use of Testing in Civil Rights Enforcement." In M. Fix and R. Struyk (eds.), *Clear and Convincing Evidence: Testing for Discrimination in America.* Washington, D.C.: Urban Institute Press, 1993.

Business Resources. *Mystery Shopper Customer Service Evaluation Report.* Austin, Tex.: Texas Department of Human Services, 2001.

Center for Excellence in Local Government. "Achieving Excellence in Customer Service: Field Assessment Report for the City of Saratoga, California." Unpublished mimeographed report, Saratoga, Calif., 1988.

Cross, H., Kenney, G., Mell, J., and Zimmermann, W. *Employer Hiring Practices: Differential Treatment of Hispanic and Anglo Job Seekers.* Washington, D.C.: Urban Institute Press, 1990.

Edley, C. "Implications of Empirical Studies on Race Discrimination." In M. Fix and R. Struyk (eds.), *Clear and Convincing Evidence: Testing for Discrimination in America.* Washington, D.C.: Urban Institute Press, 1993.

Fix, M., and Struyk, R. J. "An Overview of Auditing for Discrimination." In M. Fix and R. Struyk (eds.), *Clear and Convincing Evidence: Testing for Discrimination in America.* Washington, D.C.: Urban Institute Press, 1993.

Galster, G. "The Use of Testers in Investigating Mortgage Lending and Insurance Discrimination." In M. Fix and R. Struyk (eds.), *Clear and Convincing Evidence: Testing for Discrimination in America.* Washington, D.C. Urban Institute Press, 1993.

International City Management Association. "Measuring City Agency Responsiveness: The Citizen-Surrogate Method." *Urban Data Service Report,* 1981, *13*(5).

James, F., and Del Castillo, S. "We May Be Making Progress Toward Equal Access to Jobs: Evidence from Recent Audits." Unpublished manuscript, University of Colorado, Denver, 1992.

Pager, D. "The Mark of a Criminal Record." Working paper, Center for Demography and Ecology, University of Wisconsin, 2002.

Puhl, R., and Brownell, K. D. "Bias, Discrimination, and Obesity." *Obesity Research.* 2001, *9*(12), 788–805.

Ridley, S. E., Bayton, J. A., and Outtz, J. H. "Taxi Service in the District of Columbia: Is It Influenced by the Patron's Race and Destination?" Unpublished paper, Lawyers Committee for Civil Rights, Washington, D.C., 1989.

"Smoking and Teens: Strong Measures, Like Banning Vending Machine Sales, Limit Minors' Access to Tobacco." *Washington Post,* Sept. 3, 1992, p. 7.

"Tracking Bias in Banks." *New York Times.* Feb. 16, 1992, p. 12.

Turner, M. A., Fix, M., and Struyk, R. J. *Opportunities Denied, Opportunities Diminished: Discrimination in Hiring.* Washington, D.C.: Urban Institute Press, 1991.

Turner, M. A., and Ross, S. *Discrimination Against African Americans and Hispanics: Supplemental Results from Phase II of HDS2000.* Washington, D.C.: U.S. Department of Housing and Urban Development, 2003.

Turner, M. A., Ross, S., Galster, G., and Yinger, J. *Discrimination in Metropolitan Housing Markets: Results from Phase I of HDS2000.* Washington, D.C: U.S. Department of Housing and Urban Development, 2002.

Turner, M. A., Struyk, R. J., and Yinger, J. *Housing Discrimination Study Synthesis.* Washington, D.C.: U.S. Department of Housing and Urban Development, 1991.

Turner, M. A., and others. *Other Things Being Equal: Testing for Discrimination in Mortgage Lending.* Washington, D.C.: U.S. Department of Housing and Urban Development, 2002.

U.S. General Accounting Office. *Tax Administration: Accessibility, Timeliness, and Accuracy of IRS Telephone Assistance Programs.* Washington, D.C.: U.S. General Accounting Office, Feb. 2, 1989.

U.S. General Accounting Office. "Tax Administration: Monitoring the Accuracy and Administration of IRS' 1989 Test-Call Survey." Washington, D.C.: General Accounting Office, Jan. 4, 1990.

Weichselbaumer, D. "Sexual Orientation Discrimination in Hiring." Working paper, Department of Economics, Johannes Kepler University of Linz, Austria, Oct. 2001.

Wienk, R., and others. *Housing Market Practices Survey.* Washington, D.C.: U.S. Department of Housing and Urban Development, 1979.

Wissoker, D., Zimmermann, W., and Galster, G. *Testing for Discrimination in Home Insurance.* Washington, D.C.: Urban Institute, 1998.

Yinger, J. *Housing Discrimination Study: Incidence and Severity of Unfavorable Treatment.* Washington, D.C.: U.S. Department of Housing and Urban Development, 1991.

Yinger, J. "The 1989 Housing Discrimination Study: Results and Implications." In M. Fix and R. Struyk (eds.), *Clear and Convincing Evidence: Testing for Discrimination in America.* Washington, D.C.: Urban Institute Press, 1993.

12

Using Focus Groups

Robert Goldenkoff

Focus groups probably affect our lives more frequently, and in more ways, than any other evaluation technique. The play list of your favorite radio station, the packaging of your food, the content of political campaigns, the endings of Hollywood movies, and even a replacement for advice columnist Ann Landers are just a few examples of how focus groups shape so much of what we see, touch, taste, hear, and purchase. The reason for their influence is not hard to understand: when appropriately applied, few, if any, other methodologies are as cost-effective in drawing out peoples' thoughts and attitudes about a particular subject. On the downside, focus group results cannot be statistically generalized to larger populations.

Focus groups have been an important component of private sector market research since the mid-1950s. In the 1970s, public sector and nonprofit organizations started to use focus group research with increasing frequency, and generally for the same reasons as private industry: to understand and meet the needs of their clients better. Nevertheless, focus groups, like all other evaluation techniques, have certain strengths and weaknesses that make them better suited for some applications than for others.

What Are Focus Groups?

A focus group is a form of qualitative research where a small number of participants (typically six to ten) informally discuss a particular topic under the guidance of a trained moderator. The participants, usually unknown to one another, share certain characteristics. Depending on the nature of the study, these shared traits can include similar social or demographic attributes, employment, and some relationship to the topic under review.

The key to focus groups is participant chemistry. Indeed, the combination of similar individuals, a moderator who encourages them to share their views, and a nonthreatening, nonjudgmental environment produces a group dynamic that eliminates participants' inhibitions and emboldens them to air their true feelings on the subject at hand.

This group dynamic—and the honest responses that result—are precisely why focus groups can yield such robust information when compared to other forms of evaluation. As Krueger (1988) notes, a shortcoming of mail and telephone surveys, as well as one-on-one interviews, is that they assume that people know how they feel and form their opinions in isolation. However, people may need to hear the views of others before forming an opinion of their own (Krueger, 1988).

For example, one evening I received a call from a market researcher who was doing a survey on behalf of apple growers. The researcher wanted to know what kind of apples I bought and rank what was important to me when selecting apples, such as price, color, size, taste, and texture.

To be honest, apples were never a large part of my life, and I rarely gave my fruit purchases much thought. Not surprisingly, it was difficult for me to articulate within the structured responses to such questions as, "To what extent do you like large apples?" what was driving those decisions. A response of, "Not quite—it's more like this . . ." or, "Granny Smiths? Those are the green ones, right?" could not be recorded on the researcher's questionnaire. In later reflecting on that experience, I noted that had I been in a room with other apple eaters—perhaps some more discerning than myself—I could have listened to their reasons for selecting one type of apple over another, considered their views, reacted to them, and expressed my own thoughts. In a focus group, my response might have gone like this: "While some of the people here like large apples, I buy small apples—Macs, mainly—because they need to fit in my lunch bag." Although my response could not be used for statistical purposes, it nonetheless generated better information on the reasons for my buying behavior.

Group dynamics can also get people to reveal certain prejudices and politically incorrect or embarrassing beliefs that they might otherwise suppress in the course of a survey, even an anonymous one. Indeed, while people might provide rational or publicly acceptable reasons for their thoughts and actions when responding to a survey, in a focus group—where participants are selected on the basis of certain shared characteristics in order to generate group dynamics—they might be more inclined to disclose the real, yet socially unacceptable, motivations for their behavior.

Importantly, focus groups are not designed to develop a consensus, draw up a plan, or decide on a course of action. In fact, just the opposite is true. The explicit goal of focus group research is to extract the range of perceptions and alternative viewpoints that people might have on a particular topic.

Focus group research dates back to 1941 when social scientists Paul Lazarsfeld and Robert Merton used "focused interviews" to assess audience responses to radio programs. During World War II, Merton used his technique to investigate how army training films affected the morale of new recruits (Stewart and Shamdasani, 1990). The marketing profession picked up on the technique during the following decade, and focus groups have been a staple of the advertising industry ever since (Krueger, 1988).

In the 1970s and 1980s, public sector and nonprofit organizations began using focus groups with greater frequency as well. Under mounting pressure to improve their performance and accountability, market their services, and become more customer oriented, these entities turned to focus groups to obtain a better understanding of their clients' needs. This trend continued into the 1990s at the federal level with the enactment of the Government Performance and Results Act of 1993, which called on bureaucracies to provide better service at less cost by identifying their mission and goals, concentrating on customers, empowering employees, and eliminating inefficient practices. Although agencies typically use statistical data and surveys to inform these efforts, the use of focus groups appears to be growing. More recently, initiatives to open public sector jobs to private competition might prompt some agencies to turn to focus groups to get closer to their clients and promote their services.

What Types of Evaluations Are Best Suited to Focus Group Research?

Focus groups are extremely versatile: they can generate information before, during, or after a program or service is provided. They are particularly good at eliciting detailed, introspective responses on people's feelings, thoughts, perceptions, actions, behaviors, and motivations and are best used in evaluations aimed at determining what, how, and why. They are less effective at obtaining quantitative data or for inquiries seeking answers to such questions as "How often?" or "How many?" and probably should not be used for these purposes.

Focus groups can typically be organized more quickly and produce faster results than other data collection techniques, such as telephone surveys and mailed questionnaires. In fact, a few weeks might be all that is needed to go from design to finished report. They are also more flexible than other methodologies in that evaluators can explore different concepts by getting participants to discuss alternatives and trade-offs, and can measure the intensity of participants' feelings by taking note of their body language and other cues. Focus groups tend to be more expensive to conduct on a per respondent basis (although they are often less expensive overall), and the results cannot be generalized to a larger population.

Stewart and Shamdasani (1990), and Krueger (1988), among others, have summarized the more common applications of focus groups. As a whole, they can be grouped into four types of applications: exploratory data gathering, refining ongoing programs and services, evaluating completed programs, and validating or adding context to the results of other research methods.

Exploratory Data Gathering

Focus groups are often used before a program or service is implemented when not much is known about the subject of interest. Specific applications include identifying needs, expectations, and salient issues, and assessing the acceptability of a new program. Focus groups are also used to uncover the vocabulary and syntax that target populations use to describe subjects of interest. When employed for exploratory purposes, focus groups can be either the principal data-gathering mechanism or a tool to design or refine other data collection instruments such as mailed questionnaires. The ability of focus groups to explore important issues and how people talk about specific topics make them particularly useful for the latter application.

Following are two examples of exploratory focus groups:

• In September 2002, on behalf of the Partnership for Public Service, a polling firm held two focus groups with federal employees pegged for inclusion in the department of homeland security, the creation of which was then under consideration by Congress (Hart and Teeter, 2002). The purpose of the evaluation was to explore federal employees' perceptions of the proposed agency as well as their attitudes toward federal employment in general. One session was held with managers and supervisors at the GS-11 level or higher, and a second session was conducted with front-line workers at the GS-4 to GS-10 positions. The results of the evaluation were limited because only two focus groups were held at a single location. Still, based on comments such as, "Communication is just not out there," and, "I think people are going to be left in the dark as long as possible," the polling firm concluded, among other things, that participants felt left out of the reorganization process and, as a result, lacked confidence in the agency's future success.

• To gauge public acceptability of a new dollar coin to replace the paper note, the U.S. General Accounting Office (GAO) held a series of focus groups with members of the general public and private sector employees who handled money as part of their jobs. The results of the focus groups showed little interest in a new dollar coin. Members of the general public believed that a new coin would be confusing and inconvenient, and these negatives would offset any savings to the government. Private sector employees who handled money as part of their jobs were more inclined to accept the new coin, but they also cited a number of disadvantages, such as the expense of retrofitting vending and coin counting machines. In general, focus group participants believed that if a dollar note and a dollar coin were both available, people would opt for the paper currency (U.S. General Accounting Office, 1990b).

Interestingly, despite spending more than $67 million to market the dollar coin from 1998 to 2001, the U.S. Mint stopped circulating the coin in 2002. Although the promotional campaign was effective in raising awareness of the coin, it could not persuade people to use it instead of the paper dollar. Continued circulation of the dollar bill and reluctance on the part of retailers and banks to stock the coin were just some of the barriers to more widespread use (U.S. General Accounting Office, 2002).

Refining Ongoing Programs and Services

Focus groups are an excellent tool for fine-tuning or expanding existing programs. Specific applications include increasing client participation, adapting programs to better meet client needs, developing progress reports on the conduct of a program, and illuminating potential trouble spots.

As one example, Worksystems, a federally funded workforce investment board based in Portland, Oregon, that provides employment and training services, used focus groups as part of an effort to reach people who could benefit from its programs and products but were not using them (Worksystems, 2001). Worksystems contracted with a polling firm, which held three focus groups with Portland-area full-time workers. The focus groups were followed by a survey of five hundred full-time workers in Portland and its surrounding counties.

The first focus group session was all female, the second all male, and the third mixed-gender Hispanics. Participants were asked about their current jobs, the difference between a "job" and a "career," barriers to changing jobs, their views of job training and career counseling, and how to reach out to workers like themselves. The focus groups revealed that "careers" were viewed far more positively than "jobs," which led to a recommendation that Worksystems use the word *career* in lieu of *jobs* whenever possible in order to attract people into occupations. The focus groups also revealed that participants had a strong desire to start a small business, underscoring the need for mentor programs to help people obtain capital, develop a marketing plan, and understand legal and tax issues.

As part of an effort to make the federal government a more competitive employer of top college graduates, GAO held nine focus groups with college students majoring in a variety of fields at five randomly selected universities across the country (U.S General Accounting Office, 1990a). Students were asked to discuss their career expectations, perceptions of federal employment, and the recruiting techniques they believed could best attract graduates to federal service in the future. Students cited noncompetitive starting salaries and a complex and time-consuming hiring process that made federal employment unattractive to them. They also acknowledged knowing very little about available federal jobs or how to apply for them, which highlighted the importance of more aggressive campus recruitment efforts. One University of Arizona student explained, "There is a certain vagueness, especially within the biological sciences with respect to government. It is just like a black hole. What is there? We don't know."

Evaluating Completed Programs

At the conclusion of a program or service, focus groups can help assess what worked, what did not work (and why), customer satisfaction, and lessons learned. For example, the National Commission on the High School Senior Year, a partnership between the U.S. Department of Education and several foundations that was created to examine students' experiences in the last year of high school, sponsored a series of focus groups to obtain a better understanding of the transition from high school to the post–high school world. The communications firm that conducted the sessions held eight focus groups with young people, ages eighteen to twenty-five, across the country experiencing transition difficulties (Steen, 2000).

Participants were asked to discuss missed opportunities, reflect on their high school experience, and comment on their transitions to life after high school. These sessions were somewhat unusual in that they were conducted by conference calls as opposed to in-person interviews (the pros and cons of this approach are discussed below). Based partly on the students' comments, the commission concluded that high schools are inadequately preparing enough students for postsecondary learning or careers after college, and they called for schools to develop expanded and more rigorous alternatives to the traditional senior year (National Commission on the High School Senior Year, 2001).

Validating or Adding Context to the Results of Other Evaluation Methods

Sample surveys are extremely efficient when it comes to collecting a large volume of data across a range of topics from an enormous number of people. However, to obtain that efficiency, survey questions are typically closed-ended and provide few, if any, opportunities for respondents to explain their answers or provide responses other than the limited set of choices contained in the survey instrument.

To address this limitation, evaluators sometimes employ focus groups to confirm or expand on the information obtained in surveys. In some cases, evaluators select focus group participants from survey respondents who answered a question a certain way. In other cases, the survey results can be used to develop the questions for focus group sessions consisting of a separate cohort of individuals (this is the reverse of using focus groups for exploratory data gathering).

Worksystems did this when it used the results of an earlier survey to develop questions for a focus group session comprising twenty-five directors and managers of Oregon community development corporations, federal housing agencies, housing authorities, and workforce agencies concerned about the lack of workforce development resources available to their residents (Kristin Wolff, interview by the author, Nov. 2002).

Key Ingredients of a Successful Focus Group Session

Arranging an effective focus group session is a lot like planning a successful party. Both require the right mix of people and environment to make them work. The principal elements of a focus group session are a moderator, an assistant moderator, the facilities, the participants, and the questions.

The Moderator

The moderator guides the discussions, ensuring that all views are expressed. Although this sounds simple and straightforward in theory, in reality it requires considerable training and practice to be able to do it well during the course of a focus group session. Participants can be bashful, disruptive, dominant, or unable to stay on task. All of these behaviors can destroy the chemistry that is so important to an effective focus group session and diminish the quality of data that are collected.

Experienced moderators take a number of steps to help ensure participants will open up, beginning with their welcome to participants. The narrative that follows is fairly typical of a moderator's opening remarks. The session itself was one of several organized by the public administration department at a major university. As part of its reaccreditation process, the department obtained the perspectives of alumni on the quality of the public administration program and how it could be improved:

> Welcome to our session today. I want to tell you how much the Public Administration Department and I appreciate your participation in our discussion. My name is _____ and I'll be the moderator of today's discussion. Also with me is _____ .
>
> As part of its accreditation process, the department is studying the quality of the public administration program and ways it can be improved. Specifically, we'd like you to tell us about how well the program met your needs when you were a student and, based on your experiences since graduating, how the program can better meet the needs of today's students.
>
> Before we get started, let me point out several important issues. We are interested in your personal opinions on the topics we will discuss. There are no right or wrong answers here, and we're not trying to achieve a consensus; so please feel free to share your ideas even if they differ from what others have said. Also, keep in mind that we are just as interested in negative comments as positive comments.
>
> The discussion will be on a first-name basis. Of course, your comments are confidential, and no names will be attached to any comments in the summary report.
>
> You may have noticed the tape recorder. We're recording the discussion because we don't want to miss any of your comments, and it also makes our analysis more accurate. Please speak up, and only one person should talk at a time.
>
> Finally, we plan to finish within ninety minutes. We won't be taking a formal break, so if you need to, feel free to leave the room, but please try not to disturb the group.
>
> Let's get started by going around the room and have each of you tell when you graduated and what you're doing now.

Note how this introduction describes the purpose of the study to ensure everyone has a common understanding of why they are there, and presents a set of ground rules to encourage participants to express their views. The ground rules underscore the fact that everyone is expected to participate, their answers are equally valid, and the discussion will remain confidential. If participants know one another, as sometimes happens when the focus group takes place in a particular organization or office, participants should be asked not to disclose any of the comments they hear that day.

The moderator's introduction also explains the presence of the tape recorder. Recording equipment can inhibit people from opening up, so it is important to put them at ease whenever it is used. (With few exceptions, as when dealing with extraordinarily sensitive topics, you should record the discussion to help ensure the complete and objective capture and analysis of all comments.) After a few minutes, participants typically forget that it is there. When contractors conduct a focus group, the evaluation sponsors often observe the sessions from behind a one-way mirror. Their presence should be noted and explained as well. This is particularly important if the sponsor is a government agency. Participants might feel that they were spied on if they found out later that the observers were government representatives. If particularly sensitive topics are being discussed, the sponsors should consider not attending the session to avoid squelching the dialogue.

Note how the moderator completes the introduction and moves into the interview by asking alumni when they graduated and what they are doing now. Focus group sessions typically start with an easy question such as this as an icebreaker to get participants comfortable with speaking with a group of strangers. Some participants, if they do not speak early in the session, may never feel sufficiently comfortable to speak at all.

When participants introduce themselves, they should be asked to provide only their first names in order to preserve a measure of confidentiality. Also, the warm-up question should not cause participants to reveal information that could affect the dynamics of the group. For example, in some groups, revealing occupation could indicate some members are wealthier or better educated than the others, which could impair the discussion, depending on the purpose of the session.

Other tools have proven effective in getting participants to express their views as well. For example, each participant in the Worksystems focus groups was given a sheet of paper with the meeting agenda. This allowed participants to jot down their thoughts if they did not want to talk. Worksystems observed that women tended to be more forthcoming in writing (Kristin Wolff, interview by author, Nov. 2002). Another helpful technique is to pick up on the main points of the discussion, summarize them, and recite them to the group for further reaction, elaboration, and clarification.

If the issue being studied is particularly sensitive or personal, such as those involving race or gender, the moderator should be selected from the same demographic group as the participants. Moderators should also be familiar with and make frequent use of probing and reinforcement techniques. Probing techniques get participants to elaborate on their responses, while reinforcements demonstrate interest in the respondents' answers, thereby encouraging them to continue speaking. The box contains examples of each. In using both techniques, it is important to make only neutral comments. Remarks such as "excellent response" or even body language such as head nodding (unless used consistently after every response) could bias answers because it cues the respondent as to what is acceptable or expected. The better versed the moderator is in the subject matter and purpose of the study, the better are the probes and reinforcements.

Examples of Probes and Reinforcers

Probes

"Anything else?"

"Any other reason?"

"How do you mean?"

"Could you tell me more about your thinking on that?"

"Why do you feel that way?"

Reinforcers

"I see."

"Let me get that down."

"I want to make sure I have that right."

"It's useful to get your ideas on this."

"Thanks. It's important to get your opinion on that."

Moderators can use eye contact, facial expressions, and other body language to draw reserved participants into the discussion and, as necessary, call on people directly. Questions such as, "Steve, do you agree with that?" or "What are your thoughts on this issue, Karen?" can connect the more reserved participants with the conversation without intimidating them.

Sometime moderators encounter the opposite problem: suppressing the more talkative and dominant personalities and keeping the discussion on track. Here, moderators can again use body language (avoiding eye contact), remind everyone of the ground rules, and call on others. Moderators can also use the seating arrangement to their advantage by taking note of who the dominant people might be as participants start to arrive, and seating those individuals immediately next to them. Should the need arise, the moderator can turn away from the dominant individual. One experienced moderator even suggests leaning into the table, physically inserting yourself between the overbearing person and the rest of the group (Lynn Musser, interview by the author, Dec. 2002).

The moderator must also keep the discussion on track. Depending on the subject matter, some people may try to use the session as a venue for their own agenda, complain, or simply discuss irrelevant topics. In other cases, two or more participants might have distracting side conversations with one another. These situations need to be treated delicately because if they are cut off too quickly or harshly, it could inhibit them and others from speaking.

The excerpt that follows is from one of the focus group sessions that GAO held with college students—in this case, graduate biology students—on how to attract them to federal service. Note how the moderator lets the discussion coast a bit and allows a few seconds of personal conversation between two of the participants so as not to restrain the conversation, but reeled the entire group back in before they drifted too far by reminding people of the question they were talking about. Once they got back on track, they revealed that they were more interested in pursuing careers in the private sector or academia in part because of the stereotype they have about government work:

Moderator: To what extent do you think that the federal government can give you what you want in a job?

David: Like move to Washington, D.C.?

Moderator: Is that where federal jobs are?

David: I don't know, but that is certainly my perception . . . . Every month they send out this flier, this clipboard with these twenty or so pieces of yellow paper with all the jobs in molecular biology and microbiology that the government is offering.

Ingrid: Really? I have never seen one.

David: The government sends it, starting at like GS-11 or something.

Kevin: I have never seen that either.

David: It's always hanging on the [bulletin] board.

Kevin: Whose board is this?

David: It's in the [biology] building.

Ingrid: Third floor, right?

David: On the third floor right next to Professor Little's office.

Ingrid: Okay. We don't live on the third floor.

David: I look at [federal job announcements], and I don't know, some of the jobs are interesting, the pay surely looks decent. But working on little worms that affect some kind of, you know, bovine worms or something . . .

Ingrid: Come on, we work on yeast. How can you condemn worms?

Moderator: The question was, do you think that the government can satisfy what you are after in a position?

Ingrid: Not yet.

David: Not yet. I think the government has to change. . . . Everybody is attracted to industry or academia.

Moderator: Why? Why are they considered better places to work?

Jeff: A lot of it is the stigma that I have developed over all these years that I guess I could call it the post office workers' stigma. . . . You just get in and you never leave. [Most participants nodded their heads in agreement.]

Ingrid: You don't move up; you don't move around.

Finally, moderators must be adept at reading nonverbal communication such as head nodding, eye rolling, and frowns and factor them into the analysis of the results. All of these cues can signal agreement or disagreement with what is being said, as well as the intensity of those feelings, even if the other participants remain silent.

The Assistant Moderator

The assistant moderator has two principal jobs (Krueger, 1988): maintaining the moderator's neutrality by tending to administrative tasks and disruptions and taking notes. Administrative tasks include greeting participants, distributing name tags, handling refreshments, seating latecomers, and operating the recording equipment.

In taking notes, the assistant moderator should be alert to changes in question sequence; viewpoints held by a minority of participants; intensity levels as indicated by participants' body language, tone of voice, and enthusiasm; and new lines of questioning that should be pursued in subsequent sessions. The assistant moderator's notes also serves as a backup in case the recording equipment fails.

The assistant moderator does not typically pose any questions to the group, although in some cases, at the end of the session, the moderator will ask the assistant if he or she has any questions. Finally, the assistant helps the moderator analyze the results.

Because of the additional costs associated with them, assistant moderators are not always used in sessions that are run by contractors. However, because they contribute to so many aspects of a focus group session, evaluators should consider using assistant moderators, especially if the focus groups are conducted in-house. At a minimum, a second person—perhaps the evaluation sponsor—should be present to help take notes.

The Facilities

The facilities where the focus groups are conducted are just as important to a robust discussion as a trained moderator. They should be convenient, comfortable, and not intimidating. As one experienced moderator noted, people are more likely to express themselves if they feel at home (Lynn Musser, interview by the author, Dec. 2002).

The characteristics of the facilities that meet this threshold vary with the group and the topic being discussed. For example, if the topics are about the operations, procedures, or mission of a particular organization, a conference room and businesslike setting are appropriate. If the topic is more personal in nature, the room should be less formal—perhaps a grouping of chairs set around a low coffee table. When contractors conduct focus groups, they typically use special facilities where the moderator and participants sit in one room, and clients sit in another, observing the session through a one-way mirror.

Participants' need for public transportation, child care, wheelchair access, special scheduling, and other group-specific requirements must be considered to ensure a high participation rate. Worksystems held its focus groups at shopping malls and community colleges that attract the customers Worksystems sought to reach. The participants were familiar with the settings, parking was free, public transportation was convenient, and child care was offered (Kristin Wolff, interview by the author, Nov. 2002). Similarly, GAO held its focus groups with college students in classrooms or student lounges where they would feel at home (U.S. General Accounting Office, 1990a).

The time of day that the focus groups are held can affect attendance. GAO held its sessions with college students in the late afternoon and early evening so as not to conflict with students' work and class schedules (U.S. General Accounting Office, 1990a).

Coffee, tea, water, soft drinks, and other nonalcoholic refreshments, and perhaps light snacks, help create a more hospitable atmosphere and may in fact be a necessity during a lengthy session. More substantive fare is often provided as well, especially if the session is scheduled during mealtime. Although most people typically appreciate such offerings, they raise the cost of the sessions and sometimes require more specialized facilities, capable of properly storing, heating, and preparing the food. More elaborate catering can also be a distraction as participants concentrate on the food as opposed to discussion questions.

Some researchers have used conference calls in lieu of a facility when geographical dispersion made it impossible to bring participants together at a single site. This approach was used for the focus groups sponsored by the National Commission on the High School Senior Year (Steen, 2000). Although conference calls can elicit participants' opinions and perceptions, they may not generate the same group dynamics as face-to-face encounters. Some of the richness of the discussion might also be missed because it is impossible to pick up head nodding, fist waving, and other nonverbal signs of agreement or disagreement.

The Participants

Focus group participants are typically strangers to one another but share similar characteristics. To ensure the right people get invited, careful consideration must be given to recruiting. Krueger (1988) describes five sources of candidates:

- Existing lists of people, such as clients, members, and service recipients
- Contacting other groups for names
- Asking focus group participants to suggest the names of others
- Random telephone screening
- Recruiting people on site by inviting a sample of people using an organization's services to participate in a discussion

The simplest method is recruiting participants from existing lists of people. Organizations already have contact information on these individuals, and other information important for selection such as race, gender, income level, and services received, would likely be available as well. However, for certain types of studies, such as how to expand membership, evaluators need to go outside an existing clientele and recruit from a broader universe of people.

Market research firms and other organizations that routinely conduct focus groups can tap into a number of different databases and produce lists of people with specific demographic, economic, consumer, and other attributes, all at the neighborhood level. In addition, they typically maintain lists of people with diverse characteristics who have agreed in advance to participate in a session if they qualify. The organizations call on them when needed for a particular client. Although this can speed the recruitment process, they may not be representative of the target population, and you should be wary of "focus groupies"—people who routinely attend focus groups for the participation fees and meals that are sometimes provided.

For Worksystems' study of how to attract more people to its services, a polling firm used census and other data to identify neighborhoods meeting certain ethnic, income, and other demographic characteristics of its target population. The firm then made random calls in those areas to recruit specific people (Worksystems, 2001).

When GAO held its focus groups with college students on their perceptions of federal employment, it randomly selected five universities from across the country. From that group, GAO invited students from the sciences, engineering, business, and other academic disciplines that the government was having difficulty attracting. To obtain the names of specific students, GAO contacted the department chairs at those schools, informed them of the purpose of the study, and asked for the names of about a dozen students who might want to participate. Each of the students had to have an overall B average or higher or be in the top 20 percent of their class, be within a year of graduation, and be enrolled full time (U.S. General Accounting Office, Aug. 1990a).

Although GAO randomly selected the schools it visited, Krueger (1988) notes that scientific sampling techniques are not essential for choosing focus group participants because the purpose of focus groups is to better understand a particular phenomenon as opposed to generalizing or making inferences. Nevertheless, randomization can help reduce any selection biases that can creep into a group that is judgmentally selected. Screening questionnaires can be administered to ensure potential recruits possess the demographic or other characteristics desired for the focus group.

Ensuring people attend the session, much like ensuring high response rates to surveys, calls for a combination of multiple contacts, personalization, and tangible and intangible incentives. Following is a typical telephone script used to introduce candidates to the study and screen them for their eligibility:

> Good evening. My name is John Smith and I work for the XYZ Society, a nonprofit educational organization located in Anytown. Is this Ms. Jones?
>
> We will be conducting a series of informal discussions with people in your community about preventing teenage drug abuse and would like you to participate. Your views are important because they will be used to improve the services we provide to young adults in your neighborhood. All the information shared in the discussions is strictly confidential. The group discussions last approximately ninety minutes and will take place at 123

> Main Street at 7:00 P.M. Light refreshments will be served. May
> I ask you a few short questions to determine your eligibility?

Note how the script:

- Identifies the organization, describes the purpose of the evaluation in general terms, and explains what will be done with the information.
- Invites people to a "discussion." The term *focus group* should be avoided because it is too technical or vague. You can also ask people to "share their views" or "discuss their ideas."
- Motivates candidates to participate by stressing the value of the study and the importance of their opinions.

If people agree to participate, you should also verify the spelling of their name, obtain their house and e-mail addresses, and inform them that if selected, they will receive a formal invitation about two weeks before the session. You should also ask if they have any special needs. Because a number of people change their mind about participation, Krueger (1988) recommends overrecruiting by as much as 25 percent at this stage.

Tangible incentives can also increase participation rates. They often include refreshments or a meal, reimbursement for transportation expenses, or an honorarium that can range from around twenty-five dollars for relatively easy-to-recruit populations, to several hundred dollars for hard-to-recruit population groups or people in highly paid professions, such as doctors or executives. If a cash incentive is offered, consider whether it might introduce some type of selection bias into the sample of participants ultimately selected. For example, the people most willing to participate might be those in the greatest financial need.

To guard against no-shows, it is important to invite several more participants than the desired six to twelve attendees. Just how many more depends on your judgment of the reliability of the candidates. With some groups, such as those that are already involved with or committed to the program or topic being studied, an additional two or three invitees might be all that is needed to ensure a group of sufficient size. With others, it might be necessary to overrecruit by as much as half. Although there are drawbacks to groups that are too large or too small, it is usually better to err on the side of a larger group because groups that are too small may not have the necessary group dynamics or generate sufficient information.

The letter that is sent to candidates selected for the focus groups should restate the information conveyed in the screening calls. It should also include directions to the focus group site and the name of a contact person they can call if they have any questions or need to cancel.

For best results, the letter should not be a form letter. It should be personalized—that is, addressed specifically to each individual and signed with an original signature. The less the mass-produced look of the letter, the more likely it is that recipients will feel individually valued and attend the session. Finally, a day or so before the focus group, confirm their participation with a reminder phone call.

Focus Group Questions

Focus group questions need to be open-ended in order to generate as much discussion as possible. This is why good focus group questions often begin with such phrases as, "How do you feel about . . . ," "What is your opinion of . . . ," or "Please describe . . . ." Closed-ended questions—that is, inquiries that invite a yes-no or single word answer—are best avoided or left to other types of data collection methods.

This generally holds true even for questions that call for a numerical response, such as those that ask "How many?" or "How often?" because there is not much that can be done with the response analytically (remember that the main goal of focus groups is to understand rather than measure). However, it is possible to ask an open-ended question about a quantitative issue. For example, suppose you were assessing client satisfaction with a particular social service program, and you wanted to know how long clients had to wait before being seen by a counselor. A focus group question that asked, "How long do you typically wait before seeing a counselor?" would likely generate vague and imprecise answers. It would be better to use observational or other evaluation techniques to obtain a more accurate measure of client waiting time and use the focus group to obtain clients' views about their waiting time with a question such as, "How do you feel about the length of time you need to wait before seeing a counselor?"

That said, some focus groups use hand-held electronic voting devices that allow participants to respond to multiple-choice questions. Although the results are not useful for statistical purposes, they do provide a sense of the significance or importance of a particular item such as a service characteristic. Participants might be asked to use the devices to anonymously vote on such questions as, "Which is more important to you: shorter waiting time or extended hours?" This type of vote should come only after participants have had a chance to discuss the topic.

The sample interview guides in Exhibit 12.1 illustrate other attributes of focus group questions. They start with very general inquiries and finish up with one or two questions closely linked to the study objectives (the latter are ideally suited to electronic multivoting). For example, the focus group exploring how to attract college students to federal service first asks participants about their career expectations in general, then gets more specific with a series of questions on recruiting strategies, and then concludes with a set of questions about their specific perceptions of federal employment and how agencies can best attract them. This drill-down approach helps engage participants' interest (as noted earlier, the first question is typically an icebreaker to get people comfortable with speaking) and helps ensure that the broad issues, topics, and perceptions get drawn out.

Note the relatively small number of questions: no more than ten to twelve, and six to eight are preferred. It is difficult for a group to discuss a long list of questions in the time allotted, and a lengthy list suggests a line of inquiry that is asking too many detailed questions or trying to cover too many topics.

The questions in Exhibit 12.1 also contain possible probes to help ensure consistency across each session. Moderators will also find probes useful if they are not well versed in the topic under discussion. If aspects of the focus group significantly change, the results should not be used.

Visual aids can help participants provide more informed answers. GAO did this when it held a series of focus groups on the acceptability of the currency change. Participants were shown a Canadian dollar coin and the Susan B. Anthony dollar, as well as a chart that explained how cash transactions would be rounded up or down if the penny were eliminated. To see how checkout counter and cash register operators might react to the new coin, focus groups consisting of money handlers were shown a typical cash drawer layout before and after the currency changes (U.S. General Accounting Office, 1990b).

Before conducting the focus groups, pilot-test the questions to help ensure they will generate the needed information, are easily understood by participants, and that participants have the knowledge to respond to them. Krueger (1988) describes a three-step testing process:

Step 1: Experts familiar with both the purpose of the study and the nature of the participants review the questions and their probes.

Step 2: For the first focus group session, the moderator reviews the content and sequence of the questions, room arrangement, and group composition. The results of this first session can be used with the subsequent sessions if there were no substantive changes. However, if the questions or other aspects of the focus group change significantly, the results should not be used.

Step 3: At the end of the first focus group, the moderator should turn off the recording equipment and ask participants for feedback. Participants might be asked if they understood the questions, if there was anything that should have been asked but was not, and if they have any additional suggestions.

Exhibit 12.1. Focus Group Questions: Examples

Example 1: Evaluation of How to Attract College Graduates to Federal Service

Topic 1: Career Values and Expectations (30 minutes)

1. What are some aspects of a job that would motivate you to choose a career at one organization over another?
    Probe: Touch on the following job dimensions:
    - Selection/hiring process: Highly selective, merit based, fast decisions
    - Rewards: Salary and benefits, mobility, continuing education, flexible hours
    - Content of work: Ability to apply your education, challenges, travel, variety
    - Physical environment: Size of organization, location
    - Psychological environment: Colleagues, management style, org. stability.
2. What do you hope to gain from your first job?
3. What factors affect how long you will stay at your first job?

Topic 2: Recruiting Strategies (30 minutes)

4. What steps do you take when looking for a job?
5. When looking for a job, what specific information do you want to know? How should it be presented to you?
6. Let's talk a little about recruiters. What qualities do you think make a good recruiter?

Topic 3: Perceptions of Federal Employment (40 minutes)

7. Now let's move to a little different topic. What are your impressions of the federal government as an employer? (*Probes:* What images come to mind when you think of federal employment? How do you feel about people who work for the federal government?)
8. Early in our meeting, we discussed factors that are important to you when choosing a job. Do you believe you would find these factors in a job with the federal government?
9. If the federal government could do one thing to convince you to work there, what would it be?

Example 2: Assessment of Alumni Satisfaction with Graduate Public Administration Program

1. How do you feel about the overall quality of the education you received as a master of public administration (M.P.A.) student? How well did it prepare you for your career?
2. How satisfied were you with the public administration (PAD) faculty in terms of their teaching ability and accessibility?
3. Based on your experience since receiving your degree, what aspects of the current curriculum do you feel should be emphasized? What aspects do you feel should be deemphasized?

Probes: Computer Training	Qualitative Methods
Communication Skills	Public Administration Theory
Policy Analysis/Program Evaluation	State and Local Government
Budget Process	Other
Legislative Process	
Quantitative Methods	

4. What subjects, if any, do you feel should be added to the M.P.A. curriculum to ensure its relevance to today's public management environment?
5. How do you feel about the M.P.A. program's career counseling efforts? What can be done to improve them?
6. In thinking about all aspects of the M.P.A. program such as its academic quality, career training, and faculty interest in the students, what advice would you give to the head of the Public Administration Department to meet the needs of students better?

Deciding How Many Focus Groups to Conduct

Although evaluators often hold four to six focus groups for a particular project, more complex evaluations may require a dozen or more. Ultimately, the number of groups to conduct is driven largely by the evaluation objectives, the diversity of the target population, and resource constraints. The goal is to conduct enough groups to capture the range of views held by the population of interest. You know that you have reached this point when additional sessions fail to produce significantly new or different information.

Ideally, you should hold at least two or three sessions for each target population. The results of the second and third sessions will help corroborate or refute the findings from the first. If you held only one session, you would never know whether the group's views were prevalent in the larger population or merely the result of a dominant participant or some other unique factor. If these initial sessions yield similar results, it may not be necessary to conduct additional interviews. However, if the results of the three sessions produce vastly different views, or if two sessions generate similar data while the results of a third are dissimilar, additional sessions would be warranted to get a better sense of the range of viewpoints. You might also want to consider factors that could affect the diverse viewpoints. For example, the subject matter might be very complex and the questions might need to be narrowed, or the target population could be divided into smaller, more homogeneous subgroups. The need to cover multiple geographical areas would also increase the number of sessions needed. Of course, in studies where the population of interest is very small (for example, managers in a single office), all or most of the population can be captured with a single session.

The purpose of the focus groups can affect the number of sessions. If the focus groups are exploratory in nature, a small number of groups might be all that is needed to get a sense of "what's out there." If the purpose of the evaluation is to obtain information to refine a program, a greater degree of precision would be needed, which would argue for a larger number of groups to ensure diverse perspectives have been captured.

Analyzing Focus Group Data

The analysis of focus group data can range in sophistication from a simple summary of major themes to more complex content analyses and cross-group comparisons. The level of rigor depends on the purpose of the focus groups, the complexity of the inquiry, and the evaluator's available resources.

As Stewart and Shamdasani (1990) note, when quick decisions are needed (whether to move ahead on a proposed program, for example) or when the results of the focus groups are self-evident, a brief summary and analysis would suffice. Highlighting major themes and illustrating them with participants' comments is also cost-effective in these situations. However, if the evaluation objectives are more ambitious (for example, obtaining in-depth understanding of a complex issue), the analysis needs to be more sophisticated and rigorous.

Typically, evaluators use a verbatim transcript of each session and content analysis. This qualitative analytical tool is a formal methodology for structuring and systematically analyzing written or spoken information. (In Chapter Fifteen in this book, Caudle describes how to do content analysis.) But with specific regard to focus groups, Krueger (1988) notes that immediately after the interview, the moderator, and if appropriate, assistant moderator, should have a debriefing session in which they prepare a summary of the conversation that includes the findings and interpretations related to the issues being studied. They should also document such things as changes to the question sequence, levels of enthusiasm, themes and subthemes, and body language. These preliminary summaries and initial impressions are important because multiple sessions blur together and it is easy to forget what was said in a particular group. Once transcripts or, at a minimum, detailed write-ups of the sessions become available, you can proceed to the more formal content analysis that Caudle describes.

Working with Contractors

Organizations often contract out their focus groups to polling and public relations firms, market research companies, and similar outfits. Contractors can provide skilled moderators, databases for recruiting participants, meeting facilities, recording equipment, and analytical support. They can also do much of the labor-intensive work such as contacting participants and ensuring their attendance, preparing transcripts, and drafting a final report. To get the best results with a contractor, it is important to stay engaged throughout all phases of the project. This means working with them to ensure they understand the organization needs, the issues being researched, the types of people necessary for the sessions, and the kinds of questions and probes that need to be asked.

When Worksystems held its focus groups with full-time workers in Portland, Oregon, it worked very closely with the polling firm that conducted the sessions, ensuring that the firm understood what Worksystems did and the information it needed. Over time, a healthy relationship developed between sponsor and contractor, which was evident in the preparation of the interview questions. Worksystems and the polling firm played key roles in drafting the questions. Worksystems, because of its subject matter knowledge, identified what needed to be asked. The polling firm, because of its expertise in focus groups, knew which questions would be effective and which ones would not. In the end, Worksystems was pleased with the results, but this occurred in large part because of the time it spent with the contractor up front (Kristin Wolff, interview by the author, Nov. 2002).

The cost of contracting out focus groups can vary considerably depending on the location, the participants, and the number of sessions, but it can be as much as several thousand dollars per session. Although this may be less expensive than other data collection techniques such as mailed surveys, it can be quite expensive when measured on a per participant basis. Specific costs can include the moderator, participant meals, honoraria for the participants, room fees, recording equipment, transcription services, and project staff time.

Given these costs, is it better to conduct the focus groups in-house or contract them out? The simple answer to this is to choose the method that will produce the best-quality data. The box provides guidance on making this decision.

Tips on How to Determine Whether to Conduct a Focus Group In-House or Contract Out

• What is the evaluation budget? Although contracting out can be costly, in-house evaluation can also be expensive in terms of staff time and time spent away from other responsibilities. There might also be such out-of-pocket expenses as recruiting incentives, travel costs, recording equipment rental, and transcription services. When all of these expenses are added up, the additional costs of contracting out the focus groups may not be that much more costly.

• How accessible is the target population? If there is a readily accessible list of potential candidates, recruiting participants might be relatively easy. However, if the population of interest is a particular demographic profile as opposed to known individuals, the databases of a polling or market research firm might be needed. Depending on the nature of the population, recruiting candidates can be the most time-consuming component of focus groups.

• What level of expertise is available to conduct the focus groups, analyze the data, and report out the results? Moderating a focus group requires considerable facilitation skills and practice, and developing suitable questions that will produce the needed information is not as easy as it seems. Analyzing the data in a systematic and structured format requires skill as well, and can also be quite time-consuming, whereas contractors can produce a final report within a few weeks of the final session, and in some cases, even less time.

Conclusion

Focus groups are extremely flexible, can be completed in a matter of weeks, and can enrich other data collection techniques such as surveys. Like all other methodologies, they have limitations, are not suitable for all inquiries, and require specific expertise to design and carry out. However, when appropriately applied, focus groups are a powerful tool for generating data on how people think or feel, reasons for their behavior, exploring their experiences, and testing specific proposals.

References

Hart, P. D., and Teeter, B. "Attitudes Toward the Department of Homeland Security: Key Research Findings." Memo to the Partnership for Public Service, Oct. 10, 2002. [www.ourpublicservice.org].

Krueger, R. A. *Focus Groups: A Practical Guide for Applied Research*. Thousand Oaks, Calif.: Sage, 1988.

National Commission on the High School Senior Year. *The Lost Opportunity of Senior Year: Finding a Better Way*. Washington, D.C.: National Commission on the High School Senior Year, Jan. 2001.

Steen, B. "Opportunities Missed: Reflections on Transitions From High School." Slide presentation prepared for the National Commission on the High School Senior Year, Fleishman-Hillard Research, Oct, 30, 2000. [www.commissiononthesenioryear.org].

Stewart, D. W., and Shamdasani, P. N. *Focus Groups: Theory and Practice*. Thousand Oaks, Calif.: Sage, 1990.

U.S. General Accounting Office. *Federal Recruiting and Hiring: Making Government Jobs Attractive to Prospective Employees*. Washington, D.C.: U.S. General Accounting Office, Aug. 22, 1990a.

U.S. General Accounting Office. *National Coinage Proposals: Limited Public Demand for New Dollar or Elimination of Pennies*. Washington, D.C.: U.S. General Accounting Office, May 23, 1990b.

U.S. General Accounting Office. *New Dollar Coin: Marketing Campaign Raised Public Awareness But Not Widespread Use*. Washington, D.C.: U.S. General Accounting Office, Sept. 13, 2002.

Worksystems. "Report of Findings from Three Focus Groups and a Survey of 500 Full-time Workers in Washington, Multnomah, Clackamas, Clark, and Tillamook Counties." Unpublished paper, July 2001.

13

Collecting Data in the Field

Demetra Smith Nightingale, Shelli Balter Rossman

There is much interest among policymakers, public officials, the media, and the general public in understanding what actually occurs in programs at the ground level and learning what kinds of services or programs seem to work best for different target groups or in different localities. Evaluators are often called on to examine how local programs or agencies operate and how services are delivered. The operational inquiry might be part of a multifaceted formal evaluation, or it might occur independently as a self-contained study. The focus of analysis might be one program in a single location or several programs in multiple locations, and the study might be cross-sectional in nature (conducted at one point in time) or longitudinal (addressing operations over some time period). In addition to formal evaluations, federal and state officials and program managers routinely visit local programs to get a better sense of operational reality. Public officials with monitoring responsibilities, for example, visit programs to review specific issues.

Virtually all program evaluations are field based to some extent, meaning that researchers generally collect data in the field where programs are located. While on site, evaluators systematically collect information through surveys, focus groups, structured interviews with officials or staff, and case file reviews. One method of data collection that has become very common in program evaluations is semistructured interviews with administrators, staff, and program customers, conducted to document various aspects of a program or agency. This type of fieldwork is frequently part of process studies, implementation analyses, or organizational assessments, as well as outcome evaluations.

This chapter describes approaches to collecting data about programs in the field, including multisite studies that are part of formal evaluations, as well as separate process studies and less extensive efforts that are more appropriate for routine program monitoring and oversight. The box contains some examples of field research study objectives.

Objectives of Field Studies

The details of fieldwork depend on the objectives of the data collection, which are based on the overall objectives of the study or project within which the fieldwork occurs. It is important to fully understand what the fieldwork is intended to achieve, how it fits into the conceptual framework of the evaluation as a whole, and the categories of information it is expected to collect.

The objectives of the fieldwork determine both the focus (priorities) and the scope (intensity) of the data collection activity. At least two types of fieldwork are commonly conducted: program management and program evaluation.

Program Management Fieldwork Model

Federal, state, and local program managers routinely conduct monitoring reviews that involve field visits, reviews of records, interviews, and observations. The topics or issues reviewed depend on the needs of management (such as determining compliance with regulations or improving program performance). Analysis may be quantitative or qualitative, ideally based on predetermined management standards or criteria. The fieldwork is usually conducted by managers or staff of public agencies. However, in some cases, contractors may be engaged to carry out the management review, for example, as part of a performance monitoring project or an assessment of technical assistance needs. The results, typically presented in site reports, may lead to recommendations for corrective action or performance improvement.

Program Evaluation Fieldwork Model

Evaluators typically collect information on predetermined topics. The classification of topics is based on the overall evaluation project and its objectives. Various data collection methods might be used, including interviews, surveys, focus groups, observation, statistical compilations, and record reviews. Standard social science principles (such as validity, reliability, and objectivity) must be considered in developing the fieldwork plan. Ideally, the

Examples of Field Research Study Objectives

Implementation Evaluation of Welfare-to-Work Programs in New York City (Nightingale and others, 2002)

Performance analysis objective	Examine program participation and outcomes over eight years.
Implementation analysis objectives	Describe the organization, management and service delivery procedures in local welfare offices and in programs under contract to serve welfare recipients.
	Identify policy, bureaucratic, and political factors that influence the way local programs are structured and managed.

Program Outcome Evaluation of a Child Support Enforcement Collections System (Holcomb and Nightingale, 1989)

Performance analysis objectives	Estimate the impact of the information clearinghouse in five demonstration states on child support collections and government savings.
Implementation analysis objectives	Document and assess how the clearinghouse was planned, implemented, and operated.
	Assess the feasibility of implementing and operating the automated clearinghouse by identifying problems encountered and solutions applied.
	Identify differences in the clearinghouse across the five demonstration states and reasons for the differences.

Impact Evaluation of an Aftercare Program for Substance Abusers (Rossman, Roman, Buck, and Morley, 1999)

Impact analysis objectives	Compare substance abuse relapse and criminal recidivism of offenders randomly assigned to receive program services (OPTS clients) to the same outcomes for offenders not enrolled in the program.

Implementation analysis objectives	Document and assess the implementation of collaboration between probation and parole entities and service providers and document and assess the nature and extent of case management and core services (substance abuse treatment, employment, housing, medical and mental health treatment, and family support) provided to OPTS clients.

fieldwork and the evaluation are based on theoretical models and hypotheses. Both qualitative and quantitative analysis may be conducted. Individuals who have academic or professional training in research or evaluation usually conduct the fieldwork. Evaluators can be either staff of public agencies or researchers from outside research organizations or universities. The results of the work are presented in project reports and often are integrated into other components of the evaluation.

Each of these and other fieldwork models can potentially involve similar types of data collection methods, but each is based on somewhat different professional practices and experience. The important point is that the specific objectives of the fieldwork set boundaries or standards for the data collection effort. Although it is not essential that a study have a clearly defined fieldwork model, one usually exists, even if it is unstated. The fieldwork model—or reason for conducting the study—heavily influences specific details about how the fieldwork is designed, the types of data collection instruments used, the professional backgrounds of data collectors and analysts, and the types of quality control and analytic methods employed. These issues are discussed in the sections that follow.

Thus, fieldwork is conducted for at least two purposes:

- To describe what happens at the level being examined (local office, local program, local agency, local community, state office, state agency, and so on) by collecting information about procedures and data on outcomes
- To explain why the situations are as they are

The specific objectives of a fieldwork effort usually fall under one or both of these two general purposes. Before researchers design the detail of the fieldwork, it is critical that they articulate clearly and specifically the evaluation questions and issues that relate to the fieldwork portion of the study. Some field studies have very specific objectives, even though the overall evaluation addresses broader issues. In contrast, some field-based components of evaluations are called on to address broader programmatic issues, while other components focus on specific questions.

For example, in most large-scale program evaluations that estimate client impacts at the individual level (such as the effect a program has on individual employment or educational achievement), a field data collection component may investigate in detail specific aspects of the program being evaluated, such as organizational structure, intake procedures, management functions, and staff job satisfaction. An impact analysis component would focus on statistically estimating the change in individual outcomes. Thus, many program impact evaluations commonly include process analysis or implementation analysis components that involve fieldwork to document specific details of a program. The qualitative descriptors can then be transformed into quantitative program descriptor variables and incorporated into statistical analyses of program impacts on individual clients to explain the impact findings more fully.

In most evaluations, it is necessary to build the fieldwork design around the basic evaluation questions. An institutional analysis of the Work Incentive Program (WIN) for welfare recipients, for example, was designed to examine the organizational, managerial, and service delivery characteristics of high- and low-performing state and local programs to determine what seemed to be related to differences in performance (Mitchell, Chadwin, and Nightingale, 1979). The resulting information was used to develop performance improvement strategies for the program nationally. The study had two components: a quantitative analysis of program performance and a more qualitative analysis of programmatic features of high- and low-performing programs. The second component relied heavily on information obtained by teams of evaluators who conducted fieldwork in forty-three local communities.

Design Issues

When the evaluation questions, objectives, and issues of interest have been clearly specified, the evaluators need to make a number of design decisions:

- Determine an appropriate method for guiding the data collection and subsequent analysis
- Select sites
- Decide which types of data collection instruments to use and then develop them
- Identify and select respondents

These decisions depend greatly on any cost and time constraints that may exist. Evaluations addressing similar or even identical questions may use different fieldwork designs reflecting different cost and time constraints.

Frameworks for Guiding Data Collection

It is sometimes tempting to attempt to examine all aspects of an agency or program using unstructured data collection methods—often described as "getting into the field and finding out what is going on." While one might obtain a valuable sense of "what is going on" from a study like this, it is not based on a conceptual framework, it lacks methodological rigor, and the credibility of findings reported may be compromised. However, one of the greatest pitfalls in conducting field-based studies is the risk associated with collecting too much information; analysts can easily become overwhelmed with mounds of qualitative and quantitative information: field notes, interview transcripts, focus group reports, management reports, and site reports, among others. Unless the data collection stage is well organized, the analysis will be very difficult and subject to problems of accuracy and reliability. To avoid subsequent analytic problems, it is important to use or develop guidelines or a framework at the beginning to help focus the study.

Just as there is no common set of research questions that field-based studies are called on to address, neither is there a common framework used to guide the data collection—in other words, there is no cookie-cutter framework that can be adopted. Instead the evaluators must develop an overriding framework for each study. In some evaluations, the guidance can be based on the research questions and using them to structure the data collection. Many studies use graphical logic models to help structure data collection. In large-scale evaluations, more theoretical conceptual models often are used.

Research Questions. Here is a sampling of the many types of research questions that might be addressed in studies that are likely to involve fieldwork:

- *What are the major goals and assumptions underlying the policy that was adopted?* What are the policy's underlying premises and assumptions? What is the policy intended to accomplish? How does this vary by level of program (for example, state, local)?
- *What are the main program outcomes and performance of a program or policy?* How are outcomes and performance measured? What are the priorities among measures? How consistent are the various outcome and performance criteria? What is the trend in performance over time or across sites?
- *What are the organizational and service delivery structure and context in which the policy is operationalized?* How is the organization structured? What are

staff roles and responsibilities? What organizational arrangements and linkages are in place to deliver services? What types of interagency and interprogram interactions and collaborations are involved?

- *How are key management functions carried out, and what role do they play in the program?* How is program planning structured? Who is involved? What types of management information are used and for what purposes (planning, monitoring, performance analysis, performance improvement, evaluation, or something else)?
- *Is the program following the formally established strategy?* Are all the components implemented as required? Are all the components implemented efficiently? If linkages among components are necessary, are they all in place? Are some components weaker than others?
- *How are services delivered, and how do clients flow through the service delivery system?*

Research questions such as these are commonly posed to evaluators. A small-scale evaluation might address one specific type of issue—for example, how key management functions, such as program planning, are carried out in a particular program. The important dimensions of that general issue can be clarified in discussions with policymakers or program administrators or agency officials. Then the evaluators can specify the types of questions or data items that will have to be collected and the types of respondents in the field who might be interviewed. Thus, small-scale studies focusing on one or just a few localities and on a few related issues can usually develop a data collection and fieldwork plan by carefully specifying the various dimensions of the evaluation questions at hand. The key point is that it is important to have a clear guide for collecting information in the field, even if the evaluation question seems simple and straightforward. A study guide can help the evaluators maintain objectivity and avoid overcollection of information. A study framework based on research questions should at a minimum include:

- Clarifying each of the evaluation questions to be addressed in the study
- Identifying types of information required to address each question (for example, program procedure information, program data on outcomes, organizational information, staff perceptions on key issues, customer satisfaction)
- Specifying data collection strategies to use to collect each item of information (for example, management information data, staff surveys, administrator interviews, customer or user surveys)

Logic Models. At a somewhat higher level of methodological sophistication, evaluators often benefit from using a diagrammatic or graphic model to specify the key dimensions of the issue being addressed and how different dimensions or factors relate to each other and to the research questions and evaluation outcomes. Flowcharts and logic models have long been used by public administrators to plan and develop programs: specifying program components, client-flow procedures, management activities, and program outcomes. (See Chapter One, this volume, for more on logic models and their use in evaluations.) Logic models are used for developing programs and delivery systems to improve the quality of services, such as to ensure that mental health service treatments or interventions are appropriate and consistent with clinical practice (Hernandez, 2000). Decision points and action sequences are included in models, and some indicate when different levels of a program or organization interact around a particular activity or service.

Just as flow models have been routinely used in program planning development and administration, they are now increasingly used for program evaluations of management issues and other issues that involve sequential phenomena (Abbott, 1995). Carefully developed logic models have the potential to improve service provision or program management because the model, or plan, incorporates a theoretical understanding of how different actions or steps interact to produce certain outcomes. If outcomes are less than acceptable, staff and managers can use the logic model to diagnose problem points and suggest improvement strategies.

Implementation Models. Large-scale evaluations of public programs generally include implementation analysis components, as well as individual impact analysis, cost-benefit analysis, and program outcome analysis. Program implementation components of large evaluations often focus on the details of program processes: understanding the internal dynamics and structure of a program, the organizational context in which the program operates, how clients enter and move through the program, and how the program is structured and managed. (See Chapter Three, this volume.) Describing and analyzing the process involves delineating program services or client activities into discrete components, documenting how these components fit together in terms of client flow, and obtaining a variety of perspectives from people inside and outside the program on the strengths and weaknesses of the various components. Process analysis is considered a subcategory of implementation analysis, focusing on the specific procedures (such as provisions of services and client flow) that occur at the operational service delivery level.

Using graphic depictions similar to logic models, program implementation and process studies that are embedded into comprehensive evaluations often use conceptual framework models that are used to guide the development of hypotheses, data collection, and analysis. Implementation analysis draws from many academic disciplines, especially those related to organizational behavior, social networks, economic behavior, and group dynamics.

Implementation studies of welfare-to-work programs, for example, have drawn extensively from organizational theory and systems theory to build a conceptual framework that defines the various categories of information that will be collected in the field. Figure 13.1 shows a simplified depiction of an implementation framework used in impact evaluations documenting and assessing factors that influence program outcomes (Rossman, Roman, Buck, and Morley, 1999). The general premise is that some factors (such as the economy, funding levels, or political priorities) totally outside the control of managers and administrators affect how a program is structured and designed. The decisions about structure, design and operations in turn influence the nature of service delivery and, ultimately program outcomes.

Evaluating the implementation of a program or policy therefore requires documenting each factor or component that is hypothesized to influence outcomes. A carefully specified framework that defines the factors in each category can form the basis for organizing data collection instruments and analysis to explain how a program operates.

Large implementation studies based on theoretical understanding of how organizations and programs operate stand in contrast to less formal efforts that do not use formal fieldwork protocols and involve visiting a few convenient sites, meeting with local administrators, touring a program, and possibly speaking with clients. Some theoretical models from certain disciplines such as economics or sociology can be adapted to serve as conceptual frameworks for field studies. Systems theory and program logic models can also be used to establish conceptual frameworks for field-based studies.

Program implementation is complex. To fully understand what is happening in a program, the evaluator must examine it from different perspectives and view each component of the program separately as well as part of a whole entity. Without a guiding framework, it is very easy to become overwhelmed in the details and lose track of the program as a whole. Conceptual models and frameworks help the evaluator stay organized and avoid information overload. There is no one standard conceptual framework. Each study requires developing a framework that draws on relevant intellectual theory from established academic disciplines or from accumulated knowledge from past studies of similar programs or policies.

Site Selection and Staffing

Two issues are particularly important in selecting sites for field studies: the unit of analysis and the extent to which the findings are to be generalized to other sites. Final decisions on how many sites to include in the field study, however, depend heavily on the resources available and the staffing required. In most field studies, decisions about staffing and site selection are made simultaneously.

Figure 13.1. Simplified Components of an Implementation Analysis Conceptual Framework

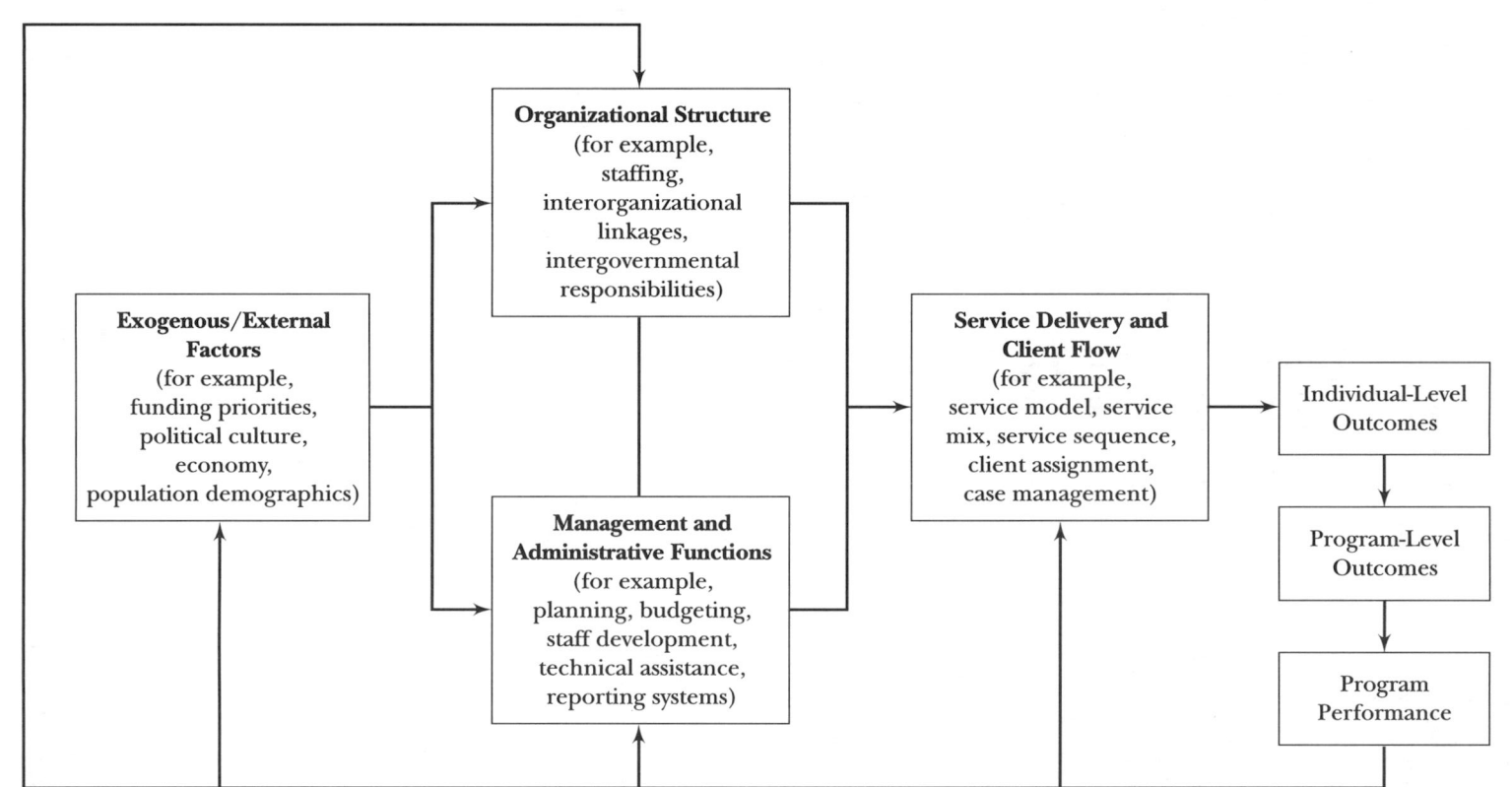

Source: Rossman, Roman, Buck, and Morley (1999).

Unit of Analysis. One of the first issues to address before selecting sites for a field study is clarifying the unit of analysis for the fieldwork portion of the evaluation. The unit, or level, of analysis will determine the types of sites that will be selected for the field data collection. The unit of analysis is usually obvious from the evaluation questions. For example, if the primary evaluation objective is to document and analyze school management and organization, the units of analysis are local schools, and the fieldwork sites will be schools. If the evaluation objective is to document local programs' exemplary approaches to serving teenage mothers, the units of analysis and the study sites are local programs serving this population.

These are fairly straightforward examples. In the real work setting of evaluation, though, the choice is usually more complicated. There are often multiple dimensions to evaluations that require different levels of analysis. For instance, if the evaluation objective is to determine how teenage mothers feel about their circumstances and the services available to them, these mothers are the units of analysis. But the evaluators must decide how—that is, from what source—to identify the mothers: schools, hospitals, local programs, welfare rolls, cities, and states. These then also become units of analysis. The final analysis might focus on mothers served by local programs in general, or on each local program (with the mothers each of them serve), or on both levels of analysis. Thus, if evaluators want to be able to discuss individual programs in their analysis, they should consider this when selecting the sites where the fieldwork is to be conducted—for example, a city, a neighborhood, or one or more institutions or programs serving the city or neighborhood.

Multiple levels of analysis are common in program organizational evaluations, that is, evaluations not just focusing on individuals. In a national evaluation of coordination between welfare programs and job training programs, for example, a number of units of analysis are possible: local communities (within which all job training and welfare programs would be examined), states (within which all job training and welfare programs would be examined), one or more specific job training programs (which could be examined at the state or local level), or one or more specific welfare programs (which could be examined at the state or local level).

When there are several possible units of analysis, decisions about site selection are typically based on how the information acquired in the fieldwork will be used by the evaluators. If the purpose is to prepare case studies, each of which can stand on its own, it is not necessary to select the same types of sites. An examination of coordination, for instance, could include one or more local communities, as well as one or more states. If the purpose is more analytical— perhaps to examine factors that encourage or discourage coordination between two programs—then the evaluators should select sites that represent as broad a range as possible of the various types of programs and situations, such as including programs of varying sizes, urban and rural locations, or programs serving populations with different demographic characteristics.

The unit of analysis for fieldwork studies should be obvious based on the overall evaluation issues specified. Common units of analysis in evaluations are local programs, local offices, individual local facilities (such as libraries or schools), cities, neighborhoods, institutions, and states.

Number of Sites. Once it is clear what units of analysis should be used, the evaluators must decide how many sites to include. This decision is usually determined by resource constraints. Four main factors affect the resource levels required for fieldwork:

- Travel distance
- Length of time on site
- Level of evaluation staff required
- Number of evaluation staff required

The cost of each of these factors will be governed by the intensity of data collection. If the field efforts are exploratory, involving unstructured data collection activities, such as discussions with key officials or staff in a program, then each site visit can probably be limited to a short period of time—one or two days—when one evaluator works alone. That person should be fairly senior to ensure that the exploration is as comprehensive as possible. At the other extreme, an evaluation that involves collecting detailed descriptions of program operations by surveying or interviewing a number of staff in each site will require more days on site, probably more than one staff person, and a longer period of time.

A number of evaluations of welfare and employment and training programs have included an implementation, or process analysis, component. Typically, the fieldwork design involves a team of two evaluators, with one fairly senior and the other either a midlevel evaluator or a research assistant. The two-person team is on site for three to five days, depending on the size of the site or city and the scope of the inquiry. Two-person teams have proved to be the most efficient for collecting accurate data and analyzing and interpreting the information. The evaluation team can discuss issues and share contextual insights that greatly strengthen the overall quality of information.

Many different activities might be carried out while on site. Site visits can be demanding and caution should be exercised to avoid placing too high a workload burden on the field staff. To provide a rough estimate of the staff resources required on site, two trained evaluators working together can be expected to accomplish any one of the following types of activities in one day:

- Each person can usually conduct three or four one-hour interviews with staff, administrators, or community officials, allowing time for preparing for each interview and reviewing notes before starting the next interview.
- Depending on the study, the team together can conduct two or three focus groups (which may last one to two hours each).
- Each evaluator can administer six forty-five-minute in-person questionnaires.
- The team can review case records. A typical welfare case record review, for example, takes between fifteen and forty-five minutes, depending on what information needs to be extracted from the files.
- A two-person team can perform a well-planned combination of two activities, such as one or two in-person interviews and one focus group session, during the same day.

Evaluations generally involve using multiple data collection methods on site, and often several types as well, such as participant observation or statistical data collection from management information systems. Thus, the resources devoted to each site visit depend on the mix of activities to be conducted. Fieldwork can become quite expensive. For example, on-site fieldwork that involves collecting data on programs in ten cities, each in a different state, using a two-person team (one senior evaluator and one midlevel evaluator) on site for one week per city, would require about one hundred person-days, at a cost of between $50,000 to $100,000 for labor, travel, per diem, and expenses. An additional 100 to 200 person-days would be required for previsit preparations and post-visit report writing.

There are lower-cost staffing configurations that may be fully satisfactory for some studies, such as program reviews, survey administration, or collection of routine statistical data. As an example, one public official (such as a state program monitor or program administrator, or a federal inspector or monitor, or an evaluator) can visit a local program for just one day and collect a substantial amount of information. The on-site time can be spent efficiently using carefully developed data collection instruments, scheduling activities in advance, and following field protocol established before the visit.

Sample Selection. The sample of sites for fieldwork can be selected in a number of ways. At one extreme, the sampling method can be random, using standard probability sampling techniques. This would require identifying a universe of possible sites, clustering or stratifying the sites on the basis of some criteria, and then randomly selecting within the strata or clusters. At the other extreme, the site selection process can be purely purposive, with specific sites or specific types of sites chosen, such as small rural sites with high-poverty populations, or award-winning programs that are considered exemplary, or large programs in high-growth economic labor markets.

Site selection for most field studies usually falls somewhere between these extremes. Evaluators examining exemplary program models might choose sites based on some feature of the program that is of particular interest—the specific populations served, unique locations, innovative program models, and special organizational structure—and choose randomly from among sites meeting those criteria.

In large part, the selection of sites depends on whether the findings from the field are intended to be representative of some larger group of programs or sites or whether they are to be used for stand-alone case studies. If the data and information from the field sites are to be generalized to a larger group of sites of programs, the selected sites should be as representative as possible of the population of sites from which the sample is drawn. If the information is to be used primarily for descriptive case studies and is intended to be illustrative only, then purposive sampling is sufficient.

Even if evaluators choose sites purposively, the selection should still be based on clear guidelines and criteria. In many cases, these resemble the types of criteria used to select sites by random stratification or clustering. Examples of selection criteria include level of program performance, rural versus urban location, level of client income, level of client ethnic concentrations, labor market condition, and geographical location.

In some field studies, site selection might evolve through the evaluators' soliciting interest from local jurisdictions, programs, or agencies. One Urban Institute study was designed to develop and then evaluate a management-oriented performance improvement model in state Work Incentive Programs serving welfare recipients (Nightingale and Ferry, 1982). The study could include only two states, and the following conditions were used to select them:

- The state agency had to have a strong potential for improvement while not currently performing at full capacity.
- The program administrators at the state level had to express a deep commitment to improving their operations.
- State officials had to be willing to participate actively in developing and implementing improvement strategies by making key staff available for the duration of the two-year project.

In the selection process, the evaluators compiled information showing how well each candidate state met the three criteria. The information was obtained through reviews of program performance reports and conversations with key state administrators.

There are no hard and fast rules about how to select sites for fieldwork studies. Site selection evolves from the general evaluation objectives. The evaluator must decide whether sites should represent maximum variation or maximum similarity. Regardless of how scientific the site selection process is, evaluators must have preestablished criteria that subsequently can be used when reporting the implications of the findings. The selection of sites should be based on the objectives of the evaluation, but the final decisions must also consider the staffing that will be required and all costs at each site.

Types and Scope of Instruments

Except in the most exploratory type of fieldwork, field evaluators will need to use one or more data collection instruments. At a minimum, the evaluation will need a field data collection guide that includes instructions for obtaining information from interviews, observations, surveys, case reviews, and focus groups. Instruments vary from highly structured to very unstructured.

The structured types of data collection instruments are best known and include surveys, questionnaires, tests, and data coding sheets. Structured instruments have specific items, questions, or codes that data collectors must use in recording information. The least structured evaluations may have no formal data collection instruments. Between are semistructured data collection instruments that consist of topical areas or subject categories, along with questions that the interviewer may use, as well as suggested wording for asking about key issues. This section examines the advantages and disadvantages of a more structured versus a less structured data collection approach.

Trade-Offs Between Semistructured and Structured Instruments. There are some important issues to consider in deciding whether to use highly structured instruments (such as questionnaires or surveys) or less structured, more open-ended interview guides. Interviewers need to be fully knowledgeable about the subject and possess strong interviewing skills if they are to use an unstructured data-gathering approach. They need to be totally familiar with the topics covered and be able to probe respondents for more or different kinds of information on a particular issue. Interviewers should also be able to guide and control the interview without leading or biasing the respondent. A more structured instrument requires less skill to administer, since it does not allow interviewers much freedom for elaboration. The main strength of a structured instrument is that data collected are easily coded and can be entered into a database relatively quickly, which means that analysis can be conducted efficiently.

A semistructured interview guide allows flexibility in the collection of data. Interviewers who are knowledgeable and well prepared can ask respondents to expand on particular issues to obtain more or different kinds of information. A skilled evaluator can gain valuable insight and data by recognizing potentially useful leads and following them to pursue details and explanations.

There are risks to allowing such flexibility. Some interviewers may seek too much information tangential to the study (for example, an interviewer may tend to focus on an issue that is of personal or professional interest to him or her) and fail to fully address the issues of concern to the evaluation. Evaluators should be cautioned about this during the data collection training.

Finally, a semistructured interview guide provides a rich amount of detail and represents a reasonable compromise between an unstructured approach (which is most appropriate for an evaluator working independently) and a highly structured approach such as a questionnaire (which does not permit the evaluator to pursue interesting or important issues that may arise during the course of the interview). Unlike structured data collection instruments, which typically are designed to collect standardized data by using close-ended responses or coded categorical responses, semistructured instruments tend to produce large volumes of qualitative notes. Unless the interview guide is carefully developed to focus directly on the required information, the evaluators may be inundated with volumes of notes that are time-consuming to organize and analyze. (See Chapter Sixteen, this volume, for more guidance on analyzing qualitative data.)

Development of Semistructured Instruments. Careful development of semistructured instruments can guard against the risk that interviewers may not fully address the issues of primary concern, and the risk of producing vast amounts of qualitative notes.

The topics in the interview guide should reflect the questions and issues specified for the study. An outline of a semistructured interview guide used in the WIN Performance Improvement Project are presented in the box. The actual interview guide had specific subtopics, probes that might help interviewers, and some sample wording of questions the interviewer might use.

Interview Guide Outline Used in the
Kentucky WIN Performance Improvement Project

Information on the person interviewed

Position, title, job responsibilities

Job expertise

Organization

Structure and staffing configuration

Host agency

Management functions

Planning and budgeting

Goals and mission

Monitoring

Reporting and management information systems

Training, staff development, and technical assistance

Management style

Communication

Distribution of authority

Interorganizational relationships

Innovativeness

Supervisory activities

Interpersonal activities

Service delivery system

Client flow

Caseload management

Provision of services

Job development and job placement

Subsidized employment

Handling noncooperative clients

Serving volunteers

Perceptions and attitudes

Job satisfaction

Perceptions of program effectiveness

Perceptions of program priorities

Source: Nightingale and Ferry (1982).

Evaluators can use one guide that contains all topics that will be addressed in the field, or they can prepare a separate interview guide for each type of respondent—for example, one guide for supervisors and one for staff, or one for personnel in one agency and another for personnel in a different agency. Separate guides allow evaluators to list specific questions that relate directly to a particular program or staff level, which reduces the amount of question modification the interviewer has to do. A general interview guide has the advantage of streamlining the data collection process and ensures maximum flexibility in each interview since the interviewer will have all possible questions readily at hand. An interviewer who realizes in the process of an interview that the respondent can address other issues can easily modify the interview.

If a general interview guide is used, it is helpful to prepare a respondent-question matrix that indicates which topics to address with each type of respondent. The respondent matrix in Exhibit 13.1 serves at least two purposes. First, the interviewer uses the matrix to prepare for each interview, and when the interview is completed, the notes are coded to correspond to the sections of the interview guide. Later in the day when the interview notes are reviewed, the field teams can ensure that all topics specified for particular respondent types were addressed; if they were not, the teams can make an effort to follow up while they are still on site. Second, once all site visits are completed, the matrix can aid the evaluators in assembling and organizing the information for analysis.

Respondent Selection. Interview guides and other data collection instruments should be developed in a way that allows straightforward identification of the types of individuals who will be interviewed—recognizing that the type of person to be interviewed will also affect the content of the instrument. This means, for example, that the interview guide should include topics delineated as clearly as necessary to help guide the interview, but not so detailed that it cannot be used easily with respondents who are not exactly of the category specified.

As with site selection, respondent selection can be done either randomly or purposively. If the focus of the field evaluation is to document or describe activities of particular types of personnel, such as managers, police officers, firefighters, social workers, or data processing clerks, then it is appropriate to select respondents randomly if all staff cannot be interviewed. Random selection may be helpful only if there is a large number of persons in the same job category, since evaluators can interview only a reasonable number of them, given time and resource constraints.

More typically, it is often necessary to interview a number of different types of individuals, possibly even from different agencies. In advance of the field visit, the evaluators should carefully identify the different types of respon-

Exhibit 13.1. Example of a Portion of a Respondent Question Matrix

Respondent Category	Subject Codes						
	Organization	Tasks	Goals	Conflict	Training	Jobs	Child Care
Local ES office manager	X	X	X	X	X	X	X
Local ES-WIN supervisor	X	X	X	X	X	X	X
Local ES-WIN staff	X	X	X	X		X	
Local SAU-WIN supervisor	X	X	X	X	X		X
Local SAU-WIN staff	X	X	X	X			X
Local welfare IMU supervisor	X		X	X			X
Local welfare IMU staff	X		X	X			X

Note: ES means Employment Service; ES-WIN refers to the staff in the ES responsible for the Work Incentive Program (WIN); SAU-WIN refers to the staff in the welfare office responsible for the WIN program, called the "separate administrative unit" or SAU; and IMU refers to the income maintenance unit in the welfare office, where intake occurs.

Source: Mitchell, Chadwin, and Nightingale (1979).

dents to be interviewed. To the extent possible, evaluators should interview more than one person in a particular category. For example, in a program that includes one manager and three supervisors, each responsible for similar work units that consist of five staff each, evaluators should interview two or three of the supervisors and a number of staff. Interviewing multiple respondents of each category will ensure that the information obtained is not biased because one person, rather than another, was selected for the evaluation. In practice, though, availability of staff during the scheduled visit is often a major selection criterion.

The fieldwork will be most efficient if preparations for the site visit interviews are made in advance. Using the respondent matrix as a guide, specific persons who will be interviewed should be identified and notified ahead of time and, if possible, interview appointments set up before evaluators arrive at the site.

Interview Guide. The interview guide can be produced in a number of different forms. Many evaluators prefer to take notes by hand during interviews, often using their own personal form of shorthand, and later type the full interview using word processing software. Most typically, an interview guide is reproduced on sheets of paper that can be bound into a booklet or stapled together. Then each interviewer can be given one of the guides to use in all interviews, recording responses in a separate notebook. Alternatively, the interviewer could use one booklet for each interview, with responses from that interview written in designated spaces on the form.

Some evaluators prefer electronic portable notepads, tablets, or notebooks—that is, small, portable personal computers. Evaluators can use traditional laptop or notebook computers and type notes during the interview, and later edit or code information as necessary. Computerized tablets or notepads allow the interviewer to write in longhand onto the special screen or tablet during the interview. The software converts the handwritten notes into standard word processing format.

Another approach is to reproduce the interview guide on index cards rather than separate sheets of paper. Each card lists one topic and all questions or issues related to it that are to be addressed in interviews. The cards can be coded to identify the type of respondent (or agency) for whom the topic is relevant, and each card can include a code that can later be used for organizing or summarizing the information from all interviews. Exhibit 13.2 presents a sample card from an interview guide (Nightingale, Holcomb, and O'Brien, 1990).

Whether to produce interview guides on paper, on cards, or in portable electronic format is a personal choice. Some evaluators prefer the index card method. The same guide (set of cards) can be used a number of times without falling apart (unlike guides on paper). This is no small benefit for multisite evaluations that might involve interviewing dozens of respondents in each site. In addition, the cards can be organized, reorganized, and reshuffled in a number of ways to allow the interviewer to streamline each interview. This allows flexibility in controlling each interview. Semistructured interviews may not follow the sequence of issues and questions in the guide; a skilled interviewer will do well to allow the respondent to continue a flow of thoughts as long as issues that are in the guide are being addressed. Using a set of cards, the interviewer can unobtrusively review all cards if necessary without distracting the respondent by flipping through pages of paper sheets. This flexibility has proven to be quite valuable in allowing the respondent to continue to discuss issues as they arise rather than saying, "We will return to that in a minute."

In large evaluations with multiple interviewers, it is usually desirable to have all interview notes recorded using the same process and topic sequence to ensure consistency. Usually the notes are typed and entered into a word processing system to systematize the interview information and allow efficient sorting of the content of text using word processing features such as "Search" and "Find." (See Chapter Sixteen, this volume, for more information on qualitative and content analysis methods.)

Exhibit 13.2. Example of One Topic in a Semistructured Interview Guide

---

[Topic]   10. Child Care   *[Sites]*   Salem, Seattle

                                                      [Respondent] Welfare staff

[Interviewer note]   [Ask of the highest-ranking person in the office, and verify with other staff]

[Subtopics]   A. Which of the following child care funding sources are available for FIP/AFDC clients?

                                     Title XX funds?
                                     WIN funds?
                                     AFDC disregard funds?
                                     Other funds? *[specify]*

                B. Which staff are responsible for authorizing the expenditure of child care funds for a particular client?

                                     ES staff?
                                     Welfare social workers?
                                     ES supervisor?
                                     Welfare supervisor?
                                     Other? *[specify]*

Note: Title XX of the Social Security Act funded child care and social services; WIN means the Work Incentive Program; AFDC is the Aid to Families with Dependent Children program; ES means the local Employment Service office.

Field Visit Protocol

Fieldwork projects require careful attention to many procedural and logistical details before, during, and after the site visits. This section discusses the protocol—the critical procedures that should be developed—for a field visit. Field evaluators should be fully trained on these details. Procedures should be followed precisely to ensure that the information collected is of high quality, that different evaluators collect information in a comparable manner, that the fieldwork is minimally obtrusive, and that confidentiality is maintained to the maximum extent possible.

Previsit Preparations

The successful completion of the on-site portion of an evaluation that includes fieldwork depends critically on careful preparation before the site visit. Evaluators should not underestimate the importance of the previsit activities. Previsit preparations include a variety of activities, from setting up site-specific files of existing materials to handling logistical arrangement and recruiting and training field staff.

During the early stages of planning an evaluation, materials should be assembled from a variety of sources, such as government program files, agency and program Internet Web sites, grant applications, existing databases, or site narratives from prior field trips or evaluation files. Where feasible, these materials should be organized into files associated with each of the designated field sites. A log of contacts (such as phone conversations with the key contact person or program director in each site) can also be included in each site file or folder.

For evaluations in which many documents are being collected from each site, attach a checklist of materials requested to the site's master folder or file. The materials should be checked off as they are received. Follow-up requests should be made and noted on the log. A log of contacts is especially important in studies that will be conducted over a long period of time and those involving several researchers because it serves as the official record for the study. All files and contacts must be carefully documented to allow the evaluation to be completed efficiently regardless of changes that might occur within the project (for example, if the evaluation team changes due to turnover or if evaluator assignments change).

Site Clearances. Initial contact with field sites should identify any constraints that might affect scheduling or data collection. For example, to gain entry into schools, evaluators may need to obtain clearances from high levels in an agency to speak to teachers and staff, or there may be other evaluations underway in the same site, which might require coordinating schedules. If entry clearance or interview authorizations are needed, the evaluator should clarify who is responsible for obtaining approvals (that is, the evaluator or the contact person in the agency), whose permission must be sought, and what information is needed to facilitate the process. Scheduling must be sufficiently flexible to accommodate delays due to bureaucratic obstacles; nevertheless, planning should include actions that can be taken to minimize schedule slippage.

Scheduling Visits and Interviews. Several factors, including travel distance and level of staffing required, affect site scheduling. Early communication should identify a primary contact person at selected sites who can serve as liaison to the evaluation and a tentative date or time period or possible alternative schedule for the visit. This scheduling will permit advance planning of logistics, such as travel reservations and field staffing assignments. Economies of scale in both travel savings and staffing often can be achieved when visits to geographically close sites can be scheduled together.

Information packages should be assembled and sent to the local contact person to provide background information about the evaluation. These should include:

- An overview of the evaluation objectives, as well as the scope of each field visit
- Assurances that confidentiality procedures will be followed (for either individuals interviewed or for the site as a whole, depending on the study)
- A sample schedule that the evaluation team would like to follow, identifying those the team wants to interview or meet with, for how long, and the times each day that the field evaluation team members will be available

Either the field visit team or the designated site contact person can schedule the interviews. The division of responsibility should be clearly established as soon as possible. During that discussion, the evaluators should review with the contact person the list of potential respondents, verifying that appropriate categories of staff have been identified, and identifying other persons who may also be important to interview. Usually the initial interview in a site should be with the key contact person, who can provide an overview of the system.

Evaluators need to decide whether they will conduct individual or group interviews and determine the appropriate setting for conducting the interviews. If interview topics are sensitive or there is a need to ensure individuals' confidentiality, one-on-one interviews rather than group interviews should be planned, with private rooms secured for each session. Even when confidentiality is not an issue, reasonable efforts should be made to secure quiet, unobtrusive settings for interviewing to minimize distractions, which can reduce the quality of responses.

Once the field visit has been scheduled, personnel at the site should be notified by phone, mail, or e-mail of the dates for the visit and the time scheduled for the interview. Several days prior to the visit, contact should be made with the key contact person and possibly with each respondent to reconfirm plans, review the proposed agenda, and ensure the scheduling of the interviews.

Defining Information Needs. Evaluators often collect program materials, agency reports, and other documents related to the study site. It is important to request copies of relevant reports in advance of the actual visit. During the initial telephone conversations regarding the site visit schedule, for example, evaluators should ask about reports, organization charts, procedure manuals, and other program descriptions, and request copies for review before the visit. If the evaluators intend to collect copies of records of documents while on site, they should discuss their needs in advance with the key contact person or respondents, and encourage site personnel to assemble the information before the visit. This is especially helpful if a large number of documents or files are needed or if the site has limited resources, such as a small number of staff or limited access to duplicating equipment, that might make it difficult to compile requested information.

Staffing Assignments. Decisions about the division of labor should be made as early as possible so that field staff know which sites they will cover, which interviews they will be responsible for conducting, and the specific issues they will be exploring. Once field assignments are established, staff should review materials already on hand, such as organization charts, management information reports, grant applications, program planning documents, and fiscal forms. At the same time, staff should review the checklist of requested documents, noting which materials still need to be collected in advance or when on site.

The issue of field staff safety bears special mention. Both real and perceived risks of working in some communities (such as high-crime neighborhoods) can make it difficult to hire qualified researchers to staff certain projects. It is crucial to consider the kinds of actions that may be taken to ensure staff safety. Following are some strategies that help:

- Use two-person teams for site visits in high-risk areas, possibly including someone on the team who is familiar with the local situation.
- Schedule interviews only in public locations, such as public offices, libraries, fast food restaurants, or other well-lit, high-traffic facilities.
- Train staff to take appropriate logistical precautions (such as having a clear set of directions and a map, a sufficient quantity of gas, accessible cell phones preprogrammed with key contact information and local numbers for assistance, and knowledge of public transportation options or how to arrange for taxicabs).
- Prepare field evaluators about watching out for their own safety. Teach them the kinds of situations to avoid (such as isolated parking locations or walking a long distance in unfamiliar territory and public displays of large amounts of cash or expensive jewelry).

Project Orientation. Unless the fieldwork is of very short duration or involves fewer than three field researchers, the team should prepare a document specifying procedures that field data collection staff are to follow. Such a document is useful for both previsit training of the teams and as a reference to use while in the field.

The project field documents should include the following:

- The overall objectives of the evaluation and the specific purpose of the field visits
- Item-by-item instructions for administering instruments, including the definition of terms used in the project
- Advice on how to gain respondent cooperation and, where necessary, procedures appropriate to obtaining informed consent

- Confidentiality requirements, including privacy during interviews
- Procedures for conducting interviews
- Procedures for collecting other data, such as structured observations, questionnaire distribution or administration, or record audits
- Quality control procedures, including instructions on how to edit field notes
- Administrative requirements, such as accounting and reporting procedures for submitting expense reports, obtaining reimbursement for travel, per diem rates, and so on
- Recommendations for managing time while on site

Training. Training for field teams should cover all aspects of the field visits, including going over the instruments and all procedures in detail. Another important topic to include in the training relates to how to gain and maintain respondent cooperation. The level of cooperation secured will be partially dependent on the interviewer's ability to listen to the respondent, being aware of any sensitivities or anxieties the respondent might have, and responding appropriately to place the respondent at ease.

Before going into the field or sending staff, evaluators should consider the kinds of issues or resistance that respondents may raise. Training should incorporate answers to anticipated questions and should include having team members practice appropriate responses to likely situations or procedures to follow in the event of unforeseen events that could pose a threat to data collection. In large evaluations, these mock interviews are sometimes videotaped to provide immediate and forceful feedback to the interviewers.

Site Packets. Before the field trip, research staff should review the planned on-site procedures to assess their need for supplies and equipment, such as writing implements, notepads, electronic devices, and other office supplies that they should bring. We have found that two long (one-hour) or three short interviews can be recorded in a notebook the size of a journalist's notebook (about six by eight inches). Staff should plan to take a few extra notebooks on each field visit to avoid running out.

If visits to several sites are linked or researchers anticipate collecting large amounts of bulky material, it may be desirable to bring along prepaid mailing labels and envelopes to send completed materials back to the home office. Since data, such as interview responses, may not be replaceable if lost, it is probably wise to use courier-type delivery services, which have sophisticated tracking capabilities, virtually guaranteeing that packages will not be lost.

On-Site Procedures

Information on important on-site activities for which evaluators should be prepared should be included in the field visit protocol (procedures) developed before conducting the site visits.

Maintaining the Schedule and Interviewing Protocol. It is not possible to guarantee a particular response rate in advance. However, with appropriate planning and effort (such as careful scheduling, guidelines for encouraging respondent cooperation, and having contingency plans for various situations), the team should be able to achieve a high interview completion rate, approaching 100 percent of those scheduled in advance. Professional demeanor and ability to conduct interviews without exhibiting judgment or excessive sympathy or emotion are particularly important.

If a respondent is reluctant to cooperate, field staff should attempt to convert reticence into cooperation. A first step is to ascertain whether the respondent has concerns or questions about the study or the interview that can be resolved, thus permitting the interview to proceed. For example, the timing may be inconvenient, in which case rescheduling the interview might resolve the impasse. In some cases, a rescheduled interview can be completed later in the visit or, if necessary, at a later time by telephone. If this does not succeed, it may be best to allow another interviewer or the evaluation supervisor to attempt the interview at a future time.

A pilot test, or pretest, should be conducted in at least one site to try out all instruments and procedures. This will help identify revisions or corrections that are needed. In most evaluations, the pilot site can also be part of the formal field evaluation since most of the same information will be collected.

Collecting and Recording Information. Field evaluators should be given materials that help them explain the purpose of the study to respondents as well as permit them to move efficiently through the planned interview. Each interview should begin with a brief introduction to the project. (An example is provided in the box.) Each respondent must understand the project and the purpose of the interview. Explaining the project takes only one or two minutes and is one of the most important parts of the interview. In these first few minutes, the interviewer should establish an environment that places the respondent at ease.

Introducing the Project to the Respondent

"I am a researcher who has been contracted by Agency A to evaluate the state's Program for Family Independence. This first wave of interviews focuses on early planning and implementation issues and any problems or special issues during start-up. We are also interested in learning about the flow of clients through your system. We are interviewing staff in this local office and staff in other related agencies. We will be back to conduct interviews approximately every six months over the next four years."

Immediately after the introduction, the interviewer should address confidentiality. If the respondent's name is going to be included in a report, that must be explained at the time of the interview. If all information is to be confidential, meaning no names will be included in the report and no findings will be attributed to anyone by name, that needs to be explained. Confidential interviews are more likely than "public" interviews to produce rich detail—if the respondent understands the confidentiality pledge and believes that the interviewer will abide by the pledge. This is true even if the information being requested is not sensitive. (See the box for an example.)

Example Statement of Confidentiality

"It is very important for us to learn how the Program for Family Independence operates here, problems or issues you may have identified, and suggestions for how a program like this should be run. This is a new program, and it is essential for us to document its implementation and ongoing development. We need your cooperation to do this, since you know the most about welfare and employment and training problems and the problems that must be overcome. We are not employees of any state agency, nor are we auditors. We will be submitting reports to the state legislature, but in these reports, there will be no way that anyone could identify what any particular individual told us. We pledge confidentiality. The sources of our interview information will not be divulged to anyone else here in this office, city, or state. No names will be included in our reports. Do you have any questions before we begin?"

The evaluation should establish procedures for handling and storing the information collected, particularly if it is confidential. The procedures for maintaining confidentiality may range from not entering respondents' names into any databases that are constructed, to devising systems of randomly generated identification numbers maintained in secured computer files.

After the introduction, it is helpful to break the ice with an initial question designed to obtain background information on the respondent and ease into the interview. This can include asking the respondent his or her official job title, length of time employed with this agency, and what he or she did before this job. After this, the evaluator should move into the substance of the interview.

There are several ways to record the information from an interview: audio- or videotaping, taking notes by hand and transcribing the information into a notebook or directly onto interview forms, or using an electronic portable notebook, where notes can be written in longhand onto the electronic pad and later converted into a standard word processing format. There are pros and cons associated with each approach, and the decision about which to use is generally a matter of personal preference. Subsequent analysis of information is generally accomplished more easily when interview notes (whether initially obtained through long-hand notes or electronic methods) are transcribed into standard word processing following an established outline or topic format.

Daily Reviews. After the day's interviews are completed, interviewers should review the material gathered to add subject codes, respondent codes, and site codes where needed. The material should be cleaned and clarified to be sure it is legible and meaningful to other members of the evaluation team. For example, only agreed-on abbreviations or those defined in the interviewer notes should be used.

Some evaluators choose to dictate each day's interview notes into a tape recorder. The tapes can later be transcribed for analysis or preparation of site reports. The taping process also allows the evaluators an opportunity to review the day's information carefully.

If there is more than one evaluator on site, the team should briefly review their respective notes, data, and experiences to identify possible areas of inconsistency, issues that may have been missed totally (such as a question none of the respondents were able to answer well because it was outside all respondents' scope of responsibility), or areas that need further clarification or detail. The end-of-day debriefings afford valuable exchanges of information that can be helpful later in the analysis. The team may want to tape-record those sessions.

The major protocol guidelines for conducting interviews, taken from on an internal field training session at the Urban Institute are summarized in the box (Holcomb, 1993). These have been found to help field evaluators conduct smooth interviews, yielding accurate information.

When an interview is finished, the respondent may express interest in knowing what the evaluators are finding. Similarly, when all interviews are completed at a site, an administrator may want to discuss with the evaluators the findings or conclusions they have drawn. Evaluators will naturally be thinking about preliminary findings before they leave the site, but they should not attempt to draw conclusions or make recommendations while in the field. Later phases of the evaluation (after the site visits) should be devoted to analysis. It is very tempting to provide immediate feedback but also extremely risky, so it should be avoided. Evaluators should be prepared to respond politely to such requests by explaining that they have accumulated a large amount of information and material that will have to be carefully reviewed and analyzed before it can be reported. This response may make the evaluator slightly

Protocol and Guidelines for Field Interviewing

Preparing for the Interview

1. Interviewer should know the questions backward and forward prior to making the field visit.
2. Interviewer should know the purpose of each question. Train interviewers properly as part of field visit preparation.
3. Identify primary and secondary questions/issues, for consistency across interviews, in case some items must be omitted to stay within time limitations. Avoid asking too many questions or questions not in the interview guide.
4. Two-person field teams offer the advantage of division of labor. If this is feasible, one person can take responsibility for ensuring comprehensive coverage of interview items while the other takes responsibility for accurate and complete recording of responses.
5. Be on time. Let the respondent know if you are running late. Allow time for getting lost.

Beginning the Interview

6. Establish a positive first impression. Be appreciative at the start of the respondent's knowledge and willingness to cooperate. Take time with the introduction (5–8 minutes, maximum).
7. Assure confidentiality and define what that means and what it includes.

Conducting the Interview

8. Note taking is important—record responses verbatim. Note any interviewer impressions, observations, or interpretations separately and set that insight off with brackets.
9. Two-person field teams offer the advantage of division of labor. If this is feasible, one person can take responsibility for ensuring comprehensive coverage of interview items while the other takes responsibility for accurate and complete recording of responses.
10. Ask the respondent to pause if necessary to permit complete recording of responses.
11. Do not contradict or correct the respondent; probe his or her position if necessary to be sure you understand it.
12. If something is unclear, do not assume the respondent's meaning and do not simply write the response down if you aren't sure what it means; take the initiative to clarify responses until you understand what is being said.

13.   Ask about references to legislation, acronyms, or names that you are not familiar with.

14.   Record information as stated even if you dislike the respondent, are offended by what is said, or if you disagree with the response.

15.   Remain alert throughout each interview, especially when you think you are starting to hear the same thing over and over again—there might be important nuances you won't understand until you go over all the notes from all respondents after the site visit. Interview time should probably be limited to about one-hour to avoid mental fatigue.

16.   Identify primary and secondary questions/issues, for consistency across interviews, in case some items must be omitted to stay within time limitations. Avoid asking too many questions or questions not in the interview guide.

Post-Interview Tasks

17.   Clean notes as soon as possible, preferably right after the interview, but definitely the same day, while the session is still fresh in your mind.

18.   When different people are conducting interviews on site, they should communicate frequently—daily, if possible—to compare information and experiences and to generate a common understanding of the overall program.

19.   After the visit, send thank you letters. Remember you might return to this site for a future study.

Source: Holcomb, P. "Field Protocol." (Staff presentation). Washington, D.C.: Urban Institute, March 1993. Reprinted with permission.

uncomfortable, but it is much better than realizing later that he or she had given a program official partial or incorrect findings.

Data Maintenance and Analysis

Once field data have been amassed, they can be used to generate several types of summaries, such as frequencies, trends, contingencies, and intensities. Qualitative information can provide rich anecdotal evidence. (Caudle, in Chapter Fifteen of this volume, describes in detail qualitative data analysis methods.)

Most important when semistructured interviews are used, the evaluators need to decide how to systematically summarize the large quantity of information collected. Analyzing qualitative data is roughly equivalent to performing analysis of more structured data collection methods such as surveys, in which the documents under scrutiny are the records of interview responses. Such analysis involves organizing the data into relevant sets of content or issue categories or topics and sets of response alternatives for each content or issue category.

Even when data sets are derived from semistructured, open-ended instruments, evaluators should identify preliminary categories of possible responses prior to data collection. This structure provides guidelines that help to orient the data collection efforts. For example, anticipating certain themes and possible responses can help field staff determine whether interviews are achieving the evaluation objectives or whether evaluators need to probe further or refocus the respondents' attention. Usually preliminary categories or topics can be proposed during the fieldwork planning stage, based on the evaluation questions or hypotheses. Often the range of response alternatives can also be anticipated. However, these predetermined coding possibilities should be viewed flexibly since new themes and insights are likely to emerge during the data collection, or some anticipated topics and responses may never materialize.

One approach to data organizing is to have field evaluators sort the information for each identified research topic or category using the response alternatives postulated prior to actual data collection. The coding scheme is finalized based on feedback from field staff who are asked to identify categories or response alternatives that do not fit the data. Adjustments can be made by expanding or collapsing the initial choices of topics or responses. As analysts sort the data, they can flag any anecdotes or quotations that might enrich the final report.

A more rigorous (and costly) approach to analyzing qualitative interview notes, if resources are sufficient, is to divide the analysts into two teams to review a sample of interviews independently. Each team develops a set of content categories and response alternatives for each category based on the interview notes. The teams convene as a single group to discuss and merge the categories and responses. Once consensus is achieved, a sample of interviews can be split into subsamples of respondents. Each team receives one subsample, which they code using the agreed-on scheme; then the teams exchange samples and repeat the categorization process. This approach tests both intracoder reliability (the degree of consistency with which a coder interprets similar responses) and intercoder reliability (the degree of consistency in interpretation among different coders).

If consistency in coding is unacceptably low, there are several options for improving reliability:

- Categories can be tightened and redefined to reduce the chances for miscoding.
- A training session can be held to increase intercoder reliability by making coders more familiar with the categorization system.
- Instead of having analysts code every item for a series of interviews, each analyst can be assigned responsibility for coding the same set of questions or topics for all interviews, thus becoming the coding specialist for specific items, and thereby increasing intracoding reliability.

The data maintenance approaches described are for use when the interview information collected in the field is manually sorted and coded. The proliferation of personal computers and specialized software packages can greatly simplify this sorting process. For instance, there are content analysis programs that generate lists of unique words in one or more documents as well as the frequency of occurrence of each word. There are search programs that permit exploration of whether and in what context certain key words or phrases are used. These and other programs have streamlined qualitative data analyses. While these possibilities are intriguing, we have not yet personally tested their utility. Therefore, we are unable to suggest which approaches are useful or what limitations might be encountered in applying these programs for evaluation purposes.

Conclusion

The fieldwork portion of an evaluation provides an opportunity to collect rich detail that can augment more quantitative data that are included in the evaluation. Too often fieldwork is approached in an informal or haphazard manner that results in massive amounts of notes that cannot be easily analyzed. Evaluators should pay careful attention to developing fieldwork procedures, designing fieldwork data collection instruments, and preparing plans for managing and analyzing the information collected. Carefully implemented, fieldwork data collection can produce valid and credible information that cannot be obtained from other sources.

References

Abbott, A. "Sequence Analysis: New Methods for Old Ideas." *Annual Review of Sociology,* 1995, *21,* 93–113.

Hernandez, M. "Using Logic Models and Program Theory to Build Outcome Accountability." *Education and Treatment of Children,* 2000, *23,* 24–40.

Holcomb, P. "Field Protocol." Staff presentation at the Urban Institute, Washington, D.C., Mar. 1993.

Holcomb, P., and Nightingale, D. S. *Evaluation of the Western Interstate Child Support Enforcement Clearinghouse.* Washington, D.C.: Urban Institute, 1989.

Holcomb, P., and Nightingale, D. S. "Conceptual Underpinnings of Implementation Analysis." In T. Corbett and M. C. Lennon (eds.), *Policy into Action: Implementation Research and Welfare Reform.* Washington, D.C.: Urban Institute Press, 2003.

Mitchell, J. J., Chadwin, M. L., and Nightingale, D. S. *Implementing Welfare Employment Programs: An Institutional Analysis of the Work Incentive Program.* Washington, D.C.: Urban Institute, 1979.

Nightingale, D. S., and Ferry, D. *Assessment of the Joint Federal-State Performance Improvement Projects in the Work Incentive Program.* Washington, D.C.: Urban Institute, 1982.

Nightingale, D. S., Holcomb, P., and O'Brien, C. T. *The Structure and Operations of the Washington State Family Independence Program.* Washington, D.C.: Urban Institute, 1990.

Nightingale, D. S., and others. *Work and Welfare Reform in New York City During the Giuliani Administration.* Washington, D.C.: Urban Institute, 2002.

Rossman, S. B., Roman, C. R., Buck, J., and Morley, E. *Impact of the Opportunity to Succeed (OPTS) Aftercare Program for Substance Abusing Felons.* Washington, D.C.: Urban Institute, 1999.

14

Using Agency Records

Harry P. Hatry

The source of data that evaluators most often use is records kept by either the agency delivering the service being evaluated or by other agencies that have records relevant to the work of the program being evaluated. The term *agency records* (also called *administrative records* and *archival records*), as used in this chapter, refers to data that are not from original data collection efforts such as surveys, interviews, and trained observer ratings. Rather, they are regularly collected and recorded by an agency, whether or not an evaluation is being conducted. Examples of agency record data include:

- Information on client characteristics
- Quantity of work done
- Response times
- Information on the disposition of the work (such as number of clients successfully completing services)
- Recidivism
- Number and type of complaints
- Number of reported crimes
- Student grades
- Number of school dropouts

Carlos Manjarrez of the Urban Institute provided important help for this chapter.

- Number of reported cases of child abuse
- Number of violations of environmental regulations as reported by inspectors

The advantage of agency records for evaluations is that the data are presumably already available, thus eliminating the need for new (and, perhaps, expensive) data collection efforts. A primary limitation to the use of agency records as a source of evaluation information is that they often do not contain the data to measure important outcomes. Thus, procedures described in previous chapters, such as surveys and trained observer ratings, will often be needed as well.

It is tempting to evaluators to accept agency records at face value and not look critically at the information they contain. But "programs differ widely in the quality and extensiveness of their records and in the sophistication involved in storing and maintaining them" (Rossi, Freeman, and Lipsey, 1998, p. 211). Thus, "Archival data are never precisely what one wants or expects. Given this, the investigator is challenged to do what is possible given time and resources, in shaping the data according to needs" (Elder, Pavalko, and Clipp, 1993, p. 11).

This chapter discusses some of the issues and problems that can arise with use of agency records and suggests ways to alleviate these difficulties.

The published literature contains little discussion of the issues and problems in collecting data from agency records. Among the few authors who address the topic, even if only briefly, are Babbie (1989), Elder, Pavalko, and Clipp (1993), Rossi, Freeman, and Lipsey (1998), Kiecolt and Nathan (1985) (primarily for use of archived survey data), Krippendorff (1980), Nachmias and Nachmias (1987), Singleton, Straits, Straits, and McAllister (1988), and Webb, Campbell, Schwartz, and Sechrest (1966). Sometimes a government agency, as part of written descriptions of its procedures, briefly describes data collection problems and their alleviation, such as the Corporation for National and Community Service (2002) and the U.S. Department of Education (2001).

Throughout this chapter, the word *client* is used in a general sense. Some programs, such as criminal justice programs, work on what they refer to as cases. Other programs may have different terms for the subject of their work; for example, road maintenance programs focus on segments of roadways and recreation programs on "customers."

Potential Problems and Their Alleviation

Table 14.1 lists a number of problems that evaluators are likely to face when using agency record information. Each problem is discussed in this section.

Table 14.1. Potential Problems in Data Obtained from Agency Records
and Possible Ways to Alleviate Them

Problem	Possible Ways to Alleviate the Problem
1. Missing or incomplete date	• Go back to the records and related data sources (such as by interviewing program staff) to fill in as many gaps as possible. • Determine whether part or all of the evaluation needs to be modified or terminated. • Exclude missing data or provide a best estimate of the missing values.
2. Data available only in overly aggregated form	• Where feasible, go back into the records to reconstruct the needed data. • Undertake new, original data collection. • Drop the unavailable disaggregations from the evaluation.
3. Unknown, different, or changing definitions of data elements	• Make feasible adjustments to make data more comparable. • Focus on percentage changes rather than absolute values. • Drop analysis of such data elements when the problem is insurmountable.
4. Data that are linked across time and clients	• Be sure that the outcome data apply to the particular clients and work elements covered by the evaluation • Track the clients and work elements between agencies and offices using such identifiers as social security numbers. • Look for variations in spellings, aliases, and so on.
5. Confidentiality and privacy considerations	• Secure needed permissions from persons about whom individual data are needed. • Avoid recording client names. Instead use unique code identifiers. • Secure any lists that link unique code identifiers to client names. Destroy these after the evaluation requirements are met. • Obtain data without identifiers from agency employees (limiting subsequent analyses).

Missing or Incomplete Data

In many, if not most, instances, information on some clients or work elements will be missing or incomplete. These gaps will affect the overall accuracy of the information. This applies whether the evaluators are attempting to obtain data on all clients (all work elements) or are drawing samples from the available records. If the proportion of missing or incomplete cases is substantial for a category of cases that is important to the evaluation, this problem will be a major evaluation concern.

Once a set of data is known to be missing, it is important to determine the extent to which the missing data are random or if they vary in a systematic fashion. For example, agencies may not have data files from a given time period or they may be missing complete client records from a subcontractor. Identifying the systematic nature of missing data is the first step in recapturing, or adjusting for, what was lost. In some rare cases, the missing data may be random and can be ignored.

The evaluator should first determine whether it will be feasible to obtain the missing or incomplete information. This may not be possible, such as when data are sought for periods of time that are far in the past. In such cases, the evaluators should determine whether the number of missing cases will prevent them from answering at least some questions important to the evaluation. The evaluators might even have to terminate the entire evaluation.

Missing data have caused substantial evaluation problems, for example, in a number of state efforts to evaluate economic development programs. For example, in some programs, lists of businesses assisted by the programs were not carefully kept. The evaluators needed the names of the businesses and their addresses in order to obtain business ratings of the services they had received. The evaluators had to ask program staff to put client lists together as well as they could, recognizing that these lists would be incomplete to an unknown extent.

The problem was even worse in a national evaluation of local programs that brought social services into schools to help reduce school dropouts. Many of the programs sampled did not have lists of clients served, data on the duration of their program, or the extent of client participation in various program activities. The evaluators had to reconstruct this information from case files and staff memories.

Evaluators can handle missing information in a number of ways—for example:

- They can leave the data out of tabulations. To calculate percentages or averages, the evaluators would not count the missing data in the numerators or denominators. Suppose the evaluators are calculating the proportion of events completed on time. They know there were one hundred cases, but the records show that sixty were completed on time, twenty-five were not, and timeliness for the other fifteen cases could not be determined. The percentage of timely completion would be 60/85, or 71 percent.

• The number of missing data items can be included in the denominator of the percentages so that the denominator represents the total number of cases, even though the case records on some may be missing or incomplete. This, in the above example, would give a percentage of 60/100, or 60 percent. The second is the more conservative figure for the on-time percentage.

• Assign values to the missing data elements. These values are estimates that the evaluators believe best represent the population of interest, such as by using the mean of the available observations. For example, if data on earnings are missing for members of a particular ethnic group, the average earning of those in the ethnic group *for whom earning figures are available* might be substituted for the missing data. The overall average earnings for all ethnic groups would then include these estimates of earnings for the missing clients. In some instances, the evaluators may want to apply more sophisticated procedures involving the use of equations that attempt to predict the values of the missing data based on a number of variables for which data are available. Each of these imputation methods, however, can result in biased estimates. (For technical discussions of these options, see Little, Rubin, and Rubin, 1987, 1990.)

• Delete the incomplete cases, but assign a weight to each complete case to compensate for the deleted cases. For example, say that other information on the population of interest indicates that males comprise 49 percent of the population, but the sample includes only 40 percent. Furthermore, suppose the percentage of males gives a 25 percent favorable response to a question but females give a 35 percent favorable response. To calculate the overall percentage of the population who have a favorable response, weight the 25 percent by 0.49 and the 35 percent by 0.51, not by 0.40 and 0.60.

In this example, the modified weighting results in an estimate of the overall population who think favorably as 30 percent rather than 31 percent. This is not much of a difference. Sometimes sophisticated weighting techniques produce little change, as in this example.

Which of the above options should be used will depend on the specific evaluation situation. Probably the best option is to analyze the data using all of these approaches to determine whether important findings are sensitive to the problem.

Data Available Only in Overly Aggregated Form

Sometimes the data are available only in aggregated form. This is a variation of the first problem. In most instances, evaluators are likely to want to obtain more detailed information. For example, they might want to assess not only overall water quality but also water quality for various segments of a body of water using agency record data on various water quality characteristics (such as dissolved oxygen, clarity, and chemical content). The data available in the records might not provide sufficient past data on each segment of interest. There may be little that evaluators can do in such instances. If time and resources permit, they can collect the new data. This will be possible if the evaluation is just beginning and the evaluator can build this data collection into the program's procedures. However, it is likely to be quite difficult, or impossible, to reconstruct past water quality data in the detail desired.

This problem can be worse if evaluators are attempting to use comparison groups (see Chapters Five and Six, this volume, on evaluation designs in this volume) and these other groups are served by another agency or even another government jurisdiction that did not collect or record the information in the detail needed. In such cases, the evaluators will likely have to forgo that breakout detail in their comparisons.

In some situations, the evaluators may be able to go back into the records to obtain the needed data. For example, public agencies often track complaints they receive but do not tabulate complaints or disaggregate them into needed categories, such as by type of complaint, location of complaint, or other characteristics that may be important to the evaluators. In this case, the evaluators may be able to delve into individual case records and obtain the desired level of detail. If the agency has changed its record-keeping procedures, such as switching from hard copy to digital records or has used multiple generations of computer data management software, this may severely restrict an evaluator's ability to recapture the past data.

Before the design phase of an evaluation is completed, the evaluators should check the availability of data needed for their proposed evaluation plan and make any needed adjustments. It will be a fortunate evaluation team that is able to obtain record data on all the disaggregations it would like to make.

Unknown, Different, or Changing Definitions of Data Elements

Evaluators should ascertain not only the availability of data but also how the major data elements they are collecting are defined and collected. This information is essential if they are to assess the accuracy and comparability of the data used. It is particularly important when the evaluators obtain information from different sites or different agencies, or collect data from several years during which data collection procedures might have changed.

A classic example of the use of different definitions by different public agencies is that of school dropout rates. Comparisons of school dropout data across school districts and states can be fraught with pitfalls. Dropout rates have been calculated in many different ways by school systems. For example, the rates may represent the ratio of the number of students graduating in a given year divided by the number of students entering at the beginning of that year. Or they may represent the number graduating in a given year divided by the number who entered as freshmen four years earlier. Agencies may or may not take into account the number of students who transferred into or out of the school system. Agencies may count GED (general educational development) students in different ways, or handle differently the number of students who graduate earlier or later than the rest of their class. Some differences in definitions are matters of judgment as to how the rate should be defined; in other cases they may involve logic errors. In any case, reasonable consistency and comparability across years and across school systems are needed when comparisons are being made.

A problem sometimes found in human service programs is that of duplicated counts. Some records of clients may count people each time they returned for service. In situations where the evaluators need unduplicated counts, this may require the evaluators to reconstruct counts from the data files or to make estimates of the amount of duplication, perhaps based on sampling the records.

A common problem are data that cover different periods of time. The evaluators might want to compare data across cities or states, but find that some report the data by calendar years and others by fiscal years, and those that report by fiscal years have different fiscal years.

Another typical situation arises with the definitions of cost elements. Currently, generally accepted standards of what to include in cost comparisons do not exist.

The following steps should help evaluators avoid, or at least alleviate, data definition problems:

1. Identify the definitions and data collection procedures that have been used by the program and check for significant changes over the time period included in the evaluation. Evaluators should identify likely problems at the start of the evaluation.
2. Where differences in definitions or data collection procedures are found, make appropriate adjustments, for example, by excluding data

elements for which data are not available in compatible definitions across comparison groups or examining the original information and identifying appropriate adjustments.

3. Work with percentage changes rather than absolute values. Compare percentage changes from one year to the next among comparison groups (for example, in the reported crime rates of various cities), even though the data that are being compared are based on somewhat different definitions and data collection procedures. This adjustment may provide roughly accurate comparisons as long as the definitions and procedures for each individual agency or office remained stable over the time period covered by the evaluation.

4. Keep a record of data definition problems that have not been fully solved, and estimate (and report) the impacts of these problems on the final evaluation findings.

Data Linked Across Time and Clients

A special variation of the problem of unknown, different, or changing definitions of data elements occurs in situations where the evaluators need to link data from different agencies, or even different offices within the same agency, to track the impacts of a public program. These offices and agencies may use different identifiers, or they may track clients (or other work elements, such as water quality or road condition) in different ways. Sometimes they do not use the same name for the same element. They may use social security numbers or other special client identifiers rather than names. Offices may use variations of clients' names. Some offices may identify clients by household and others by individual household member. All of these circumstances present problems to evaluation teams.

The evaluators need to identify the presence of such problems. Some may require special data collection efforts, close examination of names to identify name variations (for example, considering multiple identifiers such as age, addresses, and social security numbers to verify identities), and perhaps special computer runs to identify and link together the relevant data on the units of analysis for the evaluation.

For example, for a variety of employment programs, evaluators have sought to use the employment and earnings information from state unemployment insurance (UI) offices. Usually such information as social security numbers and names is used to identify the employment and earnings history of the employment program clients. Assuming the evaluators can obtain access to those files, a number of other problems typically arise:

- The data may not become available for many months, perhaps too late for the evaluation.
- Some individuals may not have been in employment covered by the UI database.
- Different names or social security numbers may have occurred for some clients, perhaps due to data entry errors.
- The clients may have worked in other states.

All of these difficulties can lead to a lower-than-desirable percentage of clients matched with the UI database. If these problems become too great, the evaluators may need to use surveys of clients to obtain the needed information. (See Chapter Nine on using surveys.)

Another problem can arise in the use of agency record data to calculate outcomes. Evaluators may want to calculate the number and percentage of clients who achieved successful outcomes in a year after the clients entered the program. Evaluators must be sure that the results data are for the clients they are tracking. The problem is perhaps best explained by an example.

One state's department of human services developed a computerized tracking system to provide information on the success rates of its clients. The agency initially calculated the number of successful case closures in each year and the number of cases served in the same year. It divided one by the other to estimate the percentage of cases successfully closed. But the numerator and the denominator represent different cases. Instead, the system needs to track cohorts of incoming clients—clients entering in a given year—over a specific duration of time to identify the percentage of clients who achieved specific outcomes by the end of the specified time period. (The time indicator might be the "percentage of children placed for adoption in the previous year who were adopted within twelve months after being placed.") An alternative is to use as the cohort those clients whose condition was assessed during the particular reporting period and determine the percentage of successful outcomes for those clients. If the evaluators find that an agency's reports provide such misleading information, they, with the agency's help if possible, will likely need to examine individual records to obtain more valid percentages of clients with successful outcomes.

A similar problem, particularly for human service programs such as social and mental health services, is the determination of when the follow-ups should be made to determine program outcomes. If samples of clients are drawn without consideration of how long a period has elapsed since service began or ended, and outcomes are not all measured for the same time interval, the measurements will yield data on clients whose length of program participation will likely have varied widely. To avoid such inconsistencies, evaluators generally should use a standard time period for obtaining outcome indicators such as "the percentage of clients starting service in 2004 who twelve months later showed significantly improved functioning." (For such indicators, the evaluators will need precise definitions of "significantly improved functioning" and of the time envelope for "twelve months later," and apply these to all clients being tracked.)

Confidentiality and Privacy Considerations

Evaluators sometimes face obstacles in obtaining information from agency records because the data are confidential. This problem occurs often when human services, education, and criminal justice programs are being evaluated. It can also arise when evaluators seek any type of sensitive information such as a person's income.

Evaluators must protect the privacy of anyone about whom they obtain data, whether from records, surveys, or interviews. This protection can be provided in a variety of ways:

• Do not record a person's name, social security number, or other identifiers obtained from the records. In some instances, it may be sufficient for the agency to provide the evaluators with a unique identifier rather than names or other identifiers, to the evaluators. However, if the evaluators need to link those data with data from other sources, this procedure will not work.

• Assign a number to each client, and carefully secure the list that cross-references the numbers to clients' names. This procedure will also be useful should the evaluator need to return to the agency records to recapture or verify lost or anomalous data after a data check. Such lists should usually be destroyed after all the evaluation needs are met.

• Report only grouped data. Do not include in evaluation reports any information that might enable a reader to link a particular finding to an individual client. Sometimes evaluators may want to cite a particular case. If so, no identifying information should be provided without obtaining permission, preferably in writing, from those able to give such permission. A classic example of this problem occurred in an evaluation of state export activities in the Northeast. Because the chemical export market in Delaware was dominated by the DuPont Corporation, the U.S. Census Bureau would not release information on the amount of chemical exports in the state. If this information were made public, business competitors could readily identify DuPont's level of activity. The evaluators therefore had to forgo using chemical export data on Delaware. Fortunately, such situations tend to be rare.

• In advance of any data exchange, the evaluator should provide the agency with a detailed memo outlining the procedures he or she will use to protect the privacy of individual clients. This demonstrates good faith on the part of the evaluator, and it reassures agency staff that the data are being handled in a responsible and professional manner.

A major problem in evaluation can be the need to obtain permission to access individual records. Evaluators of a national school dropout prevention program needed permission from local program staff, administrators of the school systems that had implemented the program, and the parents of sampled students to review agency record information on individual program clients such as grades, test scores, attendance records, and incidence of disciplinary action. Other examples of such problems occur in evaluations that seek to access state unemployment insurance records or federal social security records.

Securing such permissions can be quite time-consuming and expensive. This is especially so when consent agreements have to be obtained from each individual, such as to obtain information on individual students or for access to social security records (Olson, 1999).

When the evaluators are employees of the agency whose program is being evaluated and the needed data come from the agency's own records, obtaining permission is not likely to be a problem.

When evaluators are from outside the agency, agency employees can be asked to transcribe pertinent information for them without including individual identifiers. Such protected access can break an impasse, especially if the employees (or agency) can be paid for the time involved in collecting the needed data. Such data, however, cannot be linked to records from other agencies. When obtaining the data, convey to agency employees that certain individual characteristics may be very important to the evaluation, such as age, race, and gender. In the interest of protecting the identity of individual clients, some agencies may cleanse data files more thoroughly than necessary.

Increasingly evaluators are concerned with measuring the impact of a program in particular locations, such as a neighborhood or county. In such cases, individual identifiers such as a client's address can be important elements of the evaluation. If the evaluator is unable to obtain spatial data at the address level, the evaluator can ask that the address information on the individual record be replaced with a code representing a larger area, such as a tract or county. Recoding individual addresses at a somewhat larger jurisdictional area preserves the individual record and still provides the evaluator a spatial indicator for the evaluation.

If an agency contracts with another organization to deliver the service being evaluated, the contractor may resist access to its records on individual clients. In such situations, the evaluators should attempt to obtain voluntary compliance by working with the contractor. Organizations that anticipate such future evaluations might in the contract require the contractor to provide access to needed records.

Quality Control

Data errors can occur at any point in record keeping. To help maintain data quality, evaluators should consider the data checks for reasonableness and staff training set out in the following sections.

Data Checks for Reasonableness

The widespread use of computers and the availability of inexpensive software have greatly simplified the process of checking data for certain types of errors. Such procedures are particularly important when many people are engaged in data collection or data entry and many data are involved. Information that comes to the evaluators in the form of computer tapes can have many inaccuracies, such as missing, inaccurate, or contradictory data due to either entry errors or errors in the original data collection. Evaluators will generally need to clean the data, that is, check them for reasonableness before making computations, whether they are managed by computer or manually. Such checks could include the following:

- Identify ranges of possible values for each data element, and check to see if any of the data fall outside those ranges. For example, an entry of 110 for a person's age would be flagged either manually or by computer. Also, where applicable, make sure the computer or manual data processors can distinguish between such entries as the number zero, "not applicable," and "don't know."
- Check consistency across data elements. With computers, elaborate checks can be made. For example, persons above certain ages are not normally employed in full-time positions. A computer could readily check for such problems. In an examination of drug testing programs, evaluators found clients in the database who had the same identification number and birthday but a different race or sex. The evaluators went back to the original data source to correct what they found to be data entry errors.
- Look for missing data, flagging these instances so that decisions can be made about how to deal with them.

Staffing Considerations

Evaluators should ensure that the staff collecting the data are given sufficient instruction and training about what to look for. If different people collect information on the same elements, they should be trained to collect comparable data and identify differences that occur. They should be instructed to bring problems to the attention of the evaluation team for decisions on how to handle differences in data definitions.

One approach to alleviating data collection problems is to have data collectors specialize. For example, one person can be assigned responsibility for gathering specific data elements from agency records at all sites. This option, however, will not always be feasible.

Other Suggestions for Obtaining Data from Agency Records

The quality of data can be enhanced by actions taken prior to, during, and after the initial information has been obtained from the fieldwork. The following sections offer suggestions for quality assurance steps in each of these three phases.

Before Field Data Collection Begins

1. Get acquainted with the agency staff who originally collected the data. If evaluators are seeking data from people they do not know, making their acquaintance can be very helpful in gaining assistance and information throughout the data-gathering effort. In small agencies, typically only a few people have access to the information needed for the evaluation. These persons tend to be overburdened with multiple responsibilities. If the evaluator is able to describe the potential usefulness of the efforts, so that an investment of time will be useful to people in these positions, data requests are likely to meet less resistance.

2. Try to deal directly with those who are most familiar with the data records. If the evaluators need access to agency records, they should learn how the files are organized. They should ask those familiar with the records to identify possible problems, such as changes in definitions that have occurred over time, problems in getting the needed data, and likely reliability and validity problems. This effort gives evaluators a sense on whether their data plans are reasonable, helps them anticipate problems, and helps them assess what information they can most likely obtain.

3. If evaluators ask an agency to provide data rather than requesting access to agency files, they should make the task as easy as possible for the agency staff by such steps as the following:

- Give the agency as much advance notice as possible.
- Put the request in writing, and provide clear, full descriptions of the data needed.

- Explain to the agency people why the data are needed, but be flexible. The agency staff may be aware of problems with specific data items and be able to suggest suitable alternatives.

4. Request samples of the data formats and definitions before going into the field to gain a better perspective on what data are available.

5. In some cases, it may be necessary and appropriate to compensate the agency for the extra time and effort required to generate the requested information. This might occur, for example, if the information in the format and detail that the evaluators need requires major new computer runs on the agency's databases, or the evaluators cannot gain direct access to data files on individuals but are willing to use data without individual identifiers if agency employees are willing to transcribe the data from the records.

In the Field

1. Whether they are collecting completed agency reports or extracting data from agency files, the evaluators should, if feasible, talk with the persons who provided the data and know something of its content. They should ask about data definitions, their limitations, and especially any problems in how the data have been obtained. Even if the evaluators believe they have obtained such information before the start of field data collection, they should check again while in the field.

2. The evaluators should learn the form and detail in which the data are available. Data collectors will need to determine whether to forgo some of the information wanted, try to obtain data not currently in the desired form or detail, or accept the less-than-ideal data situation.

3. For each item of data collected, the evaluators should identify the periods of time covered by that item. Frequently, items of data apply to different time periods, requiring the evaluator to make adjustments or at least to identify the discrepancies in their reports. For example, data for some elements may refer to calendar years, some to fiscal years, and others to school years.

4. Evaluators should check to make sure that the data obtained from the agency are complete for the time period. If, for example, records of individuals who have dropped out of a given program are included in one data file but omitted from another, a simple comparison of outcomes related to the given program would likely be invalid.

5. For data elements intended to cover specific geographical areas, the evaluators should identify what areas apply to each data element. Some outcome data, for example, might be reported by organizational unit coverage (such as police precincts, fire districts, regional districts, and offices). Other outcome data might be reported by census tracts or by neighborhood.

This diversity may or may not present problems for the evaluation. Also, the geographical boundaries may have changed over the time period covered by the evaluation. Evaluators need to know the extent of such problems so they can make decisions on ways to make adjustments or at least report them.

After Initial Data Have Been Obtained

1. Determine for each data element how missing or incomplete data should be handled. Decisions to drop a certain element or case or to make a specific adjustment should be reached, when possible, prior to data analysis.

2. Check for illogical, inconsistent data. Where appropriate, ask the data source for the correct data.

3. Send data back to originators for verification—in situations where the originators are likely to be able, and willing, to make such verification.

4. Thank agency sources for their assistance. Let them know that their help has been valuable and appreciated.

5. Document and provide appropriate caveats in the evaluation report. The evaluators should provide their best judgments on the effects of these data problems on the findings.

Conclusion

Agency records will be the source of many important data in many, if not most, evaluations. At the very least, evaluators are likely to need to identify from records the amount of work that is the subject of the evaluation (for example, the number of customers or work items). Inevitably, evaluators will find less than perfect data from agency records. Whether these data come from the agency in which the program is located, another agency, a contractor, or another jurisdiction, the evaluators need to ensure that they know the definitions and content of the various data elements being collected. The evaluators will need to ascertain that the data they use are sufficiently comparable for them to compare different groups or the same group across time.

Evaluators should be aware that obtaining data from agency records will present unexpected difficulties. The challenge is to make needed adjustments that do not compromise the overall quality of the evaluation.

References

Babbie, E. *The Practice of Social Research.* (5th ed.) Belmont, Calif.: Wadsworth, 1989.

Corporation for National and Community Service. "AmeriCorps Program Applicant Performance Measurement Toolkit." Dec. 20, 2002. [www.project star.organization].

Elder, G. H., Jr., Pavalko, E. K., and Clipp, E. C. *Working with Archival Data: Studying Lives.* Thousand Oaks, Calif.: Sage, 1993.

Kiecolt, K. J., and Nathan, L. E. *Secondary Analysis of Survey Data.* Thousand Oaks, Calif.: Sage, 1985.

Krippendorff, K. *Content Analysis: An Introduction to Its Methodology.* Thousand Oaks, Calif.: Sage, 1980.

Little, R., Rubin, J. A., and Rubin, D. B. *Statistical Analysis with Missing Data.* New York: Wiley, 1987.

Little, R., Rubin, J. A., and Rubin, D. B. "The Analysis of Social Science Data with Missing Values." In J. Fox and J. S. Long (eds.), *Modern Method of Data Analysis.* Thousand Oaks, Calif.: Sage, 1990.

Nachmias, D., and Nachmias, C. *Research Methods in the Social Sciences.* (3rd ed.) New York: St. Martin's Press, 1987.

Olson, J. A. *Linkages with Data from Social Security Administrative Records in the Health and Retirement Study.* Washington, D.C.: Social Security Administration, Aug. 1999.

Rossi, P. H., Freeman, H. E., and Lipsey, M. W. *Evaluation: A Systematic Approach.* (6th ed.) Thousand Oaks, Calif.: Sage, 1998.

Singleton, R., Jr., Straits, B. C., Straits, M. M., and McAllister, R. J. *Approaches for Social Research.* New York: Oxford University Press, 1988.

U.S. Department of Education, Division of Adult Education and Literacy. *Measures and Methods for the National Reporting System for Adult Education— Implementation Guidelines.* Washington, D.C.: U.S. Government Printing Office, Mar. 2001.

Webb, E., Campbell, D. T., Schwartz, R. D., and Sechrest, L. *Unobtrusive Measures: Nonreactive Research in the Social Sciences.* Skokie, Ill.: Rand McNally, 1966.

Part Three

Analyzing Evaluation Data

The time to think about how data will be analyzed and reported is early in the evaluation planning. Conceptualizing what the audience for an evaluation will desire in terms of analytical sophistication and precision can help evaluators select among the many techniques available. Mapping out what the end product should look like provides some of the structure needed to guide planning of analysis procedures.

Constraints on evaluators' choices among analytical options go beyond what their clients will expect in reports, however. Time and resources will affect the types of data collected, and thus the sorts of analytical techniques that can be used. In many cases, evaluators must rely on data that others have collected, or on the formats that others prefer for further data collection efforts. Evaluators' skills in effectively applying and reporting analytical techniques may also limit the possibilities for analysis of evaluation data.

The chapters in Part Three present techniques for analyzing data collected in evaluation efforts. The four chapters cover (1) analysis and interpretation of data collected through qualitative data collection techniques such as interviews and site visits; (2) selection, application, and reporting of inferential statistics; (3) the application and interpretation of regression analysis; and (4) the use of cost-effectiveness and cost-benefit techniques in program evaluation.

The authors of these chapters describe analytical techniques in nontechnical terms to clarify the relative advantages and disadvantages of the various options. In each chapter, the authors describe the purpose of the analytical strategies and the types of evaluation questions that are most amenable to application of each; the assumptions or requirements of the data and the data collection methods that must be met to use each analytical technique effectively; the sorts of information that should be provided in reports about application of each technique; and the possible limitations that may accompany application of the techniques.

Sharon Caudle, in Chapter Fifteen, discusses strategies for analyzing data collected through observation, examination of documents, and interviews. Data analysis activities discussed include content analysis, abstracting and transforming raw data during the data collection process, developing data displays organizing the data, and drawing and verifying conclusions during and after data collection. She explains how to accomplish each of these qualitative data analysis activities and lists references that provide further guidance. Caudle suggest several approaches that evaluators can use to strengthen the credibility, generalizability, and objectivity of qualitative evaluation efforts—for example, triangulation, peer debriefing, informant feedback, and the use of auditors to assess the evaluation process and product.

Kathryn Newcomer and Philip Wirtz, in Chapter Sixteen, describe a variety of statistical techniques available to evaluators. They identify the most important issues that evaluators should address when applying statistical techniques to strengthen the conclusions drawn from the findings. They describe basic distinctions among statistical techniques, outline procedures for drawing samples and applying statistical tools, provide criteria for evaluators to use in choosing among the data analysis techniques available, and offer guidance on reporting statistics appropriately and clearly. Illustrations of the application of the chi-square test and the t test are provided, along with other guidance especially pertinent to the analysis of variables measured at the nominal and ordinal levels of measurement.

Dale Berger, in Chapter Seventeen, demonstrates how regression analyses can be applied to evaluate the results of a program. Berger introduces the basic regression model and defines all of the basic concepts in clear terms. The use of regression to analyze program data is illustrated for two treatment groups with and without pretests. An extension of regression, mediation analysis, which is appropriate when there is an intervening variable that mediates the relationship between the program intervention and outcome, is also explored. The chapter interprets regression analysis as it is provided in SPSS computer output and then provides guidance on audience-friendly presentation of regression analysis.

James Kee, in Chapter Eighteen, offers guidance on the application of cost-effectiveness and benefit-cost techniques in program evaluation. He outlines opportunities to apply the various options, along with the issues evaluators must address should they select one of these techniques. Kee provides guidance to evaluators as he describes cost-effectiveness analysis and its capabilities, differentiates among the various types of benefits and costs that should be arrayed in any benefit-cost analysis, offers suggestions on the valuation of benefits, identifies common problems surrounding the measurement of costs, and provides guidance on presenting cost-effectiveness and benefit-cost information to decision makers.

The chapter authors carefully delineate the issues evaluators should address as they select analytical techniques and report the results of analyses. They discuss factors affecting such decisions and the potential threats to the validity of results provided in evaluation reports. Replicability with the assurance of consistent results is the hallmark of valid and appropriate data analysis. Evaluators need to acknowledge analytical choices and unanticipated obstacles to help ensure that results are interpreted appropriately.

15

Qualitative Data Analysis

Sharon L. Caudle

Qualitative analysis means making sense of relevant data gathered from sources such as interviews, on-site observations, and documents and then responsibly presenting what the data reveal. Often the journey from raw data to what the data reveal is challenging, when, as Patton (2002, p. 431) notes, "Analysis finally makes clear what would have been most important to study, if only we had known beforehand."

This chapter's focus is on analytical strategies and practices that are easy to use, low cost, and flexible enough to apply to a wide range of routine program evaluation qualitative analysis tasks. Qualitative analysis, of course, occurs in large-scale, formal program evaluations. But it also comes into play in ad hoc, quick-turnaround analyses. For example, analysts are often called on to analyze documents quickly or present findings on a policy or program issue. For these shorter-term, high-impact qualitative analyses, following a qualitative analytical strategy and supporting practices are as important as for a large-scale, formal program evaluation.

Preanalysis Elements

The separation between research design, data sources and data collection, analysis, and presentation of findings is never clear-cut, or wanted, in qualitative research. The power of qualitative research comes in large part from the ability to move between, explore, and enhance the design, data analysis, and findings as the study proceeds. Analysis "works on" data. The quality of

analysis in a program evaluation is particularly affected by certain preanaly-
sis elements that occur before the main analytical effort: research design and
data targeting, data collection and documentation, a data organization system, and analyst team skills and knowledge.

Research Design and Data Targeting

One important element is a well-crafted research design and appropriate
data targeting to respond to the evaluation's research questions and the
research design's plan for analysis. Miles and Huberman (1994) say that study
design questions can be seen as analytical—an anticipatory data reduction—
as they constrain later analysis by ruling out certain variables and relationships and attending to others. The analysis decisions, says Maxwell (1996),
should influence, and be influenced by, the rest of the research design. For
example, as Mason (2002) describes, when the analyst team determines the
research's sampling strategy, the team will need to think ahead to what analysis the team will likely conduct, ensuring a direct link among the sampling
strategy, the data analysis, and the presentation of the findings. The program
evaluation's research design generally identifies the purpose of the evaluation, the major research questions, and the strategy for data analysis.

The analysis plan identifies data sources and analysis methods. The
research questions must be translated to detailed questions for data collection instruments. In the beginning, the detailed questions may be relatively
unstructured and then become more focused and structured toward the end
of the study as the evaluation defines key areas and findings are tested. In
addition, program events may change, forcing revisions to the research questions and data collection instruments. The quality of analysis will be hampered if the data targeting by the data collection instruments is not well done,
contains serious gaps, or drifts from the research questions over time.

One strategy to ensure good data targeting is to keep the evaluation
purpose and research questions close at hand as data collection instruments
are designed. I normally take each research question and formulate detailed
subquestions directly linked to the research question. These subquestions
then become converted to areas of coverage or questions for interviews and
document selection and analysis.

Data Collection and Documentation

A second element is adequate collection and documentation of relevant data.
Program evaluation data most often come from field interviews; documents
such as legislation and plans; other media such as videos, presentations, and
pictures; and direct or unrestricted observation, where the analyst takes note

of settings, interactions, and events. Relevant data from these sources have to be collected and documented to the maximum possible extent to be of any analytical use. Too often, analyst teams take short-cuts that short-circuit the analytical process.

For example, analysts may stop writing or recording as an interview proceeds, making immediate choices about what is relevant or not. The interview notes or recordings should be complete even if material does not appear directly relevant. Once the interview is complete, write-ups should be done immediately if they are from interview written notes and should be as complete as possible, even if some material initially appears to be irrelevant. The write-ups or transcripts should not be categorized or interpreted as they are done. Analysts who selectively decide what to document or process data into categories while writing up interview notes can make subsequent analysis difficult. Lost in this approach are the words of the interviewee and the detail of what was said. Later, if analysis indicates that one area is emerging as an important finding, there may be no way to capture similar evidence in earlier interviews if what appears to be irrelevant information has not been collected or formally documented or if categories have already reduced the data prematurely.

Data Organization System

The data organization system should organize program evaluation research design and decision-making information, collected field data, analytical commentaries, and observations and drafts from the beginning of the evaluation. Qualitative research normally translates to what seems to be mountains of interview write-ups, hard copy documents, summaries of preliminary findings, presentations, and the like. For the beginning analyst, data organization frequently is the task that will be done later. However, without a data management system, the analyst and his or her team will constantly have data identification, access, and retrieval problems.

Data organization can be fairly simple. One approach is to organize the data by purpose and source in binders, with tabs for individual documents or documents that can be bundled together. For example, one binder can hold research design and analytical documentation, such as decision rules, definitions, sampling strategies, and contact information. A second binder contains interview write-ups, and a third, documents with their summaries. Another binder contains analytical work, such as data displays, coding and categories, and data summaries. A final binder contains documents presenting findings, including early vignettes and summaries, presentations, and draft reports. Feedback on the documents is normally filed with the related document under the same binder tab. The documents are filed in chronological order with notations to cross-reference the source with other data sources.

Material can also be electronically stored in databases, which are particularly useful to share with the entire analyst team over a network. Whether the analyst team uses a manual or electronic system, or a combination, the team will need to keep records protected and secure if there are confidential issues.

Analyst Team Skills and Knowledge

A final element is the analyst team itself. According to Patton (2002), no abstract analytical processes can substitute for the skill, knowledge, experience, creativity, diligence, and work of the qualitative analyst. Each analyst, whether working as a single researcher or one of many, brings different skills and knowledge to the analytical task. Strauss and Corbin (1998) emphasize that analytical insights happen to "prepared minds"—using what analysts bring to the data in a systematic and aware way to derive meaning without forcing analyst explanations on data. Being prepared means having skills in forming questions, selecting and sampling the components to be studied, identifying data sources, collecting data, selecting data segments for analysis, and seeing patterns and themes in the data. A skilled analyst will know how to ask an interview question, listen to the answer, interpret its meaning and relevance, frame another question to respond to the answer, and keep track of what needs to be explored during the remainder of the interview, all at virtually the same time.

In addition, each analyst brings unique knowledge of theories, concepts, models, and approaches to the evaluation. At the operational level, some analysts will have conducted prior research at program sites, bringing an understanding of context and relationships that will move the analysis along. For example, the analyst will have valuable knowledge of program history, key actors, standard operating procedures, and decision-making structures. Moreover, analysts bring their own theoretical concepts, beliefs, and assumptions to the evaluation—a strength if properly focused but a weakness if they bring bias to the analysis. Overall, these skills and knowledge contribute immensely to collecting good data ready for analysis.

Analytical Subprocesses and Practices

Qualitative data analysis is a complex set of intertwined processes and practices. Data analysis has been described as the interplay between raw data, the procedures used to interpret and organize the data, and the emerging findings (for a fuller description, see Huberman and Miles, 1998; Patton, 2002;

Strauss and Corbin, 1998; Yin, 1989; Maxwell, 1996). Data analysis consists of the two major subprocesses: (1) data reduction and pattern identification and (2) producing objective analytic conclusions and communicating those conclusions.

The first subprocess of data reduction and pattern identification examines, categorizes, tabulates, compares, contrasts, or otherwise recombines and reduces the data in sifting trivia from significance. Data summaries, coding, finding themes, clustering, and writing stories help identify patterns. Tools such as data displays organize and compress the data set. The second subprocess produces objective and compelling analytic conclusions that address a study's initial propositions, rule out alternative explanations, and then communicate the essence of what the data reveal. The analyst is looking for relevant and significant findings in the identified patterns, including interpreting those findings. Techniques such as triangulation, looking for negative cases, and checking results with respondents aid in addressing objective and validity concerns.

Information technology can greatly facilitate qualitative analysis, generally known as computer-aided qualitative data analysis (CAQDAS). (A good discussion of using computers in qualitative research is provided by Patton, 2002, and Richards and Richards, 1998, including cautions regarding their use.) The most commonly used CAQDAS packages are QSR Nvivo, QSR versions of the earlier product known as NUD*IST, Ethnograph, ATLAS, and Hypersoft. The software packages can aid data storage, coding, retrieval, and comparison, particularly with large data sets where manual manipulation is difficult and time-consuming. For example, QSR N6 operates on two data sets: a document system that holds the documents and research notes and a "node" system that holds the topics and categories for analysis. The two systems are related by coding. N6 has text search and node search tools that look for words or phrases and code those passages and compare coding and relationships in various ways (QSR International, 2002).

For smaller evaluations, or where the software is not available or the analyst team does not have sufficient experience in comfortably using the packages, word processing and presentational software such as Microsoft Word and PowerPoint are good alternatives. For example, Word can be used to set up formal interview write-up and document summary formats, tables for reducing data, and more structured matrices as the data are reduced. PowerPoint can be used for developing figures, such as network data displays. Further reduced data displays can also be imported into Word documents for the final presentation of findings.

The following sections discuss key analytical practices and examples: coding basics, memos and remarks, and data displays.

The Basics: Coding

Wolcott (1990) observes that the critical task in qualitative research is not accumulating all the data possible, but getting rid of most data that have been accumulated. Content analysis facilitates sorting through the data by identifying, coding or categorizing, clustering, and labeling to identify primary themes or patterns. (For a full description and additional examples, see Maxwell, 1996; Miles and Huberman, 1994; Strauss and Corbin, 1998; Mason, 2002; Wolcott, 1990.)

Codes or categories are simply labels that assign meaning or themes to the evaluation data. An analyst defines a code for a segment of data, labels the segment, and then labels similar segments of data with the same code. Coding therefore breaks data down into discrete elements, such as events, relationships, or processes. Events could be specific activities, relationships could be connections between subjects in a study, and processes could be related steps or changes. The use of discrete element coding allows analytical comparison for similarities and differences.

There are different options for units of analysis for coding purposes—for example:

- Line-by-line analysis, closely examining phrase by phrase and sometimes word by word
- Examining a whole sentence or paragraph
- Examining an entire document and determining what makes the document the same as, or different from, other coded documents

The unit of analysis should be the same in an individual evaluation. Although not every segment of data requires coding, the analyst should be highly critical in identifying relevant information.

Analysts generally develop codes or categories in two ways, often in combination. One way is creating precodes—codes or categories the analyst team brings to the evaluation before collecting data, drawing from existing program theory, the evaluation's theories and hypotheses, research questions, and program variables. The team might develop and test an initial set of codes or phrases that sorts all available data. For example, as part of study of homeland security issues, I drew on current literature and reports to develop key concepts that were used in analyzing the data.

A second way is deriving the codes or categories from the program being evaluated. Codes are derived inductively during the data analysis, pointing to acts, activities, meanings, participation, relationships, settings, and methods. These codes reflect reoccurring concept phrases or practices overtly stated by program people being studied or those named by the analyst if those studied do not concretely name concepts. I participated in a study to provide information on individual and cross-cutting federal agency approaches to create and sustain effective state relationships in managing for results. One question was how and why state performance goals, measures, or strategies differed from those of the federal program. Exhibit 15.1 shows an excerpt of an interview write-up with coding derived from the data.

Normally, codes or categories are considered as either descriptive or interpretative (interpretative coding might also be called inferential). Descriptive codes name things, such as processes, actors, or events. For example, a descriptive code might be STPLAN, for "strategic planning." Interpretive or inferential codes provide additional meaning or identify emerging patterns, themes, or explanations. For example, an interpretive code might be GOMO, for organizations that are "going through the motions" in conducting strategic planning. In larger evaluations, the coding is generally one word or acronym, such as the STPLAN or GOMO illustrations. In smaller evaluations, a phrase might be used as the code, such as "formal strategic planning principles." This is a practice I generally follow when working alone on a smaller project since using phrases often will not require formal coding definitions, and I normally use the language provided in interviews or documents.

Exhibit 15.1. Coding Concepts Developed from the Data

Interview Excerpt	*Possible Coding Concepts*
Mr. Smith said that as he looked at the Federal Highway Administration [FHWA] goals on the Web site, he was chagrined to realize the state had never taken DOT [federal Department of Transportation] objectives into account in the SWOT [strengths, weaknesses,	Awareness of federal goals
opportunities, and threats] analysis that the state goes through in its planning process. His thought was that maybe the federal and state goals should be congruent.	Federal-state planning process congruence
The strategic planning process in the state department has been driven in the past by its directors, and the internal process is not as strong as it should be. If	Strength of state planning process
the state had been more aware of federal goals and targets, it might have changed its own direction and strategies. That just didn't happen in terms of alignment.	State direction to match federal goals
Hopefully, the state will get to the same point as FHWA, or at least in the same ballpark in many cases. But the state would not have the same position as FHWA or other	State direction driving state goals
states in many cases, because specific goals would depend on the direction of the state. The state might have the same general goals but different strategies. However, the FHWA-state dialogue never happened.	Federal-state goals match; strategies differ

The same segment of data might be labeled with both descriptive and interpretive codes or phrases, with descriptive codes generally being applied first, then the interpretative. Patton (2002) makes the point that there should be careful separation of description from interpretation. In his view, interpretation involves explaining findings, answering "why" questions, attaching significance to particular results, and putting patterns into an analytical framework. Interpreting the data should come after major descriptive questions are answered.

In managing codes, the analyst should make sure the code name closely matches the concept or practice it describes, be clearly defined, and have instructions for its application. This management concept facilitates codes' being applied consistently by individual analysts. The evaluation's research design should including testing the consistent application of codes. In addition, data management should include the thoughtful testing of the codes' ongoing usefulness. The coding scheme should be adjusted as the analysis progresses to include new codes, remove nonrelevant codes, and refine existing codes, such as further differentiating codes that capture too broad a category of data. The analyst then revisits already coded data to test previously assigned codes or apply newer codes. Later, coded data can be clustered into more general categories.

The first cut of qualitative data analysis starts with the first interview or observation or document. Depending on what data are available, the analyst reads or listens to interviews and examines documents. Any memos or notes written during the course of collecting the information are also part of the analytical mix. At some point, the evaluation will turn to what Patton (2002) calls confirmatory data collection—deepening insights into and confirming or disconfirming patterns.

As the analyst team goes through the information, each analyst looks for recurring elements and records data concepts, topics, insights, and potential coding categories and relationships. These recordings might be done directly on the data documents, such as in the margins, with sticky notes that can be easily removed later, or in a binder of observations. Each analyst works back and forth between the emerging coding categories and the data to define a coding system that appears to cover the existing data. After the first review, the team compares notes and builds the initial coding system, deciding on data segments that appear similar or related in a consistent way, can be differentiated from other categories, and appear to account for all, or virtually all, the data.

Memos and Remarks

Memos and other recording of analytical remarks during data analysis can help capture the analyst team's thinking about the data, such as questions to ask, surprises, links to other data segments, potential coding or categorizing options, or tentative interpretations. They are intended to stimulate the analysis process as data collection proceeds. The memos or remarks, says Maxwell (1996), can range from a brief marginal comment on an interview transcript or a theoretical idea recorded in a field journal to a full-fledged analytical essay. Memos can also serve as an initial draft of information that can be used in presenting findings.

My general practice is to place observations within the text as I transcribe interviews or summarize documents, using brackets, as shown in Exhibit 15.2. Later thoughts can be shown as marginal notes. I generally include analytical remarks in messages to the others of the analytic team.

Data Displays

Coding and memos and remarks are necessary, but not sufficient, for moving analysis forward. Data displays can aid further data sorting and organization. (For more information, see Maxwell, 1996; Huberman and Miles, 1998; Mason, 2002; Miles and Huberman, 1994; and Patton, 2002. Miles and Huberman, 1994, have extensive examples.) Data displays present information in visual formats such as matrices (essentially the crossing of two lists using rows and columns) and networks (which display nodes or points with links between them showing relationships). They are filled in as the analyst works back and forth from the table to the data, adjusting rows and columns and other labels.

Data displays are analytically powerful. They present a full data set's concepts and relationships in one location, opening the information to critical thinking, confirming what is displayed, or considering new relationships and explanations. Early rough data displays lead to more sophisticated displays and related elaboration of emerging findings. The analyst team can look for alternative ways to organize the data and illuminate new or variations in patterns. Matrices are especially helpful in seeing distributions in the

Exhibit 15.2. Embedding Analytical Remarks

Mr. Smith said he is not aware if the state was involved in setting any national performance goals, measures, or targets. He said the closest the state might have come to getting involved was on environmental planning, when there was some discussion with the Federal Highway Administration regarding national targets. However, that was after the targets were set, and the discussion was how to operationalize the topics. State input on the targets never occurred. *[Analyst's note: One pattern perhaps is for federal agencies to set targets, then ask states about implementation; other federal agencies might use legislation or some other means. Is state input asked for by anybody?]*

---

data—how often a particular code or category occurs. The choice of what data to display is an analytical one, and the analyst team should closely anchor the displays to the evaluation's research questions and reflect the concepts and relationships clarified by coding. As Miles and Huberman (1994) note, counting goes on in the background when judgments of data qualities are made. When the analyst team identifies a theme or pattern, the team is isolating a data segment that is occurring a number of times and in a consistent manner.

For example, in the study of federal-state results management, I took each interview question and cut and pasted from the interviews into tables by program by state in the first step of data reduction. Exhibit 15.3 provides the excerpt from the overall data display for just one question.

The next step of data reduction uses coding segments derived from the data set of all programs for this one question, but applied to each program area, and each state that matches the code pattern, shown in Exhibit 15.4.

Finally, the state observations were merged into one data set, allowing the development of distributions and comments about outliers. A summary is shown in Table 15.1.

Exhibit 15.3. Initial Data Reduction Data Display

Interview Question	*Program/Interview Excerpts*
State involvement and impact on decision making TANF [Temporary Assistance for Needy Families]	*State 1:* have provided comments, goals and have been involved with national policy decision making, at least with the ability to provide comments; ACF officials do a good job in having discussions with the states; Child Welfare League, NGA, and APHSA provide a conduit for state comments to ACF
	State 2: state involvement through voicing opinions and making recommendations and through APHSA participation; participate in APHSA-sponsored discussions of PGs, but little follow-up or follow-through on ideas presented
	State 3: goals set in legislation and set as state requirements, still finding way, state does not work closely with ACF as much
	State 4: TANF high performance bonus report is primary instrument for goals and PMs; 4 teleconferences held with ACF, where state provided recommendations; state provided comments on high performance bonus notice of proposed rulemaking; contacts usually formal

Note: ACF: Administration for Children and Families; NGA: National Governors Association; APHSA: American Public Human Services Association; PGs: performance goals; TANF: Temporary Assistance for Needy Families; PMs: performance measures.

Exhibit 15.4. Second Data Reduction Data Display

Agency/Program	State General Observations
ACF/TANF (4 states)	Opportunity to comment on draft/proposed PGs and/or PMs (State 1, State 2, State 4)
	Involved in development of PGs and/or PMs (no states)
	Use of national associations (State 1, State 2)
	Developed best goals, measures for all state capability (no states)
	Goals, measures set in statute (State 3)
	Issues about real impact (no states)

Objectivity and Validity Elements

In qualitative research, Mason (2002) says the analyst must ensure that the data are appropriate for the research questions and that recording and analysis of the data has not been careless and slipshod.

Threats to Objectivity and Validity

Although there are many threats to objectivity and validity of the evaluation research and its findings, several are particularly important (for a fuller description, see Mason, 2002, Maxwell, 1996, Huberman and Miles, 1998, and Miles and Huberman, 1994).

Inaccurate or Incomplete Data. With inaccurate or incomplete data, what the analyst team collects covers only part of story or is not accurate, for several reasons. The team might miss data, selecting what are considered relevant data, ignoring and thus not documenting other data. The team might fall in love with, and thus overvalue, particularly good data sources. Or the team might get rushed or fatigued and not go through data such as voluminous documents or be able to conduct interviews objectively as the evaluation proceeds. For example, over the course of a few months, I did over two hundred phone interviews, each lasting approximately one hour. As I did more and more interviews, the descriptions in large part seemed to represent the same thing—"I have heard that before"—and it was a constant battle to take full notes and transcribe them accurately.

Misinterpreting the Data's Meaning or Meanings. The individual analyst—or entire team—will interpret and present data according to the analyst's disciplinary background, training, and experience instead of representing the point of view of program participants and their context. In addition to presenting an analyst point of view, the analyst team might have a different

Table 15.1. Full Data Set Distribution

Question	Number	Percentage	Observations
State involvement and impact on decision making and observations			
Opportunity to comment on draft and proposed PGs and/or PMs	57	46.3	
Involved in development of PGs and/or PMs	24	19.5	Half VocRehab and MCH
Use of national associations	27	22.0	
Developed best goals, measures for all state capability	9	7.3	
Goals, measures set in statute	4	3.3	
Issues about real impact	25	20.3	

Note: PGs: performance goals; PMs: performance measures; VocRehab: vocational rehabilitation; MCH: maternal and children's health.

understanding of the meaning of terms or concepts emerging in the research and not test them within the evaluation's context. Or the analyst might "invent" data or misrepresent the perspective presented by the data source, such as an interviewee. An analyst team might take documents as factual, legitimate data, instead of viewing them as being constructed for particular purposes and agendas. Often in my work, other members of the team might discount interview descriptions because they run counter to what is said in formal documents available from the Internet. I remind the team that the formal document might be true, but alternative descriptions certainly are worth the effort in checking out what is factual and what is constructed.

Discounting Data. People tend to overweight facts they believe in or depend on, ignore or forget data not consistent with the direction of their reasoning, and see confirming instances far more easily than disconfirming instances. Furthermore, the team might come up with questionable causes and suppress other evidence. For example, a pithy quote may not reflect a clear pattern in the data and may be relevant to only a minor issue.

Failure to Sufficiently Document the Chain of Evidence. This refers to the chain of evidence concerning the evaluation's scope and methodology, key analytical decisions, and cautions about what the analysis allows a team to present, or not present, as findings. Instead, the analyst team may provide only cursory information in the formal presentation of findings, or place a jumble of information that is difficult to understand or recreate in the data management system.

Countering the Threats

The team can counter these threats by several practices:

- Quickly and completely transcribe field notes or interviews and ask for and collect all related program documents.
- Assess the available data and determine what data seem to be inconsistent or missing based on other research or the analyst's experience.
- Use triangulation to collect information from diverse sources with a variety of data collection methods.
- Solicit feedback from others on methods, data sources, and preliminary findings.
- Compare the emerging findings with similar research.
- Be alert to and rigorously follow up on unexpected data or data relationships.
- Actively look for rival or competing themes or explanations that might fit the data.
- Use negative case analysis (the active search for and examination of cases that do not fit the pattern that appears to be emerging in the evaluation). For example, in doing "best practice" research, it might be helpful to contrast the context and characteristics of those cases with best practices with others that are not known for best practices. These negative cases provide a rich source of information to discern practices that can be touted and the context in which they work.
- Use extreme cases to help verify and confirm conclusions and serve as a way to explore key factors and variables. In best practice research, this might entail rigorous study of the best organization and its practices. Unexpected data, negative cases, and extreme cases should be clearly accounted for in the analysis and the presentation of findings.
- Make sure that quotes come from a wide range of data sources, not just from sources who state issues particularly well.
- Be rigorous in examining data relationships and connections. This would involve questioning common understandings, the absence or presence of other factors that could be affecting the relationships, and if the relationships are supported by sufficient data.
- Minutely examine words and phrases that appear to be repeating in the data, and use the data to point to actual meaning versus the team's interpreting the meaning. This helps to guard against misinterpretations.
- Use team debriefings. Each analyst reviews available data, such as interview write-ups and documents, and identifies themes. In the debriefings, varying themes are reconciled or highlighted for further data collection and analysis. This process also ensures that data content is shared across the team

to give individuals knowledge of the full data set and allow for different perspectives to be brought to the data analysis.

• Use coding practices to increase validity and objectivity. Having the same analyst recode material and another analyst independently code the same material can increase coding accuracy. However, this is very time intensive, and doing interim debriefings and analytical checks might serve just as well.

• Prepare documentation of the analysis and key decisions as if it will be rigorously audited by an external party.

Interpreting the Data and Presenting the Findings

Analysis begins with the first data source and continues to the very end. There is little distinction between data collection and the analysis process. Analysis includes the data displays and related text explanations, but it can also be analytical memos that are written during the course of the evaluation. These would document meetings of the analytical team as well as analytical insights that should become more sophisticated and abstract as the evaluation proceeds. As findings begin to emerge, the analyst team should think about interim and final data presentations.

Interim Findings

As data are collected, analytical insights will occur, such as patterns and themes. At least in the early part of the evaluation, no data gathering and analytical doors are closed as the emphasis centers on complete and accurate data and developing findings. As data collection and analysis move into full swing, the analyst team should continually produce analytical products that can be presented to various audiences, such as funders and decision makers, and secure feedback to improve the evaluation. "Early and often" analysis and presentation continually informs and develops strategies for the research design, data collection instruments, sampling strategy to fill in data gaps, consideration of other methods, and testing preliminary findings against current theory or theory construction. It also serves to tease out alternative explanations. Relationships between segments of data can be explored, such as correlation or apparent cause and effect. I normally develop short paragraphs with examples of emerging findings early on that present a short analytical story. I also develop interim briefings and presentations to hone the analysis and the emerging findings.

Miles and Huberman (1994) recommend interim products such as case summaries and vignettes. Interim case summaries present what the analyst team knows about the case and what remains to be found out. These summaries present a review of findings, evaluation of the data quality supporting them, and the agenda for the next data collection. A vignette describes a series of events believed to be representative or typical of the data, done with a narrative or story approach. For example, as part of a research team, I examined how certain leading organizations approached information technology performance management, studying practices of both public and private sector organizations. The team used case study illustrations to illustrate key practices. For example, one practice was assessing performance maturity and developing complete performance definitions. An illustration of gaining experience with fundamental measures and then expanding, shown in the box, survived as a vignette during the interim analysis and became a text box used in the final report.

Example Case Vignette

Kodak is one organization that is systematically defining the maturity of each measure it plans to use in its balanced scorecard. Kodak categorizes measure maturity as fundamental, growing, or maturing. Established indicators are considered as fundamental. Growing measures are evolved from the fundamental, but are not the best they can be. Maturing measures are defined as best-in-class for whatever they are measuring. For example, for internal performance, a fundamental measure is to meet all service-level agreements, a growing measure is information delivery excellence, and a maturing measure is defect-free products and services. Kodak believes it is important to build the right fundamental practices first in developing an initial information technology performance management system.

Presenting the Final Findings

The final step of qualitative analysis is formally presenting the final findings (for a fuller description, see Yin, 1989, Patton, 2002, and Wolcott, 1990). Early and frequent analysis should make this final step less daunting as it focuses material for composing the finding presentation. In fact, Wolcott (1990) says that writing is a form of thinking that will help the analytical process.

The analyst team should have a clear strategy and responsibilities for key presentation events and processes.

Setting and Adhering to Milestones. This is a key element in presenting findings. Bounding the time of the evaluation from beginning to final delivery date is important, but more important is setting key deliverable dates and keeping to them during the course of the analysis. The analyst team should specify an evaluation's research plan that is realistic about access to data sources, time for data collection, analysis efforts, internal review and clearance, and securing feedback or comments from external sources.

I am always amazed when a research design ignores vacations, holidays, and other events that will steal time and expertise away from the analysis and presentation of findings. These can be internal to the analyst team, such as planned vacation time. However, they often affect data collection. For example, the two weeks around Christmas and New Year's are deadly for conducting interviews or other data collection in government settings. If data sources are involved in budget formulation, then budget season may delay data collection.

Determining Audience Needs. The analyst team will need to keep in mind the possible audiences and what each specific audience will want in terms of the analysis. For example, Yin (1989) says that colleagues will be interested in relationships between the findings and other research. Decision makers will want to know action implications for action. The analyst team likely will need to devise multiple products for diverse audiences that will respond to their analytical needs or make conscious decisions of what audience will not be satisfied at all or in part.

Organizing the Analytical Products. By the end of the analysis process, which has occurred since the beginning of the evaluation, the analyst team will have many data displays, summaries of interview findings, document summaries and implications, examples that can illustrate findings, and feedback comments. These analytical information sources should be organized, indexed, and protected so they can be easily retrieved and controlled as writing starts. This is particularly important if several members of an analyst team are responsible for writing and need access to the information, which they can use to illustrate draft findings. Control also comes out of organizing. This means making sure that a single data source does not overpopulate the findings and that there is balance across data sources. For example, in doing studies of homeland security, one data source was particularly robust, and each analyst wanted to use it as an example. If one data source is the primary source of examples, then it soon appears that the findings are of the one data source, not the total data set.

Outlining and Sequencing the Report Presentation. Wolcott (1990) says that one key to writing up qualitative research is a detailed written outline that will clearly identify major and subordinate points and assess if the structure will accommodate the data and an appropriate presentation sequence. In fact, he advocates writing a draft before beginning fieldwork as it will remind the analyst team about format, sequence, space limitations, and focus. In addition, the draft writing will surface and document analyst team beliefs, including biases and assumptions. Wolcott says that organizing the report has no set answers, such as if to organize the report as events occurred.

While writing a draft before collecting data is not a practice I have used, I have found preparing an outline about midway through data collection and analysis to be helpful. Decisions about the audience for the bulk of reporting should have been made, and there are generally considerable analytical products available. The outline is continually revised, with points added or deleted, as analysis comes to a conclusion.

Composing and Tightening the Findings. This element includes deciding what goes in the report and what writing style will be followed. As Patton (2002) says, reporting findings is the final step in data reduction, but decisions have to be made about what finds its way into the report. For example, the analyst team will have to decide how much description to include, such as what direct quotations, if any, should be woven into the report and what balance there will be between description, analytical products, and interpretation. In many reports I have worked on, developing tight descriptive and inferential information, collapsing data displays, and deciding on the most important examples is often difficult, but it must be well done if the report is to be well received.

For example, I developed several themes and suggested practices for the study regarding federal-state results management. The box contains an abbreviated excerpt of a paper presenting findings that integrated data from several questions regarding state involvement in and impact on federal program performance decisions and recommendations for improvement. It includes a sense of the number of officials who recommended improvements, illustrative paraphrased comments from officials, areas of disagreement, and recommendations.

Data displays are also a tool I favor in final reports. For example, I conducted research on how financial institution regulatory agencies could improve their annual performance plans. The information came from federal and state organizations that were identified as using or planning to use a variety of useful practices. One data display that was used identified different types of performance comparisons to set performance targets:

- Redefined performance expectations
- Future performance levels or changes in levels to be achieved at a later date
- Best practice benchmarks from other organizations
- Program implementation milestones

An abbreviated data display from the full data set from the final report is shown in Table 15.2.

Patton (2002) advises focusing by determining the essence—what is substantively significant—and providing enough detail and evidence, including

Reporting the Findings: An Example

A second federal agency practice was involving states as full partners in federal Government Performance and Results Act (GPRA) decision making.

Interviews indicated federal agencies should educate state officials about GPRA, including its measurement of federal and state performance. A significant number of state officials were only vaguely aware of GPRA, and others did not have any knowledge of GPRA. Many state officials did not see the connection between GPRA and the state delivery of federal programs. However, there was some state disagreement if Congress intended GPRA to measure state performance or federal performance in delivering federal programs. Some saw GPRA as intended to measure federal responsibilities, not state responsibilities. Others believed federal agencies could not mandate federal performance goals, measures, targets, or strategies, but could hold states accountable for individual state goals. State officials often became concerned if federal agencies moved beyond high-level statements to stipulate state or local goals, measures, targets, or strategies.

Many state officials involved in the GPRA decision-making process believed they had little voice in the actual formulation or finalization of national goals for programs under their responsibility. Some saw their comments on proposed national goals as largely a pro forma federal activity allowing federal officials to say they had involved the states in GPRA decision making. Most state officials believed state input could inform federal officials about goals important to states, the impact of policy decisions, and performance implementation options and capabilities. The state officials generally recommended ongoing federal-state consensual GPRA decision making. Federal officials should work with state officials or national state association officials to formulate national GPRA goals, annual performance targets, measures, or strategies, depending on the latitude in the program legislative performance requirements. Overall, the interviews indicated that if states were involved in and had impact on formulating GPRA decisions, then there was more state acceptance and ownership of the final decisions and overall GPRA process.

sufficient context, to make the case, yet not including everything that could be described. However, the initial composition of the report should include multiple examples and illustrations—more than you know you will need—and comprehensive analysis or interpretation. The analyst team should not rush too quickly to delete or synthesize material. Through additional drafting, the initial composition can be more thoroughly examined, holes filled in, and "extra" material deleted or folded into a tighter description. As the composi-

Table 15.2. Report Data Display

Performance Comparisons	Examples of Performance Comparisons	Source
Predefined	• 80% of the domestic seafood industry will be operating preventative controls in safety	Food and Drug Administration
	• Achieve a readiness index of 72 required by the Department of Defense	Coast Guard
	• Zero significant radiation exposure resulting from civilian nuclear reactors	Nuclear Regulatory Commission
Future levels	• Reduce the rate of air travel delays by 5.5% from a 1992–96 baseline of 181 delays per 100,000 activities	Federal Aviation Administration
	• Reduce three of the most prevalent workplace injuries and causes of illness by 7% from baseline in selected industries and occupations	Occupational Safety and Health Administration
Milestones	• Develop modeling techniques to assess human exposure and dose response to certain foodborne pathogens	Food and Drug Administration

Source: U.S. General Accounting Office (1999, p. 41).

tion develops in the final stages, the best examples and illustrations can be retained.

Identifying What Objectivity and Validity Tests Will Involve the Draft Findings. This final element includes the use of the tests in composing the final report. The analyst team has both internal and external choices for securing feedback on the draft findings. Internally, the team can impose a formal review of the report and its conclusions. However, the formal review should be done not by the team itself but by others as cold readers. If the team conducts its own review, too often the team members zero in on their own material, testing yet again for substance and writing style but not thinking about threats to objectivity and validity. Externally, the team asks for a review by program officials and colleagues that can add to the objectivity and validity of the findings. Externally, the team can also use an advisory committee to review and comment on draft materials.

Highlighting a Few Key Points

I am often asked how I see relevant patterns in what others may see as a hopeless morass of data. No one is born with an inner eye and instinct to conduct qualitative data analysis. This chapter has highlighted many elements, tools, and issues in qualitative analysis efforts that help in seeing relevant patterns. These are summarized in Table 15.3 in the form of practices.

These practices define a rigorous and comprehensive approach to qualitative data analysis. However, they also should be applied within a philosophical framework that values a rigorous and comprehensive approach. Qualitative data analysis can be enhanced by the analyst team's valuing a philosophical framework that stresses certain key points.

Analytical Knowledge Development. This means being a serious student of program evaluation methods, including analytical techniques and practices. While some knowledge comes from formal graduate courses, much more comes from subscribing to journals and purchasing books—and reading them. Too often, analysts get locked into techniques they have used in the past or do not refresh their knowledge. Keeping up with the literature is a constant reminder of what is possible and what are new approaches.

Obstinate Attention to the Research Questions. This means not drifting off the path of the evaluation's purpose, from a large-scale evaluation to providing comments on a document. I continually revisit the research questions and keep assessing if the data collection and analysis are answering the evaluation purpose, as stated in the research questions. It is frequently very easy to start pursuing data sources and collection that may be personally interesting but have little, if anything, to do with the intent of the evaluation. The

Table 15.3. Summary of Qualitative Data Analysis Practices

Practice Area	*Practices*
Preanalysis elements	• Well-crafted research design and appropriate data targeting • Adequate collection and documentation of relevant data • Well-designed data organization system • An analyst team with appropriate skill, knowledge, experience, creativity, diligence, and work ethic
Analytical subprocesses and practices	• Well-founded data reduction and pattern identification • Producing objective analytical conclusions and communicating those conclusions
Objectivity and validity elements	• Addressing threats to objectivity and validity • Countering the threats through practices such as triangulation, negative case analysis, and examining data relationships
Data interpretation and findings presentation	• Not closing data gathering and analytical doors too soon • Using interim products such as case summaries and vignettes • Having a clear strategy and responsibilities for presentation events and processes such as setting milestones, determining audience needs, organizing the analytical products, and identifying objectivity and validity tests

research questions keep the analyst tethered to the main goal. Changing events that make the research questions moot or in serious need of revision should necessitate a change in the evaluation's purpose.

Theoretical and Context Preparation. This means developing knowledge about two things. One is relevant theory, especially other research, that can help the research design and what might be possible avenues for analytical insights. The other is the evaluation context, most often program details, organizational settings, and governmental relationships. This knowledge leads to a better understanding of what is or could be happening in the program. Even in doing a document review, I try to understand the context and history of the document and bring that to the analytical exercise.

Insisting on Thick Data Collection and Description. An analyst is only as good as the data he or she is analyzing. If data sources are minimal or not forthcoming with description or if the description is not captured in evaluation work papers, then the analysis is on a slippery slope. The outcome is generally speculation or superficial analysis that is questionable for decision making. The bottom line is to work very hard to collect all relevant data.

Listening to and Recycling the Data. I continually try to look at different perspectives and possible alternatives as I listen to the data and recycle the data through iterative analysis as more data are collected or I start understanding what the data seem to be saying. The saying, "It's not over 'til it's over," is a good principle to follow here.

Experience. Years of doing qualitative analysis build skills in designing evaluations, preparing for and conducting interviews, organizing the data, crafting data displays, and developing interim findings. Experience also brings sensitivity to looming trouble, such as slipping milestones and findings that seem to overreach when compared to the actual data sources.

Conclusion

The final judge of qualitative analysis is the evaluation product's reception and use. I am always proud of products where the findings are meaningful and relevant to the audience, are factually correct and fully supported by the data, are well presented, and meet project time lines. Each qualitative analyst needs to develop a personal scorecard to judge the quality of his or her analysis. The strategies and techniques presented in this chapter will lead to fine ratings.

References

Huberman, A. M., and Miles, M. B. "Data Management and Analysis Methods." In N. K. Dezin and Y. S. Lincoln (eds.), *Collecting and Interpreting Qualitative Materials*. Thousand Oaks, Calif.: Sage, 1998.

Mason, J. *Qualitative Researching.* (2nd ed.) Thousand Oaks, Calif.: Sage, 2002.

Maxwell, J. A. *Qualitative Research Design: An Interactive Approach.* Thousand Oaks, Calif.: Sage, 1996.

Miles, M. B., and Huberman, A. M. *Qualitative Data Analysis: An Expanded Sourcebook.* (2nd ed.) Thousands Oaks, Calif.: Sage, 1994.

Patton, M. Q. *Qualitative Research and Evaluation Methods.* (3rd ed.) Thousand Oaks, Calif.: Sage, 2002.

QSR International Pty Ltd. *N6 Reference Guide.* Doncaster, Victoria, Australia: QSR International Pty Ltd., Mar. 2002.

Richards, T. J., and Richards, L. "Using Computers in Qualitative Research." In N. K. Dezin and Y. S. Lincoln (eds.), *Collecting and Interpreting Qualitative Materials.* Thousand Oaks, Calif.: Sage, 1998.

Strauss, A., and Corbin, J. *Basics of Qualitative Research: Techniques and Procedures for Developing Grounded Theory.* (2nd ed.) Thousand Oaks, Calif.: Sage, 1998.

U.S. General Accounting Office. *Managing for Results: Strengthening Regulatory Agencies' Performance Management Practices.* Washington, D.C.: U.S. Government Printing Office, Oct. 1999.

Wolcott, H. F. *Writing Up Qualitative Research.* Thousand Oaks, Calif.: Sage, 1990.

Yin, R. K. *Case Study Research: Design and Methods.* Thousand Oaks, Calif.: Sage, 1989.

16

Using Statistics in Evaluation

Kathryn E. Newcomer, Philip W. Wirtz

Statistics are used in a variety of ways to support evaluation endeavors. The manner in which program and pertinent contextual factors are measured greatly affects the sorts of analytical techniques and statistical tests that are available for use.

A key distinction affecting choices of statistics is the level of measurement used for coding the phenomena of interest. In 1946, Stevens identified four levels of measurement (nominal, ordinal, interval, and ratio) that have been used to describe empirical data ever since. Under Stevens's taxonomy, nominal and ordinal levels of measurement are inherently categorical, while interval and ratio variables reflect an underlying numeric continuum. Numeric distinctions are made with interval and ratio level variables that permit the values to be mathematically manipulated. Ratio measures differ from interval only in the assumption of a meaningful zero point.

Nominal-level measurement entails simply attaching numbers to data for purposes of assigning them to groups. Ordinal-level variables differ from nominal-level variables in that the categories of ordinal variables bear some ordered relationship to one another. For example, participants in a job training skills program might be identified at the end of the program as "successful" (completed training and employed within two weeks of program completion), "partially successful" (completed training but unable to find employment within two weeks of program completion), or "unsuccessful" (failed to complete training), with the distinction that ordinal variables are characterized by order), while the nominal-level categories serve only to differentiate the categories. Ordinal variables play a key role in evaluation since ordinal attitudinal scales are typically used to measure program participants' perceptions.

An enduring legacy of the Stevens taxonomy is the need to match the level of measurement to the analytical technique; it is frequently the case that the selection of the appropriate analytical technique is virtually pro forma once the levels of measurement of the key variables in the analysis have been established. In practical application of statistics, other considerations, such as the audience's comfort level, also merit attention. Matching analytical techniques to the level of measurement, audience, and evaluation questions is yet another challenge for evaluators.

Other chapters in this volume have referred to statistical decisions, such as determining an adequate sample size and selecting an appropriate measure of a program effect. This chapter offers more background for such decision making and guidance for selecting statistical techniques.

Descriptive and Inferential Statistics

When any phenomena are counted, the numbers can be tabulated according to a variety of procedures. If the resulting statistics, such as averages, are used to describe a group of items, the figures presented are called *descriptive statistics.*

In many situations, the population of program recipients, or even service providers, is so large that to survey the entire population would be too costly. Instead, a sample is drawn from the population with the hopes of generalizing the quantitative results to the population. To ensure that the statistics can be generalized with confidence, the manner in which the sample is drawn is of critical importance. If a group of units is selected in a systematic fashion such that the probability for each unit to be selected from the larger population is known, the group can be referred to as a probability sample. When statistics are computed from the sample with the intention of generalizing from the sample to the population from which the sample was drawn, the statistics are referred to as inferential statistics.

Generalizing from Samples

The accuracy of inferences drawn from a sample to a population is critically affected by the sampling procedures used. Four principles should guide evaluators when they select samples:

• *The population of interest must be reasonably known and identifiable.* This criterion presents a challenge for evaluators when records are not comprehensive. Therefore, evaluators should make efforts to ascertain whether the reason that records are not inclusive may be indicative of any bias.

- *A sampling technique should be used in which the probability for selecting any unit in the population can be calculated (probability sampling).* Evaluators should use a sampling technique such as using random numbers to select units (random sampling), perhaps using the tables of random numbers in textbooks or in statistical software, or selecting every *n*th unit in the population (systematic sampling). When there are specific subgroups within the population of particular interest, the evaluators may divide the population into such subgroups and apply probability sampling techniques within each of the subgroups, an approach called *stratified sampling.*

- *A sample should be drawn that is of appropriate size relative to the size of the population to which generalization is desired.* Basic statistics textbooks and software provide formulas that can be applied to identify appropriate sample sizes as long as the evaluators can specify how much confidence they wish to have in the results and the amount of error they are willing to accept.

- *Even though probability sampling is applied, evaluators should examine a sample to ensure that it is truly representative of the population to which the evaluators hope to generalize* on variables of critical interest, such as demographic characteristics like gender and race. Probability sampling can help rule out chance variation that may conceal true relationships or impede accurate identification of program effects, but it cannot guarantee that the sample contains certain units or people in the same proportion as they exist in the population of interest.

When the data collection strategies make the use of probability sampling techniques impossible, as when evaluators do not have access to the full population, using statistics for inferential purposes may be problematic. In such cases, statistics should not be generalized from the sample to the population; evaluators should take even greater care to test the representativeness of the sample and identify sources of bias that render the sample unlike the population from which it was drawn. The statistics might then be used for inferential purposes with explicit recognition that the statistical inferences are not as valid as the numerical representation of confidence indicates.

Statistical techniques have been developed to test whether relationships between variables in a sample can be generalized to the population from which it was drawn, given the particular sample size and the variation within the sample. Such techniques generate statistics that estimate the statistical significance, or generalizability, of relationships between variables. The chi square and the *t* test are the two statistics most frequently used to address the question of generalizability of relationships between variables. (Applications of each of these statistics appear in Appendixes 16A and 16B.)

Statistical Hypothesis Testing

To apply inferential statistics, a systematic procedure called statistical hypothesis testing should be used. First, a statistical hypothesis identifying the relationship between any two variables of interest must be specified. For two variables, a *null hypothesis* is stated. The null hypothesis in program evaluation is that the program has no effect in achieving the intended outcome. For example, "access to home health aides does not affect medical costs for emergency care" might be a null hypothesis for an evaluation of a home health aid program. When the null hypothesis is not rejected, the sample data do not permit a conclusion that the program has had the measured outcome.

When data are drawn to test the null hypothesis of no effect, if the program truly has no effect and the data support this, there is no problem. Similarly, if the program has the intended effect and the test data demonstrate this, again there is no problem.

Problems arise when there is a discrepancy between the true situation and the test results; in that case, an erroneous conclusion can be drawn. If the true situation is that the program does not have the desired effect but the statistics calculated suggest that it does, an error called a false positive, or type I error, is committed. If the true situation is that the program does have the desired effect but the test data suggest that it does not, a false negative, or type II error, is committed.

It is difficult to protect equally against both types of errors, so the costs of committing each should be considered and attention paid to avoiding the more costly one. In some cases, a false positive may be more costly to the public than a false negative. For example, when evaluators conclude a false positive that a very costly teenage pregnancy prevention program is effective when it really is not, the result may be that future funding is wasted on an ineffective program. A false-negative conclusion that an effective airline regulation is not working may mean that the regulation is not reauthorized. In any case, aspects of the evaluation design that may make either a false positive or a false negative more likely should be carefully considered. Table 16.1 identifies design features that may make an evaluation vulnerable to either a false-positive or a false-negative finding. Evaluators should weigh the consequences of committing both false-positive and false-negative errors and then identify ways in which they might minimize the more costly error.

Any measurement precaution that helps protect the evaluator from committing a false negative increases the statistical power of the test—the capability of a statistical test to accurately detect effects or differences between groups. Once the relative costs of committing a false positive and a false negative are considered, evaluators can develop a decision rule that reflects the level of confidence they wish to have in their decision to gener-

**Table 16.1. Evaluation Design Features Likely
to Generate False Positives or False Negatives**

Design Features	Raises the Likelihood of False Positives	Raises the Likelihood of False Negatives
1. Threats to validity		
a. The sample is made up of volunteers	X	
b. The same questions are used on a pretest or posttest	X	
c. Experimental mortality—only the more motivated group members remain in the program to be measured	X	
d. Hawthorne effect—the program participants are aware they are being measured and change their behavior in the desired direction	X	
e. The program is new and program staff or participants are more motivated than they might be later in the life of the program	X	
f. A control or comparison group tries to compensate for their failure to receive treatment		X
g. Staff fears harm to the control group and tries to compensate by providing more help to them		X
2. Other design characteristics		
a. Sample size too small		X
b. Time period for measurement too short		X
c. "Control" group receives "treatment" from other sources		X
d. Program not fully implemented		X

alize the existence of relationships found in their sample to the population. Since the probabilities of committing a false positive and a false negative are inversely related, the more evaluators protect against one type of error, the more vulnerable the test will be to the opposite error.

Selecting a Statistical Confidence Level

A quantified decision rule for specifying how much evidence is needed to generalize results also indicates how confident the evaluator wishes to be that a false positive will not occur. This decision rule provides the confidence level for the test.

The confidence level reflects the amount of evidence evaluators want to have to ensure that they are correct in concluding that the program does produce the observed effect. In the social sciences, a 95 percent confidence level is conventionally used as a decision rule for testing statistical hypotheses. The null hypothesis to be tested is that the treatment does not have the intended effect. If the findings are sufficiently deviant from what the probability tables predict if the null is true, the null hypothesis is rejected. This decision allows one to generalize the program effects found in the sample to the population from which it was drawn with the confidence that, over the long run, a test of this type should result in a false-positive error only five times out of one hundred.

For many, if not most, public program purposes, 95 percent may be excessive. Conclusions for which evaluators are 80 percent or 90 percent confident may be adequate and reduce the size of the sample needed, thereby reducing cost. When the costs to the public of committing a false negative are high—for example, judging an effective program to be ineffective because of obtaining data from a very small sample—it may be appropriate to go beyond convention and use even an 80 percent confidence level. While such a figure indicates that the risks of committing a false positive are greater than typically accepted, this lower confidence level helps hedge against making a false-negative error and dooming a program because the data do not seem to indicate that the program is effective.

Conducting a test that achieves significance at the 95 percent confidence level is typically interpreted in either of the following ways:

- One would obtain findings like this only five times out of one hundred samples if the null hypothesis (of no effect) was really true.
- One can be 95 percent confident that the sample findings were not simply the result of random variation.

When the null hypothesis is rejected (using the 95 percent decision rule), it is appropriate to state that the relationship in the sample data is "statistically significant at a confidence level of 95 percent." Concluding that a relationship between two variables is "statistically significant" tells the audience that, following conventional statistical hypothesis testing procedures, the relationship found in the sample reflects a real relationship in the population from which the sample was drawn. However, generalizing a relationship can be subject to many other threats, such as a selection bias, due to the evaluator's not being able to obtain data on some of those in the sample (for example, their refusal to complete surveys), or those in the sample being volunteers. Even if the numbers demonstrate that the findings are "statistically significant at the 95 percent confidence level," other problems with the representativeness of the sample may render the generalization of a relationship between two variables inappropriate.

Using a Confidence Interval to Convey Results

When the magnitude of a program effect is given, the results should be reported as a confidence interval—that is, the sample statistic should be stated with a margin of error such as plus or minus 2 percent. Reporting an effect without such a margin of error is not appropriate, for it incorrectly implies too much precision in the measures. Program effects should be given as falling within a range. For example, one might report that "the proportion of clients still receiving welfare benefits was five to ten percentage points lower for those who had completed the job training program than for the clients who did not complete the training."

Reporting of both statistical significance and the size of program effects should be clear. Both findings should be reported and interpreted for the audience. For example, a difference between treatment and control groups may be minuscule yet be statistically significant at a specified confidence level, usually due to a very large sample size. A difference may be impressive in magnitude but not statistically significant, usually because of a small sample size. Will policymakers care if a new program raises third graders' reading scores by 0.2 percent? Probably not; it is too small a gain if the program is at all costly.

Testing Statistical Significance for Nominal- and Ordinal-Level Variables

Evaluation researchers are often faced with the need to test for differences among three or more groups, or to compare two or more samples with respect to a nominal-level variable that has more than two categories. The chi-square test provides an approach for testing for the statistical significance of relationships between variables with any number of categories. Appendix 16A provides an illustration of applying the chi-square test using a commonly used software program—Statistical Package for the Social Sciences (SPSS). We demonstrate how to use software printout to develop user-friendly tables for presentation.

The chi-square test can be used whenever the objective is to determine whether a set of observed frequencies differs significantly from those that would be expected under a certain set of theoretical assumptions. Suppose we wish to know whether one or more ethnic groups tend to benefit differently from the intervention compared to the other groups. If random samples are drawn from each of the ethnic groups who received the intervention, the chi-square test can be used to determine whether the proportion of success differs across the ethnic group populations.

The chi-square test can be generalized to any situation in which we are interested in the relationship between two nominal-level variables. In fact, although the most typical application of the chi-square test pertains to nominal-level scales, chi-square tests are frequently also used with ordinal scales and sometimes even with collapsed interval and ratio scales (although more powerful tests are available and would generally be preferred over chi square in such cases).

Assumptions

The chi-square test requires that the expected frequencies are not very small. The reason for this assumption is that chi square inherently tests the underlying probabilities in each cell, and when the expected cell frequencies fall, these probabilities cannot be estimated with sufficient precision. Hence, it is essential that the sample size be large enough to guarantee the similarity between the theoretical and the sampling distribution of the chi-square statistic. Because the formula for computation of chi square includes the expected value of the cell frequency in the denominator, the chi-square value would be overestimated if this value was too small, resulting in the rejection of the null hypothesis.

To avoid making incorrect inferences from the chi-square test, a commonly applied (albeit possibly too conservative) general rule is that an expected frequency less than 5 in a cell is too small to use. Conservatively, when the contingency table contains more than one cell with an expected frequency less than 5, it is often appropriate to combine them to get an expected frequency of 5 or more. However, in doing so, the number of categories would be reduced, resulting in less information. It should be noted that the chi-square test is quite sensitive to the sample size. Table 16.2 illustrates the impact of sample size on chi square, and Table 16.3 illustrates that the same data are more likely to produce statistically significant findings when the number of cells in the table are reduced. Chi-square results do not tell us how strongly two variables are related. Measures of the strength of the relationship such as those discussed below should be used along with chi square to address the magnitude of the relationship analyzed.

Practical Significance

The terms *significance* and *statistical significance* are conventionally reserved for the judgment that sample results showing a relationship between variables can be generalized to the population from which the sample was drawn. A separate judgment should be made regarding the magnitude of the effect

Table 16.2. Effect of Sample Size on Chi Square

Rearrested Within Twelve Months of Release	Prisoner Served Full Sentence	Prisoner Released into Halfway House Six Months Prior to End of Sentence
Yes	63.3	58.6
No	36.7	41.4
	100%	100%
Sample Size	χ^2	Significance
100	.1984	NS
2000	3.97	.05
3500	7.00	.01

Table 16.3. Effect of Collapsing Tables on Chi Square

	Location of Procedure	
Level of Medicare Patient Satisfaction with Facility	Outpatient Clinics (N = 100)	Hospitals (N = 100)
1 Not at all satisfied	10	12
2	10	13
3	12	9
4	25	28
5 Extremely satisfied	43	38
	100%	100%

Since $df = 4$, you need $\chi^2 = 9.50$ for $p < .05$.

1,2	20	25
3, 4, 5	80	75
	100%	100%

Since $df = 1$, you need $\chi^2 = 3.84$ for $p < .05$.

that is being measured. In fact, the presentation and terminology used should clarify that two separate judgments are made: whether the sample data can be generalized and an evaluation of the size of the effect as slight, moderate, or strong. Judgments about the size of the effect reflect what the evaluators view as the practical importance of the measured effect. For example, if a new mathematical curriculum in a high school appears to raise students' achievement scores 1 percent, even if the large sample drawn indicates that the effect is "statistically significant," the size of the impact of the curriculum may seem inconsequential.

There are no standards available for evaluators to use when interpreting the magnitude of the size of the observed effect (or observed relationship between two or more measures). For example, most statistics measuring the magnitude of relationships between measures range from 0 to 1, or −1 to +1, and the closer to 1 (or −1) a number falls, the stronger the relationship is. There are no conventionally accepted rules to indicate what number is high enough to call "high." The best way to evaluate such numbers is to compare them to appropriate referents, such as comparable figures for previous years, other administrative units, or comparable programs. However, interpreting the comparisons is a judgment call. Appropriate and meaningful comparisons are absolutely essential to lend credibility to measures of magnitude. Statistical tests of the strength of the relationship between two variables are available that reflect how the two variables are measured and whether the analyst can convincingly argue that one of the variables is dependent on (affected by) the other. Table 16.4 provides a list of measures of association.

Measures of Association: Nominal-Level Variables

Phi Squared. The computation of chi square reveals that its value is directly influenced by the number of observations in the analysis. This suggests that chi square divided by the number of observations would provide a better measure of association. It turns out that this ratio, called ϕ^2 (and pronounced "fee-squared"), obtains the value 0 when there is absolutely no relationship between the two variables (for example, when all the samples have exactly the same proportion of successes). Furthermore, when the problem of interest involves two dichotomous variables, ϕ^2 takes on the value 1 when the relationship between the two variables is perfect (all of the successes are in one of the two groups, and all of the failures are in the other). However, in the more general case when both variables have more than two values, ϕ^2 can attain values that are considerably larger than unity: in fact, the upper bound of ϕ^2 is one less than the number of categories in the variable with the fewer categories.

Cramer's V. By a simple manipulation of ϕ^2, we get a measure (Cramer's V) that ranges from 0 to 1 regardless of the number of categories in either of the two variables, and can attain the value 1 even when the number of categories of the two variables is not equal. Furthermore, V and ϕ^2 are identical when at least one of the two variables is dichotomous. Thus, the upper limit of V depends solely on strength of the relationship, not on the number of categories in either variable or on the sample size. The interpretation of V is less intuitive than lambda (considered subsequently) but can be compared across tables of different size.

Contingency Coefficient. Like Cramer's V, Pearson's contingency coefficient is a chi-square-based measure of the relationship between two nominal

**Table 16.4. Statistics Useful for Measuring the Strength
of Relationships Between Two Variables**

How Are the Variables Measured?	Appropriate Coefficient	Range
Both are nominal	Phi squared	0 to ∞
	Cramer's V	0 to 1
	Pearson's contingency coefficient	0 to 1
Both are nominal and it is clear which variable is "dependent" on the other, that is, asymmetric	Goodman and Kruskal's tau	0 to 1
	Lambda	0 to 1
Both are rankings	Spearman's r	−1 to +1
Both are ordinal	Goodman and Kruskal's T	−1 to +1
	Kendall's T–b	−1 to +1
	Stuart's T–c	−1 to +1
Both are ordinal and it is clear which variable is "dependent" on the other, that is, asymmetric	Somers' D	−1 to +1
Both are interval	Pearson's r	−1 to +1

variables. Although the range of the contingency coefficient is always limited to 0 through 1, it can reach the limit of 1 only if the number of categories is unlimited. Unlike lambda, this statistic has no operational interpretation and cannot be interpreted across tables of different sizes.

Goodman and Kruskal's Tau. All of the association measures previously introduced suffer from the nonintuitive interpretability of the index. Although it makes sense conceptually to reflect on 0 representing "no association" and 1 representing "perfect association," it is unclear how to interpret an index value of, for example, .87. This limitation of the preceding measures of association led to the development of a class of proportional reduction in error (PRE) measures of association, all of which can be interpreted in a more intuitive manner. Goodman and Kruskal's τ_B is an example of one such measure of association.

To employ τ_B, it is necessary to distinguish between a dependent variable (the variable you wish to predict) and an independent variable (the variable on which you wish to base the prediction). In the previous example, the outcome of the intervention (success or failure) would typically constitute the dependent variable, and preintervention characteristics (such as below versus above the poverty line) would typically constitute the independent variable. The τ_B associational measure represents the reduction in the proportion of errors you would make as a result of knowing the value of the independent variable, and thus ranges between 0 and 1. For example, a τ_B of .87 would carry the interpretation that by knowing the value of the independent variable, you are making 87 percent fewer errors when predicting the value of the dependent variable than you would if you did not know the value of the independent variable. Note that τ_B is categorized as asymmetric since its value depends on which of the two variables you choose as dependent. For many applications in evaluation research, this is often not a limitation.

Lambda. Lambda is very similar to τ_B: it is an asymmetric PRE measure that ranges between 0 and 1. The definition of "error" is somewhat less conservative than that used in τ_B, and as a result τ_B values are typically somewhat lower than λ values. A major problem associated with λ occurs in the circumstance that one of the dependent variable categories has many more observations than the others, resulting in a λ of zero when none of the other association measures we have considered would have been zero and where we would typically not want to refer to the variables as being unrelated. For these reasons, τ_B is typically viewed as preferable to λ when the number of observations is not approximately equal across the categories of the dependent variable.

Measures of Association: Ordinal-Level Variables

The measures of association considered thus far will work with any level of measurement but are best suited to nominal scales. In this section, we focus on measures of association that are appropriate whenever the relationship between the two discrete variables is either monotonic increasing or monotonic decreasing. Although the concept of a linear relationship between two variables is limited to interval- and ratio-level variables, it is appropriate with ordinal variables to identify a relationship in which as one variable increases, the other increases (or, conversely, as one variable increases, the other decreases).

Spearman's r_s. Spearman's r_s is used to compare the rankings on two sets of scores, for example, when people or administrative units are ranked from best to worst on two different criteria. Conceptually, calculating Spearman's r_s involves nothing more than taking the differences of ranks, summing the squares of those differences, and then manipulating the measure so that its value will be 1 when the rankings are in perfect agreement, −1 if they are in perfect disagreement, and 0 if there is no relationship. If the sample size is at least 10, the sampling distribution of r_s is approximately normal with known standard error, leading to the application of the standard normal distribution (z) for tests of significance.

Measures of Concordance. The following are measures of ordinal association that consider whether the variable Y tends to increase as X increases:

gamma, Kendall's τ_b, Stuart's τ_c (also known as Kendall's τ_c), and Somers' D. These measures are appropriate for ordinal variables, and they classify pairs of observations as concordant or discordant. A pair is considered to be concordant (C) if the observation with the larger value of X also has the larger value of Y. A pair is considered to be discordant (D) if the observation with the larger value of X has the smaller value of Y. For example, if income and education are related, if a has a higher income than b, then we predict a will also have a higher education level than b. (Refer to Agresti, 1990, for additional information.)

Goodman-Kruskal Gamma. The estimator of gamma is based on the number of concordant and discordant pairs of observations. (It is also a PRE measure of ordinal table association.) It ignores tied pairs (that is, pairs of observations that have equal values of X or equal values of Y). Gamma is appropriate only when both variables lie on an ordinal scale. It has the range −1 to +1. If the two variables are independent, then the estimator of gamma tends to be close to zero. Gamma is symmetric so one need not specify which variable is dependent on the other. Gamma is estimated by

$$G = [(C - D) / (C + D)].$$

For 2×2 tables, gamma is equivalent to Yule's Q. (Refer to Goodman and Kruskal, 1979; Agresti, 1990; and Brown and Benedetti, 1977.) Gamma is preferable to Spearman's rho and Kandall's tau when the data contain many tied observations.

Kendall's τ_b. Kendall's τ_b is similar to gamma except that τ_b uses a correction for ties. It is appropriate only when both variables are dichotomous or lie on an ordinal scale. It is best used in square contingency tables (where the number of rows equals the number of columns). It is symmetric and has the range −1 to +1. (Refer to Kendall, 1955, and Brown and Benedetti, 1977.) There is no well-defined intuitive meaning for τ_b, which is the surplus of concordant over discordant pairs as a percentage of concordant, discordant, and approximately one-half of tied pairs. The rationale for this is that if the direction of causation is unknown, then the surplus of concordant over discordant pairs should be compared with the total of all relevant pairs, where those relevant are the concordant pairs, the discordant pairs, plus either the X ties or Y ties but not both, and since direction is not known, the geometric mean is used as an estimate of relevant tied pairs. It reaches 1.0 (or −1.0 for negative relationships) only for square tables when all entries are on one diagonal and equals 0 under statistical independence.

Stuart's τ_c. Stuart's τ_c, also a non-PRE measure of ordinal table association, makes an adjustment for table size in addition to a correction for ties. It can be used in nonsquare tables and does not require specifying one variable as dependent. It is appropriate only when both variables lie on an ordinal scale. It has the range −1 to +1.

Somers' D. Somers' *D* differs from τ_b in that it uses a correction only for pairs that are tied on the independent variable. Somers' *D* is appropriate only when both variables lie on an ordinal scale. It has the range −1 to +1. (Refer to Somers, 1962; Goodman and Kruskal, 1979; and Liebetrau, 1983.) If you have a clear dependent variable that you are trying to predict, report Somers' *D* for predicting *y* (assuming *y* is the variable you are trying to predict). This is preferable because it includes ties only on *y* and ignores ties on *x* that are irrelevant for your purposes anyway.

Selecting Appropriate Statistics

Evaluators should use several criteria to ensure selecting the most appropriate statistics in a particular situation. The three categories of criteria that evaluators should use in deciding which statistical technique will be most appropriate are provided in the box listing these criteria.

The substantive questions identified to guide an evaluation, the data collection decisions made about how to measure the phenomena of interest, and the type of audience the evaluator is addressing all affect selection of statistical techniques.

Sample data are usually selected with the intention of generalizing results to the population from which the sample units were drawn. Statistics that test generalizability include chi square and *t*. Which of these statistics is selected depends on how the variables were measured. Chi square can be used no matter how the variables are measured, but the *t* test requires that the dependent variable (typically the program effect) be measured at the interval-ratio level—for example, unemployment rate. Appendix 16B provides an illustration of applying the *t* test using SPSS software.

No matter which analytical technique is selected, both the statistic used to assess statistical significance and the magnitude of an effect or strength of the relationships analyzed should be reported. Table 16.5 displays objectives evaluators may have in analyzing data and statistical techniques frequently used to address them.

Selecting a Technique to Estimate Program Impact

When evaluators address impact questions and wish to estimate or predict an impact by measuring the relationship between the alleged cause—the program—and the alleged effect, the manner in which the variables were measured limits the number of statistics appropriate for use. The most fundamental constraint is whether the variables were measured at the nominal,

Criteria for Selecting Appropriate Data Analysis Techniques

Question-Related Criteria

- Is generalization from the sample to the population desired?
- Is the causal relationship between an alleged cause and alleged effect of interest? Is it an impact question?
- Does the question (or statutory or regulatory document) contain quantitative criteria to which results can be compared?

Measurement-Related Criteria

- At what level of measurement were the variables measured: nominal (for example, gender), ordinal (for example, attitudes measured with Likert-type scales), or interval (for example, income)?
- Were multiple indicators used to measure key variables?
- What are the sample sizes in pertinent subgroups?
- How many observations were recorded for the respondents: one, two, or more (time series)?
- Are the samples independent or related? That is, was the sample measured at two or more points in time (related)?
- What is the distribution of each of the variables of interest, such as bimodal or normal?
- How much precision was incorporated in the measures?
- Are there outliers affecting calculation of statistics, that is, extremely high or low values that skew the mean and other statistics?

Audience-Related Criteria

- Will the audience understand sophisticated analytical techniques such as multiple regression?
- Will graphic presentations of data (such as bar charts) be more appropriate than tables filled with numbers?
- How much precision does the audience want in numerical estimates?
- Will the audience be satisfied with graphs depicting trends or desire more sophisticated analyses such as regressions?
- Will the audience understand the difference between statistical significance and the practical importance of numerical findings?

Table 16.5. Matching Statistical Techniques to Analytical Objectives

Purpose of the Analysis	How the Variables Are Measured	Appropriate Technique	Appropriate Test for Statistical Significance	Appropriate Measure of Magnitude
To compare a sample distribution to a population distribution	Nominal/ordinal	Frequency counts	Chi- square	NA
	Interval	Means and medians Standard deviations/ interquartile range	Chi square	NA
To analyze a relationship between two variables	Nominal/ordinal	Contingency tables	Chi square	See Table 16.2 and difference in column percentages
	Interval	Contingency tables/ test of differences of means or proportions	Chi square or t	Difference in column percentages or in means
To reduce the number of variables through identifying factors that explain variation in a larger set of variables	Interval	Factor analysis	NA	Pearson's correlations; Eigenvalues
To sort units into similar clusters or groupings	Nominal/ordinal/ interval	Cluster analysis; discriminant function analysis	F; Wilks' Lambda	Cannonical/ correlation coefficient[2]
To predict or estimate program impact	Nominal/ordinal dependent variable	Log linear regression	t and F	Odds estimates
	Interval dependent variable	Regression	t and F	R^2, beta weights
To describe or predict a trend in a series of data collected over time	Nominal, ordinal, or interval independent variables but interval dependent variable	Regression	t and F	R^2, beta weights

ordinal, or interval level of measurement. With nominal measures, contingency tables that array frequency counts are the most often used technique for analyzing data to assess the impact of one variable on another. In fact, if any of the variables of interest are nominal, contingency tables are the best option. Table 16.6 presents a model contingency table.

With ordinal measures, contingency tables and frequency distributions are still the most likely choice for analysis. Some researchers prefer to treat ordinal measures as if they are equivalent to interval measures, and they choose analytical techniques typically reserved for interval measures such as regression. However, unless an ordinal scale contains at least five values, it is probably best to treat the scale as a nominal measure. Even if the scale contains five or more values, it is best first to examine the observed frequencies and then determine whether the range in the actual responses is sufficient for the scale to be treated as an interval measure. For example, if the vast majority of clients rated services 4 or 5 on a five-point scale, the measure should not be treated as if it were interval when a statistical technique is selected.

With interval measures, evaluators have the widest range of alternatives. When evaluators wish to explain an effect (what analysts call a dependent variable) by other variables, regression is often used. (Application of regression is discussed in Chapter Seventeen.)

Table 16.6. Model Contingency Table with Two Ordinal Variables: Reported Incidence of Bouts of Depression by Participation in Morning Art Classes

	Level of Participation of Homeless Clients in Art Class		
	Never Participated in After-Breakfast Art Class	*Participated in After-Breakfast Art Classes About Once a Week*	*Participated in After-Breakfast Art Classes Two or Three Times per Week*
Reported number of bouts of depression:			
More than once a week	53	33	29
At least weekly	21	33	33
Never	26	33	38
	100%	99%	100%

Gamma = −.15

Chi square is statistically significant at 95% confidence level.

[a]Totals may not add up to 100 percent due to rounding.

Selecting Techniques to Sort Measures or Units

When multiple indicators have been used to measure a phenomenon of interest, such as a program effect, there are two basic approaches to reducing the data to a smaller number of factors: aggregating measures that are prespecified to capture the effects (or variables) of interest or using analytical techniques to identify patterns in the measures that indicate, post hoc, that there are observable patterns in the measures.

When criteria for measuring a program effect, such as quality of services, are set for evaluators, the measures used can simply be aggregated. A summary index can be used that weights different measures and then sums the total.

When evaluators are unsure of what basic factors best express the criterion of interest, they can use analytical techniques that sort through the indicators to identify covariation that might permit the creation of indices. Factor analysis is the technique most frequently used for such data reduction purposes.

The logic supporting factor analysis is that there are underlying factors that explain the observed variation in the indicators. The correlations among the indicators are examined to identify patterns suggesting independent groups of covarying measures that might actually be reflecting more fundamental factors. An evaluation of air controllers' responses to new regulations might start with a set of forty-five indicators, but with factor analysis, the number may be reduced to five basic concerns.

Sometimes evaluators wish to sort units such as delivery sites into groups to identify characteristics of high or low performers. If the criterion on which the units are evaluated as low and high is known beforehand, discriminant function analysis can be used to identify the other characteristics of the units that will best predict which units will score high on the criterion measure. Discriminant function analysis is similar to regression in that it identifies linear combinations (models) of other variables that best predict the groupings—of high and low performers, for example. To illustrate, suppose evaluators were trying to identify key characteristics of parolees who commit crimes versus those who do not commit crimes after release. Discriminant function analysis might allow them to use five indicators describing the parolees to identify characteristics most likely to predict recidivism.

When the criterion on which units are to be disaggregated is not known beforehand, cluster analysis can be used to identify similar groupings. Cluster analysis differs from factor analysis in that the objective is to group objects, typically people or units, rather than to identify groupings among variables. Characteristics of programs such as the level of administrative workload and other contextual characteristics might be used to identify clusters. An evaluator of an interjurisdictional program, such as legal services to the poor, might be interested in identifying clusters of offices that appear to operate under many of the same constraints. In this case, cluster analysis might be applied to identify characteristics that seem to differentiate most consistently across the offices. (See Hair, Anderson, Tatham, and Black, 1998, for more on factor analysis, discriminant function analysis, and cluster analysis.)

Other Factors Affecting Selection of Statistical Techniques

In addition to considering how statistics will be used in an evaluation, evaluators must consider other criteria when selecting a statistical technique. Sample size, for instance, may have a dramatic effect on an analysis; a small sample may fail to demonstrate an effect of a program, thus precluding any further analysis of subgroup differences.

In addition to the actual size of a sample, the number of observations recorded for the units of interest is pertinent to decision making regarding statistical techniques. For example, when two or more observations are taken on the same units, change over time may be analyzed, and the notion of related samples is introduced, leading to the selection of statistics created just for such situations. When many observations are available on a specific phenomenon, such as traffic fatalities over a series of years or infant mortality rates for specific jurisdictions over a period of years, time-series techniques employing regression may be applied.

Before employing any statistical technique, evaluators should examine the distribution of the units along each of the variables or measures. Such basic frequency analysis will indicate how much the units vary on each of the variables. For example, if race is of interest in an analysis of the impact of a management training course on managers, and only two of fifty-six training participants are minority group members, it will be impossible to use race as a variable in any analysis. If age of program participant is of interest in an evaluation but a sample contains only fifteen and sixteen year olds, the low variation on age rules out many analytical techniques. When a variable is measured at the interval level but the sample range is very narrow, the techniques available are limited to those appropriate for ordinal variables.

Similarly, if measurement was intended to be expressed in intervals but responses indicate that respondents could not make such fine differentiation, then techniques requiring interval measures are again ruled out. For example, survey questions asking researchers to report the percentage of their time devoted to research, administration, and teaching are intended to yield interval measures given in percentages. However, if almost all respondents respond "about half" or "about one-third" to these questions, this level of precision suggests that these variables should be analyzed as ordinal, not interval, measures.

The question of how to handle outliers frequently arises. Basic statistics such as the mean and standard deviation can be skewed by extreme values (outliers). It may be tempting to report statistics without the inflating effect of units that vary wildly from most other units. One option is to select statistics that are not affected by outliers, such as a median in place of a mean or an interquartile range (the interval capturing the middle 50 percent of the scores) in place of a standard deviation. When applying more sophisticated techniques, such as regression, a good option is to conduct and report analyses both with and without outliers.

Evaluators should ascertain whether highly sophisticated techniques with numerical statistics will be accessible and desirable for their clients. Anticipating clients' preferences may automatically disqualify some techniques. Evaluators should use a statistician to help make decisions about specific statistical techniques. The most frequently used statistical software, SPSS, SAS, and STATA, are quite user friendly and well documented, but they do not obviate the need for consulting a statistician.

Reporting Statistics Appropriately

Clarity is essential when statistical results are reported. The level of detail provided is again contingent on clients' expectations and preferences. The box below contains a number of suggestions for reporting statistical analyses.

Tips for Presenting Data Analyses

Identify Contents of All Tables and Figures Clearly

- Use the title to identify the variables or measures used.
- Label all variables or measures with adequate detail.
- Provide the exact wording of questions on the table or figure.
- Identify program components and program results (alleged causes and alleged effects).

Indicate Use of Decision Rules in Analysis

- State whether missing or inapplicable responses are included in the analysis.
- If values of variables were collapsed, such as low and high, state where the cutoffs were made.
- If the term *average* or *midpoint* is used, state whether this means mean or median.

Consolidate Analyses Whenever Possible

- Present only the percentage reporting yes for questions to which the possible responses are yes or no.
- Present in one table percentages for a series of substantively related questions.
- Collapse responses to contrast *agrees* versus *disagrees,* or similar opinions, omitting *unsure* responses if appropriate.

Do Not Abbreviate

- Do not present shortened titles or labels used during data processing in tables and figures.
- Do not use acronyms.
- Do not use statistical symbols to represent statistics.

Provide Basic Information About Measurement of Variables

- Give the minimum and maximum value for each variable used.
- Give the sample size (or number or respondents reporting) for each variable displayed in the table or figure.
- Provide complete information about the scale or measurement mechanism used—for example, "scale ran from 1 (meaning Not at All Relevant) to 5 (meaning Completely Relevant)."

Present Appropriate Percentages

- Provide percentages, not raw figures.
- Clearly identify the base from which percentages were calculated.
- Calculate percentages on the appropriate base, for example, "85 percent of the treatment group scored high on the criterion," *not,* "32 percent of those scoring high were in the treatment group."

Present Information on Statistical Significance Clearly

- Present the confidence level used in each table, such as 90 percent or 95 percent.
- Be consistent in reporting confidence levels across all tables in a report.
- Show which statistics were statistically significant through the use of asterisks with clear legends.
- Do not simply present raw values of statistics, such as chi square or standard errors, and expect readers to calculate statistical significance.

Present Information on the Magnitude of Relationships Clearly

- Distinguish between statistics showing the statistical significance of relationships, and statistics measuring the strength of relationships or the magnitude of effects.
- Present the confidence interval or error band around measures of strength or magnitude in a user-friendly manner, such as, "Program participants' scores were from 20 percent to 24 percent higher than those of the comparison group."
- Comment on the importance of the magnitude of the relationship or effect, as well as noting whether it was statistically significant.

Use Graphics to Present Analytical Findings Clearly

- Use zero as the starting point for axes in graphs.
- Use appropriate scales so that figures will not be unduly distorted.
- Use colors whenever possible to present more than one line on the graph.
- Label lines on the graph, not in the legend.
- Do not use more than four different patterns or colors to represent groups if at all possible.

The degree to which the tables and graphs providing statistical results are user friendly is also quite important. To assist readers, consolidation of numerous analyses is helpful. Unfamiliar abbreviations, acronyms, and software jargon are often confusing to readers. Complete information about how variables were measured should accompany tables, with sufficient information to allow the reader to assess the adequacy of measurements used.

A good reality test of completeness is for the evaluators to examine the statistics reported and the explanatory information provided, and ask themselves whether an analyst outside the project could write a report on the data provided without needing any additional data. Replicability is a hallmark for any analysis.

The last step in completing a thorough analysis of quantitative data is to report any threats to the statistical validity of the information provided. Common weaknesses are samples that are too small and application of techniques without meeting all assumptions or criteria appropriate for their use. The challenge of the evaluator is to provide a user-friendly explanation of all decisions made and a critical assessment of the statistical accuracy that the test can reasonably be expected to provide. (Chapter Nineteen provides guidance on acknowledgment of threats to validity.)

Reporting Statistical Results to High-Level Public Officials

The advice offered here for reporting statistical results applies in most situations. However, reports for high-level officials, such as mayors and legislators, present a special case. Typically these clients are not concerned with technical issues such as statistical confidence and confidence intervals. In fact, they may not want to hear evaluators' findings diluted by statements specifying that the numbers may (or may not) fall within a range.

The unique challenge to evaluators reporting directly to the highest-level decision makers is to convey the tentative nature of statistical results accurately without excessive hedging. Certainty is simply not part of a statistician's vocabulary; statistical inference offers best estimates, not specific answers.

When high-level decision makers request specific answers, evaluators should attempt to prepare their audience to receive less than certain data. Detail about confidence levels need not be offered in a briefing or an executive summary as long as it is provided somewhere in a written report. Confidence intervals are actually not too exotic, since politicians are accustomed to hearing their popularity polls reported as percentages plus or minus a margin of error. An estimate with a range of uncertainty (plus or minus 10 percentage points, for example) may be acceptable.

A distinction between statistical and practical importance may be too much to provide to high-level decision makers. Instead, only findings that are of practical importance should be presented. Whether it is statistically significant or not, a small change in an effectiveness or efficiency measure should probably be omitted from a report. For a high-level audience, graphic presentations showing trends typically are preferable to tables filled with numbers. For example, a time trend will be more impressive than a set of regression coefficients.

Conclusion

Planning for statistical analyses begins when the planning for any evaluation effort starts. Opportunities and decisions regarding which techniques may be appropriate and which statistics should be reported are affected by decisions made early in evaluation planning. As evaluators make decisions about how to analyze data, they must have in mind the sort of reporting format (for example, should it be highly quantitative? rich in detail?) that their clients will want in an analytical report. In addition to clients' expectations, the questions that are addressed, the measurement decisions made, and the need to depend on samples to generalize quantitative results to larger populations all shape evaluators' decision making regarding statistics. Statistics never speak for themselves, but evaluators must take great care to ensure that they speak with statistics accurately and clearly.

Appendix 16A

An Application of the Chi-Square Statistic Calculated with SPSS

The Problem. Evaluators interviewed children participating in YMCA youth programs as part of an analysis to help the YMCA target programming more effectively. Although the sample of respondents is not totally random, since there were virtually no refusals, the evaluators assume they can apply chi square to test whether they can generalize their findings for differences in programming preferences of the boys compared to the girls they interviewed to all target participants (whom they did not interview). Their sample has fifty participants. They decided to use the conventional decision rule of 95 percent. Thus, the null hypothesis being tested is: *Gender has no effect on programming preferences.* And the alternative hypothesis is: *Gender does affect programming preferences.*

Exhibit 16A.1 provides the computer printout produced by SPSS to analyze the bivariate relationship between program participants' preferences and gender. The SPSS printout produces too much information, and you would not want to provide all of it to readers. The essential data are presented more clearly in Table 16A.1.

The Solution. A chi square of statistical significance can be calculated for these data. The chi square tests the null hypothesis that there is no difference in YMCA program preferences expressed by boys and girls. Calculation of chi square first involved computing what would have been the expected frequencies in the table if the null hypothesis were true, then comparing these expected frequencies with the observed frequencies. A chi-square distribution can be consulted to identify the value of chi square that would be needed to reject the null hypothesis and allow 95 percent confidence in this conclusion. To use a chi-square table, one must calculate the degrees of freedom; for the chi square, this number is calculated as (the number of rows in the table − 1) multiplied by (the number of columns in the table − 1). For the problem at hand, the degrees of freedom is $(3 − 1) \times (2 − 1)$, or 2. For a 95 percent confidence level and 2 degrees of freedom, a chi-square table indicates 5.99 as the number that must be exceeded in order for the null hypothesis (that there is no generalizable difference between the preferences for the groups) to be rejected. Thus, the decision rule for this

Exhibit 16A.1. SPSS Printout of Analysis of the Bivariate Relationship Between YMCA Program Preferences and Gender

Case Processing Summary

| | Cases | | | | | |
| | Valid | | Missing | | Total | |
	N	Percent	N	Percent	N	Percent
Gender of Child* Favorite Type of Programming	50	100.0%	0	0%	50	100.0%

Gender of Child * Favorite Type of Programming Cross-Tabulation

| | | | Favorite Type of Programming | | | |
			Science and Technology	Sports	Creative and Performing Arts	Total
Gender of Child	Male	Count	6	10	6	22
		% within Gender of Child	27.3%	45.5%	27.3%	100.0%
		%within Favorite Type of Programming	66.7%	71.4%	22.2%	44.0%
		% of Total	12.0%	20.0%	12.0%	44.0%
	Female	Count	3	4	21	28
		% within Gender of Child	10.7%	14.3%	75.0%	100.0%
		%within Favorite Type of Programming	33.3%	28.6%	77.8%	56.0%
		% of Total	6.0%	8.0%	42.0%	56.0%
Total		Count	9	14	27	50
		% within Gender of Child	18.0%	28.0%	54.0%	100.0%
		%within Favorite Type of Programming	100.0%	100.0%	100.0%	100.0%
		% of Total	18.0%	28.0%	54.0%	100.0%

Chi-Square Tests

	Value	df	Asymp. Sig. (2-sided)	Exact Sig. (2-sided)
Pearson Chi-Square	11.348[a]	2	.003	
Likelihood Ratio	11.780	2	.003	
McNemar Test				b
N of Valid Cases	50			

[a]1 cells (16.7%) have expected count less than 5. The minimum expected count is 3.96.

Directional Measures

			Value	Asymp. Std Error[a]	Approx. T[b]	Approx. Sig.
Nominal by Nominal	Lambda	Symmetric	.289	.146	1.743	.081
		Gender of Child Dependent	.409	.168	1.946	.052
		Favorite Type of Programming Dependent	.174	.158	1.010	.312
	Goodman and Kruskal tau	Gender of Child Dependent	.227	.119		.004[c]
		Favorite Type of Programming Dependent	.145	.077		.001[c]
	Uncertainty Coefficient	Symmetric	.140	.077	1.829	.003[d]
		Gender of Child Dependent	.172	.094	1.829	.003[d]
		Favorite Type of Programming Dependent	.118	.065	1.829	.003[d]
Ordinal by Ordinal	Somers'd	Symmetric	.423	.121	3.494	.000
		Gender of Child Dependent	.386	.112	3.494	.000
		Favorite Type of Programming Dependent	.468	.133	3.494	.000

[a]Not assuming the null hypothesis.
[b]Using the asymptotic standard error assuming the null hypothesis.
[c]Based on chi-square approximation.
[d]Likelihood ratio chi-square probability.

Symmetric Measures[d]

		Value	Asymp. Std Error[a]	Approx. T[b]	Approx. Sig.
Nominal by Nominal	Phi	.476			.003
	Cramer's V	.476			.003
	Contingency Coefficient	.430			.003
Ordinal by Ordinal	Kendall's tau-b	.425	.121	3.494	.000
	Kendall's tau-c	.461	.132	3.494	.000
	Gamma	.667	.151	3.494	.000
Measure of Agreement	Kappa	.[c]			
N of Valid Cases		.50			

[a]Not assuming the null hypothesis.

[b]Using the asymptotic standard error assuming the null hypothesis.

[c]Kappa statistics cannot be computed. They require a symmetric 2-way table in which the values of the first variable match the values of the second variable.

[d]Correlation statistics are available for numeric data only.

Table 16A.1. Contingency Table: Participants' Preferences for YMCA Programming by Gender of Child

Reported Favorite Type of YMCA Programming	Boys (N = 22)	Girls (N = 28)
Science and technology	27.3	10.7
Sports	45.5	14.3
Creative and performing arts	27.3	75.0
	100.1%[a]	100%

Note: Chi square is statistically significant at the 95 percent confidence level. The lambda measure of Strength of Relationships is .174.

[a]Totals may not add up to 100 percent due to rounding.

problem is as follows: If the calculated chi square exceeds 5.99, the null hypothesis of no difference in the program preferences of boys and girls will be rejected.

Following are the steps in testing the hypothesis of no relationship between gender and program preferences:

Step 1. We compute chi square (see the Exhibit 16A.1). Chi square is the sum of the squared difference between the expected frequency and the observed frequency divided by the expected frequency for each cell.

Step 2. We compare the computed chi square for this table (shown as the Pearson chi square) to the decision rule set earlier. In this case, our computed chi square of 11.348 is greater than 5.99, so we can reject the null hypothesis of no difference between the boys' and girls' program preferences.

Step 3. To convey our finding in an appropriate manner, we would use wording such as the following: "Based on our sample of fifty participants, there was a difference between the boys and girls in terms of their program preferences, and this difference in the sample is large enough for us to conclude that differences exist in the population at the 95 percent confidence level." Note that a generalization of gender-based differences from the sample to the population, our alternative hypothesis, is supported. In fact, boys were more than twice as likely as girls to identify science and technology and sports programs as their favorite programs, while girls were almost three times as likely as boys to select creative and performing arts as their favorite YMCA program.

Note for Appendix 16.A

Running Crosstabs: To develop a contingency table, select Analyze from the top pull-down menu. From there, select Descriptive Statistics, followed by Crosstabs. Choose the appropriate variables for the "row" and "column" categories. Clicking on Statistics will allow you to identify how you will measure statistical significance (in this case, we have used chi square). Clicking on Cells will allow you to decide how the data will be displayed (here we have selected Rows, Columns, and Totals). Click on OK to run the crosstabs.

Appendix 16B

An Application of the t Test Procedure

The Problem. The interview data from YMCA program participants discussed in Appendix 16A are again analyzed. The evaluators want to know if there is a difference in the number of years boys and girls participate in the YMCA programs, and they also want to know if the difference is the same or not depending on which programs the boys and girls prefer. Thus, the dependent variable is the number of years the children report having participated in the YMCA programs, and the independent variable is gender (boys versus girls). In addition, a third variable, called the control variable, is introduced to see if the original relationships between gender and years of participation change related to programming preferences. The null hypothesis is: *Gender does not affect the length of time (in years) participants attend YMCA programs, even when controlling for their preferred programs.* And the alternative hypothesis is: *Gender does affect the length of time (in years) participants attend YMCA programs, even when controlling for preferred programs.*

The Data. The SPSS printout for the *t* test appears in Exhibit 16B.1. Again, for presentation purposes, you would not provide all of the data reported on the SPSS output. Table 16B.1 provides the essential data from the four *t* tests performed: one for the entire sample and one for each of the three categories of "favorite program."

The Solution. The *t* test of statistical significance can be calculated for these data. This technique tests the null hypothesis that there is no difference between boys and girls in the number of years they have participated in YMCA programs. A *t* distribution can be used to identify the value that the observed *t* statistic should exceed to support the conclusion that the observed difference in the two sample means is large enough to generalize to the population from which the program participants were drawn. In other words, if the null hypothesis is rejected in this sample, the evaluators may generalize the difference they observed to the larger population using an appropriate vehicle, such as a confidence interval placed around the observed difference, to convey their best estimate of the difference in years one might expect in the population to which they wish to generalize.

In consulting a table showing the *t* distribution, one first must calculate the degree of freedom for this problem, which is computed as the size of the

Exhibit 16B.1. SPSS Printout for a *t* Test of the Difference in Years of Participation Between Boys and Girls, Controlling for Program Preferences

T-Test

Group Statistics

	Gender of Child	N	Mean	Std. Deviation	Std Error Mean
Number of Years Participating in YMCA Programs	Male	22	4.0909	2.82690	.60270
	Female	28	5.6071	3.05916	.57813

Independent Samples Test

		Levene's Test for Equality of Variances		t-test for Equality of Means							
										95% Confidence Interval of the Difference	
		F	Sig.	t	df	Sig. (2-tailed)	Mean Difference	Std. Error Difference	Lower	Upper
Number of Years Participating in YMCA Programs	Equal variances assumed	.287	.595	−1.798	48	.078	−1.5162	.84325	−3.21170	.17923
	Equal variances not assumed			−1.816	46.684	.076	−1.5162	.83515	−3.19664	.16417

T-Tests with Controls

Favorite Type of Programming = Science and Technology

Group Statistics

	Gender of Child	N	Mean	Std. Deviation	Std Error Mean
Number of Years Participating in YMCA Programs	Male	6	2.0000	.63246	.25820
	Female	3	7.0000	2.00000	1.15470

Independent Samples Test

		Levene's Test for Equality of Variances		t-test for Equality of Means							
										95% Confidence Interval of the Difference	
		F	Sig.	t	df	Sig. (2-tailed)	Mean Difference	Std. Error Difference		Lower	Upper
Number of Years Participating in YMCA Programs	Equal variances assumed	3.500	.104	−5.916	7	.001	−5.0000	.84515		−6.99847	−3.00153
	Equal variances not assumed			−4.226	2.203	.044	−5.0000	1.18322		−9.66718	−.33282

Favorite Type of Programming = Sports

Group Statistics

	Gender of Child	N	Mean	Std. Deviation	Std Error Mean
Number of Years Participating in YMCA Programs	Male	10	5.8000	3.19026	1.00885
	Female	4	8.0000	4.16333	2.08167

Independent Samples Test

		Levene's Test for Equality of Variances		t-test for Equality of Means							
										95% Confidence Interval of the Difference	
		F	Sig.	t	df	Sig. (2-tailed)	Mean Difference	Std. Error Difference	Lower	Upper
Number of Years Participating in YMCA Programs	Equal variances assumed	.158	.698	−1.075	12	.304	−2.2000	2.04654	−6.65903	2.25903
	Equal variances not assumed			−.951	4.492	.390	−2.2000	2.31325	−8.35441	3.95441

Favorite Type of Programming = Creative and Performing Arts

Group Statistics

	Gender of Child	N	Mean	Std. Deviation	Std Error Mean
Number of Years Participating in YMCA Programs	Male	6	3.3333	1.75119	.71492
	Female	21	4.9524	2.78345	.60740

Independent Samples Test

		Levene's Test for Equality of Variances		t-test for Equality of Means							
									95% Confidence Interval of the Difference	
		F	Sig.	t	df	Sig. (2-tailed)	Mean Difference	Std. Error Difference	Lower	Upper
Number of Years Participating in YMCA Programs	Equal variances assumed	2.101	.160	−1.340	25	.192	−1.6190	1.20814	−4.10725	.86915
	Equal variances not assumed			−1.726	13.115	.108	−1.6190	.93811	−3.64390	.40580

Table 16B.1. *t* Test of Difference: Reported Number of Years Participating in YMCA Programs by Gender of Child by Favorite Type of Programming

	N	Mean Reported Number of Years Participating in YMCA Programs	Is t Test of Difference in Means Statistically Significant at 95%?	95% Confidence Interval Around the Difference
Total sample				
Boys	22	4.09	No	NA
Girls	28	5.61		
Among those whose favorite programs are science and technology				
Boys	6	2.0	Yes	3–7 years
Girls	3	7.0		
Among those whose favorite programs are sports				
Boys	10	5.8	No	NA
Girls	4	8.0		
Among those whose favorite programs are creative and performing arts				
Boys	6	3.3	No	NA
Girls	21	4.6		

sample in group 1 minus one plus the size of the sample in group 2 minus one. In this example the degrees of freedom equal $(22 - 1) + (28 - 1)$, or 48. As the evaluators wish to test for a significant difference in either direction and they have chosen a 95 percent decision rule, the value that the observed *t* must exceed to demonstrate statistical significance is 2.00 or –2.00. Thus, the decision rule for this problem is the following: If the calculated *t* statistic exceeds 2.0 or is less than –2.0, the null hypothesis (there is no difference between boys' and girls' mean years in YMCA programs) will be rejected.

The steps in conducting the *t* test for this problem are as follows:

Step 1. Calculate *t*. Here *t* equals the difference of the means for the two groups divided by the joint standard error. SPSS allows us to test whether we can assume that the variance in the dependent variable is equal in the two groups using the F test first. Here the F is not statistically significant, so we use the *t* value where the variances are assumed to be equal.

Step 2. Compare the computed *t* statistic to the decision rule set earlier. In this case, the *t* statistic equals –1.8, which does not exceed the criterion level specified in the decision rule. Thus, the null hypothesis cannot be rejected.

Step 3. To convey the findings appropriately, we can start by stating: "Based on our sample of 50 YMCA participants, there is insufficient evidence to say there is a statistically significant difference in the number of years boys and girls have participated in YMCA programs, that is, we cannot generalize a relationship between gender and years of participation to the population. When we examine the t tests for the three subgroups, we find we can reject the null at a 95 percent confidence level only for participants who prefer science and technology. Since we rejected the null hypothesis of no difference for that group, the next question to be addressed is this: How big is the difference between the groups? To address this question, we may use the standard formula for a confidence interval to place around the observed difference between the means reported for the two groups. The observed difference is 5 years. The interval to be placed around this value is the joint standard error multiplied by the t value for a 95 percent confidence level for this problem. Thus, the interval will be 3 to 7 years.

"We can then conclude that based on this sample of 50 participants, using a 95 percent confidence level, among participants who prefer science and technology programs, girls have participated 3 to 7 years longer than boys in these programs."

In this example, a relationship between gender and length of participation is statistically significant for only one of the three subgroups,

Note for Appendix 16B

Running a t *test analysis:* To run t tests, select Analyze, then Compare Means, and then Independent Samples T-Test from the menu at the top of the screen. Choose the appropriate variables for Test Variable and Grouping Variable. The grouping variable will need to be a dichotomous variable that you define in the space provided (in this example our grouping variable is gender). Select OK to run the t test.

To run a t *test with controls:* Before following the t test directions, you will need to split the file, which will allow the data to be analyzed within specified categories (in our example, we have split the file by programmatic preferences). Select Data and then Split File from the top of the computer screen. Select Organize Output by Groups and define which groups you would like to use organizing the data from the menu on the left. When you are finished, select OK and run the t test.

indicating that, at least based on the numbers, the relationship is not generalizable to the broader population and the magnitude of the observed difference in years is large enough for us to suggest that there is a difference in boys' and girls' participation time only for those who prefer the science and technology programs. And there are other questions that evaluators should ask about the findings. For example, how comfortable do we feel that the sample truly represents all YMCA program participants? With such a small sample and, with a statistically significant difference in only one subgroup that has a really small sample size, we would definitely want to be cautious in presenting our findings.

References

Agresti, A. Categorical Data Analysis. New York: Wiley, 1990.

Brown, M. B., and Benedetti, J. K. "Sampling Behavior of Tests for Correlation in Two-Way Contingency Tables." *Journal of the American Statistical Association*, 1977, *72*, pp. 309–315.

Goodman, L. A., and Kruskal, W. H. *Measures of Association for Cross Classification*. New York: Springer-Verlag, 1979.

Hair, J. F., Anderson, R. E., Tatham, R. L., and Black, W. C. *Multivariate Data Analysis*. Upper Saddle River, N.J.: Prentice Hall, 1998.

Kendall, M. *Rank Correlation Methods, Second Edition*. London: Charles Griffin, 1955.

Liebetrau, A. M. *Measures of Association, Quantitative Application in Social Sciences, 32*. Thousand Oaks, Calif.: Sage, 1983.

Somers, R. H. "A New Asymmetric Measure of Association for Ordinal Variables." *American Sociological Review*, 1962, *27*, pp. 799–811.

Stevens, S. S. "On the Theory of Scales of Measurement." *Science*, 1946, *103*, 677–680.

Further Reading

Textbooks

Anderson, A.J.B. *Interpreting Data*. London: Chapman and Hall, 1989.

Bohrnstedt, G. W., and Knoke, D. *Statistics for Social Data Analysis*. Itasca, Ill.: Peacock, 1982.

Cohen, S. S. *Practical Statistics*. London: Edward Arnold, 1988.

Foreman, E. K. *Survey Sampling Principles*. Vol. 120: *Statistics: Textbooks and Monographs*. D. B. Owen and others (eds.). New York: Dekker, 1991.

Godfrey, M. G., Roebuck, E. M., Sherlock, A. J. *Concise Statistics*. London: Edward Arnold, 1988.

Goodman, L. A. *Analyzing Qualitative/Categorical Data.* J. Magidson (ed.). Lanham, Md.: University Press of America, 1978.

Groninger, L. D. *Beginning Statistics Within a Research Context.* New York: HaperCollins, 1990.

Healey, J. *Statistics: A Tool for Social Research.* (2ⁿᵈ ed.) Belmont, Calif.: Wadsworth, 1990.

Hedderson, J. *SPSS/PC + Made Simple.* Belmont, Calif.: Wadsworth, 1990.

Jaccard, J. *Statistics for the Behavioral Sciences.* Belmont, Calif.: Wadsworth, 1983.

Loether, H. J., and McTavish, D. G. *Descriptive and Inferential Statistics: An Introduction.* (4ᵗʰ ed.) Old Tappen, N.J.: Allyn & Bacon, 1992.

Meier, K. J., and Brudney, J. L. *Applied Statistics for Public Administration.* (2ⁿᵈ ed.) Boston: Duxbury Press, 1987.

Renner, T. *Statistics Unraveled: A Practical Guide to Using Data in Decision Making.* Washington, D.C.: International City Management Association, 1988.

Runyon, R. P., and Haber, A. *Fundamentals of Behavioral Sciences.* (7th ed.) New York: McGraw-Hill, 1991.

Sharp, V. F. *Statistics for the Social Sciences.* Boston: Little, Brown, 1979.

Siegel, S. *Nonparametric Statistics for the Behavioral Sciences.* (Rev. ed.) New York: McGraw-Hill, 1988.

Walsh, A. *Statistics for the Social Sciences: With Computer Applications.* New York: HarperCollins, 1990.

Welch, S., and Comer, J. *Quantitative Methods for Public Administration.* (2ⁿᵈ ed.) Chicago: Dorsey, 1988.

Special Topics

Achen, C. H. *Interpreting and Using Regression.* Sage University Paper series on Quantitative Applications in the Social Sciences, series no. 07–029. Newbury Park, Calif.: Sage, 1982.

Asher, H. B. *Causal Modeling.* Sage University Paper series on Quantitative Applications in the Social Sciences, series no. 07–003. Newbury Park, Calif.: Sage, 1976.

Berry, W. D., and Feldman, S. *Multiple Regression in Practice.* Sage University Paper series on Quantitative Applications in the Social Sciences, series no. 07–050. Newbury Park, Calif.: Sage, 1985.

Cohen, J. *Statistical Power Analysis for the Behavioral Sciences.* New York: Academic Press, 1977.

Converse, J. M., and Presser, S. *Survey Questions: Handcrafting the Standardized Questionnaire.* Sage University Paper series on Quantitative Applications in the Social Sciences, series no. 07–063. Newbury Park, Calif.: Sage, 1986.

Edwards, W., and Newman, J. R. *Multiattribute Evaluation.* Sage University Paper series on Quantitative Applications in the Social Sciences, series no. 07–026. Newbury Park, Calif.: Sage, 1982.

Hartwig, F., and Dearing, B. E. *Exploring Data Analysis.* Sage University Paper series on Quantitative Applications in the Social Sciences, series no. 07–016. Newbury Park, Calif.: Sage, 1979.

Henkel, R. E. *Tests of Significance.* Sage University Paper series on Quantitative Applications in the Social Sciences, series no. 07–004. Newbury Park, Calif.: Sage, 1976.

Hildebrand, D. K., Laing, J. D., and Rosenthal, H. *Analysis of Ordinal Data.* Sage University Paper series on Quantitative Applications in the Social Sciences, series no. 07–008. Newbury Park, Calif.: Sage, 1977.

Klecka, W. R. *Discriminant Analysis.* Sage University Paper series on Quantitative Applications in the Social Sciences, series no. 07–019. Newbury Park, Calif.: Sage, 1980.

Levine, M. S. *Canonical Analysis and Factor Comparison.* Sage University Paper series on Quantitative Applications in the Social Sciences, series no. 07–006. Newbury Park, Calif.: Sage, 1977.

Lewis-Beck, M. S. *Applied Regression: An Introduction.* Sage University Paper series on Quantitative Applications in the Social Sciences, series no. 07–022. Newbury Park, Calif.: Sage, 1980.

Lodge, M. *Magnitude Scaling: Quantitative Measurement of Opinions.* Sage University Paper series on Quantitative Applications in the Social Sciences, series no. 07–025. Newbury Park, Calif.: Sage, 1981.

McDowall, D., McCleary, R., Meidinger, E. E., and Hay, R. A., Jr. *Interrupted Time Series Analysis.* Sage University Paper series on Quantitative Applications in the Social Sciences, series no. 07–021. Newbury Park, Calif.: Sage, 1980.

Ostrom, C. W., Jr. *Time Series Analysis: Regression Techniques.* Sage University Paper series on Quantitative Applications in the Social Sciences, series no. 07–009. Newbury Park, Calif.: Sage, 1978.

Reynolds, H. T. *Analysis of Nominal Data.* Sage University Paper series on Quantitative Applications in the Social Sciences, series no. 07–007. Newbury Park, Calif.: Sage, 1977.

Schrodt, P. A. *Microcomputer Methods for Social Scientists.* Sage University Paper series on Quantitative Applications in the Social Sciences, series no. 07–040. Newbury Park, Calif.: Sage, 1984.

Wildt, A. R., and Ahtola, O. T. *Analysis of Covariance.* Sage University Paper series on Quantitative Applications in the Social Sciences, series no. 07–012. Newbury Park, Calif.: Sage, 1978.

Statistical Software

Minitab, Inc. *Minitab Reference Manual for DOS, Release 8.* State College, Pa.: Minitab, 1991.

Norusis, M. J. *SPSS/PC + Studentware.* Chicago: SPSS, 1990.

Norusis, M. J. and SPSS, Inc. *SPSS/PC + 4.0 Base Manual.* Chicago: SPSS, 1990.

Norusis, M. J. and SPSS, Inc. *SPSS/PC + 4.0 Statistics.* Chicago: SPSS, 1990.

SAS Institute, Inc. *SAS User's Guide: Basics, Version 5 Edition.* Cary, N.C.: SAS Institute, 1985.

SAS Institute, Inc. *SAS User's Guide: Statistics, Version 5 Edition.* Cary, N.C.: SAS Institute, 1985.

Stata Corporation. *Stata Release 8.* College Station, Texas: Stata Corporation, 2003.

17

Using Regression Analysis

Dale E. Berger

Correlation and regression are extraordinarily powerful tools that find frequent use in evaluation and applied research. Regression analysis is used to describe relationships, test theories, and make predictions with data from experimental or observational studies, linear or nonlinear relationships, and continuous or categorical predictors. The user must select specific regression models that are appropriate to the data and research questions. Many excellent books provide extended discussion of regression analysis (Campbell and Kenny, 1999; Cohen, Cohen, West, and Aiken, 2003). In this chapter, I focus on concepts, vocabulary, computer commands and output, and presenting results to a nontechnical audience in the context of basic applications relevant to evaluation, including group comparisons, analysis of change, and mediation analysis.

Introduction to the Multiple Regression Model

Many practical questions involve the relationship between a dependent or criterion variable of interest (call it Y) and a set of k independent variables or potential predictor variables (call them $X_1, X_2, X_3, \ldots, X_k$), where the scores on all variables are measured for N cases. For example, we might be interested in predicting performance (Y) using information on years of experience (X_1), an aptitude test (X_2), and participation in a training program (X_3). A multiple regression equation for predicting Y can be expressed as follows:

$$\hat{Y} = B_0 + B_1 X_1 + B_2 X_2 + B_3 X_3.$$

To apply the equation, each X score for an individual case is multiplied by the corresponding B value, the products are added together, and the constant B_0 is added to the sum. The result is $\hat{Y}$, the predicted Y value for the individual case. The correlation between observed Y and predicted $\hat{Y}$ is the multiple correlation coefficient, R.

Can performance be predicted better than chance using this regression equation? Does the training program improve our ability to predict performance, or can we do as well with only the first two predictors? Could we improve prediction by including an additional variable? Is the relationship between performance and years of experience linear, or is the relationship curvilinear? Is the relationship between aptitude and performance stronger or weaker for people who participated in the training program? Regression models can be designed to address these questions and more.

Comparing Two Groups

The examples that follow illustrate applications of regression analysis using SPSS. We begin with a test of the difference between means of two groups. A comparison of regression analysis with a conventional *t* test for independent groups is provided to enhance our understanding of regression analysis.

Example 1: Testing the Difference Between Two Group Means

We wish to compare the efficacy of two training programs, each designed to teach sixth-grade children about healthy living. A group of eighty sixth-grade children was randomly split into the two training conditions: a thirty-minute study period using a brochure prepared for the project and a thirty-minute video presentation. After completion of training, we administered a POST test of knowledge, with possible scores from 0 to 200. Using hypothetical data, SPSS produced the results shown in Table 17.1.

The performance of these two groups on the posttest can be compared using a *t* test for independent groups. Assumptions for this test are that we have random and independent sampling from the two populations, reasonably normal distributions of data around the two population means, and approximately equal variances in the two populations. Degrees of freedom for this test is $(N_1 - 1) + (N_2 - 1) = (38 - 1) + (42 - 1) = 78$.

The independent samples *t* test results in $t(78) = 1.898$, $p = .061$. The group difference is not statistically significant at the conventional $p = .05$ level. (To increase the sensitivity of the test, but with a higher risk of false significance, we may choose to use a more liberal value, such as 10 percent, and

Table 17.1. Group Means and Standard Deviations

	GROUP	*N*	*Mean*	*SD*	*SE Mean*
POST	Brochure	38	102.97	19.530	3.168
	Video	42	111.10	18.769	2.896

construct a 90 percent confidence interval.) In the sample, the Video group performed 8.13 points better than the Brochure group, but the lack of statistical significance implies that we cannot be confident that children with the video program would do better if the study were extended to the population of all comparable sixth-grade children. The population mean may be larger for children who receive the brochure program.

Next, we examine the difference between the brochure and video populations with regression analysis. Group membership is indicated by the nominal variable GROUP that takes on only two values, 0 = Brochure and 1 = Video. A variable that takes on values of only 0 or 1 is called a dummy variable. In evaluation, it is common to code a control group as 0 and the intervention as 1. With dummy-coded group membership as the independent variable (X = GROUP) and posttest knowledge as the dependent variable (Y = POST) in a regression analysis, we obtain the results shown in Figure 17.1 and Table 17.2.

Figure 17.1 shows a plot of the POST test scores for each value of GROUP membership (0 = Control; 1 = Treatment). The line represents the predicted value of POST for values of GROUP. The vertical distance between

Figure 17.1. Regression of POST Test Scores on GROUP Membership

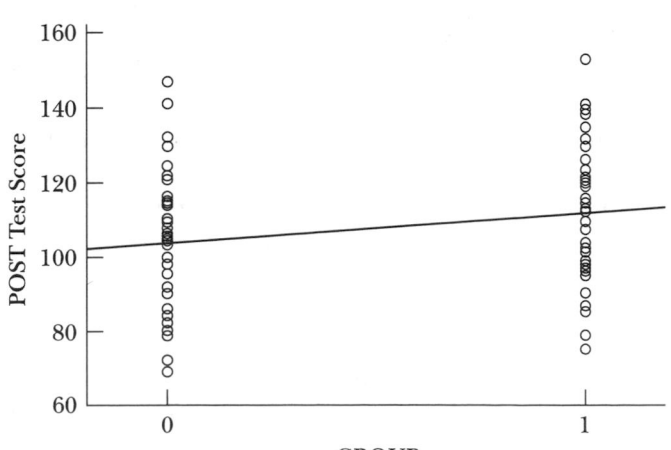

Table 17.2. SPSS Regression Summary Using GROUP to Predict POST

	Unstandardized Coefficients		Standardized Coefficients			95 Percent Confidence Interval for B	
	B	SE	Beta	t	Significance	Lower Bound	Upper Bound
(Constant)	102.974	3.104		33.175	.000	96.794	109.153
GROUP	8.131	4.284	.210	1.898	.061	−.397	16.659

Note: The dependent variable is POST.

a point and the regression line is the residual, or error in prediction. Some of the observed POST test scores are above the regression line, and some are below. Mathematically, to minimize the sum of squared deviations from the regression line, the line passes through the two group means.

The unstandardized coefficients are the B coefficients for the raw score regression equation to predict Y from X. Thus, our prediction equation is $\hat{Y} = B_0 + B_1 X_1 = 102.974 + 8.131\ X_1$, which means that the Predicted Posttest Score = 102.97 + 8.131*GROUP. The variable GROUP takes on values of 0 (for the control group) or 1 (for the treatment group).

When we use this model to predict the posttest score for someone who receives the brochure treatment (GROUP = 0), we find the prediction to be 102.97 + 8.131*0 = 102.97. Note that this is the mean for the brochure group. The predicted score for someone who receives the video treatment (GROUP = 1) is 102.97 + 8.131*1 = 111.10, which is the mean for the video group. The B_1 regression coefficient of 8.131 is the difference between the two group means in our sample. B_0 is called the intercept because it is where the regression line "intercepts" Y when X = 0; it is the predicted value of Y when X is zero. B_1 is called the slope because it is "rise over run" for the regression line, or the predicted change in Y (POST) when X (GROUP) increases by one unit. In our example, the slope is 8.131, the value of B_1.

If there is no difference between the group means in the population, then group membership is not a useful predictor of the POST test score, and we expect the slope (B_1) in a sample would not differ significantly from zero. We can compute a t test for B_1 by dividing the value of the B coefficient for GROUP by its standard error. The null hypothesis is that the population B coefficient is zero. The *t* test for the GROUP coefficient is $t = 8.131/4.284 = 1.898$. The number of degrees of freedom for the *t* test is the total N minus the number of B coefficients that are estimated from the data (including the constant). In our example, this gives df = 80 − 2 = 78. The computer output shows that p = .061 for this test, and if we use a conventional decision rule of 5 percent, we are led to conclude that we cannot be confident that the population B coefficient is greater than zero. The 95 percent confidence interval for B provided by SPSS in Table 17.2 leads to the same conclusion; this interval ranges from −.397 to +16.659. Our data are compatible with B = 0 or even with a negative B in the population; we cannot be confident that either population group mean is larger than the other.

We can compare this test to the standard independent samples t test. The t test is based on the assumptions that our samples are randomly selected from the populations of interest, that the residuals (errors in prediction) are reasonably normally distributed, and that the variance of these errors is about the same at each level of X. The test results, conclusions, and assumptions for the regression analysis are identical to those from the t test analysis. It is important to see that the regression test does not require that the predictor variable X be normally distributed, but it does require that the residuals from the model be normally distributed.

Figure 17.2 shows the pooled distribution of standardized residuals from the regression line. This distribution is important because it allows us to assess the assumption that these residuals are normally distributed in the population. A more thorough approach is to examine the distribution of residuals for each group separately. A visual inspection of Figure 17.1 assures us that the distributions of residuals above and below the line are comparable at the two levels of GROUP.

Figure 17.2. Pooled Distribution of Standardized Residuals from the Regression Line

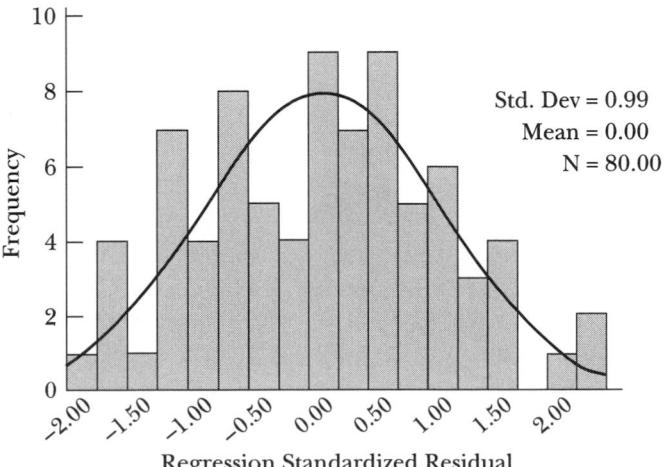

Example 2: Compare Treatment Effects in Two Groups, Controlling for Pretest

A more powerful research design includes a measure of knowledge before treatment as well as knowledge after treatment. This allows an assessment of change for individuals. Table 17.3 shows the means and standard deviations on PRE and POST tests overall and for each group separately. The SPSS syntax for this analysis is in the box on page 485.

With regression analysis, we first use PRE to predict POST. Figure 17.3 shows a scattergram of posttest scores by pretest scores. As we will soon see (when we discuss Table 17.5), the regression equation from SPSS is $\hat{Y} = B_0 + B_1 X_1 = 54.348 + .537 X_1$, so Predicted Posttest Score = 54.348 + .537*PRE. When $X_1 = 0$, the predicted value of Y is the intercept, $B_0 = 54.348$. In our example, there are no cases with values of PRE near zero, so the intercept may not be useful for interpretation. B_1 is the slope of the regression line, telling us that as PRE increases one unit, the predicted value of POST increases .537 units.

This equation, $\hat{Y} = B_0 + B_1 X_1 = 54.348 + .537 X_1$, is represented by the regression line in Figure 17.3. Someone with a PRE score of 40 would have a predicted POST score of 54.348 + .537*40 = 54.348 + 21.480 = 75.8. Errors in prediction from this model are represented visually in Figure 17.3 as the vertical distance between each point and the regression line. This residual "error" for a case can be interpreted as that part of posttest performance that cannot be predicted from pretest performance. Cases above the regression line have positive residuals, which indicates better posttest performance than

Figure 17.3. Scattergram of Posttest Scores by Pretest Scores

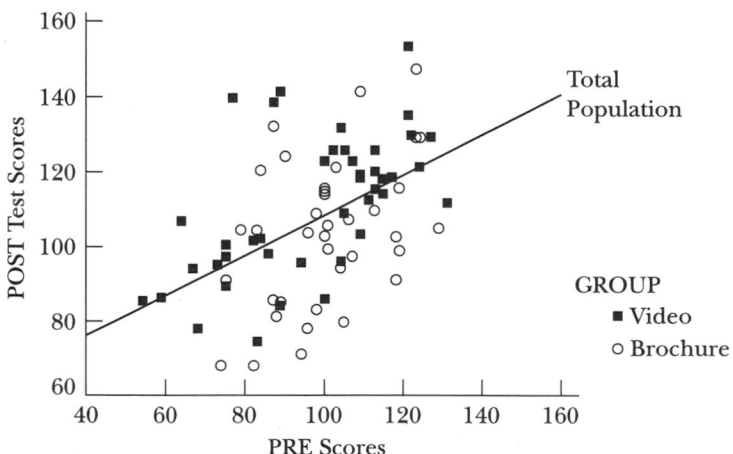

SPSS Syntax for Analysis of Change

REGRESSION

/DESCRIPTIVES MEAN STDDEV CORR SIG N

/MISSING LISTWISE

/STATISTICS COEFF OUTS CI R ANOVA CHANGE

/CRITERIA = PIN(.05) POUT(.10)

/NOORIGIN

/DEPENDENT post

/METHOD = ENTER pre /METHOD = ENTER group

/SCATTERPLOT = (post,*ZPRED) (*ZRESID,*ZPRED)

/RESIDUALS HIST(ZRESID) NORM(ZRESID)

/CASEWISE PLOT(ZRESID) OUTLIERS(3) .

Table 17.3. Group Means and Standard Deviations on PRE and POST Tests

GROUP	PRE	POST
Brochure		
Mean	99.92	102.97
N	38	38
SD	14.929	19.530
Video		
Mean	97.10	111.10
N	42	42
SD	20.287	18.769
Total		
Mean	98.44	107.24
N	80	80
SD	17.888	19.446

would be predicted from their pretest performance; cases with negative residuals performed worse on the posttest than expected for someone with their level of pretest performance. Cases from a group with a more effective treatment will tend to have more positive residuals than cases with a less effective treatment. A test of the group difference on residuals is a test of the treatment effect, controlling for differences on PRE scores. In Figure 17.3, it appears that the Video group (black dots) tends to have more positive residuals than the Brochure group (white dots).

We can test the statistical significance of group difference on these residuals by fitting two models, where model 1 uses only PRE as a predictor and model 2 uses both PRE and GROUP as predictors (the SPSS syntax is shown in the "SPSS Syntax for Analysis of Change" box on page 485). This analysis produces the model summary shown in Table 17.4. Let us consider the information provided by this summary.

In model 1, multiple R is .494, the absolute value of the Pearson correlation between PRE and POST. R^2 is commonly used as an index of the effect size, measuring the strength of the relationship between the predictor and the dependent variable. This statistic, also called the coefficient of determination, has the desirable property that it varies between 0 and 1, and it can be interpreted as the proportion of variance in the dependent variable that can be predicted from the predictor variables in the sample. In our example, $R^2 = .244$, so 24.4 percent of the variance in POST can be predicted from PRE in our sample.

Because the regression coefficients are calculated to maximize the R^2 for the sample data, R^2 overestimates the strength of the relationship in the population. Adjusted R^2 is an estimate of the proportion of variance in POST that can be predicted from PRE in the population from which the sample was drawn. In our example, adjusted $R^2 = .235$, only slightly smaller than the sample $R^2 = .244$. Adjusted R^2 is always smaller than R^2, and the amount of

Table 17.4. Summary of Hierarchical Regression Models

					Change Statistics				
Model	R	R^2	Adjusted R^2	SE of the Estimate	R^2 of Change	F Change	df1	df2	Sig. F Change
1	.494[a]	.244	.235	17.013	.244	25.218	1	78	.000
2	.554[b]	.307	.289	16.399	.063	6.952	1	77	.010

Note: The dependent variable is POST.

[a]Predictors: (Constant), PRE.

[b]Predictors: (Constant), PRE, GROUP.

shrinkage is greater for smaller samples and models with more predictors. If the relationship in a sample is weaker than chance, the sample R^2 will still be positive, but the adjusted R^2 will be negative. In this situation, the population R^2 can be estimated to be zero. An alternative approach that uses a maximum likelihood estimate for the population R^2 is provided by Alf and Graf (2002) in an Excel workbook (which can be downloaded from www.sci.sdsu.edu/alfagrafics). This approach is more accurate and avoids negative estimates.

The standard error of estimate = 17.013 is the estimate of the standard deviation of residuals (deviations of points around the regression line) in the population. The variance of the residuals is 17.013^2, or 289.442. This variance of residuals is the variance in POST that is unexplained by the model. The estimated population variance of POST is 19.446^2, or 378.147. Thus, the proportion of POST variance that is unexplained is 289.442/378.147 = .765. The proportion of variance in POST that is explained by PRE using the model is 1 −.765 = .235. This is equivalent to the adjusted R^2 = .235, an estimate of the proportion of population variance in POST that is explained by PRE using a regression model.

Change statistics provide an estimate and a test of the additional contribution of the variables entered on each step to predicting POST. On the first step (model 1), the only predictor is PRE. The contribution of PRE alone is R^2 change = .244, the same as R^2 for model 1. The test of this contribution is highly significant, $F(1, 78) = 25.218$, $p < .001$. The null hypothesis for this test is that the population R^2 change is zero. We can reject this null hypothesis and conclude that PRE test scores significantly predict POST test scores.

In the second model in Table 17.4, we add GROUP membership as a predictor. R^2 increases from .244 to .307. This R^2 change of .063 is statistically significant, $F(1,77) = 6.952$, $p = .010$. We conclude that GROUP is predictive of POST test scores, after controlling for scores on the PRE test. Treatment group membership accounts for about 6 percent of the variance in posttest scores beyond variance that can be predicted from pretest scores in our sample.

Table 17.5 provides additional information about our models, including estimates of individual regression coefficients and tests of their statistical significance. In model 1, where PRE test is the only predictor of POST, the unstandardized regression model is = $B_0 + B_1 X_1 = 54.348 + .537\ X_1$, as described earlier. The slope of the regression line for standardized scores is the standardized regression coefficient, beta = .494. If X_1 is increased by one standard deviation, the predicted Y score is increased by .494 standard deviations. As a formula, $Z_{\hat{Y}} = \beta Z_{x_1} = .494\ Z_{x_1}$. When we have a single predictor, beta is equal to the Pearson correlation (r = .494). The t test for PRE in

Table 17.5. Coefficients for Hierarchical Regression Models

Model	Unstandardized Coefficients		Standardized Coefficients		
	B	SE	Beta	t	Significance
Model 1					
(Constant)	54.348	10.703		5.078	.000
PRE	.537	.107	.494	5.022	.000
Model 2					
(Constant)	47.119	10.675		4.414	.000
PRE	.559	.103	.514	5.403	.000
GROUP	9.711	3.683	.251	2.637	.010

Note: The dependent variable is POST.

model 1 tests the null hypothesis that PRE is not predictive of POST test scores in the population, $t(78) = 5.022$, p <.001. This t test is equivalent to the F test for Change in model 1 in Table 17.4.

Model 2 in Table 17.5 uses both PRE test scores and GROUP membership to predict POST test scores. The unstandardized regression model is $\hat{Y} = B_0 + B_1X_1 + B_2X_2 = 47.119 + .559*PRE + 9.711*GROUP$. When there is more than one variable in a regression model, it is important to recognize that the test of statistical significance for a regression coefficient is a test of the unique contribution of that variable beyond all other variables in the model. Thus, the test of GROUP in model 2 is not a test of the observed group difference on the POST test but a test of the group difference in that part of the POST test that cannot be predicted from the PRE test, that is, the residual of POST with PRE removed. This is also described as a test of the relationship between GROUP and POST, controlling for PRE, holding PRE constant, or beyond PRE. Here we see that GROUP contributes significantly beyond PRE in predicting POST test scores, $t(77) = 2.637$, p = .010. In example 1, we saw that the Video and Brochure groups did not differ significantly on the observed POST scores. However, when we control for individual differences on the pretest, we do find a statistically significant advantage for the Brochure group.

The B coefficient of 9.711 for GROUP indicates that when we control for differences on the PRE test, the mean for the Video group (GROUP = 1) is 9.711 greater than the mean for the Brochure group (GROUP = 0), and this difference is statistically significant with p = .010. The degrees of freedom for each t test is N minus the number of B coefficients estimated from the data, including the Constant. In our example, N = 80 so df = 78 for model 1 and df = 77 for model 2.

The equivalence of a t test (df = v) to an F test (df = 1, v) can be demonstrated by squaring the t value to get the F value. Thus, the F test for R^2 Change contributed by GROUP in the Model Summary for model 2 is equivalent to the t test of the B coefficient for GROUP in the table of coefficients [$t^2 = (2.637)^2 = 6.954 = F$] for model 2. These two tests address exactly the same issue: Does GROUP contribute significantly to predicting POST test scores when we control for PRE test scores?

Mediation Analysis with Regression

Regression can be used to describe and test conceptual models of how a program works, providing a useful framework for examining and improving key components of the program. A simple test of the effects of a program might be focused on the relationship between the level of program implementation (X) and an outcome (Y). This relationship can be conceptualized as a causal model where the program has a direct causal impact on the outcome, as shown in Figure 17.4.

A limitation of this simple black box model is that it provides little understanding of how the program produces its effects or why the program fails if no effects are found.

A more sophisticated theoretical analysis identifies processes by which the program is presumed to have effects. This analysis can be conceptualized as a causal model where the program (X) has an impact on an intervening mediator variable (M), which in turn has an impact on the outcome (Y), as shown in Figure 17.5. The notation for variables and regression coefficients in this section is conventional for mediation analysis (Baron and Kenny, 1986).

If the entire effect of the program operates through the mediator, the regression coefficient c' is zero. If c' is smaller than the regression coefficient c in the first model, then M is said to partially mediate the effects of X on Y.

Mediation analysis can help us understand how programs work and guide development and modification of programs to make them more effective. Donaldson (2001) provides an excellent discussion of applications of mediation and moderation analysis in program development.

Figure 17.4. Black Box Model

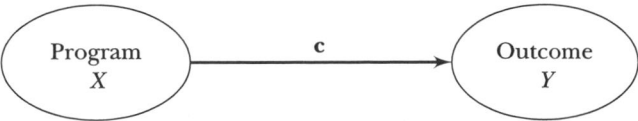

c = regression coefficient on X when predicting Y

Figure 17.5. Mediation Model

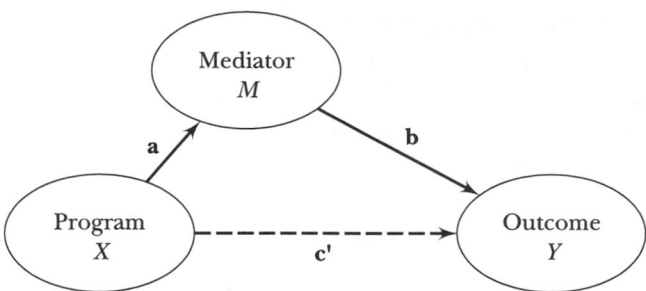

a = regression coefficient on X when predicting M

b and **c'** are the regression coefficients on M and X, respectively, when both are used together to predict Y

Tests of Significance of Mediation

The amount of mediation is measured by the difference between **c** and **c'**. This difference is also equal to the product of the paths to and from the mediator. Thus, **c − c' = ab**. The total effect of X on Y (**c**) can be decomposed into a direct component (**c'**) and an indirect component (**ab**).

A common test of statistical significance of the indirect component **ab** uses an approximation of the standard error of **ab** proposed by Sobel (1982): $S_{ab} = \sqrt{b^2 s_a^2 + a^2 s_b^2}$ where **a** and **b** and their standard errors can be taken from the regression analyses. The ratio $\mathbf{ab}/S_{ab}$ is distributed approximately as a standardized normal z.

A somewhat more liberal test that has common application and intuitive appeal is simply to test both **a** and **b**. If both paths are statistically significant, we conclude that there is mediation. More powerful tests have been developed recently, but they are not yet used widely (MacKinnon and others, 2002; D. P. MacKinnon, personal communication, Oct. 26, 2002).

An on-line calculator of the Sobel test and other tests is available from K. J. Preacher and G. J. Leonardelli at http://quantrm2.psy.ohio-state.edu/kris/sobel/sobel.htm. Several additional methods are available to test the indirect component ab (MacKinnon and Dwyer, 1993). Recent work on mediation by MacKinnon is available on his Web site (MacKinnon, 2002).

Example 3: Estimating and Testing Mediating Effects

One goal of a school drug prevention program is to reduce the intention of adolescents to use marijuana. The program, based on education, is presumed to increase knowledge about the effects of marijuana, which in turn is presumed to decrease intention to use marijuana. As evaluators, we are interested in testing the validity of this model.

We will analyze hypothetical data on knowledge of the effects of marijuana (M) and intention to use marijuana (Y) from 150 ninth-grade students who completed a six-week drug prevention program and from 180 comparable ninth-grade students who did not take the course (Program = X). X = 1 for students who completed the program, and X = 0 for students in the control group. Tables 17.6 and 17.7 provide information needed for mediation analysis. The SPSS syntax for these tables is in the box.

Table 17.6. Regression of Training Program on Knowledge

Model	Unstandardized Coefficients		Standardized Coefficients			95 Percent Confidence Interval for B	
	B	SE	Beta	t	Significance	Lower Bound	Upper Bound
Model 1							
(Constant)	44.368	1.132		39.203	.000	42.142	46.595
Program (0 = no; 1 = yes)	10.913	1.591	.354	6.860	.000	7.784	14.043

Note: The dependent variable is Knowledge.

Table 17.7. Regression of Training Program and Knowledge on Intention to Use

Model	Unstandardized Coefficients		Standardized Coefficients			95 Percent Confidence Interval for B	
	B	SE	Beta	t	Significance	Lower Bound	Upper Bound
Model 1							
(Constant)	3.696	.073		50.329	.000	3.552	3.841
Program (0 = no; 1 = yes)	.620	.103	.315	6.004	.000	.417	.823
Model 2							
(Constant)	3.348	.174		19.231	.000	3.006	3.691
Program (0 = no; 1 = yes)	.534	.110	.271	4.868	.000	.318	.750
Knowledge	7.844E-03	.004	.123	2.202	.028	.001	.015

Note: The dependent variable is Intent to Use.

Mediation Analysis with SPSS

In the first regression analysis, we use the predictor variable (X = program) to predict the mediator variable (M = knowledge). To make sure that we use exactly the same cases in this analysis that uses only two variables, and in the subsequent analysis that uses all three variables, we tell SPSS to limit the analyses to cases that have complete data for all three variables. This is easily done by pasting the command /variables = . . . into the syntax window before running the program from the syntax window. (Check the sample size for each analysis to make sure that the proper cases are used.)

Regression

```
/VARIABLES = program, know, intent

/DESCRIPTIVES MEAN STDDEV CORR SIG N

/MISSING LISTWISE

/STATISTICS COEFF OUTS CI R ANOVA CHANGE

/CRITERIA = PIN(.05) POUT(.10)

/NOORIGIN

/DEPENDENT know

/METHOD = ENTER program

/SCATTERPLOT = (know,*ZPRED )

/CASEWISE PLOT(ZRESID) OUTLIERS(3) .
```

In the second regression analysis, we use both X and M to predict Y. The only changes are as follows:

```
/DEPENDENT intent

/METHOD = ENTER program /METHOD = ENTER know

/SCATTERPLOT = (intent,*ZPRED )
```

The two /METHOD commands request two hierarchical models. The first uses PROGRAM to predict INTENT, and the second uses both PROGRAM and KNOW to predict INTENT.

To establish that our data are consistent with the hypothesis of mediation (Baron and Kenny, 1986), we need to show the following:

Step 1: Show that X is related to Y (path **c** in the causal model shown in Figure 17.4). From model 1 in Table 17.7, $B_1 = c = .620$, $t(328) = 6.00$, $p < .001$.

Step 2: Show that X is related to M (path **a** in Figure 17.5). From model 1 in Table 17.6, $B_1 = a = 10.913$, $t(328) = 6.86$, $p < .001$.

Step 3: Show that M is related to Y in the presence of X (path **b** in Figure 17.5). From model 2 in Table 17.7, $B_2 = b = .00784$, $t(327) = 2.20$, $p = .028$.

Step 4: For complete mediation, show that X is not related to Y when we control for M (path c' in Figure 17.5 is zero). For partial mediation, path c' is less than path **c**. From model 2 in Table 17.7, $B_1 = c' = .534$, $t(327) = 4.87$, $p < .001$.

Presenting Mediation Analyses

Figure 17.6 provides a conceptual and quantitative summary of our model and findings. The unstandardized coefficients on each path are expressed in the units of the variable at the point of the arrow. If the units of the variables are interpretable, then unstandardized units add useful information. For example, in Figure 17.6, we can see that adolescents who participated in the Program scored 10.913 points higher on the Knowledge scale and .620 higher on the Intention to Use scale.

If units on the variables are not meaningful, it is better to report standardized (beta) coefficients than unstandardized (B) coefficients. The beta coefficients apply to variables expressed in standardized form. For example, in model 2 in Table 17.7, the beta coefficients for Program and Knowledge are .271 and .123, respectively. The unstandardized coefficients (B) are influenced by scaling, such that $[SDy/SDx]*beta = B$. In our example, SD for the 7-point Knowledge is .9863 and SD for the 100-point Intention to Use scale is 15.427. Calculations show $(.9863/15.427)*.123 = .00786$. The beta coefficients do not depend on scaling, because standardized variables all have SD = 1.

The mediation effect can be measured as the reduction in the regression coefficient for X on Y when M is included: $c - c' = .620 - .534 = .086$. Alternatively and equivalently (within rounding error), the mediation effect can be calculated as the product of the indirect paths from X to Y through M: $(10.913) * (.00784) = .086$.

Figure 17.6. Effects of Program and Knowledge on Intention to Use Marijuana

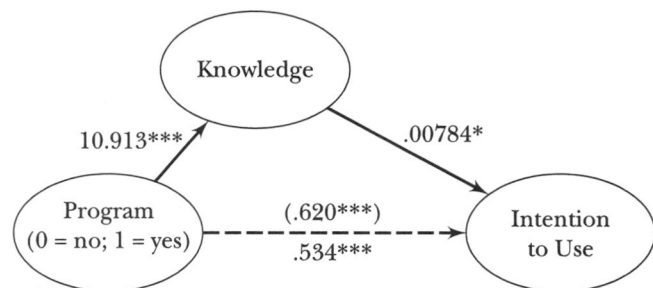

Note: Total effects are shown in parentheses.

*p < .05; **p < .01; ***p < .001.

Paths **a** and **b** are both statistically significant, which we take as evidence consistent with a partial mediating effect of knowledge on the relationship between the Program and Intention to Use. The more conservative Sobel test of the indirect path **ab** (Sobel, 1982) gives z = 2.098, two-tailed p = .036. [ab = (10.913)(.007844) = .08560; $S_{ab} = \sqrt{b^2 s_a^2 + a^2 s_b^2} = \sqrt{(.007844)^2(1.591)^2 + (10.913)^2(.00356)^2}$ = .04081; z = (.08560)/(.04081) = 2.209.]

We conclude that the large observed Program effect on Intention to Use can be explained only in small part by the increase in knowledge for adolescents in the Program. The effects of the Program on Intention to Use apparently are largely due to features other than the increase in knowledge, even though the program does produce a substantial increase in knowledge.

Presenting Results from Regression Analysis in a Table

Regression results can also be presented in a table, as shown in Table 17.8. Reasonable people may choose to report different statistics, depending on the goals of the study (see Nicol and Pexman, 1999, for examples).

Table 17.8 summarizes key information with four conceptually distinct types of data, each of which can be useful. First, we have the simple correlations (r), which tell us how each individual predictor variable is related to the criterion variable, ignoring all other variables. We can see that both predictors are individually related to the dependent variable.

The second type of information comes from R^2 change at each step. Here the order of entry is critical if the predictors overlap each other. R^2 change for the first term entered into a model is simply its r^2. If Knowledge

Table 17.8. Program and Knowledge as Predictors of Intent to Avoid Marijuana

Step	Variable	r	R^2 Change	B	SE_B	Beta
1	Program	.315***	.099***	.534***	.110	.271***
2	Knowledge	.219***	.013*	.00784*	.00356	.012*
	(Constant)			3.348***	.174	

*p < .05; **p < .01; p < .001; cumulative R^2 = .112; adjusted R^2 = .107.

had been entered first, its R^2 change would have been $(.219)^2 = .048$, p < .001. Because of partial overlap with education, Knowledge adds only .013 R^2 change (p < .05) when it is entered after Program is in the model.

The third type of information comes from the unstandardized B coefficients in the final model. These coefficients allow us to construct the raw score regression equation. The tests of statistical significance test the unique contribution of each variable beyond every other variable in the model. The test of B for the last term entered into the model is equivalent to the test of R^2 change for the final term.

The fourth type of information comes from standardized regression coefficients for the final model. These also test the unique contribution of each predictor beyond all other predictors. If the predictors do not overlap at all, the beta coefficient for each variable is identical to its r value. Here we see that the beta for Knowledge (.012) is much smaller than its correlation (.219), reflecting the overlap of Program with Knowledge in predicting Intent.

Other Issues

Comprehensive textbooks (such as Cohen, Cohen, West, and Aiken, 2003) describe additional topics that may be important in specific applications of regression. The following section provides a very brief introduction to special concepts that are likely to be useful in evaluation applications.

Categorical Variables

Categorical variables, such as religion or ethnicity, are often coded numerically where each number represents a specific category (for example, 1 = Protestant, 2 = Catholic, 3 = Jewish). It is meaningless to use a variable in this form in correlation or regression because the order of groups is arbitrary and the size of the numbers does not represent the amount of some characteristic. However, it is possible to capture all of the predictive information in the original variable that has g categories by using $(g - 1)$ new variables, each of which captures part of the information.

For example, suppose a researcher is interested in the relationship between ethnicity (X_1) and income (Y). If ethnicity is coded in four categories (1 = European Americans, 2 = Latino Americans, 3 = African Americans, and 4 = Other), the researcher could create three new variables that each picks up one aspect of the ethnicity variable. A good way to do this is to

> ### SPSS Syntax for Creating Dummy Variables from a Categorical Variable
>
> RECODE ETHNIC $(1 = 1)$ (ELSE $= 0$) INTO D1.
>
> RECODE ETHNIC $(2 = 1)$ (ELSE $= 0$) INTO D2.
>
> RECODE ETHNIC $(3 = 1)$ (ELSE $= 0$) INTO D3.

use dummy variables, where each dummy variable (D_j) takes on values of only 1 or 0, as shown in Table 17.9. The SPSS syntax is provided in the box.

In this example, $D_1 = 1$ for European Americans and $D_1 = 0$ for everyone else, $D_2 = 1$ for Latino Americans and $D_2 = 0$ for everyone else, $D_3 = 1$ for African Americans, and $D_3 = 0$ for everyone else. A person who is not a member of one of these three groups is given the code of 0 on all three dummy variables. One can examine the effects of ethnicity by entering all three dummy variables into the analysis simultaneously as a set of predictors. The R^2 added for these three variables as a set can be measured and tested for significance. The F test for significance of the R^2 added (R^2 change) by the three ethnicity variables is identical to the F test one would find with a one-way analysis of variance on ethnicity. In both analyses, the null hypothesis is that the ethnic groups do not differ in income or that there is no relationship between income and ethnicity.

If there are four groups, any three can be selected to define the dummy codes. Tests of significance for R^2 added by the entire set of $(g - 1)$ dummy variables will not be affected by the choice. Intermediate results and the regression coefficients will depend on the exact nature of the coding, however. Other methods of recoding will produce the identical final R^2 but provide different intermediate results that may be more interpretable in some applications.

Table 17.9. Dummy Coding of a Categorical Variable

	(Dep Var)	Ethnicity	Dummy Variables		
Case	Y	X_1	D_1	D_2	D_3
1	25	1	1	0	0
2	18	2	0	1	0
3	21	3	0	0	1
4	29	4	0	0	0
5	23	2	0	1	0
6	13	4	0	0	0
7	31	1	1	0	0
:	:	:	:	:	:

Correlation and Causation

Inferring causality in correlational studies requires strong knowledge or assumptions about relationships (Campbell and Kenny, 1999; Kenny, 1979). Many different models may be consistent with a given set of data. Models that assume causal flow in different directions may fit data equally well. If we ignore an important causal variable, an observed correlation may be spurious and not be evidence for causality in either direction. For example, the positive correlation between shoe size and spelling ability among elementary school children is spurious because it can be explained by the relationship of each of these variables with age. A model that assumes bigger feet cause better spelling would fit the data, but so would a model that assumes better spelling causes bigger feet!

Multicollinearity

If a certain predictor can itself be predicted very well by the other predictors in the model, we have a problem identified as high multicollinearity. For example, suppose X_1 and X_2 are nearly perfectly correlated with each other. Even if X_1 is a good predictor of Y, X_1 cannot make a large, unique contribution in the presence of X_2. The regression model could equally well assign the predictive weight to either X_1 or X_2, or split the weight between them. Thus, B and beta coefficients are very unstable and difficult to interpret when we have high multicollinearity. When two predictors are highly correlated, it is likely that neither one will make a unique contribution to the model, even if each is a good predictor by itself. In this case, it may be desirable to eliminate one of the predictors or to make a composite of the two. Multicollinearity for an independent variable (IV) is measured by R^2 for predicting that IV from all other IVs. The proportion of variance in an IV that cannot be predicted from other IVs is (1 – multicollinearity) = tolerance. The variance inflation factor (VIF) is the reciprocal of tolerance, and it indicates the proportionate inflation in the error term for testing a B weight or a beta weight, relative to the error term when all predictors are uncorrelated.

Interactions

If two predictor variables interact, then the relationship between one predictor and the dependent variable is conditional on the level of the other predictor. An example of an interaction between predictors is if there is a stronger relationship between knowledge and intent to use marijuana for people who have completed a training program than for those who have not. In this example, the program is said to be a moderator of the relationship between knowledge and intent.

We can test the statistical significance of an interaction by creating an interaction variable as the product of the values for the two predictor variables. The contribution of the interaction can be assessed as R^2 change by the interaction term after the two predictor variables have been entered into the analysis. Detailed guidance for analysis of interactions is available in Aiken and West (1991).

Centering Continuous Predictor Variables

Interpretability of regression coefficients often can be improved by centering continuous predictor variables. Centering is accomplished by subtracting the mean from the variable for each case. Thus, a centered score is a deviation score. Cohen, Cohen, West, and Aiken (2003) recommend that continuous predictor variables be centered before interaction terms are computed, unless the variable has a meaningful zero (also see Marquardt, 1980). Centering reduces multicollinearity or overlap of the interaction term with the variables from which it is calculated. Centering X before computing X^2 reduces collinearity between X and X^2 in polynomial analysis. For a centered variable, $X = 0$ indicates a score at the mean of X. If all predictors are centered, then the intercept (the constant) is the predicted value for Y when all predictors are at their mean.

Nonlinear Relationships

If the relationship between two variables is nonlinear, then a linear model is not appropriate. A log or square root transformation to one or both variables may produce variables that can be appropriately modeled with linear relationships. A polynomial relationship can be modeled by including powers of X. For example, if both X and X^2 are included in a model, the result is of the form $\hat{Y} = B_0 + B_1X + B_2X^2$. This model is appropriate for a quadratic function. If B_2 is significant, then there is a nonlinear component in the relationship between X and Y.

Outliers

One or more cases that do not fit with the rest of the model may be from a different population. Extreme scores can distort the results of a model substantially, especially if the sample is not large. An essential first step in data analysis is to plot the data to assess the appropriateness of the models. Outliers may be errors that can be corrected or cases that can be omitted for separate analysis. Sometimes outliers are the most interesting and important cases; they should not be discarded automatically. Graphic representations of the data can be very helpful in identifying outliers and guiding decisions for dealing with them.

Missing Data

Missing data cause problems because multiple regression procedures require that every case have a score on every variable that is used in the analysis. There are multiple ways to deal with missing data (for example, listwise deletion or pairwise deletion), but none is entirely satisfactory. The best advice is to take strong precautions to minimize missing data.

Schafer and Graham (2002) offer a practical discussion of issues involved with missing data. They recommend maximum likelihood and multiple imputation methods, which have only recently become available in popular statistics programs. These methods are especially useful when a large portion of cases have missing data and when data are missing at random.

It is important to consider why data are missing on a variable. If data are missing systematically, the model may not be representative of the target population. With only a small portion of missing data with large samples, it generally does not matter which method is used. With a substantial portion of data missing, decisions on how to deal with missing data can have a substantial impact on analyses.

Power Analysis and Sample Size

The power of a statistical test is the probability of rejecting the null hypothesis when it in fact is not true. Low power is a problem in much research on the effects of programs. Lipsey and Wilson (1993) reviewed 111 meta analyses that covered more than ten thousand program evaluation studies. They found that average power to detect a typical effect size was only about 50 percent. Power can be increased by increasing sample size, but also by reducing error (better measures or better statistical control), increasing effect size (more powerful treatments), or increasing the alpha error rate, as from .01 to .05 (see Lipsey, 1990).

It is desirable to use a few relatively independent predictors with many cases. With k independent predictors, Green (1991) recommended $N > 50 + 8k$ when testing R^2, and $N > 104 + k$ when testing individual B_j. Larger samples are needed when predictor variables are correlated. If all population correlations between predictors (ρ_{xx}) and with the dependent variable (ρ_{xy}) are medium (all ρ_{xy} and $\rho_{xx} = .3$), $N = 419$ is required to attain power = .80 to test the unique contribution of each of five predictors, but if all $\rho_{xy} = .3$ and $\rho_{xx} = .5$, then required $N = 1,117$ (Maxwell, 2002). Statistical significance may not be very meaningful with extremely large samples, but larger samples are desirable because they provide more precise estimates of parameters and smaller confidence intervals.

Stepwise versus Hierarchical Selection of Variables

If the best predictors are selected from a larger set of potential predictors, the sample R overestimates the relationship in the population. A common villain here is the stepwise regression option that is included in many statistical programs. It is very easy for the novice to use stepwise procedures where the computer program is allowed to identify a small set of the "best" predictors selected from the set of all potential predictors. A serious problem is that the significance tests reported by SPSS do not take into account the number of variables that were considered for inclusion in the model. Stepwise methods should be reserved for exploration of data and hypothesis generation, and results should be interpreted with proper caution. It would be prudent to replicate the findings with new data.

Another problem with stepwise regression is that the program is likely to enter the variables in an order that makes it difficult to interpret R^2 added at each step. For example, it may make sense to examine the effects of a training program after the effects of previous ability have already been considered; the reverse order is less interpretable.

In practice, it is almost always preferable to use hierarchical analyses whereby the researcher determines the order of entry of the predictor variables based on theoretical considerations. The researcher must plan the analysis with care, prior to looking at the data. The double advantage of hierarchical methods over stepwise methods is that there is less capitalization on chance, and the careful researcher will be assured that results such as R^2 added at each step are interpretable.

For any complete set of variables, multiple R and the final regression equation do not depend on the order of entry. However, at intermediate steps, the B and beta values as well as the R^2 added, partial, and semipartial correlations can be greatly affected by variables that have already entered the analysis.

Final Advice

Look at the data! An essential first step in data analysis is to plot data to assess the appropriateness of contemplated models. It is good practice to examine the plot of residuals as a function of Y. An assumption of regression analysis is that residuals are random, independent, and normally distributed. A plot of residuals as a function of predicted scores can help you spot extreme outliers or departures from linearity. Bivariate scatter plots can also provide helpful diagnostics, but a plot of residuals is a better way to find multivariate outliers. A transformation of data (for example, log or square root) may reduce the effects of extreme scores, make relationships more linear, and make the distributions closer to normal (see Tabachnick and Fidell, 2001). Models and descriptions must be appropriate for the data.

It is risky to assume that a relationship holds beyond the range in which observations were made. Prediction is less accurate for cases that are further from the center of the joint distributions.

Regression estimates and tests are based on assumptions. In particular, we must assume that residuals from the regression model are reasonably normally distributed. In addition, sampling must be random and independent in order to generalize to the population from which the sample was selected.

If there are data on many variables and you examine the data to help you find the variables that are the best predictors of your criterion, be sure that the tests of statistical significance take into account the total number of variables that were considered. This concern is even more serious with stepwise regression where the computer selects the best variables.

Watch for multicollinearity where one predictor variable can itself be predicted by another predictor variable or set of variables. Estimates and tests of effects of individual variables may be quite misleading. It is often useful to reduce the number of predictor variables by forming composites of variables that measure the same concept. A composite can be expected to have higher reliability than any single variable. It is important that the composites are formed on the basis of relationships among the predictors, not on the basis of their relationship with the criterion. Factor analysis can be used to help formulate composites, and reliability analysis can be used to evaluate the cohesiveness of the composite.

Keep in mind that alternate models may also account for the data. A model that hypothesizes causal flow in a different direction may also produce statistically significant effects and fit the data equally well.

Report findings with enough detail that the data can be used in subsequent meta analyses. This means to include sample size with each analysis and a measure of effect size, such as R^2 values. Confidence intervals are very useful to show effect sizes and precision of estimation. It is not enough to report results as "significant" or "p < .05."

Finally, be thoughtful rather than mechanical with data analysis. A big advantage people have over the computer is that they can ask, "Does this make sense?" Do not lose this advantage. Do not trust the computer to do justice to data. Get close to your data: the data are your friends.

Glossary

Adjusted R^2 or shrunken R^2. An estimate of R^2 in the population for a given set of predictors; shrinkage is greater with more predictors and with smaller samples.

B coefficient. The weight assigned to a variable in a raw score regression equation.

Beta coefficient. The weight assigned to a standardized variable in a standardized score multiple regression model.

Centering. Subtracting the mean of X from each X score. The mean of a centered variable is zero.

Coefficient of determination. Multiple R^2, which is the proportion of variance in the dependent variable that can be predicted with the multiple regression model in the sample.

Confidence interval (CI). The range within which a population parameter is expected to lie with a specified level of confidence, $1 - \alpha$. If CIs are constructed from many independent samples, we expect $1 - \alpha$ of the intervals to contain the true population value.

Dummy variable. A variable that takes on values of only 0 or 1. A categorical variable with g levels can be fully represented by $g - 1$ dummy variables, which can be used in regression.

Effect size (ES). A measure of the magnitude of a relationship, such as r or R^2, in contrast to measures that depend on sample size such as statistical significance (p) or t from a t test.

Hierarchical regression. A regression analysis where predictor variables are entered sequentially in an order designed to address specific questions.

Intercept. The predicted value of the independent variable Y when all predictors (X) are equal to zero; B_0 in a raw score regression equation.

Leverage. A measure of multivariate extremeness of a case in a set of independent variables.

Listwise deletion. Omission of a case if data are missing on any variable for that case. Only cases that have data on all variables are included in the computation of multiple correlations.

Mediator. A variable that lies on the causal path between a predictor (X) and an outcome (Y), and accounts for some or all of the relationship between X and Y.

Moderator. A predictor variable that is related to the strength of the relationship between another predictor and the dependent variable Y. Moderation is an interaction between two predictors, whereby the relationship of each predictor with Y is conditional on the level of the other predictor.

Multicollinearity. The multiple correlation predicting one independent variable from all other independent variables. The dependent variable is not considered in multicollinearity.

Multiple correlation. The correlation between a variable and the predicted value for that variable, using a weighted composite of predictor variables; symbolized by R.

Pairwise deletion. Estimation of each pairwise correlation by using all cases that have data on both of those variables, even if the cases are missing data on other variables.

Power. The probability of rejecting a false null hypothesis. Power depends on the sample size, the actual effect size in the population, and the alpha error rate.

R². Multiple R^2 is the proportion of variance in the dependent variable that can be predicted with the multiple regression model in the sample; also called coefficient of determination.

R² change or R² added. The increase in R^2 associated with a variable or set of variables added to a regression model.

Raw score multiple regression model. The prediction equation for the dependent variable using predictor variables in their unstandardized form.

Residual. The difference between an observed score and the predicted value for that score.

Slope. The B or beta weight on an independent variable in a regression equation; with a single independent variable as a predictor, B indicates the change in the predicted value of the dependent variable when the independent variable increases one unit.

Standard error; standard error of estimate. The standard deviation of an estimate of a population parameter.

Standardized regression coefficient. The weight assigned to a standardized variable in a standardized score multiple regression model; a beta coefficient.

Stepwise regression. A sequence of regression models where variables are selected or rejected solely on the basis of their contribution to the model, capitalizing on chance.

Tolerance. One minus the multiple correlation for the prediction of one independent variable from all other independent variables; one minus multicollinearity.

Unstandardized regression coefficient. The weight assigned to an unstandardized variable in a raw score multiple regression model; a B coefficient.

References

Aiken, L. S., and West, S. G. *Multiple Regression: Testing and Interpreting Interactions.* Thousand Oaks, Calif.: Sage, 1991.

Alf, E. F., Jr., and Graf, R. G. "A New Maximum Likelihood Estimator for the Population Squared Multiple Correlation." *Journal of Educational and Behavioral Statistics,* 2002, 27, 223–235.

Baron, R. M., and Kenny, D. A. "The Moderator-Mediator Distinction in Social Psychological Research: Conceptual, Strategic, and Statistical Considerations." *Journal of Personality and Social Psychology,* 1986, *51,* 1173–1182.

Campbell, D. T., and Kenny, D. A. *A Primer on Regression Artifacts.* New York: Guilford Press, 1999.

Cohen, J., Cohen, P., West, S. G., and Aiken, L. S. *Applied Multiple Regression/Correlation Analysis for the Behavioral Sciences.* (3rd ed.) Mahwah, N.J.: Erlbaum, 2003.

Donaldson, S. I. "Mediator and Moderator Analysis in Program Development." In S. Sussman (ed.), *Handbook of Program Development for Health Behavior Research.* Thousand Oaks, Calif.: Sage, 2001.

Green, S. B. "How Many Subjects Does It Take to Do a Regression Analysis?" *Multivariate Behavioral Research,* 1991, *26,* 499–510.

Kenny, D. A. *Correlation and Causality.* New York: Wiley, 1979.

Lipsey, M. W. *Design Sensitivity: Statistical Power for Experimental Research.* Thousand Oaks, Calif.: Sage, 1990.

Lipsey, M. W., and Wilson, D. B. "The Efficacy of Psychological, Educational, and Behavioral Treatment: Confirmation from Meta-Analysis." *American Psychologist,* 1993, *48,* 1181–1209.

MacKinnon, D. P. "Statistical Mediation." [http://www.public.asu.edu/~davidpm/ripl/mediate.htm]. 2002.

MacKinnon, D. P., and Dwyer, J. H. "Estimating Mediated Effects in Prevention Studies." *Evaluation Review,* 1993, *17,* 144–158.

MacKinnon, D. P., and others. "A Comparison of Methods to Test the Significance of the Mediated Effect." *Psychological Methods,* 2002, *7,* 83–104.

Marquardt, D. W. "You Should Standardize the Predictor Variables in Your Regression Models." *Journal of the American Statistical Association,* 1980, *75,* 87–91.

Maxwell, S. E. "Sample Size and Multiple Regression Analysis." *Psychological Methods,* 2002, *5,* 434–458.

Nicol, A.A.M., and Pexman, P. M. *Presenting Your Findings: A Practical Guide for Creating Tables.* Washington, D.C.: American Psychological Association, 1999.

Schafer, J. L., and Graham, J. W. "Missing Data: Our View of the State of the Art." *Psychological Methods,* 2002, *7,* 147–197.

Sobel, M. E. "Asymptotic Intervals for Indirect Effects in Structural Equations Models." In S. Leinhart (ed.), *Sociological Methodology.* San Francisco: Jossey-Bass, 1982.

Tabachnick, B. G., and Fidell, L. S. *Using Multivariate Statistics.* (4th ed.) Needham Heights, Mass.: Allyn and Bacon, 2001.

18

Cost–Effectiveness and Cost–Benefit Analysis

James Edwin Kee

A significant challenge for program evaluation is the comparison of total program costs to total program benefits. Developing accurate costs and relating those costs to specific measures of effectiveness or to total benefits, can greatly assist decision makers but can prove difficult for the program evaluator. Cost-effectiveness analysis is a technique that relates total costs to some measure or measures of program effectiveness. Cost-benefit analysis takes that process one step further and seeks to place dollar values on all (or most) costs and benefits.

Cost-effectiveness analysis identifies and provides information on the full costs of a program and relates these costs to specific measures of program outcomes, such as so many lives saved per unit of cost or the reciprocal, so many dollars of program costs per life saved: for example, the number of lives saved per \$1 million of expenditures or so many dollars per life saved. The users can then compare the cost-effectiveness of various similar programs to determine which program is most cost-effective, that is, which program cost less per unit of outcome or achieves the most outcome per unit of cost.

Cost-benefit analysis also identifies and provides information on the full costs of programs and further weighs those costs against the dollar value of all program benefits. The evaluator can then calculate the net benefits (or costs) of the program, examine the ratio of benefits to costs (the benefit-cost ratio), and determine the economic rate of return (ERR) to society on the government's original investment. Users can then compare the program's benefits and costs with those of other programs or proposed alternatives.

These analyses can take place at different points in policymaking. As a program is being considered, an ex ante (or prospective) analysis of costs and benefits can be evaluated to see if a program should be undertaken or to compare alternative prospective programs aimed at a common policy objectives. At any point during a project, costs and benefits can be compared. A current year or snapshot analysis provides data on whether the program's current benefits are worth the costs. Finally, an ex post (or retrospective) analysis provides decision makers with total program costs and benefits to date so they can evaluate a program's overall success. Each of these types of analyses has its usefulness, peculiarities, and issues. For example, in the analysis of proposed programs, the estimation of costs and benefits is most difficult because they have not yet occurred. Those costs and benefits are largely known in a retrospective analysis, but determining which cost and benefits to attribute to the project is often challenging because the observed outcomes may have been the result of programs or events other than the one being analyzed.

Framework for Analysis

In conducting a cost-effectiveness or cost-benefit analysis as part of a program evaluation, whether ex ante or ex post, the first step is to identify all of the known benefits and costs of the program to the government, the program clients or beneficiaries, and others not directly involved in the program. There also are several distinct categories of benefits and costs: real versus transfers, direct and indirect, and tangible and intangible.

For each benefit or cost, direct or indirect, it is important to clearly state its nature, how it is measured, and any assumptions made in the calculations of the dollars involved. The statement of the assumptions is particularly critical because the decision maker needs to understand the analysis behind the numbers. Those assumptions need to be made clear to decision makers and also subjected to a sensitivity analysis to determine to what extent the outcome of the analysis is controlled by certain assumptions made.

Real Benefits and Costs Versus Transfers

Real benefits and costs represent net gains or losses to society, whereas transfers merely alter the distribution of resources within the society. Real benefits include dollars saved and dollars earned, lives saved and lives enriched, increased earnings and decreased costs to the taxpayers, and time saved and increased quality of life. In contrast, some societal gains are directly offset by other losses and are considered transfers. For example, a local tax abatement program for the elderly will provide a tax-saving benefit to some but a cost (of equal amount) to others (higher taxes or lower services). Transfers also

Key Terms

Benefit-cost ratio. The net present value of a stream of benefits of a program or project divided by the net present value of a stream of costs.

Cost-effectiveness ratio. The net present value of a stream of costs divided by a measure of outcome. Alternatively, a measure of outcome divided by the net present value of a stream of costs.

Discount rate. The interest rate used to convert future benefits and cost to their present value in year 1.

Marginal cost. The incremental (additional) cost of producing one more unit of output.

Marginal benefit. The incremental benefit generated by one unit of output.

Market value. The value (cost or benefit) of an item that would represent a willing buyer and seller under perfect market conditions.

Net present value. The conversion of a stream of future benefits less future costs to their equivalent benefits and cost in year 1, at the beginning of the project or program.

Opportunity cost. The value of using a resource (such as land or money) for one thing instead of another.

Sensitivity analysis. The calculation of how various indices (cost-effectiveness or cost-benefits) would change based on a change of key assumptions of costs or benefits.

Shadow pricing. An attempt to value a benefit or a cost where no competitive market price exists.

Sunk cost. Investments previously made in a program or project, such as original research and development costs, that cannot be recouped, as compared to ongoing costs.

occur as a result of a change in relative prices of various goods and services as the economy adjusts to the provision of certain public goods and services. Transfers are often important to policymakers. Many government programs involve the subsidizing of one group by another in the society and thus should be clearly identified where possible. But from an overall societal perspective, transfers do not increase total welfare; they merely redistribute welfare within society.

Direct and Indirect Benefits and Costs

Direct benefits and costs are those that are closely related to the primary objective of the project. Indirect or secondary benefits and costs are by-products, multipliers, spillovers, or investment effects of the project or program. An often cited example of indirect benefits from space exploration is the numerous spin-off technologies benefiting other industries. Direct costs include the costs of personnel, facilities, equipment and material, and administration. Indirect costs are intended (such as overhead) and unintended costs that occur as a result of a government action. For example, a dam built for agricultural purposes may flood an area used by hikers, who would lose the value of this recreation. This loss might be partially offset by benefit gains to those using the lake created by the dam for recreation. In all cases, the benefits and costs must be traced to the government action. For example, if a claimed benefit is the creation of new jobs, the benefit is the new jobs created at the margin over what new jobs would have occurred without the government action.

Marginal Benefits and Costs. An important, and often missed, distinction for the program evaluator is the difference between total and marginal benefits and costs. In assessing the overall profitability of a program or project, an analyst will need to consider the total costs in getting the project started through its operation's cycle. But at any point when an agency is deciding whether to continue or discontinue a project or program, it will consider only its marginal costs and benefits.

Marginal cost is defined as the incremental (additional) cost of producing one more unit of output. Marginal benefit is the incremental benefit generated by that one unit of output. Although in practice, analysis is not done on single incremental units, the evaluator attempts to analyze the program at the margin in determining whether to continue production of a product or program: What are the benefits that the program is now generating versus its costs?

In considering any program or project, the analyst must always start with the status quo: no change in the current level of expenditure for a program or project. In the case of a new program or project, the analysis should always contain a "do nothing" alternative to provide a baseline. So the only costs and benefits that would be considered are those that would occur in addition to those that would have occurred anyway without any action (the baseline).

Fixed versus Variable Costs. Sometimes it also is useful to consider the distinction between fixed costs (those that do not vary with the size of the program) and variable costs (those that vary depending on the size of the program). This may be particularly important in sizing a program or project, as marginal benefits may increase or decrease with increasing program size.

Tangible and Intangible Benefits and Costs

Tangible benefits and costs are those that the analyst can readily identify in unit terms and can convert to dollars for a cost-benefit analysis. In contrast, intangible benefits and costs include such things as the value of wilderness or increased sense of community. It is especially difficult to place a dollar value on many intangible benefits. This is perhaps the most problematic area of cost-benefit analysis and why cost-effectiveness analysis might be more appropriate for some types of benefits.

Determining the Geographical Scope of the Analysis

Although the focus of an analysis may be within a certain geographical area (a political jurisdiction such as a state, for example), some benefits or costs may spill over to neighboring areas (another jurisdiction). This may be an important consideration and should be identified in both cost-effectiveness and cost-benefit analysis. One method of dealing with these spillovers or externalities is through transfer pricing, or estimating the value of the subsidy or cost prevention measure, if deemed important for the analysis. There is a tendency for evaluators of existing projects to ignore spillover costs and benefits if they are not costed in some fashion; however, these spillovers often have political consequences. Thus, efforts to measure (or at least identify) these benefits or costs provide insight into the project's full effects.

For example, if one thousand persons from a neighboring jurisdiction use the county mass transit system, paying a daily fare of three dollars for a round trip, one benefit to the county government is the user fee revenue generated by the out-of-county riders. However, in a cost-benefit analysis, the benefit to those riders might well exceed the three dollars when calculating the value of the riders' time saved, reduced gasoline usage, and automobile (and personal) wear and tear. To the extent that total benefits to the out-of-county riders exceed the three dollars, politicians might be able to argue for a subsidy from the neighboring jurisdiction to support the county's transit system. This would be particularly true if the transit system was not self-supporting (as few are) and required a subsidy from in-county taxpayers. Thus, unless the neighboring county contributed to the transit system, in-county taxpayers would also be subsidizing out-of-county riders.

Table 18.1 provides a breakdown of some common benefit and costs by type and approaches to estimating costs and, for cost-benefit analysis, valuing the benefits.

Table 18.1. Framework for Analysis

	Illustration of Benefit and Cost	Valuation Approaches
Benefits		
Direct, tangible	Goods and services	Fair market value or willingness to pay
	Increased productivity or earnings	Increased production or profits or life-time earnings
	Time saved	After-tax wage rate
Direct, intangible	Lives saved	Lifetime earnings (if valued)
	Healthier citizens	
	Quality of life	(Implicit or contingent valuation using survey data or other techniques)
	Aesthetics	
Indirect, tangible	Cost savings	Difference between before and after action
	Spillover impacts to third parties	Estimated impact or mitigation of impact
	Multiplier effects	Additional indirect jobs created by proposal
Indirect, intangible	Preservation of community	
	Increased self-esteem	
Costs		
Direct, tangible	Personnel	Wages and benefits
	Materials and supplies	Current expenses
	Rentals (facilities, equipment)	Fair market rents
	Capital purchases	Depreciation plus interest on undepreciated part or annualized cost of depreciation and interest
	Land	Next best use or market value times interest rate
	Volunteers	Market or leisure value
Direct, intangible	Fear of harm	
Indirect, tangible	General overhead	Standard allocation formula or activity-based costing
	Spillover costs to third parties/Environmental damage	Estimation of impact or mitigation cost
	Compliance or client costs	Resources required of others (for example, money, time)
Indirect, intangible	Loss of aesthetics	Surveys of valuation
Transfers	Taxes and subsidies	While pure transfers result in no net gains or losses to society, they may be important for decision makers because of their distributional consequences
	Changes in profitability of businesses and industries	
	Changes in relative land value	

Estimating Costs

The first step in cost-effectiveness or cost-benefit analysis is to account for all program costs. In examining various types of program costs, both direct and indirect, the following broad categories are often used:

- One-time or up-front cost: Planning, research and development, pilot projects, and computer software
- Ongoing investment costs: Land, buildings and facilities, equipment and vehicles, and other expenditures whose useful life exceeds one year
- Recurring costs: Operations and maintenance; personnel salaries, wages, and fringe benefits; materials and supplies; and overhead costs
- Indirect and secondary costs, including mitigation measures and compliance cost and costs to other government agencies or to third parties—for example, costs to business of new health and safety regulations or relocation costs for persons or animals affected by a program

Case Study: Dropout Prevention Program

To illustrate the evaluation of costs, assume an analyst is asked by a high school principal to evaluate an existing program to reduce the incidence of early dropouts, aimed at at-risk high school students. The principal might be concerned as to whether the prior costs have been worth the results (an ex post analysis) or may be considering alternative programs to achieve the stated objective or other educational programs that might have a higher priority (an ex ante analysis). The Dropout Prevention Program example involves the creation of a special academy aimed at students at risk for dropping out. The academy has access to space, teachers, and equipment. In order to create the program, a consultant was hired to train the teachers and provide a curriculum for the academy—an example of a one-time, up-front cost. One full-time teacher was hired to manage the academy, and three other teachers were paid extra compensation to work after school in the program. Their salary (or extra compensation) plus benefits would be a recurring cost.

The box sets out a cost breakdown for a typical program dealing with high school students who are at risk for dropping out prior to graduation.

Pricing Costs

In the Dropout Prevention Program illustration, accounting or budgetary information would provide data on teachers' salaries, capital costs and materials used in the program, and other expenditures. Nevertheless, some costs will not be as easily identified from project documents but must be developed

Dropout Prevention Program Cost Breakdown

Several categories of cost categories need to be considered.

One-Time or Up-Front Costs

- Cost of a consultant who provided teacher training and information on how to set up the academy (direct, tangible)
- Computer software purchased for use in the program (direct, tangible)

Ongoing Investment Costs

- Use of classroom facilities (direct, tangible)
- Purchase of computers for use in the academy (direct, tangible)
- Academic texts that are used for more than one year (direct, tangible)

Recurring Costs

- Full-time salaries and benefits of teachers dedicated to the academy (direct, tangible)
- Part-time salaries and benefits for teachers receiving extra compensation for after-class programs associated with the academy (direct, tangible)
- Extra maintenance costs associated with after-school use of the facilities (indirect, tangible)
- Materials and supplies, including workbooks and other material used up during the program (direct, tangible)
- Travel expenditures for field trips (direct, tangible)
- Overhead costs, such as general supervision and finance (indirect, tangible
- Increased insurance (indirect, tangible)
- Cost of volunteers (indirect, tangible or intangible)

There are also secondary and compliance costs:

- Opportunity cost to students participating in the after-school program (indirect, tangible)
- Opportunity cost to parents if required to participate in the program (indirect, tangible)

Finally, there may be unintended indirect costs or mitigation measures (indirect, tangible or intangible) or there may be none. If the program had a negative aspect, then the cost of that negative aspect would have to

> be included or the costs of measures taken to prevent the negative occurrence. For example, in the Dropout Prevention Program, the existence of a special program, even if voluntary and open to all, might trigger some negative effects on students not in the special program and actually increase the rate of their dropping out of school. This could be accounted for as an indirect cost, or, alternatively, if the school attempts to mitigate the adverse effects, the costs could be those mitigation measures.

using best estimates, or shadow pricing. For example, if the academy uses dedicated classroom space, whether during the school day or after school, there is no cash outlay for the school, but the classroom use would represent an opportunity cost. The use of this space for the academy means it cannot be used for other educational activities. Should the evaluator place a dollar value on that opportunity cost? If the school could rent the space for other after-school activities, then the opportunity cost would be measured by the rental income forgone. If the classrooms would otherwise be vacant, then the opportunity cost for the space would be zero. Some additional cost would have to be assigned to the program for the additional maintenance cost of the facility caused by the extra use. This could be charged to the program by the school.

Cost of Capital

The cost of capital assets should be spread out over their expected useful life. There are many standard depreciation schedules for buildings and other capital equipment; sometimes there are different rates used for accounting or tax purposes. For government programs, an estimate needs to be made of the useful life of the asset considering physical deterioration, potential for obsolescence, salvage value at the end of the program, and other factors. Normally the asset (less its final salvage value) is depreciated equally per year over the life of the asset (straight-line depreciation). In addition to depreciation, the government loses the opportunity to use the money that is tied up in the undepreciated asset. This opportunity cost is expressed as an interest rate times the undepreciated portion. Spreadsheets and numerical tables also provide an amortization or annualized cost of depreciation plus interest (see Levin and McEwan, 2001).

In the Dropout Prevention Program illustration, the cost of computers and textbooks that have a useful life of more than one year should be amortized over the expected life of the asset. Computers typically would be amortized over a five-year period and textbooks over three years. Thus, the purchase of ten computers in year 1 of the project at two thousand dollars per computer would cost twenty thousand dollars; however, the actual costs per year assigned to the program would be the depreciation (over five years) plus the interest cost on the undepreciated portion. This number can be annualized by using a payment function in a calculator or spreadsheet: payment (PMT in Excel) is a function of interest rate (r), time period or number of payments (nper), and the present value of the capital cost (pv). In the case illustration, the interest rate is assumed to be 5 percent, the capital cost is $20,000, and the time period is five years. This leads to an annual cost of $4,619 for the computers. Similarly, the textbooks with a useful life of three years would have an annual cost of $367.

Land is not consumed as other capital facilities and equipment, and it is not depreciated; however, it has alternative uses. Land used for one activity cannot be used for another, and it cannot be sold to raise funds for other activities. Its value for a particular program is its opportunity cost to the government, normally expressed as the market value of the land times the prevailing rate of interest cost for government (for example, long-term U.S. Treasury bill or municipal bond rate).

The cost of interest payments is sometimes counted as a program or project cost if the project required the issuance of debt to finance it. This is particularly true if the program or project is designed to be self-sufficient, with revenues paying for total costs (for example, a specific recreational facility or a water or sewer project). From a budgetary perspective, interest payments are clearly a cost. However, if the analyst is doing a comparison of programs across jurisdictions, the inclusion of interest payments from borrowing would give a faulty comparison of program efficiency.

Indirect Costs

Indirect or secondary costs are by-products of the program. They include intended items, such as overhead, and unintended items, such as negative environmental effects.

Overhead. Many consulting firms and other profit and nonprofit agencies, such as colleges and universities, employ a standard indirect cost allocation figure on top of their direct costs, often computed at 30 to 60 percent of the total direct costs or a subset of direct costs, such as personnel expenditures. State and local governments also use an indirect cost allocation figure in determining reimbursement for certain federal grants-in-aid programs. These percentages are based on total administrative overhead costs compared with all other expenditures (or all personnel expenditures) from all other programs.

The major controversy with indirect cost allocations is whether a specific program really adds marginal cost to the overhead agencies. That is, does the program cause increased administrative burdens on the central administrative staff? A state government will have an office for the governor and attorney general, a legislature, and certain overhead agencies (finance, personnel, purchasing) whether or not a particular program exists; most of these expenses are sunk costs. However, additional programs do cause additional workload on some of those agencies that may lead to an increase in personnel and other needs. The application of the appropriate overhead rate is significant judgment call for the evaluator; the analysis might be highly sensitive to the choice made.

Rather than estimating an overhead rate, an evaluator might use a method called activity-based costing. In this method, overhead costs are allocated based on certain cost drivers. For example, if a proposed program was going to use summer help and involve significant personnel actions, then the additional cost assigned to the project would be the additional costs to the personnel or human resource office, perhaps as a function of program employees versus total employees.

Costs to the Private Sector. Government often shifts costs to the private sector, especially in regulatory activity. When the Environmental Protection Agency mandates the installation of scrubbers on electric utilities or the purchase of higher-cost low-sulfur coal in order to reduce acid rain (as legislated in the 1991 Clean Air Act), the costs of the program are not just the regulatory agencies' costs of enforcement of the new requirements. The costs to the electric utilities, which will likely be passed forward to the consumers of the utilities' power, must also be considered.

Sometimes costs to the private sector are easy to identify, such as the increased cost to car manufacturers when passive restraint systems are installed. At other times, regulations impose additional reporting requirements, causing an increase in clerical staff for business or a loss of time to individuals who must wade through the additional bureaucratic red tape. If substantial, these costs should be identified and, if possible, valued in dollars. Time lost should be valued just as time saved is valued on the benefit side of the analysis.

Costs to Participants and Volunteers. One other indirect cost of programs is the cost to participants and volunteers. Although these are not cash outlays, they are considered real costs of the program. For example, in the Dropout Prevention Program illustration, the academy for at-risk students operates after school. For the students involved, this represents an opportunity cost for their time, which should be identified even if the analyst chooses not to place a dollar value on it.

Many government programs also employ the use of volunteers as part of the program. They can provide a real benefit to a program and may relieve the agency from spending money for part-time staff. Levin and McEwan

(2001) argue that the value can be determined by estimating the market value of the services that a volunteer provides. This approach seems correct where the volunteer has specific skills and the agency would otherwise have to employ someone of the same skills. Otherwise, the cost might be viewed as the opportunity cost to the volunteer. That might be significant if the volunteer must take off work to participate and loses money by volunteering, or it may be negligible, where the volunteer is giving up leisure time. Furthermore, the volunteer may gain something by volunteering—a sense of participation or civic virtue, for example—that may outweigh the opportunity cost. In the case of student volunteers, they may gain more knowledge and expertise as they volunteer, or they may be fulfilling some community service requirement, thus canceling out any cost to them. Therefore, although it is important to recognize the participation of volunteers, it is not always clear that a specific cost should be assigned to their use.

Indirect costs to the private sector and to participants and volunteers are controversial and their valuation sometimes problematic. Because of this, it is useful to separate costs to government from costs to others in society or to identify costs to participants and costs to all others (including government). In this fashion, the decision maker can more readily determine the most important costs to consider.

Sunk Costs. Sunk costs are defined as investments previously made in a program or project, such as original research and development costs, as compared to ongoing costs. In an ex post evaluation of total benefits and costs of a program, the evaluator will consider all previous costs. However, when recommending future action on a program or project (an ex ante analysis), sunk costs should be ignored, because they have no impact on the marginal costs and benefits of the continuation of the project or program.

Dropout Prevention Program Illustration. Table 18.2 follows the illustration of the Dropput Prevention Program for high students at risk of dropping out of school. It provides an estimate of costs for a program involving fifty students and one full-time teacher in a special academy created for these students. Table 18.3 displays those costs over the life of the program, in constant dollars (that is, not reflecting inflation).

Displaying Cost Information. Table 18.3 allows the analyst to display the full costs of the Dropout Prevention Program. If the program is in its fifth year and the principal is attempting to decide whether to continue it, the evaluator can present cost information to the principal on an annual basis and the total costs for the five years the program was operating. Where the analyst chooses not to place a dollar value on a cost (as in the cost of volunteers), the category of cost can at least be indicated in the analysis.

Examining the data, we find total costs, through year 5, for the program are approximately $643,000, and the annual cost (in year 5) is $127,887. The

Table 18.2. Costing an Existing Dropout Prevention Program

Cost	Estimate and Method of Valuation
Up-front costs: Use of consultants; program software	Actual costs of program in its first year (for example, $3,000 for consultants and $500 for software)
Facilities: Use of classroom after school	Opportunity cost of classroom use (could it be used for other purposes or rented out?). Assume there is no other use: $0.
Capital expenses: Purchase of material with use longer than one year—computers and texts	These costs are generally spread out over their useful life; for computers and texts, 3 to 5 years. Assume 10 computers at $2,000 for 5 years (annual cost: $4,619) and 20 texts at $50 with a 3-year life (annual cost: $387).
Salaries: Both full-time and part-time salaries include annual costs plus benefits.	Assume one full-time faculty at $35,000 plus 30 percent benefits ($10,500); plus three part-time faculty—9 months at $2,000 per month plus benefits (part-time benefits might be lower, say, 10 percent). Annual cost: $104,900.
Maintenance: Extra costs of maintaining facilities after normal hours; may include energy costs, janitorial, and maintenance.	These would be the marginal costs incurred over what the costs would have been without the program: Assume $1,000 a month for 9 months. Annual cost: $9,000.
Materials and supplies:	Annual costs: Assume $100 per participant, with 50 participants. Annual cost: $5,000.
Travel:	Cost of buses for field trips, car mileage, and so on. Annual assumed costs: $3,000.
Overhead: Administrative, including any costs of supervision; insurance	Appropriate measure is marginal cost; for example, if insurance went up because of the new program or cost of auditing program increased cost of annual audit. Annual assumed costs: $1,000.
Participants' cost: Includes both students and parents if they are required to participate. Volunteer cost: opportunity cost if applicable	Although this is a nonbudget cost, it may represent a real cost to participants (for example, the ability to earn money after school or the cost to parents of taking off from work or driving to school to participate). Even if the analyst chooses not to place a dollar value on the opportunity cost, it should be identified in the analysis.

Table 18.3. Dropout Prevention Program Lifetime Costs, in Constant Dollars

	Year 1	Year 2	Year 3	Year 4	Year 5	Total
Costs to the school						
Up-front cost						
Consultants	$3,000					$3,000
Software	$500					$500
Capital expenses						
Classroom	$0	$0	$0	$0	$0	$0
Computers	$4,619	$4,619	$4,619	$4,619	$4,619	$23,097
Texts	$367	$367	$367	$367	$367	$1,836
Salaries						
Full time	$45,500	$45,500	$45,500	$45,500	$45,500	$227,500
Part time	$59,400	$59,400	$59,400	$59,400	$59,400	$297,000
Maintenance	$9,000	$9,000	$9,000	$9,000	$9,000	$45,000
Materials and supplies	$5,000	$5,000	$5,000	$5,000	$5,000	$25,000
Travel	$3,000	$3,000	$3,000	$3,000	$3,000	$15,000
Overhead						
Administrative	$500	$500	$500	$500	$500	$2,500
Insurance	$500	$500	$500	$500	$500	$2,500
Total cost to school	$131,387	$127,887	$127,887	$127,887	$127,887	$642,934
Costs to others (no dollar estimate)						
Participants	$0	$0	$0	$0	$0	$0
Parents	$0	$0	$0	$0	$0	$0
Volunteers	$0	$0	$0	$0	$0	$0
Total costs to others	$0	$0	$0	$0	$0	$0
TOTAL COSTS	$131,387	$127,887	$127,887	$127,887	$127,887	$642,934
Number of participants	50	50	50	50	50	250
School cost per participant	$2,628	$2,558	$2,558	$2,558	$2,558	$2,572
Other cost per participant	$0	$0	$0	$0	$0	$0
Total cost per participant	$2,628	$2,558	$2,558	$2,558	$2,558	$2,572
Net present value at 3 percent						
School cost	$606,754					
Other cost	$0					
Total cost	$606,754					
School cost per participant	$2,427					
Other cost per participant	$0					
Total cost per participant	$2,427					

principal now understands the full cost and various components of the cost of the program. Although opportunity costs to participants, parents, and volunteers were not valued in this illustration, they were noted and should be explained in the narrative. This is also true of the opportunity cost of the space used in the school.

The spreadsheet provides cost data per participant. The principal can weigh those costs against the costs of other proposed programs to accomplish the same objective or against other competing programs aimed at other educational objectives. However, total cost to the school and participants, even on a cost per participant basis, may not provide sufficient information to the principal. In order to compare various programs aimed at the same objective—preventing high school dropouts—it is important to develop some common measures of effectiveness.

Cost-Effectiveness Analysis

Cost-effectiveness analysis relates the cost of a given alternative to specific measures of program outcomes, for example, dollars per life saved on various highway safety programs. Cost-effectiveness analysis is sometimes the first step in a cost-benefit analysis, though it stands alone as an effective evaluation tool. It is especially useful when the program's objectives are either singular or sufficiently related so that the relationship between the objectives is clear. For example, if the goal of the Dropout Prevention Program is to prevent high school dropouts, alternative programs can be compared by analyzing the costs per dropout prevented (or per increase in percentage of students graduating) without valuing those benefits in dollars.

The analyst can simply present the benefits per x dollars and allow the decision makers to assess whether the benefits are worth the costs. However, government programs often generate more than one type of benefit. One approach is to simply compare costs to various measures of program benefit. However, this becomes problematic when comparing multiple programs with various benefits. In that case, the analyst might have to weight the various benefits to achieve a common denominator. In cost-benefit analysis, it is dollars that are the common denominator. Nevertheless, when valuing in dollars is impossible or impractical or there is a dominant measure of effectiveness, cost-effectiveness analysis often provides a superior economic technique.

Measures of Effectiveness

Everyone is attempting to do a better job of measuring program effectiveness. It is the focus of performance-based budgeting and the Government Performance Results Act. Measures of performance are idiosyncratic to each program. In all cases, they must be related to the objectives of the program. Thus, in the Dropout Prevention Program example, the objective is to increase graduation rates through a decrease in the number of dropouts prior to graduation. Thus, "dropouts prevented" becomes an outcome measure for the program.

Levin and McEwan (2001) provide a number of other examples of program measures from various studies. A program with the objective of improving the functioning of disabled infants and toddlers was measured based on some common behavioral tests, and a Brazilian program to improve achievements in elementary schools used test scores in basic skills in Portuguese and mathematics.

Dropout Prevention Program Illustration

In the example, we might consider a number of potential measures of benefits. Staying in high school through graduation will lead to more productive lives, higher earnings, less reliance on government assistance (such as welfare programs), and perhaps fewer criminal and other negative behaviors. In a cost-effectiveness analysis, the goal is to come up with one or more measures that will serve as a proxy for program success. In this case, that measure seems obvious. The program goal is to prevent dropouts. Therefore, the program measure of effectiveness can be number of dropouts prevented.

In an ex post analysis to determine the number of dropouts prevented as a result of the program, an analyst would examine data on dropouts for at-risk high school students. In the example, the analyst determines that of 50 at-risk high school students, 20 typically drop out before graduation. However, those enrolled in the academy (the Dropout Prevention Program) were more likely to stay in school. Data indicate that over the five years of the program, of 250 participants, 69 dropped out before graduation compared to the expected 100 with no program. Thus, the number of dropouts prevented by the program can be estimated at 31.

The analyst can now compare the 31 dropouts prevented with the program cost. Those costs can be displayed on an annual basis and totaled over the five years. Since costs in year 1 are more costly than costs in later years, the stream of costs should be discounted by the appropriate interest rate for the school district. The role of discounting is discussed in more detail later in the chapter. For this analysis, the costs in years 2 through 5 are discounted by 3 percent annually. The costs per dropout prevented are calculated as $19,573 of costs to the school. No costs were calculated for the participants or volunteers, but they could be identified. Table 18.4 provides a summary of cost-effectiveness information. For the principal, knowing the cost per dropout prevented is obviously of more value than simply knowing the cost per participant (derived from Table 18.3).

Table 18.4. Dropout Prevention Program Cost-Effectiveness Analysis

Year	1	2	3	4	5	Total
Dropouts per 50 students	20	20	20	20	20	100
Dropouts per 50 participants	17	15	13	12	12	69
Dropouts prevented	3	5	7	8	8	31
Program costs						
Total cost to school	$131,387	$127,887	$127,887	$127,887	$127,887	$642,934
Total cost to others	$0	$0	$0	$0	$0	$0
TOTAL COSTS	$131,387	$127,887	$127,887	$127,887	$127,887	$642,934
Cost per dropout prevented						
To school	$43,796	$25,577	$18,270	$15,986	$15,986	$20,740
To others (participants)	$0	$0	$0	$0	$0	$0
Total cost per dropout prevented	$43,796	$25,577	$18,270	$15,986	$15,986	$20,740
Net present value at 3 percent						
School cost per dropout prevented		$19,573				
Other cost per dropout prevented		$0				
Total cost per dropout prevented		$19,573				

Usefulness of Cost-Effectiveness Analysis

The major advantage of cost-effectiveness analysis is that it frees the evaluator from having to express all benefits in monetary terms. Program outcomes can be addressed according to their multiple attributes. For education programs, for example, student learning can be assessed in terms of improved test scores, physical education programs can be assessed in terms of improvements in various physical skills of the participants (or percentage passing a physical fitness exam), and programs to increase college placement can be assessed in terms of numbers of students placed in various colleges (Levin and McEwan, 2001). In none of these cases does the evaluator have to weigh the costs against a dollar value of benefits. The evaluator simply presents the results to the decision maker, who then decides whether the various outcomes are worth the dollar cost. This often is a very effective, and low-cost, method of providing comparative program cost data to decision makers.

Government programs, however, frequently generate more than one type of cost and benefit. A weapons system might have both offensive and defensive uses; an education program might target more than one population group in the school system or have more than one beneficiary effect. The mix of benefits may depend on how the program is designed and implemented. When conducting a cost-effectiveness analysis comparing programs having multiple objectives, the evaluator may need to assign weights on the relative benefits in order to assist the decision maker's comparisons.

Weighting Benefits. Musgrave and Musgrave (1989) provide an illustration using expenditures on education. Expenditures on elementary education might contribute more to literacy than outlays on higher education do; however, expenditures on higher education might contribute more to advancing scientific knowledge than a similar amount spent on elementary education.

Suppose a $3 billion expenditure on elementary education produces a 12 "unit" gain in literacy and a 3 unit gain in scientific knowledge, whereas a $3 billion expenditure on higher education produces only a 3 unit gain in literacy but a 15 unit gain in scientific knowledge. Units might be a function of percentage increases in the literacy rate or new patents. Can the evaluator compare the two programs? If the units are valued equally—a 1 percent increase in literacy equaling a 1 percent increase in patents—the clear winner is the higher education expenditure. If, however, because of distributional reasons (literacy programs would help disadvantaged people) or other value judgments, a literacy unit is "valued" at 25 percent greater than a scientific knowledge unit, the evaluator might conclude that the elementary education program is preferable. Ultimately, the key issue is the valuation of the unit for both programs, which ultimately must be decided by the policymaker. An evaluator can help the decision maker by comparing the costs to various units of output and indicating any explicit or implicit valuation.

Disadvantages to Cost-Effectiveness Analysis. There are two major disadvantages of cost-effectiveness analysis compared to benefit-cost analysis:

- In considering programs with multiple benefits, unless the evaluator assigns weights to each benefit to obtain a common denominator for comparison purposes, the comparison may be of less use to decision makers. Yet assigning weights often becomes at least as problematic as assigning dollar values to each benefit.
- A cost-effectiveness analysis does not produce a single bottom-line number, with benefits exceeding costs or costs exceeding benefits. Thus, if a program costs $1 million and produces 10 units of outcome x, 12 units of outcome y, and 20 units of outcome z, how is the evaluator to make a judgment concerning the cost-effectiveness of the program? This must be left to the judgment of the decision makers. The question for the decision maker is often whether the total outcomes produced are worth the $1 million expenditure.

Cost-benefit analysis attempts to value the outcomes in monetary terms. If it is possible to do so, that valuation may be of more assistance to a decision maker than a simple listing of program outcomes that can be compared to total costs.

Cost-Benefit Analysis

Cost-benefit analysis is an applied economic technique that attempts to assess a government program or project by determining whether societal welfare has or will increase (in the aggregate more people are better off) because of the program or project. Cost-benefit analysis can provide information on the full costs of a program or project and weigh those costs against the dollar value of the benefits. The analyst can then calculate the net benefits (or costs) of the program or project, examine the ratio of benefits to costs, determine the rate of return on the government's original investment, and compare the program's benefits and costs with those of other programs or proposed alternatives. Cost-benefit analysis has three rather simple-sounding steps:

1. Determine the benefits of a proposed or existing program and place a dollar value on those benefits.
2. Calculate the total costs of the program.
3. Compare the benefits and the costs.

These steps, however, can be very challenging for the analyst. Even when benefits can be calculated in unit terms, such as so many lives saved, it is often difficult to place a dollar value on each unit. For many intangibles (national security, wilderness values, quality of life), determining both the unit of analysis and its dollar value is problematic. Nevertheless, even when the analyst cannot capture all of the benefits and costs in quantitative terms, the procedure can uncover important issues for judging a program's success or failure.

Use of Cost-Benefit Analysis

In many respects, cost-benefit analysis of government programs is similar to financial analysis conducted in the private sector as existing and potential investment opportunities are considered. Government and its taxpayers are investing funds to achieve certain societal benefits, just as a firm is investing to achieve profit. Public agencies and their evaluators must ask:

- For a proposed program or project: Do we expect this project or program to create net benefits to society?
- For an existing program: Is the program a success, that is, has it improved societal welfare?
- At any given decision-making point, should the program be continued when weighed against alternative uses for the government's funds?

While similar questions are asked in a cost-effectiveness analysis, the attempt in a cost-benefit analysis is to provide a bottom line similar to a private sector financial analysis, though with some key differences.

Most government programs are not priced, at least not to maximize profits. Although revenue may be important from a budgetary perspective, benefits are broader than any monetary return to the government and may occur over decades. In assessing the success or failure of the project, a government should also consider the opportunity cost of using the funds in the proposed project. Governmental policymakers have alternative uses for tax dollars or borrowing capacity, such as other programs or returning the money back to its citizens in the form of tax reductions and thus allow more spending in the private sector.

Analysis of the Dropout Prevention Illustration

In the analysis of the Dropout Prevention Program for the high school principal, measures of cost-effectiveness alone may not be sufficient. The principal may want to compare this program with other options that produce dissimilar benefits, for example, expanding the advising and counseling program to assist students in gaining college admissions. Therefore, the principal may want a dollar value placed on the benefits of the Dropout Prevention Program so that he can compare that program to others under consideration. Table 18.3 has provided the cost information, the first step in the analysis. The next step is to consider the range of benefits from the program and to place dollar values on those benefits:

- The major benefit of completing high school is to the participants themselves: an increase in lifetime earnings because of the diploma. To calculate this number, an evaluator would need to compare similar individuals who have completed high school with those who have dropped out. These data might be available from the U.S. Bureau of Labor Statistics. In the illustration, it is assumed that this increase in earnings averages $8,000 a year, with a net present lifetime value of $136,000 per dropout prevented.
- There may be benefits to the rest of society as a result of an individual's completing high school. Those might include less crime, less government support (welfare and other transfers), and increased taxes paid to the government. Some of these benefits to the rest of society are costs to the participants. Thus, taxes gained by government are a cost to the participants (in effect, a transfer that must be netted out in the analysis).
- The analysis makes the assumption that lower crime costs are primarily a benefit to the rest of society (less detention and judicial system cost and less cost to victims). This includes the "gain" to potential victims (they avoid a loss of their property) offset somewhat by the "loss" to the participants (they lost the value of goods stolen and fenced).
- It is clear that there are some benefits that are difficult to put a monetary value on. For example, the cost of stolen goods to victims does not cover the full cost of pain and suffering to the victims, but those other costs may be difficult to place a dollar value on. Similarly, graduating from high school may create a self-confidence in the students that enhances their lives beyond lifetime earnings. In addition, better-educated citizens may benefit society in other nonmonetary ways.

Although costs begin in year 1 of the project, benefits do not occur until the students have actually graduated at the end of year 1 or beginning in year 2, though it is possible that some benefits (such as lower crime) might begin immediately. Furthermore, the benefits continue to occur long after the program is being analyzed.

At the end of the five-year period, the school has spent $642,934 with a net present value (in year 1) of $606,754 at a 3 percent discount rate. Benefits have just begun to accrue to those who successfully completed high school. In fact, in four of the first five years, the costs of the program exceed the benefits. This is typical in many government programs that have a long-term benefit.

Net present value (NPV) of benefits minus costs or costs minus benefits is the most traditional format for government agencies to present the results of the analysis; however, a benefit-cost ratio is sometimes used when comparing similar programs. The benefit-cost ratio is determined by dividing the total present value of benefits by the total present value of costs. In the dropout program illustration, benefits are expected to equal $4,172,651 discounted at 3 percent over the thirty-year period of the analysis, with net benefits over costs of over $3.5 million.

Table 18.5 provides a summary of the information—a further breakdown of the benefits and costs for the participants and for the rest of society on an aggregate basis and on a per-dropout-prevented basis. It combines both cost-effectiveness and cost-benefit data. It also considers an alternative that estimates a cost to the participants: a loss of time that they could have been working. This is useful to see whether the cost-benefit numbers are still positive if this opportunity cost is calculated. The alternative assumes that 50 students could work 15 hours a week for 36 weeks at a wage rate of $5 an hour. Over the five years, this results in a net present value cost of $636,808 for the participants.

Whether viewed from the total societal perspective (participants and all others) or from each perspective, the Dropout Prevention Program can be considered a success: benefits exceed the costs even under the alternative that costs the participants' time. The analyst can also develop benefit-cost ratios for the program. They are calculated by dividing the net present value (NPV) of benefits by the net present value of costs, for society as a whole and individually for the participants and the rest of society:

- NPV benefits to others ($1,288,848, excluding participant gains) divided by NPV costs to others ($606,754) equals a benefit-cost ratio of 2.12 to 1.
- NPV total social benefits ($4,172,101) divided by NPV total social cost ($606,754) equals benefit-cost ratio of 6.88 to 1.
- The alternative, which costs participants' time, also has a positive benefit-cost ratio: 4.53 to 1 for participants, 2.12 to 1 for others, and 3.35 to 1 for society as a whole.

The benefit-cost ratios are useful in two respects. First, they enable the decision maker to compare similar programs. For example, if another proposed dropout prevention program of similar scale had an estimated benefit-cost ratio of 8 to 1, it might be considered superior (more efficient) to the current program (all things else remaining the same). Second, a decision

**Table 18.5. Cost-Effectiveness and Cost-Benefit Summary
of the Dropout Prevention Program**

Net Present Value at 3%	30-Year Impact		Costing Participant Time	
	Total	*Per Dropout Prevented*	*Total*	*Per Dropout Prevented*
Costs				
Costs to school	$606,754	$19,573	$606,754	$19,573
Costs to participants	$0	$0	$636,808	$20,542
Total costs	$606,754	$19,573	$1,243,562	$40,115
Benefits				
Number of dropouts prevented		31		31
To participants				
Increase in earnings	$4,193,822	$135,285	$4,193,822	$135,285
Less gain from crime	($52,423)	($1,691)	($52,423)	($1,691)
Less welfare payments	($1,048,456)	($33,821)	($1,048,456)	($33,821)
Less taxes	($209,691)	($6,764)	($209,691)	($6,764)
Total to participants	$2,883,253	$93,008	$2,883,253	$93,008
Net benefits (costs) Part	$2,883,253	$93,008	$2,246,445	$72,466
Benefit-cost ratio	NA		4.53	
To others				
Cost savings—crime	$30,702	$990	$30,702	$990
Cost savings—welfare	$1,048,456	$33,821	$1,048,456	$33,821
Taxes	$209,691	$6,764	$209,691	$6,764
Total to society	$1,288,848	$41,576	$1,288,848	$41,576
Net benefits (cost) others	$682,094	$22,003	$682,094	$22,003
Benefit-cost ratio	2.12		2.12	
Total benefits	$4,172,101	$134,584	$4,172,101	$134,584
Net benefits (costs)	$3,565,347	$115,011	$2,928,539	$94,469
Benefit-cost ratio	6.88		3.35	

maker can decide whether a 6.88 to 1 overall societal benefit-cost ratio is sufficient given other investment or budget alternatives. From an economic efficiency perspective, any program with benefits exceeding costs, or with a benefit-cost ratio of better than 1, would be considered an efficient allocation of resources. In reality, decision makers seldom use benefit-cost ratios unless they are examining two similar projects in size and scope.

Unlike the private sector, government evaluators usually do not conduct return on investment or economic rate of return (ERR) analysis; however, that also can be computed. It is the discount rate that would yield total present value benefits equal to costs. In the Dropout Preventin Program illustration, it is approximately 33 percent. The government agency or political decision maker can then assess the success or failure of the project based on whether a 33 percent rate of return is satisfactory given other opportunities the agency might have had in year 1. (Calculating an ERR is not used very often in the United States; it is more common with international organizations.)

It is important for the analyst to conduct a sensitivity analysis of key assumptions to see which have the greatest impact on the analysis. What is the probability that those assumptions will occur? The analyst should examine a range of alternative assumptions and determine their impact on the analysis.

Opportunity Cost and Net Present Value

It is important to recognize that the school, by spending $642,934 on the Dropout Prevention Program, did not have those dollars to spend for other programs, and thus there is an opportunity cost that should be recognized in the analysis. In order to incorporate the concept of opportunity cost, cost-benefit analysis employs NPV analysis that converts all costs and benefits to their present value at the beginning of the project, in year 1.

The opportunity costs to the agency are expressed as the real rate of return (r) appropriate to the agency at the beginning of the project. The benefits (B) less costs (C) in year 2 can be expressed as $B - C/(1 + r)$; year 3 as $B - C/(1 + r)(1 + r)$ or $B - C/(1 + r)^2$; year 4 as $B - C/(1 + r)^3$; and year 5 as $B - C/(1 + r)^4$. For the thirty-year period, the net benefits less costs of the project can be calculated using the following formula:

$$NPV = B^{y1} - C^{y1} + \frac{B^{y2} - C^{y2}}{1 + r} + \frac{B^{y3} - C^{y3}}{(1 + r)^2} \ldots \frac{B^{yx} - C^{yx}}{(1 + r)^{x-1}}$$

Present value analysis is often extremely sensitive to the choice of the appropriate interest rate (usually referred to as the discount rate) for the agency. If in the Dropout Prevention Program, illustration, the school's opportunity costs were reflected by a 7 percent interest rate instead of a 3 percent rate, then the NPV decreases from $3.5 to $1.9 million. The higher the discount rate is, the greater the future benefit streams are discounted. Since cost-benefit analysis is often very sensitive to the choice of a discount rate, a range of alternatives should be used and the results presented to the decision makers.

Continuing or Not Continuing the Program

Should the principal continue the program in the illustration? By year 5, the program is costing $127,887 a year and is preventing eight dropouts a year for a cost per dropout prevented of $15,986. If the principal is considering whether to continue the program (an ex ante analysis), certain costs incurred by the school (for example, the original cost of consultants) are now sunk costs, that is, funds have already been spent and resources used. They have no relevance for decisions about whether to continue the project. They have achieved (or not achieved) benefits. Thus, the previously spent funds on start-up and on capital costs are not considered by the agency in deciding whether to continue the project. The agency is concerned only with its current and future costs and expected continued benefits:

- Will it need to spend additional dollars to modify the program?
- Will it need to upgrade its facilities and equipment or buy new computers?
- What is the salvage value of current capital involved in the project or its opportunity costs for alternative uses, if any?
- Is there still a need or demand for this program?

Thus, the program's continuation faces a different evaluation from an ex post analysis of the project's net benefits. One of the challenges for the analyst is determining whether program projections are realistic. Agency policymaker support for a project may lead to an underestimation of future costs and an overestimation of future benefits.

The cost-benefit illustration reinforces an important distinction for the analyst: the difference between total and marginal benefits and costs. In assessing the overall "profitability" (or net benefits) of a proposed or existing project, an agency will consider the total costs of getting the program or project started through its operation's cycle. But at any point when an agency is deciding whether to continue or discontinue a project or program, it should consider only its marginal costs and benefits.

Problems in the Valuation of Benefits

Evaluating benefits is much more difficult for government than business because benefits and costs may not be reflected or easily measured in market prices. Furthermore, while cost issues pose some problems, the measurement of program benefits is generally more difficult than the cost side of the analysis. The more complex the program objectives (for example, urban renewal), typically the more difficult the benefit analysis is because it often involves multiple objectives aimed at different beneficiary groups (business interests, the poor, the middle class, and many others).

There are a number of potential sources of data for analyzing program benefits:

- Existing records and statistics kept by the agency, legislative committees, or agency watchdogs such as the U.S. General Accounting Office.

- Feedback from the program's clients—either the general population or the subset of the population the program is serving. This might be obtained through a questionnaire or focus group.
- Ratings by trained observers.
- The experience of other governments, private or nonprofit organizations.
- Special data gathering.

More detailed discussion of evaluation design and data collection procedures is contained in other chapters in this book. However, a caveat is in order: data collection is not a cost-free exercise. Although the evaluator wants to have as many data as possible on both benefits and costs, he or she must weigh the value of the increased accuracy gained from the accumulation of new data against the costs associated with the data collection. Thus, the first order of priority for the evaluator is to assimilate existing data and determine whether they are sufficient for the analysis. The more costly the project or program is, the more the evaluator may want to supplement existing data with new data collected through questionnaires, experiments, surveys, or other evaluation techniques.

Most economists argue that despite their imperfections, market prices are the best valuation of a benefit. Therefore, the evaluator should use a market value when one is available or a surrogate, such as willingness to pay. For most government programs, the recipients are not fully paying for the benefits received; therefore, the evaluator must make an alternative assessment of value. For example, the value or shadow price of a "free" outdoor swimming pool might be the amount people are willing to pay for a similar swimming experience in a private or nonprofit pool. The difficulty with the concept of willingness to pay is that a person's willingness may vary significantly depending on circumstances. Therefore, it is important to subject any valuation to a sensitivity analysis to see how dependent the results are on the choice of a specific valuation. Using a range of values is one approach to dealing with this uncertainty.

In developing nations, there often are market distortions (tariffs, monopolies, subsidies, and others) and no true competitive market. In this case, attempts are made to find a shadow price, such as a world market price, that approximates a competitive market value.

Cost Avoidance. Cost avoidance or cost savings are also benefits. Thus, an anticrime program analyst could measure dollars saved from avoided burglaries. An antiflood program analyst could measure dollars saved from avoiding flood damage. A health program analyst could measure avoided costs such as medical care expenditures and loss of productivity. To determine the amount of cost avoidance, the evaluator would have to look at historical data and trends before and after implementation of the government program and estimate the effect of the program on other government spending and the general public.

For example, if a new dam built for flood control purposes prevented a loss of $10 million from flooding that periodically occurred in the community, the $10 million is a cost savings. The annual benefit to the community would be expressed as $10 million times the risk that such a flood would occur in any given year. If on average the community was flooded every ten years, than the yearly benefit would be $1 million ($10 million times 1/10).

Often a government program can be justified solely on the basis of savings to the government itself. In our illustrative Dropout Prevention Program, the benefits include cost savings to the criminal justice system, lower welfare payments, and increased taxes from the more productive high school graduates. Those benefits alone might exceed the costs of the program.

Time Saved. Time saved is a tangible benefit. However, measurement of its dollar value is more subjective. Each person may value his or her time differently. A common method of estimating the value of time is by using the economists' theory of work-leisure trade-off. When people have control over the hours they are working, they will work (including overtime) until their subjective value of leisure is equal to the income they would gain from one more hour of work—their after-tax wage rate.

Using the after-tax wage rate is not without problems. Many people cannot choose their hours of work, and not all uses away from the job are equally valuable. For example, to avoid spending time in rush-hour traffic, persons who dislike driving might be willing to pay to avoid such driving at a rate exceeding their wage rate. Those who use the road for non-rush-hour pleasure driving might not care about the opportunity cost of their time. Thus, the value of a person's time will vary with when the time saved occurs and the particular circumstances.

An alternate valuation of time is to look at willingness to pay for faster transportation. If commuting by train is more expensive but quicker than commuting by bus, we can infer how much travelers are willing to pay—at a minimum—to reduce their commuting time and therefore their valuation of their time. In another example, if people pay to use a new toll road at a cost of one dollar and save fifteen minutes in travel time, than we can infer that the value of time saved to them is at least four dollars per hour. The average benefit may be higher; some commuters would be willing to pay more than one dollar to save fifteen minutes. On the basis of several such studies, one proposed estimate of the effective value of traveling time is about 60 percent of the before-tax wage rate (Rosen, 1992). Average nonagricultural wages is generally used as the wage rate measurement.

Valuing Lives. Lives saved is clearly a tangible benefit—an unestimatable value to the person whose life was saved—and the justification for many government health and safety programs. Our religious and cultural values suggest that life is priceless, and there are numerous examples (the child who fell into the well hole in Texas) where people have gone to an enormous extent of time and money to save a single life. But this poses a problem for the evaluator. Rosen (1992) phrases the issue in this fashion: if the value of life is infinite, any project that leads to even a single life being saved has an infinitely high present value. This leaves no sensible way to determine the admissibility of projects. If every road in the United States were a divided four-lane highway, it is doubtless true that traffic fatalities would decrease. Would this be a good project?

Similarly, we could save many lives if we reduced the speed limit nationwide to twenty-five miles an hour. What is the cost here? It is the lost time for movement of people and goods. Since we have chosen not to do this, does this mean that we do not value lives saved as much as the cost of time? Implicitly yes, so lives do not have an infinite value. The question for the evaluator is how to value a life.

Economists have developed two methods to value a human life. The first, which is often used in civil court cases, estimates the individual's lost earnings for his or her remaining life. The problem is that this would cause us to value a young college graduate on the verge of a career more highly than a senior citizen who has retired or has few work years remaining. A second approach looks at people's acceptance of higher-risk jobs and their related higher salaries as payment for a higher probability of death. Thus, it is possible to impute a value of life based on a willingness to forgo the higher salary. The problem with this approach is the uncertainty surrounding the job risk and whether persons have a knowledge of the death probability versus the salary rewards. In addition, persons differ widely as to their risk aversion.

Does this mean that the evaluator's task is hopeless? Certainly if the chief benefit of a government program is to save lives, a benefit-cost analysis will be extremely sensitive to the evaluator's choice of a dollar figure per life saved. In such a case, it is not clear that a benefit-cost analysis is superior to a cost-effectiveness analysis that would simply calculate the cost of the program per life saved, without making a judgment on the value of life. But what if the program also has other objectives, such as the saving of serious injuries or preventing property damages? One approach is to relate total program costs to several measures of effectiveness, some of which might be quantified in dollar terms (property damages prevented) while others would be quantified in nondollar terms (so many lives saved or serious injuries prevented). Although this does not produce one bottom line, it does provide the decision maker with all of the relevant information about the program.

In another approach, the National Highway Traffic Safety Administration (U.S. Office of Regulatory Analysis, 1990) has converted injuries prevented to "equivalent" fatalities prevented based on "willingness to pay" (determined by a study of what individuals typically pay for small increases in their safety) and the cost that the rest of society bears when an individual is killed or injured. Their values per injury ranged from $4,000 to $1.5 million (in 1986 dollars) depending on the severity of injury, with an average value of about $100,000. Assuming a fatality cost of $2 million, they determined that twenty injuries were "equivalent" to one fatality and have analyzed programs (such as passive restraint requirements) on a cost per "equivalent" life saved.

Even using this approach, the National Highway Traffic Safety Administration needed to use a figure ($2 million) for loss of life in order to convert injuries to equivalent fatalities. Although it may seem insensitive to place a value on life, we may have no choice in a world of scarce resources. One approach is to determine the value of life required for the analysis to indicate a positive net benefit and simply leave to the decision makers the question of whether that amount is appropriate. In any case, where lives saved are a major component of the benefit equation, the specific assumptions on the valuation of a life must be made clear and a sensitivity analysis conducted to determine how sensitive the final benefit-cost results are to the choice of valuation.

In estimating how many lives were saved or injuries avoided, evaluators typically use before and after studies to determine the effectiveness of certain government programs or health and safety requirements. This often is a major evaluation problem, however, as program outcomes may be affected by other concurrent factors, such as use of alcohol and drugs or willingness to use seat belts. (See Chapter Five, this volume, on quasi-experimental design.)

Increased Productivity. Increased productivity is a common benefit goal of many government investment programs—both capital investments, such as roads, bridges, water projects, and other infrastructure developments, and human capital investments, such as education and job training. These benefits might be measured in increased profits or lifetime earnings.

Economic development projects are often justified on the basis of the creation of new jobs. Furthermore, some jobs are viewed more favorably than others. "Export" jobs (those that produce goods and services that extend beyond the jurisdiction) are thought to create additional jobs within a community. Economists use multipliers to determine total new job creations, and the choice of an appropriate multiplier is often subject to debate—and clearly is a key assumption that must be identified for the decision maker. If the new jobs reduce the level of unemployment in a jurisdiction, they clearly produce measurable benefits for both those previously unemployed and for government (increased taxes and decreased transfer payments). However, if the new jobs create an in-migration of families, the net benefits to the jurisdiction are not as clear. New families create costs to the community in terms of increased service demands as well as the benefit of new revenues. Evaluators often fail to consider those community costs sufficiently.

Chain Reaction Problem. A common error often made in benefit-cost analysis is to make the project or program appear successful by counting secondary benefits that arise from it while ignoring secondary costs. For example, if a government builds a road, the primary benefits are the reduction in transportation costs (time spent and fuel) for individuals and businesses. Profits of adjacent restaurants, motels, and gas stations may also increase due to the traffic. This may lead to increased profits in the local food, bed linen, and gasoline production businesses. Economist Harvey Rosen (1992) calls this the chain reaction game: if enough secondary effects are added to the benefit side, "eventually a positive present value can be obtained for practically any project" (p. 258).

Rosen notes that this process ignores the fact that there are likely losses as well as gains from building the road. Profits of train operators may decrease as some of their customers turn to cars for transportation, and increased auto use may bid up the price of gasoline, increasing costs to many gasoline consumers. At the very least, secondary costs must be counted as well as secondary gains. In many cases, these transfers are often washes, with the gains to some equaling the losses to others. Since this is very complex, the analyst might want to restrict the analysis to the most significant secondary effects.

Recreational Values. Recreational values are typically based on the concept of willingness to pay. The evaluator first must determine the number of people who have visited a particular recreational area and then attempt to value each "user day" of recreation. Several techniques are used.

One approach is asking recreational users what they would be willing to pay to use a particular recreational area (a park, wilderness, or something else). The problem with this technique is that respondents may answer strategically. If they think they may have to pay to use a favorite park, they may give a lower value than the true value to them. If they think the response may influence the continued provision of the recreation, they may place a higher value than their true value. In many cases, statements of willingness to pay have differed from actual behavior.

A second technique is to estimate what it costs users to travel to the recreation area—plane fares, rentals, gasoline, travel time, and so forth. This works best for recreational sites that draw visitors from a wide area, such as a national park.

Finally, evaluators sometimes look at similar recreational experiences in the private sector. The value of a public swimming pool or tennis courts might be assessed at rates similar to the costs to users of similar private facilities in the area. As with the value of life saved, if recreational days are the primary benefit of a proposed project, a cost-effectiveness analysis, identifying cost per user day of recreation, may be as useful to decision makers as a more detailed cost-benefit analysis.

In addition to the value to users, recreational areas may have some indirect benefits that should be valued. The availability of urban recreation may reduce the incidence of juvenile delinquency and the cost of the local criminal justice system. Major recreational areas may draw out-of-state visitors, who increase local profits in hotels, restaurants, and related establishments. There also may be some indirect costs, including road congestion and increased recreational injuries.

Option or Existence Value. Option or existence value is an offshoot of the willingness-to-pay concept for certain types of recreation. Even if a person does not intend to visit a wilderness area, for example, that person may desire to preserve some wilderness areas in the country in order to maintain the option (for self or others) of visiting them at some time in the future, or a person may simply value knowing of the existence of wilderness areas. Putting a price tag on these values is difficult, although surveys have attempted to ascertain the value to individuals.

Land Values. Increased land values may be a benefit, depending on the geographical scope of the analysis. The larger the scope, the more likely there is a transfer of wealth rather than a net increase in value. Thus, if a government investment decision increases the valuation of one parcel of land because it has made it more accessible (perhaps with a highway interchange), the effect is to make other parcels of land relatively less valuable, assuming the interchange has not increased the total demand for land in the jurisdiction.

A new local community park may increase the value of the residences near the park relative to those residences farther away from the park, but it is unlikely to have an overall impact on the demand for housing in the community.

Taxes. Taxes are sometimes thought of as a benefit, and from a budgetary perspective they are important, especially if the program or project is designed to produce revenues equal to expenditures. But from a societal perspective, taxes are transfers: the gain to the government is a loss to the individual paying the taxes. The individual does gain from the services that the government provides with taxes but loses dollars that could have been spent on private purchases. One approach is to show the gain to government offset by the loss to the party being taxed. This is the approach taken in the Dropout Prevention Program illustration, where taxes paid to government are offset by the loss to those benefiting from the higher employment opportunities.

Common Issues and Problems with Cost-Effectivness and Cost-Benefit Analysis

There are a number of issues common to both types of analysis. These include choice of discount rate and environmental and other unintended effects.

The Discount Rate

The choice of an appropriate discount rate for government is subject to considerable debate. Many economists argue for the use of a before- or after-tax private sector interest rate based on the theory that government expenditures require taxation or borrowing that takes money out of the private sector, and therefore government should be held to a similar investment standard. Others argue that government exists to operate programs the private sector will not. Therefore, a low social discount rate, of 2 to 3 percent, is the appropriate standard. Still others suggest using the rate government can borrow funds, such as the "real" long-term Treasury bill rate or municipal bond rate for state-local projects. Unless mandated otherwise, analysts should use a range of discount rates to determine how sensitive the net benefits, benefit-cost ratio, or cost-effectiveness is to the choice of a particular discount rate.

It is important for the analyst to recognize that conducting a present value analysis is not the same as adjusting for inflation. Most cost-effectiveness and cost-benefit analysts use constant dollars, in effect, removing inflation as a factor in the analysis. In this case, the discount rate should reflect a real market rate, that is, the full market rate less anticipated inflation. If benefits and costs include inflation, the discount rate must reflect the full market rate, that is one that includes an inflation factor.

Spillovers and Unintended Effects of Government Actions

Private firms are unconcerned with costs or benefits to third parties (non-buyers). For example, if a local community has built a new road to a plant or if effluent from the plant pollutes the downstream locality or places strains on the government's wastewater treatment plant, these spillover costs (or externalities) are not taken into account by a private firm when it analyzes its profit margin. The firm will "internalize" these costs only if government taxes, regulates, or otherwise holds the firm accountable. Regardless of government action, however, any program evaluation must consider the cost of these spillovers to society.

Unfortunately, not all government actions have beneficial effects; some have an adverse impact on the environment, and others may have unintended consequences on certain populations. A new dam may flood a wildlife habitat, or an urban renewal program may displace low-income housing. Often government tries to mitigate adverse consequences of their action, and those costs are considered in the analysis. However, even if it has not taken action to mitigate damages to others, those damages should be counted. If it is impossible to calculate the dollar value of the damage (such as certain environmental consequences), one method of evaluating the damage is to calculate what it would have cost the government to mitigate the damage had it chosen to do so.

Equity Concerns

It is not just the total benefits and costs but also who benefits and who pays that are of concern to policymakers. This is not always easy to determine if there are strong distributional consequences to the program, but where there are, they should be noted. In general, government taxpayers subsidize the beneficiaries of specific government programs. One approach to dealing with distributional issues is to weight the benefits and costs. For example, the analyst could weight a benefit or cost to a low-income family as twice the value of a similar benefit and cost to a middle-income family and three times as much as a similar benefit to an upper-income family. The issue is the appropriate weights—one more subjective factor that must ultimately become a judgment by policymakers. Perhaps a better alternative is to attempt to identify the costs and benefits to each significant group that is affected by the project. That approach is illustrated in the Dropout Prevention Program case.

Sensitivity Analysis

It is important for the program evaluator to test the sensitivity of the analysis to particular assumptions; that is, what is the probability that those particular assumptions will occur? The advantage of Excel and other computer-run spreadsheets is that they now allow the evaluator to examine a range of alternative assumptions and determine their impact on the analysis.

For example, an analysis of a highway safety program to prevent drunk driving will make certain assumptions about the number of lives saved and injuries prevented by the program. How confident is the evaluator of those numbers? If there were other nonprogrammatic factors that influenced the results (such as safer cars), how are those considered in the assumptions. Is $2 million the correct value to use for a life saved? What if a higher or lower figure was used? Where key assumptions are critical to the results of the analysis, they should be clearly identified for the decision maker.

Intangibles

No matter how creative the evaluator is, there will be some benefits and costs that defy quantification. Even if you can value the cost of an injury, that dollar figure will not fully capture the pain and suffering involved, and financial savings from burglaries prevented does not fully capture the sense of security that comes with crime prevention. These are often important components of the benefit-cost equation and should be identified and explained as clearly as possible. There is a tendency to relegate these issues to an afterthought or footnote. The danger with this approach is that benefits and costs that are easily identified and valued tend to drive the evaluation.

The best method for identifying issues surrounding intangible benefits and costs is to relate them to the dollar results. For example, if the analysis reveals net costs over benefits of $2 million but also reveals certain environmental benefits that could not be converted to dollars, then the question of whether the environmental benefits over the period studied were worth the $2 million cost can be highlighted. If there were intangible costs as well as benefits, then the benefits would have to be worth $2 million plus the intangible costs for the program to be considered a success. By juxtaposing dollars against the intangibles, the evaluator asks the decision maker to weigh the intangibles against the known costs (or costs over dollar value of benefits).

Conclusion

Cost-benefit or cost-effectiveness analyses are not panaceas that will provide decision makers with the answer. However, if the analyst provides an accurate framework of benefits and costs—attempting to identify them, measure them, and value them—the decision maker is provided a wealth of information on which a better decision can be made. Other alternatives to cost-benefit and cost-effectiveness analysis include cost-utility analysis, risk analysis, and a variety of decision-making grids that value and weight various aspects of program alternatives

The biggest danger in any such analysis is the black box syndrome. Instead of laying out the relevant issues, assumptions, and concerns, the analyst may be tempted to hide the messiness of the analysis from the decision maker, presenting a concise answer as to net benefits or costs, or cost-effectiveness. However, two honest, careful analysts might arrive at opposite conclusions on the same set of facts if their assumptions about those data differ. A Scotsman once proclaimed that the "devil is in the detail," and it is the detail—the assumptions and the sensitivity of the analysis to particular assumptions—that may be of

Exhibit 18.1. **Cost-Benefit Summary of the Dropout Prevention Program**

Baseline analysis: Benefits exceed costs by $3.6 million

Key assumptions:

- 31 dropouts prevented over 5 years of program
- Increased earnings of high school graduates at $8,000 a year
- No opportunity cost for participants' time in the program
- Real discount rate of 3 percent

Effect of changes in key assumptions of baseline analysis:

• One fewer/additional dropout prevented per year:	+/–$0.7 million
• Earnings of high school graduates, $1,000 more/less than baseline:	+/–$0.5 million
• Opportunity cost to participants—$20,542 over 5 years:	–$0.6 million
• Discount rate of 1 percent higher/lower than baseline:	+/–$0.5 million

---

most use to the decision maker in judging the value and usefulness of the evaluator's work.

One method of highlighting information for decision makers is to use a table that identifies assumptions made in the baseline analysis and provides data on the effect of a change in the key assumptions. Exhibit 18.1 provides an example of such a table. It follows the Dropout Prevention Program and provides a baseline cost-benefit number and the key assumptions behind the number. It then provides the effects of a change in the assumptions on the baseline analysis.

From this information, the decision maker can easily determine that the analysis is most sensitive to the actual number of dropouts prevented per year; however, a small change in any of the assumptions would not have a dramatic impact on the analysis. By providing these types of data, the analysis can assist the policymaker to focus on the key questions and assumption and their relationship to a range of possible outcomes by either a cost-effectiveness or cost-benefit analysis.

References

Levin, H. M., and McEwan, P. J. *Cost-Effectiveness Analysis.* (2nd ed.) Thousand Oaks, Calif.: Sage, 2001.

Musgrave, R., and Musgrave, P. *Public Finance in Theory and Practice.* New York: MCGraw-Hill, 1989.

Rosen, H. S. *Public Finance.* (3rd ed.) Homewood, Ill.: Irwin, 1992.

U.S. Office of Regulatory Analysis. *Final Regulatory Impact Analysis, Extension of the Automatic Restraint Requirements of FMVSS 208 to Trucks, Buses, and Multi-purpose Vehicle Weight Rating of 8,500 Pounds or Less and an Unloaded Vehicle Weight of 5,500 Pounds or Less.* Washington, D.C.: Office of Regulatory Analysis, National Highway Traffic Safety Administration, Nov. 1990.

Part Four

Getting Evaluation Results Used

Program evaluation presents many challenges beyond the issues that arise in evaluation design, data collection, and data analysis. Evaluators should make all reasonable efforts to (1) gain and hold the interest, confidence, and support of policymakers, managers, and other intended users of evaluation information; (2) maintain the cooperation of program managers, staff, clients, and others who provide needed evaluation data; (3) present evaluation findings and improvement options clearly; and (4) stimulate the actions needed to improve public programs and communicate their value to policymakers and the public.

The six chapters in Part Four describe methods for planning and managing evaluation projects as well as ways to present evaluation results and get those results used. These chapters discuss:

- Potential pitfalls in evaluation
- Management of evaluation projects
- Effective reporting of evaluation results
- The use of organizational report cards
- The use of evaluation by small nonprofit organizations

Evaluation leadership and management are still more art than science. Those in charge of evaluation programs and projects face difficult challenges in producing credible findings and in getting their findings used by policy-makers, managers, and other stakeholders. Since procedures for these areas are far less formalized than are the procedures for research design, data collection, and data analysis, it is not surprising that differences appear among the authors of these chapters. In these less than fully charted waters, there is helpful guidance in each chapter.

Harry Hatry and Kathryn Newcomer, in Chapter Nineteen, provide a checklist to help evaluators and those reviewing evaluations to assess how potential pitfalls in planning and implementing evaluations may hinder the validity, reliability, and credibility of evaluation findings and conclusions. Recognizing that all evaluations have limitations, the authors note that recognition and explanation of those limitations can add to the credibility of evaluation work.

James Bell, in Chapter Twenty, discusses how evaluation project managers can design and implement useful evaluation projects—projects that, for example, contribute to improved program performance. Bell shows how evaluation project managers can develop rational proposals, gain and maintain agreement with sponsors clarifying the evaluation mandate, staff and organize their projects for results, make productive assignments to evaluation staff, monitor the progress of individual assignments and the project as a whole, and ensure the quality and usefulness of the evaluation products.

George Grob, in Chapter Twenty-One, discusses how evaluators can write compelling evaluation reports that convince readers of the study's findings and promote their taking action in response. He shows how evaluators can craft their core message, communicate their findings and improvement options, and briefly describe their methodology and its limitations.

William Gormley Jr., in Chapter Twenty-Two, discusses the growing use of organizational report cards: regular efforts by an organization to collect data on other organizations, transform the data into information relevant to assessing performance, and transmit the information to audiences external to those organizations. The chapter provides examples of organizational report cards used by consumers, public sector and corporate purchasers, and elected officials. Gormley focuses on report cards that rate the performance of hospitals, physicians, schools, and employment and training agencies.

Mary Kopczynski and Kathleen Pritchard, in Chapter Twenty-Three, discuss the use of evaluation by small nonprofit organizations including service delivery and advocacy organizations. They explore unique barriers to conducting evaluation at the community level and offer options for overcoming those barriers, showing ways in which small, nonprofit organizations can involve volunteers in community-level assessments and how such organizations can make productive use of the data that they do collect.

In the final chapter, the book editors discuss quality control of the entire evaluation process: the selection and training of evaluators, evaluation standards and ethics, and incentives for the conduct of program evaluations and use of evaluation findings. They discuss trends in program evaluation and use of evaluation information and conclude with suggestions for minimizing evaluation costs and documenting the results of evaluation activities.

19

Pitfalls of Evaluation

Harry P. Hatry, Kathryn E. Newcomer

Two key issues in program evaluation are to attempt to determine what the effects (outcomes) of the program have been over a specific period of time and to determine the extent to which the specific program, rather than other factors, has caused the effects. Both issues are typically subject to considerable uncertainty, particularly since the great majority of evaluations are not undertaken under controlled laboratory conditions. Program effects are often unclear, are often ill defined, and can be quite messy to measure. Dealing with the second issue—to what extent the effects identified can be attributed to the specific program—also presents considerable difficulties: outcomes can be affected by numerous other factors in addition to the program itself, and the effects of these external factors will generally be difficult to determine without careful analysis.

Strong methodological integrity is critical to support efforts to measure both the programs (treatments) and the outcomes (effects) in all evaluation projects. The integrity of evaluation findings rests on how well design and data collection choices strengthen the validity and reliability of the data. The best time to anticipate limitations to what we can conclude from evaluation work is when designing the research and developing the instruments. Unfortunately, we can never anticipate everything, and the best-laid plans may not work out.

This chapter draws material from Harry P. Hatry, "Pitfalls of Evaluation," in G. Majone and E. S. Quade (eds.), *Pitfalls of Analysis*. New York: Wiley, 1980.

When reporting findings, in addition to following the good advice given about design and data collection provided in this book, evaluators should carefully assess how pitfalls that occur in the conduct of the work may hinder the validity, reliability, and credibility of their findings and conclusions. This chapter provides a checklist of pitfalls to help evaluators or those reviewing evaluations assess how pitfalls in planning and executing evaluations constrain what can be concluded about the programs studied. The implications of each pitfall for the validity, reliability, and credibility of the findings are identified. Many of the pitfalls are discussed in detail in various texts on program evaluation, such as the classic Riecken and Boruch (1974).

The primary touchstones of methodological integrity discussed in social science methods texts are measurement validity (sometimes referred to as construct validity), external validity, internal validity, statistical conclusion validity, and reliability (Singleton, Straits, Straits, and McAllister, 1988; Stangor, 1998; O'Sullivan, Rassel, and Berner, 2003). We have added credibility to our list because evaluation findings are not likely to be used if program staff or funders do not find the findings believable. The definitions are set out in the box.

The pitfalls discussed here are arranged according to the time at which the pitfall generally occurs: before the beginning of actual data collection for the evaluation: during the process of data collection, or after the data have been collected (when findings are to be presented and use is to be made of the findings). A summary of the pitfalls and the methodological concerns each addresses is presented in Tables 19.1, 19.2, and 19.4.

Pitfalls Before Data Collection Begins

If the evaluation does not get off to a good start, the whole evaluation can be undermined.

Pitfall 1: Failure to Assess Whether the Program Is Evaluable

Not doing an assessment of the potential utility and evaluability of evaluation candidates to ensure that it is likely that the program can be evaluated in sufficient time for the evaluation findings to be useful, and within available resources, can severely limit what can be learned. Programs probably should not be subject to substantial program evaluation effort when:

- The program has vague objectives.
- Although the objectives are reasonably clear, the current state of the art in measurement does not seem to permit meaningful measurement of impacts.

The Touchstones of Methodological Integrity

Credibility. Are the evaluation findings and conclusions believable and legitimate to the intended audience? Evaluation findings are more likely to be accepted if the program stakeholders perceive the evaluation process and data to be legitimate and the recommendations to be feasible.

External validity. Are we able to generalize from the study results to the intended population? Evaluation findings are generalizable (or externally valid) if we can apply the findings to groups or contexts beyond those being studied.

Internal validity. Are we able to establish whether there is a causal relationship between a specified cause, such as a program, and the intended effect? Attributing program results to a program entails ensuring that changes in program outcomes covary with the program activities, that the program was implemented prior to the occurrence of outcomes, and that plausible rival explanations for the outcomes have been ruled out to the extent reasonable.

Measurement validity. Are we accurately measuring what we intend to measure? Measurement validity is concerned with the accuracy of measurement. The specific criteria for operationalizing concepts, such as program outputs and outcomes, should be logically related to the concepts of interest.

Reliability. Will the measurement procedures produce similar results on repeated observations of the same condition or event? Measures are reliable to the extent that the criteria and questions consistently measure target behaviors or attitudes. Measurement procedures are reliable to the extent that they are consistently recording data.

Statistical conclusion validity. Do the numbers we generate accurately estimate the size of a relationship between variables or the magnitude of a specific criterion measure? Numerical figures are valid if they are generated with appropriate statistical techniques supported by reasonable assumptions.

Table 19.1. Pitfalls Occurring Before Data Collection Begins

	Methodological Concerns					
	Measurement Validity	*External Validity*	*Internal Validity (Causal Inference)*	*Statistical Conclusion Validity*	*Reliability*	*Credibility*
Program or theory feasibility						
1. Failure to assess whether the program is evaluable		X	X	X		X
2. Starting data collection too early in the life of a program		X	X	X		X
3. Failure to secure input from program managers and other stakeholders on appropriate evaluation criteria	X	X	X			X
4. Failure to clarify program managers' expectations about what can be learned from the evaluation						X
Preparation for collection						
5. Failure to pretest data collection instruments appropriately	X	X	X	X	X	X
6. Use of inadequate indicators of program effects	X	X	X	X	X	X
7. Inadequately training data collectors	X	X	X	X	X	X

- The program's major impacts cannot be expected to show up until many years into the future, by which time the information is not likely to be useful (when, for example, it seems likely that by the time the evaluation is completed, all relevant important decisions will already have been made and whatever is found cannot be acted on).

In many instances, evaluability problems can be alleviated, as Wholey discusses in Chapter Two through use of an evaluability assessment. The evaluability assessment should be careful not to overreact to apparent hurdles. For example, with persistence, it is often possible to identify major specific objectives for programs that seem vague at first. It is often possible to obtain rough but adequate impact information about characteristics that at first glance appear to be too subjective (such as by using structured interviewing of systematic samples of clients on various aspects of program services). Often, even evaluations conducted over prolonged periods may be useful for decisions in later years even though they are not useful to the current funders or sponsors.

Proper evaluation requires adequate staff, money, and time, and the evaluation plan clearly needs to be compatible with the resources available. However, although some corner-cutting and less sophisticated approaches can often be used when resources are scarce, too many such compromises can weaken an evaluation to the point where it is not worth doing.

Seldom discussed in the literature is the need to distinguish whether the program to be evaluated is under development or is operational. Evaluations of projects in a developmental stage in general seek less definite information on impacts and are likely to be more concerned with determining the characteristics of the preferred program and its basic feasibility. Ignoring this distinction appears to have resulted in inappropriate expectations and inappropriate evaluation designs in some instances, especially for U.S. federal agency evaluations.

Pitfall 2: Starting Data Collection Too Early in the Life of a Program

Not allowing enough time to assess stable program operations is a pitfall frequently encountered in the evaluation of new programs. There seems to be a chronic temptation to begin collecting program outcome data for evaluation as soon as the initial attempt at implementation begins. For many new programs, however, the shakedown period may last many months. During this time, program procedures stabilize, new people become adjusted to the new procedures, and the new program begins to operate under reasonably normal conditions. Thus, enough time should be allowed before beginning collection of the postprogram data, and enough time after, for an adequate test of the new program. Evaluation periods of less than a year may not provide enough program experience and can be affected by seasonal differences. For example, tests of a new street repair procedure might not cover the special effects of the bad weather season. The appropriate timing will depend on the nature of the program and the setting into which it is introduced. To illustrate a likely typical timing, a minimum period of perhaps six months might be appropriate before the program is assumed to have been implemented, and at least one year of subsequent program operations should be covered by the evaluation.

Pitfall 3: Failure to Secure Input from Program Managers and Other Stakeholders on Appropriate Evaluation Criteria

A complaint sometimes voiced by program stakeholders about evaluation conclusions and recommendations is that the evaluators did not measure the right things. Evaluators should seek input from program staff, funders, and program clients to ensure that they employ criteria of both the program treatment and the more relevant program effects, or outcomes, that staff and funders consider relevant and legitimate.

As McLaughlin and Jordan describe in Chapter One and Love recommends in Chapter Three, logic modeling is a highly useful tool for involving program staff in identification of appropriate measures of program activities and short- and longer-term outcomes. Participation of program stakeholders before data collection in identification of what is most relevant to measure and what are the most accurate operational indicators to employ is critical in ensuring the findings will be deemed credible.

Pitfall 4: Failure to Clarify Program Managers' Expectations About What Can Be Learned from the Evaluation

Program staff are typically not receptive to evaluation and may need to be convinced that evaluation efforts can produce information useful to them. Evaluators may also find that program staff are leery of opening up programs to analysis of how they are working. Thus, one of the major obstacles to the undertaking and use of evaluation is that evaluators too often pay too little attention to helping program staff identify constructive ways in which programs can be improved. Unfortunately, this is easier said than done. Usually a large number of factors, in addition to the program procedures, can affect program success. These include such elements as the quantity and quality of the staffing used to operate the program, the success in motivating the employees who will implement it, and the organizational structure in which the program operates. Program staff often are in a particularly good position to obtain insights into reasons for problems. If the evaluators can draw on this understanding and act as a constructive force for program improvement, the credibility and utility of the evaluation function will increase over the long run. Then, perhaps, the innate hostility of program managers to being evaluated will be diminished.

Evaluations of any kind seldom give definitive, conclusive, unambiguous evidence of program success (or failure). Even with experimental designs, numerous problems inevitably arise in keeping the experiment uncontaminated and, subsequently, in extrapolating and generalizing the results beyond the experimental scope and time period. The evaluators should be careful to make it clear from the start to their customers, and to potential users of the evaluation findings, that such limitations exist. Unrealistic expectations by program managers about what they can learn from evaluation findings may discourage future evaluation support.

Pitfall 5: Failure to Pretest Data Collection Instruments Appropriately

An essential task for evaluators prior to beginning data collection is to pretest all collection instruments. Whether data are observational or perceptions, the instruments used to measure conditions, behaviors, or attitudes should be carefully tested to ensure they will capture the intended phenomena. As Greiner describes (Chapter Eight) and Newcomer and Triplett emphasize (Chapter Nine), all instruments for recording data need to be pretested in the specific program context in which they will be applied.

Pitfall 6: Use of Inadequate Indicators of Program Effects

The credibility and usefulness of an evaluation can be called into considerable doubt if inadequate measures are used. Variations of this pitfall include limiting the assessment to only one criterion or a very few criteria when others are also relevant (perhaps because a decision is made to evaluate only those criteria agreed on ahead of time with program officials), and neglecting possible unintended consequences of the program (sometimes beneficial and sometimes detrimental). For example, an evaluation of a program for placing mental patients in their own homes and communities rather than in government institutions should consider not only changes in the condition of the clients, but also the effects on clients' families and the community into which the clients are transferred. Economic development programs sometimes have adverse effects on the environment, and environmental programs sometimes have adverse effects on economic development.

Before establishing the final evaluation criteria, evaluators should review the objectives of the program from the viewpoint of the agency installing the program and the clients of the program and look for significant effects that were not initially anticipated. Evaluators should strive to identify various perspectives on the objectives (both explicit and implicit) of the program to be evaluated. For example, opinions might be sought from supporters and opponents, program operators and clients, and budget officials and program managers. (This assumes that evaluators will have sufficient leeway from the sponsors of the evaluation to try to be comprehensive.)

An important variation of this pitfall is failure to assess the impact of the program on the various major client groups. Inevitably, programs have different effects on various groups, helping some groups significantly more than others and perhaps harming other groups. Insufficient identification of the effects on different groups of program recipients will hide such differences and prevent users of the evaluation findings from considering equity issues. The lack of an assessment of program financial costs can also be an important omission. Evaluators often neglect costs, but such information can be of considerable use to funders.

Finally, when attitudinal data are being collected from program participants, care should be taken to word survey questions in a clear, unbiased manner to assess program effects fairly. Pretesting surveys and questionnaires should reduce the use of slanted questions. However, it is still possible that users of evaluation findings may view the questions as skewed in a way that either inflates or reduces effects. Guidance on question wording is provided by Newcomer and Triplett (Chapter Nine).

Pitfall 7: Inadequately Training Data Collectors

Regardless of the type of data collection employed in an evaluation, sufficient time must be given to training the evaluation staff used to visit sites, review files, or conduct interviews. The length of time needed for training, and the frequency of the retraining, will vary depending on the type of collection activity, as Nightingale and Rossman (Chapter Thirteen) and Greiner (Chapter Eight) discuss. Typically, consultation among data collectors should continue throughout the collection phase of the evaluation. Initial training may not adequately anticipate all context-specific challenges for data collectors.

Pitfalls During Data Collection

A number of pitfalls can occur during an evaluation's operation.

Pitfall 8: Failure to Identify and Adjust for Changes in Data Collection Procedures That Occur During the Measurement Period

As discussed in Chapter Fourteen, evaluators need to look for changes in agency record keeping, such as changes in data element definition or data collection procedures that affect the relevant data. Data definitions and data collection procedures can change periodically and in the process cause important differences in the meaning of those data. Evaluators using data for which they themselves have not determined the data collection procedures should be careful to look for, and adjust for (if they can), such occurrences. As has been noted (Riecken and Boruch, 1974), "Too often a new program is accompanied by changes in record-keeping" (p. 107).

Pitfall 9: Collecting Too Many Data and Not Allowing Adequate Time for Analysis of the Data Collected

These two problems go hand in hand. They are all too prevalent when tight timetables exist for evaluations, which usually seems to be the case. The temptation seems to be prevalent to collect data on any characteristic of the client or situation that conceivably could be relevant and then not allow enough time for analysis of the data. The temptation to collect data is a difficult one to overcome, particularly since it is not possible at the beginning of an evaluation to know which data will be useful in the study. The argument is often advanced that evaluators can always exclude data later. However, once collected, data pile up, with a pyramiding effect in terms of data processing and analysis effort (as well as adding to the costs of data collection)

Allowing enough time for data analysis is complicated by the tendency to impose overly tight deadlines for evaluations. When implementation difficulties delay the start of the program, when data come in later than anticipated, and when computer processing is later than promised, these delays all lead to squeezing the amount of time available for analysis before the deadline for the evaluation. To help alleviate these problems, schedule for unforeseen contingencies and include fewer data elements to be processed.

Pitfall 10: Inappropriate Conceptualization or Implementation of the Intervention

Adequately capturing program activities can be challenging due to fluctuations in program implementation that occur, which is frequently the case. The best-laid plans of evaluators may not come to fruition when they are placed in real-life settings. The longer the period of observation, the greater is the chance of deviation from the original intentions.

Table 19.2. Pitfalls Occurring During Data Collection

	Methodological Concerns					
	Measurement Validity	External Validity	Internal Validity (Causal Inference)	Statistical Conclusion Validity	Reliability	Credibility
Research Procedures						
8. Failure to identify and adjust for changes in data collection procedures that occur during the measurement period	X	X	X	X	X	X
9. Collecting too much data and not allowing adequate time for analysis of the data collected			X			X
Measurement Constraints						
10. Inappropriate conceptualization and/or measurement of the "intervention"	X	X	X	X	X	X
11. Beginning observation when conditions (target behaviors) are at an extreme level		X	X	X		
Reactivity						
12. Inappropriate involvement of program providers in data collection	X	X	X	X	X	X
13. Overly intrusive data collection procedures that change behaviors of program staff or participants	X	X	X		X	

Table 19.2. Pitfalls Occurring During Data Collection, *continued*

	Methodological Concerns					
	Measurement Validity	External Validity	Internal Validity (Causal Inference)	Statistical Conclusion Validity	Reliability	Credibility
Composition of Sample						
14. Failure to account for drop off in sample size due to attrition		X	X	X		X
15. Failure to draw a representative sample of program participants		X	X	X		X
16. Insufficient number of callbacks to boost response rates		X	X	X		X
Flawed Comparisons						
17. Failure to account for natural maturation among program participants		X	X			X
18. Failure to provide a comparison group		X	X			X
19. Failure to take into account key contextual factors (out of the control of program staff) that affect program outcomes			X			X
20. Failure to take into account the degree of difficulty of helping program participants		X	X			X

For example, in evaluations of neighborhood police teams, the assignment of teams to specific neighborhoods may depart from the plan if dispatchers assign those police officers too frequently to other neighborhoods. In some cases, if the program planners and evaluators watch carefully, such deviations can be corrected, but in other situations, this may not be possible. Another example involves the difficulties of maintaining random assignment procedures in an experiment when assignments have to be made throughout the period by personnel other than the evaluation team. In an experiment to test the effects of requiring appearances for moving traffic violations before a judge, the court clerk who had responsibility for the random assignments had firm ideas about the need for a court appearance for young drivers and did not adhere to the random assignment procedure (Conner, 1977). Random assignments of clients in controlled experiments may initially be done appropriately, but subsequently be altered under the pressure of heavy workload.

Because of such challenges to defining the treatment, it is important that the evaluators carefully monitor the program over the period of the evaluation. At the least, they should check periodically to ascertain that there have been no major departures from the plan during implementation. When substantial deviations occur, adjustments should be made (such as, in effect, beginning a "new" evaluation if a major overhaul of the program occurs during the evaluation). If such adjustments cannot be made satisfactorily and the changes are of major importance, the evaluation should be terminated, or at least the alterations should be explicitly considered when assessing the findings.

Pitfall 11: Beginning Observation When Conditions (Target Behaviors) Are at an Extreme Level or Not Adjusting for This

Timing is crucial in evaluation. Evaluators need to investigate, to the extent feasible, the target behavior among program participants (or communities) prior to implementation of the program treatment. When new program activities are introduced because conditions have risen to undesirably high levels (perhaps birthrates among unwed teenage mothers have soared) or undesirably low levels (perhaps the percentage of substance abuse treatment clients staying sober has plummeted), it is likely that assessment of program effects will be inflated. This "regression to the mean" phenomenon implies that if the target behaviors have risen (or fallen) to extreme levels, a natural shift toward improvement (or deterioration) can be expected even without the new program. Clients who at the outset have the greatest need (they may be in a crisis situations) are likely to show a greater amount of improvement than others. Conversely, the less needy, most able clients may tend to show little, no, or even negative improvement, regardless of the program (Conner,

1977). For example, a program initiated because of a recent rash of problems, such as a high traffic fatality rate, might show an improvement merely because the chances of recurrence are small (Campbell and Ross, 1968).

Ways to alleviate this problem include projecting time trend lines (see Chapter Sixteen) and categorizing clients as to their degree of difficulty and then analyzing the outcomes for each level of difficulty. Such approaches enable better and fairer comparisons.

Pitfall 12: Inappropriate Involvement of Program Providers in Data Collection

This well-known pitfall nevertheless is often ignored. Government agencies with tight resources, especially subnational governments such as state and local governments in the United States, and small, nonprofit service providers, are particularly tempted to use program staff to provide ratings of program success.

It is desirable for any agency, as a matter of good management, to undertake some internal evaluation of its own programs. For example, mental health and social service agencies frequently use caseworkers' ratings to assess the progress of the caseworkers' clients. This procedure is reasonable when the information is solely for internal purposes, such as for use by the caseworkers themselves and their immediate supervisors. Such procedures, however, do not provide data on client improvement after clients have left the programs to determine the longer-term effects of the services, and such procedures seem to be expecting too much of human nature (asking employees to provide objective information that will be used to make judgments about continuation of their own programs).

Pitfall 13: Overly Intrusive Data Collection Procedures That Change Behaviors of Program Staff or Participants

When program staff or participants are aware that their program is being evaluated, they may behave differently than they do normally. The Hawthorne effect may mean that several providers or recipients act in ways that lead to overestimation of program effects. For example, program staff may try harder to ensure that a new program activity demonstrates positive results.

Program personnel who are handpicked to staff a new program may make the outcomes of the test unrepresentative and nongeneralizable. Using specially chosen personnel may be appropriate in the developmental stages of a program, but it is to be avoided when the program is to be evaluated for its generalizability. For a representative test, personnel who would ordinarily be operating the program after the evaluation period should be used. Otherwise, any observed advantage to the treatment period might be due to the use of the special personnel.

Recipients of benefits who are aware that the program is being evaluated may provide overly positive feedback about services and effects or try harder to demonstrate their achievement of desired changes.

Pitfall 14: Failure to Account for Drop-Off in Sample Size due to Attrition

For many social services, it is difficult to track program participants for an adequate length of time to assess intermediate or long-term program outcomes. Sometimes this pitfall occurs due to the transient nature of the target population, such as homeless people or youth released from juvenile detention centers. In some cases, follow-up efforts to survey program beneficiaries fail due to the provider's failure to maintain up-to-date contact information for those served. And in other cases, beneficiaries of services, such as mental health or reproductive health services, may refuse to acknowledge that they received the services. Small sample sizes may result from these obstacles, leading to less precision in the findings. Unrepresentative samples may also result that are skewed toward participants who are more motivated or stable. Evaluators need to acknowledge whatever "completion" rates occur and identify the implications.

Pitfall 15: Failure to Draw a Representative Sample of Program Participants

The inability to locate program beneficiaries at points of time some period after their receipt of services, or refusals from beneficiaries to be surveyed, present only two potential constraints on the representativeness of samples. Other flaws in sampling procedures may hinder efforts to generalize results, such as sampling in a way that omits or undersamples a key group, such as persons without phones, those with unlisted telephone numbers, persons with answering machines, those living in trailers, or those living in multiple dwelling units or having more than one telephone number.

Survey procedures that are based solely on self-selection, such as placing survey questionnaires on tables or in tax bills, are likely to result in very low response rates and highly unrepresentative samples. The possibility that program participants who submit surveys or participate in interviews or focus groups differ from those who do not participate, in ways relevant to their responses, is virtually always a concern in evaluation work. Efforts to test for differences between sample respondents and those who choose not to participate in data collection efforts are necessary, yet not fully sufficient to eliminate suspicions of nonresponse biases.

Pitfall 16: Insufficient Number of Callbacks to Boost Response Rates

An inadequate number of callbacks or making calls during limited time periods in the day or in the week can result in too small and unrepresentative samples of program participants. Unfortunately, evaluation resources often are not sufficient to do all that is ideally desirable to reach participants. As noted in Chapter Nine, the increasing use of answering machines presents a new challenge to evaluators hoping to conduct telephone interviews as part of their research.

Pitfall 17: Failure to Account for Natural Maturation Among Program Participants

In some cases, "maturation" can occur, in which the participants served improve normally even without program intervention, perhaps because of aging. For example, as criminals, alcoholics, or drug addicts age, reductions in their adverse behavior may occur even without treatment programs. As another example, an evaluation of community alcoholic treatment centers included a follow-up eighteen months after intake of a comparison sample of persons who had an intake record but for whom only nominal treatment was provided (Armor, Polich, and Stambul, 1976). Of this group, a large percentage, 54 percent, were identified as being in remission even without more than normal treatment(compared to 67 percent of the treatment group).

Pitfall 18: Failure to Provide a Comparison Group

The lack of a comparison group or use of an inappropriate comparison group can distort the interpretation of evaluation findings. Even if randomized controlled experiments are used, examining groups that were not part of the intervention can often provide evidence about whether the outcomes were due to the program. In the classic evaluation of the Connecticut highway speeding crackdown, the large reduction in fatalities in Connecticut was compared with other nearby, and presumably similar, states to see if similar reductions had occurred (Campbell and Ross, 1968). Such a comparison helped rule out some other possible causes of reduced fatalities in Connecticut, such as special weather conditions in the region during the period or the introduction of safer automobiles.

The evaluation of community alcoholism treatment centers followed up not only those who received significant amounts of treatments but samples of two comparison groups: persons who had made only one visit to a treatment center and who received no further treatment and clients who had received minimal services (usually detoxification) but then left the center and never resumed contact (Armor, Polich, and Stambul, 1976). The evaluators identified 67 percent of all treated clients as being in remission at the time of an eighteen-month follow-up. But even the nominal treatment group showed a 54 percent remission rate. Thus, it appears likely that a substantial portion of the remission in the treatment group would have occurred without the program. Considering only the 67 percent would lead one to overstate the effects of the treatment.

Comparison groups should be used with considerable care. If the program's clients differ from the comparison group in some critical characteristic (such as the motivational levels of persons entering the program), differences in outcomes could be due to those characteristics and not to the program. Therefore, it is important, when possible, to check the comparison groups for similarity of key characteristics. Unfortunately, opportunities to observe useful comparison groups are not always available.

Pitfall 19: Failure to Take into Account Key Contextual Factors (Out of the Control of Program Staff) That Affect Program Outcomes

A wide variety of possible circumstances or factors affect participants' behavior or other program effects and can lead to unrepresentative and misleading findings. For example, changes in the employment status of persons given training programs can occur because of changes in general economic conditions, regardless of participation in the training programs. The greater the number of different agencies, jurisdictions and service providers involved in program implementation, the more opportunities there are for contextual factors to affect outcomes (U.S. General Accounting Office, 1998).

Pitfall 20: Failure to Take into Account the Degree of Difficulty of Helping Program Participants

Not explicitly considering and controlling for workload-client difficulty when assessing program results can lead to misinterpretation of what has occurred. The difficulty of the incoming workload can cause success (or failure) rates to be misleading (Hendricks, 2002). Higher success rates for programs that have a larger proportion of easier-to-help clients than other programs should not necessarily be labeled as being more effective. Consider the hypothetical outcomes shown in Table 19.3.

Based on the totals alone, the results for unit 1 appear superior because success was achieved in 60 percent of the cases as contrasted with 47 percent. Unit 2, however, shows a higher success rate for both high-difficulty clients (25 percent, compared to 0 percent for unit 1) and routine clients (80 percent, compared to 75 percent for unit 1). The overall higher success

Table 19.3. Consideration of Workload Difficulty

	Unit 1	Unit 2
All cases	500	500
Number helped	300	235
Percentage helped	60%	47%
Difficult cases	100	300
Number helped	0	75
Percentage helped	0%	25%
Routine cases	400	200
Number helped	300	160
Percentage helped	75%	80%

Source: Adapted from Hatry (1999, p. 112).

rate for the first unit stems from its having a larger proportion of clients with lower difficulty.

Thus, the difficulty of the incoming workload can be a major explanation for observed effects. In controlled experiments, even if workload difficulty is not explicitly controlled in making random assignments (such as by stratifying the sample), randomization would likely result in assigning similar proportions to each of the groups. Nevertheless, the control and treated groups should be examined after they are chosen to determine if they are indeed sufficiently similar on difficulty.

Pitfalls After Data Collection

Even fine-quality evaluations can be wasted if care is not taken when reporting the findings.

Pitfall 21: Overemphasis on Statistical Significance and Underemphasis on Practical Significance of Effect Size

Too narrow a focus on too much precision and too much reliance on statistical significance can lead to excessive costs in resource allocation (such as by encouraging the use of larger samples than needed at the expense of other evaluation tasks) and even to misleading findings. Statistical significance levels at the 95 to 99 percent significance levels will often be overkill

Table 19.4. Pitfalls Occurring After Data Collection

	Measurement Validity	External Validity	Internal Validity (Causal Inference)	Statistical Conclusion Validity	Reliability	Credibility
	Methodological Concerns					
Inappropriate Use of Analytical Techniques						
21. Over emphasis upon statistical significance and under emphasis on practical significance of effect size		X	X	X		X
22. Focusing only on overall results with inadequate attention to disaggregated results		X	X			X
Insufficient Link Between Data and Conclusions						
23. Generalizing beyond the confines of the sample, or the limits of the program sites included in the study		X	X			X
24. Failure to acknowledge the effects of multiple program components	X		X			X
25. Failure to submit preliminary findings to key program staff for reality testing		X	X			X
26. Failure to adequately support conclusions with specific data						X
27. Poor presentation of evaluation findings						X

for programs other than those with important safety or health elements. Typically, the information gathered in evaluations and other factors in making program decisions are not precise, and for most management decisions, a high level of precision is not needed. "It doesn't pay to lavish time and money on being extremely precise in one feature if this is out of proportion with the exactness of the rest" (Herzog, 1959).

Whatever the significance levels used, the use of statistical significance as the only criterion for detecting differences can be misleading to officials using the information. What may be a statistically significant finding (at a given significance level) can, particularly when very large samples are involved, suggest that important program effects have occurred even though the effects may be small in practical terms and may be unimportant to public officials. With large sample sizes, differences of even two or three percentage points between the outcomes of the treatment and comparison groups can be statistically significant, but they may not be significant to officials making decisions based on that information.

Good advice is to present the actual differences and the level of statistical significance, so that users of the information can judge for themselves. All too often, summaries of findings indicate whether findings are statistically significant without identifying the actual size of the program effects.

Pitfall 22: Focusing on Only the Overall (Average) Results with Inadequate Attention to Disaggregated Results

Examination of the aggregate data is useful for assessing a program's aggregate effect. However, in general, the analysis should not be limited to presenting the aggregate effects. It will often be highly useful to examine subsets of the data. For example, when a number of projects are included in the evaluation, the evaluators should consider whether certain projects or groups of projects tended to have greater effects than others. Variations in conditions among projects are likely, and an examination may be able to shed light on possible reasons for variations, possibly suggesting variations that should be considered further, even though the overall program does not appear successful.

Some types of clients served by the program may be more (or less) successfully served than others, even though such differences were not anticipated in the original evaluation design. Therefore, in general, evaluators should examine various subgroups to detect whether some groups were substantially better (or worse) served than indicated by the aggregate figures. For example, a particular type of program may work well with more severe cases than with less severe cases, or with older clients than with younger clients, or with female clients than male clients.

Sometimes subgroups to be followed up in the evaluation may be stratified at the beginning to ensure adequate consideration of different characteristics. If this is not done, an after-the-fact analysis of outcomes for various types of clients might not be possible if those subgroups are underrepresented in the sample.

Pitfall 23: Generalizing Beyond the Confines of the Sample or the Limits of the Program Sites Included in the Study

Even when the evaluation is well done and well controlled, there are numerous pitfalls in trying to generalize results to other sites or situations. "Too many social scientists expect single experiments to settle issues once and for all" (Campbell, 1969). "The particular sample from which control and experimental group members are drawn . . . may be idiosyncratic in that other potential target populations are not represented. If the conditions . . . in the experiment . . . differ markedly from conditions which prevail in other populations, then it is reasonable to believe that additional testing of the program is required" (Riecken and Boruch, 1974). There are several variations of this pitfall; recognizing them should temper statements about the generalizability of findings:

• The trial's results may represent only one sample point—that is, one trial under one set of conditions. Replication may be needed in other sites and at other times before one can state with confidence the general effectiveness of the program. Of course, to the extent that the initial trial covers a variety of sites and the evaluation of the program covers the entire target population, this will be of less concern. Often, however, there will be limitations on the size and coverage of the trial. Not all locations, not all potential client groups, and not all other potentially important conditions are likely to be covered. Such limitations of the evaluation should be clearly stated in the findings. For example, the New Jersey Graduated Work Incentive experiment examined only one type of geographical location on the U.S. urban East Coast. It covered only male-headed households, and it varied only the level of income guaranteed and the tax rate (Roos, 1975). The applicability of the findings to other conditions would need to be judged accordingly. As another example, if a test of a new street-patching material happens to be undertaken during a year with an unusually low amount of rain, the validity of the findings would be in question for periods of normal rainfall.

• A special variation of the overgeneralizing pitfall can occur when explicit or implicit statements are made about the particular characteristics of the intervention that "caused" the observed impacts. This problem arises particularly where only one site (and one set of program intervention characteristics) is used in the trial of the program. As discussed under Pitfall 10, it is vital that evaluators know what was actually implemented and that they be alert for features of the trial that appear to be significant in the program's apparent success or lack of it, even though they were not initially intended to be tested during the trial. For example, in evaluations of the effectiveness of social service casework, such characteristics as the particular technique used, the caseworker's personality, the amount of time spent with the client, and the caseworker's style could all affect the outcomes (Fischer, 1976). Unless the evaluation procedures attempted to isolate these characteristics in the test, evaluators would be unable to generalize about the extent to which these characteristics affect the outcomes. They would not be able to state whether, for example, apparent successes (or failures) were the result of the techniques used or the caseworkers' style and personality. This might be less of a problem if a large number of sites and many different caseworkers were involved in the test. Otherwise there would be substantial ambiguity about what was driving the observed outcomes and what should be done about the program. The conclusion might be reached that casework is (or is not) effective, whereas what was actually evaluated was only one combination of casework characteristics.

• Behavior may change when the novelty of a new program wears off (for either program operators or their clients). And client behavior may alter from that in trials undertaken on only part of the population when the program is established so that everyone can receive the program. For example, a program to determine the effects of the use of group homes rather than large institutions for caring for children with juvenile delinquency records might be tested in one or two locations. The finding might not be representative of other settings if the program's scale was expanded. For example, citizens might become antagonistic to a larger number of homes in their community. Or if the locations are chosen because of the communities' willingness to test the group homes, other communities might be more resistant.

• Some groups may turn out not to have been covered by the evaluation. In some instances, this may have been part of the plan; in others, it may be unintentional. The evaluators should determine which types of clients were included and which were not. They should avoid attributing observed effects to those not covered in the evaluation unless a logical case can be made for it. Many evaluations will not be able to cover all the major target groups that were initially intended for coverage and are intended to be covered by the program after it goes into full-scale operation. If this is found to be the case, the findings should be qualified. The New Jersey Graduated Work Incentive experiment, as noted, was limited to male-headed households and those located in only one geographical location; thus, its generalizability was limited.

Pitfall 24: Failure to Acknowledge the Effects of Multiple Program Components

In many areas of social services, program participants benefit from many activities. For example, in many homeless shelters, participants may receive meals, counseling, basic health services, shelter, and even religious guidance in faith-based organizations. They may also receive services from multiple agencies. For example, youth may receive messages regarding the effects of drug use and unsafe sex from many sources. The evaluation may attempt to isolate the effectiveness of the different program components, but sometimes this is too costly. Identifying other related services received by beneficiaries should be part of initial work. However, if it is beyond the scope of the evaluation to sort out their effects, subsequent generalizations about program effectiveness need to acknowledge the possible influence of these other services.

Pitfall 25: Failure to Submit Preliminary Findings
to Key Program Staff for Reality Testing

Permitting key program personnel to review the findings before promulgation of the evaluation findings is generally a matter of courtesy and good practice. It also has an important technical purpose: to provide a review of the findings from a different perspective. This practice appears to be regularly followed by audit agencies in the United States and many government-sponsored evaluations, but is less common in evaluations undertaken by others.

Program people may be aware of situations and factors that the evaluators have missed, and they can often add considerable insight into the interpretation of the data, sometimes identifying misinterpretations and misunderstandings by the evaluators. Even when program managers are defensive and hostile, they may offer comments that will indicate that the evaluators have indeed made misinterpretations or even errors that should be corrected. In one evaluation in which one of us was involved, drug treatment program personnel reviewing the draft report pointed out to the evaluation team that an important group of program clients had been left out, requiring the evaluators to follow up what would otherwise have been a neglected group of clients. Finally, the opportunity to suggest modifications may reduce defensiveness by program personnel, thereby enhancing the likelihood that the evaluation findings will be used.

Pitfall 26: Failure to Adequately Support Conclusions with Specific Data

In presenting the findings of an evaluation, whether orally or in writing, evaluators should be careful to clearly link objective findings and objective data to the conclusions offered. Program staff and others will be quick to question the nature of the supporting evidence for findings, especially when findings are not positive.

This caveat also applies to recommendations. The basis of each recommendation should be identified. When evaluators attempt to provide insights into why programs are not as effective as they might be and then provide recommendations to improve the program, there is a tendency not to distinguish those recommendations that follow from the major technical examination from recommendations that have emerged from the more subjective, qualitative insights the evaluators obtained during the technical evaluation. Preferably, such insights would be obtained through technical analyses. However, even when these are obtained through more qualitative means, it is important that evidence supporting recommendations be clearly presented.

Pitfall 27: Poor Presentation of Evaluation Findings

Program evaluation findings, whether presented orally or in writing, should be clear, concise, and intelligible to the users for whom the report is intended. This should not, however, be used as an excuse for not providing adequate technical backup (documentation) for findings. The technical evidence should be made available in writing, in either the body of the text, appendixes, or a separate volume, so that technical staffs of the program funders and other reviewers can examine for themselves the technical basis of the findings. (See Chapter Twenty-One for suggestions for effective report writing.)

In addition, pitfalls encountered throughout the evaluation process, even those identified too late during the process of evaluation to address fully, should be discussed. The amount of uncertainty in the findings should be identified not only when statistical analysis is used but in other instances as well. Information about the impact of pitfalls encountered by evaluators on the magnitude or relative certainty of program effects should be provided, even if only in the form of the evaluators' subjective judgments.

Conclusion

The checklists of pitfalls provided here should not be considered to cover all pitfalls. There are always evaluation-specific problems that can confront evaluators. Focusing on how decisions made throughout the evaluation process affect the different kinds of validity, reliability, and credibility of findings and recommendations is essential. The care with which potential limitations are identified and explained serves to strengthen the credibility of the evaluator's methodological expertise. Recognizing pitfalls should not be considered a weakness but rather a strength of rigorous evaluation work.

References

Armor, D. J., Polich, J. M., and Stambul, H. B. *Alcoholism and Treatment.* Santa Monica, Calif.: Rand Corporation, 1976.

Boruch, R. F. "On Common Contentions About Randomized Field Experiments." *Evaluation Studies Review Annual,* 1976, *1,* 158–194.

Campbell, D. T. "Reforms as Experiments." *American Psychologist,* 1969, *24,* 409–429.

Campbell, D. T., and Ross, H. L. "The Connecticut Crackdown on Speeding." *Law and Society Review,* 1968, *8,* 33–53.

Conner, R. F. "Selecting a Control Group: An Analysis of the Randomization Process in Twelve Social Reform Programs." *Evaluation Quarterly,* 1977, *1,* 195–244.

Fischer, J. *The Effectiveness of Social Casework.* Springfield, Ill.: Charles C. Thomas, 1976.

Hatry, H. P. *Performance Measurement: Getting Results.* Washington, D.C.: Urban Institute Press, 1999.

Hendricks, M. "Outcome Measurement in the Nonprofit Sector: Recent Developments, Incentives and Challenges." In K. Newcomer, E. Jennings Jr., C. Broom, and A. Lomax (eds.), *Meeting the Challenges of Performance-Oriented Government.* Washington, D.C.: American Society for Public Administration, 2002.

Herzog, E. *Some Guide Lines for Evaluative Research.* Washington, D.C.: U.S. Department of Health, Education, and Welfare, Welfare Administration, Children's Bureau, 1959.

O'Sullivan, E., Rassel, G., and Berner, M. *Research Methods for Public Administrators.* White Plains, N.Y.: Longman, 2003.

Riecken, H. W., and Boruch, R. F. (eds.). *Social Experimentation: A Method for Planning and Evaluating Social Intervention.* Orlando, Fla.: Academic, 1974.

Roos, N. P. "Contrasting Social Experimentation with Retrospective Evaluation: A Health Care Perspective." *Public Policy,* 1975, *23,* 241–257.

Singleton, R., Straits, B., Straits, M., and McAllister, R. *Approaches to Social Research.* New York: Oxford University Press, 1988.

Stangor, C. *Research Methods for the Behavioral Sciences.* Boston: Houghton Mifflin, 1998.

U.S. General Accounting Office. *Managing for Results: Measuring Program Results That Are Under Limited Federal Control.* Washington, D.C.: Government Printing Office, 1998.

20

Managing Evaluation Projects

James B. Bell

The theory and methods of public program evaluation meet the reality of policymaking and program management and operations through the conduct of individual evaluation projects. Uncertainty about current performance and narrow political interest challenge an evaluator to maintain focus and political neutrality while undertaking the difficult technical task of carrying out an evaluation. Managers and policymakers often view evaluation initially as an unknown that can block their own progress while providing support for their competitors.

Against a backdrop of demanding technical requirements and a dynamic political environment, the goal of evaluation project management is to develop, with available resources and time, valid and useful measurement information products that achieve the intended purpose of the project. Typically, such an evaluation supplies information on program performance, and decision makers are expected to use this information to enhance program performance. Secondary aims of evaluation project management are development of evaluation staff and education of the project sponsor and other stakeholders about program evaluation.

This chapter uses several definitions that are clarified here:

- *Evaluation project management:* A process of considerations, decisions, and activities engaged in by the leadership of an evaluation project to facilitate its conduct. The evaluation managers must transform the mandate, resources, and schedule for the project into valued evaluation products (tangible and intangible).

- *Project director:* The leader of evaluation management, who is directly accountable to the project sponsor for successful completion of the evaluation.
- *Evaluation staff* or *evaluators:* The individuals who conduct the evaluation, that is, those whose work is facilitated by evaluation leadership. At times, the evaluation staff includes the project director and other senior evaluators who have major roles in carrying out an evaluation as well as responsibilities for project management.
- *Evaluation mandate:* The direction on the analytical purpose and intended use of evaluation findings given to evaluation management by the project sponsor.
- *Sponsor:* The organization paying for the evaluation.
- *Client:* Usually also the sponsor, but sometimes a client organization other than the sponsor is identified and is expected to use the evaluation products.
- *Stakeholders:* Besides the sponsor and direct clients, there are generally multiple audiences who hold a stake in the substance of an evaluation—groups whose vying interests complicate the evaluation environment.
- *Program:* The evaluation subject, which encompasses the environment, policies, practices, resources, activities, organizations, and individuals being evaluated.

At its core, program evaluation is a human discovery process. One of the most important challenges of day-to-day project management is to create an atmosphere that fosters insight and creativity among project staff and other evaluation participants. Simultaneously, there must be sufficient focus and discipline to accomplish the evaluation mandate on schedule with available resources. Because evaluation takes place in a complex and unpredictable environment, project management is more art than science; no generic prescription for successful management exists. The advice in this chapter focuses on six areas that are essential to effective project management, set out here with their aims:

1. Developing rational proposals, which aims at optimal correspondence between the proposed work plan and budget and the sponsor's evaluation requirements
2. Clarifying the evaluation mandate, which seeks to achieve agreement between sponsor and evaluation management about the purpose, scope, resources, method, work plan, and schedule
3. Staffing and organizing for success, which refers to a demonstration by staff, through past efforts, of the mix of qualifications needed to con-

duct the evaluation. Staff are organized into a structure that maximizes each member's contribution and ensures control of evaluation expenditures and schedule.

4. Making assignments productive, which aims at assignments that are product oriented, well defined, and agreed on by evaluation managers and the staff who will undertake the effort. The sum of all assignments equals completion of all evaluation products. Each assignment is appropriate to the capabilities of the individuals or groups undertaking it.

5. Monitoring interim progress, designed to provide project monitoring information that accurately portrays and links technical progress on evaluation products, expenditures, and schedule status. A monitoring process contributes to and sustains project momentum

6. Ensuring product quality and usefulness, which aims at evaluation products given high ratings for usefulness. The evaluation products are used by policy and program management decision makers to accomplish the purpose of the evaluation.

The aims are ideals that are not likely to be fully achieved in the context of an individual evaluation. They emphasize the state that should be sought in each area of project management. Considered together, they encourage evaluation management to be dynamically responsive to the mandate for each evaluation by finding opportunities to ensure and enhance the value of the sponsor's evaluation investment throughout the course of the project.

This advice on evaluation management is not novel. Nonetheless, to achieve these aims in an evaluation project is very difficult. Constraints, such as inadequate or inappropriate evaluation staff or an individual representing the sponsor organization who is difficult to work with, tend to overwhelm efforts to pursue optimal management of evaluation resources and activities. By examining the specified areas of evaluation management and providing practical suggestions on ways to accomplish the aims listed, this chapter is intended to aid evaluation project managers.

Evaluation projects differ greatly in purpose, scope, size, method, and complexity. They also differ according to the nature of the program or organization being evaluated, the type of sponsor, and the affiliation, working style, and qualifications of staff conducting the evaluation. The differences in characteristics presented by each evaluation set unique bounds for management of that project. For example, there are managerially significant distinctions between evaluations conducted by in-house staff and those conducted by outside organizations. An in-house project may be constrained by the depth and range of the capabilities of in-house evaluation staff. Outside evaluators may possess better technical capability but less working knowledge of the subject program, and they may be insensitive to existing political relationships in and around the program.

Besides the organizational relationship between the sponsor and evaluator, other characteristics of an evaluation project influence evaluation management. A program's prior history of evaluation is significant. Must new measures be developed and tested, or will evaluators use existing well-accepted tools? How were prior evaluations viewed by this sponsor and other stakeholders? Managing the first evaluation of a program presents more challenges than an evaluation that replicates well-established and accepted protocols. In the latter, management seeks high-quality execution without expecting to develop new methodology in the process. In contrast, methodology development usually is the dominant activity in first-time evaluations. These evaluations are more difficult to manage because the activities are less amenable to routinization. Finally, the scale of the evaluation and the amount of professional staff effort greatly affect evaluation management, logistics, and operations.

This chapter provides a discussion of each of the areas of evaluation management and offers practical suggestions for realizing the aims in that area of project management.

Developing Rational Proposals

Like most other types of proposals, evaluation proposals are unique documents because there is competition. There is usually an absolute deadline and no credit for a late or a partial submission. As such, there is a heightened need for a timely commitment of sufficient resources to meet the submission deadline with a high-quality, competitive proposal. Moreover, a proposal situation demands sound technical and budget decision making, effective time management, and coordination of a group effort. The focus here is on creation of rational evaluation proposals that seamlessly integrate the technical and budget components. Besides being responsive, high-quality documents, rational proposals have a strong correspondence between the proposed type and amount of staff and other resources and the evaluation requirements.

This chapter emphasizes creating proposals for competition, but most of the guidance applies to noncompetitive situations as well. The advice also applies when an evaluation component is part of a proposal for a larger project, such as when a service-providing agency seeks a government or foundation grant and must explain how funded services are evaluated.

Most competed evaluation projects begin with the creation of a request for proposal (RFP) that contains a technical statement of work (SOW) describing the sponsor's expectations for the evaluation. The RFP may be posted for general response or distributed to preselected group of candidate evaluators. Sometimes an evaluator is invited to suggest an evaluation approach in the absence of an RFP. Usually the budget parameters are already set.

Not all proposals win support. Based on experience, the odds of success are increased when the following guidelines are seriously considered and applied:

1. Make a sound decision about whether to commit to submitting the proposal.
2. Assemble a competitive team. Make sure the senior team agrees there is a rational fit between technical requirements and the resources proposed for the project.
3. Write a responsive, high-quality technical proposal that explains how the evaluation will be done (not how much you want to do the project).
4. Make sure the budget and administrative materials are complete and accurate.
5. Maintain, and if possible ratchet up, quality and responsiveness during the postsubmission phase. Many highly contested evaluations are decided on this last round of competition.

RFP Content

As the centerpiece of an RFP, the technical SOW typically contains evaluation goals or objectives, a list of expected deliverable products with a delivery schedule, and a list of expected evaluation tasks and activities. There may be statements about the intended evaluation design that specify features of the analytic structure, such as a random assignment controlled experiment, longitudinal intergroup comparison, participant outcome tracking, or, in the case of a qualitative evaluation, the mechanisms for assessment (for example, focus groups, case studies, or semistructured in-person interviews).

As part of the SOW, the RFP may also contain the following information:

- Background and context of the subject program
- Descriptions of prior evaluations, perhaps with citations to reference materials
- Criteria that will be used to review and score evaluation proposals
- Applicant eligibility criteria and restrictions
- Award mechanism type (for example, grant or contract)
- Proposal content instructions or outline (sometimes with page limits)
- Other items, such as various administrative forms that might be required by the sponsor (also known as representations and certifications, or "reps and certs")

The format and level of detailed required for the budget, as well as the proposal submission date and time and delivery instructions, are noted in the RFP or a cover letter.

Phases of Proposal Development

There are many different routes to a completed proposal and certainly no proven standard process. Nevertheless, it seems apparent that there are five identifiable phases of proposal development. More important, perhaps, there are crucial interrelationships between the work undertaken in the different phases that, if managed well, will increase the likelihood of a rational proposal that is also highly competitive.

Contemplation Phase. The contemplation phase is usually a short period of intense scrutiny of the RFP in which questions like the following are addressed:

- What are the features of the requested evaluation?
- Do we [the applicant] have the necessary qualifications to conduct the evaluation as described in the SOW?
- Do we have the availability of qualified evaluation staff and other resources needed to conduct the evaluation?
- Does the SOW fit the subject program and situation?
- Do the resource amounts allowed for evaluation match the labor requirements for conducting the technical SOW?
- Is there a moderately complete understanding of the competitive situation [if applicable]?

Only those well positioned because of their evaluation training and experience should attempt to answer these questions. If they cannot answer these questions adequately, they should decide not to create a proposal.

Applicants typically are able to ask the sponsor questions about the RFP. Technically appropriate questions asked in a courteous, constructive manner can clarify key points about the planned evaluation and simultaneously begin to demonstrate the applicant's positive style of communication. Of course, the opposite may also be true: inappropriate questions communicated poorly could start to build a negative image of the applicant. Any communication that takes place in a competitive context, no matter how seemingly trivial, is part of the competition.

If all else points to a decision to launch a proposal, then the final issue is level of commitment to the task. Is there enough resolve to finish the proposal among the staff who will write the document? Are they motivated to work hard to succeed? Will they have the necessary support in areas such as literature search, copyediting, document production, copying, and delivery? The authors of the technical approach sections of a proposal are often already busy on existing projects. The RFP due date may conflict with pressing demands on existing projects, such as finishing a report that is due the same week the proposal is due. It is critical to discuss the proposal writing team's schedule of other work so the final decision takes these associated proposal risk factors into consideration.

Draft Staffing Plan, Budget, and Schedule. The decision to start writing a proposal is informed by conclusions about the availability of appropriate staff and seeming match between RFP work requirements and amounts and types of resources and schedule allowed by the RFP (if provided) and available through the applicant. The beginning of the writing phase focuses on developing a draft staffing plan and budget. Usually this involves assigning types and amounts of staff labor and other resources to each task and deliverable product in the SOW. There is an advantage to constructing the staffing plan, budget, and schedule early in the process: the resource parameters for the evaluation are set before much effort is devoted to the technical approach.

In formulating the staff budget, the following questions should guide the assignments of labor:

- Is the task or product well specified in the SOW—enough to allow accurate assignment of labor?
- Do the senior staff members assigned to the task or product agree that the task or product can be successfully completed with the allotted labor?
- Is the schedule realistic?

Presumably, those writing the technical sections, particularly the work plan that describes task and activities, will be able to ensure that the budget and schedule are feasible. As a practical matter, this phase is when budget and schedule concerns not noticed earlier arise. For example, many RFPs have overly optimistic schedules. Typically, the following areas are where the RFP schedules are unrealistic:

- Development of primary data collection instruments and protocols
- Gaining agreement on the key measures and audiences for evaluation findings
- Conducting site visits
- Completing multiple iterations of data analysis
- Gaining necessary clearances approvals
- Writing a final report that will be widely disseminated

The problem of unrealistic budget and schedule assumptions seems to follow from whether the sponsor has prior experience conducting an evaluation of the same or a very similar program. Unfortunately, the evaluation situation that presents the greatest challenge—a previously unevaluated program—is also the situation where unrealistic budget and schedule assumptions often occur.

Technical Content Phase. Assuming the decision to develop a proposal is reinforced by the draft staffing plan and budget, the watchwords for creating the technical content of the proposal are responsiveness, quality, and ease of use:

• *Responsiveness.*A sure way to create a noncompetitive evaluation proposal is to be unresponsive to the RFP. In fact, some sponsors will not review proposals that do not pass an initial screening for inclusion of required elements. From the sponsor's perspective, it is perhaps natural to conclude that an evaluator's inability to be responsive to the RFP foreshadows his or her inability to be responsive during the conduct of the evaluation.

Putting nonresponsiveness aside, there are two basic categories of responsiveness: responsiveness to the letter of the RFP and responsiveness to the intent of the RFP (even if the letter omits important considerations). Generally, the most competitive proposals fall into the second category. If omissions in the RFP are addressed constructively, the applicant demonstrates a command of the subject evaluation. Nonetheless, there is a risk that one or more proposal reviewers, especially those with a strong investment in creating the SOW, may be put off by such exceptional responsiveness, regardless of its methodological soundness. After all, an evaluation has both technical measurement and interpersonal and political dimensions, which naturally imbue the proposal review process.

The steps to achieving responsiveness start with the development of the proposal outline that conveys careful attention to all proposal instructions in the RFP. However, sometimes there is important information that should be in the proposal that was not in the RFP. For example, the instructions may not call for sample size estimates, but if sampling and data collection are involved in the evaluation, the proposal should be very clear about the study universe and intended number of cases or observations. There are implications for budget size that attend the sample size issue.

Once the proposal outline is settled and the number of pages in each section is determined, the process of ensuring responsiveness has just begun. Proposal writers may unknowingly drift away from the outline, so there should be periodic checks of proposal responsiveness leading up to the seminal review of the nearly final draft. Without planned, periodic monitoring of responsiveness to the RFP and midcourse correction, the likelihood of proposal writer drift increases. This problem can be exacerbated as the number of writers contributing to the proposal increases, especially when the writers are not well experienced working together to create an evaluation proposal. In short, responsiveness should be monitored throughout proposal creation.

• *Quality.* Superior quality may trump mediocre responsiveness, but the opposite is usually not true because mediocre proposal quality is generally viewed as a harbinger of the mediocre quality of future evaluation products. It is important to grasp that those reviewing a proposal will be likely to project proposal quality onto any reports or other products that will be forthcoming from the evaluation.

Some exceptions to the rule of superior quality may occur for particularly well-regarded evaluators who have a strong record of developing superior evaluation products. Sponsors and reviewers may be inclined to overlook proposal quality weaknesses because, for example, they assume the evaluator was too busy to mount a high-quality proposal in the time frame required by the RFP.

Quality in an evaluation proposal is multidimensional, beginning with the simplest elements of spelling, grammar, and formatting. A collection of issues like logical presentation, elimination of redundancy, and use of proper terminology can be quality-compromising faults or weaknesses.

In addition to writing skills, assigning section authors who are truly knowledgeable about the subject matter in their section ensures quality. For example, statistical methodologists should write the sampling plan and statistical analysis procedures, at least in part. Someone who has relevant knowledge and experience should write the description of the subject program and policy, including background and context. The necessary ability to write clearly permeates and cross-cuts the multiple areas of technical and subject matter expertise that are needed in the evaluation process itself.

Even well-articulated sections written by knowledgeable subject matter experts can be undercut if readers perceive the sections are a patchwork rather than whole cloth. Therefore, it is essential to allow time to work editorially with all sections together in the context of creating a near final draft proposal. Of course, this vital step must be enabled by well-developed drafts of all substantive sections. These should be completed with enough time remaining before submission to allow the "one coherent voice" editorial process to be completed.

• *Ease of Use.* Since some RFPs are very strict with regard to acceptable outline, page limits, and other conformities, the proposal writers may have no leeway to ease the reviewer's job. If leeway exists, this can be done by, for instance, providing a proposal summary or creating separate technical attachments in which a sampling plan or data collection instrumentation is provided.

Finalized Budgets and Administrative Materials. The technical requirements of an evaluation project and the resources needed to fulfill those requirements meet in the proposed budget, usually in the form of a spreadsheet in the business part of the proposal. However, without sufficient alignment between technical requirements of the SOW and the proposed resource allocations, the project is likely to underperform technically (except in the rare cases of excess resources). Inevitably, some aspect of the evaluation protocol will be compromised to conserve labor or another expense. In turn, this will undercut the final evaluation products and cause the evaluation to be less valuable than it should have been.

An RFP typically includes a statement of total resources in terms of gross monetary value (dollars) or gross labor amount (person-years of effort). In constructing the proposed budget, the evaluator usually starts with this total resource value and then disaggregates it systematically to create a task- or product-level budget, while always being mindful of the correspondence between RFP technical requirements and available resources. When a total resource amount is not in the RFP, proposal writers face an exceptional challenge: instead of trying to fit the technical requirements to the prescribed budget, they must simultaneously guess the total amount the sponsor wants to spend on the evaluation and then fit the technical requirements to that unsubstantiated budget amount.

The flexibility to fit budgets to technical requirements stems from the simple reality that a typical evaluation activity will consume different amounts of resources depending on how it is conducted. For example, if a start-up meeting is one of the proposed evaluation activities, under different planning assumptions, one could estimate a budget as modest as under $100 for a telephone meeting or as great as $10,000 or more. The difference in cost is accounted for by variation in cost-influencing factors:

- The number of evaluation team members who will attend
- The extent of the preparation of new documents that will be required for the meeting
- The number of cycles of client review and comment on materials that will be presented or discussed in the meeting
- Whether long-distance travel is involved
- The number of clients who will attend and whether it is the evaluation team's responsibility to organize their participation
- Whether the evaluation team will host the meeting at their facility
- Other special considerations

In essence, proposal budget construction is an exercise in clarifying the detailed plan for each evaluation activity to the maximum feasible extent.

This means specifying each person's individual activities (what she or he will be doing) as well as the full cost of each person. In addition, nonlabor costs, such as travel, printing, and copying, must be accounted for. Typically, an RPF will specify some aspects of an activity such as a start-up meeting, but since not all budget-relevant aspects are covered, the applicant should lay out an explicit plan to remove as much ambiguity as possible. If one extrapolates from the start-up meeting example across all the evaluation activities in a typical RFP, it is clear very quickly that conceptually similar SOWs can have dramatically different budgets.

The flexibility to rationally fit resources and requirements is present during proposal budget development, and it should be exercised to head off resource issues when the evaluation is conducted. Moreover, in the absence of strict cross-disciplinary standards of conduct for such activities as data collection, evaluators are free to propose work plans that align resource outlays to technical requirements, without necessarily proposing the optimal methodological protocol. The procedures to minimize data entry errors illustrate this point. While it is widely accepted by many leading evaluators, the practice of double entry of written survey data is not universally proposed because of the additional resources that will be required.

Finally, there are often overlooked uncertain situations that plague evaluation budget formulation. The following seem prevalent and particularly consequential:

- The extent to which new data collection instruments and protocols must be developed
- The extent to which the collection of data is dependent on the cooperation of parties outside the control of the evaluator or client
- The extent to which proposed staff have a strong record of undertaking similar tasks successfully
- The extent to which the client is likely to be heavily involved in all phases of the evaluation.

Postsubmission. Generally, evaluation proposal review includes a phase when the funders ask questions about the most competitive proposals. This certainly is not always the case, but it is rare that no questions are forthcoming from the sponsor to the applicants with the most competitive proposals. If nothing else, there are usually some administrative and budget matters to address before a final decision is made.

Experienced evaluators realize that this phase can be extremely important in determining the final outcome of a proposal competition, especially if the sponsor has narrowed the field to a handful of competitors. In any case, the response to the sponsor's inquiries must at least match the quality and responsiveness of the original proposal and, ideally, even exceed that level. This last round of competition probably will influence the sponsor's final decision.

Usually these final questions come with short turnaround times—the answers may be due in days or even hours—so it is important to plan for the possibility of such "best and final" questions, which means making sure that key people are available to respond to any forthcoming questions. It is a good idea to put the dates when questions might arrive on the calendars of key people and, if possible, plan vacations and professional travel accordingly.

The questions themselves should convey the sponsor's true concerns about the proposal. Questions that go to the heart of the proposed technical approach may signal a serious problem with the proposal in the sponsor's view. Relatively benign questions may signal that little is wrong with the proposal from the sponsor's perspective, but this is not always the case. Of course, the sponsor's true viewpoint is revealed through the final funding decision.

If at all possible, it is advisable to request a debriefing about a failed proposal. Without knowing what weaknesses the sponsor saw, it is very difficult for the evaluator to correct them. Moreover, the debriefing is another opportunity to engage the sponsor, learn more about what the sponsor is looking for, and thereby improve the chances of success on a subsequent proposal. Thus, a sponsor's willingness to provide a debriefing may offer useful insights for the future. For example, the sponsor may reveal future projects for which the evaluation team is well qualified and may want to encourage continued involvement of the evaluator. An unwillingness to provide a debriefing or discuss future evaluation may be a sign the sponsor does not view the applicant as a positive candidate for future assignments, a useful (albeit somewhat painful) insight for the future. This interpretation would be reinforced if it was learned that other unsuccessful applicants received a debriefing.

Responding to RFPs can be stressful and usually calls for periods of unexpected, intensive effort, but it also provides an opportunity to expand technical knowledge and hone the team's problem-solving, planning, and writing skills. The proposal experience should translate into improved professionalism that is immediately obvious. If nothing else, an evaluator's ability to address skillfully the next proposal opportunity is enhanced.

Clarifying the Evaluation Mandate

Imagine a meeting in which the project sponsors present their review of the draft final report for the evaluation and realize, too late, that the report does not match the expectations of the sponsor. The deficiencies identified in the report cannot be corrected by altering the way the evaluation results are presented. The problem stems from unresolved differences between evaluation management and the sponsor about the interpretation of the evaluation mandate.

The evaluation director and staff who had this experience did not fully comprehend the need to establish and maintain agreement with the sponsor (and the client if different from the sponsor) about the evaluation mandate. Evaluators should not misread the sponsor's tacit acceptance of the original project plan and interim progress reports. Evaluation management cannot assume that a fundamental difference about the mandate will surface through these pro forma activities. While there may be a solid agreement at the start of the evaluation, either the sponsor or the evaluation management may change their expectations during the project period. If this happens, this shift must be discussed and a revised agreement forged.

Gaining Initial Agreement

Depending on the depth and complexity of the evaluation and the differences between sponsor and evaluators about the evaluation mandate, clarification of the expectations of both sides concerning the evaluation results should be formalized orally or in writing. When a written clarification is needed, it should be created in the least expensive manner possible. For example, evaluation management may document key points about the mandate in a memorandum for the record, with a copy forwarded for review by the evaluation sponsor

When clarifying the evaluation mandate, the primary evaluation user, purpose, scope, design and method, resources, schedule, and other technical requirements must be elicited from the sponsor and others who originally shape an evaluation. This is done by the evaluation management—those most directly responsible for success of the evaluation. The same understanding of the evaluation mandate must be shared by those funding and those managing the evaluation.

As the evaluation management and the sponsor gain and maintain agreement about the evaluation mandate, their shared understanding establishes a framework for considering next steps in project management. Failure to agree on the scope and primary purpose of the evaluation or to resolve potentially troublesome issues of approach, schedule, or budget are common problems that cause evaluations to falter. For example, the sponsor may wish to avoid placing a data collection burden on certain individuals or groups or may want to develop findings based on a regionally representative stratified sample. Evaluation management must be aware of such preferences at the start of the evaluation, or resources and time may be wasted.

Many evaluations are justified on the basis of serving multiple purposes; this goal, however, may impede clarification of the mandate. The separate purposes for an evaluation range from identifying ways to improve program organizational performance to developing new evaluation methodology. When multiple purposes exist, evaluation management should discuss with the sponsor the relative importance of the different purposes. Inevitably, there are resource trade-offs; optimal achievement of the most important purpose may be jeopardized if multiple purposes are pursued.

Sometimes there is a single purpose for an evaluation, but there are differences about the implication of that purpose for the scope of measurement. In a common example, the sole purpose is to identify ways to improve program performance, but there are two or more views about the implications of "ways to improve program performance." Under one view of the evaluation scope, program operations (process) is a peripheral focus of measurement—the program is to be treated as a black box in an analysis of the outcomes of individual participants. Program operations are subject to little or no independent investigation during the evaluation. A contrasting interpretation of the scope of this evaluation sees the program operations as a measurable process. Program performance might be improved if program operation is examined. According to this view, a major focus of the evaluation is the inner workings of the program.

Continuing this example, the evaluators must work with the sponsor to resolve whether the focus of analysis will be solely on participant outcomes or will also include the program operations. Evaluation management might suggest how this difference can be resolved by reconciling the two interpretations to shape an optimally feasible and useful evaluation mandate. The scope of the evaluation can be defined to encompass program operations and participant outcomes. In this case, the agreed-on purpose is clarified to find ways to improve participant outcomes by investigating the relationship between participant outcomes and program operations.

Checking the Mandate During the Evaluation

Both the sponsor and evaluation management may, with good reason, change their interpretation of the mandate during the course of the evaluation. This change must be disclosed to the other party, and agreement should be reached on any shift in the evaluation mandate. The sponsor may respond to a changed agenda for decision making during the course of the evaluation: a new legislative proposal or an executive initiative may cause the sponsors to shift their views of the preferred measurements taken during the evaluation. Often sponsors fail to communicate effectively with evaluation management when their expectations for the evaluation change.

Evaluation management can defend against unknown shifts in the evaluation mandate by involving the sponsors in discussions of the evaluation mandate throughout the project period. They can accomplish this involvement by integrating checks on the mandate into routine evaluation activities such as the sponsor's review of an evaluation data collection and analysis plan. By describing to the sponsor the data that will be collected, evaluation management creates an opportunity for discussing possible shifts in the sponsor's expectations for the evaluation. Regardless of whether changes are identified, the project record should note that the sponsor has rechecked the mandate.

The sponsor's review of the evaluation data collection and analysis plan must be structured to draw attention to how the evaluators have operationalized the evaluation mandate. Table 20.1 is from an evaluation sponsored by the Administration for Children and Families, a component of the U.S. Department of Health and Human Services. It shows how evaluators translated the evaluation mandate into action by presenting the measures and data sources for eight program outcomes. This evaluation is designed to address several family court improvement evaluation questions and outcomes through a combination of interviews and analysis of secondary data, such as those maintained by child welfare agencies and courts' management information systems.

Finally, sometimes a shift in the evaluation's mandate is so great that a separate and distinct effort to renegotiate the project purpose, budget, and schedule is required. A change in program leadership, for example, might precipitate such major renegotiations.

Staffing and Organizing for Results

Imagine that the evaluation project director is chairing a staff meeting. The agenda is planning for a major project activity: a series of in-depth qualitative case studies. Case study execution requires intimate knowledge of the characteristics of the subject program and its environment and context and a keen understanding of the nuances of administering in-depth case studied. The project director realizes that the level of knowledge and skill of the staff members with case study responsibilities does not meet the requirements of the project. What happened? Why is the project on the verge of a crisis? There was a misjudgment about staffing. Even if the problem can be corrected, the evaluation will fall behind schedule and waste resources because individuals with the wrong qualifications were selected for the evaluation.

With a clarified evaluation mandate, the next area essential to evaluation management is staffing and organization. Who will conduct evaluation activities? How will they be organized to carry out their project responsibilities?

Table 20.1. Linking Evaluation Outcomes, Measures, and Data Sources

Outcomes	Measures	Data Sources
Output		
Mediated case plans developed	Number of sessions held, completed agreements, full agreements, partial agreements, and participants Type of participants.	Child welfare agency case records
Initial outcomes		
Better relations with child welfare workers	Level of communication, trust, and openness between parents and child welfare agency workers from perspective of parents	Structured interview with families in treatment and comparison groups
Greater compliance with case plans	Compliance with case plan of treatment versus comparison cases	Telephone interview with (or survey completed by) child welfare worker or case plan review
Parents more cooperative with child welfare workers	Level of cooperation of parents in preparing and completing child welfare treatment plan for treatment and comparison	Structured interviews with child welfare staff to discuss level of cooperation experienced with families
Intermediate outcomes		
Reduction in number of continuances	Number of continuances taking place after mediation for treatment cases versus number of continuances taking place after the same stage in court processing for matched members of the comparison group	Court management information system (MIS)
Reduction in number of trials	Number of trials held for mediated versus nonmediated cases	Court MIS
Reduction in length of time to disposition	Length of time between case opening and disposition for treatment and comparison cases	Court MIS
Permanency	Length of time between date of initial petition for this episode in custody and case closure Number of cases reopened in child welfare agency after closure	Return home: Use court MIS system for date child returned home permanently Adoption: Use court MIS to collect date of the order of termination of rights. Permanent placement with relative: Gather from the child welfare agency the date the agreement for permanent placement with relative was signed

Table 20.1. Linking Evaluation Outcomes, Measures, and Data Sources, *continued*

Outcomes	Measures	Data Sources
		Guardianship: Use court MIS system to collect the date guardianship ordered by court
		Permanent foster care placement: Use both the date the foster parent signs contract with child welfare agency regarding permanent placement and the date the court approves the permanent plan
		Independent living: Gather from child welfare agency the date the child enters independent living.
		Gather from child welfare agency number of cases re-entering foster care (rate of recidivism).
Child safety	Number of allegations of abuse and neglect taking place after mediation for treatment cases versus number of allegations taking place after the same stage in court processing for matched members of the comparison group	Welfare agency records

Source: James Bell Associates (June 2003).

A simple answer is that the project staff should embody the qualifications needed to conduct the planned evaluation activities on schedule in a high-quality and effective manner. The staff should be available and motivated. If the evaluation has more than three staff members, they should be organized into teams with well-defined roles. The number of teams, team size, and the scope of team responsibility should be consistent with the number of project staff, the evaluation purpose, and the expected products and general work plan of the evaluation. In short, evaluation staff who possess the appropriate qualifications are needed. They should work under an organizational structure that facilitates full use of their capabilities. In many evaluations, individuals from the sponsor and subject program or outside experts also are part of the evaluation project organization. The effective involvement of internal or external advisory groups can enhance evaluation performance.

Selecting Appropriate Staff

The range of qualifications available among candidate evaluation staff varies depending on project circumstances. An evaluation assigned to an in-house evaluation unit usually presents staffing choices that are defined by the evaluation qualifications and competing duties of the staff of that unit. If the same project becomes an external evaluation, the pool of potential evaluators expands, and the process of selecting individuals is altered. Regardless, the same general approach to project staffing should apply.

As a first step, a staffing matrix should aid decisions about staffing. Typically, the substantive and methodological qualifications needed to conduct the project are arrayed in rows in the matrix, and the identities of candidate staff members are listed in the columns. The cells of the matrix are then marked for individuals whose qualifications demonstrated in past similar or related evaluations match those needed to conduct the tasks and activities required for this evaluation. Table 20.2 shows the staff qualification matrix for the multidisciplinary evaluation of family court adjudication of child welfare cases discussed previously. The qualifications on the left reveal the nature of the evaluation and provide a starting point for staffing decisions: the substantive and methodological qualifications needed for this evaluation and who among those individuals available for this project has demonstrated these capabilities. Substantive qualifications are the knowledge, skills, and experience that demonstrate familiarity with the program and subject area. They indicate whether enough basic understanding of the program and environment is present in professional staff to provide a foundation for executing the evaluation. The ideal substantive qualifications encompass knowledge of all pertinent aspects of the subject area within and around the scope of the evaluation.

In the national court improvement evaluation, staff needed to understand quickly both the intentions of the federal program guidelines for court improvement and the operations of child welfare and family court systems. Knowledge was also needed about the philosophical and historical underpinnings of child welfare case adjudication and the variations in systems across state and local jurisdictions. Prior experience working with child welfare case workers and attorneys was advantageous.

In assessing family court judges and staff substantive qualifications, managers should make allowances for the transfer of substantive knowledge across subject areas. For example, a current initiative in many social programs is services integration, or the coordination of services from different organizations. Knowledge gained about services integration in one program should apply in evaluations of other social programs with services integration objectives. Similarly, common functions and processes are present in most social

Table 20.2. Staff Qualifications Matrix

Qualification Requirements	Staff Member Qualifications						
	A	B	C	D	E	F	G
Substantive							
Court improvement initiatives	X	X				X	X
Child welfare and family court systems' general operations	X	X	X	X	X	X	X
Variations in state and local structure and practice among child welfare agencies	X	X	X	X	X	X	
Methodological							
Evaluation design for complex programs in a child welfare environment	X	X			X		
Primary and secondary data collection including interviews, surveys, and extracting data from hard copy and electronic records	X	X		X	X	X	X
Data analysis including use of quantitative and qualitative methods	X	X	X	X	X	X	X
Formulating and reporting plausible and workable recommendations for program redesign	X	X	X	X	X	X	

Source: James Bell Associates (June 2003).

programs. Administration and management, financing, client intake, case management, and management information systems are functions found in many social programs. Knowledge in these functional areas is transferable across programs.

Successful evaluations can be conducted by evaluation staff with a low level of substantive knowledge, although this alternative is not initially appealing. This is possible if the project allows for an evaluation learning period; evaluators can be among the fastest learners.

Without staff who have training and experience in data collection and analysis methods, the evaluation will flounder. Assessment of needed methodological qualifications may reflect the requirements of each stage of a project: evaluation design and instrument development, data collection, data analysis and interpretation, and report writing. It is useful also to consider distinctions among quantitative social science methods such as survey research, statistical and mathematical modeling, and qualitative research. Identifying staff candidates who have capabilities in quantitative and qualitative methods is helpful. Typically, an evaluator possesses one or the other of these methodological capabilities but not both.

In addition to substantive and methodological qualifications, strong interpersonal relations and communication capabilities are essential to successful evaluations. Many evaluations suffer because staff lack the interpersonal skills needed to facilitate evaluation activities. Individual staff members should have interpersonal skills and experiences appropriate to their roles in the project.

Because they are less likely to be formally documented, these personal qualifications are also less likely to be codified in a staffing matrix. For example, some individuals who appear to have solid substantive qualifications may be too doctrinaire or zealous. They may have rigid preconceptions of program strengths and weaknesses or may be otherwise ill suited to conducting an objective evaluation. Neutrality and objectivity are necessary so that the evaluation can be fair and incisive in assessing the knowledge gained through data collection and analysis activities. The critical importance of interpersonal and communications skills is emphasized throughout Part Four of the book.

Finally, in staffing decisions, the level, and not just the type, of training, knowledge, and experience required is crucial. There should be a mix of senior and junior staff that is appropriate to the problem-solving challenge of the project. For example, a pioneering analysis of a previously unevaluated program or policy requires a greater share of effort by senior staff. In contrast, in a project that is a replication of an earlier study, junior professional and support staff may play a larger role. The senior professionals will retain technical leadership and other overarching responsibilities, but their share of total project labor should decline in an evaluation where the detailed technical approach has been tested.

Organizing for Performance

Organizing evaluation staff into teams or groups with mutually exclusive but complementary project responsibilities is central to effective project management. The use of teams, and especially the exchange of information among them, suggests a nonhierarchical, collegial structure that still allows the narrower focus needed to accomplish project tasks and responsibilities. The number and size of teams is dictated by the number of staff participating in the evaluation. A team has at least two members, but an individual may serve on more than one team. There should also be a synthesis group if there are technical teams. Technical teams can be defined by their functions in the evaluation process such as data collection or analysis. They may also be differentiated by method, subject matter, or another organizing concept suited to that evaluation. Effective team configurations reflect a workable division of responsibilities among staff considering the types of effort needed to carry out the evaluation and the qualifications of individuals on the staff. When evaluation teams are organized by method, for example, one team may carry out the quantitative research while another team performs qualitative research.

While each team conducts the work for which it is responsible, there is also a constant exchange of information between the teams. In fact, there should be project staff members who bridge methods by participating on different teams. In addition, as shown in Figure 20.1, it is advisable to form a synthesis group to shepherd the efforts of the technical teams. A synthesis team is suggested for all evaluations that have more than one technical team. Working closely with the evaluations director, the synthesis group plays a key role in project management. It is involved in most aspects of planning evaluation assignments, monitoring technical progress, and interpreting and integrating products and results from completed evaluation activities. Thus, in the synthesis group, the evaluation parts are brought together and shaped through internal peer review into the information products that will present the evaluation results. Building on the example depicted in Figure 20.1, the qualitative team leaders in the synthesis group will review and approve plans for qualitative analyses for relevance and importance.

For many projects, an internal work group and an external advisory group are also advantageous (see Figure 20.1). A client-sponsor work group helps to promote an exchange of information among the project staff and key individuals representing the sponsor or subject program. Program policymakers and managers should be involved if they are expected to use evaluation findings to improve program performance. These work groups primarily facilitate active involvement of evaluation sponsors and users in planning and reviewing evaluation progress. Work group members may also be first reviewers of draft products developed by the core evaluation staff. An internal work group also is an effective mechanism for gaining access to program staff or data sources and resolving project issues, such as dissimilar views of the evaluation mandate.

An external advisory panel is composed of experts on the evaluation subject or methodology who are independent outsiders to the evaluation. Their effort usually is applied to project quality assurance. External advisory group composition should reflect the evaluation purpose. For instance, top methodologists should oversee decisions on evaluation design if rigorous methodology is emphasized in the evaluation mandate. Their role is to ensure that evaluation design and execution meet applicable standards.

Making Assignments Productive

Imagine that three-quarters of the project schedule and budget have been spent but that only half of the evaluation work has been done. The evaluation staff has put forth good effort, but one reason for the slow and more expensive pace is the way evaluation activities were initially conceived and assigned. Ambiguous, uncoordinated assignments sap project resources and undercut the knowledge contribution possible through an evaluation.

Figure 20.1. Organization of an Evaluation Project

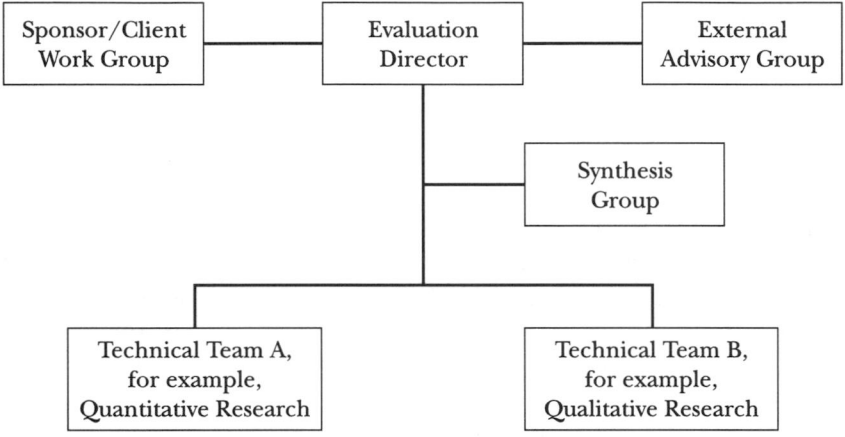

Source: James Bell Associates (June 2003).

In evaluation projects in which the results and experiences of one activity are integrally related to many other activities, a careful and coherent procedure for making assignments is needed to achieve optimal relatedness among activities and a productive evaluation overall. Evaluation management must ensure that each staff member has at all times a clear and well-defined assignment governing his or her efforts on the evaluation. In combination, the results of the individual assignments must equal the intended evaluation products. Size, schedule, and other evaluation characteristics influence the mechanism through which project assignments are made. In large evaluations, assignments usually occur at multiple echelons, with the number of organizational levels dependent on the number of participating staff and the level of staff effort in a typical month.

A national program evaluation with seven to ten professional staff members, for example, may have three echelons: the project director makes assignments to team leaders, who make assignments to small groups within their teams, who then fashion assignments for individuals in the group. The role of an echelon more than one level above the individual or group receiving an assignment varies among projects. The tighter the project budget and schedule are, the greater is the need for the top echelon to agree on the details of the assignments at all echelons.

Effort spent gaining well-conceived and agreed-on assignments should not strain the evaluation resources and schedule. A project must maintain momentum by integrating the effort required for planning and initiating assignments into daily, weekly, and monthly activities. Only a very small share of total project labor and a moderate share of total evaluation management effort should be devoted solely to assignment making.

Shaping Individual Assignments

To shape assignments for individual staff members, evaluation management should first determine the set of interim products needed for the next period of the evaluation. This set of needed products then must be parceled into mutually exclusive assignments. Each staff member should know his or her boundaries and the boundaries of the most nearly related assignments of other staff members. The instructions or guidelines for the assignments should be ordered rationally for each staff member, with considerable attention given to the preconditions and interrelationships among individual steps in carrying out the assignment. The product, resources, completion date, and other provisions of an assignment also should match the capabilities of the individuals receiving the assignment. Evaluation management should keep the scope and requirements of each assignment within or very near the capabilities actually demonstrated on other evaluations by the individuals receiving the assignment. Sometimes junior professionals, for example, underestimate the complexity of an activity and enthusiastically seek assignments that they are too inexperienced to complete.

In making assignments, evaluation management should encourage open discussions between those who will oversee the assignment and those who will carry it out. The result should be agreed-on assignments. The person conducting an assignment should believe he or she can deliver the product stipulated in the assignment. It also is advisable to establish ground rules about reporting unanticipated problems in carrying out evaluation assignments. When a staff member has trouble with an assignment, project resources are wasted unless management knows and adjusts quickly.

Evaluation management also should encourage staff development by including some new challenges in individual assignments. Each evaluation staff member needs the opportunity to grow professionally without being overwhelmed by the new challenges. Evaluation management should know the next level of challenge suitable for each staff member, including the managers themselves.

Formalizing Assignments

When making an assignment, evaluation management should formalize an agreement about the assignment with the affected evaluation staff members. Assignments should be codified in an oral or written agreement in which the level of detail is roughly consistent with the amount of resources to be employed for the assignment, its relative importance, and the certainty that the assigned individuals will accomplish the desired product on schedule and within budget. The agreement should concentrate on specifying the expected product, the major milestones in product development, the resources set aside for the assignment, and the expected completion date.

While the provisions of an assignment agreement are important, examples that illustrate the expected product of the assignment are invaluable. They facilitate clear dialogue and decisions about executing an assignment and show how the work was or might be carried out. The best illustrative materials are products of assignments from similar studies, such as a spreadsheet used to track survey follow-up or a sample analysis output report. If actual examples are not available, sketches and outlines expressing the content of the assigned product should be substituted.

The flowchart in Figure 20.2 is a schematic representation of the placement process for child abuse and neglect cases. The flowchart was used to guide the effort of evaluators assigned to develop a written description of foster care placement avoidance programs in five localities. The flowchart emphasizes the common core elements of case placement operations: the points where the evaluators' descriptions should focus. Describing each local placement avoidance program using a common definition of core elements sets the stage for identifying meaningful differences in operations among the five programs.

The form of the assignment agreements will vary, depending on the management style of those making the assignment. The use of written agreements has the advantage of creating a record and reference source for the future. Oral agreements are suitable when the purpose and scope of the assignment are very clear to all parties and the assignment is routine for that staff member or group. Such agreements are also suitable when a history of effective unwritten agreements exists for a similar assignment to the same individual or group. However, when evaluation management has any doubt about assignment completion, it is better to have written notes documenting key aspects of the assignment. Initiating a project activity based solely on word of mouth and attempting to recall an assignment from memory can create unnecessary confusion and uncertainty.

Finally, the written terms of an assignment agreement can be used again in other evaluations, but there must be safeguards against inappropriate use of the assignment language in a later project. Once an assignment has been documented, there may be a tendency to reuse the language just because it was already written, without regard for how it should be tailored for its use in a current evaluation.

Figure 20.2. Flowchart to Guide Descriptions of How Local Child Welfare Programs Work

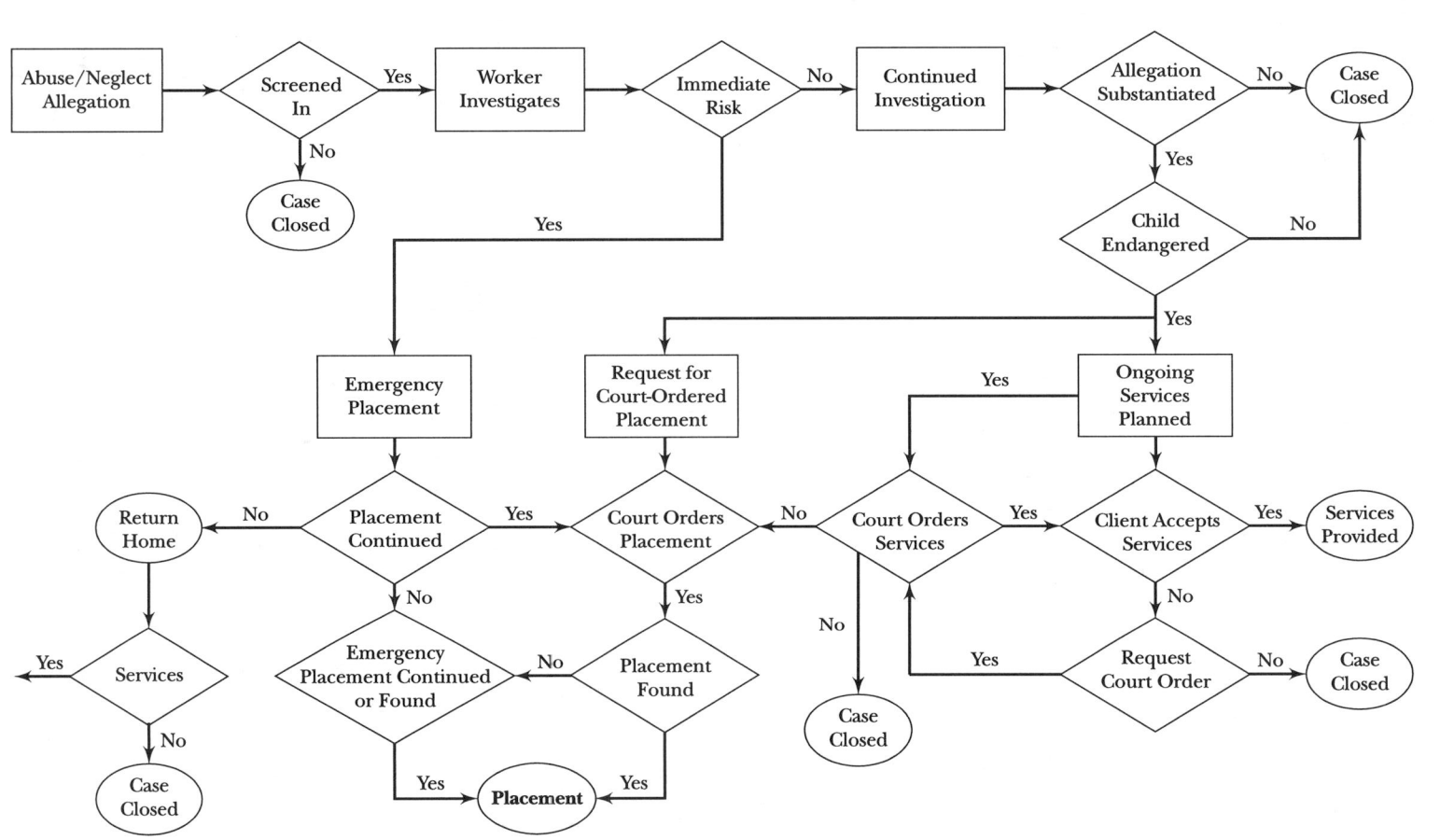

Source: Kaye and Bell (Feb. 1993).

Monitoring Interim Progress

Imagine that despite monitoring reports indicating timely progress, evaluation management discovers that data collection will not be completed until well after the planned completion date because interim monitoring has not been penetrating enough to detect the true extent of technical progress. Was the most common progress monitoring error committed: Did management mistakenly accept the appearance of originally planned levels of effort and expenditures as commensurate levels of technical progress? Interim monitoring should accurately assess the status of an evaluation at specific points in time. In addition to the technical progress on evaluation products, the monitoring reports should inform evaluation management about the calendar time and labor spent and remaining for each product.

Systematic monitoring also should provide incentives for staff to accomplish evaluation products. Interim progress monitoring should be a constructive endeavor that encourages creativity and recognition of evaluation opportunities and problems. In short, the monitoring process should help evaluation management and staff to complete a high-quality, useful evaluation on budget and schedule. It also should identify opportunities to enhance the value of the evaluation product. The following suggestions should help readers avoid common monitoring problems by focusing on well-specified product milestones, well-timed monitoring reports, and effective use of monitoring information.

Well-Specified Milestones

Evaluation assignments should have progress milestones for each evaluation product covered by the assignment. The milestones should be part of a description of the monitoring process for that assignment. When errors of omission or commission made during assignment lead to poorly specified product milestones, interim monitoring may be ineffective in pinpointing the true status of evaluation product completion. In other words, if the milestone events for completing an evaluation product are wrong, it is likely that the product will be incomplete, delayed, or flawed. For example, when an evaluation spans more than one agency, the completion of a cross-agency data collection protocol is specified as the next-to-last milestone in creating data collection plans. Presuming that creation of a cross-agency data collection protocol is feasible, the last milestone is a brief, low-intensity period of initial data acquisition during which individual agencies try to transfer the data stipulated in the cross-agency protocol. Such a trial often reveals that a separate milestone is needed to complete agency-specific data collection protocols because of the unique characteristics of local data systems. It simply may not be possible to use a generic data collection protocol without carefully tailoring it to each agency's circumstances.

Well-Timed Monitoring

Interim progress monitoring absorbs evaluation resources. Too much monitoring can cause unwarranted loss of resources, but too little monitoring may permit the squandering of project resources on unproductive efforts. Progress monitoring is appropriate when the forward momentum of the project is maintained or enhanced through monitoring. Effort should not be distracted from productive project activity for monitoring purposes, nor should evaluation resources be wasted on unproductive efforts because monitoring did not detect a difficulty.

To establish the monitoring schedule, start with the intended completion dates for major products, such as completion of a literature review or a data collection and analysis plan, and move backward. Monitoring milestones for each major product should be defined by considering the steps in product development. Consider the time and effort needed previously to accomplish each step. Sometimes a step may involve a small amount of labor but require substantial calendar time. An example of a calendar-sensitive activity is acquisition of data from a government agency. However, any activity requiring support and effort outside the span of control of evaluation management should be more carefully considered in setting a monitoring schedule.

A monitoring approach based solely on elapsed time (such as monthly progress markers unrelated to product completion) should be avoided. Such an approach complicates efforts to establish coherent staff assignments because monitoring by elapsed time disregards the natural development cycle for evaluation products. For some assignments, monthly or quarterly monitoring will create opportunities for an inexperienced staff member to flounder for lengthy periods because the time between monitoring reports is too long. For other assignments, progress will be reported prematurely, or no progress will be reported because the monitoring date has arrived before a natural point of closure has been reached in developing the evaluation product. Both occurrences may lead to missed opportunities for evaluation management to digest interim findings and redirect the project effort accordingly. These are forgone chances to optimize the evaluation investment.

Ineffective Use of Monitoring

Well-defined interim milestones and well-timed monitoring do not guarantee effective use of progress monitoring information. The managers who conduct the monitoring must be able to interpret monitoring information and respond appropriately. They must be able to engage in constructive discussions with those whose work is being monitored and know how to revise subsequent assignments in response to monitoring findings. It is not enough for senior management to establish a workable monitoring process. In a larger evaluation, it is especially important that the mid- and lower-level management staff also be able to establish workplace monitoring processes. They must be able to interpret monitoring data and adjust staff assignments accordingly.

A common failing of evaluation monitoring is that the project director and senior project management assume that their monitoring approach will translate automatically into effective monitoring by lower-echelon evaluation management staff. They should appreciate the need to orient and train these staff and understand the level monitoring involvement required of senior evaluation management staff. When there is uncertainty about the quality of monitoring, senior management staff should heighten their own participation at all levels of the project. Since carrying out an evaluation is a dynamic activity, it is unlikely that a monitoring plan can be used without adaptation during the life of the project.

There are many other ways interim progress monitoring can derail. Milestones may be well defined but the indicators of milestone achievement flawed (an irony for an evaluation project). A common mistake, for example, is acceptance that an assignment is completed because of the existence of a draft document. Without a careful review of the document, managers cannot establish that the assignment is complete.

Ensuring Product Quality and Usefulness

Imagine that it is six months after an evaluation was completed. The project director is inquiring about the response to program recommendations included in the final report. These alternatives were well received initially by the evaluation sponsor, but no action to implement program changes has occurred. Through further inquiry, the evaluation director learns that the program staff were unable to plan implementation of the recommendations. They were uncertain about how to conceptualize change in their operating system without harming performance. They also were reluctant to accept certain crucial findings contained in the report that established the rationale for the suggested alternatives. In short, although methodology experts had attested to the competence of the evaluation, key people who had to act on the evaluation did not accept its credibility or could not implement the recommendations easily.

How should evaluation management ensure that those who must act on the recommendations perceive them as valuable and useful? Certainly appropriate methodology and high-quality execution are central to evaluation quality, but they are not sufficient standards if program policy and management decision makers are expected to act on the evaluation findings and recommendations. These groups will want to see convincing evidence that the evaluators understand the subject program, that the evaluation is based on appropriate data, that recommendations are clear about why and how to modify the program, and what is likely to happen if the recommended changes are made. When an evaluation offers ill-founded recommendations, these often demonstrate that the evaluators did not understand the program's purpose and operations. For example, evaluation management may not comprehend that operational objectives for a program are set at the local level. If this is so, the evaluators may mistake the lack of strong national objectives as a sign of a weak program performance and recommend formulation of clearer national objectives. In such a case, if evaluation management had used appropriate quality assurance steps such as checking carefully with program staff at both the national and local levels early in developing the evaluation, the findings and recommendations might not have been so divorced from the program reality. The quest for high-quality, useful evaluation products should permeate all facets of evaluation management, from clarifying the evaluation mandate to the final polishing of the last deliverable report. Report outlines, preliminary briefings, and draft reports are useful for gaining agreement about the content and style of written documents. These practices help to shape evaluation reports so they can be used by sponsors and program staff.

Usually the written reports developed in an evaluation are the main tangible evidence that an evaluation has occurred. The reports must convey the essence of an evaluation in informative and understandable terms. An effective approach to ensure that project reports meet this requirement is to develop written reports in four steps, with involvement in each step by the sponsor, subject program staff, and, if warranted, outside experts. This approach is predicated on establishing agreement about the content of the report through outlines and a briefing before extensive effort is spent writing the report text.

Step 1: Outline the Project Report

The outline explains the project purpose, the titles and intended contents of the chapters and sections, and the planned length and style of the document. Agreement on this outline should be accomplished very early in the project, or as part of the original clarification of the evaluation mandate. In fact, one way to codify the technical aspect of the mandate, such as the evaluation, purpose, and scope, is to develop a detailed outline of the planned evaluation report. Each report outline should be referenced as a source of guidance often in the early preparation stages and throughout data collection and analysis.

The possible need to modify the outline of a report should be part of the dialogue among evaluation management and evaluation staff, as well as sponsor and subject program representatives.

Step 2: Construct a Briefing Package

At the earliest possible point in the project, construct a briefing package following the outline that covers the key points to be contained in each chapter and section of the report. The objective is to summarize the essence of the report before it is written. In a briefing format using exhibits and other short forms of written communication, such as bulleted lists, the content of the forthcoming report can be discussed without spending the time required in developing high-quality narrative text. With the project results presented as early as possible in preliminary form, the evaluation staff and sponsor can identify strengths and weaknesses while time and resources are still available for making corrections.

Step 3: Producing the Draft Report

The first two steps of report development are comparatively inexpensive, designed to convey report contents without incurring the cost of writing fully developed documents. The third step is normally one of the most expensive evaluation activities because it involves producing a full-scale draft report.

Although this report should be complete and readable, the emphasis should be on technical content. Editing and polishing the document should not be done until the technical contents of the final report are reviewed and confirmed. The draft final report should be subjected to intensive review by the sponsor, subject program staff, and any outside experts included in the project as advisers. However, dissemination of the draft report should be carefully controlled; evaluation management should limit reviewers to those who are familiar with the project and understand that the draft report is not a final product.

Step 4: Polishing the Final Document

The final step in report development is polishing the written document to ensure effective communication of the evaluation results to the intended evaluation audience. Since this phase can absorb resources that might have been more usefully spent in other project activities, it is wise to avoid overpolishing. Some reports have very limited audiences that do not require the same level of editing needed for a high-profile document distributed to the public. At one extreme, this final step in evaluation may involve restructuring and rewriting the draft report to strengthen its power to communicate to the general public. This is done without altering the essential meaning of the technical evaluation information contained in the accepted draft report. It requires a combination of well-developed technical knowledge of the evaluation and sound writing skills. At the other extreme, polishing may involve only light editing to address grammar, spelling, and punctuation and to correct other minor mistakes that may appear in text or exhibits.

Conclusion

Although attention to the six areas of project management examined in this chapter will not guarantee a well-managed evaluation, it should help to avert many of the most common causes of ineffectively managed evaluations. Even so, evaluation management must be alert to other problems that may compromise achievement of the evaluation mandate. Lapses in general work planning, record keeping, or data collection and analysis supervision, for example, may also affect the way an evaluation turns out.

Exhibit 20.1 summarizes the practical suggestions for the six areas of evaluation management discussed in this chapter. The seventeen suggestions listed in the exhibit should be addressed by evaluation project management regardless of the size of an evaluation. The cost of evaluation management activities should be accepted as an integral and necessary part of the cost of conducting an evaluation. Wherever possible, evaluation management costs should be contained by imaginatively integrating evaluation management and technical evaluation activities. In a well-managed project, there is a tight connection between evaluation management and the technical conduct of the evaluation.

The cost of evaluation management must be appropriate. Small-scale evaluations cannot afford the burden of overly rigorous evaluation management activities, such as extensive written documentation of the evaluation mandate or staff assignments. More difficult evaluations require higher levels of evaluation management. If the sponsor is inconsistent about the evaluation mandate, more attention will be needed in this area. Similarly, if there are concerns that evaluation staff are not optimally qualified, more attention must be paid to whether the proper expertise is being applied to each important evaluation assignment.

The goal of evaluation management and the aims in each management area apply even in very small-scale evaluations. Suggestions must be adapted depending on the type, size, duration, and other distinguishing characteristics of the evaluation project. A small project conducted in fewer than thirty days by a single evaluator would not involve use of a staff qualifications matrix, for example. Nevertheless, a solo evaluator needs to carry out a careful review of

Exhibit 20.1. Practical Suggestions for Evaluation Management

---

Developing rational proposals
1. Develop proposals that satisfactorily match staff and other resources to the evaluation products that are promised.

Clarifying the evaluation mandate
2. Gain agreement on the evaluation mandate before or very early in the evaluation.
3. Check this agreement periodically during contacts with evaluation clients and sponsors.
4. Minimize the cost of maintaining agreement by integrating checks on the mandate with technical evaluation activities, such as client review of a draft data collection and analysis protocol.
5. Beware of tacit agreements.

Staffing and organizing for results
6. Use a staffing matrix and observations about interpersonal communication skills to facilitate initial selection of staff members.
7. Organize evaluation staff members into teams based on project tasks, evaluation methodology, or subject matter responsibilities.
8. In evaluations with two or more teams, form a synthesis group to foster coherent effort across the technical teams.

Making assignments productive
9. Be very clear about each assignment's product, outcome, or end point, as well as resources and expected completion date.
10. If possible, use well-chosen examples from similar projects to illustrate expected products.
11. Formalize assignment agreements.

Monitoring interim progress
12. Don't confuse expected activity and expenditure levels with commensurate technical progress.
13. Time monitoring episodes to complement and not impede product development.
14. Ensure that project management staff are effective monitors.

Ensuring product quality and usefulness
15. Involve the sponsor, program, and other representatives of the evaluation audience in a four-step report development process.
16. Start early in the project with an outline, and then use a briefing to gain agreement about the content of the report.
17. Solidify the agreement on report content through follow-up briefings on draft products. Reserve polishing and editing resources until the technical content is finalized.

---

his or her personal qualifications for the evaluation at hand. It is necessary to gauge the presence of shortcomings in substantive, methodological, or interpersonal qualifications, even if only one person is conducting the evaluation. In a one-person evaluation, qualification deficits can be compensated for through the use of publications and the help of others who have the needed expertise. Discussions with the client can be structured to fill gaps in the evaluators' substantive knowledge of the policy or program being evaluated.

Ineffective management can dramatically influence the contribution made by an evaluation. If the aim of the evaluation remains in focus and appropriate staff and other evaluation resources are applied to well-defined activities consistent with those aims, the possibility that the evaluation will generate valuable knowledge and spark improvements in policies and programs should increase. Put simply, a valid and useful evaluation depends as much on effective management as on elegant study design.

References

James Bell Associates. "Feasibility of Evaluating the State Court Improvement Program," Vol. 2: "Evaluability Assessment Site Visit Summaries." Arlington, Va.: James Bell Associates, June 2003.

Kaye, E., and Bell, J. "Evaluation Design for Family Preservation Programs." Arlington, Va.: James Bell Associates, Feb. 1993.

21

Writing for Impact

George F. Grob

The objective of this chapter is to explain how to write compelling evaluation reports that convince readers of the findings and promote taking action in response. Evaluators take great pride in their work. What is especially rewarding for them is knowing that their studies make a difference, that positive changes will result from their clients' taking action based on their findings and recommendations. Of course, the best way to achieve such results is to produce rock-solid reports with strong evidence and practical advice. However, the way the reports are written also matters. That is what this chapter is all about—not just writing well but also writing for impact.

Effective writing involves an interplay and command of three facets of communication:

- The message: What the writer wants people to remember after they have read the report
- The audience: Individuals the writer wants to read or hear about the study
- The medium: The many factors that carry the message—words, pages, reports, typeface, graphics, paper, ink, color, computer screens, slides, newsletters, panel discussions, and the like.

This article was written by George F. Grob in his private capacity. No official support or endorsement by the Office of Inspector General, U.S. Department of Health and Human Services, is intended or implied.

These three facets of effective writing are highly interrelated, but it is convenient to discuss them one at time.

The Message

The message is the most important of the three facets. This is what the writer wants people to remember—the core message and the related findings and recommendations.

The Mom Test

No report will matter much unless it passes what I call the "Mom Test." Imagine that you have just finished nine months of work on an evaluation of community policing. You have delivered the report and are waiting to hear from the client, your home town local government. You stop by to see your family while you are in town and bring with you a fresh printed copy, with its back spine as yet uncracked, and slide it across the table to your mother, who is serving your favorite cookies and home-brewed coffee. She looks at it lovingly and says: "We're all so proud, Chris. What does it say?" And you answer, "Mom, it says . . . "

That's the "Mom Test": being able to finish the sentence. You can add one more short sentence if you need to, but no more. You have to do it in a way that your mother can easily understand you. Your summary has to be simple but also specific, insightful, inspiring, and interesting, and it must elicit a response something like: "Well I sure hope they do something about it."

Here are some examples that pass the test:

> "Police officers on the beat in a community make a big difference. Now is not the time to cut funding for them."

> "Only 80 percent of children entering school in our town are fully inoculated against common childhood diseases. The average in our state is 90 percent."

> "The reading improvement program started last year in our schools seems to be working. Reading levels are up significantly in every classroom where it was tried."

Failure to pass the Mom Test is the most common and significant weakness in evaluation reports that fail to inspire action. The main reason for failing the test is not the difficulty finding words to succinctly express the report's message. *It is because there is no message.* The author may have provided lots of findings and good recommendations, but no kernel, no unforgettable nub that attracts attention and compels the reader's interest. This point cannot be emphasized enough:

- An evaluation report can have impact only if readers can discern its main message.
- They can do so only if the evaluator expresses it.
- The evaluator cannot express it without having one.

Findings

Much more is needed to convey the results of an evaluation study than a simple one- or two-sentence main message. Clients and stakeholders expect to see detailed findings. From the perspective of writing for impact, the following principles should guide the formulation of findings.

- Tell them something they don't already know.
- Be reasonable.
- Be concise.

Most of an evaluator's clients and readers understand their field of work very well. Still, they are hoping that an independent, creative, intelligent professional can help them find what has eluded them: new insights. Hence, the first principle is to tell them something new. The reaction that evaluators want to obtain from other stakeholders is, "Thanks. This was helpful." Stakeholders who react that way will give the findings and recommendations serious attention, and the evaluators will make a difference. If not, they will harvest indifference at best and resistance at worst.

The principle of reasonableness does not mean, "Tell them what they want to hear." Clients can handle criticism. In fact, it is independence and professionalism that they most value in the evaluator. That is the reason they are willing to pay good money to obtain the evaluator's assistance. So evaluators should tell it like it is—but be measured and reasonable in doing so.

The third principle, conciseness, is the child of the Mom Test. Readers can remember about two to five key ideas, and no more. If there are too many findings to reduce to five, they can be grouped into categories. Then the writer can summarize the findings in each category into a single broad finding and let the detailed findings be part of the explanation of the broad ones.

Options and Recommendations

To have impact, an evaluator usually needs to offer solutions to the problems discussed in the findings, although there are some exceptions. For example, a finding may be so startling that just stating it and letting others deal with its consequences might be the most effective way to generate solutions. Or the study may find no problems to correct, just a big misunderstanding. But these are exceptions. Most of the time, recommendations are needed and appreciated. Here are a couple of principles to use in formulating them.

- Be practical. Temporarily step into your clients' shoes while formulating solutions.
- Give lots of options. Big decisions are almost never made by just a few people. Broad consultation and ultimately consensus are needed to gain acceptance of ways to solve problems that have eluded the very best professionals in any field of endeavor. It is far better to offer a half-dozen ideas than to insist on just a couple. In fact, the evaluator might well want to label the solutions as "Options for Improvement" instead of "Recommendations." Everyone wants the former; sometimes they resent the latter.

Methodology

Evaluation reports need to describe the methods used to obtain findings. The goal here is to explain just the right amount—not too much, not too little. The advice is:

- Don't get carried away.
- Still, describe the whole thing.
- Briefly discuss its shortcomings.

Evaluators are naturally keenly interested in their methodologies and need no encouragement to talk about it. However, clients and stakeholders are mostly interested in findings and recommendations. They will start by assuming that the evaluator has done a professional job and are not interested in plowing through page after page of methodology.

At the same time, advocates or defensive managers who do not like the findings and recommendations will immediately attack the methodology. A full description of the methodology will uphold the findings in the report, the integrity of the evaluator, and even the evaluation profession itself. Hence, to have impact, the evaluator faces a significant challenge: keeping the description of methodology succinct yet complete and compelling. Here are some hints on how to achieve this balance:

- Keep the description of methodology very brief in the executive summary—no more than one paragraph.
- Put a page or two in the body of the report.

- Provide a full description in an appendix.
- Offer ways for the reader to contact the author for more information about the methods.

Evaluators sometimes take too narrow a view of their own methodologies. They focus on their surveys, correlation analyses, focus groups, and other such techniques. They sometimes regard their literature reviews, stakeholder consultations, and analyses of laws and regulations as background work that precedes the formulation of their methodology. However, their clients think that these chores are important too, and the simple recitation that these tasks have been performed adds much credibility to the report.

No methodology is perfect. There are always shortcomings, and if the evaluator does not acknowledge them, others certainly will highlight them in the public comments that will inevitably follow. But if the evaluator discusses them briefly, the report comes across as quite professional. It is ironic that pointing out the flaws of one's own methodology gives it greater credibility, but that is the case. At the same time, the "shortcomings" section does not have to be lengthy or exhaustive. There is no point in going on and on, telling readers why they should not believe anything they read in the report.

The Audience

A report's audience is the set of people the evaluator wants to read it and be influenced by it. From the perspective of obtaining impact, the audience can be more precisely defined as the set of people who are or should be involved in deciding matters covered in the report. They consist of two groups: thought leaders and other interested persons.

Thought Leaders

In every field of endeavor is a group of people recognized as the movers and shakers. They are the thought leaders. An understanding of the existence and functioning of thought leaders is extremely important:

- An evaluation report will have no impact unless it impresses the thought leaders.
- Thought leaders will not be impressed unless they read the report.

For an evaluation report to have impact requires persuading the movers and shakers of the merits of its findings and recommendations. No significant action will occur until they all agree, or at least agree to disagree. But action *will* occur if they do.

The set of thought leaders for a particular evaluation is concrete. Their names can be listed. In a large corporation, they include board members, the chief executive officer, the chief financial officer, key stockholders, and heads of large operating departments or services sectors. In an accounting or law firm, they are the partners and administrators. In the federal government, they consist of key members of Congress and their staff, executives of affected federal agencies, representatives of industry and beneficiary groups or activists, and the Office of Management and Budget. In a nonprofit foundation, they are the board members and top staff. On a smaller scale, the thought leaders are the owners and managers of a small business.

In order for a report to have impact, the evaluator must make sure that the evaluation results are known by the thought leaders. The following actions are therefore essential in getting the thought leaders to read the report:

- Make a list of the thought leaders having influence on matters discussed in the evaluation report.
- Send them all a copy of the report.
- Make the report very easy for them to read.

Other Interested Persons

In addition to the thought leaders, numerous individuals who are not influential might very well become so—such as students and researchers. Many others will not care about the topic of the report—until they read it. Through reports, evaluators can inspire others to become movers and shakers. Think back on your own development and recall the things that influenced you to become an evaluator or a leader in a subject that you are now evaluating. Chances are these included reports, articles, and books.

The problem is that evaluators cannot make a list of these people, yet need to get the report to them. The way to do this is to get reports published and disseminated through professional journals, newsletters, and books. Electronic outlets are now ubiquitous. More on this later.

The Medium

Reports and other publications convey a message using several different carriers simultaneously, each one interacting with the other and all of them important. I am using the word *medium* to refer not to the general, classic type of publication—television, newspapers, radio—but to cover anything necessary to deliver the message: the color of the ink, the grammar of the sentence, the size of the paper, the method of binding the reports, the writing style, the U.S. mail, the Internet, the type size, the fonts, overheads, television sets, newspapers, newsletters, panel discussions, and much more. All of these are important.

The Six Basic Formats

If I were writing this chapter ten years ago, I would have started by describing a convenient standard report format—something to follow and deviate from. Today, however, electronic information technology has completely changed the way we communicate. Almost anyone can produce, and virtually everyone consumes—and expects to find material on—videos, overhead projector slides, PowerPoint presentations, audio recordings, Web pages, and CD-ROMs, among many choices. Newsletters abound, all hungry for material to fill in the white spaces before deadline. Cottage advocates open Web sites, publish newsletters using Internet listservs, and send messages to worldwide audiences. How can an evaluator efficiently get the message of a report out to the world through all the different media that are available?

The answer is to concentrate on the message and to become facile at using electronic processors to adjust it to the publication format and medium at hand. To do so requires mastering communication at approximately six levels of detail and format styles:

- The Mom Test summary
- The killer paragraph
- The outline
- The two-page executive summary
- The ten-page report
- Technical reports

We will look at the six basic formats. As an aid to the discussion, I have created examples of the formats using material from a hypothetical evaluation of a low-income energy assistance program of the mythical Cobalt Electric Power Company. I will illustrate the first four of the six basic formats as I explain each one. The last two formats—the ten-page report and technical reports—are too long for this book. However, the principles for writing them will hopefully be clear enough when we get to those topics. We begin with an eclectic set of notes embodying various facts about the methodology, findings, recommendations, and other initial material. This set of facts, shown in the box, is not an example of effective writing. Rather, I will select from this material and recast it to shape various pieces of the basic formats.

Cobalt Low-Income Energy Assistance Program Study Facts

We analyzed a stratified random sample of five thousand records from the Cobalt County Electric Power Company's (CCEPC) Customer Billing and Payment Accounting and Control (CBPAC) System. Half of the records were drawn from records of customers whose bills were reduced because of their participation in an energy assistance program that was designed to mitigate the burden of electric heating and air-conditioning costs for low-income families; the other half were drawn from families not receiving such relief. The bills we looked at were for the coldest months of the fiscal year (December 2001 and January and February 2002). We also sent a mail questionnaire to each customer in the sample. The response rate was 72 percent for those receiving relief and 66 percent for regular customers.

Based on a projection of our sample, we found that 2.5 percent of all CBPAC bills had one or more errors. This included 0.8 percent mailed to incorrect addresses, 1.3 percent with incorrect personal identifiers, 0.5 percent returned as undeliverable with no forwarding address, 0.5 percent delivered after payment due date due to original misrouting, 1.2 percent billed for the incorrect amount, 1.0 percent with excess billing amounts. Excess billing amounts averaged $24 ($16 to $32 at the ninetieth percent confidence level).

Differences in error rates between the energy assistance beneficiaries and other customers were not statistically significant at the 90 percent level in all categories. CCEPC customer satisfaction ratings were 74 percent (62 to 86 percent) for customers receiving billing relief and 72 percent (59 to 85 percent) for all others. Ninety-two percent (85 to 99 percent) of CCEPC customers not receiving relief said they understood CCEPC's Customer Billing Appeal and Conflict Resolution (CPACR) procedures; 4.5 percent (2.7 to 6.3 percent) had contacted the customer service department during the preceding year, with 68 percent of these satisfied that they had been treated competently by CCEPC appeals and customer relations personnel. However, only 60 percent (54 to 78 percent) of customers receiving energy assistance said they understood the CPACR system. Only 1.5 percent (0.6 to 2.4 percent) had contacted the customer service department, with 48 percent of these satisfied that CCEPC personnel had treated them competently. Twenty percent (15 to 25 percent) of regular customers and 48 percent (36 to 60 percent) of the assisted customers reported that they had difficulty understanding key details of their monthly bills such as stepwise changes in utility rates based on consumption levels, seasonally differentiated rates, methods and amounts for calculating penalties for late payment, and how to call for more information.

> We recommend that CCEPC: (1) set performance goals to improve billing accuracy and customer relations; (2) establish refresher training courses for CPACR ADP operations staff to ensure that all current procedures are routinely followed; (3) institute sampling-based quality control reviews to detect and correct CBPAC systems programming and other error sources for incorrectly labeled billing addresses; (4) immediately obtain qualified outside technical assistance to review and correct all programming and administrative errors leading to errors on billing amounts, with particular attention to overbilling; (5) institute sampling-based quality control reviews to detect and correct such errors; (6), based on points 4 and 5, establish appropriate internal controls to prevent errors on billing amounts; (7) rewrite information materials regarding the CPACR appeal rights and procedures to ensure that they can easily be understood by CCEPC customers; (8) conduct case reviews to determine the reasons for dissatisfaction of CCEPC customers with respect to appeal procedures, especially lower-paying customers; (9) based on point 8, provide training for CCEPC staff who interface with customers on appeal matters; and reformat and rewrite monthly bill statements to make them more understandable to CCEPC customers, especially lower-paying customers receiving energy assistance relief.

The Mom Test Summary. If you skipped the section on the Mom Test, go back and read it now. The following box provides a Mom Test summary for Cobalt's energy assistance program.

The Mom Test Summary for the Cobalt Report

The Cobalt Low-Income Energy Assistance Program suffers from shortcomings of the power company's billing system, which is riddled with errors. Some beneficiaries get charged too much, and they have difficulty understanding their bills and appeal rights.

The Killer Paragraph. The one or two sentences written to pass the Mom Test are needed mostly for oral presentation of the study results—the quick statement at the beginning of the meeting and the explanation in the hallway on the way to the meeting, for example. The equivalent written version is the killer paragraph.

A compelling paragraph can be useful on many occasions. For example, delivery of the report to the client is typically done by letter or memo. The place for the killer paragraph is after the "Dear So-and-So" and the line that says "I am happy to send you the report." At this point, a good, concise paragraph is far more compelling than one or two pages of text. A strong paragraph, because of its short, stand-alone format, cries out: "Bottom line, here's what we found." Once that point is made, don't dilute it with more words. Anyone who wants more can read the report.

The killer paragraph is a lot more too: It is the abstract that appears first in the version of the report that gets published in a professional journal. It is the first paragraph in the news article that someone else writes about the findings. It is the brief summary that appears on the first page of a trade group's or professional organization's newsletter that talks about the report on the inside pages. It is the description that appears as a compilation of studies being sent to some important person. It is what shows up in a literature review. It is what makes it on the computer screen when someone does a word search and the report makes the list.

The killer paragraph may be the only thing that most people will ever know about all that work the team accomplished. It had better be good. Here are some tips on how to write this paragraph and an example.

Tips on Writing the Killer Paragraph

- Findings and recommendations. These are the most important parts of the report. Use most of the words on them.
- Methodology. The least important part of the paragraph is the methodology. Try to make only a passing reference to it.
- Concreteness. Do not just serve up sweeping generalities. Include concrete facts—numbers and examples.
- Prioritize. There is no need to mention every finding and recommendation, just the major ones.
- No abbreviations. Do not use any abbreviations or technical language.
- Brevity. Aim for about twelve lines or a quarter of a page of text. Never exceed one-third of a page.

Killer Paragraph for the Cobalt Report

In response to concerns raised by family welfare advocates about billing errors, we reviewed the low-income energy assistance program of the Cobalt County Electric Power Company. We found that errors were commonplace, not just for needy customers whose bills were reduced, but for all customers. Fully 2.5 percent of bills in our random sample had some kind of error, such as the wrong amount, incorrect address, or incorrect personal identifier;

1.2 percent of customers were overbilled an average of $24. Forty percent of those receiving relief told us they did not understand their appeal rights, and almost half of them said they had trouble reading their bills. We recommend stronger internal controls to reduce errors and a consumer education initiative to make billing statements and explanations of appeal rights easier to understand.

The Outline. Few other instruments achieve emphasis and clarity of thought as effectively as outlines do. Outlining helps the writer decide what is important and helps the listeners or readers. A topic outline provides a visual reinforcement of an oral presentation. It makes it easier for clients to organize their own thoughts, and it helps them remember what has been said or written. These features make a one-page outline highly useful to pass around the table at the start of the presentation on the report's findings and recommendations.

A sentence outline, in which the first thought (at least) of each major section is a sentence, is a very handy briefing document that can stand on its own. Forcing yourself to render the main thoughts in sentences is a good discipline to promote clarity, precision, and emphasis. More important, it will become the backbone of the executive summary and the report itself, and a powerful tool for communicating its findings and recommendations.

A topic outline, which uses phrases instead of sentences for key ideas, is useful as the table of contents for the report and as a briefing document or visual aid when giving an oral briefing. It is less tedious to read than a sentence outline, and sometimes makes it easier to follow major threads of thought.

For all these reasons, it is worthwhile to take the trouble to prepare an outline. The topic outline for the Cobalt report in the shaded box below and on the next page illustrates how integral the outline is to the report itself and to other documents derived from it.

Topical Outline for the Cobalt Report

Methodology
    Billing Records
        Random sample, 5,000 records
        Stratified by assistance status
    Customer Experience
        Mail Survey
Findings

Errors
   Billing Errors
      2.5 Percent Error Rate Overall
      1.2 Percent Billed for Wrong Amount
      1.0 Percent Overbilled
   Other Errors
      Addresses
      Personal Identifiers
  Customer Perspectives
   Most Customers Coping
   Problems for Needy Payers
      Appeals
      Difficulty Understanding Bills
Recommendations
  Set Performance Standards
  Strengthen Internal Controls
  Clarify Appeal Rights
  Make Bills Easier to Understand

The Two-Page Executive Summary. For serious readers, the two-page executive summary is the most important part of the study. The principles for writing it are generally the same as for the paragraph-length version, but with more room to elaborate. The shaded box contains some additional tips. For the entire executive summary for the Cobalt report, see Exhibit 21.1.

Tips on Writing the Executive Summary

- Prioritize. Concentrate on the findings and recommendations.
- Start the findings a third of the way up from the bottom of the first page, or higher.
- Flesh out the recommendations, starting them about the middle of the second page.
- Limit discussion of the methodology. Use no more than a short paragraph to describe the methodology. Use plain language.
- Do not squeeze material in by using small type sizes or narrow margins. The idea is to make the report easy to read, not hard to read.
- Do not use footnotes. Save those for the body of the report (if you need them at all).
- Use headlines, and put the main point of each paragraph in the first sentence.

Exhibit 21.1. Executive Summary for the Cobalt Electric Power Company Low-Income Energy Assistance Program

---

PURPOSE: To evaluate the effectiveness of and client experience with the Cobalt Electric Power Company's low-income energy assistance program.

BACKGROUND: We conducted this study in response to concerns raised by family welfare advocates. We received full cooperation and support from the Cobalt County Electric Power Company, which had voluntarily established a program to reduce the bills of needy families in order to mitigate the burden of heating and air conditioning costs. We analyzed a stratified random sample of 5,000 records from the company's billing and payment system. Our sample was stratified to distinguish low-income families receiving billing relief from other customers. The sample was drawn from bills for the three coldest months of the year. We also sent a mail questionnaire to each customer in the sample. We conducted a literature review of studies on billing systems and customer satisfaction surveys.

FINDINGS

Billing Errors Were Commonplace

We found that errors were commonplace, not just for needy customers whose bills were reduced, but for all customers. Two and a half percent of all bills had one or more errors. Of particular significance, 1.2 percent of customers were billed for the incorrect amount, including 1.0 percent with excess billing amounts. Excess billing amounts averaged $24. Other errors included 0.8 percent mailed to incorrect addresses, 1.3 percent with incorrect personal identifiers, 0.5 percent returned as undeliverable, and 0.5 percent delivered after payment due date due to original misrouting.

The Customer Satisfaction Rate Was 73 Percent

Customer satisfaction rates were 74 percent for customers receiving assistance and 72 percent for all others.

Regular Customers Were Coping with Billing Errors; Needy Families Less So

Reactions to Cobalt's appeals system were mixed. Ninety-two percent of regular customers said they understood the billing appeals procedures; 4.5 percent had called the customer service department during the preceding year, with 68 percent of these satisfied that they had been treated competently by Cobalt's customer relations personnel. But only 60 percent of the needy families receiving assistance said they understood the appeals system; only 1.5 percent had contacted the customer service department for any reason, and 48 percent of these were satisfied that they had been treated competently. These low-income customers also had more

Exhibit 21.1. Executive Summary for the Cobalt Electric Power Company Low-Income Energy Assistance Program, *continued*

---

problems understanding their bills. Twenty percent of regular customers but 48 percent of assisted customers reported that they had difficulty understanding key details such as stepwise changes in utility rates based on consumption levels, seasonally differentiated rates, methods and amounts for calculating penalties for late payment, and how to call for more information.

Options for Improvement

Set Performance Goals

While many specific steps can and will be needed to correct operational problems, a broader initiative may be needed to set the overall framework for improvement and to maintain attention to problems until they are solved and more effective practices are ingrained. We suggest that Cobalt establish long- and near-term goals for such things as:

Overall errors	Customer satisfaction
Address error	Satisfaction with appeal experience
Payment error	Reading levels and fog factor for
Personal identifiers	Billing documents and
Overpayments	Explanation of appeal rights

Strengthen Internal Controls

Provide refresher training for information technology and billing operations staff to ensure that all current procedures are routinely followed. Obtain outside technical assistance to correct all computer programming errors. Use quality control sampling to detect and correct systems programming and other error sources on an ongoing basis.

Clarify Appeal Rights and Strengthen Their Administration

Rewrite information materials regarding the appeal rights and procedures to ensure that they can easily be understood by customers, especially low-income customers. Conduct case reviews to determine the reasons for dissatisfaction of customers with respect to appeal procedures, especially low-income customers. Provide training for Cobalt staff who interface with customers.

Make Bills Easier to Understand

Reformat and rewrite monthly bill statements to make them more understandable, again with special attention to the needs of low-income customers.

The Ten-Page Report. Dollar for dollar, minute for minute, the best investment any of us will ever make in reaching our goal to make a difference in this world is in writing a compelling ten-page report. It will reach more thought leaders than anything you do. It will outlast every speech you ever make. It may reach people not yet born. It can easily be mounted on the Internet, and people may read it without even printing it out. Except for the following section on technical reports, almost everything else discussed in this chapter is how to produce this document.

The ten-page report can be thought of as an extended version of the executive summary. Just flesh out the summary with key facts, explanations, and context.

Technical Reports. For some audiences, a ten-page report is not enough. This is particularly true of researchers, academics, policy analysts, program staff, and specialists, who need context and details about methodology. They won't believe anything in the report unless it contains these additional layers of information and discussion for them. However, there is considerable room in how finely honed and polished this material needs to be, which depends on the subject matter and the field of inquiry. Depending on who you are trying to reach, you may need none, one, or more than one technical report, each tailored to a specific client or audience. The shaded box contains tips about how hard to work and how to package these deeper layers of knowledge.

Tips on Producing Technical Reports

- For executives and senior program managers, skip the appendixes.
- Program and policy staff typically want detailed tables, frequency distributions of responses to survey questions, list of survey recipients, and published guides gathered over the course of the evaluation. Give it to them, but skip the step of writing a high-quality tome. Send them copies of file tables, e-mail them the database versions of this material, or send it to them on a CD.
- For technical experts and some researchers, it is probably worthwhile preparing formal, professional-looking technical reports that look good and are easy to use.
- For the research community at large, the world of academics, and serious policy researchers, take the time to prepare solid, comprehensive reports. Then take the ten-page report, and rename it Executive Report. Now everyone will be pleased. The executives get a report especially written for them; the deep thinkers get what they want—thoughtful context and careful methodology.

Writing Style and Layout

Because evaluators write for impact, they have to capture the reader's attention, hold it, and focus it. However, important people who read a lot also read fast, so evaluators have to write for the way they read, that is, skimming. To really understand how busy people read reports, we first have to understand how they see them.

Layout and Typography. The executive reader, skimming a report, initially reads everything but the plain text. Therefore, the report writer needs to make sure that the important material in the report is announced by the layout, the typography (font characteristics like styles, sizes, bold, and underlining), and the graphics. The general principle for such enhancements is as follows:

- Use layout and typographic enhancements to highlight your main points.
- Don't use such enhancements for anything else.

The box provides tips on what kind of enhancements to use and what kind to avoid.

Tips on Report Enhancements

Enhancements to Use

- Outline. The message is in the outline, so make it jump off the page by using the topic outline as the headlines for the text.
- Bold text. Put the three to five key findings and recommendations in boldface type.
- Type size. Increase the type size a couple of points for the major findings and key recommendations.
- Lists. Put the subfindings and subsidiary recommendations or options into lists.

Enhancements to Avoid

- Excess. Using layout and text enhancements is like shouting. If you shout everything, you shout nothing. Only three to five thoughts should jump off each page.
- Footnotes. Do not put footnotes in the executive summary. Otherwise, a side remark may claim the attention of executive readers.
- All caps. Do not use all caps for more than one or two short words. They are hard to read.

- Abbreviations. Abbreviations, usually written in all caps, look like enhanced text. They are not what the writer wants skim-reading executives to pay attention to.
- Italics. Do not use italics in subheads. Italics are ambiguous enhancements: to some people they appear emphatic; to others they seem more parenthetical. Thus, they may deemphasize things to some people instead of emphasizing them. Instead, use them within the body of the text to distinguish or emphasize words or phrases.

Graphs, Tables, and Other Large Graphics. Graphs, tables, formulas, and pictures, collectively referred to as graphics, are often used in evaluation reports. Readers like them because they highlight and explain complex and important subjects. Readers also like to analyze and interpret them themselves. These kinds of graphics can also be visually interesting, artful, and attractive. Evaluators like them because they are helpful in analyzing data, are effective tools of presentation, and are an expression of their professions. They also like pictures, because they provide entertaining backdrop for what might otherwise be professional-sounding but otherwise dull prose.

Unfortunately, with one exception, these are all reasons evaluators should not put these particular types of graphics in their reports. Here is why not.

Large graphics are far more noticeable than any of the other enhancements already discussed: type size, bold and italic type, lists, and so on. Imagine that you are skimming a report and what you notice are the large graphics—the graphs, pictures, cartoons, tables, and formulas. Now apply the fundamental principal of enhancements: "Use graphics to highlight and clarify your message. Don't use them for anything else." Is the graph you notice while skimming the report about the main message? Is it about the major finding? Is it about the most important recommendation? If so, it should be there. If not, it should not be used.

Graphs and tables are tools for analyzing. They can reveal relationships, distinctions, trends, significant differences, and inconsistencies. They can also be useful for describing and emphasizing. But graphs that are good for analyzing may not be best for describing or emphasizing. For example, a key correlation might have been revealed with the help of a graph with one independent and four dependent variables, dozens of data points, and four different families of curves. But the best graph for emphasizing and explaining the correlation might be a simple straight line that illustrates the general nature and magnitude of the relationship between two variables. Clearly, the second one should go in the report, even if the evaluator is prouder of the first one. The shaded box on the next page gives more advice about graphics.

Figure 21.1 shows a set of slides that illustrate how graphs can be used to tell the story of the report in this chapter.

Tips on Using Large Graphics in Reports

- If you use graphics at all, include one for the most important finding. Otherwise do not use any because anything with a graphic automatically becomes a major finding in the reader's mind, even if it is not one.
- Use one or two graphics in the ten-page report. Put lots more in technical reports, where they are more useful analytically.
- Keep graphics simple. For graphs, use standard types with few bars, lines, and slices. Limit their detail and style to the default versions available in commonly available grant-producing software. They are easy to produce and read.
- Instead of noun phrases, use abbreviated versions of the major findings as titles of graphs and tables in order to drives the point across. See the examples on the next page.
- In a short report, limit the number of rows and columns in tables to two or three each. This creates emphasis. Omit interior lines for demarking rows and columns. They are not needed for short tables and are visually distracting.
- Long, complicated tables can be useful in long, technical reports, although even there they can be boring and exhausting to the reader.
- Make graphs and tables large enough to read. Watch out for tiny text or numbers in the keys, source notes, and axis data points.

Power Writing

Power writing is a writing intended to be very easy to understand and emphatic. It is defined by this purpose and by the techniques that it uses to achieve them. It lends itself very well to use in evaluation reports because it forces the writer to get to the point and enables the reader to grasp the main message and the thread of logic underlying the findings and recommendations. It provides simple explanations but without superficiality. The box explains how to do power writing.

Tips on Power Writing—How to Do It

- The most important sentence of any paragraph is usually the first; sometimes it is the last.
- Try to express the principal thought of each paragraph in the first sentence, which makes skim reading easy.
- Use the last sentence as the power sentence if you need the paragraph

Figure 21.1. Graphs That Tell the Cobalt Story

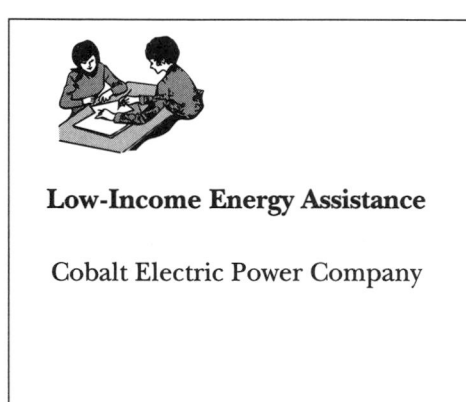

Low-Income Energy Assistance

Cobalt Electric Power Company

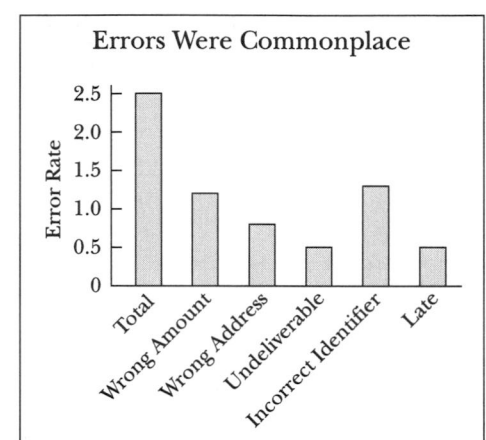

Errors Were Commonplace

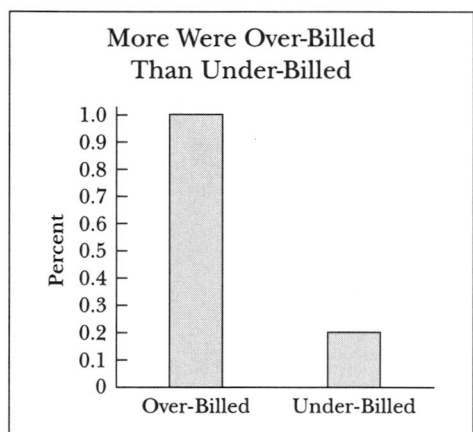

More Were Over-Billed Than Under-Billed

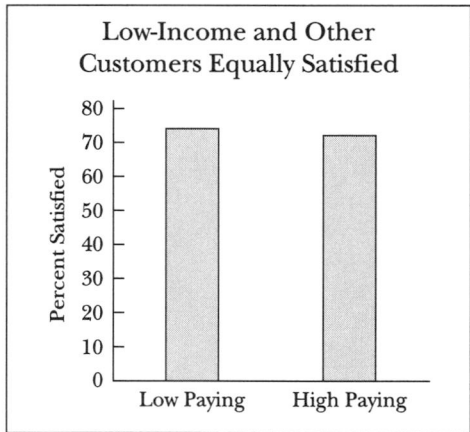

Low-Income and Other Customers Equally Satisfied

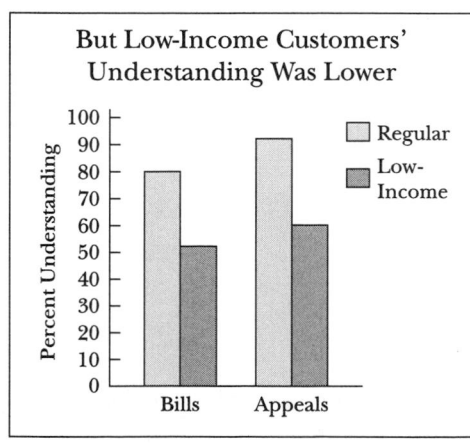

But Low-Income Customers' Understanding Was Lower

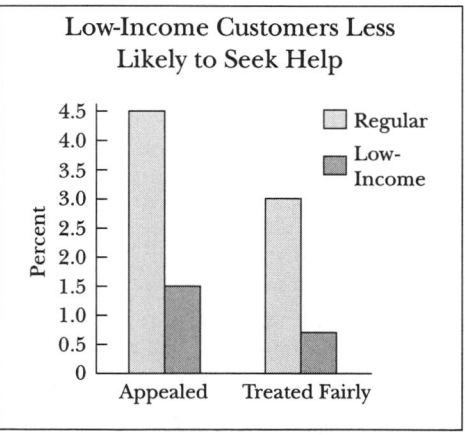

Low-Income Customers Less Likely to Seek Help

itself to introduce the power thought, lead the readers up to it, or surprise them with it.

- Use the body of the paragraph to elaborate on or introduce the power sentence. Elaboration includes evidence, explanation, effects, and pros and cons.
- Readers are put off by long sections of unrelieved type. Try to keep paragraphs down to a quarter of a page, and never more than a third of a page.
- Break sentences into small chunks. Try to avoid more than two lines each. Long sentences are a real put-off for skim readers and can be confusing.
- Avoid technical jargon. Executives are able to express complex thoughts in common language and appreciate others who can do the same thing.
- The passive voice leads to ambiguity and complex sentence structure. It obfuscates. Use it when that is what you want to do (as you may sometimes deliberately and legitimately choose to do). Otherwise use the active voice.
- Do not use abbreviations. Instead, use common nouns, pronouns, and substitute expressions. The context will usually make it clear what you are talking about.

Physical Considerations

Even the best report that serves up insightful findings and practical recommendations using cogent and unforgettable prose and mind-grabbing graphics can be forgettable if some simple but crucial physical considerations have been ignored.

Paper Copies. Most of the thought leaders and key staff will read a paper copy of the report—a copy that someone other than you has given them, a fact that leads to two fundamental principles:

- Make it easy for others to copy the report.
- Make it hard for them to ruin it in the process.

The following box has tips for these principles.

Tips on Getting Others to Make Great Copies of Reports

- Others are far more likely to copy the shorter than the longer technical versions.
- Make it easy to remove the cover. Staple it on, or put the report in a folder or three-ring binder.

- Although copy machines can easily print both sides, more than half the time, it does not happen. If you print on both sides of the paper, odds are high that many readers will get a copy with every other page missing.
- Do not use color, which copies as various shades of gray. It is boring and indistinguishable and gets muddy looking after the third or fourth generation of copying.
- Let the first inside page be a black and white version of the cover. The recipient will instinctively use it for making copies, and all other readers will not be introduced to a murky version of the report with an illegible title, the inevitable result of copying the colored cover.
- Use standard business-size paper so no one has to fuss with different paper trays in copying the report.

Electronic Reports. It is now easy to e-mail the report to others or to get it on the Internet. But the electronic version will also get mangled when opened unless precautions are taken. Remember that the message has to be carried by the graphics, yet that is the part that is least likely to come out as it originally looked.

Even if recipients have the same word processor, even the same version, it will not necessarily come out as in the original on the other end. That is because the font may be slightly different on different computer screens and printers. Even a slight difference can cause a word to slip to the next line, or one from the next line to move up to the previous one. That one word can shorten a paragraph or page by a line, which can leave the reader at the other end with orphan text (the last line of a paragraph at the top of the next page) and widow headers (a header at the bottom of the page whose associated text start on the next page). Far worse, it can cause an entire graph or table to slip to the next page, leaving a huge white space on one page and totally destroying the pagination and layout of the entire rest of the report. Other things can go wrong too. In lists, for example, the tabbing distance will not be the same, and the wraparound programming will be foiled, turning carefully crafted lists into unreadable jumbles of words and spaces.

Evaluators may have to do some extra work to avoid all these problems, but given the pervasive use of e-mail and the Internet, it may be well worth the effort. See the shaded box for some tips on how to do this.

Tips on Producing Reliable Electronic Reports

- Acrobat. Produce an Acrobat version if possible. Almost all computers include at least a read-only version of this program. It can also be readily downloaded for free. It preserves text almost exactly as you see it.

- Web version. Many word processors give the option of saving reports in Web format (HTML). Although it looks different from the written report, you can edit the Web version to make it clear and attractive.
- Web posting. If you can, post a Web version of the report on the Web and send recipients the Web address. You can also e-mail a click-on Web link quite easily, which is universally readable and transmits quickly, or copy it into an e-mail, relieving recipients of the chore of pulling down an attachment. Be careful with the spacing, though. Do not use the computer's tab, insert, or centering features. Instead, type spaces one at a time to achieve these effects.
- Plain text. Produce a plain text version of the report, relying on spacing and capital letters for formatting and text enhancements. This is easy to do for the short version of the report. The plain text version is universally readable and transmits quickly. You can also copy it into your e-mail.

Presentations. A speech or presentation can make a powerful impression on others. If these are stakeholders or other important people, this is an unparalleled opportunity to persuade them of the wisdom of the report.

Speech is also ephemeral. Word of mouth about how good a speech or presentation was can extend its effects, but only to a few people, and only so far as the person relating what was said can also speak or write effectively and can represent the presentation accurately. All the ideas in the presentation will go through the sieve of others' minds and will be bent and colored by their interests, biases, and how their minds work. Make it easy for them to get the story right. Give them a piece of writing that they can copy and attach to the minutes or use as an outline and reminder of the concepts when they write articles based on it.

Evaluators can also greatly enhance their speech with writing projected on a screen through slides or overheads. And they can get their point across effectively at a briefing if they give everyone a handout that emphasizes the important points. The shaded box has suggestions for doing both. An example of a slide presentation for the Cobalt study is found in Figure 21.2.

Tips on Preparing Overheads and Handouts

- Six-page limit for overheads. If you need more, put them in a handout. This is not a hard and fast rule, though. Much depends on the pace and style of presentation.
- Five-line limit per slide. With more lines, the type is too small to be read. Nevertheless, there is much room for exceptions. The size of the room and the screen make a big difference.

Figure 21.2. Slide Presentation of the Cobalt Story

Low-Income Energy Assistance

Cobalt Electric Power Company

Methodology

- Billing records
  - Random Sample, 5,000 Records
  - Stratified by Assistance Status
- Customer Experience
  - Mail Survey

Billing Errors

- 2.5% Overall Error Rate
- 1.2% Billed for Wrong Amount
- 1.0% Over-Billed
- Other Errors: Addresses, Identifiers
- Same for Low-Income and Others

Customer Perspectives

- Most Customers Coping
- Problems for Low-Income Families
  - Appeals
  - Difficulty Understanding Bills

Solution: Set Standards

- Errors
  - Overall
  - Incorrect Payments
  - Over-Payments
  - Wrong Addresses
  - Personal Identifiers
- Customer Satisfaction
- Appeal Process
- Readability of
  - Bills
  - Appeal Rights

Take Corrective Action

- Strengthen Internal Controls
- Clarify Appeal Rights
- Make Bills Easier to Understand

- Topic phrases only. Do not use complete sentences.
- Color slides. Use the color in the overhead slide projections to advantage, but be careful that the text is readable. Dark backgrounds make this difficult.
- Black and white handouts. Make handouts in black and white.
- Pictures. Add a cartoon or picture to each slide to set the mood and make them more interesting. However, make sure the pictures are related to the message. Otherwise, the audience will enjoy the slide show and forget your message.
- Backup. Use PowerPoint-type programs to produce full-page color transparencies as a backup to the slide show presentation. If something goes wrong with the computer projector, old-fashioned projectors are universally available.

Conclusion

Be sure to break any of the above rules and ignore any hints that do not make sense for the situation. There are many cases where what has been suggested in this chapter does not apply. To put things in perspective, the last two shaded boxes set out a simple formula and a golden rule for writing for impact.

Formula for Success

- The Mom Test. Summarize the report in one or two simple, compelling sentences.
- Findings. Provide two to five findings that bring new facts or insights to the subject matter.
- Options and recommendations. Offer numerous practical options for solving the problems raised by the findings.
- Power writing. Get to the point, and use simple, clear sentences.
- Layout, typography, and graphics. Use these to highlight the message.
- Thought leaders. Get the report into the hands of all the key stakeholders.

Golden Rule

- Make the message jump off the page.
- Make sure nothing else does.

22

Using Organizational Report Cards

William T. Gormley Jr.

Organizational report cards have proliferated, especially in the fields of education and health. They have many purposes but two are particularly important: in economic terms, they help to correct information asymmetries between organizations that provide services and outsiders who purchase or appraise such services; in political terms, they help to make service delivery organizations more accountable to public officials and to citizens.

Several trends have encouraged the development of organizational report cards:

- The privatization of certain services makes it all the more important to have trustworthy measures of the performance of nonprofit and for-profit organizations that deliver services on behalf of the government.
- Greater sensitivity to budget deficits encourages public officials to demand good value for money as they seek to control costs without diminishing the quality of public services.
- The expansion of consumer choice in such realms as education and health care has generated greater consumer interest in comparative performance data.
- Both citizens and public officials are better educated and thus better equipped to use and understand performance data
- The growing popularity of the Internet has produced an ideal forum for easy access to data on organizational performance.

Although they have grown dramatically over the past decade or so, organizational report cards are not new. In education, the first report card dates back to Horace Mann, who promoted standardized testing within Boston's public schools in the 1840s. In health, the first report card dates back to Florence Nightingale, who in the 1860s convinced several London hospitals to publish mortality statistics (Gormley and Weimer, 1999). These rudimentary initiatives paved the way for more sophisticated and more extensive undertakings in the late twentieth century, when organizational report cards were rediscovered.

Report cards today differ quite a bit from each other in their technical sophistication. Some, which may be described as scientific, include elaborate risk adjustments to ensure that client characteristics are taken into account. Risk-adjusted performance measures use statistical controls for client background characteristics to estimate the effects of a particular program or organization on desired outcomes. A good example is New York State's coronary artery bypass graft (CABG) surgery report card, which takes patients' preexisting characteristics, or comorbidities, into account before calculating mortality rates. Others, of a more popular nature, stress comprehensibility more than validity—for example, the ratings of colleges and universities by *U.S. News and World Report,* which Frederickson (2001, p. 53) has described as "a postmodern wedding of simplified social science and pop entertainment." A third, hybrid, category is more valid than the popular report cards and more comprehensible than the scientific report cards. An example is a rating of health maintenance organizations (HMOs) by the California Cooperative HEDIS Reporting Initiative (CCHRI), which presents several discrete quality measures in a visually appealing way.

Because there are lots of ways to assess organizational improvements and societal progress over time, it is important to distinguish between organizational report cards and other performance measures. My colleague David Weimer and I view an organizational report card as "a regular effort by an organization to collect data on two or more other organizations, transform the data into information relevant to assessing performance, and transmit the information to some audience external to the organizations themselves" (Gormley and Weimer, 1999, p. 3). Given that definition, organizational report cards are indeed different from other performance measures (see Table 22.1).

For example, program evaluations seldom involve regular data collection and may or may not involve an organizational focus, an external assessment, an external audience, or multiple organizations. The Government Performance and Results Act (GPRA), which requires almost all federal agencies to prepare annual indicators of progress toward important goals, is another case in point. Because performance measures required by GPRA are

Table 22.1. Organizational Report Cards and Other Performance Measures

	Organizational Focus	Regular Data Collection	External Assessment	Data Transformation	External Audience	Multiple Organizations
Organizational report cards	Yes	Yes	Yes	Yes	Yes	Yes
Government Performance and Results Act	Yes	Yes	Maybe	Yes	Yes	No
Benchmarking	Yes	Maybe	Maybe	Yes	Yes	Yes
Balanced scorecards	Yes	Yes	No	Yes	Maybe	No
Program evaluations	Maybe	No	Maybe	Yes	Maybe	Maybe
Social indicators	No	Yes	Yes	Yes	Yes	No
Disclosure requirements	Yes	Yes	Yes	No	Yes	Yes

Note: GPRA: A 1993 law requiring federal agencies to measure their own performance annually; and some agencies include external assessments in their performance measures. Benchmarking: Comparing organizations to the best of their kind or to standards established by knowledgeable professionals. Balanced Scorecards: Organizational self-assessments developed by managers of for-profit firms. Program evaluations: Assessments of the policy impacts of government programs. Social indicators: Measures of social conditions, such as poverty, divorce rates, and out-of-wedlock births. Disclosure requirements: Government requirements that manufacturers and distributors of products disclose health and safety risks.

Source: Adapted from Gormley and Weimer (1999, p. 4). Reprinted by permission of the publisher from *Organizational Report Cards* by William T. Gormley, Jr., and David L. Weimer, p. 4, Cambridge, Mass.: Harvard University Press. Copyright © 1999 by the President and Fellows of Harvard College.

designed by each agency as part of a self-evaluation exercise, they too are different from organizational report cards.

Ideals and Realities

In an ideal world, organizational report cards serve multiple audiences and help them to make difficult choices. Individual consumers weigh the evidence in organizational report cards before selecting an HMO, a hospital, a college, or a graduate school. Corporate purchasers and government agency purchasers examine organizational performance as they decide whether to renew a contract with a particular service delivery organization. Governors ask how their state compares with other states as they decide how to reallocate scarce resources.

In that same ideal world, organizations that deliver services pay attention to report cards and adjust their behavior in an effort to compete more effectively with other organizations that produce the same services. Organizations change their production processes, reallocate resources, focus on problems that need to be corrected, and change the incentives that managers face. In other words, organizational learning occurs in an ideal world, resulting in improved performance.

In the real world, that may not occur. Individual consumers may not be aware of organizational report cards or may prefer to rely on word of mouth, or they may prefer to focus on cost considerations. Corporate purchasers may be highly sensitive to cost and largely insensitive to quality as they pursue profits. Government agency purchasers may behave the same way if their political overseers impose tight budget constraints. As for governors, they may not care how other states are doing unless the electorate also cares. And the electorate may care more about taxes than about the quality of public services.

In the real world, organizations that deliver services may engage in dysfunctional behavior after receiving a "bad" report card. If participation in a report card project is voluntary, an organization that has performed badly or expects to perform badly may decline to participate. To create the illusion of a strong performance, an organization may engage in cream skimming—selecting as clients those who are most likely to succeed rather than those who are most in need of help. To guarantee good indicators, an organization may teach to the test, focusing on the measures that the report card focuses on rather than broader, more abstract goals, such as students' critical abilities. To beat the system, an organization may engage in unfair or deceptive practices. Or it may practice denial, blaming everyone but itself (including the messenger) rather than taking responsibility for its own poor performance.

Do people actually use report cards? If so, who does, and when and how? Is report card use common or rare? Are some consumers or some professionals more likely to use report cards than others? What are the consequences of report card use for consumer behavior and purchaser behavior and professional behavior? And what are the consequences for the targeted organizations? Do they pay attention to report cards? Do they improve their practices as a result?

In the sections that follow, I consider evidence from several fields, but especially health care, and I differentiate between "good" and "bad" organizational report cards and cite some examples of the former.

Consumer Use of Report Cards

Pennsylvania publishes one of the three best hospital report cards in the United States. It also publishes data on the performance of cardiac surgeons who perform CABG surgery at Pennsylvania hospitals. A telephone survey of 474 heart patients found that 12 percent were aware of the report card at the time of their surgery and that 20 percent of that group (or a total of 2.3 percent) said that the report card had a "moderate" or "major" impact on their decision making as to which hospital and surgeon to choose (Schneider and Epstein, 1998). An even smaller subset of professed "users"—just under 1 percent—could recall with accuracy the categorical mortality rating of the hospital, surgeon, or surgical group. The authors attribute low utilization rates in this instance to several factors: a limited amount of time for a heart patient to make a decision on where to have the surgery, perceptions of no alternative cardiac surgery hospital within a reasonable distance of the patient's home, and the viewpoint that it is better to rely on relatives and friends for advice than some other source, such as a newspaper article or a report card (Schneider and Epstein, 1998).

New York also publishes one of the three best hospital report cards in the United States. Indeed, it may well be the best of the lot. Like Pennsylvania, it also publishes information on the performance of cardiac surgeons who perform CABG surgery at New York hospitals (surgeons who perform a small number of operations are excluded from the list for statistical reasons). In a quasi-experimental study of hospital and physician market shares before and after the publication of the report card, Mukamel and Mushlin (1998) found that hospitals and physicians with better outcomes experienced higher rates of growth in market share. Clearly, this suggests that patients were gravitating toward hospitals and surgeons with better track records.

In 1995, the Agency for Healthcare Research and Quality (AHRQ) initiated the Consumer Assessment of Health Plans Study (CAHPS), which helps consumers make choices among managed care organizations by publishing customer satisfaction survey statistics for different health plans. Because state Medicaid agencies have aggressively promoted managed care in recent years, it was expected that such surveys would be especially beneficial to Medicaid clients. A New Jersey evaluation, which mailed CAHPS surveys to one-half of new Medicaid clients during a four-week period in 1998, found no differences in the plan choices of those receiving and those not receiving the CAHPS report. However, when the researchers focused on Medicaid clients who reported receiving and reading the CAHPS report, they found that readers were somewhat more likely to choose better-rated plans than nonreaders (Farley and others, 2002). This finding was even clearer when the researchers focused on readers who enrolled in a plan other than the dominant managed care plan. These results are consistent with experimental studies, where investigators have documented differences in the quality of plans chosen by individuals who do and do not read the CAHPS reports (Farley and others, 2002). The key, the authors conclude, is to ensure that clients read the reports.

At least thirty-five states publish report cards on individual public schools (Gormley and Weimer, 1999). Louisiana is one of them. A survey conducted by the Louisiana Department of Education found that a majority of parents agreed that the report cards provide useful information and have the potential for improving education (Caldas and Mossavat, 1994). At the other end of the spectrum, only 22 percent of parents thought that the report cards were "a waste of time and money" (Kochan, Franklin, Crone, and Glasock, 1993, p. 4). This report leaves much to the imagination. How exactly do parents use these report cards? Do they use them to put pressure on principals and teachers for curriculum reform or staffing changes? Do they occasionally switch schools or school districts because of the information they read in a report card? Unfortunately, these questions were not asked or answered.

Corporate or Government Purchasers

Many decisions to purchase services are made not by individual consumers but rather by corporate or government purchasers that sign contracts with a limited number of service providers. This is especially common in health care, given the explosion of HMOs, preferred provider organizations, and other organizations that serve as intermediaries between patients and those who pay for their services.

A particularly useful source of data, for companies and government agencies that sign contracts with managed care organizations, is the Health

Employer Data Information Set (HEDIS), prepared by the National Committee for Quality Assurance (NCQA). This data set was originally designed by employers, among other participants; it was also funded by employers, with additional financial support from what was then the Health Care Financing Administration. Therefore, one might expect that companies would make extensive use of the data, which include interval-level data on the extent to which managed care clients have taken advantage of preventive medicine, such as breast cancer and prostate cancer screenings and child immunization. Also available is information on which managed care organizations have been accredited by NCQA, a rough surrogate for health care quality.

According to one study (Gabel, Hunt, and Hurst, 1998), a growing percentage of employers are familiar with NCQA accreditation, but approximately two-thirds are not. Furthermore, only 11 percent of employers considered NCQA accreditation to be very important, and only 5 percent considered HEDIS data to be very important. Another study reached more positive conclusions, perhaps because the focus was on thirty-three employers with large workforces. Specifically, the authors found that 78 percent of the firms had access to HEDIS data, and 54 percent of that group used the data; 75 percent of the firms had access to consumer satisfaction data, and 59 percent of that group used the data (Hibbard, Jewett, Legnini, and Tusler, 1997). Some of the biggest original backers of HEDIS were employers with large workforces. This study suggests that purchasers with a higher number of employees are more likely to use quality-relevant data on managed care organization performance.

We saw previously that individual consumers pay some attention, though not a great deal, to report cards that rate hospitals and physicians in Pennsylvania and New York. But what about managed care organizations that contract out with particular surgeons at particular hospitals? Mukamel and others (2000) found that 64 percent of New York's managed care organizations were familiar with the state's cardiac surgery reports but only 20 percent said that the reports were a "major" factor in their contracting decisions (32 percent of the 64 percent). In terms of actual behavior, managed care organizations seemed to prefer surgeons identified as "high-quality outliers" (unusually strong performers) and "those who have a high procedure volume" (Mukamel and others, 2000, p. 329) The authors found no evidence that managed care organizations were steering business to surgeons with lower risk-adjusted mortality scores, perhaps because the organizations found other quality indicators easier to use. A national study of HMO contracting with hospitals for bypass surgery found that risk-adjusted mortality scores help to predict contracting decisions, with HMOs preferring hospitals with lower scores, and thus higher quality (Gaskin, Escarce, Schulman, and Hadley, 2002). However, that study did not look at report cards; it is simply consistent with the proposition that report cards, where available, help to furnish HMOs with information that they value.

State Medicaid agencies purchase health care services from HMOs on a regular basis. After identifying some HMOs as suitable, they usually allow Medicaid clients to choose from among the suitable plans. However, some clients, for whatever reason, refuse to choose. Under such circumstances, state Medicaid agencies must "auto-assign" a client to a particular plan. Some states have recognized that this auto-assignment process presents an opportunity to reward quality. Since 1999 Michigan has auto-assigned a larger share of clients to plans with better track records, as measured by certain HEDIS indicators, such as child immunization measures. Similarly, Arizona auto-assigns clients based on such factors as child immunizations and preventive health care for women. These proactive uses of report cards should help to shift Medicaid clients away from low-performing plans and toward high-performing plans in the long run.

Some private firms use another technique to encourage their employees to sign up with a superior health plan. General Motors, for example, rates a variety of health plans based on several quality factors, such as NCQA accreditation, preventive care, medical and surgical care, women's health, and patient satisfaction. The actual price of each plan to employees depends in part on quality: employees pay less out of pocket for better health plans (General Motors, 1997). This strategy appears to have had a striking impact on employee behavior. In December 1996, 26.5 percent of the plans selected by GM employees were "strong" and 8.0 percent were "poor"; in January 1998, 32.2 percent of the plans selected by GM employees were strong and 1.3 percent were poor (T. Cragg, personal communication to the author, Feb. 25, 1998). Within a short period time, GM achieved a substantial shift of employee health plan preferences away from weak plans and toward superior ones.

In child care, one indicator of superior quality is whether a day care center is accredited by the National Association for the Education of Young Children (NAEYC). Studies show that such centers do a better job of caring for young children (Helburn, 1995; Whitebook, Sakai, and Howes, 1997). Since approximately 1990, state governments have been using federal and state dollars to help poor and near-poor parents to meet their child care needs. To encourage enrollments at accredited day care centers, twenty-one states now provide for differential reimbursement, whereby accredited centers are reimbursed at a somewhat higher rate for every subsidized child they enroll. Research in ten of these states shows that differential reimbursement has increased the number of applications for NAEYC accreditation by day care centers (Gormley, 2002). Statistically significant effects are more likely in states with relatively large reimbursement differentials. Thus, day care centers seem to be responding to financial cues from government purchasers. The next step is to get parents, especially poor or near-poor parents, to seek out accredited day care centers.

Professionals as Advisers

Whether individual consumers use organizational report cards depends in part on how seriously professionals who advise consumers take such instruments. In health care, for example, patients seek advice from physicians, who routinely refer patients to other physicians (such as surgeons) and to hospitals. In education, students seek advice from guidance counselors, who urge high school students to apply for admission to certain colleges and universities. In child care, parents sometimes seek advice from resource and referral agencies (R&Rs) that maintain a roster of licensed child care facilities.

In this area as elsewhere, more is known about health professionals than about other professionals. According to one survey, 22 percent of New York cardiologists routinely discussed data from New York's CABG surgery report card with patients, and 38 percent said that the data influenced their referrals to surgeons "somewhat" or "very much" (Hannan, Stone, Biddle, and DeBuono, 1997). In Pennsylvania, 13 percent of cardiologists said the state's CABG report card had a "moderate" or "substantial" impact on their referrals (Schneider and Epstein, 1996). A larger percentage of Pennsylvania cardiologists—(35 percent) and cardiac surgeons—(25 percent) reported discussing the CABG report card with at least one patient during the previous year (Schneider and Epstein, 1996). In both states, cardiologists expressed concern that report cards might discourage cardiac surgeons from performing surgery on high-risk patients.

In child care, authentic organizational report cards are hard to find, despite the fact that information asymmetries between parents and providers are substantial enough to justify them. Part of the problem is that few parents turn to R&Rs for help in choosing child care—Approximately 9 percent, according to one careful study (Hofferth, Brayfield, Deich, and Holcomb, 1991). The deeper problem is that the R&Rs themselves are extremely reluctant to gather, store, or share quality-relevant information about individual facilities. Afraid of alienating providers, wary of potential lawsuits, and aware of a considerable margin for error, most R&Rs are willing to share little more than the identity, location, and capacity of individual facilities, plus the number of vacancies (Gormley, 1995). In an ideal world, R&Rs would also share information on each facility's regulatory history, including code violations and substantiated complaints. However, only Colorado and Texas have computerized such information and made it available to parents through local libraries or the Internet.

Organizational Change

There are at least two ways in which organizational report cards might result in an improvement in the quality of services that consumers receive. Under the first scenario, report cards shape the choices that consumers or purchasers make, resulting in a shift of organizational market shares. If P.S. 32 performs well and P.S. 24 performs poorly, students shift from P.S. 24 to P.S. 32, and social welfare improves. If St. Mary's hospital performs well and St. Bartholomew's hospital performs poorly, patients shift from St. Bartholomew's hospital to St. Mary's hospital, and social welfare improves. Under the second scenario, report cards directly shape the behavior of organizations that deliver services, without any change in market shares. P.S. 24, embarrassed by its poor performance, replaces key personnel or changes key procedures and does better as a result. St. Bartholomew's hospital, stunned by its poor rating, appoints a task force that makes a series of recommendations to improve performance; within a year or two, hospital outcomes begin to change for the better. Of course, there is also another possibility: instead of making meaningful reforms, a public school may accelerate drills for the standardized tests that undergird report cards. Students may know more facts, while their ability to interpret the facts suffers. Similarly, a hospital may shift resources from renal and gastrointestinal divisions to the cardiac division in order to improve its rating in the CABG surgery report card. Heart patients may fare better, while renal and gastrointestinal patients fare worse.

A review of the literature on organizational impacts suggests that report cards do have direct effects on the behavior of organizations that deliver services. Some of these effects are functional (or positive), but others are dysfunctional (or negative).

A careful study has shown that following the introduction of the first CABG surgery report card in New York, the observed mortality rate for New York declined by 22 percent, as opposed to 9 percent elsewhere (Peterson and others, 1997). The same pattern applied to risk-adjusted mortality rates, which declined 10.5 percent for New York, as opposed to 5.8 percent elsewhere (Peterson and others, 1997). As suggested earlier, market shares appear to have increased for hospitals and physicians with better report cards. But other forces were also at work. After being ranked the third-worst hospital for CABG surgery, St. Peter's Hospital in Albany, New York, launched an internal investigation, which revealed a poor record of treating high-risk cases in particular. Following an internal review, St. Peter's discovered that medical personnel used intra-aortic balloons to stabilize weak hearts only 20 percent of the time. They increased the rate of use to 85 percent, altered procedures for drug use and heart numbing, and witnessed a sharp decline in mortalities for high-risk patients in 1993 (Montague, 1996). After receiving disappointing ratings in a series of CABG surgery report cards, the Strong Memorial Hospital in Rochester, New York, hired new cardiac surgeons and reorganized its heart surgery program. As a result, its performance improved (Smith, 1997). In these instances, report cards triggered a process that resulted in improved procedures and, ultimately, improved outcomes as well.

In contrast to New York, which invested heavily in a scientific report card for CABG surgery, Missouri has issued hybrid report cards on a range of subjects, such as outpatient procedures, obstetrical services, and emergency departments. According to a survey of state hospital administrators conducted in 1994, a substantial number of Missouri hospitals altered their policies after the obstetrical services guide was published. Cesarean deliveries declined at hospitals with relatively high c-section rates, and vaginal birth after c-section rates improved at hospitals with relatively low rates (Longo and others, 1997). Interestingly, the authors of this study found that positive changes were more likely in localities with competitive hospital environments than in localities with hospital monopolies.

A North Carolina study suggests that public school report cards have had a positive impact on the performance of public schools. After comparing schools rated below average with schools rated above average in 1990, Clotfelter and Ladd (1994) found that the schools rated below average showed larger relative gains in student test scores between 1990 and 1992 than schools rated at or above average. They also found some evidence that principal turnover rates were higher for schools rated below average, which could help to explain their greater performance gains. A Florida study points in the same direction. As part of a broader school reform plan, Florida law required that all public schools be graded from A through F, based on student achievement. If a school receives two Fs within four years, its students are eligible for vouchers to attend private schools. One year after the first test scores were reported, public schools that received an F raised their test scores significantly more than comparable schools (cited in Ladd, 2002). Although experts disagree on whether this strengthens the case for vouchers or for report cards, it certainly indicates that report cards have had an effect.

A Texas study suggests that public school report cards can be particularly effective when combined with financial incentives. In Dallas, which combined a report card with strong financial incentives, seventh-grade pass rates in reading and mathematics were higher than in Austin, El Paso, Fort Worth, San Antonio, and Houston, which used neither report cards nor financial incentives (Clotfelter and Ladd, 1996). This study offers support to advocates of high-stakes testing, which has spread to twenty states (Koretz, 2002). In Kentucky, which initiated high-stakes testing in 1990, some positive results have also been reported. For example, Elmore, Abelmann, and Fuhrman (1996) found that Kentucky students wrote more and better as a result of financial rewards for superior student writing.

The Kentucky case, however, offers a sobering reminder of the pitfalls that can accompany high-stakes testing schemes. During the initial implementation period, some Kentucky teachers indulged in substantial grade inflation when grading their students' writing samples, while others reviewed tests in advance or even rewrote their students' essays (Stecklow, 1997). Once these problems came to light, they were corrected. But they are not unique. In Dallas, for example, at least two cases were reported where school staff members were caught tampering with test results in order to boost ratings (Gormley and Weimer, 1999). More broadly, a study of Chicago's elementary schools concluded that 4 to 5 percent of classroom test scores were tainted by some form of cheating (Jacob and Levitt, cited in Kane and Staiger, 2002).

The Job Training Partnership Act and its successor, the Workforce Investment Act, require states to prepare performance measures to show how well local employment and training agencies have done in placing trainees and boosting their earnings. Although states enjoy some discretion in how they define success, all are supposed to provide financial rewards to employment and training centers that do a better job. Unfortunately, Heckman, Heinrich, and Smith (2002) found evidence of both self-selection and cream skimming in their study of employment and training agencies. Specifically, blacks, persons with less than a high school education, persons from poorer families, and individuals without recent work experience are less likely to be enrolled. Although cream skimming appears to have diminished over time (Gormley and Weimer, 1999), another problem persists: the short-term performance measures on which financial rewards are based appear to be very poor predictors of long-term employment and earnings (Heckman, Heinrich, and Smith, 2002). In effect, employment and training agencies are being rewarded for the wrong kind of behavior.

Another dysfunctional response to report cards has arisen in the criminal justice field as a response to crime statistics reported by the Federal Bureau of Investigation (FBI). Every city police force wants to show progress over time, as manifested by a reduction in serious crimes. Homicides leave little room for creative interpretation, but property crimes lend themselves to manipulation. For example, thefts can be classified as "missing property" or "lost property," effectively reducing a city's reported property crimes. Auditors for the Philadelphia police department once estimated that approximately one out of every ten serious crimes was downgraded or dropped from the ledger altogether (Matza, Fazlollah, and McCoy, 1998). A follow-up report by the *Philadelphia Inquirer* documented numerous cases of abuse. In one instance, a complainant stated that her wallet was stolen, but the police listed the wallet as "lost." In another instance, someone reported an attempted burglary; the police investigated but characterized the episode as "vandalism." Attempted burglary is one of the seven major crimes that the FBI uses in its official reports; vandalism is not. In short, it would appear that Philadelphia police adapted to the FBI's annual report card on crime by classifying crimes disingenuously to create the illusion of progress.

Politicians

The most neglected of all report card users are public policymakers and especially politicians. Despite the undeniable importance of politicians, no one has studied their use of organizational report cards in any systematic way.

To shed some light on the extent and manner of report card use by politicians, I analyzed state of the state addresses by governors in January 2002 (Table 22.2). Of thirty-six governors whose addresses were available, 55.5 percent made explicit ranked comparisons with other states. For example, Lincoln Almond, the governor of Rhode Island, noted with pride his state's number one ranking in prenatal care and, more broadly, in comprehensive health care. Governor Don Sundquist of Tennessee crowed over his state's number one ranking in the percentage of eighth-grade math teachers with access to computers in the classroom.

An additional 19.4 percent of the governors made looser, less explicit comparisons with other states. For example, Bob Wise, the governor of West Virginia, claimed to have "one of the most successful drug discount programs in the nation." And Tony Knowles, the governor of Alaska, made this rather vague assertion: "While other states are reeling from high unemployment and recession, Alaska's economy is moving forward."

**Table 22.2. Governors' Use of Organizational Report Cards,
State of the State Messages, January 2002**

Type of Use	Frequency of Use
None	22.2%
Loose comparison with other states	19.4
Ranked comparison with other states, without attribution	36.1
Ranked comparison with other states, plus explicit reference to organizational report card	19.4

Source: Data from National Governors Association, http://www.nga.org.

Most commonly, governors cited statistics that cast their state—and the gubernatorial administration—in a favorable light. For example, Governor Parris Glendenning of Maryland boasted that Maryland ranked first in the percentage of high school graduates. Interestingly, Governor Angus King of Maine made precisely the same claim.

Less frequently, governors cited statistics that suggest an urgent need for change. For example, Scott McCallum, the governor of Wisconsin, complained that his state ranked among the top five in taxes. He also lamented that Wisconsin workers' earnings lagged behind those in neighboring states. In Vermont, Howard Dean expressed regret at his state's high electricity rates, which were seventh highest in the nation. In Colorado, Governor Bill Owens complained that his state's auto insurance rates were twelfth highest in the nation.

Although most governors who used report cards cited them without attribution, several explicitly mentioned a particular report card. Five governors cited education statistics—three from *Education Week,* one from *U.S. News & World Report,* and one from the *Digital Survey.* A sixth governor cited homelessness statistics from the Department of Housing and Urban Development, and a seventh cited *Governing* magazine's fiscal stewardship rankings.

Without interviewing governors or other public officials, it is difficult to know with certainty how politicians perceive organizational report cards when they cite them. Judging from their rhetoric, they seem to be using interstate comparisons to make a case for public approval or for policy reform. In either instance, they are probably engaging in what Whiteman (1985) would call "strategic" use of policy information. In other words, the role of the statistics is to try to persuade others to support the politician's point of view: that the incumbent is to be praised, that existing budgets ought to be undisturbed, or that the incumbent's proposed reforms ought to be adopted.

Conceivably, however, there is also some substantive use. One can imagine Vermont's governor learning that his state's electricity rates are seventh highest in the nation and vowing to do something about this. One can imagine Oklahoma's governor learning that his state's college entrance scores are below average and concluding that this is unacceptable.

Factors Facilitating Use of Report Cards

Consumers or purchasers are most likely to use organizational report cards under the following circumstances:

- Information is accessible. Most state governments have made great efforts to make data on public school performance available to parents. Some state governments have made data on hospitals' performance available to patients. Very few state governments have made data on child care facilities' performance available to parents. If data accessibility does not guarantee use, the lack of access does guarantee nonuse.

- There is sufficient lead time to integrate report cards into decision making. Consumers' limited use of CABG mortality data may be more a function of the time constraints facing cardiac patients than anything else. Someone who experiences chest pains probably needs to choose a hospital and a physician quickly, and under duress. The choice of an obstetrician and a hospital to deliver a baby may be a better candidate for report card use, because there is enough lead time to make a decision.

- There is competition, which means that consumers have real choices to make. In this sense, the child care market is a better candidate for report card use than the public school market, because parents typically have several child care facilities within close proximity, as opposed to only one neighborhood school. Similarly, in health care, report card use is probably more likely in urban areas than in rural areas, because of the greater number of hospitals and managed care organizations in urban areas.

Organizations that deliver services are most likely to use organizational report cards under the following circumstances:

- Mandatory participation in a report card project. This element promotes a good, diverse grade distribution, with enough strong participants to serve as role models and enough weak participants to inspire some embarrassment. Without mandatory participation, some organizations will evade the glare of unfavorable publicity by opting out. With mandatory participation, the best way to avoid embarrassment in the future is to change practices and policies.

- Financial incentives, which encourage organizations to take report cards seriously. Bonuses or rewards for superior performance can act as powerful motivators, whether the organization is a public agency, a nonprofit organization, or a for-profit firm. Every organization needs more money, or at least thinks it does. The specifics of the financial incentives undoubtedly matter too—whether the rewards accrue to organizations or individuals, whether the rewards are large or small, whether the rewards apply to outputs or outcomes. But the bottom line is that financial incentives magnify the influence of organizational report cards.

- Organizations are relatively immature. At the beginning of the 1990s, managed care organizations were devoted to preventive medicine in theory but had not come close to reaching their potential, offering a full set of immunizations to two year olds, offering mammograms to middle-aged women, and offering prostate exams to middle-aged men. Since that time, managed care organizations have steadily improved their track records along these and other dimensions. Bigger, more difficult challenges loom ahead. It will be harder to improve so quickly in the future.

Ideals and Realities Revisited

Implicit in this chapter is the assumption that report cards can improve consumer choice and organizational performance, if given a fair chance. But what if a report card is poorly designed or contains misleading information? What if it makes a bad organization look good or a good organization look bad? What if it takes other organizations off the hook because they chose not to participate or because of missing data?

Fortunately, it is possible to distinguish between good and bad report cards. A good report card has the following characteristics (Gormley and Weimer, 1999):

- Validity. The report card measures what it claims to measure: organizational performance.
- Comprehensiveness. This characteristic refers to breadth of coverage, as when a hospital report card covers several surgical procedures or a school report card covers both academic performance and social behavior.
- Comprehensibility. A report card can be easily understood.
- Relevance. The report card focuses on matters that are of real concern to real people, such as life and death or how much children are learning in school.
- Reasonableness. This refers to the time and money required to comply with data requests from the organization producing the report card.
- Functionality. A report card has impact, specifically, positive impact. It is functional if it encourages good organizational behavior.

Based on these criteria, it is possible to identify some exceptionally good report cards:

- New York State CABG surgery report card. At the technical end of the spectrum, the New York State CABG surgery report card is one of the best (www.health.state.ny.us). Although it is relatively narrow in scope and thus not very comprehensive, it meets all the other criteria well or extremely well. Most notably, its use of logistic regression analysis with risk-adjusted data helps to ensure high validity. Heart patients care about mortality, so its relevance is high. The use of bar graphs helps to make it comprehensible to a lay audience. It relies on data that hospitals must already gather, so its reasonableness is also high. And examples of use, the ultimate test of functionality, have already been cited.

• Business school ratings produced by *U.S. News & World Report*. This report, at the popular end of the spectrum, is generally praiseworthy. Unlike some other ratings published by the same magazine, they are updated annually, which makes them more valid and more relevant. Also unlike other ratings, they include both behavioral measures (such as the starting salaries of their recent graduates) and perceptual measures (two separate ratings by peers and by employers). The absence of risk adjustment is a problem. How much credit should the Harvard Business School get for the starting salaries of students so superb that they might have commanded relatively high salaries even without the benefit of a Harvard degree? Nevertheless, despite some imperfections, the business school ratings are among the best college and university report cards currently being produced (www.usnews.com).

• The California Cooperative HEDIS Reporting Initiative. This hybrid report card, between the two ends of the popular-technical spectrum, has produced an admirable report card on HMOs that encompasses virtually all health plans doing business in California. The data are audited by a respected independent firm, which contributes to the report card's validity. Both the print version and the Internet version of the report card (www. healthscope.org) are user friendly, with icons that make it easy to distinguish between above average and below average performance.

• The Environmental Defense. This organization, formerly known as the Environmental Defense Fund, produces a good report card for environmental performance, available on the Internet (www.scorecard.org). One of its distinctive features is its versatility. Users may access data by state, county, or postal code. Available is an abundance of information on criteria air pollutants, hazardous air pollutants, lead hazards, land contamination, and other environmental threats. The Web site encourages political action and donations to environmental causes.

• National Center for Public Policy and Higher Education. This good report card on higher education, published every two years, provides useful information on six performance dimensions for each state: preparation, participation, affordability, completion, benefits, and learning. Thus, the report card is fairly comprehensive, and it is highly relevant: it addresses issues of undeniable importance, such as the capacity of all citizens to share in the economic benefits that flow from higher education. It is quite reasonable, because it relies on data already gathered and published by others, such as the Census Bureau and the U.S. Department of Education. It is also highly comprehensible, with letter grades that facilitate comparisons across states.

The absence of controls for the demographic characteristics of the state population is a weakness.

Who is best equipped to design and produce an organizational report card, and how should they go about it? Perhaps the best answer to this question is that the production of a report card has five distinct stages: data gathering, data verification, data analysis, information presentation, and information dissemination (Gormley and Weimer, 1999). In general, the public sector has certain advantages in the early stages, and the private sector has some strengths in the later stages. In data gathering, for example, many private firms or nonprofit organizations will not gather appropriate, comparable data without a government mandate. The government can play an indispensable role in extracting data from reluctant organizations. By contrast, consider information dissemination. The most effective communicators in society are journalists, advertising executives, and public relations experts, most of whom work for the private sector. Although each case is unique, there is no reason to assume that the same organization should handle all five stages of report card production. In fact, it often makes more sense for the public and private sectors to work in tandem, playing to their respective strengths.

An interesting question is whether report cards should be produced by advocacy groups. Because these groups have an action orientation, they may be better able to facilitate report card use. They may also be more diligent in the effort to make sure that their report cards are comprehensible and user friendly. The key stumbling block, if there is one, is validity. Because advocacy groups have a strong point of view, they may be less interested in producing a credible, objective report card. If they do produce a report card, they should avoid inflammatory rhetoric and exaggerated claims. They should also work hard to produce a range of indicators that will be relevant to persons with diverse points of view.

Conclusion

Clearly, report cards have begun to shape behavior. Just as clearly, they have yet to revolutionize the delivery of health care, education, child care, or vital social services.

What are we to make of this limited use? I would argue that even a relatively small number of users can have a large impact on the quality of social services that consumers receive. If opinion leaders such as politicians pay attention to report cards, then ordinary citizens who are otherwise unaware of these report cards may nevertheless be influenced by them. If large employers pay attention to report cards, then HMOs and hospitals may change their practices in response. If professionals who advise consumers (physicians, high school guidance counselors, child care resource and referral agencies) pay attention to report cards, a critical mass of consumers may change their preferences. If even 2 percent of consumers shift their behavior, that may be sufficient to induce substantial organizational change.

Producers of organizational report cards should not be discouraged by findings that direct use of report cards by consumers is not widespread. Ultimately, the indirect effects of report cards may matter more than the direct ones. Just as the mass media have effects on public opinion through a two-step flow of communication (from the mass media to opinion leaders, from opinion leaders to citizens), so too report cards are likely to influence social service delivery through a multistep flow of information.

References

Caldas, S., and Mossavat, M. "A Statewide Assessment Survey of Parents', Teachers', and Principals' Perceptions of School Report Cards." Paper presented at the annual meeting of the American Educational Research Association, New Orleans, La., Apr. 4, 1994.

Clotfelter, C., and Ladd, H. "Information as a Policy Lever: The Case of North Carolina's School 'Report Card.'" Paper presented at the Annual Conference of the Association for Public Policy Analysis and Management, Chicago, Oct. 28, 1994.

Clotfelter, C., and Ladd, H. "Recognizing and Rewarding Success in Public Schools." In H. Ladd (ed.), *Holding Schools Accountable: Performance-Based Reform in Education*. Washington, D.C.: Brookings Institution, 1996.

Elmore, R., Abelmann, C., and Fuhrman, S. "The New Accountability in State Education Reform: From Process to Performance." In H. Ladd (ed.), *Holding Schools Accountable: Performance-Based Reform in Education*. Washington, D.C.: Brookings Institution, 1996.

Farley, D., and others. "Effects of CAHPS Health Plan Performance Information on Plan Choices by New Jersey Medicaid Beneficiaries." *Health Services Research*, 2002, *37*, 985–1007.

Frederickson, H. G. "Getting Ranked." *Change*, Jan.–Feb. 2001, pp. 49–55.

Gabel, J., Hunt, K., and Hurst, K. *When Employers Choose Health Plans Do NCQA Accreditation and HEDIS Data Count?* New York: Commonwealth Fund, Sept. 1998.

Gaskin, D., Escarce, J., Schulman, K., and Hadley, J. "The Determinants of HMOs' Contracting with Hospitals for Bypass Surgery." *Health Services Research*, 2002, *37*, 963–984.

General Motors. *Flex Enrollment Decision Guide for GM Salaried Employees*. Detroit, Mich.: General Motors, Oct. 1997.

Gormley, W. Jr. *Everybody's Children: Child Care as a Public Problem.* Washington, D.C.: Brookings Institution, 1995.

Gormley, W. "Differential Reimbursement Policies and Child Care Accreditation." Unpublished manuscript, Georgetown University, 2002.

Gormley, W. Jr., and Weimer, D. *Organizational Report Cards.* Cambridge, Mass.: Harvard University Press, 1999.

Hannan, E., Stone, C., Biddle, T., and DeBuono, B. "Public Release of Cardiac Surgery Outcomes Data in New York: What Do New York State Cardiologists Think of It?" *American Heart Journal,* 1997, *134,* 55–61.

Heckman, J., Heinrich, C., and Smith, J. "The Performance of Performance Standards." *Journal of Human Resources,* 2002, *37,* 778–811.

Helburn, S. (ed.). "Cost, Quality and Child Outcomes in Child Care Centers." Denver: University of Colorado-Denver, 1995.

Hibbard, J., Jewett, J., Legnini, M., and Tusler, M. "Choosing a Health Plan: Do Large Employers Use the Data?" *Health Affairs,* 1997, *16,* 172–180.

Hofferth, S., Brayfield, A., Deich, S., and Holcomb, P. *National Child Care Survey, 1990.* Washington, D.C.: Urban Institute Press. 1991.

Kane, T., and Staiger, D. "The Promise and Pitfalls of Using Imprecise School Accountability Measures." *Journal of Economic Perspectives,* 2002, *16,* 91–114.

Kochan, S., Franklin, B., Crone, L., and Glasock, C. "How Do Parents and Teachers 'Grade' Louisiana's School Report Card Program?" Paper presented at the Mid-South Educational Research Association meeting, New Orleans, La., Nov. 9, 1993.

Koretz, D. "Limitations in the Use of Achievement Tests as Measures of Educators' Productivity." *Journal of Human Resources,* 2002, *37,* 752–777.

Ladd, H. "School Vouchers: A Critical View," *Journal of Economic Perspectives,* 2002, *16,* 3–24.

Longo, D., and others. "Consumer Reports in Health Care: Do They Make a Difference in Patient Care?" *Journal of the American Medical Association,* 1997, *278,* 1570–1584.

Matza, M., Fazlollah, M., and McCoy, C. "The Big Write-Off: When Stolen Goods Are 'Lost.'" *Philadelphia Inquirer,* Nov. 2, 1998.

Montague, J. "Report Card Daze." *Hospitals and Health Networks,* 1996, *5,* 33–38.

Mukamel, D., and Mushlin, A. "Quality of Care Information Makes a Difference." *Medical Care,* 1998, *36,* 945–954.

Mukamel, D., and others. "Do Quality Report Cards Play a Role in HMOs' Contracting Practices? Evidence from New York State." *Health Services Research,* 2000, *35,* 319–332.

Peterson, E., and others. *The Effects of New York's Bypass Surgery Provider Profiling on Access to Care and Patient Outcomes.* Durham, N.C.: Duke University Medical Center, 1997.

Schneider, E., and Epstein, A. "Influence of Cardiac-Surgery Performance Reports on Referral Practices and Access to Care." *New England Journal of Medicine,* 1996, *335,* 251–256.

Schneider, E., and Epstein, A. "Use of Public Performance Reports: A Survey of Patients Undergoing Cardiac Surgery." *Journal of the American Medical Association,* 1998, *79,* 1638–1642.

Smith, S. "Strong Hospital Heart Surgery Safer," *Rochester Democrat and Chronicle,* Sept. 5, 1997, p. 1.

Stecklow, S. "Kentucky's Teachers Get Bonuses, But Some Are Caught Cheating." *Wall Street Journal,* Sept. 2, 1997, pp. A1, A5.

Whitebook, M., Sakai, L., and Howes, C. *NAEYC Accreditation as a Strategy for Improving Child Care Quality.* Washington, D.C.: National Center for the Early Childhood Work Force, 1997.

Whiteman, D. "The Fate of Policy Analysis in Congressional Decision Making: Three Types of Use in Committees." *Western Political Quarterly,* June 1985, pp. 294–311.

23

The Use of Evaluation by Nonprofit Organizations

Mary E. Kopczynski, Kathleen Pritchard

Evaluation at the community level takes place in several forms. It occurs in nonprofit organizations that provide specific services to a particular population (for example, programs serving the elderly, a neighborhood, or people with disabilities). It sometimes occurs when funders such as foundations, governments, and United Ways wish to evaluate individual programs or groups of programs that provide a particular type of service (mental health, counseling, employment-related, or housing services). Evaluation also occurs in nonprofit organizations that provide indirect services, such as information, referral, advocacy, planning, and assessment services to the community at large. Evaluation by service delivery organizations is undertaken primarily to measure progress in service delivery (an outcome focus). In the second group of organizations, evaluation is often undertaken more broadly, such as to assess community-level need or monitor community-level conditions. A general finding, in both cases, is that evaluation by nonprofit organizations suffers from lack of use. This chapter explores some of the reasons and some of the strategies that might improve the use of evaluation in community-based nonprofit organizations.

Barriers to the Use of Evaluation by Community-Based Nonprofit Organizations

In the case of service-providing nonprofits, the appeal and approach to evaluation may differ significantly from a governmental approach. In contrast to the large-scale evaluation efforts or substantially funded evaluation units of government programs, most community-based nonprofits lack the will, expertise, and resources to conduct such efforts. However, the same rationale that drove the public sector to be more accountable has driven the nonprofit sector to look more seriously at the results of its programs and to assess their impact and effectiveness. And the demand for evaluation (particularly outcome-focused monitoring) is high, whether it stems from enlightened board members, donors, or funders, including government, foundations, and, notably, United Ways.

Clearly, the demand to evaluate cannot be answered without resources and training. But in community programs in the nonprofit world, the necessary orientation and training may not be there. The researchers, scientists, and analysts who best lend themselves to evaluation work and are employed by the public sector (see Chelimsky, 1994) are unlikely staff in the nonprofit world. Although some program areas, such as health care and counseling, do have staff who are trained in measurement and the use of data, such training is less common among people in human service or grassroots programs operating in the community.

Demands for evaluation instead are often seen as intrusive takeaways from the "real work" of the organization. Community groups are often annoyed or indignant that when they are working so hard and being paid so little, anyone would question what they "know in their hearts" to be true. The challenge is to make evaluation useful to nonprofits and to allow them to see the benefits. As Chelimsky (1994) notes, the first requisite to useful evaluations is an appreciation that the evaluation is worth doing and that the findings will be useful. In the real world of busy service providers who are not predisposed to appreciate this work, evaluators have a long way to go to convince nonprofits that the benefits outweigh the costs.

In the mid- to late 1990s, United Way of America undertook an effort to encourage and train staff at local United Ways across the country to focus on a practical approach to measuring program outcomes (Plantz, Greenway, and Hendricks, 1977). The resulting manual and materials have profoundly affected the nonprofit world by changing the focus from inputs and outputs to a focus on outcomes. To date, the manual, *Measuring Program Outcomes: A Practical Approach*, has sold over 120,000 copies. As Affholter (1994) notes, there is a difference between outcome monitoring and outcome evaluation. Outcome monitoring and program evaluation overlap. Outcome monitoring focuses on outcomes or results, while evaluation "extends beyond the tracking and reporting of program outcomes into examination of the extent to which and the ways in which outcomes are caused by the program" (p. 96). The true benefits may be more obvious as one moves from the former to the latter.

One of the harsh realities uncovered in the implementation of this changed focus is the stark contrast between program design and reality. In one United Way, for example, when program providers were invited to a working session to discuss their outcomes, they reviewed the grant proposals that the development officers and grant writers in their own agencies had written to describe their programs. In most instances, the service providers had not seen the grant proposals and were unaware of the lofty promises that grant writers had made to funders. There was often little connection between what service providers viewed as the program's intent or measure of success and what the grant writers had promised to their funders. It is not surprising that attempts at evaluation would reveal disappointing results.

This demand for program outcome reporting has also highlighted the lack of quality data systems in many nonprofit organizations. Seldom are agency records set up for evaluation purposes. When data are not valued, there is little incentive to keep them accurately. In small nonprofits, there are often no baseline data and no tradition of keeping accurate records. In many cases, data collection systems are not connected to outcomes. Although most nonprofits have long-standing requirements to report to funders on client demographics, often the demographic data are not linked to their outcome reporting systems. A community-based organization might be able to report how many males and females it serves, and it may be able to report what number of the total clients served achieved their outcomes. But because data collection methods are not established or information systems are not linked, it may be a challenge to report what percentage of the men achieved their outcomes or what percentage of those achieving their outcomes are women.

For many nonprofit organizations, the perceived purpose of data collection is completing the forms required by funders. The objective is filling in the required boxes with numbers. Although highly unlikely, it would not be uncommon for a nonprofit to report that exactly 50 percent of the participants in any program are male and 50 percent are female, or that exactly 5 percent live in each identified postal code, or that each of four income categories contains 25 percent of the total clients served. The failure to link data with their potential use for learning, planning, and service improvement is common.

When organizations fail to report credible data, it may be a sign that they put no effort into collecting the data, assign no value to the information, or that there is no consequence for failing to report accurate information. It might also be a reflection of the fact that tracking clients in difficult situations may be an extremely difficult task. Getting follow-up data on homeless clients, for example, is indeed a challenge. Whatever the reason, nonprofits need ways to recognize and flag poor-quality data. Often the nonprofit's executive director and board members have not seen the information, and the people who filled out the reports this year have no idea what was said by the people who filled out the reports last year.

Even if the data were accurate, few agencies have the capacity to look at data over time. They may be challenged to compare previous years' data to the current year's data and see that numbers in a certain category changed by X percent. Combine the lack of information systems with staff turnover, generally exceedingly high in the nonprofit world, and it is easy to see why few agencies can demonstrate empirically whether they are doing better or worse than last year. Of course, good comparative data could be the antidote to the lack of institutional memory that is common because of the high turnover rates among staff.

Beyond the lack of appreciation of data, lack of training, poorly developed information systems, and high turnover rates, budget constraints of nonprofits often limit the potential for quality evaluations. When organizations believe they must choose to apply resources to either providing service or evaluation research, the answer is predictable.

Although there are many barriers to the effective use of evaluation, there is also evidence that in many cases, benefits are being reaped from evaluation in nonprofit organizations. Several national organizations such as Big Brothers Big Sisters, Boys and Girls Clubs, and Girls Inc. are assisting local affiliates in developing measurement tools and methodologies to assist in outcome measurement. United Ways in Minneapolis, Milwaukee, New Orleans, and Santa Fe, among others, can demonstrate meaningful changes that have occurred as a result of program outcome measurement efforts. Both United Ways and the agencies they fund are beginning to realize and document the benefits they have seen by adapting this new approach. For example, a survey by United Way of America found that nearly three-fourths of the implementing United Ways were using the data to enhance marketing and fundraising (73 percent) and to increase accountability with donors and the community (73 percent). They also reported that it improved United Way's image and helped them become more visible (70 percent) and that using the information helped United Ways retain, maintain or increase financial support (68 percent) (United Way of America, 2003).

One of the key learnings of local United Ways that implement program outcome measurement is that agencies often lack the know-how or capacity to do much with the data once collected. Similarly, very few United Ways are using the findings to their fullest extent. Fewer than half (49 percent) of the United Ways implementing program outcome measurement used the results in their own planning, only one-third used the information to support planning and budgeting, and only one-quarter were using the information to identify trends or make other comparisons to inform their work. Although significant strides have been made in exposing nonprofits to the methods of outcome measurement, challenges remain in expanding the use and the benefits of evaluation in this sector.

Strategies for Improving Quality and Use

For outcome measurement and evaluation findings to lead to program improvement, nonprofits and their funders need to go beyond the challenge of reporting on the score and take steps to get at the potential factors that influence success. To do that, programs need to start in simple ways. One local United Way, for example, asks funded programs to report their outcome successes in relation to targets that they set, but also to explain why the target was set at that level and what important lessons were learned from the data.

Still, looking at the results only from single programs makes it difficult to note patterns, trends, or factors that might be explored on a larger scale. Hatry and Lampkin (2001) offer several useful suggestions for local service organizations about managing outcome data to increase their use. Among the most beneficial are these recommendations:

- Identify client characteristics such as age, gender, and education that seem likely to affect client success in achieving the intended outcomes.
- Break out (disaggregate) data by client characteristics and other factors likely to affect outcomes.
- Work with other organizations that provide similar services to identify a core set of common outcome indicators and ways of taking into account differences in program and client characteristics that will allow instructive comparisons.
- Generate reports on outcomes at regular intervals.
- Hold "how are we doing? sessions" soon after performance reports become available.

For example, in analyzing the relationship between client characteristics and outcomes, the boxed text shows an example from the United Way of Greater Milwaukee that helps to illustrate the point that looking at breakout data in relation to outcomes can help agencies increase their use of the data.

The recommendation to identify instructive comparisons to improve the use of the data is significant. As Morley, Hatry, and Cowan (2002) note, caseworkers in community-based nonprofits may review individual client outcomes for service improvement for individual clients, but very few supervisors or managers review tabulated data on even a sample of client data for comparison. This is also the case with funders where program officers may review individual program results, but seldom see the data in ways that would allow them to discern patterns across programs delivering similar services or serving similar populations. As Affholter (1994, p. 111) notes, "As with most evaluations, outcome data must be comparative if they are to be useful."

In the funding world, where much of the drive for program outcome measurement evolved, program officers could benefit from looking at results

Programs had been encouraged from the start to look at possible "influencing factors" or things that might affect outcome achievement, such as client characteristics or demographics, location of service delivery, and so on. Despite the fact that this was part of the formal training promoted by United Way of America, and that programs were required to collect and report basic demographic information, programs seldom reported or explained any of the variation in outcome achievement based on demographics or other influencing factors. In fact, encouraging programs to look at possible influencing factors, revealed the need to improve the overall quality of the client data itself. Because the easiest and most straightforward of these characteristics was gender, the United Way of Greater Milwaukee secured a small grant that would permit a closer look at client data, with a special emphasis on women and girls.

At the same time, a local neighborhood organization that received funds from United Way for a youth development program noted in its review of its own program outcomes that, at certain ages, boys seemed to be outperforming girls on some of the outcomes they were measuring. What, asked an astute executive director, might explain this? As he raised the question in a regular "lessons learned" session among similar programs, understanding heads nodded. They didn't have the data, but thought if they broke it down that way, they would see a similar pattern. A closer look by United Way at the aggregate youth programs uncovered some interesting patterns. While the average female participation rate in all programs was 63 percent, participation in youth programming by girls was only 48 percent? What would explain this difference?

Again, the experience of service providers offered many possible explanations:

- "Boys' programming is cheaper and easier."
- "Girls need special services."
- "Our outreach is to boys because we think they need the most help."
- "The culture we serve believes the opportunities should go to boys first."
- "The programs offered come from our history when we originally served only boys, then just more recently, we changed our name and opened our doors to girls."

Further analysis found, in part, it was a question of unequal resources, revealing a "gender gap" in funding. Programs serving girls were receiving more than a quarter of a million dollars less than programs serving boys. It also revealed that the nonprofit organizations had actually given very little thought to whether programming was gender-appropriate. But, service providers were eager to learn more. Research unveiled criteria of successful girls' programming, and a fundraising effort to achieve parity in funding was undertaken.

This special effort to ask programs to look at the impact of gender on their outcomes had many payoffs. It allowed programs to see the benefits of applying breakout data to their analysis. It challenged many "thought we knew" explanations, and spurred many new questions.

across funding categories, types of programs, and among programs. Government funders, foundations, and United Ways might begin to set the example by encouraging program monitors to use outcome data in different ways. In addition to looking at whether program X is complying with reporting requirements and achieving its intended outcomes, funders might use the data to look for patterns and similarities and differences in programs X, Y, and Z, getting leads that encourage more in-depth analysis and explanation. Figure 23.1 shows examples from the United Way of Greater Milwaukee (2001, 2002) that highlight ways that individual program outcome data might be reviewed.

In Figure 23.1A, funded programs were grouped by community impact areas, and the percentage of the total declared and measured targets achieved was reported. For example, during 2000, 81 percent of the outcomes measured by programs providing services to deliver basic needs reached their performance target, 73 percent of the outcomes measured by programs providing services to promote strong families met or exceeded their performance targets, and 69 percent of the outcomes measured by programs promoting self-sufficiency hit their targeted goals. These simple findings could indicate several things, of course. They may simply reflect that meeting basic needs for food, clothing, and shelter tends to be a short-term outcome, while achieving self-sufficiency is a longer-term outcome, and one might expect lower levels of outcome attainment, Note that when the data are compared to the following year, outcome achievement was reduced in each of the categories, indicating the need for further analysis.

Figure 23.1B suggests another way to look at the grouped data, including levels of outcome achievement by specific types of programs. In 2000, the fact that all of the performance targets set by programs in the areas of homelessness and health maintenance were achieved may simply indicate that the targets were set too low and the programs need assistance in stretching their targets or identifying and measuring outcomes beyond the shortest-term, immediate outcomes. Comparing results with the following year reveals significant

Figure 23.1. Outcome Achievement by (A) Impact Area and (B) Program Type

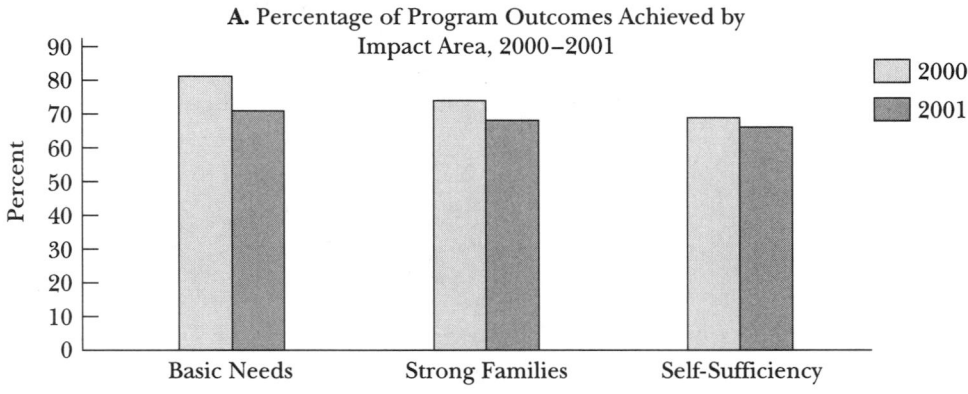

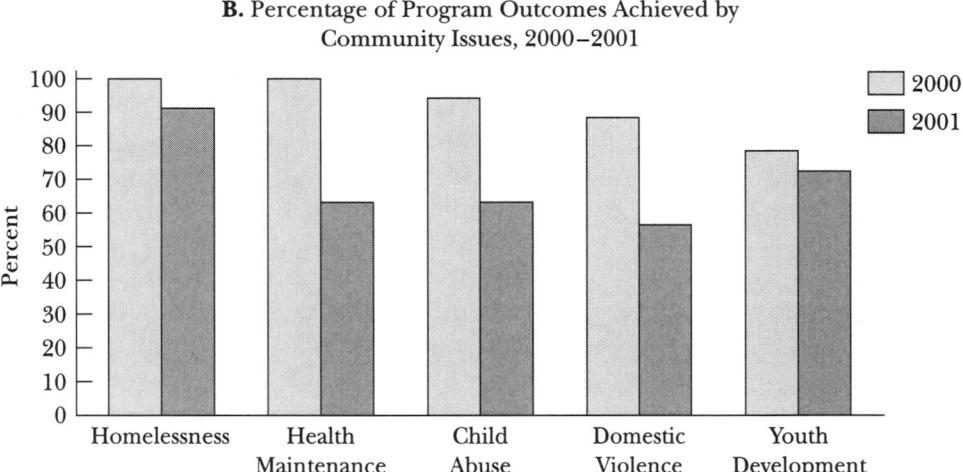

Source: Adapted from United Way of Greater Milwaukee (2001; 2002). Reprinted by permission of United Way of Greater Milwaukee.

reductions in the level of achievement that might be explained by more sophisticated measurement practices, more realistic performance standards, and better data, among others.

How Can Evaluators Help?

The question is how to build a critical mass of users so that evaluation in nonprofits makes an impact. How could the evaluation community target efforts that pay off? How can evaluation be integrated and used? Sanders (2002) argues that for evaluation to be mainstreamed into an organization, it must be seen as a means for learning, changing, and becoming more effective. Some clues to how evaluators could help this to happen within community-based nonprofit organizations may be found in recommendations from empowerment and participatory evaluation.

The theoretical framework underlying various participatory and empowerment evaluation approaches suggests that explicit involvement of key stakeholders in various aspects of the evaluation process will yield a greater appreciation for the value of, and enhance the usefulness and utilization of, evaluation results (Dawson and D'Amico, 1985; Greene, 1988; Fetterman, 1996). Empowerment evaluation recasts the role of evaluators from expert to coach or facilitator. Evaluators work with organizations to teach individuals to conduct their own evaluations and to help "organizations internalize evaluation principles and practices, making evaluation an integral part of program planning" (Fetterman, 1996, p. 9). Others maintain that "only extensive involvement in evaluation design, exploration of findings, interpretation of results and drawing up final recommendations will increase utilization" of findings and results (Papineau and Kiely, 1996, p. 82). Greater ownership of the results is expected to promote greater potential for accomplishing individual and collective goals at the program or community level.

How, then, do we overcome the practical and perceived obstacles to engaging service providers and other community stakeholders in using evaluation? Several specific suggestions are noted in the box.

The empowerment evaluation literature also explicitly addresses evaluation at the community level. This type of evaluation attempts to empower neighborhood groups or residents to achieve any of a variety of community goals: better services, more accessible government, or improved access to information. Nonprofit organizations increasingly are playing important roles in facilitating evaluation efforts that benefit an entire community or neighborhood, and in so doing, they seek to involve residents in a variety of ways.

Engaging Volunteers in Community-Level Assessments

This chapter has thus far focused primarily on evaluation from the perspective of nonprofit organizations that provide direct services to clients. A second type of nonprofit organization, sometimes referred to as community intermediaries, often has a broader mandate to shape or influence a wider community agenda. These organizations face similar challenges and constraints as their direct service counterparts in terms of limited financial and staff resources, evaluation expertise, and desire to undertake such efforts at the cost of deferring other activities perceived as more critical to the mission of the organization.

How Evaluators Can Help

- Promote evaluation as something of benefit even to small nonprofits. Evaluators can help to demonstrate that evaluation should be undertaken to benefit nonprofits rather than to appease funders. The common appeal is service improvement. Evaluators can promote principles of learning in the use of data.

- Establish an evaluation team to work with nonprofit staff to determine the real state of data. Evaluators could help to identify the right questions to ask and suggest potential uses of data. Board members and local United Ways can be helpful in accessing connections at local universities. By building relationships with the evaluation community, nonprofits could benefit from the needed expertise, and faculty and students would have access to real-world examples.

- Help to determine where to focus capacity-building efforts within nonprofits, since one size does not fit all and there are uneven payoffs in developing evaluation capacity.

- Help to uncover inexpensive and easy ways to get better data and establish protocols to document ways the data are treated. Evaluators can model ways to show the value of data and encourage systems that link outcome data to demographic data or information systems that permit a look at previous year's performance.

- Encourage the publication and dissemination of information that is received so that there is some sense of quality assurance and possible reality checking, knowing there is public review.

- Let data collectors know that their work is appreciated and used, and get results to workers who collect the data, the volunteers on the board, clients, and executive directors who need to nurture and encourage the appreciation of evaluation.

- Involve a wide range of individuals as volunteers in a variety of evaluation activities to provide important feedback to the organization, help to stretch scarce organizational resources, or strengthen ties between the nonprofit organization and the clients served or other important stakeholders in the community.

Community intermediaries typically serve the community by convening stakeholders, coordinating planning and community assessment services, and providing information, referral, or advocacy services. They also have immediate access to a range of constituents who might be encouraged to assist in any variety of evaluation activities. These community intermediaries are often expected to be responsive to information requests from residents or constituent groups and to help level the playing field in terms of access to information and its use in advocating for a changed or improved condition.

A number of these organizations have leveraged the support of volunteers to assist in community evaluation or assessment activities (see the box for examples of their activities). Although direct service organizations also engage volunteers, some of the key differences in approach have to do with how volunteers are solicited and for what purpose. Empowerment and participatory approaches notwithstanding, the typical role of a volunteer in program evaluation is focused on a limited set of activities, such as sitting on an advisory board, providing input on a set of desirable outcomes for a service or organization, or attending a community meeting where evaluation findings are presented and discussed. These activities, although important, fail to tap the full potential of interested volunteers and often lead to an incomplete understanding and use of evaluation results by the participants. Volunteer involvement in a broader range of evaluation activities, including data collection, review of data, and participation in various reporting and communication activities, offers the potential for greater ownership of the process, enhanced credibility of the results, and stronger commitment to participate in improving outcomes.

The term *volunteer* in its purest sense refers to individuals who voluntarily commit to participating in one or several evaluation activities without the expectation of monetary compensation. They are often motivated by a sense of civic responsibility or desire to serve others. Practically, however, they are often solicited with a promise of a modest stipend or other incentive for their participation. This is usually sufficient for community-level assessments, since the volunteer experience is often tied to an expectation that the activity will translate into a tangible benefit for the participants themselves or the broader community.

Nonprofit service organizations, however, sometimes take a broader view of these definitions, especially in cases where the volunteer is helping to provide a particular service that the organization or its staff could not supply. In these cases, it seems entirely appropriate for the organization to retain and compensate an individual for his or her time and contribution. For example, an organization might solicit assistance from a college or graduate student to enter data from intake forms and periodically tabulate and summarize basic statistics. (For the remainder of this discussion, we characterize volunteers as individuals who wish to participate in evaluation activities for reasons that go beyond financial incentives and are not employed by the organization sponsoring or administering the evaluation activity.)

Volunteers have participated in a variety of program evaluation techniques discussed throughout this book. For example, when an organization is trying to identify various aspects of service delivery that are most meaningful to clients or customers, it may sponsor a series of focus groups to understand

> ## Sample Roles of Volunteers in Nonprofit Evaluation Activities
>
> - The subject of a particular intervention using an experimental or quasi-experimental design
> - A provider of information through interviews, surveys, focus groups, complaints, or other feedback technique
> - A passive recipient of information from an evaluation study (a news story, community pamphlet, or evaluation report, for example)
> - A data collector, such as through trained observer ratings or interviewing neighbors or other study participants
> - A critical consumer or user of evaluation information, such as by working to help secure government or community response to a concern raised by the data

and prioritize these needs better. Volunteers have also been used by nonprofit organizations to help administer customer surveys. One demonstration project, for example, trained ushers at performing arts venues in several major cities to distribute questionnaires randomly to members of the audience of live performing arts events.

Increasingly, community-based organizations are initiating their own evaluation activities. A key feature of these activities is the involvement of community stakeholders and volunteers in many aspects of the evaluation, including design, refining outcomes and indicators to be monitored, collecting data, and using information to consider appropriate community (public and private) action.

The case study in the box provides an illustration of how resident volunteers can participate in projects designed to collect information about community conditions and resident perceptions of those conditions. The model used in this case study is an adaptation of similar efforts undertaken by organizations such as the Fund for the City of New York (COM-NET project) and the Connecticut Policy and Economic Council (City Scan project).

Considerations Regarding the Use of Volunteers

As eager as any organization may be to stretch scarce resources by engaging volunteers or to respond to stakeholders' requests to play a more meaningful role in the design and implementation of an organization's mission, attention should be given to several considerations prior to making the decision to use volunteers in program or community evaluations. The Fort Worth demonstration project, along with others that have sought to engage volunteers in

Case Study: Engaging Resident Volunteers in the Collection and Use of Quality of Life Indicator Data

In the spring of 2001, adult and youth residents from the Near Northside neighborhood in Fort Worth, Texas, came together to identify a variety of community conditions in need of improvement. Mobilized by staff from the Near Northside Partners Council (NNPC) and using a framework developed by an outside evaluation organization, residents participated in a demonstration effort designed to engage local residents in the collection and use of outcome data. Key evaluative components of the effort were centered around trained observer ratings, a neighborhood survey, and the use of results to develop an action plan for the neighborhood. Hand-held computer technology was used as the central means by which data were collected.

In addition to obtaining a better understanding regarding the feasibility of engaging residents in data collection activities and how the data obtained could be used to contribute to improved neighborhood conditions, the demonstration effort was designed with the following secondary goals in mind:

- To raise awareness among adult and youth residents about their ability to have an impact on community-based outcomes
- To provide residents with access to information and specific skills for monitoring local conditions
- To improve communication between residents and local government actors about the provision of local services
- To improve accountability of local governments to residents regarding the provision of public services
- To provide a workable model that can be expanded locally and replicated in other neighborhoods

Local Partner Roles

The NNPC serves as an advocacy and community organizing council, focusing on issues such as improving city services, reducing crime, increasing citizen participation, rehabilitating neighborhood housing, supporting economic development, and providing leadership development services to residents. NNPC was the lead local convener and coordinator for this effort, helping to identify local volunteers, convene meetings of local working groups, coordinate various aspects of data collection activities, and bring together the larger community to consider demonstration results and next steps.

NNPC assembled two working groups of neighborhood residents to participate in this demonstration: an adult group to provide general oversight and direction to the project and a youth group that would have primary responsibility for collecting the data. The working groups were asked to participate in three core activities: (1) identifying and prioritizing desirable community conditions for neighborhood residents, (2) participating in training activities for use of hand-held technology and procedures for undertaking trained observer ratings and resident survey data collection activities, and (3) reviewing findings and results from data collection activities and participating in a community forum with other residents to seek initial ideas for developing an action plan.

Demonstration Results

This project began in March 2001 and concluded with a community forum in March 2002, during which results were presented to local residents and other stakeholders. The demonstration effort had the following core activities:

1. Assemble a local working or advisory group.
2. Identify and prioritize conditions to be measured.
3. Translate conditions into specific indicators.
4. Develop data collection instruments.
5. Program hand-held computers, and design reporting formats.
6. Develop data collection procedures and training materials.
7. Train resident volunteers to use hand-held computers.
8. Collect data and transfer to database.
9. Produce reports and review data.
10. Report findings to the community and take action.

   In addition to convening two groups of adult and youth volunteers, NNPC also identified a field coordinator to work with the outside evaluators to cofacilitate or implement most of these remaining tasks. The evaluators had primary responsibility for the technical tasks related to the design of the data collection instruments and report formats, programming the hand-held computers, sample design, and design of procedures and training materials for resident data collectors. The field coordinator and volunteers had lead responsibility for coordinating and implementing data collection activities, maintaining hand-held computers, and transferring data periodically to the evaluators for processing the data. Review of data and presentation to the community were shared responsibilities.

   Data collection activities for both the trained observer ratings and resident survey in Near Northside concluded in November 2001. In total, physical conditions such as road surface, street cleanliness, housing, and yard conditions were rated for ninety blocks, and one hundred residents were interviewed about these conditions and knowledge of various community resources. Sample block reports were prepared and shared with the community. The evaluators prepared a memo that summarized key findings from the data collection activities. Local project participants reviewed these findings and prepared a community pamphlet in English and Spanish, "Community Palm Pilot Survey Results." The field coordinator and two youth volunteers participated in a national conference, Neighborhood Surveys and Community-Building Tools, in November 2001. Key findings were shared at a community forum in March 2002 attended by residents, community police officers, city council representatives, and other local representatives. NNPC has since been working to implement a similar demonstration in two neighborhood communities. Findings have been shared with local officials, and fundraising efforts are underway to support follow-up data collection activities.

evaluation activities, offers many useful insights to community-based nonprofits. These experiences help to clarify limitations as well as opportunities for maximizing the potential contributions of volunteers to nonprofit evaluation activities. We identify a number of key questions to consider.

What Are the Purpose and Scope of the Evaluation Activity, and How Will the Information Be Used?

The purpose and scope of the evaluation activity to be undertaken will help to inform whether it would be appropriate to enlist the assistance of volunteers. For direct service organizations, for example, it might not be appropriate to ask volunteers to review confidential case files of clients who reside in the community. In other cases, the nature of the task defined by the evaluation might be so technical that the effort to train volunteers would not be cost-effective. Generally, internal audits or special studies that are not intended for public use might not be appropriate opportunities for engaging volunteers. Alternatively, community assessments or other studies that attempt to improve accountability and service delivery from the perspective of key stakeholders would likely be enhanced though the use of volunteers.

What Is the Role of the Evaluator in Relation to the Organization and Its Volunteers?

Some organizations have in-house research directors or an individual with a background in evaluation or assessment and therefore do not need outside help to undertake evaluation activities. Whether the evaluator resides in-house or is retained as a consultant, the organization needs to define whether the evaluator will serve as a facilitator, technical director of the evaluation, trainer, or some combination of these roles. This consideration is particularly important for community-level evaluations, where the evaluator may be perceived as an outsider to the community. Particularly when the goal of the evaluation is to help residents become more knowledgeable and effective users of community data, the process and subsequent results will be improved when the evaluator adopts the role of facilitator or coach and works closely with the sponsoring organization to develop and implement the evaluation.

How Broad or Limited Is the Intended Scope of Volunteer Involvement?

Volunteers can participate in evaluation activities in many ways. In some cases, the organization may not have the capacity to train volunteers to collect data but is very interested in obtaining feedback from clients or other community stakeholders. One of the key ways in which volunteers can play an important role is to help identify relevant program or community outcomes. Such information can be solicited through focus group discussions, customer feedback forms, or periodic surveys. Although the use of volunteers, particularly to assist in activities that could not be undertaken by the organization due to limited human resources, can save time, involving volunteers in data collection activities can necessitate additional levels of coordination and thus take more time to complete the activity. Given the dual purposes of many community assessment activities to obtain information while also building skills of resident volunteers or engaging community members in finding solutions, the additional time spent is not likely to be considered an obstacle.

How Will Volunteers Be Recruited? Are Special Skills or Training Required?

Nonprofit organizations typically have ready access to a variety of constituent groups that might be tapped as volunteers. For direct service organizations, this task might be as simple as posting a note to a bulletin board or picking up the telephone to ask for assistance from individuals. Community-based organizations might have access to a youth leadership group or neighborhood action committee. Initial recruitment efforts are typically relatively easy. The greater challenge is in maintaining the volunteers' interest and involvement later. Evaluation activities in which volunteers participate are typically accompanied by one-time on-the-job training. Thus, organizations should consider in advance whether specific training procedures need to be developed, such as training residents to interview neighbors or in the use of trained observer rating guides (or photographs) to maximize inter-rater reliability. Other skills that may be desirable, depending on circumstances, are basic computer skills and the ability to translate, read, or interpret in different languages.

Who Is Responsible for Coordinating Volunteers?

This task is usually reserved for the organization sponsoring the evaluation activity, often through the assignment of a field coordinator. The field coordinator is perhaps the most critical ingredient in a successful effort to engage volunteers in evaluation activities. This individual is responsible for coordinating the various tasks, scheduling and motivating volunteers, and troubleshooting, especially if the evaluator is not accessible on a regular basis. The field coordinator is also often attuned to the volunteers' perspective and can step in when certain problems are detected. For example, in Fort Worth, the field coordinator noted that some volunteers were more conscientious than others. He experimented with various pairings of individuals until the right fit could be found. He also worked with some of the more dedicated volunteers to increase their level of responsibility by sharing some of the scheduling tasks.

What Role Will Other Stakeholders Have in the Evaluation?
How Will the Community Be Prepared for the Evaluation?

Particularly in community-level evaluation, there is a tendency for nonprofit organizations (particularly those with an inclination toward advocacy) to prefer not to engage a wide variety of stakeholders at the outset. This is in part due to past experiences or perceptions of advocacy groups about how data might be used to undermine the community or a simple distrust of agencies or organizations external to the community. It is important for nonprofits, community advocates, and other stakeholders to recognize that the best solutions to community concerns will likely result from a transparent process. Community groups can often strengthen their evaluation activities by partnering with other organizations that may have access to a wider range of resources and technical ability for obtaining credible data. These organizations may also have experience to guide community groups in the use of evaluation results to identify priorities and appropriate strategies to be undertaken by various constituent groups. The best way to accomplish this is to keep all relevant parties informed at the outset and throughout the process and to consider what each group is willing to contribute to the effort. Similarly, outreach efforts to the community or neighborhood in which the evaluation is taking place are likely to help maximize participation and response to various data collection activities, as well as commitment to the findings once they are made known.

What Is the Availability and Role of Technology versus Traditional Paper-and-Pencil Approaches to Data Collection and Record-Keeping Activities?

Understandably there is concern in the nonprofit community about costs. Trade-offs exist between resource requests and the need to obtain and report credible information. Recent efforts to experiment with technology demonstrate potential for greater efficiencies in data collection. This must be balanced with considerations about equipment costs and the availability of in-house expertise to program and maintain databases and reporting formats. The main advantages of newer technologies, such as hand-held or pocket computers, are the ability to eliminate the need for additional data entry and to generate data reports in a matter of minutes rather than waiting days or weeks or months for data entry and error checks to take place. Technology has also provided an incentive to volunteers who are eager to learn how to use the new devices, particularly young people raised in the electronic age. Several corporations have demonstrated a willingness to donate equipment to communities as part of their commitment to public service. In addition, some communities are beginning to contemplate the idea of lending libraries for slightly older models of technology. Handheld or pocket PCs currently range from about $250 to $500 per unit. For example, a Dell Axim 5 with 32 MB of RAM, USB cradle, carrying case, and a three-year warranty will cost $330. Units have become considerably more affordable over the past several years. The units used in Fort Worth a couple of years ago (Casseopeia Model E-125 which is no longer available) cost approximately $450. Additional accessories such as digital cameras, wireless modems, and GPS receivers can be purchased for between $300 and $500 per unit.

What Will Motivate Volunteers to Stay with the Effort?

Volunteers most often choose to get involved because they wish to make a tangible contribution to an organization, their community, or a cause. Thus, it is imperative to demonstrate a connection between the assigned tasks or activity and a tangible product or result. (By and large, the same logic tends to apply to nonprofit staff asked to participate in evaluation activities.) Other interim incentives for volunteers include the opportunity to develop new skills, participate as a member of a group or committee, and interact with other residents or individuals who share similar ideas about the community. These interim incentives often bring someone to the table and sustain his or her interest at the outset. Beyond these incentives, cash stipends are still likely to be the most popular, particularly if working with youth or in lower-income neighborhoods. Cash incentives can be structured in a number of ways, such as to compensate individuals for successful completion of a specific activity (such as attending an orientation meeting, community forum, or training session) or for completing an agreed-on package of activities over the course of a three- or six-month project period. In Fort Worth, $250 was allotted for each youth participant and $125 for each adult adviser. Additional funds were held in reserve to reward more dedicated volunteers at the end of the project.

Regardless of the type of incentive offered, volunteers may lose interest as the evaluation wears on and unexpected challenges arise. Again, the volunteer coordinator is an important source for gauging the level of commitment of the volunteers, keeping individuals focused on the end result and helping to keep the process running as smoothly as possible. The volunteer coordinator, working with the evaluator, can provide periodic updates or status reports as well as share preliminary results as they are available. By and large, however, as with any other volunteer endeavor, the organization should expect some level of attrition.

Volunteers and Evaluation

Clearly there are numerous trade-offs to consider in determining whether to use volunteers in community-level evaluation. There is great promise and potential for nonprofits to leverage additional human capital. However, this assumes that resources and skills are available to the organization to train and coordinate volunteers. Many intangible and unexpected benefits resulted from the use of youth volunteers in Fort Worth: a strengthened sense of community among project participants, increased understanding of the needs and concerns of residents, and the opportunity for youth to interact with city council representatives.

The goal will always be to develop a model for volunteer involvement in community evaluation that can be easily replicated at low cost. Several models are already in place. The next challenge will be to document successful processes and procedures and seek ways to sustain these efforts. Evaluators need to find ways to transfer the skills and expertise required to undertake resident data collection activities to individuals within community-based organizations. A model for replicating and sustaining these efforts might be to work with one or more high school instructors (or college professors) willing to incorporate these skills into a civics curriculum, class project, or ongoing community service program. This approach would access new groups of students each year who could be trained in the techniques and facilitate data collection on a recurring basis.

Conclusion

Nonprofit organizations face a unique set of challenges that have historically contributed to an underappreciation for the value and utility of program evaluation. As real and valid as many of these concerns remain, however, these organizations must find practical ways to overcome their inexperience with evaluation: their very survival may depend on it. This chapter began with an overview of many of the challenges that small nonprofits encounter in their attempts to create and use evaluation data. Some of these challenges are philosophical (such as organizational reluctance to divert resources from service delivery to data collection and monitoring efforts), but most are practical (such as insufficient familiarity or technical ability to undertake evaluation activities) and thus more amenable to some of the potential solutions discussed.

The demand for credible evaluation information from nonprofit organizations is high. Increasingly, board members, donors, and community stakeholders are asking more sophisticated questions and expecting data-driven responses. Nevertheless, many community-based nonprofits continue to lack the internal capacity to obtain or interpret program data readily. We considered strategies for making evaluation activities relevant to an organization by looking at client characteristics, seeking instructive comparisons, and leveraging assistance from the evaluation community and volunteers. The solutions offered throughout this chapter are designed to increase the confidence and proficiency of small nonprofits in maximizing the quality and use of evaluation techniques and results.

References

Affholter, D. P. "Outcome Monitoring." In J. Wholey, H. Hatry, and K. Newcomer (eds.), *Handbook of Practical Program Evaluation*. San Francisco: Jossey-Bass, 1994.

Chelimsky, E. "Making Evaluation Units Effective." In J. Wholey, H. Hatry, and Newcomer, K. (eds.), *Handbook of Practical Program Evaluation*. San Francisco: Jossey-Bass, 1994.

Dawson, J. A., and D'Amico, J. J. "Involving Program Staff in Evaluation Studies: A Strategy for Increasing Information Use and Increasing the Data Base." *Evaluation Review,* 1985, *9*(2), 173–188.

Fetterman, D. M. "Empowerment Evaluation: An Introduction to Theory and Practice." In D. M. Fetterman, S. J. Kaftarian, and A. Wandersman (eds.), *Empowerment Evaluation: Knowledge and Tools for Self-Assessment and Accountability.* Thousand Oaks, Calif.: Sage, 1996.

Greene, J. G. "Stakeholder Participation and Utilization in Program Evaluation." *Evaluation Review,* 1988, *12*(2), 91–116.

Hatry, H., and Lampkin, L. (eds.). *An Agenda for Action: Outcome Management in Nonprofit Organizations.* Washington, D.C.: Urban Institute, 2001.

Morley, E., Hatry H., and Cowan, J. *Making Use of Outcome Information for Improving Services: Recommendations for Nonprofit Organizations.* Washington, D.C.: Urban Institute, 2002.

Papineau, D., and Kiely, M. "Participatory Evaluation in a Community Organization: Fostering Stakeholder Empowerment and Utilization." *Evaluation and Program Planning,* 1996, *19*(1), 79–93.

Plantz, M. C., Greenway, M. T., and Hendricks, M. "Outcome Measurement: Showing Results in the Nonprofit Sector." In K. E. Newcomer (ed.), *Using Performance Measurement to Improve Public and Nonprofit Programs.* New Directions for Evaluation, no. 75. San Francisco: Jossey-Bass, 1977.

Sanders, J. R. "Presidential Address: On Mainstreaming Evaluation." *American Journal of Evaluation,* 2002, *23*(3), 253–259.

United Way of America. *Measuring Program Outcomes: A Practical Approach.* Washington D.C.: United Way of America, 1996.

United Way of America. *Indicators That a United Way Is Ready to Plan for, Implement, Sustain, Use and Benefit from Program Outcome Measurement.* Washington D.C.: United Way of America, 2003.

United Way of Greater Milwaukee. *Funded Program Characteristics and Outcomes for the 1999/2000 Fiscal Year.* Milwaukee, Wis.: United Way of Greater Milwaukee, 2001.

United Way of Greater Milwaukee. *A Demographic Profile of Clients Served by Funded Agencies in 2000–2001.* Milwaukee, Wis.: United Way of Greater Milwaukee, 2002.

24

Other Issues and Trends in Evaluation

Harry P. Hatry, Joseph S. Wholey,
Kathryn E. Newcomer

Many opportunities exist to use evaluation to improve program design and program performance. This handbook presents a variety of approaches for evaluating program performance and getting evaluation results used. In this final chapter, we discuss important related topics: (1) quality control of the evaluation process, (2) selection and training of evaluation personnel, (3) standards and ethics in evaluation work, (4) incentives for the conduct and use of program evaluation, and (5) the relationship between program evaluation and performance monitoring. Finally, we discuss trends in program evaluation and present some concluding observations.

Quality Control of the Evaluation Process

A major purpose of program evaluation is to examine the quality of public services. Evaluators should be concerned with the quality of the evaluation work as well in individual evaluations and across evaluations. Earlier chapters in this book suggest a number of quality control steps to take in managing evaluation activities—for example, checking for missing data and checking for consistency in the definitions of data items when data are collected from different offices or different years.

Here we are concerned with quality control of the entire evaluation process. Public and private agencies that undertake evaluation activity, whether in-depth studies or ongoing performance monitoring, might implement such quality control processes as the following (more detailed suggestions, with criteria for judging the quality of a performance monitoring system, are provided in Wholey, 1999):

- Provide for peer review of evaluation designs and draft evaluation reports. The peer review might be undertaken by evaluators in the agency, evaluators in another part of government, or experts from universities or consulting firms. These peer reviews should be done by people familiar with the type of program being evaluated; many evaluation problems can occur because evaluators lack knowledge of the program.
- Give staff in the agencies and programs that have been evaluated the opportunity to respond to draft evaluation findings. This step is valuable both politically and for quality control. The feedback can identify important problems in the evaluation itself. In an evaluation of drug programs in Dade County, Florida, for example, the agencies whose programs were evaluated noted after reviewing the draft report that an important group of client records had been overlooked by the evaluators. This required the evaluation team to reopen its data collection and analysis activities and rework its findings.
- Provide for periodic outside, independent reviews of the evaluation activities, as the U.S. General Accounting Office (2003) has suggested. Such reviews should identify any patterns of weakness in evaluation design, data collection procedures, or report presentations and suggest steps to increase the technical quality and usefulness of the evaluation findings. Reviewers might also identify alternative approaches not currently being used by the evaluation office. Any office tends to slip into standard modes of operation. Outside critics may be in the best position to identify the need for changes.
- Regularly review the work of evaluation contractors and provide oversight of the evaluation contractor's work while it is under way, including review of evaluation designs and draft evaluation reports (see Chapter Twenty, this volume). After the final report has been submitted, the quality and timeliness of the contractor's performance should be assessed, taking into consideration the time and resources that were available.
- Place primary responsibility for data quality on the program managers and staff who oversee collection of the evaluation data elements. This is the first line of defense against bad data. While evaluation contractors and independent evaluators may collect new data, inevitably some important data will come from the program staff.

Evaluator Selection and Training

Getting skilled, trained evaluators is an important prerequisite for quality evaluations An evaluation usually requires a team rather than a single individual. The team is likely to need an understanding of organizational contexts, legislative mandates, evaluation designs, data collection, data processing, analysis methods, and the ability to listen and communicate evaluation findings and recommendations, both orally and in writing. All the needed knowledge and skills, however, need not, and usually will not, reside in a single individual. An evaluation team can also use outside members for services such as survey research, data processing, and editing.

Educational background is informative but by no means likely to be conclusive in selecting evaluation personnel. Good grades in evaluation-related courses will likely increase the probability that candidates know what they are doing, at least with regard to the technical aspects of evaluation work. But some individuals with such training do not adapt well to operating environments in which resource constraints preclude elaborate designs such as controlled experiments. We have worked with many fine evaluators whose backgrounds may seem quite surprising, such as history majors. Program evaluators most need logical, systematic approaches to their work; such abilities can be found in people with many different backgrounds. Examples of past evaluation work should be sought to help determine the skill levels of candidates for evaluation positions.

Agencies should provide periodic training opportunities for both experienced and newer evaluation staff. Training should cover such topics as detailed evaluation designs, statistical techniques for selecting samples and analyzing the data, questionnaire design, working with program personnel, and the effective presentation of evaluation results.

Standards and Ethics

Certain norms should guide all evaluators' work, regardless of their discipline. In planning their work, for example, evaluators should ensure that evaluation criteria are relevant and that evaluation findings will be available in time for important policy and management decisions. Within available resource constraints, evaluators should ensure that their data and conclusions are valid. They should ensure adequate training for data collectors, pretests of data collection schemes, ongoing quality control testing of data collection, and security of the resulting data. The bases for decisions about who, what, when, and how to measure should be clear to evaluation clients.

Standards exist for certain segments of the evaluation profession (Davis, 1990). U.S. General Accounting Office "Yellow Book" standards (2003) guide the work of its auditors and evaluators as well as those in agency offices of inspectors general. In 1982, the Evaluation Research society promulgated general standards for evaluation work (Rossi, 1982). In 1992, its successor, the American Evaluation Association, began efforts to develop a new set of standards for evaluation practice. The Joint Committee on Standards for Educational Evaluation (1994) has published a set of standards for evaluation of education programs. The American Evaluation Association developed a set of guiding principles for evaluation and endorsed the joint committee's evaluation standards.

One of the most difficult dilemmas for evaluators is ensuring that the benefits of evaluation exceed its costs. Evaluators may be asked to expend resources on evaluation projects that they believe are unlikely to yield useful data. Evaluators and auditors may be asked to answer evaluation questions that they consider unanswerable given realistic time and resource constraints or the realities of program design. Under such conditions, evaluators should consider segmenting the problem (conducting small pilot studies designed to clarify what is knowable in the short term, what additional information is likely to be useful, and what it would cost to get and use additional information) or, at the extreme, not attempting the evaluation.

If evaluation findings are likely to influence public support for the program or have other political repercussions, evaluators may face pressures to slant their findings in one direction or another. They may receive more or less subtle cues from evaluation sponsors indicating that such slanting is desired. These situations are always difficult. An evaluator who faces such pressures and is unable to resolve them may be forced to move elsewhere. One possible solution is for the evaluator to indicate the assumptions that would lead to a particular conclusion and then show in a sensitivity analysis how different assumptions would lead to different conclusions. Another option the evaluator can take in extreme circumstances is whistle-blowing, such as reporting to the agency's inspector general that such pressures have been exerted. If the pressures are subtle, however, whistle-blowers may find themselves in untenable situations later.

Information obtained in evaluations should not violate program participants' anonymity, confidentiality, or privacy rights. If the evaluators want to quote or refer to particular individuals, they should usually obtain the written permission of the people to be cited. For some evaluations, the evaluators will be required by a federal agency to obtain informed consent prior to obtaining records on or conducting interviews with individuals. The Education Commission of the States (1991) defines such informed consent as follows: "A person must voluntarily give his or her consent before information about that person can be released to someone else, and consent must be based on a full understanding of what information will be exchanged, with whom it will be shared, and how it will be used" (p. 2). The commission's report on information sharing is a good source for a comprehensive discussion of the meaning of confidentiality. Sieber (1992) offers useful guidance on working on internal review boards to ensure that research is done ethically.

Obtaining informed-consent forms can become quite cumbersome and time-consuming. Evaluators should determine in advance what requirements apply to a particular evaluation. Evaluators may need to consider alternatives such as requesting data without any personal identifiers or requesting group data only. Both options, however, preclude linking data on the same individuals from different sources.

A major concern arises if courts subpoena evaluators' records: these may include data permitting identification of individuals who have been guaranteed confidentiality. This possibility poses a legal question that evaluators should refer to their own legal advisers. Evaluators should not automatically provide such subpoenaed information before determining their legal rights. In some cases, the confidentiality of the responses is protected under law.

Incentives for Undertaking Program Evaluation and Using Evaluation Findings

For evaluation to be worth the effort, evaluation findings and recommendations need to be used by executives, managers, or legislators. Evaluators can provide information that may guide decisions to improve performance, but political and bureaucratic will is also needed for change to occur.

Evaluation is often threatening to the administrators whose programs are being evaluated. Evaluations may provide ammunition for those who want to reduce program expenditures or dramatically change the program's direction. Many so-called summative evaluations performed by the federal government fall into this category. We believe, however, that a major purpose of most program evaluations should be to provide information that helps program managers and staff to improve their programs. This more constructive approach should be emphasized by agencies—public and private—and by evaluators themselves. To get the most out of evaluation, those at higher levels should create incentives for—and remove disincentives to—performance-oriented management and management-oriented evaluation. Here we suggest some incentives for constructive use of program evaluation:

• Involving potential users in the evaluation can encourage use. Regardless of who sponsors the evaluation, evaluators should seek input from program managers and staff on evaluation objectives and criteria. Where appropriate, evaluators should include the program manager and key program staff as reviewers of the evaluation design and draft reports or even on the evaluation team. Program managers should be kept aware of the progress of evaluations and be given the opportunity to review evaluation findings before they are made public. These steps increase the likelihood that program personnel accept and use the findings.

- The legislative body, chief executive, or agency head can mandate periodic program evaluations or regular monitoring and reporting of program outcomes. Congress has mandated in-depth evaluations for a number of programs. The Government Performance and Results Act of 1993 (GPRA) requires federal agencies to report annually on the performance of each of their major programs and develop evaluation plans (U.S. Congress, 1993). As of the end of 1999, at least thirty-three state legislatures had required some form of performance measurement by the executive branch (Liner and others, 2001). Many states require regular reporting of a variety of indicators of school district and individual school performance. Although these activities primarily focus on performance monitoring, such activities sometimes lead to more in-depth evaluation studies.

- The legislative body, chief executive, or agency head can ask program managers to set target levels of performance in terms of key service quality and outcome indicators at the beginning of the year and to report progress in achieving those targets quarterly or at the end of the year. (Since 1998, the federal government has undertaken such planning and reporting as required by the 1993 Government Performance and Results Act.) This step is most applicable in situations where regular performance monitoring is used rather than in-depth program evaluations.

- To the extent feasible, the chief executive or agency head can take steps to build achievement of program results into performance appraisal systems for executives, managers, and supervisors. (We do not recommend that government agencies jump quickly into linking staff members' pay to program results, however. When money is brought into the picture, the chances of hurting morale and being counterproductive escalate considerably.) If achievement of organizational objectives is included in managers' performance appraisals, both those appraised and those doing the appraising should recognize that factors outside the managers' control can affect program results. The managers appraised may have been the beneficiaries of windfalls or the victims of "pitfalls" due to external factors. (For example, the outcomes of job training programs can be affected by changes in the local economy that are beyond the control of the program manager.) Such problems can be alleviated if performance targets are adjusted to reflect the influence of factors beyond the control of program managers, such as client characteristics and local economic conditions. Governments can use performance contracts (or grants), with rewards or penalties tied to success in meeting targets included in the contract or grant. This is already becoming more common.

- Legislators or chief executives can give agencies and programs more flexibility in how they do their work if they have regularly met, or exceeded, their performance targets. For example, programs could be given more flexibility over personnel controls, and restrictions could be reduced on line item or object class fund transfers—in exchange for meeting performance targets based on evaluation results.

Most of the above items are steps that program managers and evaluators cannot take by themselves. They require actions by higher-level officials in governing bodies of private organizations or in the executive and legislative branches of government.

Relation Between In-Depth Program Evaluations and Performance Monitoring

Considerable differences in opinion exist among evaluators as to how performance monitoring and in-depth evaluation studies are related, in particular the extent to which they are at odds with or complement each other.

In-depth evaluations seek to provide information on the linkage of a program's intervention to the outcomes that occurred. They seek to provide information on the outcomes of the intervention and explanations as to why the outcomes occurred, particularly the extent to which the intervention contributed to the outcomes. Such evaluations may require relatively large resources. Thus, only a portion, and usually a very small portion, of the programs of an organization are evaluated in any given year.

Performance monitoring seeks primarily to assess the outcomes of a program without any in-depth examination of the program. Typically, organizations apply performance monitoring to a wide number of the organization's programs, and the outcome information is available at frequent intervals, such as quarterly, or monthly.

In-depth evaluations are considerably more informative and provide considerably more information for major policy and program decisions. Performance monitoring tends to be much more of a management tool because of the frequency, and thus timeliness, of the information.

We believe that these processes are complementary. We believe that performance monitoring can and should be considered an important subset of program evaluation. Thus, a chapter on performance monitoring has been included in both editions of this book. Performance monitoring has the advantage of maintaining a focus on outcomes in a wide variety of service areas.

Furthermore, we believe that the presence of performance monitoring tends to encourage the use of in-depth evaluations. This occurs in two ways. First, the information on outcomes from a performance measurement system often raises questions as to why the outcomes are as good or bad as they are. This is likely to occur particularly in situations where the outcomes failed to meet targets or were much better than targets. Having performance data inevitably leads to questioning as to why the significant results have occurred and thus to greater support for evaluation studies, at least in selected programs. Usually, however, because of a lack of time and resources, public organizations seek less expensive ways to obtain such data. However, when the stakes are large, public organizations are likely to press for an in-depth evaluation, particularly at the federal level of government.

Second, if an organization regularly collects outcome information, this can enhance the ability of evaluators to undertake in-depth evaluations by providing ready-made outcome data. For example, if an outcome monitoring system has been regularly obtaining feedback from clients of health and social service programs at regular intervals, subsequent evaluations can use such information and not rely solely on after-the-fact data collection, saving time and funds and perhaps providing better evaluation information.

Not widely recognized is that the availability of regularly collected outcome information also has the potential for encouraging small-scale randomized, controlled experiments. For example, if a program is regularly collecting outcome information and program officials want to test a new intervention without immediately applying it across the board, evaluators would need only to develop the process for randomization of future clients and add to the database information as to which clients received which intervention. This possibility applies primarily to relatively small-scale interventions and interventions that are limited to one organization. (However, various matched-pair designs might be used involving multiple locations in the country.) This randomization option has very rarely been used to date, but we believe it represents an untapped considerable potential. Such randomized evaluations might even be undertaken by organization staff with little outside assistance. (Note, however, that the outcome information from performance monitoring systems will not likely exactly match the needs of a particular in-depth evaluation. However, if the program's performance monitoring process includes customer outcome data identified by demographic and service characteristics, the evaluators are likely to be able to obtain a great deal of the information that they need.)

What appears needed by public organizations is a combination, a balance, of in-depth evaluations and performance monitoring. The GPRA, for example, with its focus on results, specifically calls for performance monitoring and indirectly for program evaluation (such as by requiring that findings from completed program evaluations be reported in each federal agency's annual performance report). These requirements strengthen the demand for both. Indeed, the introduction of GPRA, and to a lesser extent state government legislation that calls for performance monitoring, appears likely to stimulate the demand for in-depth program evaluations, particularly large-scale evaluations at the federal government level.

Retrospective versus Prospective "Evaluation"

Program evaluation looks backward. It seeks to provide information to stakeholders that assesses past success. An important use for this evaluation information is to help decision makers make decisions about the future. The evaluators may provide their recommendations about changes that are desirable given the findings from their evaluation. However, as usually defined, program evaluation does not examine future options.

Examining future options as to their likely effects and costs is another, and quite different, type of analysis. It involves looking into the future, an even more difficult subject than program evaluation, This future-looking analysis is called by such names as *policy analysis, systems analysis,* or *program analysis.* Performance budgeting also focuses on the future. Budget decisions should consider past outcomes and in-depth program evaluation findings as bases for estimating the future results that would be achieved by particular funding levels. However, this falls more into the realm of future analysis rather than that of program evaluation.

Some cost-effectiveness and cost-benefit analyses focus on past results (See Chapter Eighteen). Most cost-effectiveness and cost-benefit analyses focus on future results.

Trends in Program Evaluation

Here we provide our thoughts as to likely trends in program evaluation over this decade.

Ever-tighter budgets are likely to continue. The environment in which managers and evaluators work has become more challenging as taxpayers and legislators continue to be insistent on economy, efficiency, and identifying what they are getting for their money. This will continue to encourage public officials at federal, state, and local levels, and others responsible for providing funding to service organizations to justify their funding with some form of evaluation information. This applies to each of the following types of organizations:

- Federal and state legislation has led to requirements for some form of performance monitoring, with over thirty-three states having some sort of performance monitoring legislation.
- Nonprofit service organizations have begun facing pressure to provide evidence that they have made a difference in the lives of their clients.

United Way of America led this effort, with many local United Ways introducing requirements for outcome information, usually with some form of performance monitoring.

- Many private foundations have increasingly been requiring evaluation efforts, including in-depth program evaluations.

- Internationally, a number of countries have begun developing evaluation capabilities. Australia, Canada, Sweden, New Zealand, and the United Kingdom have had some form of evaluation for many years. Japan has begun to develop its evaluation capacity at the national government and prefecture levels (approximately the equivalent of U.S. counties) and has formed a national evaluation society. Efforts in international cooperation are likely to continue to grow, such as the Cochrane Collaboration and Campbell Collaboration processes (which involve meta-analyses and research syntheses in various service areas such as health and education). The latter bodes well for the likelihood of strengthening worldwide interest in quality program evaluations and the use of that information to identify successful practices.

- Developing countries are being pressed by the international donor community to focus on results, rather than primarily on funds and activities, and this has become a major theme of the international donor community in its efforts to help developing countries. This appears highly likely to continue. The major multilateral banks such as the World Bank, the Asian Development Bank, and the Inter-American Development Bank, and individual country donors such as those of the United States (Agency for International Development), Canada, United Kingdom, Sweden, and Germany, for example, have begun to encourage funded countries to develop evaluation processes. This effort is still in its infancy. We expect that university faculty members in many of these countries will become increasingly interested in in-depth program evaluations encouraged by this focus on identifying the results of government-sponsored programs.

It is inevitable that controversy will continue over such performance monitoring and evaluation requirements. Many service organizations believe that evaluation activities reduce funding for their direct services to clients and thus are harmful. In addition, questions about the capacity of service organizations to undertake such efforts are, and will continue to be, a major concern. These concerns are legitimate. If funders, and the service organizations themselves, are to make evaluation effort worthwhile, they need to use the evaluation information to help them improve their programs. Both service organizations and funders need help in developing their capacity to support evaluation efforts. We expect that more will be done in future years to alleviate both of these concerns.

Emphasis on Evaluation for Government Audits and Program Reviews

Evaluation procedures will likely be used increasingly in government auditing and program reviews. Both federal and state-level auditing in the past has primarily focused on fiscal auditing and searching for waste, fraud, and abuse. However, performance auditing and related external reviews of agency performance have been growing with their emphasis on what results programs are getting for their funds. The U.S. General Accounting Office has been a major leader in this "value for money" auditing, along with similar offices in Canada and United Kingdom. The current comptroller general of the United States has even proposed changing the name of the U.S. General Accounting Office to the U.S. Government Accountability Office. At the state level, the National Legislative Program Evaluation Society of the National Council of State Legislatures was formed. In 2001, it reported on forty-four states that had some form of office outside the executive branch that undertook at least some evaluation activity (National Conference of State Legislatures, 2001). (These efforts are limited to after-the-fact evaluations, precluding randomized controlled experiments.)

Continued Expansion of the Use of Customer Surveys as a Major Data Collection Procedure

Use of customer surveys as a major data collection procedure for evaluating public programs will be a growth industry. Their use has already grown considerably in the government sector. (Of course, evaluators have used customer feedback as a data collection procedure for many years.) GPRA has led to a sizable increase in the number of surveys sponsored by the federal government and its agencies. For a large number of programs, feedback from households and program customers is necessary to obtain meaningful information on the condition, attitudes, and behaviors of clients after they have completed service (whether the condition relates to their employment status, heath, extent of risk behavior, or something else). The survey research industry has benefited greatly from this trend. It appears highly likely that the use of such surveys will continue to grow. This same trend is beginning to occur in the nonprofit sector, where organizations are increasingly seeking outcome information on service results and in other countries.

New Technology Will Speed Up and Enrich Evaluation Data

New technology, some of which we can only guess at, is likely to add to the richness of the data available and the increasing ability to process large amounts of data in a practical way. For example, as indicated in Chapter

Eight on trained observers, the use of hand-held calculators, bolstered by the use of photography and videotaping (and perhaps even holographic devices), is likely to be used increasingly to track the physical condition of a variety of service elements, such as roads, parks, buildings, housing, and neighborhoods. These devices can be used to obtain more accurate ratings as well as more comprehensive information useful to evaluation users.

Data entry and analysis are almost certain to become much faster and less expensive for evaluators (balanced by the cost of the new technical equipment). Technology is already available that permits direct real-time entry of field-collected data into computers, such as to translate observations of problems in the field directly into work orders for repair and maintenance crews. Advances in computer and copying technology will increasingly allow easier production of attractive, multicolored reports and fancier forms. The accessibility of such tools will enhance the capability of evaluators to draw attention to their data. A danger here is that overdone visuals may confuse readers or deflect questions about the accuracy and validity of the evaluation findings. These technological developments seem likely to increase the quality and richness of the evaluation information that can be obtained. The danger still exists that evaluators may overcomplicate their reports and miss the forest for the trees of technology.

Increased Understanding of the Use of Evaluation Information in Improving Programs

A major issue in making evaluation, including performance monitoring, useful is the inadequate use of the findings by decision makers. Thus far, the primary use of outcome information in performance monitoring efforts at all levels and in all sectors has been for accountability purposes, not for program improvement. This mirrors the in-depth evaluation distinction between summative and formative evaluation. For example, the large amount of data resulting annually from the GPRA appears to be greatly underused by program managers, primarily concerned with meeting higher-level requirements for the reports. This need appears to have distracted agency officials and their program managers from using the data to make improvements.

Exceptions exist, but on the whole, this lack of use of evaluation to improve programs appears to be a major gap. We expect this will change as program personnel become more familiar with outcome data, and managers will be encouraged to use the data for improvement purposes. The availability of regularly collected outcome information through performance monitoring procedures has already begun to stimulate the use of the outcome information for a number of other purposes, such as:

- Use of incentives based at least in part on measured program outcomes as a basis for monetary awards for public managers. Monetary incentives, based at least in part on program outcomes, are controversial. This is due in part because they usually have been based primarily on the judgments of supervisors, with resulting concerns about supervisor favoritism and biases. In the past, performance appraisals have been handicapped by the lack of objective outcome information. As government employees become more comfortable with the relevance and reliability of outcome information, the use of outcome data for both monetary and nonmonetary incentives is likely to increase. An essential element, not well understood, is that when using outcome information, the government and its employees need to accept that causality is not established by outcome information alone. Thus, all parties need to accept that windfalls will happen that cause good outcomes and that external factors will arise that produce poor outcomes.

- Use of performance information in program reviews. For example, a supervisor can regularly hold program review meetings, that is, "How are we doing? sessions" with staff to go over the latest performance reports. These sessions would be used to identify where the program is doing well and where badly, seek suggestions for making improvements, and in later review sessions identify the extent to which, after changes have been made, improved outcomes have or have not occurred. The reports reviewed would include information from both regular performance monitoring reports and any in-depth evaluation reports that had become available during that reporting period. Major versions of this approach have been used in New York City and Baltimore (see Henderson, 2003). In both cities, high-level officials review organizational performance with their personnel at regular intervals, clearly signaling the interest of these top officials in the performance data. We expect to see some form of this process expand considerably as evaluation data become more regularly available.

University Education Will Increasingly Include Evaluation Material

It seems likely that university training in such subjects as public administration, public policy, and specific program areas such as health, education, and criminal justice will increase attention in their curricula to evaluation because of the increased interest in these fields. In the long run, this should build the demand for evaluation, including performance monitoring. Student understanding of evaluation will likely, more often than not, make them less fearful of it and make them better future users of such information. Similarly, more in-service training in evaluation is likely to occur on evaluation in government and nonprofit service agencies.

Final Thoughts

At the beginning of this handbook, we suggested two primary reasons for evaluation activities: to achieve greater accountability in the use of public or donated funds and to help agency officials to improve their programs. We believe that the second purpose should usually be the primary one. In the long run, improving services should be the main rationale for allocating resources to evaluation activities, whether for ad hoc, in-depth evaluations or for regular, ongoing monitoring of program results. This is the cost-effectiveness test for program evaluation, whether the benefits to citizens ultimately received by improved programs is worth the cost of the programs.

Given the trend toward increased monitoring and evaluation of government and private sector performance, the challenge for evaluators will be to respond to these new opportunities and help ensure that evaluation leads to more effective programs. Because most government and nonprofit agencies operate under severe financial constraints, evaluation funds will always be vulnerable. Thus, it is vital that evaluators demonstrate beneficial results from their work. Evaluators should document the effects that their evaluations have and develop case studies of evaluations that have been used to add value to government programs.

Evaluators should devise practices that are as low cost as possible, both to reduce their vulnerability to budget cuts and to get the most product from limited resources. Throughout this handbook, we have attempted to identify low-cost evaluation options. Evaluators should consider such approaches as the following:

- Using agency records to the extent possible
- Using focus groups to help identify evaluation criteria, collect evaluation data, and help interpret evaluation data
- Using less powerful evaluation designs
- Using smaller sample sizes
- Resisting the temptation to seek unnecessarily large amounts of information
- Using mail and telephone surveys rather than in-person interviews (with follow-ups to increase response rates), and accepting lower response rates than ideally desired if necessary
- Avoiding excessive precision in sampling and statistical analysis (for example, 95 percent confidence levels may be too costly; such precision may not be needed in many program evaluation efforts)
- Using technology where appropriate to save time and money in data collection, entry, processing, and analysis

Program evaluation, whether low cost or high cost, is by no means a panacea. It does not substitute for quality implementation of programs. It is not likely to provide definitive information as to benefits or causality. What evaluation can do is provide reasonably reliable, reasonably valid information about the merits and results of particular programs operating in particular circumstances. Necessary compromises will inevitably mean that the users of the information will be less than fully certain of the validity of the evaluation findings. In a world full of uncertainties and hazards, however, it is better to be roughly right than to remain ignorant.

References

Davis, D. F. "Do You Want a Performance Audit or an Evaluation?" *Public Administration Review,* 1990, *50*(1), 35–41.

Education Commission of the States. *Confidentiality and Collaboration: Information Sharing in Interagency Efforts.* Washington, D.C.: Education Commission of the States, Jan. 1991.

Henderson, L. J. "The Baltimore CitiStat Program: Performance and Accountability." Arlington, Va.: IBM Endowment for the Business of Government, May 2003.

Joint Committee on Standards for Educational Evaluation. *The Program Evaluation Standards.* (2nd ed.) Thousand Oaks, Calif.: Sage, 1994.

Liner, B., and others. *Making Results-Based State Government Work.* Washington, D.C.: Urban Institute Press, 2001.

National Conference of State Legislatures. "Ensuring the Public Trust: How Program Policy Evaluation Is Serving State Legislatures." Denver, Colo.: National Conference of State Legislatures, July 2001.

Rossi, P. H. (ed.). *Standards for Evaluation Practice.* New Directions for Program Evaluation, no. 15. San Francisco: Jossey-Bass, 1982.

Sieber, J. E. *Planning Ethically Responsible Research.* Thousand Oaks, Calif.: Sage, 1992.

U.S. Congress, Senate, Committee on Governmental Affairs. "Government Performance and Results Act of 1993. " 103rd Cong., 1st sess., June 16, 1993.

U.S. General Accounting Office. *Government Auditing Standards.* Washington, D.C.: U.S. Government Printing Office, 2003.

Wholey, J. S. "Quality Control: Assessing the Accuracy and Usefulness of Performance Measurement Systems." In H. Hatry (ed.), *Performance Measurement: Getting Results.* Washington, D.C.: Urban Institute Press, 1999.

Name Index

Subject Index

Airport screeners, 334

Alaska: governor's use of report cards in, 640; nationwide surveys and, 261

Alcohol abuse services evaluation, 140–141

Alexandria, Virginia, trained observer ratings in, 232, 233

Alfagrafics Web site, 487

American Association of School Administrators, 179

American Education Research Journal, 193

American Evaluation Association, 672–673

American Federation of Teachers, 179

American Psychological Association, 193

American Red Cross, 10

Analysis of covariance, 138

Analyst team skills and knowledge, 420

Analytical memos and remarks, 424–425

Answer machines, 257, 562

Antecedent variables, 10

Apian, 279

Archival records. *See* Agency records

Arizona, Medicaid assignments in, 635

Asian Development Bank, 679

Association, measures of, 448–452

Assumptions: in chi-square test, 501; expert judgment procedures that reveal, 304; in regression analysis, 501; sensitivity testing of, 538, 539–540, 673; of validity, linking, 79, 80, 81. *See also* Logic models; Program theory

ATLAS, 421

Attitudinal data, 557

Attrition effects: literature review criteria and, 184; in quasi-experimental designs, 129, 131, 134; in randomized experiments, 163–164

Audience: as data analysis presentation criterion, 432; report writing for, 608–609; as statistical technique selection criterion, 452, 453. *See also* Sponsor; Stakeholders

Audiotaping, 389–390

Auditing, 680

Auditors, 414

Australia, 679

Autocorrelations, 135–136

Autoregressive integrated moving average (ARIMA), 136

B

B coefficients, 494, 495, 502

Backcoding data, 286

Backward mapping, 19, 20

Balanced scorecard, 104, 106, 107, 108–109, 110, 630

Baltimore, Maryland, program reviews in, 682

Beach maintenance, trained observer ratings of, 216

Before-after designs, 1, 127–130, 135, 147, 197

"Before and After: Streets and Parks and the Returnable Container Law," 215, 253

Benchmarking, 102, 117–119, 120, 630

Benefit-cost ratios, 508, 527–528

Benefits: cost savings as, 531–532; data sources for analyzing, 530–531; direct, 509, 510, 511; examples of, 511; increased productivity as, 534–535; indirect, 509, 510, 511; intangible, 510, 511, 539; lives saved as, 532–534; marginal, 509, 530; real, 507–508, 511; tangible, 510, 511; taxes as, 536; time savings as, 532; transfer, 507–508, 511, 536; types of, 511; valuation of, 415, 511, 530–539; weighting, 523–524. *See also* Cost-benefit analysis

Best practice research, 429

Beta coefficient, 502

Beta weights, 454

Bias: in before-after designs, 128–130, 177; in client feedback surveys, 93; in coverage, 82–83; defined, 177; in expert judgment, 299–300; in interrupted time-series designs, 131, 133–134, 135–136; literature review criteria and, 183–184; in nonequivalent group designs, 136–139, 142; in performance measures, 110; in randomized experiments, 162–164; in regression-discontinuity designs, 144–145, 146; selection, 444–445; systematic review and, 177

Big Brothers Big Sisters, 652

Binders, data organization, 419–420

Bivariate scatter plots, 501

Black box paradigm, 65, 76, 489, 539–540

Blueprints, 198

Body language, 349

Boston, Massachusetts, public schools, 629

Bottom-line number, 524, 525. *See also* Cost-benefit analysis

Boys and Girls Clubs, 652

Briefing package, 600

Briefings: in evaluability assessment, 51–52; in implementation evaluation, 95–96

British Breathalyzer effects study, 134

British Medical Journal, 193

Budgets and budgeting, evaluation, 577–578, 580–581

Building maintenance, trained observer ratings of, 216, 221, 224, 244

Bureau of Prisons (BOP), 298

Business Resources, 311, 335, 338

Design changes, program: evaluability assessment for, 40–41, 53; implementation evaluation for, 90–95

Design embellishments, for quasi-experiments, 127, 147–148; in interrupted time-series designs, 131–135; in nonequivalent group designs, 137–141, 142; in regression-discontinuity designs, 145–146

Design, evaluation: approaches to, 1–5; data analysis planning and, 417–418; evaluability assessment for, 1–2, 3, 33–60, 549, 550, 554; exploring options for, 41, 47, 53, 56–57; of field studies, 367–383; of implementation evaluation, 63–96; issues in, 1–2; logic modeling for, 1, 2, 3, 7–29; meta-analysis, systematic review, and research synthesis, 176–200; for one-shot studies, 1–2, 269; of performance monitoring systems, 98–122; pitfalls in, 548, 550–554; quasi-experimental, 126–148; randomized experimental, 150–173; selection of, in evaluability assessment, 41–42, 47–48, 56–57; with threats to validity, 443

Design matrix for surveys, 258–260, 262–263

Design, program: evaluability assessment of, 39–41; implementation evaluation of, 68, 70, 73–80

Developing nations: evaluation pressures on, 679; market distortions in, 531

Developmentally disabled persons, Individual Program Planning (IPP) process for, 94–95

Devil's advocate (DA), 300, 302–304

Dialectical inquiry (DI), 300, 302–304

Dictionary of Epidemiology, 176

Difference in means, 454

Difference-of-means test, 331–332

Diffusion effects, 159–160

Digest of Social Experiments (Greenberg and Shroder), 152

Digital cameras, 238, 240, 251, 666

Digital Survey, 641

Disability support services evaluation, 75–76, 94–95

Disaggregation: of agency record data, 401; inadequate attention to, pitfall of, 565–566; of survey data, 261, 287–288; of trained observer ratings, 222, 223–224, 247–248

Disclosure requirements, 630

Discount rate, 508, 528, 537

Discounting, 428, 521

Discrepancy evaluation model, 13

Discrete element coding, 422

Discriminant analysis, 454, 456

Discrimination assessment role playing, 207, 310,

311–313; systematic *versus* random, 332–334. *See also* Employment discrimination role-playing studies; Gender discrimination role-playing studies; Housing discrimination role-playing studies; Latinos role-playing studies; Minority role–playing studies

Disinterestedness, Mertonian norms of, 299–300, 301

Distributional issues, in cost-benefit analysis, 538

Documentation, program: for evaluability assessment of program intent, 37; for evaluability assessment of program reality, 39–40, 46–47, 52–53; for fieldwork, 385; for implementation evaluation, 82, 86–88; for performance monitoring systems, 106–107, 111–112; in quasi-experiments, 135. *See also* Agency records

Dollar coin acceptability study, 343–344, 357

Dose response studies, 139–140

Double coding, 185

Drill-down approach, 356–357

Driver education review, 195

Dropout prevention programs: agency record evaluation of, 402, 406; cost-benefit analysis of, 512–516, 517–520, 525–530, 532, 536, 540; cost-effectiveness analysis of, 521–522, 538

Drug courts, 298

Drunk driving prevention, 538

Dry land, 178–179

Dummy variables, 496–497, 502

Duplicated counts, 402

DuPont Corporation, 405

E

Early Head Start, 152, 157, 161

Early randomization, 165

Early Reading First, 153, 154, 157

Economic development projects, benefits of, 534–535

Economic rate of return (ERR), 506, 528–529

Education Commission of the States, 673, 684

Education literature reviews. *See* Campbell Collaboration

Education Week, 641

Educational programs: expert judgment evaluation of, 293; uncertainty of, 293

Educational software effect studies, 184, 185

Effect sizes (ES): defined, 503; estimation of, for literature reviews, 184–185, 187, 192, 199; interpretation of magnitude and, 446–448; statistical power and, 160–162, 499–500